The Original Aramaic New Testament in Plain English
(An American Translation of the Aramaic New Testament)
Translated (with notes and commentary) by Rev. Glenn David Bauscher

Glenn David Bauscher
Lulu Publishing

The Original Aramaic New Testament in Plain English
(An American Translation of the Aramaic New Testament)
by Glenn David Bauscher

Editor- Timothy Mitchell, New South Wales Australia
Copyright © 2007; 7th edition Copyright © 2011

Lulu Publishing

The Original Aramaic New Testament in Plain English

Table of Contents

The Gospel According to The Apostle Matthew.. 15
The Gospel According To Saint Mark.. 56
The Gospel According To Saint Luke.. 81
The Gospel according to The Apostle John... 136
The Acts of The Apostles.. 169
The Epistle of The Apostle Paul to the Romans... 210
The First Epistle of The Apostle Paul to the Corinthians... 228
The Second Epistle of The Apostle Paul to the Corinthians.. 246
The Epistle of The Apostle Paul to the Galatians... 258
The Epistle of The Apostle Paul to the Ephesians.. 266
The Epistle of The Apostle Paul to the Philippians.. 272
The Epistle of The Apostle Paul to the Colossians... 277
The First Epistle of The Apostle Paul to the Thessalonians.. 282
The Second Epistle of The Apostle Paul to the Thessalonians...................................... 287
The First Epistle of The Apostle Paul to Timothy... 290
The Second Epistle of The Apostle Paul to Timothy... 296
The Epistle of The Apostle Paul to Titus.. 300
The Epistle of The Apostle Paul to Philemon.. 303
The Epistle of The Apostle Paul to the Hebrews... 305
The Epistle of The Apostle James.. 324
The First Epistle of the Apostle Peter... 330
The Second Epistle of The Apostle Peter.. 336
The First Epistle of The Apostle John... 340
The Second Epistle of The Apostle John... 345
The Third Epistle of The Apostle John.. 346
The Epistle of The Apostle Jude... 347
The Revelation of Yeshua The Messiah... 349
Epilogue... 377
Appendix.. 378
Bibliography:... 384

Introduction

This volume is a translation of what this author believes to be the original Aramaic New Testament as first written by The Apostles and Evangelists Matthew, Mark, Luke, John, Paul, Peter, James and Jude.

This translation of The New Testament is different from most New Testament translations in that most are translated from Greek or Latin, whereas this is from Aramaic. Aramaic was the language of Jesus of Nazareth ("Yeshua Netsari" in Aramaic) and of his twelve disciples. The Peshitta New Testament is the only complete Aramaic New Testament known today which is held by a significant Christian denomination to be the original text written by the Apostles. **The Church of The East** has always held to this text as the original writing of the Apostles, preserved with word for word accuracy by its Scribes for nearly two thousand years with meticulous care and reverence.

This prose translation is taken from the author's **The Aramaic-English Interlinear Translation of The New Testament** (a very literal translation with the Aramaic words side by side with their English translations in parentheses in the same word order as the Aramaic, which reads right to left).

Why should anyone be interested in such a translation? The answers are manifold and I cannot address them all here. The most important reason is that the original Gospels (and Epistles as well) were written in Aramaic and later translated into Greek for Greek speaking Romans. Josephus addresses the language of the first century Israelites in his 1st century volumes of Jewish history. He wrote in Aramaic and translated his works into Greek later. He also testifies plainly that Greek was not the language of his Israeli countrymen (born AD 37 and died after AD 100) and that Greek was not spoken by the vast majority of Jews at that time.

Josephus provides almost all the historical information of first century Israel available today. Every serious student of the New Testament has consulted Josephus for background information on that time period in Israel.
Here is a statement from Josephus : _**"I have also taken a great deal of pains to obtain the learning of the Greeks, and to understand the elements of the Greek language, although I have so accustomed myself to speak our own tongue , that I cannot pronounce Greek with sufficient exactness. For our nation does not encourage those that learn the language of many nations. On this account, as there have been many who have done their endeavors, with great patience , to obtain the Greek learning, there have hardly been two or three who have succeeded herein , who were immediately rewarded for their pains."**_ _– Antiquities XX, XI 2.(published circa A.D. 93)_
Josephus, a learned Priest and Pharisee of his time, wrote that he did not know Greek well enough to speak it fluently; he knew a few who had learned it well. The main truth to be gleaned here is that Greek was not the language of Israel, nor a second language. It had to be studied deliberately to be learned, and it was apparently discouraged by the Jews.
In A.D. 77, Josephus wrote his Jewish Wars in Aramaic and later translated it into Greek for the Greek- speaking Roman citizens. Even his later Antiquities, quoted above, shows that Josephus was not fluent enough in Greek to compose his several volumes in that language. The Jewish rabbis of that time forbade the teaching of pagan tongues to their young men. They taught that it was preferable to feed one's son the flesh of swine than to teach him Greek.
Josephus elsewhere wrote that he wrote his works "in the language of his country" and later "translated his history into Greek". This establishes that Greek was not the language of Israel.
This historical information is valuable in determining what the language of the original NT was. The New Testament was **written by Jews** in Israel, for the most part, and **to Jews originally**, since they were the original Christians. Even the church in Rome was established by Jewish converts who had been dispersed from Israel and spoke Aramaic. Aramaic had been the language of the Holy Land and the Middle East since the 7th century BC. It was imposed on that part of the world by The Assyrians when The Assyrian Empire ruled that area of the world in the ninth through seventh centuries BC. Greek never supplanted Aramaic in that area.

Greek did spread in the western empires of Alexander The Great and the Caesars. That is why the Hebrew Old Testament was commissioned by Greek King Ptolemy of Egypt around 285 BC to be translated into Greek, so he and Greek speaking people of Alexandria, Egypt, could read the Jewish scriptures in their own language.
It makes no sense whatever to suppose the original Gospels were written in Greek. The first Christian churches were established by Jewish disciples and converts of The Messiah Yeshua (Jesus) in Israel, Samaria , in Asia Minor, Syria and Mesopotamia, and later in the cities of Rome, Corinth, Ephesus, Galatia, Philippi, etc. , all of which were inhabited by colonies of Jews who had been dispersed there centuries before by the Babylonian, Persian and Greek persecutions of each respective empire over a period of seven centuries. A careful reading even of the epistles of Paul reveals that **he was writing to churches comprised of Jews familiar with the Old Testament Hebrew writings and laws and to whose ancestors Paul refers as "our fathers"** (See 1 Corinthians 10:1, Romans 2:17-4:25 , Galatians 2:15 and of Gentiles as well. **The Jews took the Aramaic language with them wherever they went, as it had replaced Hebrew as the language of Israel in the Babylonian captivity in the 6th century BC.**
Aramaic was the lingua franca of the Holy Land, Syria, Mesopotamia, Asia Minor from 700 BC to AD 700. The Jews of first century Israel would have been unable to read Greek gospels (not to mention unable to write them). The order of gospel preaching and writing

was always "**To the Jews first and also to the Gentiles.**" Every church would have wanted a copy of the original readable by Jews and Gentiles, which would require Aramaic first to the Jews, Syrians, Assyrians, Persians and most Asians, and Greek for most Roman Gentiles.

The Greek New Testament testifies that Aramaic was spoken by the Judeans of Christ's time. The New International Version uses the word "**Aramaic**" seven times in the Gospels and Acts to indicate the language of Israel and its inhabitants. Greek is never mentioned as the language spoken by any of the disciples or any Israelite. The Apostle Paul is referred to as knowing at least some Greek in Acts 22:37, but a few verses later he is speaking to the Jews in Aramaic. Paul was not from Israel; he was from Tarsus of Cilicia, a center of Greek learning in the Eastern world. Serious study of the above seven references to Aramaic makes clear the fact that the Jews of Israel spoke Aramaic as their native language.

For an extensive discussion and evidence supporting Aramaic originals, please see my web site: **aramaicnt.com**
I have written three books which bear on the subject : Divine Contact-The Original NT Discovered , The Aramaic-English Interlinear New Testament and Jegar Sahadutha-"Heap of Witness".

One question many ask about the Aramaic text is, "Are there major differences in this text as compared to other translations? The answer is that about 95% of the text is the same as other New Testaments, but the 5% difference is a really interesting , significant and powerful 5% content!

Let me give an example in Mark 14:61-64:
61.   But he was silent, and he did not answer him anything. And again, The High Priest asked him and said, "Are you The Messiah, The Son of The Blessed One?"
62.   But Yeshua said to him, "I AM THE LIVING GOD, and you shall behold The Son of Man sitting at the right hand of Power and coming on the clouds of Heaven."
63.   But The High Priest ripped his tunic and he said, "Why now do we need witnesses?"
64.   "Behold, you have heard the blasphemy from his own mouth. How does it appear to you?" But they all judged that he deserved death.

Do you see what I mean? Our Lord used the Aramaic phrase, "Ena Na", which signifies a Divine utterance in 97% of the places it is found in The Peshitta Old Testament- "I am The **LORD** your God", "I am The **LORD** who heals you", etc, in hundreds of references. Yet Our Lord used this phrase of Himself about thirty times. Let me give one more example, this one in John's Gospel:

1.   Therefore Yehuda led a troop also from the presence of the Chief Priests and the Pharisees. He led the guards and came there with torches and lamps and weapons.
2.   But Yeshua, because he knew all these things had come upon him, went out and said to them, "Whom are you seeking?"
3.   They were saying to him, "Yeshua the Nazarene." Yeshua said to them, "I AM THE LIVING GOD." But Yehuda the traitor was also standing with them.
4.   And when Yeshua said to them, "I AM THE LIVING GOD", they went backward and they fell on the ground.

Again we find Our Lord used the same phrase, "**Ena Na**", and the band of soldiers fell backward to the ground! This is powerful testimony that Yeshua claimed to be God Himself, when He was to be arrested and later when put under oath by The High Priest of Israel. It was the testimony of Jesus, quite literally, and when He would have chosen His words precisely and appropriately. The common people may have been ignorant of the significance of this phrase, but Caiaphas surely was not, as He knew the scriptures quite well. John's Gospel has 25 instances of Jesus uttering these "I AM" statements: **I AM THE LIVING GOD**, The Good Shepherd; **I AM THE LIVING GOD**, The Bread of

Truth, and "Unless you believe **I AM THE LIVING GOD**, you shall die in your sins", etc..

As far as the wording, grammar and historical statements in The Peshitta New Testament, I challenge anyone to find one error of any kind in the accepted Peshitta text upon which my translation is based. If it were actually a translation of Greek, as is commonly supposed by scholars, it represents an error free translation. One cannot say the Greek NT is error free. It has quite a few Greek grammatical errors in Revelation. The original should be better than the translation, not vice versa, especially considering that we are discussing Divinely authored writings!

Many Greek scholars will take issue with this view of The Peshitta as original, but most of them have no knowledge of Aramaic and have not read one verse of Aramaic, hence they cannot speak with authority against The Peshitta's primacy or for the Greek NT's claim for primacy over The Peshitta. Greek is taught in most seminaries; Aramaic is hardly taught anywhere. I have studied and learned Greek and Aramaic well and have read the New Testament in both languages. Beyond this, I have studied the merits and evidence cited for both positions. I believe very few Greek primacy advocates can honestly make the above claims.

There is abundant evidence I have found in The Peshitta via computer which I can honestly say is unprecedented and which is shockingly powerful support for not only the position that The Peshitta NT is the original, but for something even more dramatic: **The Peshitta NT was written by God Himself!**

As I said earlier, I cannot go into the evidence here, but I have done so elsewhere and it is a fascinating study. It amounts to an evaluation of the text using the scientific method in an experiment which produced abundant supporting data.*(Please see my website* **aramaicnt**.**com** *for information.)*

Apart from the analytical examination of The Greek and Aramaic texts is another and perhaps just as compelling testimony for an original Aramaic New Testament; that is simply reading the text itself. I found this extremely moving and powerful. The next best thing to reading the Aramaic is reading a good English translation of the Aramaic. This I believe I have provided in this volume of The New Testament (and in my interlinear New Testament).

The word of God is its own best witness. Sinner (pre- Saint) Augustine was converted to Christ when he heard someone in the street crying out ,"Take and read." , and he got hold of a Bible and began reading The New Testament. He became arguably the most ardent and influential theologian - philosopher since The Apostle Paul.

So the best advice I can give are those simple words:

"Take and read."

A word about proper names is in order. The reader will notice differences in name spellings in this version from other Greek and Latin based versions. That is because the Greek and Latin languages adapt Semitic names of the Hebrew and Aramaic Old and New Testaments into Western Greek and Latin forms and these show up in the English translations. Translating from Aramaic directly into English circumvents the middle step and gives a more accurate representation of the actual Hebrew and Aramaic names in English.

I have attempted to respect the familiarity of well known NT names such as Mary, Joseph, David, Jacob, Paul, etc, by retaining enough semblance of the familiar spelling to keep them recognizable and at the same time to give a very accurate rendering of the original name. The one name which represents a blatant exception to that rule is "**Yeshua**", which is the original behind "**Jesus**".

There are other exceptions as well: "Yohannan" is "John"; "Kaypha" is "Peter"; "Yaqob" is "Jacob" and also "James". "Yehudah" is "Judah". "Yoseph" is Joseph. Most others are recognizable, being similar to the Greek forms.

I have also preserved Old Testament names in their familiar forms for the most common names: Moses, Elijah, Isaiah, David, Ruth, Joshua, Solomon, etc. ,as well as OT place names: Jerusalem, Bethlehem, Galilee (Galila) , etc.. These were derived from Hebrew, not Greek, and are very similar to Aramaic spellings. I have not discarded Greek altogether in determining how to represent proper names, however, especially those not referring to Old Testament persons. The Greek NT is a first century production and represents , in my view, a window into how the Aramaic names were pronounced. I have consulted Greek transliterations of the many Aramaic names in rendering the English spelling of those names, while also giving faithful Aramaic renderings of those names. I also have kept the layman reader in mind, trying not to confuse with some completely alien sounding names that would be totally unrecognizable, especially when the person or place named is a familiar one to Bible readers ("Pharisees" is "Preesha"; "Sadducees" is "Zaduqia" ; **Jehovah**" is "MarYah") , so I have chosen to render those familiar names in the familiar forms, with some exceptions, which I have mentioned in the previous paragraph.

Divine Names and titles are generally translated, not transliterated like human names or place names. "**Jehovah**" is used to translate the Aramaic "**MarYah**" , which is The Aramaic for The Hebrew -"**Yahweh**", and always refers to The Deity. This Name, very interestingly, is applied to Yeshua (Jesus) in the Peshitta New Testament at least 32 times! "**MarYah**" literally means "**LORD JEHOVAH**". It is first applied to the infant Jesus in Luke 2:11. The last reference is in Rev. 22.20.

*Greek has no equivalent for "**Yahweh**" ; instead it uses "**Kurios**", which is not a name, but a title, and can refer to a human or to God. I cannot believe the original NT would lack the most sacred Old Covenant Name revealed to man, but the Greek does lack it! This alone disqualifies the Greek as the original.*

*The Peshitta NT has "**MarYah**" (always the Divine Name) 239 times! This the Jews understood and used as the sacred Name of God in their Aramaic tongue. It always refers to The Deity.*

I believe what I have in my possession and <u>from which</u> I have translated here (The Aramaic text, not the translation itself) is the exact, word for word, letter for letter, original and Divinely authored New Testament! It contains no errors of any kind historical, grammatical, orthographical, textual, geographical, scientific, or theological! It answers to Our Lord's promise:
שמיא וארעא נעברון ומלי לא נעברן -Matthew 24:35
"Heaven and earth may pass away, but **My words shall not pass away**".

פשיק הו דין דשמיא וארעא נעברון או אתותא חדא מן נמוסא תעבר- Luke 16:17
And it is easier for heaven and earth to pass away, than for **one letter** to pass from the law.
"The Law" is a term referring to the written word of God, as John 10:34 reveals, since Jesus refers to Psalm 86 as "The Law".
תורת יהוה תמימה משיבת נפש עדות יהוה נאמנה מחכימת פתי Psalms 19:7
The law of the LORD is perfect, converting the soul:
the testimony of the LORD is sure, making wise the simple.

<u>The following is one of eight long messages encoded in The Aramaic New Testament. Each letter in this 25 letter Hebrew message is separated by exactly 18,474 letters, and spans almost the entire New Testament!</u>

in a manger Yeshua will blossom of God The Son where ? to lodge
להלן אהי בן אל יניץ ישוע באיבוס

Where should The Son of God be lodged? Jesus shall blossom forth in a manger.

The sense and symmetry in this code is unparalleled among other Bible codes I have seen which were found by others. It is poetic and powerful, as are all the codes I have found in The Peshitta New Testament. The imagery used here :Lodging The Son of God in a manger, Jesus budding forth as a flower in His birth, these are a signature poetic language found in all six of the long codes I have found and which I display in this book. They possess and convey a beauty rare among Christian and secular literature. All these codes also center around the Gospel story of The Messiah's birth, suffering, death and resurrection.

How could such design and beauty be accidental ? That means there are approx. ten chapters separating each letter of the code, which code letters stretch essentially from Matthew to Revelation. There are exactly 18,474 letters between each of the 25 code letters !

If one letter of This Aramaic NT were deleted or one letter added to it, this Christmas code about The birth of Christ would not exist!

Codefinder, using the frequency statistics for each letter of the code, calculates an R factor of 20, which essentially is the number of decimal places after the decimal point in the probability figure ! - 0.00000000000000000001 or 1 in 100,000,000,000,000,000,000
That is approximately 1 in 100 million-trillions.

To see more codes in The Peshitta and info. about them, get my book, **Divine Contact-Discovery of the Original New Testament** at aramaicnt.com

Philosophy of Translation

"For the words that you gave me I have given them, and they have received them and known truly that I have proceeded from unity with you." John 17:8

"The words that I speak with you are spirit and life." John 6:63

"Father, hallow them in Your truth, because Your Word is The Truth". John 17:17

But as it is written: "Eye has not seen, ear has not heard, and upon the heart of man has not come up that which God has prepared for those who love him.
But God has revealed it to us by his Spirit, for The Spirit searches into everything, even the depths of God.
And who is the man who knows what is in a man except only the spirit of the man that is in him? So also a man does not know what is in God, only The Spirit of God knows.
But we have not received The Spirit of the world, but The Spirit that is from God, that we may know the gift that has been given to us from God.
But those things we speak are not in the teaching of the words of the wisdom of men, but in the teaching of The Spirit, and we compare spiritual things to the spiritual.
For a selfish* man does not receive spiritual things, for they are madness to him, and he is not able to know, for they are known by The Spirit. * ("d'vanphesh" comes from Napsha –"soul", "self", "animal life", and can mean, "soulish", "selfish", "brutish".)
But a spiritual man judges everything and he is not judged by any man.
For who has known the mind of THE LORD JEHOVAH that he may teach him? But we do have the mind of The Messiah." - 1 Corinthians 2:9-16

"Every writing which is written by The Spirit* is profitable for teaching, for correction, for direction and for a course in righteousness,
that the man of God will be perfect and perfected for every good work." 2 Timothy 3:16,17

Translation is a tricky business. The translator, to be most effective, needs to know the meaning of the source he is translating and be able to communicate that in the language of the audience. Translation of scripture is much trickier than translation of the words of man, as a theological-philosophical component exists not encountered in secular sources, for what human can know the meaning of the mind of God? It is not simply a matter of knowing two human languages; it is a matter of knowing the infinite mind of Deity and interpreting and conveying it to humans.

"And who shall be worthy for these things?", wrote Paul The Apostle,
"For we are not like others who blend the words of God, but according to that which is in the truth and according to that which is from God, before God in The Messiah we speak". 2 Corinthians 2:16,17

In his second letter to the Corinthians, speaking of ministering the word of God, Paul wrote:

"But in this way we have trust in The Messiah toward God, not that we are sufficient to think anything as from ourselves, **but our power is from God, He who made us worthy to be Ministers of The New Covenant,** not in The Scripture, but in The Spirit, **for The Scripture kills, but The Spirit gives life**."- 2 Corinthians 3

All the above translations are from this translation -<u>The Original Aramaic New Testament in Plain English,</u> by David Bauscher.

The Bible is a paradox among all literature. It is a book, or collection of books which says that mere words cannot convey truth of themselves, only error and death, and that The Spirit of God alone is Truth and Life. So the Bible is the written word of God which cannot be known by mortal minds. Only God Himself can convey it, and it must also be received by a spiritual mind like God's mind *(Refer back to 1 Cor. 2:16)*

Effective Bible translation, then, must be primarily the work of The Holy Spirit executed through a human instrument. To some extent, effective translation depends on the inspiration of God as did the writing of the original scriptures, though not to the same extent, of course.

The translation will invariably contain errors, as the target language will not exactly convey the meaning of every original word or phrase. That kind of error is unavoidable and part of the confusion of languages which God decreed the world at Babel, as recorded in Genesis 11.

If the reader or hearer has The Spirit of God within, then The Spirit can bridge the language gap, and what is more important, the mind gap, between God and man.

This translation is not perfect, I really don't believe there is such a thing as a perfect translation of The Bible. I do believe, as Paul, that "we are not sufficient to think anything as of ourselves, but our power is from God."

I can honestly say that while translating the New Testament, I experienced Divine help, power and inspiration all the way through. I have a good mind for learning languages, but I was an apprentice watching his Master taking me through the process of using Aramaic vocabulary and grammar to unveil His Mind and Heart in the English language. I was "along for the ride", as it turns out.

Because of my novice status as an Aramaic scholar, I actually have greater confidence in the results than I might have had if I were a native Aramaean, as George Lamsa was, speaking Aramaic fluently. Lamsa did not need to rely on God nearly as much as I did, and frankly, I think the resulting translation shows that to be true.
 This reveals another paradox.

What men call expertise, superior ability and learning, often prove to be a disappointment and lose the contest to the upstart and underdog who had tremendous challenges to overcome and who went beyond his own capacity and resources to conquer those challenges.

"The race is not to the swift, nor the battle to the strong." – Ecclesiastes 9:11

The Old Testament teaches this principle very well: "And Saul said to David, You are not able to go against this Philistine to fight with him: for you are but a youth, and he a man of war from his youth." 1Sa 17:33

But we know what happened, though the odds seemed a hundred to one against David, he killed Goliath, for as he said: "The LORD does not save with sword and spear, for the battle is The LORD's, and He will deliver you into our hands."

The Apostle Paul wrote that scripture is of The Spirit of God and must be understood with the aid of The Spirit Who authored scripture. Reading scripture without The Spirit can kill a person! Interpret that as you will; the point is that we must have The Holy Spirit to speak to us directly in order to understand scripture and receive spiritual life. This principle applies to a translator as well as to every reader of scripture.

Knowledge of a language can be a hindrance to properly translating scripture. Let me explain. A person who speaks Aramaic fluently (which I do not, nor did Murdock or Etheridge) may trust in his knowledge of the language and may not feel a need to seek God's help and trust Him to guide him in the translation. Thus his knowledge of the language would be a serious impediment and mitigate the spiritual nature and accuracy of the translation. I know that sounds like a contradiction, and I am not arguing that greater knowledge of the language is undesirable, only that it can be a stumbling block. It does not need to be, and should not be so.

But ask yourself this question: How many translations of The Bible were done by native speakers of Hebrew or Greek? One would think, for example, that the Greek New Testament would be best translated by Greeks who grew up speaking Greek and also know English.
I know of no such translation that is commonly used in the churches.
How can this be, that none of the known translations of the Greek N.T. is done by native Greek speakers? I submit that it is a testament (pun unintended) to human nature. Translators fluent in the language tend to trust in their fluency, in their translation of a spiritual and Divine text; those who study the language in adulthood are less inclined to be over confident in their ability and more inclined to seek Divine help and to emphasize the spiritual element rather than the linguistic component in translating the Bible text.

Sound understanding of a language is often insufficient in determining the original meaning of scripture, especially when so many words have several different meanings which may make sense in a particular scriptural context.
Here is how I applied this principle to my translation of The Peshitta New Testament: I was always asking myself, "What is God saying to me here? How does this speak to my spirit?" Very often, there are several different meanings for an Aramaic word or phrase, as is the case with English and all languages. Of course, a spirit of prayer is the only spirit in which to approach the holy task of translating the very words of The Living God, and it was in that spirit and in His Spirit I believe I did approach my task, from start to finish. I did perceive powerful Divine guidance, inspiration, help and confidence in the work. That does not mean I did perfect work, as I know there are errors of all sorts in the translation. What it does mean, as I see it, is that God is pleased with the results and that this translation effectively represents His intended meaning and purpose in writing to us in the first century through His Apostles and Evangelists.
Some look for a translation by one fluent in the source language, i.e. Aramaic, as an indication of the trustworthiness of the translation. Ignoring the issue of the target language, let's focus on the matter of fluency. Fluency generally pertains to the speaking of a language, nothing more. We must consider the matter of literacy first and foremost, when discussing translation of a language. A four year old American boy may be a fluent English speaker, but most likely would be illiterate-i.e., he cannot read or write English, or any other language. The success of translating a written source per se is dependent on the ability of the translator to read and understand the source language, not on ability to speak it. He or she must learn the grammar, vocabulary, sentence structure and idioms of the language.

Consider that Josephus wrote his Antiquities and Jewish Wars in Aramaic and later translated them into Greek. He also wrote in his Greek translation of Antiquities that he could not speak Greek well enough to converse in it. This was because Greek was not his native tongue and he was so used to speaking with his countrymen in Aramaic and not hearing Greek, that he never became fluent in Greek. He was quite literate in Greek, however! His Greek writing is excellent, some of the best compositional Koine Greek ever.

Let me now give an example of how I approached selecting between different possible translations of a verse of scripture: James 2:18

אמר 18 (says) גיר (for) אנש (a man) לך (to you) את (is) לך (to you) הימנותא (faith) ולי (& to me *)
את (is) לי (to me) עבדא (works) חוני (show me) הימנותך (your faith) דלא (without *) עבדא (works *)
ואנא (& I) מחוא (showing) אנא (am) לך (to you) הימנותי (my faith *) מן (from) עבדי (my deeds)

"For a man says to you, 'You and I have faith; I have deeds; Show me your faith without deeds and I shall show you my faith by my deeds.'"

All other translations of this verse that I can find start out basically —"Someone says, you have faith, I have works..." The Greek text has this, as do the translations of The Peshitta Aramaic I have read. The Aramaic text can be understood to mean "**You and I have faith; I have works**", or "**You have faith and I have works**". There is a subtle difference here, though I believe it is an important one. In the common rendering, it can sound like James is pitting works against faith, almost as the Law keeping Jews who had no faith in Jesus as The Messiah may have argued against Christians who did not live by the Law of Moses but believed in Jesus for salvation. One could come away from verse 18 with the idea that James was arguing with The Apostle Paul about "Faith versus works". Actually, the context shows that this is not the case, but I believe my rendering is in better agreement with the context than the conventional translation.

James assumes "**You and I have faith**", which is assuming both parties lay claim to faith. It is thus not a dispute between faith and works, or one group claiming to have faith and another laying claim merely to works; it is two parties both claiming to have faith. Only one, however, also claims to have works- good deeds. This makes the choice of translation easy for me, as it removes all doubt that James' position is exactly the same as Paul's and that he is reinforcing the necessity of faith, but only of practical and practicing faith, not of a mere claim to faith or a mental exercise called faith.

Another example is in Hebrews 11:1-
Here are two other translations of The Peshitta of Hebrews 11:1-
"Now FAITH is the persuasion concerning things which are in hope, as if they were in reality, and a revelation of those which are not seen." -JOHN WESLEY ETHERIDGE
"Now faith is the substance of things hoped for, as it was the substance of things which have come to pass; and it is the evidence of things not seen." —George M. Lamsa
Here is my translation:
11:1 איתיה (is) דין (but) הימנותא (faith) פיסא (the conviction) על (concerning) אילין (those things)
דאיתיהין (that are) בסברא (in hope) איך (as if) הו (it) דהוי (were) להין (these things)
בסוערנא (in action *) וגלינא (& the revelation) דאילין (of those things) דלא (that not) מתחזין (are seen)

"Now faith is the conviction concerning those things that are in hope, as if it were these things in action, and the revelation of those things that are unseen."

Needless to say, the translation I have produced is what my spirit hears God's Spirit saying in the Aramaic text (aside from the fact that the primary sense of סוערנא - "surana", is "action"); it is clear and rings true to me. I could give many such examples in the New Testament.

I ask the reader to "Explore everything and hold what is excellent." 1 Thessalonians 5:21

This translation is derived from my Aramaic-English Interlinear NT, which is as literal as a translation can be. There are idioms in Aramaic, of course; these I highlighted in the color interlinear editions in purple, though not always translating idiomatically, but usually word for word. Here in this *New Testament in Plain English* I have translated most of the idioms as such, which makes it much easier to understand. I have attempted,

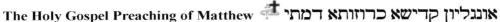
however, to retain as much of the literal sense as is reasonable in English, though not always in the best English grammar. This is because I am more concerned that the reader get the benefit of the original word order and emphasis, which in Semitic languages (Hebrew,Aramaic,Ethiopic,Arabic) is often quite different from Western non-Semitic languages. Often, Aramaic will rename a subject or object with a pronoun for emphasis; sometimes this will be translated as reflexive: "He himself", "himself", "themselves", instead of the simple personal pronoun. Sometimes a verb is doubled or even tripled for emphasis; this may result in: *"The sower, who sowed, sowed the word."*–Mark 4:14. The Aramaic root "Zara" is used three times in that short verse, once as a noun and two as a verb. The Greek verse has only one verb and one participle ("the sower"), hence the English translations also have one verb: "The sower sows the word." Another example is: *"And he stretched his hands toward his disciples and said, "Behold my mother and behold my brothers!"*-Matthew 12:49. The Greek has simply, "Behold my mother and my brothers." Not a big difference here, but I have retained the redundant "behold", simply because it is there in the Aramaic text. Such idiosyncrasies and others are common to Aramaic and Hebrew and are alien to English. It is a difficult balancing act to translate literally and idiomatically simultaneously, while rendering all in good English grammar as well. I am sure improvements can be made and will be forthcoming.

So the translation is very literal, yet idiomatic. I have left the English readable, yet rough, to convey the sense of the original as accurately as possible. I hope the reader will forgive the raw style of some of the translation. I do believe it better conveys the simplicity and power of the Peshitta New Testament. I believe The Aramaic Peshitta is unparalleled in both respects among all New Testament texts.

Many, no doubt, will still want to know my qualifications for doing this translation and presenting it as preferable to that of others who had studied Aramaic longer and were recognized scholars and professors in the field. To such, I present the following from my Original Aramaic New Testament in Plain English:

1 Corinthians 1

26.For you see also your calling my brethren, that not many among you are wise in the flesh, neither are many among you mighty, neither are many among you children of a great family line.

27.For **God has chosen the foolish** of the world to shame the wise, and **he has chosen the weak of the world** to shame the mighty.

28.And **he has chosen those of low descent** in the world and **the rejects** and **those who are nothing**, to nullify those who are,

29.**That no one will boast before him**.

30.But you also are from him in Yeshua The Messiah, he who has become for us the wisdom of God and the righteousness and the holiness and the redemption,

31.According to what is written: "**Whoever boasts, let him boast of** THE LORD JEHOVAH."

"Foolish, weak, of low descent, rejects, those who are nothing"- I think I have attained those credentials, for I have chosen to value what Jesus values and have given up my desire to be "somebody" in the world, so that I may follow my LORD and please Him.

With God's help, inspiration and encouragement, I have completed two translations of the Peshitta New Testament and am in the process of translating the Peshitta Old Testament.
I have included translations of Peshitta Psalms and Proverbs in most editions of the NT. Most Eastern Peshitta scholars and many Western scholars date the Old Testament Peshitta as a first century A.D. translation from the Hebrew Old Testament.

I also can say that I have endeavored always to honor The Triune God, and believe my translation glorifies The Author of all scripture:
Alaha Ava, Brah MarYah Yeshua Meshiakha, w'Rookha d'Qoodsha Breeka, Khath Alaha, Breek lalam almeen. Ameen.
(God The Father, His Son THE LORD JEHOVAH Yeshua The Messiah and The Blessed

Spirit of Holiness, One God, Blessed to the eternity of eternities. Amen.

The Gospel According to The Apostle Matthew

Chapter 1

1. The book of the genealogy of Yeshua The Messiah, The Son of David , The Son of Abraham.
2. Abraham begot Isaaq, Isaaq begot Jaqob, Jaqob begot Yehuda and his brothers.
3. Yehuda begot Pharez and Zarah from Tamar. Pharez begot Hezron, Hezron begot Aram .
4. Aram begot Aminadab, Aminadab begot Nahshon, Nahshon begot Salmon
5. Salmon begot Boaz from Rahab, Boaz begot Obayd from Ruth, Obayd begot Jesse.
6. Jesse begot David the King, David begot Solomon from the wife of Uriah.
7. Solomon begot Rehoboam, Rehoboam begot Abia, Abia begot Asa.
8. Asa begot Jehoshaphat, Jehoshaphat begot Joram, Joram begot Uzaya.
9. Uzaya begot Jotham, Jotham begot Ahaz, Ahaz begot Hezekiah.
10. Hezekiah begot Manashe, Manashe begot Amon, Amon begot Joshaiah.
11. Joshaiah begot Jokania and his brothers in the captivity of Babel.
12. After the captivity of Babel, Jokania begot Shelathiel, Shelathiel begot Zorubabel.
13. Zorubabel begot Abiud, Abiud begot Eliakim, Eliakim begot Azor.
14. Azor begot Zadoq, Zadoq begot Akin, Akin begot Eliud.
15. Eliud begot Eliazer, Eliazer begot Matthan, Matthan begot Yaqob.
16. Yaqob begot Yoseph the guardian of Maryam, her from whom was begotten Yeshua, who is called The Messiah.
17. Therefore all generations from Abraham until David were fourteen generations, and from David until the captivity of Babel, fourteen generations, and from the captivity of Babel until The Messiah, fourteen generations.
18. The birth of Yeshua The Messiah was thus: when Maryam his mother was engaged to Yoseph before they would have a conjugal relation she was found pregnant from The Spirit of Holiness.
19. But Yoseph her lord was righteous and did not want to expose her, and he was considering divorcing her secretly.
20. But as he considered these things, The Angel of **THE LORD JEHOVAH** appeared to him in a dream and said unto him, "Yoseph, son of David, do not be afraid to take Maryam your woman, for he who is begotten in her is from The Spirit of Holiness."
21. "And she shall bring forth a Son, and she shall call his name Yeshua, for he shall save his people from their sins."
22. Now all this happened, that the thing which was spoken from **THE LORD JEHOVAH** by the Prophet would be fulfilled:
23. "Behold the virgin shall conceive, and she shall bear a son, and they shall call* his Name Emmanuail, which is translated, 'Our God is with us' ".

* 2 ancient Greek mss.(**B,D**) have "you shall call"; Here are the two readings in Aramaic:

נֶקְרוֹן-"& they shall call"

תֶקְרוֹן-"you shall call"

Can we wonder where the alternate Greek reading came from?

24. And when Yoseph arose from his sleep, he did according to that which The Angel of **THE LORD JEHOVAH** had commanded him, and he took his wife.
25. And he did not know her sexually until she delivered her firstborn son, and she called his name Yeshua.

Chapter 2

1. Now when Yeshua was born in Bethlehem of Judaea, in the days of Herodus the King, The Magi came from The East to Jerusalem.
2. And they were saying, "Where is The King of the Judaeans who has been born"? For we have seen his star in The East and we have come to worship him.
3. But Herodus The King heard and he was troubled and all Jerusalem with him.
4. And he gathered the Chief Priests and the Scribes of the people together and was asking them, "Where would The Messiah be born?."
5. And they said, "In Bethlehem of Judaea", for thus it is written in The Prophets:
6. "You, Bethlehem of Judea, were not the least among the Kings of Judaea, for from you shall proceed The King who shall shepherd my people Israel."
7. And then Herodus secretly called The Magi and learned from them at what time the star had appeared to them.

8. And he sent them to Bethlehem and said to them, "Go inquire about The Boy very carefully and when you find him, come show me, so that I also may go worship him."

9. But when they heard from the King, they went, and behold, that star which they had seen in The East went before them, until it came and stood over where The Boy was.

10. And when they saw the star, they rejoiced with a very great joy.

11. And they entered the house and saw The Boy with Maryam his mother, and they fell *and* worshiped him and opened their treasures and offered him gifts: gold, myrrh, and frankincense.

12. And it was seen by them in a dream that they should not return to Herodus, and they went to their country by another road.

13. And as they went, The Angel of **THE LORD JEHOVAH** appeared in a dream to Yoseph, and said to him, "Arise, take The Boy and his mother, and flee to Egypt and stay there, until I speak to you, for Herodus is going to seek The Boy to destroy him."

14. So Yoseph arose, took The Boy and his mother in the night, and fled to Egypt.

15. And he was there until the death of Herodus, that the thing might be fulfilled that was spoken from **THE LORD JEHOVAH** through the Prophet which says, "From Egypt I have called my Son."

16. And Herodus, when he saw that he was mocked by The Magi, was greatly enraged, and he sent and killed all the boys of Bethlehem and of all of its borders, from two years old and under, according to the time he had searched out from the Magi.

17. Then the thing was fulfilled which was spoken by Jeremiah the Prophet which says:

18. "A voice was heard in Ramtha, weeping and great lamentation, Rachel weeping over her children, and she is unwilling to be comforted, because they are not."

19. But when Herodus The King died, The Angel of **THE LORD JEHOVAH** appeared in a dream to Yoseph in Egypt.

20. And he said to him, "Arise, take The Boy and his mother, and go to the land of Israel, for those who were seeking the Boy's life have died."

21. And Yoseph arose, took The Boy and his mother, and came to the land of Israel.

22. But when he heard that Arkilaus was The King in Judaea, in the place of Herodus his father, he was afraid to go there, and it

appeared to him in a dream that he should go to the region of Galilee.

23. And he came to dwell in a city that is called Nazareth, so that the thing would be fulfilled which was spoken by the Prophet, "He shall be called The Nazarene."

Chapter 3

1. * And in those days Yohannan The Baptizer came and was preaching in the desert of Judaea.

2. And he said, "Return *to God*, the Kingdom of Heaven has come near."

3. For this was he of whom it was said by Isaiah the Prophet, "A voice that cries in the desert, 'Prepare the way of **THE LORD JEHOVAH** and level his paths'."

4. And this Yohannan had his garment of camel hair and wore a leather garment around his waist, and his food was locusts and honey of the field.

5. Then Jerusalem and all Judaea were going out to him, and the whole region, which is around the Jordan.

6. And they were being baptized by him in the Jordan River while confessing their sins.

7. But when he saw many of the Pharisees and the Sadducees who came to be baptized, he said to them, "Offspring of vipers, who has instructed you to flee from the wrath that is coming"?

8. "Produce therefore fruit that is fitting of repentance."

9. "And do not think and say in yourselves, 'Abraham is our father', for I say to you, God can raise up from these stones children to Abraham."

10. * "But behold, the axe is laid at the root of the tree; every tree, therefore, that has not produced good fruit is cut down and falls into the fire."

11. "I am baptizing you in water for repentance, but he who comes after me is mightier than I, for I am not worthy to pick up his sandals; he is to baptize you in The Spirit of Holiness and in fire."

12. "For the winnowing fan is in his hand and he purges his threshing floor, and he gathers the wheat into his barns, and the chaff he will burn in fire that is not extinguished."

13. Then Yeshua came from Galilee to the Jordan unto Yohannan to be baptized by him.

14. But Yohannan had refused and said to him, "I need to be baptized by you, and you have come to me?"

15. But Yeshua answered and said to him, "Allow this now, for it is proper for us to fulfill all justice", and then he allowed him.

16. But when Yeshua was baptized, at once he came up from the water, and Heaven was opened unto him, and he saw The Spirit of God descending like a dove and coming upon him.

17. And behold a voice from Heaven that said, "This is my Son, The Beloved, in whom I am delighted."

Chapter 4

1. Then Yeshua was led of The Spirit of Holiness to the wilderness to be tempted by The Devil.

2. But he fasted forty days and forty nights, and afterward he was hungry.

3. And The Tempter approached him and said to him, "If you are The Son of God, tell these stones to become bread."

4. But he answered and said, "It is written: 'A man does not live by bread only, but by every word that proceeds from the mouth of God.'"

5. Then The Devil brought him to The Holy City, and stood him on the pinnacle of The Temple.

6. And he said to him, "If you are The Son of God, cast yourself down, for it is written: 'He will command his Angels concerning you, and they will carry you upon their hands, lest you strike your foot on a stone'."

7. Yeshua said to him, "Again it is written: 'You shall not tempt THE LORD JEHOVAH your God.'"

8. Again The Devil brought him to a very high mountain, and he showed him all the Kingdoms of the world and their glory.

9. And he said to him, "All these things I will give to you if you will fall down to worship me."

10. Then Yeshua said to him, "Depart Satan, for it is written: 'You shall worship THE LORD JEHOVAH your God and him alone shall you serve.'"

11. And The Devil left him, and behold Angels approached and they were serving him.

12. But when Yeshua heard that Yohannan had been delivered up, he departed to Galilee.

13. And he left Nazareth, and came to dwell in Kapernahum, by the side of the sea, in the borders of Zebulon and of Naphtali.

14. That the thing which was spoken by Isaiah the Prophet would be fulfilled which says:

15. "The land of Zebulon, the land of Naphtali, the way of the sea, the crossings of Jordan, Galilee of the Gentiles."

16. "The people who sat in the darkness have seen The Great Light, and those who were sitting in the region and in the shadow of death, to them The Light has dawned."

17. From then on, Yeshua began to preach and to say, "Return to God, for The Kingdom of Heaven has come near."

18. And as he was walking on the side of the Sea of Galilee, he saw two brothers, Shimeon who was called Kaypha, and Andraeus his brother, for they were casting a net into the sea, for they were fishermen.

19. And Yeshua said to them, "Come after me, and I shall make you to become fishers of men."

20. And at once they left their net and they went after him.

21. And when he passed from there, he saw two other brothers: Yaqob Bar Zebedee and Yohannan his brother, in a boat with Zebedee their father, who were setting their nets in order, and he called them.

22. And at once they left the boat and their father and they went after him.

23. And Yeshua was traveling about in all Galilee and he taught in their assemblies and was preaching The Gospel of the Kingdom and curing every sickness and disease among the people.

24. And his fame was heard in all Syria, and they brought to him all those who had become ill with various diseases, those who were afflicted with severe pain, and the demon possessed, and lunatics and paralytics, and he healed them.

25. And great crowds went after him from Galilee and from the Ten Cities and from Jerusalem and from Judaea and from the other side of the Jordan.

Chapter 5

1. But when Yeshua saw the crowds, he went up into a mountain and when he sat down his disciples came near to him.

2. And he opened his mouth and he was teaching them and he said:

3. "Blessed by The Spirit are the poor, because theirs is the Kingdom of Heaven. (See Matthew 22:43, the only other place in The Gospels where the

same form of the Aramaic word "**b'Rukh**" (in,by spirit) is used, refers to The Holy Spirit. See also Luke 6:20 : **"And he lifted his eyes upon his disciples, and said: Blessed are ye poor; for the Kingdom of God is yours"**. He was talking about the poor, not "the poor in spirit". God does not want us poor in spirit; He wants us to be spiritually rich.)

4. Blessed are they who mourn, for they will be comforted.

5. Blessed are they who are meek, for they will inherit the earth.

6. Blessed are those who hunger and thirst for righteousness, for they will be satisfied.

7. Blessed are they who show mercy, for mercies will be upon them.

8. Blessed are those who are pure in their hearts, for they shall see God.

9. Blessed are they who make peace, for they will be called the children of God.

10. Blessed are those who have been persecuted for the cause of righteousness, for theirs is the Kingdom of Heaven.

11. Blessed are you whenever they revile you and persecute you and they say every evil word against you for my sake, in falsehood.

12. Then rejoice and triumph, because your reward is great in Heaven, for just so they persecuted The Prophets who were before you.

13. You are the salt of the earth, but if salt becomes insipid, with what will it be salted? It is good for nothing except to be thrown outside and to be trodden upon by people.

14. You are the light of the world. You cannot hide a city that has been built upon a mountain.

15. And they do not light a lamp and set it under a basket, but on a lampstand, and it gives light to all those who are in the house.

16. Thus your light will shine before the children of men that they may see your good works, and may glorify your Father who is in Heaven.

17. Do not think that I have come to revoke The Written Law or The Prophets; I am not come to revoke but to fulfill.

18. Amen, I say to you that until Heaven and earth will pass away, one Yodh or one Taag and will not pass away from The Written Law until everything will happen.

19. Everyone therefore who violates one of these small commandments and will teach thus to the children of men will be called small in the Kingdom of Heaven, but everyone who will do and will teach the same will be called great in the Kingdom of Heaven.

20. For I say to you, that unless your goodness will exceed that of the Scribes and the Pharisees, you will not enter the Kingdom of Heaven.

21. You have heard that it was said to the ancients, "Do not murder, and whoever murders is condemned to judgment."

22. But I am saying to you, that everyone who will be angry against his brother without cause is condemned before the judge, and everyone who will say to his brother, 'I spit on you', is condemned before the assembly, and whoever will say 'You fool.' is condemned to the Gehenna of fire.

23. If therefore you bring your offering to the altar, and there you remember that your brother holds any grudge against you,

24. Leave your offering there before the altar and go, first be reconciled with your brother, and then come, bring your offering.

25. Be allied with your plaintiff quickly, while you are with him in the street, lest the plaintiff delivers you to the judge and the judge delivers you to the Tax Collector and you fall into prison.

26. And truly I say to you, you will not come out from there until you give the last quarter cent.

27. You have heard that it was spoken, "You shall not commit adultery."

28. But I am saying to you, everyone who looks at a woman so as to lust for her, immediately commits adultery with her in his heart.

29. But if your right eye subverts you, pluck it out and cast it from you, for it is profitable for you that your one member be lost, and not that your whole body should fall into Gehenna.

30. And if your right hand causes you to stumble, cut it off, cast it from you, for it is profitable for you that one of your members be lost, and not that your whole body fall into Gehenna.

31. It has been said, "Whoever divorces his wife, let him give her a writing of divorce."

32. But I am saying to you that everyone who divorces his wife, apart from the report of fornication, he causes her to commit adultery, and whoever takes her who is divorced is committing adultery.

33. Again you have heard that it was said to the ancients, "Do not lie in your oath, but you will fulfill to THE LORD JEHOVAH your oath."

34.But I say to you, Do not swear at all, not by Heaven, for it is the throne of God

35.Neither by the earth, for it is his stool for his feet, nor by Jerusalem, for it is the city of the great King.

36.Neither shall you swear by your head, because you cannot make in it a certain hair black or white.

37.But your statement shall be, "Yes, yes" and, "No, no"; anything more than these is from The Evil One.

38.You have heard that it was said, "An eye in exchange for an eye, and a tooth in exchange for a tooth."

39.But I am saying to you, you shall not rise up against an evil person, but whoever strikes you on your right cheek, turn to him also the other.

40.And whoever wants to sue you and take your coat, leave for him also your cloak.

41.Whoever compels you to go one mile *with him*, go with him two *miles*.

42.Whoever asks you, give to him, and whoever wants to borrow from you, do not refuse him.

43.You have heard that it was said, "Show kindness to your neighbor and hate your enemy."

44.But I say to you, love your enemies and bless the one who curses you, and do what is beautiful to the one who hates you, and pray over those who take you by force and persecute you.

45.So that you will become the children of your Father who is in Heaven, for his sun rises on the good and upon the evil and his rain descends on the just and on the unjust.

46.For if you love those who love you, what benefit is it to you? Behold, do not even the Tax Collectors the same thing?

47.And if you pray for the peace of your brethren only, what excellent thing are you doing? Behold, are not even the Tax Collectors doing the same thing?

48.Be therefore perfect, just as your Father who is in Heaven is perfect."

Chapter 6

1.Pay attention in your charity giving, that you do it not in front of people so that you may be seen by them, otherwise there is no reward for you with your Father in Heaven.

2.When therefore you do your charity giving, you should not blast a trumpet before you like the pretenders in the synagogues and in the streets, so that they may be glorified by the children of men; truly I say to you, they have received their reward.

3.But you, whenever you do charity giving, let not your left know what your right is doing.

4.So that your charity may be in secret, and your Father who sees in secret will reward you in public.

5.And when you pray, be not like the pretenders who like to stand in the synagogues and in the corners of the streets to pray, that they may be seen by the children of men, and truly I say to you, they have received their reward.

6.But you, when you pray, enter into your closet and lock your door, and pray to your father who is in secret, and your Father who sees in secret will reward you in public.

7.And whenever you are praying, you shall not be verbose like the heathen, for they think that they are heard by speaking much.

8.Therefore you shall not be like them, for your Father knows what you need before you ask him.

9.Therefore pray in this way: 'Our Father who are in Heaven, hallowed be your name,

10.Let your Kingdom come, let your will be done also in the earth, just as it is in Heaven.

11.Give us our necessary bread today.

12.And forgive us our debts, just as we also forgive our debtors.

13.And lead us not to temptation but deliver us from evil, for yours is the Kingdom and the power and the glory, for the eternity of eternities.'

14.For if you forgive the children of men their faults, your Father who is in Heaven will also forgive you your faults.

15.But if you will not forgive the children of men, neither has your Father forgiven you your faults.

16.And when you are fasting, do not be gloomy like the pretenders, for they disfigure their faces, so that they may appear to the children of men to fast, and truly I say to you, that they have received their reward.

17.But you whenever you fast, wash your face and anoint your head.

18.So that you may not appear to the children of men to be fasting, but to your Father who is in secret, and your Father who sees in secret will reward you.

19.Do not place treasures for yourselves on the earth, where moths and corrosion disfigure and where thieves break in and steal.

20.But place treasures for yourselves in Heaven, where neither moths nor corrosion disfigure and where thieves neither break in nor steal.

21.For where your treasure is, there is your heart also.

22.But the lamp of the body is the eye; therefore if your eye shall be sound, your whole body also will be illuminated.

23.But if your eye shall be bad, your entire body will be darkness; if therefore the light that is in you is darkness, how great will be your darkness!

24.No man can work for two masters, for either he will hate one and will love the other, or he will honor one and the other he will ignore. You cannot work for God and for money.

25.Because of this I say to you, you shall not take pains for yourselves with what you will eat, or what you will drink, neither for your body, what you will put on; behold, is not the soul greater than food, and the body than clothing?

26.Behold the birds of the sky, that they neither sow nor reap, neither do they gather into barns, and your Father who is in Heaven sustains them; behold, are you not better than they?

27.But who of you, while taking pains, is able to add a foot and a half to his stature?

28.And why are you taking pains about clothing? Consider the lilies of the field, how they grow without laboring or weaving.

29.But I say to you, not even Solomon in all his glory was clothed like one of these.

30.But if God so clothes the grass of the field that is today and will fall into the oven tomorrow, does he not multiply more to you, Oh small of faith?

31.Therefore do not be concerned or say, "What will we eat?' , or "What will we drink?', or ,"What will we wear'?

32.For the Gentiles are seeking all these things, but your Father who is in Heaven knows that all these things are necessary for you.

33.But seek first the Kingdom of God and his righteousness, and all these things will be added to you.

34.Therefore you shall not be concerned about tomorrow, for tomorrow will be concerned for itself. A day's own trouble is sufficient for it.

Chapter 7

1. You shall not judge, lest you be judged.

2. For with the judgment that you judge, you will be judged, and with the measure that you measure, it will be measured to you.

3. Why do you notice a chip that is in your brother's eye, and you do not observe the plank that is in your own eye?

4. Or how do you say to your brother, 'Let me cast out the chip from your eye', and behold, a plank is in your eye?

5. Hypocrite! First cast out the plank from your eye, and then you will see to cast out the chip from your brother's eye.

6. Do not give a sacrifice to dogs; neither throw your pearls before wild boars, lest they trample them with their feet, and return to run you through.

7. Ask and it will be given to you, seek and you will find, knock, and it will be opened to you.

8. For everyone who asks receives, and he who seeks finds, and to him who knocks it is opened.

9. And who is the man among you whose son will ask him for bread *and* will hand him a stone?

10. And if he will ask him for a fish, will he hand him a snake?

11. If therefore you who are evil know to give good gifts to your children, how much more will your Father who is in Heaven give good things to those who ask him?

12. Everything whatsoever you desire that people should do for you, do likewise for them, for this is the Law and The Prophets.

13. Enter the narrow gate, for the gate is wide and the road is spacious which leads to destruction, and many are those who are going in it.

14. How narrow is the gate and strict the way that leads to life, and few are those who find it!

15. Beware of false Prophets who come to you in lambs' clothing, but from within they are plundering wolves.

16. But by their fruit you will know them. Do they gather grapes from thorns or figs from thistles?

17. So every good tree produces good fruit, but a bad tree produces bad fruit.

18. A good tree is not able to produce bad fruit, neither a bad tree to produce good fruit.

19. Every tree that does not produce good fruit is cut down and falls into the fire.

20. Therefore by their fruit you will know them.

21. It is not everyone that says to me, 'My Lord, my Lord", who enters the Kingdom of Heaven, but whoever does the will of my Father who is in Heaven.

22. Many will say to me in that day, 'My Lord, my Lord, have we not prophesied in your name, and in your name have cast out demons, and have done many mighty works in your name?'

23. And then I will confess to them, 'I have never known you, remove yourselves far from me, you workers of evil.'

24. Everyone therefore who hears these my words, and does them, will be likened to the wise man who built his house on solid rock.

25. And the rain descended and the floods came and the wind blew, and they rushed against the house and it did not fall, for its foundation was laid on solid rock.

26. And everyone who hears these my words, but does not practice them, will be likened to the foolish man who built his house on sand.

27. And the rain descended and the floods came, and the wind blew, and they rushed against that house, and it fell, and its fall was great."

28. And when Yeshua had finished these words, the crowds were marveling at his teaching.

29. For he was teaching them as one having authority and not as their Scribes and the Pharisees.

Chapter 8

1. But when he came down from the mountain, great crowds followed him.

2. And behold a certain leper came worshiping him, and he said, "My lord, if you are willing, you are able to purify me."

3. And Yeshua, stretching out his hand, touched him, and he said, "I am willing. Be purified", and at that moment his leprosy was purged.

4. And Yeshua said to him, "Take heed that you speak to no one, but go show yourself to the priest and bring a gift as Moses commanded for their testimony.

5. But when Yeshua entered Kapernahum, a certain Centurion approached him and he prayed to him.

6. And he said, "My Lord, my boy is lying in the house and is paralyzed and he is badly tormented."

7. Yeshua said to him, "I shall come and heal him."

8. That Centurion answered and said, "My lord, I am not worthy that you should enter under my roof, but only say in a word and my boy will be healed."

9. "I also am a man under authority and soldiers are under my hand, and I say to this one, 'Go', and he goes, and to another, 'Come', and he comes, and to my servant, 'Do this', and he does."

10. But when Yeshua heard, he was amazed, and he said to them that came with him, "Truly I say to you, that not even in Israel have I found faith like this."

11. "But I say to you, that many will come from The East and from The West and will recline with Abraham and Isaaq and Jaqob in the Kingdom of Heaven."

12. But the children of the Kingdom will be cast out to outer darkness; there will be weeping and gnashing of teeth."

13. And Yeshua said to that Centurion, "Go, it will be done for you just as you have believed", and his boy was healed at that moment.

14. And Yeshua came to Shimeon's house, and he saw his mother-in-law who lay, and a fever had seized her.

15. And he touched her hand, and the fever left her, and she arose and she was waiting on him.

16. But when it was evening, they brought many demon possessed before him, and he cast their demons out with a word, and all those who had become ill, and he healed them.

17. So that would be fulfilled which was said by Isaiah the Prophet, who said: "He will take our pains and he will bear our sicknesses."

18. But when Yeshua saw the great crowds surrounding him, he ordered that they go to the shore.

19. One scribe came near and said to him, "Rabbi, I shall come after you, wherever you go."

20. Yeshua said to him, "Foxes have lairs and birds of the sky have shelters, but The Son of Man has nowhere to lay his head."

21. But another of his disciples said to him, "My Lord, allow me to first go bury my Father."

22. But Yeshua said to him, "Come after me and let the dead bury their dead."

23. And when Yeshua came up into the ship, his disciples came up with him.

24. And behold, a great earthquake occurred in the sea, so that the galley would be covered from the waves, but Yeshua was asleep.

25. And his disciples approached to awaken him and they were saying to him, "Our Lord, save us, we are being destroyed!"

26. And Yeshua said to them, "Why are you afraid, you small of faith?" Then he arose and rebuked the wind and the sea, and there was a great calm.

27. But the men were shocked and were saying, "Who is this, that the wind and the sea obey him?"

28. And when Yeshua came to the other side to the region of the Gadarenes, two demoniacs met him, who came out from the graveyard, extremely evil, so that no man could pass on that road.

29. And they cried out and they were saying, "What do we have to do with you, Yeshua, Son of God? Have you come here before the time to punish us?"

30. But there was distant from them a herd of many pigs grazing.

31. But those demons were begging him and saying, "If you cast us out, allow us to go into the herd of pigs."

32. And Yeshua said to them, "Go", and at once they came out and they entered into the pigs. And that whole herd went straight over the cliff and fell into the sea and died in the water.

33. But those who had been herding them fled and went to the city and revealed everything that had happened and about the demoniacs.

34. And the whole city came out to meet with Yeshua, and when they saw him, they begged him to depart from their borders.

Chapter 9

1. And going up into the ship and crossing over he came to his city.

2. And they brought him a paralytic as he lay in the pallet, and Yeshua saw their faith, and he said to the paralytic, "Take heart my son, your sins are forgiven you."

3. But some of the Scribes said among themselves, "This man blasphemes."

4. But Yeshua knew their thinking, and he said to them, "Why do you think evil things in your heart?"

5. "For which is easier, to say, "Your sins are forgiven you", or to say, "Arise and walk?"

6. But that you may know that The Son of Man has authority in the earth to forgive sins, I say to this paralytic, "Stand up, take your pallet and go to your house."

7. And he stood up and he went to his house.

8. But when those crowds saw, they were awestruck, and they glorified God who gave authority like this to the children of men.

9. And when Yeshua passed by from there, he saw a man sitting at a tax collection booth, whose name was Mattay, and he said to him, "Come after me", and rising, he went after him.

10. And when they reclined in the house, tax gatherers and many sinners came, and they reclined to eat with Yeshua and with his disciples.

11. And when the Pharisees saw, they were saying to his disciples, "Why does your master eat with Tax Collectors and sinners?"

12. But when Yeshua heard, he said to them, "The healthy do not need a doctor, but those who have become ill."

13. "Go learn what this says, 'I require mercy and not a sacrifice', for I have not come to call the righteous but sinners."

14. Then the disciples of Yohannan approached him, and they were saying, "Why are we and the Pharisees fasting much, and your disciples are not fasting?"

15. And Yeshua said to them, "How can the children of the bridal chamber fast as long as the groom is with them? But the days are coming when the groom will be taken from them and then they will fast."

16. "No man places of new patch of cloth on an old coat, lest its fulness tears from that coat, and the rip would be greater."

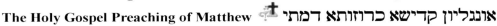
17."Neither do they put new wine in old wineskins, lest the wineskins burst and the wine is spilled and the wineskins are destroyed; but they put new wine in new wineskins, and both are preserved."

18.But as he was speaking these things with them, a certain ruler approached, bowing to him, and he said, "My daughter is dying * even now, but come, lay your hand on her, and she will live." * (Greek has, "is dead"; Aramaic can mean "is dying"; see Mark 5:22,23 & Luke 8:41,42)

19.But Yeshua arose and his disciples and they went after him.

20.And behold a woman who had a flow of blood for twelve years, came from behind him and she touched the hem of his garment.

21.For she was saying in herself, "If only I may touch his clothes, I shall be healed."

22.But Yeshua turned, and saw her, and he said to her, "Take heart my daughter, your faith has saved you." And the woman was healed from that moment.

23.And Yeshua came to the house of the ruler, and he saw chanters and a crowd that was upset.

24.And he said to them. "Get out, for the girl is not dead, but she is asleep", and they were laughing at him.

25.And when he had sent the crowd out, he entered, he took her by her hand, and the girl arose.

26.And this report went out into all that land.

27.And when Yeshua passed from there, two blind men followed him who cried out and they were saying, "Have pity on us, son of David."

28.But when he had come to the house, those blind men came near to him; Yeshua said to them, "Do you believe that I am able to do this?" They were saying to him, "Yes, Our Lord."

29.Then he touched their eyes, and he said, "Just as you have believed, let it be done to you."

30.And at once their eyes were opened and Yeshua admonished them and he said, "See that no man will know it."

31.But they went forth and they announced it in all that area.

32.And when Yeshua went out, they brought to him a deaf mute who had a demon upon him.

33.And when the demon went forth, that deaf-mute spoke, and the crowds were astonished, and they were saying, "Never has it been seen thus in Israel."

34.But the Pharisees were saying, "By the prince of demons he casts out demons."

35.And Yeshua was traveling about in all the cities and in the villages and he was teaching in their assemblies and preaching The Gospel of the Kingdom and was healing all diseases and all ailments.

36.But when Yeshua saw the crowds, he felt pity for them, for they were weary and wandering, like sheep without a shepherd.

37.And he said to his disciples, "The harvest is great, and the labourers are few."

38."Request therefore of The Lord of the harvest to send out laborers to his harvest."

Chapter 10

1. And he called his twelve disciples and he gave them authority over foul spirits to cast them out, and to heal every ailment and disease.

2. But the names of the twelve Apostles were these: the first of them, Shimeon who was called Kaypha, and Andraeus his brother, and Yaqob Bar Zebedee, and Yohannan his brother,

3. And Philippus, Bar Tolmay, and Thoma, and Mattay the Tax Collector, and Yaqob Bar Halphi, and Lebai who was called Thadi,

4. And Shimeon The Zealot, and Yehuda Skariota, he who betrayed him.

5. These twelve Yeshua sent and he commanded them and he said, "You shall not go by a road of the heathen and you shall not enter a city of the Samaritans."

6. "But go especially to the sheep that have been lost of the house of Israel."

7. "And as you are going, preach and say "The Kingdom of Heaven has come near."

8. "Heal the sick, purify the lepers and cast out demons; freely you have received, freely give."

9. "You shall not retain gold, neither silver, nor copper in your moneybags,"

10."Neither wallet for the way, nor two coats, neither shoes, nor staff, for a laborer is worthy of his provisions."

11."Whichever city or village you enter, ask who is worthy in it and stay there until you leave."

12. "And when you enter a household, invoke the peace of the household."

13. "And if that household is worthy, your blessing of peace will come upon it, but if not, your blessing of peace will return unto you."

14. "But whoever does not receive you, neither listens to your words, when you depart from the house or from the village, shake the sand from your feet."

15. "And truly I say to you, it will be tranquil in the day of judgment for the land of Sadom and Ammora compared to that city."

16. "Behold, I am sending you as lambs among wolves; be therefore crafty as snakes and innocent as doves."

17. "But beware of the children of men, for they will deliver you to the courts and they will scourge you in their synagogues."

18. "And they will bring you before Governors and Kings because of me, for their testimony and that of the Gentiles."

19. "But when they arrest you, do not be anxious how or what you will speak, for it will be given to you in that hour what you should say."

20. "For it will not be you speaking, but The Spirit of your Father speaking in you."

21. "But brother will deliver his brother to death, and a father his son, and children will rise against their parents and will put them to death."

22. "And you will be hated by everyone because of my name, but whoever will endure until the end, he will be saved."

23. "But when they persecute you in this city, flee to another, for truly I say to you, you will not have finished all the cities of the house of Israel until The Son of Man come."

24. "No disciple is greater than his master, neither a servant than his lord."

25. "It is enough for a discile to be like his master and for a servant to be like his lord. If they have called the lord of the house Beelzebub, how much more the children of his household?"

26. "Therefore you shall not be afraid of them, for there is nothing covered that will not be revealed, and hidden, that will not be known."

27. "Whatever I tell you in the darkness, say it in the light, and whatever you hear with your ears, preach on the rooftops."

28. "And you shall not be afraid of those who kill the body that are not able to kill the soul; rather be afraid of him who can destroy soul and body in Gehenna."

29. "Are not two sparrows sold for a penny, and not one of them falls to the ground apart from your Father?"

30. "But your hairs of your head are all numbered."

31. "You shall not be afraid, therefore; you are better than many sparrows."

32. "Everyone, therefore, who will confess me before children of men, I shall confess him also before my Father who is in Heaven.

33. But whoever will deny me before the children of men, I shall deny him also before my Father who is in Heaven.

34. Think not that I have come to bring peace in the earth; I have not come to bring peace, but a sword.

35. I have come to divide a man against his father and a daughter against her mother and a daughter-in-law against her mother-in-law,

36. And a man's enemies will be the members of his household.

37. Whoever loves father or mother more than me is not worthy of me; and whoever loves son or daughter more than me is not worthy of me.

38. And everyone who does not take his cross and come after me is not worthy of me.

39. Whoever will lose his life for my sake will find it; whoever will find his life will lose it.

40. Whoever receives you receives me, and whoever receives me receives him who sent me.

41. Whoever receives a Prophet in the name of a Prophet receives the reward of the Prophet, and whoever receives The Righteous One in the name of The Righteous One receives the reward of The Righteous One.

42. "And everyone who gives one of these little ones a cup of cold water only to drink, in the name of a disciple, amen, I say to you, he will not lose his reward."

Chapter 11

1. So it was that when Yeshua had finished charging his twelve disciples he moved from there to teach and to preach in their cities.

2. But when Yohannan had heard in prison of the works of The Messiah, he sent by his disciples,

3. And he said to him, "Are you he who comes, or is it another we expect?"

4. Yeshua answered and he said to them, "Go relate to Yohannan those things that you hear and see."

5. "Those who were blind see, and those who were lame walk, and lepers are being purified, and those once deaf are hearing, and those who died are rising and those who were poor are given The Good News."

A series of participles (except for "The lepers") is used to describe those who experienced miracles; the participle can describe past, present or future condition. I choose to use the past tense to describe each subject, otherwise we have Our Lord stating nonsense: "The blind see", "The deaf hear","The dead rise." The Greek text has not the flexibility of the Aramaic here. Simple nouns are used: "The blind", "The lame", "The deaf", "The dead", "The poor." See Luke 7:22 Also.

6. "And blessed is he who will not be suspicious of me."

7. But when they departed, Yeshua began to say to the crowds about Yohannan, "What did you go out to the wilderness to see, a reed shaken by the wind?"

8. "Otherwise, what did you go out to see; a man who wears a long soft robe? Behold those who wear soft things are in the house of the King."

9. "Otherwise what did you go out to see? A Prophet? Yes, I say to you, and more than a Prophet."

10. "For this is he about whom it is written: 'Behold, I am sending my messenger before your presence that he may prepare the road before you.' "

11. "Amen, I say to you, that among them born of women there has not arisen a greater than Yohannan The Baptizer, but a little one in the Kingdom of Heaven is greater than he."

12. "From the days of Yohannan The Baptizer until this hour the Kingdom of Heaven is led by force and the violent are seizing it."

13. "All The Prophets and The Written Law have prophesied until Yohannan.

14. And if you will, he is Elijah who was to come.

15. Whoever has an ear to hear, let him hear.

16. But to what shall I liken this generation? It is like children sitting in the street and calling their playmates,

17. And saying, 'We sang to you, and you did not dance, and we cried for you, and you were not sad.'

18. For Yohannan came who ate nothing and drank nothing, and they said: 'He has a demon.'

19. The Son of Man came eating and drinking and they said, 'Behold the man is a glutton and a wine drinker, a friend of Tax Collectors and of sinners.' And wisdom is justified by its works*."

• The Greek has two readings: The Majority of mss. have, "**Works**" and the Critical Text (2 mss.) has **Children**". עבדיה can mean either "**Works**" or "**Servant**". The Greek word "**Teknon**"("Child") can refer to a disciple or pupil as well:

5043 τεκνον teknon tek'-non
    from the base of 5098; TDNT-5:636,759; n n
    AV-child 77, son 21, daughter 1; 99
1.   offspring, children
    1a) child
1a) a male child, a son
1b) metaph.
1b1) the name transferred to that intimate and reciprocal relationship formed between men by the bonds of love, friendship, trust, just as between parents and children
1b2) in affectionate address, such as patrons, helpers, teachers and the like employ: my child
1b3) in the NT, **pupils or disciples are called children of their teachers**, because the latter by their instruction nourish the minds of their pupils and mould their characters
1b4) children of God: in the OT of "the people of Israel" as especially dear to God, in the NT, in Paul's writings, all who are led by the Spirit of God and thus closely related to God
1b5) children of the devil: those who in thought and action are prompted by the devil, and so reflect his character
1c) metaph.
1c1) of anything who depends upon it, is possessed by a desire or affection for it, is addicted to it
1c2) one who is liable to any fate
1c2a) thus children of a city: its citizens and inhabitants
1c3) **the votaries (adherents) of wisdom**, those souls who have, as it were, been nurtured and moulded by wisdom
1c4) cursed children, exposed to a curse and doomed to God's wrath or penalty
For Synonyms see entry 5868 & 5943 .

One Greek synonym is Παις-"Pais":
3816 παις pais pahece
perhaps from 3817; TDNT-5:636,759; n m/f

AV-servant 10, child 7, son (Christ) 2, son 1, manservant 1, maid 1, maiden 1, young man 1; 24
i.   a child, boy or girl
1a) infants, children
2) servant, slave
2a) an attendant, servant, spec. a King's attendant, minister

Since the Aramaic עבדיה can mean servant, a Greek translator may easily use a Greek synonym such as "**teknon**" to translate it. Codices Alep and B have "**ergown**"-"Works", which also can be the meaning of עבדיה. The Peshitta can explain the origin of both Greek readings and why two readings exist. These kinds of **split spin-off** readings in Greek that match dual or multiple Aramaic word meanings in The Peshitta are fairly common. We do not find the opposite phenomenon, however. The Peshitta mss. do not have such variant readings. Indeed, The Peshitta mss. have practically no variant readings of significance to mention, except in approximately ten places in the entire NT ! There is also no Greek type that regularly agrees with The Peshitta. In one place the Critical Text of Vaticanus and Sinaiticus may favor it and in the next verse, The Majority text. And the results will alternate. Often The Peshitta will disagree with all Greek readings. This is a highly unlikely scenario if The Peshitta is a translation of the Greek NT. It is a natural result of and easily explained by an original Peshitta NT and Greek translation of that original.

20. Then Yeshua began to reproach those cities in which his many mighty works had occurred, and they did not repent.

21. And he said, "Woe to you Chorazin, woe to you Bythsaida, for if those powerful works which have occurred in you had occurred in Tsur and Tsidon, they doubtless would have repented in sackcloth and in ashes.

22. Yet I say to you, that for Tsur and for Tsidon it will be tranquil in the day of judgment compared to you.

23. And you Kapernahum, which have been exalted unto Heaven, you will descend unto Sheol, for if the mighty works had been done in Sadom, which have been done in you, it would have remained until today.

24. But I say to you, it will be tranquil for the land of Sadom in the Day of Judgment compared to you."

25. At that time Yeshua answered and said, "I thank you my Father, Lord of Heaven and Earth, that you have hidden these things from the wise and the intelligent and you have revealed them to infants.

26. Yes, my Father, for so it was desirable before you.

27. Everything has been given up to me by my Father and no man knows The Son except The Father only; also no man knows The Father except The Son only, and he to whom The Son desires to reveal him.

28. Come unto me, all of you who labor and are forced to bear burdens, and I shall give you rest.

29. Take my yoke upon you and learn from me, for I am peaceful and meek in my heart and you will find rest for your souls.

30. For my yoke is pleasant and my burden is light."

Chapter 12

1. At that time Yeshua was walking on the Sabbath in the grainfields, and his disciples were hungry and they began plucking the ears of grain and they were eating.

2. But when the Pharisees saw them, they were saying to him, "Behold, your disciples are doing something that is illegal to do on the Sabbath."

3. But he said to them, "Have you not read what David did when he was hungry and those who were with him?

4. How he entered the house of God, and he ate the bread of the table of THE LORD JEHOVAH, that which was not legal for him to eat, neither for those who were with him, but rather for the priests only?

5. Or have you not read in The Written Law that the priests in The Temple profane the Sabbath and are blameless?

6. But I say to you, one greater than The Temple is here.

7. But if you had known what this is, 'I want mercy and not a sacrifice', you would not have condemned those who are blameless.

8. For The Son of Man is Master of the Sabbath."

9. And Yeshua departed from there and he came to their synagogue.

10. One man was there whose hand was withered, and they were asking him, and they were saying, "Is it legal To heal on the Sabbath", so that They might accuse him.

11. He said to them, "Who is the man among you who has one sheep, and if it falls into a pit on the Sabbath day, will not take hold and lift it out?"

12. "How much greater is a man than a sheep? Therefore it is legal to do good on the Sabbath."

13. And then he said to that man, "Stretch out your hand", and he stretched out his hand and it was restored like his other.

14. And the Pharisees went out and they took council against him so that they might destroy him.

15. But Yeshua knew, and he moved from there, and great crowds went after him and he healed all of them.

16. And he warned them that they should not reveal him.

17. That the thing would be fulfilled that was spoken by Isaiah the Prophet which says:

18. "Behold, my servant, in whom I delight, my beloved, for whom my soul has longed, I shall put my Spirit upon him, and he will preach judgment to the nations.

19. He will not dispute neither will he cry out, nor will a man hear his voice in the streets.

20. He will not break off a fractured reed, and the lamp that flickers he will not extinguish until he will bring the verdict of innocence,

21. And in his name the nations will hope."

22. But then they brought to him a certain demoniac, mute and blind, and he healed him so that the mute and blind man could speak and could see.

23. And all the crowds were astounded and they were saying, "Is this not The Son of David?"

24. But the Pharisees, when they heard, they were saying, "This one does not cast out demons except by Beelzebub the prince of demons."

25. But Yeshua knew their designs, and he said to them, "Every Kingdom that is divided against itself will be destroyed and every house and city that is divided against itself will not stand.

26. And if Satan casts out Satan, he has been divided against himself; how therefore will his Kingdom stand?

27. And if I am casting out demons by Beelzebub, by whom do your sons cast them out? Therefore they will be your judges.

28. And if I am casting out demons by The Spirit of God, the Kingdom of God has come near to you.

29. For how can a man enter the house of the mighty man and plunder his goods unless first he bind the mighty man? Then he may plunder his house.

30. Whoever is not with me is against me; whoever does not gather with me truly is scattering.

31. Therefore I say to you, all sins and blasphemies will be forgiven to the children of men, but the blasphemy that is against The Spirit will not be forgiven to the children of men.

32. Everyone who will say a word against The Son of Man, it will be forgiven him, but whoever will speak against The Spirit of Holiness, it will not be forgiven to him, not in this world, neither in the world that is being prepared.

33. Either make the tree good and its fruit good or make the tree bad and its fruit bad, for the tree is known by its fruit.

34. Offspring of vipers! How can you who are evil speak good things? For from the fulness of the heart the mouth speaks.

35. A good man from a good treasure brings good things, and an evil man from evil treasure brings evil things.

36. For I say to you that every idle word that people will speak, they will give an answer for it in the day of judgment.

37. For by your words you will be justified and by your words you will be condemned."

38. Then some of the Scribes and Pharisees responded and they were saying to him, "Teacher we wish to see a sign from you."

39. But he answered and said to them, "An evil and adulterous generation seeks a sign and a sign will not be given to it except the sign of Jonah the Prophet.

40. For just as Jonah was in the belly of the fish three days and three nights, thus The Son of Man will be in the heart of the earth three days and three nights.

41. The Ninevite men will arise in the judgment with this generation and will condemn it, for they repented at the preaching of Jonah, and behold, one greater than Jonah is here.

42. The queen of The South will arise in the judgment with this generation and will condemn it, for she came from the ends of the earth to hear the wisdom of Solomon, and behold, one greater than Solomon is here.

43. But whenever a foul spirit goes out from a man, it wanders about in places without water in them, and it seeks rest and does not find it.

44. Then it says, 'I shall return to my house from where I came out', and it goes finding that it is empty, swept and decorated.

45. Then it goes bringing with it seven other spirits worse than itself, and they enter and dwell there, and the end of that man becomes worse than his beginning. Thus will it be done to this evil generation."

46. But while he was speaking to the crowds, his mother and his brothers came standing outside and desired to speak with him.

47. And a man said to him, "Behold, your mother and your brothers are standing outside and want to speak with you."

48. But he answered and said to him who told him, "Who is my mother and who are my brothers?"

49. And he stretched his hands toward his disciples and said, "Behold my mother and behold my brothers!"

50. "For everyone who does the will of my Father who is in Heaven, the same is my brother and my sister and my mother."

Chapter 13

1. **But** that day Yeshua went out from the house and he sat down by the seaside.

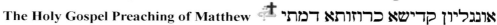
2. And great crowds were assembled to him so that he embarked, seating himself in a ship, and all the crowds were standing on the beach by the sea.

3. And he was speaking much with them in parables and he said, "Behold, a sower went out to sow.

4. But as he sowed, some *seed* fell on the side of the road and a bird came and ate it.

5. And others fell on the rock where there was not much soil, and within the hour it sprouted because there was no depth of soil.

6. But when the sun rose, it became hot, and because there were no roots, it dried up.

7. And others fell among the thorns and the thorns came up and choked it.

8. And others fell in the good soil and it yielded fruit, some a hundredfold and some sixtyfold and some thirtyfold.

9. Whoever has an ear that hears, let him hear."

10. And his disciples approached and they were saying to him, "Why are you speaking with them in parables?"

11. But he answered and said to them: "It has been given to you to know the secrets of the Kingdom of Heaven, but to them it has not been given.

12. For to one who has it, it will be given, and it will be increased.

13. And from him who has it not, will be taken even that which he has, therefore I am speaking to them in parables because they who see do not see, and those who hear neither hear nor understand.

14. And the prophecy of Isaiah is fulfilled in them, which says, 'Hearing you will hear, and you will not understand, and seeing you will see and you will not know.

15. For the heart of this people has become dense, and they have hardly heard with their ears and their eyes they have shut, lest they would see with their eyes and they would hear with their ears and they would understand in their hearts and they would be converted and I would heal them.'

16. But you have blessings to your eyes, for they are seeing, and to your ears, for they are hearing.

17. For I say to you that many Prophets and righteous ones have yearned to see the things that you are seeing and they did not see them, and to hear the things that you are hearing, and they did not hear them.

18. But hear the parable of the seed.

19. Everyone who hears the word of the Kingdom and does not understand, The Evil One comes into him and snatches the word that was sown in his heart; this is that which was sown upon the roadside.

20. But that which was sown upon the rock is the one who hears the word, and immediately with joy he receives it.

21. But there are no roots in him, but he is temporal, and when there is distress or persecution because of the word, immediately he falls apart.

22. That which was sown among the thorns is the one who hears the word, and the cares of this world and the deception of wealth choke the word, and that one is fruitless.

23. But that which was sown on the good soil is he who hears my word and understands and he yields fruit, and produces some by the hundreds and some by sixty's and some by thirty's."

24. He told them another parable and he said, "The Kingdom of Heaven is likened to the man who sowed good seed in his field.

25. And while men slept, his enemy came and sowed tares among the wheat, and he left.

26. But when the grass sprouted it produced fruit; then the tares also appeared.

27. And the servants of the lord of the house approached and said to him, 'Our Lord, did you not sow good seed in your field? From where are the tares in it?'

28. But he said to them, 'An enemy has done this'; his servants said to him, 'Do you want us to go select them out?'

29. But he said to them, 'When you collect the tares, would you not uproot the wheat with them?'

30. 'Let both grow together until the harvest, and in the time of the harvest, I shall say to the reapers, "Select out the tares first and bind them into bundles to burn, but gather the wheat to my granary."'

31. He told another parable to them and said, "The Kingdom of Heaven is likened to a grain of mustard seed which a man had taken and sown in his field.

32. And this is the smallest of all seeds, but whenever it has grown, it is greatest of all small herbs and it becomes a tree so that the birds of the sky may come settle in its branches."

33. He told them another parable: "The Kingdom of Heaven is likened to yeast which

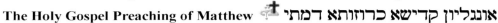
a woman took and hid in three measures of meal until all of it had fermented."

34. Yeshua spoke all these things in parables to the crowds and without a parable he was not speaking with them.

35. So that the thing that was spoken by the Prophet would be fulfilled which says, "I shall open my mouth in parables and I shall declare things hidden from before the foundation of the world."

36. Then Yeshua left the crowds and came to the house and his disciples came to him and they were saying to him, "Explain to us that parable of the tares and of the field."

37. But he answered and said to them, "He who sowed the good seed is The Son of Man.

38. The field is the world but the good seed is the children of the Kingdom and the tares are the children of The Evil One.

39. The enemy who sowed them is Satan, but the harvest is the end of the world and the reapers are the Angels.

40. Therefore, just as the tares are gathered and burn in the fire, so it will be in the end of this world.

41. The Son of Man will send his Angels and they will select from his Kingdom all of those stumbling blocks and all of those evil doers.

42. And they will cast them into the essence of fire; there will be weeping and gnashing of teeth.

"Athuna" can mean, "A furnace"; It can also mean "the essence of a thing". The latter seems more fitting, since Our Lord spoke of eternal realities, not temporal. A furnace is merely an earthly type for an eternal reality, as is earthly fire. Eternal fire is more real than earthly fire, and is the reality behind it. Paul writes later, "Our God is a consuming fire." Jastrow's Dictionary gives the following entry for this Aramaic word, with an example from The Targum of Proverbs 20:20.

אַתּוּנָא (אַתּוּנָא, אֲתוּנָא, Ms. אַתּוּנָא) m. (v. preced.,=h. אִישׁוּן) density, intensiveness, essence. Targ. Prov. XX, 20 אֲרִיךְ אֵי חֲשׁוֹכָא as darkness itself (h. text בָּאישׁוּן with בּ). Cmp. אֲרִיךָן.

43. Then the righteous will shine as the sun in the Kingdom of their Father. Whoever has an ear that will hear, let him hear.

44. Again the Kingdom of Heaven is likened to treasure that was hidden in a field which a man found and hid, and for his joy he went selling everything that he had and he bought that field.

45. But again the Kingdom of Heaven is likened to the merchant man who was searching for precious pearls.

46. But when he found a certain obviously valuable pearl, he went and sold everything he had and bought it.

47. Again the Kingdom of Heaven is like a net that was cast into the sea, and it collected from every kind.

48. But when it was full they brought it up to the seashore, and they sat and selected out and they placed the good in vessels and the bad they threw out.

49. Thus it will be in the end of the world. The Angels will go forth and they will separate the wicked from among the righteous.

50. And they will cast them into the essence of fire; there will be weeping and gnashing of teeth.

51. Yeshua said to them, "Have you understood all these things?" They were saying to him, "Yes, Our Lord."

52. He said to them, "And because of this, every scribe who is instructed for the Kingdom of Heaven is like the man, a house owner, who brings from his treasure new and old things."

53. And it was that when Yeshua had finished these parables, he departed from there.

54. And he came to his city and he taught them in their synagogues so that they would marvel and they would say, "From where does he have this wisdom and the miracles?"

55. "Is not this the carpenter's son? Is not his mother called Maryam, and his brothers, Yaqob and Yose and Shimeon and Yehudah?"

56. "And are not all his sisters with us? From where does he have all these things?"

57. And they were suspicious of him; but Yeshua said to them, "There is no Prophet who is despised except in his city and in his home."

58. And he did not do many miracles there because of their suspicion.

Chapter 14

1. But at that time Herodus the Tetrarch heard of the fame of Yeshua.

2. And he said to his servants, "This is Yohannan The Baptizer; but he has arisen from the grave, therefore miracles are done by him."

3. For Herodus had seized Yohannan and bound him and cast him into prison because of Herodia the wife of Philippus his brother.

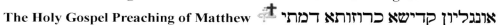
4. For Yohannan had said to him, "It is not lawful that she should be your wife."

5. And he had wanted to kill him and he was afraid of the people who were holding him as a Prophet.

6. But when Herodus' birthday came, Herodia danced before the dinner guests and she pleased Herodus.

7. Because of this, he swore an oath to her that he would give her anything that she would ask.

8. But because she had been instructed by her mother, she had said, "Give me here in a dish the head of Yohannan The Baptizer."

9. And it saddened the King, but because of the oath and the guests, he commanded that it be given to her.

10. And he sent, cutting off the head of Yohannan in the prison.

11. And his head was brought in a dish and it was given to the girl and she brought it to her mother.

12. And his disciples came, took his corpse*, performed a burial and came and informed Yeshua.

* Greek mss. B-Vaticanus (4th cent.) & א (4th cent.) have πτωμα- "Corpse"; The Majority Greek text (most mss.) have σωμα-"Body". Here are the Aramaic words "Shlada"(Corpse) and "Pagra"(Body) in Aramaic characters : שלדא , פגרא . In Estrangela, they are: ܫܠܕܐ , ܦܓܪܐ. Either one Greek translator mistook "Shlada" for "Pagra", or we have a case of split meanings of an Aramaic word , "Shlada" , being translated "Corpse" by one Greek translator and "Body" by another; It can have either meaning. Mark 15:45 has the same word split phenomenon in the Greek texts with Aramaic word Pagra!There, the Critical text of Westcott and Hort has πτωμα- "Corpse"& The Majority text has σωμα-"Body", as in this verse !

13. But when Yeshua heard, he departed from there by ship to a desert region alone, and when the crowds heard, they went after him by land from the cities.

14. And Yeshua came down, seeing the great crowds, and he was moved with pity for them and he healed their sick.

15. When it was evening, his disciples came to join him and they said to him, "This is a desert place and the time is late. Dismiss the crowds of people so they will go to the villages and buy food for themselves."

16. But he said to them, "It is not necessary for them to go. You give them to eat."

17. But they said to him, "There is nothing here with us but five loaves and two fish."

18. But Yeshua said to them, "Bring them here to me."

19. And he commanded the crowds to recline on the ground and he took those five loaves and two fish and he gazed into Heaven and he blessed and he broke and he gave to his disciples and the disciples placed those things before the crowds.

20. And they all ate and were satisfied and they collected the remainder of the fragments twelve baskets full.

21. But those men who ate were 5,000, apart from the women and children.

22. And at once he compelled his disciples to embark the ship and to go before him to the other side while he sent the crowds away.

23. And when he had sent the crowds away, he went up to a mountain alone to pray and when it was dark he was there alone.

24. And the ship was many furlongs distant from the land while it was tossed greatly by the waves, for the wind was against it.

I am going to display the first line of The Peshitta verse here in Ashuri Aramaic on top and ancient Aramaic script used in the Dead Sea Scrolls 2100 years ago underneath it:

Ashuri: (land) ארעא (from) מן (it was) הות
Dead Sea Scroll: ארעא מן הות
(distant) רחיקא (& the ship) ואלפא
ואלפ א רחיקא
Ashuri: (many) סגיאא (furlongs) אסטדיותא
Dead Sea Scroll: סגיאא אסטיותא

Most Greek mss. omit "many furlongs" and have "was in the midst of the sea". A few, like Vaticanus and Beza, agree with The Peshitta here. The Peshitta does not conform to any particular Greek text type , in fact, often it disagrees with all Greek readings. This controverts the Greek primacy theory and is explained by Greek translation of The Peshitta. The different Greek text types are simply different translation versions of The Peshitta. Greek can in no wise do justice to Aramaic word meanings and idioms with just one translation of such a pregnant language and text. Either The Peshitta is edited and selected **from all Greek readings and text types and many unique non-Greek readings**, or the converse is true,i.e.-All Greek text-types are spin offs of this original Aramaic Parent Text. The evidence overwhelmingly supports the latter and refutes the former proposition.

Ashuri Aramaic אסטדיותא סגיאא is "Many furlongs" ;
DSS Script : אסטיותא סגיאא- "Many furlongs"
Estrangela: ܣܓܝܐܐ ܐܣܛܕܘܬܐ-"Many furlongs"
Ashuri Aramaic: במצעתא דימא is "in the midst of the sea";
DSS Script: במצעתא דימא - "in the midst of the sea"
Estrangela ܕܝܡܐ ܒܡܨܥܬܐ- "in the midst of the sea"

I have also displayed the Estrangela script just for comparison. I can see a scribe looking at the Old DSS type script shaded blue and misreading the top two words for the two underneath them.

He had just written the last א in ארעא , then his eye went to ס in אסטיותא-"furlongs" , but since he had just written an א, he mistakenly skipped the following א and proceeded to read

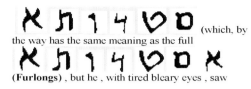 (which, by the way has the same meaning as the full

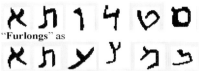 **(Furlongs)** , but he , with tired bleary eyes , saw

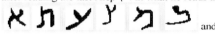 "Furlongs" as

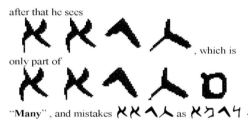 "In the midst" . Each word has the same number of letters , since he skipped an Alep **א**, and most of the letters are similar enough that they could trick a bleary eyed scribe who has stay up too late translating by lamplight. He sees the word "**Stadotha**" with his eyes, but his mind sees "**B'Metsatha**",and so he writes "**μεσον**" –"**the midst**", and now he needs a noun to finish the thought, and his eye again skips a letter **ס** after reading the last Alep **א** in what he reads as

and

after that he sees

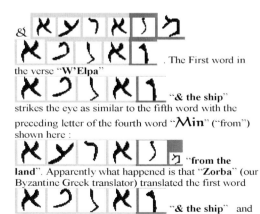 , which is only part of

"**Many**" , and mistakes ... as ... –

("**The Sea**"), so he writes **της θαλασσης** – "**The Sea**" .
Why did the Byzantine translator omit the whole phrase, "**distant from the land**"? The answer is in the highlighted words:
(land) **ארעא** (from) **מן** (it was) **הות**
(distant) **רחיקא** (& the ship) **ואלפא**

& 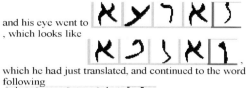 . The First word in the verse "**W'Elpa**"

"**& the ship**" strikes the eye as similar to the fifth word with the preceding letter of the fourth word "**Min**" ("from") shown here :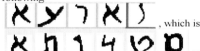

"**from the land**". Apparently what happened is that "Zorba" (our Byzantine Greek translator) translated the first word

"**& the ship**" and then when he looked back at the Aramaic manuscript

and his eye went to , which looks like

which he had just translated, and continued to the word following

, which is

as I have outlined previously. This he read as "**In the midst**", as I have illustrated.

<u>Here is the graphical evidence explaining this Majority Greek reading:</u>

"**& The Ship**"- 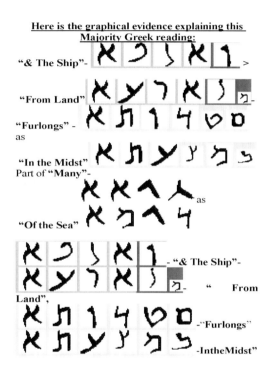 >
"**From Land**"
"**Furlongs**" - as
"**In the Midst**" Part of "**Many**"-
as
"**Of the Sea**"

- "**& The Ship**"-
" From Land",
-"**Furlongs**"
-IntheMidst"

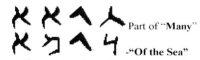 Part of "**Many**"
-"**Of the Sea**"

25. But in the fourth watch of the night, Yeshua came unto them while he was walking on the water.
26. And his disciples saw him, that he was walking on the water, and they were alarmed and they were saying, "It is an illusion!", and they cried out in fear.
27. But Yeshua immediately spoke with them and he said, "Take heart; I AM THE LIVING GOD*. Do not be afraid."

- **אנא אנא** "Ena Na" is an idiom which 97% of the time indicates speech from The Deity in The Old Testament Peshitta text (144 of 148 times in five O.T. books). It is equivalent to the Hebrew "**Ahiah Asher High**", in Exodus 3:14- "**I AM WHO I AM**". Lamsa translates this "Ahiah Asher High" in Exodus 3:14 as "**I Am The Living God**", which I have chosen as a translation for this phrase where it indicates

28. And Kaypha answered and he said to him, "My Lord, if you are He, command me to come unto you on the water."

29. And Yeshua said to him, "Come", and Kaypha went down from the ship and he walked on the water to come to Yeshua.

30. And when he saw the wind was violent, he was afraid, and he began to sink, and he raised his voice and he said, "My Lord, save me!"

31. And immediately Our Lord stretched out his hand and he held him and said to him, "Oh small of faith! Why did you doubt?"

32. And when they came up into the ship the wind stopped.

33. And those who were in the ship came and they worshiped him, and they said, "Truly, you are The Son of God!"

34. And they traveled and they came to the land of Genessar.

35. And the men of that place recognized him and they sent to all the villages around them and brought all of those who were very sick to him.

36. And they were begging him that they may touch even only the hem of his garment, and those who touched were healed.

Chapter 15

1. And the Pharisees and the Scribes who were from Jerusalem came unto Yeshua and they were saying:

2. "Why do your disciples violate the tradition of the Elders? They do not wash their hands whenever they eat bread."

3. Yeshua answered and said to them, "Why do you also violate the commandment of God for the sake of your traditions?"

4. "For God has said, 'Honour your father and your mother,' and 'Whoever reviles his father and his mother shall surely die.'"

5. "Now you are saying, 'Everyone who will say to father or mother, 'My offering is anything by which you made a profit from me', should honor neither his father nor his mother*."

*   The Critical Greek text of Westcott and Hort (א,B,D) omits "or his mother" at the end. "Old Syriac" Curetonian ms. also omits this. Nestlé's Greek NT contains this reading ("or his mother") in the text.

6. "And you nullify the word of God because of your traditions."

7. "Phonies! Isaiah prophesied well against you and said:"

8. 'This people is honouring me with their lips but their heart is very far from me.'

9. 'And they revere me in vain while they teach the doctrines of the commandments of man.'"

10. And he called the crowds and he said to them, "Hear and understand."

11. "It is not the thing that enters the mouth that defiles a man, but the thing that proceeds from the mouth that defiles a man."

12. Then his disciples approached and they were saying to him, "Do you know that the Pharisees who heard this saying were indignant?"

13. But he answered and said to them, "Every plant that my Father who is in Heaven has not planted will be uprooted."

14. "Let them alone. They are blind guides of the blind*; but if a blind man leads a blind man, both will fall into a pit."

*   The Critical Greek text of Westcott and Hort (א,B,D) omits "of the blind".

15. And Shimeon Kaypha answered and said to him: "My Lord, explain to us this parable."

16. But he said to them, "Are you still also not understanding?"

17. "Do you not know that anything that enters the mouth goes to the belly and is cast out from there in excretion?"

18. "Anything that proceeds from the mouth proceeds from the heart and it defiles the man."

19. "For from the heart proceed evil thoughts, adulteries, murders, fornications, thefts, lying testimonies, blasphemies."

20. "These things are those that defile a man, but if a man will eat after not washing his hands, he is not defiled."

21. But Yeshua went out from there and he came to the borders of Tsur and of Tsidon.

22. And behold a Canaanitess woman from those borders came forth crying out and she said, "Have pity on me my lord, son of David, my daughter is badly driven by a demon."

23. But he did not give her an answer, and his disciples came and begged him, and they were saying, "Send her away, for she is crying after us."

24. But he answered and said to them, "I am not sent except to the sheep that have strayed from the house of Israel."

25. But she came and worshiped him and she said, "My Lord, help me."

26. He said to her, "It is not good to take the children's bread and cast it to the dogs."

27. But she said, "Yes, my lord, even the dogs eat from the crumbs that fall from their master's table and they live."

• All the Greek texts omit, **"& they live"**. Why, if The Peshitta were a translation of Greek, would a translator add, **"& they live"**, since it occurs in no Greek manuscript?

28. But then Yeshua said to her, "O woman, great is your faith; it will be done for you as you will." And her daughter was healed from that moment.

29. And Yeshua departed from there and he came by the seaside of Galilee and he went up the mountain and sat down there.

30. Many crowds came to him who had the lame and the blind and dumb and the crippled and many others, and they laid them at the feet of Yeshua and he healed them.

31. So that the crowds would be amazed who saw those who had been mute speaking, and those who had been crippled who were healed*, and those who had been lame walking, and those who had been blind who were seeing, and they glorified the God of Israel.

• The 4ᵗʰ cent. Greek ms. ℵ (Sinaiticus), both "**Old Syriac** mss. and the Latin mss. omit " **& the crippled who were healed**". **Nestlé's Greek NT** contains this phrase.

32. Then Yeshua called his disciples and said to them: "I am moved with pity for this multitude; they have remained with me three days and they have nothing to eat, and I am not willing to send them away fasting, lest they should faint in the road."

33. His disciples were saying to him, "Where is bread for us in the wilderness that will satisfy this whole crowd?

34. Yeshua said to them, "How many loaves do you have?" And they said to him, "Seven, and a few small fish."

35. And he ordered the crowd to sit for a meal on the ground.

36. And he took up those seven loaves and the fish and he gave praise, and he broke and he gave to his disciples and his disciples gave to the crowd*.

• The Critical Greek text of Westcott and Hort (ℵ,B) has "to the crowds", whereas the rest of the Greek mss. has "to the crowd". The Aramaic word כנשא ("Kensha") of The Peshitta can have plural or singular meaning in its unpointed form (Early mss.

have no vowel points),hence this kind of phenomenon is not uncommon. Most Aramaic nouns have the same spelling for singular and plural forms. Some Greek translators will interpret a noun as singular and others as a plural, as here. This explains why often Greek mss. will differ in this regard.

37. And all of them ate and were satisfied and they took up the remnants of fragments, filling seven baskets.

38. But they who ate had been 4,000 men, apart from women and children.

39. And when he sent the crowds away, he went up into the ship and he came to the border of Magdo.

"**Magdo**" could be **Magadan** or **Magdala**, on the Western shore of The Sea of Galilee.

Chapter 16

1. And the Pharisees and the Sadducees approached, testing him and asking him to show them a sign from Heaven.

2. But he answered and said to them, "Whenever it is evening you say, 'It will be fair weather, for the sky is red'."

3. "And in the morning you say, 'There will be a storm today, for the sky is gloomily red.' Respecters of persons! You know how to observe the appearance of the sky; do you not know how to distinguish the signs of this time?"

4. "A wicked and adulterous generation seeks a sign, and a sign is not given to it, but the sign of Jonah The Prophet." And he left them and departed.

5. And when his disciples came to the other side, they had forgotten to take bread with them.

6. And he said to them, "Take heed; beware of the leaven of the Pharisees and the Sadducees."

7. But they were reasoning among themselves, and they were saying it was because they had not taken bread.

8. But Yeshua knew and said to them, "Oh, small of faith! Why do you think among yourselves it was because you have not taken bread?"

9. "Have you not yet understood? Do you not remember those five loaves of the 5,000? How many large baskets did you take up?"

10. "Neither those seven loaves of the 4,000 and how many round baskets you took up?"

11. "But how do you not understand that it was not about bread that I spoke to you, but

to beware of the leaven of the Pharisees and the Sadducees?"

12. But then they understood that he did not say to beware of the leaven of bread, but of the teaching of the Pharisees and of the Sadducees.

13. But when Yeshua came to the region of Caesarea Philippi, he asked his disciples, "What is it people say about me that I The Son of Man am?"

14. But they said, " Some say Yohannan The Baptizer, but others Elijah, and others Jeremiah or one of The Prophets."

15. But he said to them, "Who is it you say that I am?"

16. Shimeon Kaypha answered, "You are The Messiah, The Son of **THE LIVING GOD**".

17. Yeshua answered and said to him, "You are Blessed, Shimeon Bar Yona*, because flesh and blood has not revealed this to you, but my Father who is in Heaven."

* ברה-דיונא ("Bar-Jonah") is reproduced in all Greek mss. .transliterated from the Aramaic letters into Greek letters: "βαριωνα". This is different from borrowed words, one language from another. This is very telling about the native language and culture of the Jews of Palestine in the first century and of the source of the thousands of Greek mss. we have today. This occurs throughout The Greek NT with many names, words and phrases.

In John 1:42 , the Greek reads: συ κληθηση κηφας ο ερμηνευεται πετρος- ("You will be called Kephas, which is translated Petros".) "Petros" is the Greek for "Peter". Here the Greek writer of John tells the reader that he is translating when he writes "Petros" and that Petros is not the original name of this apostle; it is the Aramaic "Kephas". I reproduce here part of the note I have for John 1:42 :

[Here the Greek text declares that the name "Petros" is a translation of the Aramaic name "Kaypha".Here in The Greek NT, then, we find hard evidence, and in 160 other places where this Greek name occurs, that The Greek NT is translated from Aramaic! Naturally, the Peshitta has no similar translation from Greek to Aramaic, here or anywhere else. Repeat the above statement several times and ponder it: The Greek text declares itself to be translated from Aramaic !]

18. "Also I say to you, that you are Kaypha, and upon this stone I shall build my church, and the gates of Sheol will not withstand it."

19. "To you I shall give the keys of the Kingdom of Heaven; everything that you will bind in the earth will have been bound in Heaven, and anything that you will release in the earth will have been released in Heaven."

20. Then he ordered his disciples to tell no man that he is The Messiah.

21. And from then Yeshua began to inform his disciples that he was prepared to go to Jerusalem and he would suffer many things from the Elders and from the Chief Priests

and the Scribes and he would be murdered, and the third day he would rise.

22. And Kaypha took him aside and he began to rebuke him, and he said, " Far be it from you, my Lord, that this should happen to you."

23. But he turned and said to Kaypha, "Get behind me, Satan; you are a stumbling block to me because you do not reason of God but of humans."

24. Then Yeshua said to his disciples, "Whoever wants to come after me, let him deny himself and take up his cross and let him come after me."

25. "For whoever wills to save his life will lose it and whoever will lose his life for me will find it."

26. "For what does a person benefit if he gains the whole world and lacks his soul? Or what will a person give to regain his soul?

27. For The Son of Man is going to come in the glory of his Father with the Holy Angels and then he will repay each man according to his works.

28. Amen, I say to you, that there are men who are standing here who will not taste death until they will see The Son of Man who comes with his Kingdom."

Chapter 17

1. And after six days Yeshua took Kaypha, Yaqob and Yohannan his brother and brought them up to a high mountain by themselves.

2. And Yeshua was transformed before them and his face shone like the sun but his garments became white like light.

3. And Moses and Elijah appeared to them as they were speaking with him.

4. But Kaypha answered and said to Yeshua, "My Lord, it is beautiful for us that we should be here, and if you wish, we will make here three booths, one for you and one for Moses and one for Elijah."

5. And while he was speaking, behold, a bright cloud overshadowed them and a voice came from the cloud, which said, "This is my Son, The Beloved, in whom I delight; hear him."

6. And when the disciples heard, they fell on their faces, and they were very afraid.

7. And Yeshua came to them and he touched them and said, "Arise, do not be afraid."

8. And they lifted their eyes and did not see anyone except Yeshua by himself.

9. And as they descended from the mountain, Yeshua ordered them and he said to them, "Do not tell this vision in the presence of any man until The Son of Man will rise from the dead."

10. And his disciples asked him and they were saying to him, "Why do the Scribes therefore say that Elijah must come first?"

11. Yeshua answered and he said to them, "Elijah does come first so that everything may end."

12. But I say to you, behold, Elijah has come, and they did not know him, and they have done unto him everything whatsoever they wished; likewise also The Son of Man is going to suffer from them.

13. Then the disciples understood that he spoke to them about Yohannan The Baptizer.

14. And when they came to the multitude, a man came unto him and knelt on his knees.

15. And he said to him, "My lord, have mercy on me, my son has a lunatic demon and has become ill, for he has fallen many times into fire and many times into water."

• בר אגרא ("Bar agra") is an Aramaic idiom (idioms are colored purple in the interlinear text) meaning "A Lunatic". The literal wording means, "Son of a rooftop", describing an activity of praying to demons on the rooftop on the first and last days of the month by those wishing to placate demons and avert any evil from their households.

16. "And I brought him to your disciples and they were not able to heal him."

17. Yeshua answered and he said, "Oh, faithless and twisted generation! How long shall I be with you, and how long shall I endure you? Bring him here to me."

18. And Yeshua rebuked it and the demon went out from him and The Boy was healed from that moment.

19. Then the disciples came to Yeshua himself alone and they said to him, "Why were we not able to heal him?"

20. Yeshua said to them, "Because of your unbelief, for amen, I say to you, that if you had faith like a grain of mustard seed, you may say to this mountain, 'Move from here', and it will move, and nothing will be difficult for you".

• Greek mss. ℵ & B omit Ihsous - Ιησους ("Jesus") . These are the basis for the modern Greek editions and most English and other translations. **Most Greek mss**. have Iaysous -Ιησους ("Jesus"). This Greek phenomenon of omission **occurs in half of the 176 Peshitta occurrences of the Name**

Yeshua ישוע (Jesus) among those mss. (ℵ & B) and 45% of the same in the Majority Text Greek mss. of The Gospel of Luke !

21. "But this kind does not go out except by fasting and by prayer."

22. When they were traveling in Galilee, Yeshua said to them, "The Son of Man will be betrayed to the hands of men."

23. And they will murder him, and the third day he will arise." And it grieved them greatly.

24. And when they came to Kapernahum, those who take the two-each quarter-shekels head tax, came to Kaypha and said to him: "Does not your Rabbi pay the two quarter-shekels?"

25. And he said to them, "Yes." And when Kaypha entered the house, Yeshua anticipated him and he said to him, "How does it seem to you Shimeon? From whom do the Kings of the earth take taxes and head money? From their children or from strangers?"

26. And Shimeon said to him, "From strangers." Then Yeshua said to him, "Then the children are free."

27. "But lest we give offense to them, go to the sea and cast a fish hook, and the first fish that comes up, open its mouth and you will find a shekel. Take that and give for me and for you."

Chapter 18

1 And in that hour the disciples approached to join Yeshua and they were saying, "Who is truly the greatest in the Kingdom of Heaven?"

2 And Yeshua called a boy and stood him in their midst.

3 And he said, "Truly I say to you, unless you will be converted and become like children, you will not enter the Kingdom of Heaven."

4 "Whoever therefore humbles himself like this boy, he will be greatest in the Kingdom of Heaven."

5 "And whoever will receive one such as this boy, in my name, receives me."

6 "And everyone who commits an offense against one of these little ones who believe in me, it were profitable for him that a donkey's millstone would be hung around his neck and he be sunk in the depths of the sea."

7 "Woe to the world because of offenses, for it is necessary that offenses will come, but woe to the man by whom the offenses will come."

8 "But if your hand or your foot subverts you, cut it off and cast it from you, for it is better for you that you enter life as lame or as maimed, rather than having two hands or two feet, that you would fall into eternal fire."

9 "And if your eye commits an offense against you, pull it out and throw it from you, for it is better for you that you would enter life with one eye, rather than having two eyes, that you would fall into The Gehenna of fire.

* "Gehenna" is an Aramaic name, which is **transliterated into Greek letters in all the Greek mss.** in **Matthew, Mark and Luke.** It occurs 12 times in the **Greek NT**. Interestingly, "Gehenna" occurs 11 times in the Peshitta NT. In James 3:6 ,The Greek has γεεννης -"Gehenna", where **The Peshitta** has בנורא – "In fire".

Here are the Aramaic words" by Gehenna" and "in fire" :

בנורא & בגהנא

In Estrangela script, they are: ܒܓܗܢܐ "By Gehenna" & ܒܢܘܪܐ "In fire" . If the Resh ܪ were touching "Alap" - ܐ in the ܒܢܘܪܐ "In fire" of the Peshitta ms. , "Resh" ܪ could look like "Nun" - ܢ . The "He" – ܗ is similar to "Waw" ܘ and "Nun" ܢ to "Gimal" ܓ . A smudge or a bleary eye could easily transform ܒܓܗܢܐ into ܒܢܘܪܐ . Aramaic seems to account for the Greek reading "In Gehenna" in James 3:6 as well. The Greek γεεννης -"Gehenna" certainly cannot account for ܒܢܘܪܐ "In fire" in all the Peshitta mss, if one hypothesizes a Greek original behind a Peshitta translation.

10 Take heed that you do not despise one of these little ones, for I say to you that their Angels in Heaven do always see the face of my Father who is in Heaven.

11 For The Son of Man has come to save whatever has been lost.

12 How does it seem to you? If a man has a hundred sheep and one of them will go astray, does he not leave the ninety-nine in the mountain and go on searching for that lost one?

13 And if he should find it, certainly I say to you, that he rejoices in it more than in the ninety-nine that did not stray.

14 Just so, it is not the will before your Father who is in Heaven that one of these little ones should perish.

15 But if your brother wrongs you, reprove him between you and him alone; if he hears you, you have gained your brother.

16 And if he does not hear you, take one or two with you, that in the mouth of two or three witnesses every word will be established.

17 But if he will not hear them, tell the assembly, and if he does not hear the assembly, let him be to you as a tax gatherer and as a heathen.

18 And truly I say to you, everything whatsoever you will bind in the earth will have been bound in Heaven, and anything that you will release in the earth will have been released in Heaven.

19 Again I say to you, that if two of you will agree in the earth about any matter which they will request, it will be done for them from the presence of my Father who is in Heaven.

20 For where two or three are assembled in my name, there am I in the midst of them."

21 Then Kaypha approached him, and he said, "My Lord, "If my brother commits an offense against me, how many times shall I forgive him? Seven times?"

22 And Yeshua said to him, "I do not say to you until seven times, but until seventy times seven each * ."

* Lamsa's translation of The Peshitta has "Seventy times seventy seven." The literal reading is "Seventy times seven seven". This doubling of a number is an idiom, meaning here- "Seventy times seven seven each:.

23 Therefore the Kingdom of Heaven is compared to a man who was a King, wanting to take an account of his servants.

24 And when he began to take it, they brought him one who owed ten thousand talents * .

* A talent at about AD 1900 (100 years ago) was estimated by one source to be 125 British pounds. Another puts it at about 1100 dollars US. The latter would put 10,000 talents at 11,000,000 US dollars! Factoring in inflation and using the modern American average of 100 dollars for a day's wages gives 6 billion dollars as the man's debt!

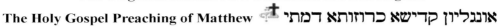
25 And when he had nothing to pay, his lord commanded that he would be sold, and his wife and his children, and everything that he had, and he would pay.

26 And falling down, that servant worshiped him, and he said, "My Lord, be patient with me, and I shall pay you everything."

27 And the lord of that servant was moved with pity, and he released him, forgiving his debt.

28 But that servant went out and found one of his associates who had owed him a hundred denarii *, and he seized him and throttled him, and he said to him, "Give me that which you owe me."

* A denarius was roughly one day's wage, so in modern American terms 100 denarii would be about 10,000 dollars.

29 And that associate fell down before his feet*, begging him and saying to him, "Be patient with me and I shall pay you."
 *The Critical Greek texts omit "**before his feet**". The Majority Greek text agrees here with The Peshitta.

30 But he was not willing, but he went and he cast him into prison until he would give him whatever he owed him.

31 But when their associates saw all what happened, it was very grievous to them, and they came and revealed to their lord everything that had happened.

32 Then his lord called him, and said to him, "You wicked servant, I forgave you that entire debt because you begged me."

33 "Was it not incumbent upon you also for you to have mercy on your associate just as I had mercy on you?"

34 And his lord was angry, and he delivered him to the scourgers until he would pay everything that he owed him.

35 So my Father who is in Heaven will do to you unless each of you forgives his brother his offenses from your heart.

Chapter 19

1 And so it was when Yeshua had finished these sayings, he picked up from Galilee, and he came to the borders of Judea to the other side of the Jordan.

2 And great crowds came after him and he healed them there.

3 And the Pharisees came to him and they were testing him, and they were saying, "Is it legal for a man to divorce his wife for any cause?"

4 But he answered and said to them, "Have you not read that he who made from the beginning, made them male and female?"

5 And he said, "Therefore a man shall leave his father and his mother and shall cleave to his wife and the two of them shall be one flesh."

6 "Therefore they were not two, but one flesh. The things therefore that God has united let not a man separate."

7 They were saying to him, "Why therefore did Moses command to give a writing of divorce and to send her away?"

8 He said to them, "Moses, confronting the callousness of your heart, let you divorce your wives, but from the beginning it was not so."

9 But I say to you, "Whoever divorces his wife apart from adultery and will take another, commits adultery, and whoever will take her who is divorced commits adultery."

10 His disciples were saying to him, "If the accusations are thus between a man and a wife, it is not expedient to take a wife."

11 But he said to them, "Not every man can receive this saying, except he to whom it is given."

12 "For there are eunuchs who were born so from their mother's womb and there are eunuchs who became eunuchs by men and there are those who have made themselves eunuchs for the cause of the Kingdom of Heaven. Whoever can receive it let him receive it."

13 And they brought children to him that he might lay his hand upon them and pray, and his disciples rebuked them.

14 But Yeshua said to them, "Let the children come to me and do not forbid them, for the Kingdom of Heaven belongs to such as these."

15 And he laid his hand upon them and went on from there.

16 And one came near and said to him, "Good teacher, what good thing shall I do that I may have eternal life?"

17 But he said to him, "Why do you call me good? There is none good except God alone. But if you want to enter life, keep the commandments."

18 He said to him, "Which ones?" But Yeshua said to him, "You shall not murder, You shall not commit adultery, You shall not steal, You shall not testify falsely."

19 "Honor your father and your mother", and "You shall love your neighbor as yourself."

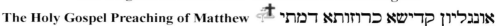
20 That young man said to him, "I have kept all these from my childhood; what am I lacking?"

21 Yeshua said to him, "If you want to be perfect, go sell your possessions and give to the poor and you will have treasure in Heaven, and come after me."

22 But that young man heard this saying and he went away, as it was grievous to him, for he had many possessions.

23 But Yeshua said to his disciples, "Amen, I say to you, that it is difficult for a rich man to enter the Kingdom of Heaven."

24 "And again I say to you that it is easier for a camel to enter the eye of a needle than for a rich man to enter the Kingdom of God."

25 But the disciples when they heard, they were greatly amazed and they were saying, "Who then can have life?"

26 Yeshua gazed at them and he said to them, "This is impossible with the children of men, but everything is possible with God."

27 Then Kaypha answered and said to him, "Behold, we have left everything and we have come after you. What then will happen to us?"

28 Yeshua said to them, "Surely, I say to you who have come after me, in The New World when The Son of Man sits on the throne of his glory, you also will sit on twelve thrones and will judge the twelve Tribes of Israel."

*Our Lord refers to the coming of "**The New World**" after His resurrection and glorification. The twelve disciples would receive authority to reign with Him in Heaven while they served Him on earth. "**All things are new**" because He, The **LORD** of Heaven and earth has died and ended all the old creation under sin and the curse; That was the judgment of the world (John 12:31-33). He has risen, raising all things from the oblivion of destruction and death into a new creation in The risen God (See 2 Cor. 5:14-17). Only a believer can see this truth, however. Instead of "**In The New World**", the Greek mss. have "εν τη παλιγγενεσια"("in the regeneration").

παλιγγενεσια occurs also in The Greek of Titus 3:5, "washing of regeneration" where the Peshitta has, דריש

בסחתא דמולדא דמן —"in the washing of the new birth"; "**In birth**" in Aramaic can be בילדא or במולדא Let's compare the Aramaic words for "in the world" and the first for-"**In birth**" :

בעלמא How about in Dead Sea Scroll script? – ⅄ℓⅩⱯ
-"in the world"

בילדא   ⅩⅬⅬⱯⱵ-
"in the birth"

Kinda' eerie, aint it?

So it looks like a Greek saw ⅄ℓⅩⱯⱵ -"in the world"

and read it as ⅩⅬⅬⱯⱵ -"in the birth", in Matthew 19:28.

Some things are too good to be true, and then some are so good, they have to be true!
God does not regenerate old things, He makes all things new:
2Co 5:17 Therefore if any man be in Christ, he is a <u>new</u> creature: old things are passed away; behold, <u>all</u> <u>things</u> are become <u>new</u>.
Ephesians 1:9,10 And he has taught us the mystery of his will, that which he had before ordained to perform in himself, for the administration of the end of time, that all things which are in Heaven and in Earth would be made new again by The Messiah.
Re 21:5 And he that sat upon the throne said, Behold, I make <u>all</u> <u>things</u> new. And he said unto me, Write: for these words are true and faithful. 6 And he said unto me, **It is done**. I am Alpha and Omega, the beginning and the end. I will give unto him that is athirst of the fountain of the water of life freely.

29 "And every man who leaves a house or a brother or sister or father or mother or wife or children or towns for my name's sake, each will receive a hundredfold and will inherit eternal life.

30 But many are first who will be last and the last ones will be the first."

Chapter 20

1 "For the Kingdom of Heaven is like the man, the lord of a household, who went out at dawn to hire laborers for his vineyard.

2 And he made an agreement with the laborers for a denarius for the day and he sent them to his vineyard.

3 And he went out at the third hour and saw others who were standing in the marketplace and were idle.

4 And he said to them, 'You go also to the vineyard; whatever is appropriate I shall give you.'

5 But those departed and he went out again at the sixth and at the ninth hours and did likewise.

6 And towards the 11th hour he went out and he found others who were standing and were idle, and he said to them, 'Why are you standing and are idle all day?'

7 They were saying to him, 'Because no one has hired us.' He said to them, 'You go also to the vineyard, and whatever is appropriate you will receive.'

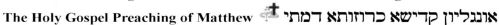
8 But when it was evening, the owner of the vineyard said to his custodian, 'Call the laborers and give them their wages, and start from the last ones up to the first ones.'

9 And those of the 11th hour came and they received a denarius each.

10 And when the first ones came they had hoped that they would receive more, and they received a denarius each also.

11 And when they received it, they complained to the lord of the estate.

12 And they were saying, 'These last ones have worked one hour and you have made them equal to us who have borne the burden and the heat of the day.'

13 But he answered and said to one of them, 'My friend, I do no evil to you. Did you not agree with me for a denarius?'

14 Take yours and go. But I wish to give to this last *group* even as to you.

15 Or is it illegal for me to do whatever I want to do with my own? Is your eye evil because I am good?'

16 So the last will be first and the first last, for the called are many and the chosen ones are few."

17 But Yeshua was prepared to go up to Jerusalem and he took aside his twelve disciples privately on the road and he said to them:

18 "Behold, we are going up to Jerusalem, and The Son of Man will be delivered to the Chief Priests and to the Scribes and they will condemn him to death.

19 And they will deliver him to Gentiles, and they will mock him, and they will scourge him, and they will crucify him, and the third day he will arise."

20 Then the mother of the sons of Zebedee came near to him, she and her sons, and she worshiped him and she was asking him something.

21 But he said to her, "What do you desire?" And she said to him, "Say that these my two sons will sit, one at your right and one at your left, in your Kingdom."

22 Yeshua answered and he said, "You do not know what you are asking. Are you able to drink the cup that I am prepared to drink or to be baptized in the baptism in which I am to be baptized?" They were saying to him, "We are able."

23 He said to them, "You will drink my cup and you will be baptized in the baptism in which I am baptized, but for you to sit at my right and at my left is not mine to give except to those for whom it is prepared by my Father."

24 But when the ten heard it, they were angry with those two brothers.

25 And Yeshua called them and said to them, "You know the rulers of the Gentiles are their lords and their great ones have authority over them."

26 "It will not be so among you, but whoever wants to be great among you, let him be one who waits on you."

27 "And whoever wants to be first among you let him be a servant to you."

28 "Just as The Son of Man came, not to be ministered to, but to minister, and to give himself a ransom in the place of the many."

29 And when Yeshua went out from Jericho, a great crowd was coming after him.

30 And, behold, two blind men were sitting on the side of the road and when they heard that Yeshua was passing by, they gave a cry, and they were saying, "Have mercy on us my Lord, son of David."

31 But the crowds were rebuking them that they would be silent, and they raised their voices all the more and they were saying, "Our Lord, have mercy on us, Son of David."

32 And Yeshua stopped and he called them and he said, "What do you want me to do for you"?

33 They were saying to him, "Our Lord, that our eyes may be opened."

34 And Yeshua was moved with pity for them and he touched their eyes, and immediately their eyes were opened and they went after him.

Chapter 21

1. And then as he approached Jerusalem and came to Bethphage, by the side of the Mount of Olives, Yeshua sent two of his disciples,

Verse one differs from **The Majority Greek text** in the name of "**BethPhage**"- most Greek mss. have βηθσφαγη- "BethSphage", while some Byzantine and (א,B) & **TR** have βηθφαγη- "BethPhage", in agreement with The Peshitta. However, the Vaticanus ms.(B) also has "εις το ορος των ελαιων" ("**unto** the Mount of Olives"), whereas **the Majority text** has "προς το ορος των ελαιων"("**toward** the Mount of Olives"). Finally, all Greek texts omit the personal pronoun in ,"**His** disciples" . Thus it looks like The Peshitta, if it were a translation of Greek, translated **The Critical Greek represented by Vaticanus**, in the first reading, then **the Byzantine Majority Text in the next reading,** and finally, **no Greek ms. in the last reading- all in one verse !**

2 And he said to them, "Go to this village that is opposite you and at once you will find a donkey that is tied and a colt with her; loose them and bring them to me."

3 "And if a man says anything to you, say to him, 'They are needed by Our Lord', and immediately he will send them here."

4 But this that happened was so that the thing that was spoken by the Prophet would be fulfilled which says:

5 "Say to the daughter of Zion, 'Behold, your King comes to you meek and riding on a donkey and upon* a colt, the foal of a she donkey.'"

- *The text here agrees with 4ᵗʰ cent. mss. (א,B)-The Critical Greek text.*

6 And the disciples went and did just as Yeshua had commanded them.

- **The Majority Greek text** agrees better here; The Critical text has "**appointed**", a derivative of the Aramaic passive verb; but the active form is used here, so it looks like the Critical Greek text translator read his Aramaic grammar wrong here, but nevertheless is witness to an Aramaic original.

7 And they brought the donkey and the colt and they placed their garments on the colt and Yeshua* rode upon it.

- *"**Jesus**" is missing in all the Greek mss.*

8 And a multitude of crowds were spreading their clothes on the road and others were cutting down branches from trees and laying them in the road.

9 But the crowds which were going before him and coming after him were crying out and they were saying, "Hosanna to The Son of David; blessed is he who comes in the name of **THE LORD JEHOVAH**; Hosanna in The Highest."

- מריא –"**Mar-Yah**" means "**LORD JEHOVAH**" or "**Lord Yahweh**". The Greek does not distinguish this name from other titles and the Greek Κυριος - "**Kurios**" may simply mean "**Sir**" or "**Master**". Thirty two times Jesus is named "מריא – "**Mar-Yah**"- "**LORD JEHOVAH**" in **The Peshitta NT** text! **The Greek N.T.**, of course, has no such references.

- * "**Oshanna**"- אושענא is not Greek, it is Aramaic; even the Greek mss. have this Aramaic word in the text, indicating that the people of Israel spoke Aramaic, not Greek. "Oshanna" means ,"**Save now!**"Here is **Barne's NT Notes** for this verse: "The word hosanna means, "Save now," or, "Save, I beseech thee." It is a **Syriac** (**Aramaic**) word, and was the form of acclamation used among the Jews. It was probably used in the celebration of their great festivals. During those festivals they sang the 115ᵗʰ, 116ᵗʰ, 117ᵗʰ, and 118ᵗʰ psalms."

10 And when he entered Jerusalem, the whole city was stirred and they were saying, "Who is this?"

11 But the crowds were saying, "This is Yeshua the Prophet who is from Nazareth of Galilee."

12 And Yeshua entered The Temple of God* and cast out all of those who sold and bought in The Temple and upset the tables of the money changers and the seats of those who sold doves.

- "**of God**" is omitted by 4ᵗʰ cent. Mss. (א,B) & **The Critical Greek text**. Sometimes it agrees with The Peshitta and sometimes not.

13 And he said to them, "It is written: 'My house will be called the House of prayer, but you have made it a den of robbers.' "

14 And they brought to him in The Temple the blind and the lame, and he healed them.

- The Greek mss. all have **προσηλθον αυτω** -"**came to Him**", where **The Peshitta** has "They brought to Him". The Aramaic verb קרב "**Qareb**" can mean "**Approach**" or "**Bring**". Think about it: "The blind and the lame **came** to him" ?

15 But when the Chief Priests and the Pharisees saw the wonders that he did and the children shouting in The Temple and saying, "Hosanna to The Son of David", it seemed evil to them.

16 And they were saying to him, "Have you heard what these are saying?" Yeshua said to them, "Yes. Have you never read, 'From the mouth of children and infants you have composed a song of praise?' "

This quotation from Psalm 8:2 agrees with neither **The Hebrew OT** nor **The LXX** Greek OT, nor **The Peshitta OT**, nor **The Greek NT**. It seems to follow a hybrid text similar to that of **The Dead Sea Scrolls**, which sometimes is similar to **The LXX** text and other times like **The Massoretic Hebrew** text. Often, (especially in **Hebrews**' frequent OT quotations), it follows **The Peshitta OT** translation text, which has some unique readings.

17 And he left them and he went outside the city to Bayth-Ania and spent the night there.

18 But at dawn when he returned to the city he was hungry.

19 And he saw one fig tree by the road and came to it and he found nothing on it except leaves only, and he said to it, "There will be no fruit on you again forever", and at once that fig tree withered up.

20 And the disciples saw and they marveled and they were saying, "How quickly the fig tree withered up!"

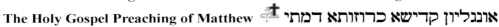
21 Yeshua answered and said to them, "Amen, I say to you, if you have faith and you will not doubt, you will do not only this of the fig tree but also if you will say to this mountain, 'Be lifted up and fall into the sea', it will be done."

22 "Everything that you will ask in prayer and believe, you will receive."

23 And when Yeshua* came to The Temple, the Chief Priests and the Elders of the people approached him as he taught them, and they were saying to him, "By what authority do you do these things and who gave you this authority?"

* *"Jesus" omitted in all Greek mss .*

24 Yeshua answered and said to them, "I also shall ask you something and if you will tell me, I shall also tell you by what authority I do these things."

25 "From where was the baptism of Yohannan, from Heaven or was it from men?" But they were counseling among themselves and saying, "If we say, 'From Heaven', he will say to us, 'And why did you not trust him?'"

26 "And we are too afraid of the crowds to say, 'From men', for they all hold Yohannan as a Prophet."

27 They answered and they were saying to him, "We do not know." Yeshua said to them, "Neither am I telling you by which authority I do these things."

* All Greek mss. have "They answered **Jesus**" here and omit **"Jesus"** later in the verse where The Peshitta has "**Jesus** said to them".

28 "But how does it seem to you? A certain man had two sons and* he called the first and said to him, 'My son, go work today in the vineyard*.'"

** The Majority Greek Text agrees with "and he called" ; The Critical Greek Text (ℵ) omits ,"And". The Critical Greek Text (ℵ) agrees with "the vineyard" where the Majority Greek has "my vineyard".

29 "But he answered and said, 'I don't want to', but afterward he was moved with regret and he went."

30 "Then he came to the other and said to him likewise, but he answered and said, 'I will, my lord', and he did not go."

31 "Which of these two did the will of his father?" They were saying to him, 'The first.' Yeshua said to them, "Amen, I say to you, that Tax Collectors and prostitutes precede you to the Kingdom of God."

32 "For Yohannan came to you in the way of righteousness and you did not trust him, but Tax Collectors and prostitutes trusted him, and even when you saw it, you were not moved with regret afterward to trust him."

33 "Hear another parable: there was a certain man, a landowner, and he had planted a vineyard enclosed by a fence and he had dug a wine press and had built a tower in it, and had given its care to laborers, and he went abroad."

34 "But when the fruit season had arrived, he sent his servants to the laborers so that they would send some of the fruit of the vineyard to him."

35 "And the laborers seized his servants; they beat one and another they stoned and another they killed."

36 "And he sent again more servants than the first time, and they did the same to them."

37 Finally, he sent to them his son as he said, 'Doubtless they will reverence my son.'"

38 "But when the laborers saw the son, they said among themselves, 'This is the heir, come, let us kill him and seize his inheritance.'"

39 "And they seized and led him outside of the vineyard and killed him."

40 "Therefore, when the Lord of the vineyard comes, what will he do to those laborers?"

41 They said to him, "He will ruthlessly destroy them and he will give the care of the vineyard to other laborers, who will give him the fruits in their season."

42 Yeshua said to them, "Have you never read in the scriptures, 'The stone which the builders rejected has become the head of the corner; this was from the presence of THE LORD JEHOVAH, and it is a wonder in our eyes.'"?

43 "Therefore, I say to you, the Kingdom of God will be taken from you and will be given to a people who will produce fruit."

44 "And whoever falls on this stone will be shattered, and it will pulverize to dust everyone upon whom it will fall."
The "**Old Syriac**"(5th cent.) Sinaiticus Aramaic ms. omits verse 44!

45 And when the Chief Priests and the Pharisees heard his parables, they knew that he had spoken against them.

46 And they sought to seize him and they were afraid of the crowds, because they were holding him as a Prophet.

Chapter 22

1 Again, Yeshua answered in a parable, and he said:

2 "The Kingdom of Heaven is compared to a man who was a King who made a wedding feast for his son.

3 And he sent his servants to call those invited to the wedding feast, and they chose not to come.

4 Again he sent other servants, and he said, "Tell those invited, 'Behold, my banquet is ready, and my oxen and my fatlings are killed, everything is prepared; come to the wedding feast.'"

5 And they showed contempt and went, one to his field, and another to his commerce.

6 But the rest seized, abused and killed his servants.

7 But when the King heard, he was angry and he sent his armies, destroyed those murderers, and burned their city.

8 Then he said to his servants, 'The wedding feast is ready, and those who were invited were not worthy.'

9 'Go therefore to the ends of the roads and call everyone whom you find to the wedding feast.'

10 And those servants went out to the roads, and they gathered everyone whom they found, bad and good, and the place of the wedding feast was filled with guests.

11 And the King entered to see the guests and he saw a man there who was not wearing a wedding garment.

12 And he said to him, 'My friend, how did you enter here when you did not have a wedding garment?' But he was speechless.

13 Then the King said to the attendants, 'Bind his hands and his feet and cast him out into outer darkness; there will be weeping and gnashing of teeth.'

14 "For the called are many and the chosen are few."

15 And the Pharisees went, and they took counsel how they might catch him in discourse.

16 And they sent their disciples to him with those of the house of Herodus and they were saying to him, "Teacher, we know that you are true and that you teach the way of God in truth and you do not take caution for man, for you do not accept the persons of men."

17 "Tell us therefore, how does it seem to you? Is it lawful to give the head tax to Caesar or not?"

18 Yeshua knew their evil and he said, "Why are you testing me, you accepters of persons?"

19 "Show me a denarius of the head tax money", and they brought a denarius to him.

20 And Yeshua said to them, "Whose is this image and inscription?"

21 And they were saying, "Caesar's"; he said to them, "Give therefore what is Caesar's to Caesar, and what is God's to God."

22 And when they heard, they were amazed, and they left him and departed.

23 That day the Sadducees approached, and they were saying to him*, "There is no life for the dead", and they asked him,

The Greek mss. omit "to Him": "The Sadducees, who say there is no resurrection", giving the impression the Sadducees said nothing about their belief, but did not believe in resurrection; The Peshitta states that they told Jesus, "There is no resurrection of the dead".

24 And they were saying to him, "Teacher, Moses said to us that if a man dies while he has no sons, his brother may take his wife and raise up seed to his brother.

25 Now, there were seven brothers with us; the first took a wife and he died, and he had no children, and he left his wife to his brother.

26 Likewise also the second and also the third, even unto the seventh of them.

27 And after all of them the woman died also.

28 In the resurrection therefore, which of these seven will have the woman, for they all had taken her?"

29 Yeshua answered and he said to them, "You do err, because you do not understand the scriptures, neither the mighty works of God.

30 For in the resurrection of the dead, they do not take wives, neither do men have wives, but they are* like the Angels of God in Heaven.

* "They are" tells us that the resurrection spoken of here is life after death. Those alive after death are even now as the angels of God.

31 But concerning the resurrection of the dead, have you not read what was spoken to you by God, who said:

32 'I AM THE LIVING GOD*, The God of Abraham, The God of Isaaq, and The God of Jaqob?' He is The God, not of the dead, but of the living."

* See note at 14:27 on "Ena Na"-"I AM The Living God"

33 And when the crowds heard, they were dumbfounded at his teaching.

34 But when the Pharisees heard that he had silenced the Sadducees, they assembled together.

35 And one of them who knew The Written Law asked him while testing him:

36 "Teacher, which commandment in The Written Law is the greatest?"

37 Yeshua said to him, "You shall love THE LORD JEHOVAH your God from all your heart and from all your soul and from all your power and from all your mind."

• This quote follows the Hebrew text of Deuteronomy 6:5 and then adds another phrase "**and from all your mind**". No OT text has these four stipulations as does **The Peshitta NT** in all three NT quotes of Deut. 6:5. **The Peshitta OT** text does use an unusual word in its final phrase: כלה קנינך וּמן – "**w'min kalah qninak**" ("**with all your faculties**").Our Lord apparently preferred that the "**all your mind**"condition be included in our love to God. Almost all Greek mss. omit "**all your strength**" in this verse, but include it in the parallel passages of Mark 12:30 and Luke 10:27 (However, **The Critical Greek** text also omits "**with all your soul**" in Mark 12:33.

38 "This is the great and the first commandment."

39 "And the second which is like it is, 'You shall love your neighbor as yourself.'

40 On these two commands depend all The Written Law and The Prophets."

41 But as the Pharisees were assembled, Yeshua asked them,

42 And he said, "What are you saying about The Messiah? Whose Son is He?" They were saying to him, "The Son of David."

43 He said to them, "And how did David by The Spirit call him THE LORD JEHOVAH, for he said:"

44 'THE LORD JEHOVAH said to my Lord, 'sit at my right hand until I place your enemies under your feet'?

See Psalm 110:1-5. In Hebrew and in The Peshitta text, the original of verse 5 has Yahweh at Yahweh's right hand! The Massoretes changed the reading to Adonai (Lord) but made a note of it in the Massorah.

45 "If therefore David called him THE LORD JEHOVAH, how is he his son?"

If one were to read The Massoretic notes of the Hebrew text of Psalm 110, one would find that the Massorete scribes changed the Name of "Yahweh"(Jehovah) in 110:5 to "Adonai"(The Lord) ; this they did in 133 other places as well. But Ps. 110, verse five would read : "Jehovah at your right hand will strike through Kings in the day of His wrath…". **The Peshitta OT** has the same reading. Our Lord's quotation of verse one suggests the whole

Psalm of seven verses. If **Jehovah** **is at God's right hand** in verse 5, then **He** must be the very same **Jehovah at His right hand in verse 1** ! No Greek ms. indicates this Divine **Tetragrammaton** Name (**Yahweh**) in verses 43-45. **The Peshitta has it three times** ! It also names "**Yeshua**" as "Yahweh" 32 times in the NT ! The **Greek has no word for Yahweh**, though the **Greek** translator might have substituted "**Kurios Theos**"("Lord God") or , "**Theos**" ("God") to indicate The Deity, since **the Name** ("THE LORD JEHOVAH") מריא – "**MarYah**" is referenced 239 times in the NT quotations of OT scripture & etc. Actually, that probably happened only five or six times out of 239 in **The Greek NT**. All other places simply have "**Kurios**" "(Lord"), which can refer to The Deity **or to a mere man. The Aramaic** מריא – **MarYah** ("THE LORD JEHOVAH") never refers to anyone but The Deity .

46 And no man could give him an answer, and no man dared again from that day to question him.

Chapter 23

1 Then Yeshua spoke with the crowds and with his disciples:

2 And he said to them:"The Scribes and the Pharisees have sat on the throne of Moses."

3 Everything therefore that they will tell you to observe*, observe* and do*, but you should not do according to their works, for they are saying, and they are not doing.

*** The Critical Greek text (א,B) omits "to observe" ; B (Vaticanus) also reverses "observe & do" to "do & observe", while א (Sinaiticus) has only "do". The Majority Greek text agrees here with The Peshitta.

4 And they bind heavy burdens and place them on the shoulders of men, but they are not willing to touch them with their fingers.

5 And they do all their works to be seen by the children of men, for they enlarge their phylacteries and they extend the blue fringes of their robes.

6 And they love the first class places at feasts and first class seats in the synagogues

7 And greetings in the marketplaces, and to be called, "Rabbi"*, by the people.

* C The Majority (Byzantine) Greek text has "ραββι ραββι"- "**Rabbi, Rabbi**". The Critical Greek text (א,B) has "ραββι" – "**Rabbi**", in agreement with **The Peshitta**. This is also another case of an Aramaic word transliterated into **The Greek NT**.

8 But you shall not be called "Rabbi", for One is your Rabbi, but you are all brothers.

• The Majority Greek Text & (א,D) have "υμων ο καθηγητης" – "**your Guide, Leader**"; (B-Vaticanus) & others have "υμων ο διδασκαλος" "**your Teacher**". The Majority Greek text has also "ο χριστος" (**The Christ**) after "ο καθηγητης". The

Critical Greek text (ℵ,B) does not have "ο χριστος" (The Christ). Both Greek readings: "υμων ο καθηγητης" – "your Guide, Leader"; (B-Vaticanus) & "υμων ο διδασκαλος" "your Teacher" can be explained by **The Peshitta** reading – רבכון ("**Your Rabbi**"). רבא "**Rabba**" means "**Great one**", & can also mean "**Teacher**" or "**Master, Ruler**"

9 And you should not call yourselves "Father", in the earth, for one is your Father who is in Heaven.

All Greek mss. but D,Θ (5th century,9th century) have: "και πατερα μη καλεσητε υμων επι της γης"-"**And do not call your Father upon earth**…." D,Θ agree with The Peshitta reading.

10 And you will not be called Leaders, because one is your Leader, The Messiah.

11 But he who is great among you will be a servant to you.

12 Whoever will exalt himself will be humbled and whoever will humble himself will be exalted.

13 Woe to you Scribes and Pharisees, impostors, who consume the houses of widows with offerings for making your long prayers! Because of this you will receive greater judgment.

The Critical Greek Text (ℵ,B) has this verse and verse 14 in switched order. The Majority Greek Text has them as The Peshitta has them.

14 Woe to you Scribes and Pharisees, pretenders, for you shut the Kingdom of Heaven before the children of men, for you are not entering, and those who are entering you do not permit to enter!

15 Woe to you Scribes and Pharisees, impostors! For you travel around sea and land to make one convert, and when it has happened, you make him doubly the son of Gehenna that you are!

• **The Greek NT** has "Gehenna" transliterated again here – an Aramaic term designating a place in Israel and a metaphor for death in sin & eternal judgment. More evidence of an Aramaic original. See note at Matthew 18:9 on **γεεννης.**

16 Woe to you blind guides, for you say, 'Whoever swears by The Temple, it is nothing', but 'Whoever swears by the gold of The Temple is liable!'

17 Fools and blind men! Which is greater, gold, or The Temple, which sanctifies the gold?

18 And ,'Whoever swears by the altar, it is nothing' ,but 'Whoever swears by the offering upon it, he is liable.'

19 Fools and blind men! Which is greater, the gift or the altar that sanctifies the gift?

20 Whoever swears therefore by the altar swears by it and by everything that is upon it.

21 And whoever swears by The Temple swears by it and by The One dwelling in it.

22 And whoever swears by Heaven swears by the throne of God and by him who sits upon it.

23 Woe to you Scribes and Pharisees, impostors, for you tithe mint and dill and cummin and you forsake the weighty things of the law: justice, mercy and faith! It is necessary for you to do these things and you should not forsake them.

24 Blind guides who strain out gnats and swallow camels!

25 Woe to you Scribes and Pharisees, pretenders, who wash the outside of the cup and of the dish, but within are full of plunder and evil* !

• The Critical Greek Text has "**ακρασιαν**" – akrasian ("excess, lack of self control"). The Majority Greek Text has "**αδικιας**" - adikiav ("unrighteousness, iniquity") . Following are two Aramaic words parallel to the Greek reading "**ακρασιαν**" – akrasian ("excess, lack of self control") in the Critical Greek NT text & "**αδικιας**" - adikiav ("unrighteousness, iniquity"):

• ורגתא, ועולא

• ܪܓܬܐ , ܘܥܘܠܐ

• ܪܓܬܐ , ܘܥܘܠܐ

The first pair is in square Aramaic script; the 2nd pair is Estrangela script & the 3rd is **Dead Sea Scroll Aramaic** script. The second Aramaic word in each pair is "w'Regta"(& Lust). It appears that the Estrangela pair are most similar of the three. If the word ܘܥܘܠܐ -"w'Awala" had the second Waw ܘܥܘܠܐ (blue) pushed half through the **Lamed** ܠ to its left , the **Waw- Lamed** pair ܠܘ would look like **Tau** ܬ . An Ayin ܥ could easily be taken for a **Gamal** ܓ if it were extended a bit at the bottom by an inadvertent stroke or smudge downward, and the first letter Waw ܘ , if not fully formed in its bottom half of the downward curve stroke, could look like a Resh ܪ . I performed these processes on an original ܘܥܘܠܐ -"w'Awala" ("& iniquity") and reproduce here the graphic result: ܪܓܬܐ . Compare the word ܪܓܬܐ "Regta" ("Lust"). The only thing missing in this scenario is the initial conjunction ܘ ("Waw"- "&") , represented in Greek by the word **και** ("kai"-&) before **ακρασιαν**. These are so common however, that even when missing in Aramaic, are supplied in translations as understood.

• Thus The Peshitta's Aramaic word ܘܥܘܠܐ - "w'Awala" ("& iniquity") can account for both Greek readings, "**ακρασιαν**" – akrasian ("**excess, lack of self control**") & "**αδικιας**" - adikiav ("**unrighteousness, iniquity**") .No singular Greek text can account for The Peshitta. The Greek "**ακρασιαν**" ("excess, lack of self control") would not give rise to ܘܥܘܠܐ-"w'Awala" ("&

iniquity").The Greek "αδικιας" - adikiav ("unrighteousness, iniquity") could do so, however, the agreement between the distinct Greek texts and The Peshitta alternates so frequently and erratically , often within the same verse, that it is not feasible that an Aramaean translator was translating Greek mss. into Aramaic, choosing a different Greek text several times within a verse, and sometimes simply adding or changing readings without any Greek source ! "Occam's Razor" would decide this matter very easily: The data are much more easily accounted for by Peshitta Primacy than by Greek Primacy. Indeed, Greek Primacy requires consistent and willful ignorance and neglect of the facts for its support, because it cannot account for the facts. The facts support a Peshitta original NT !

26 Blind Pharisees, wash first the inside of the cup and dish that their outside may also be clean.

27 Woe to you Scribes and Pharisees, impostors, who are like white tombs, which from the outside appear lovely, but from within are full of the bones of the dead and all corruption!

28 So also you from the outside appear to the children of men as righteous, and from within are filled with evil and hypocrisy.

29 Woe to you Scribes and Pharisees, pretenders, who build the tombs of The Prophets and adorn the tombs of the righteous!

30 And you say, 'If we had been in the days of our forefathers, we would not have been partakers with them in the blood of The Prophets.'

31 Therefore you testify against yourselves that you are the children of those who murdered The Prophets.

32 So fulfill the standard of your forefathers.

33 Snakes! Offspring of vipers! How will you escape from the judgment of Gehenna?

34 Because of this behold, I am sending to you Prophets and wise men and scribes; some of them you will murder and you will crucify, and some of them you will scourge in your synagogues and you will persecute them from city to city

35 So that all the blood of the righteous may come upon you that has been shed upon the earth, from the blood of righteous Abel, even unto the blood of Zechariah the son of Barachiah, whom you murdered in the midst of The Temple and the altar.

36 Amen, I say to you, all these things will come upon this generation.

37 Jerusalem, Jerusalem, you that murdered The Prophets and stoned those who were sent to it! How many times have I desired to gather your children, as a hen gathers her chicks under her wings, and you were not willing!

38 Behold, your house is left to you desolate!*

* The Critical Greek Text (B) omits "ερημος" ("desolate").

39 For I say to you that you will not see me from now on, until you will say, 'Blessed is he who has come in the name of THE LORD JEHOVAH.'"

Chapter 24

1 Yeshua went out from The Temple to depart, and his disciples approached, showing him the buildings of The Temple.

2 But he said to them, "Behold, do you see all these things? Amen, I say to you that not a stone will be left here standing, which will not be pulled down."

3 And when Yeshua sat on Tor d'Zaytha ("Mount of Olives"), his disciples came and they were saying among themselves and to him: "Tell us when these things will be and what will be the sign of your advent and of the end of the world."

4 Yeshua answered and said to them, "Beware that no man will deceive you."

5 "For many will come in my name, and they will say, 'I AM THE LIVING GOD*, The Messiah', and they will deceive many."

אנא אנא -"Ena Na" almost always refers to Divine speech. It is unclear here that these false Prophets will claim to be Divine, though a comparison with Mark 13:6 shows they would say simply : דאנא אנא –("I AM") and would deceive many. That is a claim to Deity.

6 You are going to hear battles and reports of wars.Take heed that you will not be troubled, for it is necessary that all these things should happen, but it will not yet be the end.

7 For nation will arise against nation, and Kingdom against Kingdom, and there will be famines and plagues and earthquakes in various places.

8 But all these things are the beginning of sorrows.

9 And then they will deliver you to suffering, and they will kill you and you will be hated by all the nations because of my name.

10 Then many will be subverted, and they will hate one another and will betray one another.

11 And many false Prophets will arise and will deceive many.

12 And because of the abundance of evil, the love of many will grow cold.

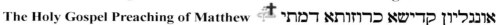
13 But whoever will persevere until the end will have life.

14 And this gospel of the Kingdom will be preached in the whole world for the testimony of all the nations, and then the end will come.

15 But whenever you will see the desecrated sign of desolation that was spoken by Daniel the Prophet, standing in the holy place, (he who reads should consider)

16 Then those who are in Judea should flee to the mountains.

17 And the one who is on the roof should not come down to take what is in his house.

18 And he who is in the field should not return to take his clothes.

19 But woe to pregnant women and to those who are nursing in those days.

20 But pray that your escape will not be in winter, neither on the Sabbath.

21 For then there will be great suffering, which has not been from the beginning of the world even until now, neither will be.

22 If those days are not cut short no one would live, but because of the chosen ones, those days will be cut short.

23 Then if someone will say to you, "Behold, The Messiah is here or there", you should not believe.

24 For false Messiahs will arise and Prophets of lies, and they will give great signs so as to deceive, if possible, even the elect.

25 Behold, I have told you beforehand.

26 If therefore they will say to you, "Behold, he is in the desert", you should not go out, or "Behold, he is in an inner room", do not believe it.

27 For just as lightning goes out from The East and appears unto The West, so will the coming of The Son of Man be.

28 Wherever the body will be, there will the eagles be gathered.

29 But immediately after the suffering of those days, the sun will darken and the moon will not show its light, and the stars will fall from the heavens and the power of the heavens will be disturbed.

30 And then the sign of The Son of Man in Heaven will appear and then all the families of the earth will mourn, and they will see The Son of Man who comes on the clouds of Heaven with miracles and many praises.

31 And he will send his Angels with great trumpets, and they will gather his own elect from the four winds, from all the ends of the heavens.

32 * But learn a parable from the fig tree: As soon as its branches bow low and its leaves bud forth, you know that summer has arrived.

33 So also, whenever you see all these things, know that he has approached the door.

34 Amen, I say to you that this generation will not pass away until all these things happen.

35 Heaven and Earth will pass away, and my words will not pass away.

36 But about that day and about that hour no one knows, not even the Angels of Heaven, but The Father alone.

37 But just as the days of Noah, so will the coming of The Son of Man be.

38 For just as they were eating and drinking before the flood, and they were taking wives, and they were taking husbands, until the day that Noah entered the ark,

39 And they did not perceive until the flood came and took them all away, thus will be the coming of The Son of Man.

40 Then two will be in the field; one will be taken captive, and one will be left.

41 Two women will be grinding at the mill; one will be taken captive and one will be left.

42 Wake up therefore, for you do not know in what hour your Lord will come.

43 But know this: if the house owner had known in what watch the robber would come, he would have been awake and would not have allowed his house to be broken into.

44 Because of this, be also ready, because at the hour in which you are not expecting, The Son of Man will come.

45 Who then is the servant who is faithful and wise, whom his Lord has appointed over the children of his household, to give them food in his time?

46 Blessed is that servant, whom, when his master will come, will find doing this.

47 Amen, I say to you, he will set him over everything that he has.

48 But if an evil servant will say in his heart, "My Lord delays to come",

49 And will start to beat his associates and eat and drink with drunkards,

50 The Lord of that servant will come on the day that he does not expect it, and in the hour in which he is not aware.

51 And he will cut him off, and he will set his portion with the phonies. There will be weeping and gnashing teeth."

Chapter 25

1. "Then the Kingdom of Heaven will be compared to ten virgins; the same took their lamps and went to meet the groom and the bride.

2 But five of them were wise and five were foolish.

3 And those fools took their lamps, and did not take oil with them.

4 But those wise ones took oil in their vessels with their lamps.

5 But when the groom delayed, all of them grew tired and slept.

6 And in the middle of the night there was an outcry, "Behold, The groom has come, go out to meet him."

7 Then all those virgins arose and trimmed their lamps.

8 The fools said to the wise, "Give us some of your oil, behold, our lamps have gone out."

9 But the wise answered and said, "Why? There is not enough for us and for you; go to those who sell and buy for yourselves."

10 And when they went to buy, the groom came and those who were ready entered with him into the wedding place, and the door was barred.

11 But afterward, those other virgins came and they were saying, "Our Lord, Our Lord, open to us."

12 But he answered and said to them, 'Amen, I say to you, that I do not know you.'

13 Wake up therefore, for you know neither the day nor the hour. Most Greek mss. have "in which The Son of Man comes" at the end of the verse. Look at the following Dead Sea Scroll script Aramaic comparisons:

אתא ברה דאנשא –"The Son of Man comes"
איך ברה דאנישין –"For as a man who journeyed"

-(beginning of next verse, with some spaces rearranged) Might this strange similarity account for the majority Greek reading? Apparently a translator double read the beginning of the next verse, first as the top reading, and then again as the second reading in Aramaic. This seems to have occurred in quite a few places in the NT.

14 Like the man who journeyed and called his servants and delivered to them his property.

15 To one he gave five talents, and to another two, and to another one, each man according to his power, and he immediately went abroad.

16 But he who received five talents went and traded them and gained five others.

17 So also he of the two gained two others.

18 But he who received one went and dug in the ground and buried the money of his lord.

19 After much time, the lord of the servants came and took an account of them.

20 And he called him who had received five talents and brought five others, and he said, "My lord, you gave me five talents behold, I have gained five other talents on top of them."

21 His master said to him, "Well done, good and faithful servant. You have been faithful over a little; I shall set you over much; enter the joy of your Lord.'

22 And he of his two talents came and he said, "My lord, you gave me two talents, behold, I have gained two other talents on top of them."

23 His lord said to him, "Well done, good and faithful servant. You have been faithful over a little; I shall set you over much; enter the joy of your Lord."

24 He also who had received one talent came, and he said, "My lord, I had known you that you are a hard man, and that you reap where you have not sown and that you gather from where you have not threshed,

25 And I was afraid, and I went and buried your talent in the ground. Behold, it is yours."

26 His master answered and said to him, "You evil and lazy servant; you knew that I reaped where I had not sown, and I gathered from where I have not threshed.

27 And it was incumbent upon you to cast my money to the exchange, so that when I would come, I could require my own with its interest.

28 Take therefore the talent from him and give it to him who has ten talents."

29 For to the one who has it, it shall be given, and it will be increased to him. But whoever does not have it, that which he has will be taken from him.

30 And they cast the worthless servant into outer darkness. There will be weeping and gnashing teeth.

31 But whenever The Son of Man comes in his glory and all his Holy Angels with him, then he will sit upon the throne of his glory.

32 And all the nations will be assembled before him and he will separate them one from another, as a shepherd who separates sheep from goats.

33 And he will place the sheep at his right and the goats at his left.

34 Then The King will say to those who are at his right, 'Come, blessed ones of my Father, inherit the Kingdom that was prepared for you from the foundation of the universe.'

35 For I was hungry and you gave me food, and I was thirsty and you gave me drink. I was a stranger and you took me in.

36 I was naked and you clothed me. I was sick, and you took care of me. I was in prison, and you came to me.'

37 Then the righteous will say to him, 'Our Lord, When did we see you that you were hungry and we fed you, or that you were thirsty and we gave you drink?

38 And when did we see you, that you were a stranger and we took you in, or that you were naked and we clothed you?'

39 'And when did we see you sick or in a prison, and we came to you?'

40 And The King answers and says to them, 'Amen, I say to you, as much as you have done to one of these my little brothers, you have done that to me.'

41 Then he will say also to those who are at his left, 'Depart from me, you cursed ones, into eternal fire, that which was prepared for The Devil and for his Angels.

42. For I was hungry and you gave me no food. I was thirsty and you gave me no drink.

43. I was a stranger and you did not take me in; I was naked, and you did not clothe me. I was sick, and in prison and you did not take care of me.'

44. And those will answer, and they will say, 'Our Lord, when did we see you hungry or thirsty or a stranger or naked or sick or in prison, and we did not minister to you?'

45. Then he will answer and he will say to them, 'Amen, I say to you, as much as you have not done to one of these little ones, neither have you done *that* to me.'

46. And these will go into eternal torture, and the righteous into eternal life."

Chapter 26

1 And it was, that when Yeshua had finished all these words, he said to his disciples:

2 "You know that after two days it is Passover and The Son of Man will be betrayed to be crucified.

3 Then the Chief Priests and the Scribes and the Elders of the people were gathered together to the court of The High Priest, who is called Qaiapha,

• The Critical Greek text omits "**and The Scribes**".

4 And they held a council about Yeshua, so that they might seize him by deceit and murder him.

5 And they were saying, "Not during the feast lest there be a riot among the people."

6 And when Yeshua was in Bayth-Ania in the House of Shimeon the Potter,

* "Garba" can mean "**Leper**" or "**Pot**". It can also mean, "**One who makes pots**", even as "**Bsama**" in the next verse can mean "**Ointment**" or "**Maker of ointment**". I am grateful for Paul Younan pointing this out in his interlinear of Matthew. There can be no doubt that <u>Shimeon was not a leper with The Messiah in his house as a dinner guest</u>. This is probably another case where the Greek translator misconstrued the Aramaic original. All Greek texts have "Leprou", from "Lepros"- "A Leper".

7 A woman came near to him who had with her a vase of oil of sweet spices, very expensive, and she poured it on Yeshua's head as he reclined.

8 But his disciples saw it and it displeased them and they said, "Why this waste?"

9 "For it would have been possible to sell this for much and it might have been given to the poor."

● The Majority Greek Text has "**This ointment** might have been sold for much". "Ointment" in Aramaic is משהא "Meshakha"- very similar to the first Aramaic word in the verse משכה "Meshkakh"("Possible"). I conjecture that the Greek scribe saw משכה (Meshkakh-"Possible) and reread it as משהא (Meshakha-"Ointment) the second time , translating it as Μυρος – "Ointment". The Aramaic explains the Greek variant reading.
The Critical Greek agrees with the Peshitta here.

10 But Yeshua knew and he said to them, "Why do you trouble the woman? She has done a beautiful deed for me.

11 For you have the poor always with you, but you do not have me always.

12 But she who has poured this ointment on my body has done *it* as for my burial.

13 And amen, I say to you, that wherever this my gospel will be preached in all the world, this also that she has done will be told for her memorial."

14 Then one of the twelve who is called Yehuda Scariota went out to the Chief Priests,

15 And he said to them, "What are you willing to give me if I shall deliver him to you?' Then they promised him thirty silver coins.

16 And from then on, he sought opportunity to betray him.

17 But on the first day of Unleavened Bread, the disciples came to Yeshua and they said to

him, "Where do you want us to prepare for you that you may eat the Passover?"

18 But he said to them, "Go to the city to a certain man and say to him, 'Our Rabbi says, 'My time is come. I will perform the Passover at your place with my disciples'."

19 And his disciples did just as Yeshua ordered them and they prepared the Passover.

20 And when it was evening he reclined with his twelve Disciples.

21 And as they ate he said to them, "Amen, I say to you, that one of you will betray me."

22 And it grieved them greatly, and they began to say to him, each one of them, "Is it I, my Lord?"

23 But he answered and said, "Whoever dips his hand with me in the dish, he will betray me."

24 "And The Son of Man goes just as it is written about him, but woe to that man by whom The Son of Man is betrayed; it would have been better for that man if he had not been born."

25 Yehuda the traitor answered and he said, "It is I, Rabbi?" Yeshua said to him, "You have said."

26 But as they ate, Yeshua took bread and blessed and broke and he gave to his disciples, and he said, "Take eat; this is my body."

27 And he took a cup, and he gave thanks and he gave to them, and he said, "Take, drink from it, all of you.

28 This is my blood of the new* covenant, which is shed in exchange for the many for the release of sins.

● The Critical Greek text omits "New" ; The Majority Greek + (C,D) have it.

29 But I say to you that I shall not drink again from this fruit of the vine until the day in which I shall drink it with you new in the Kingdom of my Father."

30 And they sang praises and they went out to Tor Zaytha. ("The Mount of Olives.")

31 And Yeshua said to them, "All of you will be offended at me this night, for it is written: 'I shall strike The Shepherd, and the sheep of his flock will be scattered.'

32 But after I am risen, I shall go before you to Galilee."

33. Kaypha answered and said to him, "Even if every man will be offended at you, I will never be offended at you."

34 Yeshua answered him and said, "Amen, I say to you that in this night, before a cock will crow three times, you will deny me."

35 Kaypha said to him, "If I should die with you, I would not deny you." So also all the disciples said.

36 Then Yeshua came with them to the place that is called Gethsemane and he said to his disciples, "Sit here while I shall go and pray."

37 And he took Kaypha and the two sons of Zebedee, and he began to be saddened and to be disheartened.

38 And he said to them, "My soul has sorrow even to death; wait for me here and keep watch with me."

39 And he withdrew a little and he fell upon his face and he prayed and he said, "My Father, if it is possible, let this cup pass by me, however not as I will, but as you will."

40 And he came to his disciples and he found them as they slept and he said to Kaypha, "Could you not keep watch with me one hour?"

41 "Watch and pray lest you enter into temptation. The Spirit is ready, but the body is weak."

42 Going again the second time, he prayed and he said, "My Father, if this cup cannot pass unless I drink it, your will be done."

43 And coming again, he found them while they slept, for their eyes were heavy.

44 And he left them and going on again, he prayed the third time, and he said the same thing.

45 And he came to his disciples and he said to them, "Sleep now and rest; behold the hour is come; The Son of Man is betrayed into the hands of sinners."

46 "Arise, let us go; he has arrived who betrays me."

47 While he was speaking, behold, Yehuda the traitor, one of the twelve, came and a great crowd with him, with swords and clubs from the presence of the Chief Priests and the Elders of the people.

48 And Yehuda the traitor had given them a sign, and he had said, "Him whom I shall kiss is the one; seize him."

49 And at once, he called Yeshua, and he said, "Shalom, Rabbi", and he kissed him.

50 Then Yeshua said to him, "Have you come to this, my friend?" Then they came and they laid their hands on Yeshua, and they took him.

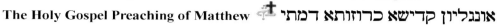
51 And behold, one of those who were with Yeshua reached his hand and drew his sword and struck the servant of The High Priest and cut off his ear.

52 Then Yeshua said to him, "Return the sword to its place, for all of those who take up swords will die by swords.

53 Do you think that I cannot ask my Father and he would raise up for me now more than twelve Legions of Angels?

54 How then would the Scriptures be fulfilled, that it must be so?"

55 At that moment Yeshua said to the crowd, "Have you come out as against a robber with swords and with clubs to seize me? I was with you every day in The Temple sitting and teaching, and you did not arrest me."

56 But this happened that the scripture of The Prophets may be fulfilled; then all the disciples forsook him and fled.

57 And they who arrested Yeshua led him to Qaiapha the High Priest, where the Scribes and the Elders were gathered.

58 But Shimeon Kaypha was going after him from a distance unto the court of The High Priest, and entering he sat down inside with the guards to see the outcome.

59 But the Chief Priests and the Elders and all the assembly were seeking witnesses against Yeshua, so that they might put him to death.

60 And they did not find them, though many false witnesses had come, but finally two came forth,

61 And they were saying: "This one said, 'I can destroy The Temple of God and in three days I shall build it.'"

62 And the High Priest stood and said to him, "Do you not return an answer? What are these testifying against you?"

63 But Yeshua was silent, and The High Priest answered and said to him, "I adjure you by **THE LIVING GOD** that you tell us if you are The Messiah, The Son of God."

64 Yeshua said to him, "You have said; but I say to you that from this hour, you will see The Son of Man who sits at the right hand of power and comes on the clouds of Heaven."

65 Then the High Priest ripped his garment, and said, "Behold, he has blasphemed. Why now do we need witnesses? Behold now, you have heard his blasphemy.

66 "What do you think?" They answered, and they said, "He deserves death."

67 And they spat in his face, and they were beating his head. But others were striking him

68 And were saying, "Prophesy to us, Messiah; who is it that hits you?"

69 But Kaypha had sat outside in the courtyard, and a maid servant came near him, and she said to him, "You also were with Yeshua the Nazarene."

70 But he denied before all of them and he said, "I do not know what you are saying."

71 And when he went out to the porch, another Maidservant saw him and she said to them who were there, "This one was also there with Yeshua the Nazarene."

72 And again he denied with an oath, "I do not know the man."

73 After a bit, those standing there came and they said to Kaypha, "Certainly, you also are one of them, for your speech reveals you."

74 And he began to curse and to swear, "I do not know the man", and at that moment, a cock crowed.

75 And Kaypha remembered the word of Yeshua that he had told him, "Before a cock will crow three times, you will deny me"; and going forth outside, he wept bitterly.

Chapter 27

1 **B**ut when it was dawn, all the Chief Priests and the Elders of the people took counsel against Yeshua, how they would put him to death.

2 And they bound him and they led him and delivered him to Pilate*, the Governor.

> * The Majority Greek text has **Pontius** Pilate; The Critical Greek text, like The Peshitta, has simply, "**Pilate**".

3 Then when Yehuda the traitor saw that Yeshua was condemned, he was moved with regret and went and brought those thirty pieces of silver to the Chief Priests and to the Elders.

4 And he said, "I have sinned, for I have betrayed innocent blood", but they said to him, "What is that to us? You know us."

> * זכיא -"Zakaia" can mean "victorious", "innocent" or "just"; The Majority Greek text has "αθωον"- "innocent" & the Critical Greek has "δικαιον" –"righteous". The Peshitta reading can explain the Greek readings.

5 And he cast the silver into The Temple and departed, and he went and hanged himself.

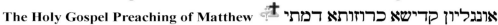
6 But the Chief Priests took the silver, and they said, "It is not legal to put it into the treasury, because it is the price of blood."

7 And they took counsel, and they bought with it the field of a potter as a graveyard for the burial of strangers.

8 Therefore that field has been called, "The Field of Blood", until this day.

9 Then was fulfilled what was spoken by the Prophet* who said, "I took thirty silver coins, the price of the Precious One on which they of the children of Israel had agreed.

• **All but 3 Greek mss.** have "**ιερεμιου του προφητου**"- "**Jeremiah the Prophet**". Those three agree with The Peshitta in reading "The Prophet", however they are 6th to 9th century mss. There are no earlier Greek witnesses for this reading, making it highly unlikely The Peshitta is a translation of the Greek in this place. Besides, "**Jeremiah**" is clearly a false reading. The quotation in this verse is from Zechariah, not Jeremiah, which means the Greek is incorrect and The Peshitta reading is not, since it does not name the Prophet quoted.

10 And I gave them for the potter's field as THE LORD JEHOVAH commanded me."

• The quotation of verses 9 & 10 in The Peshitta agrees not with **The LXX (Greek) Version** of Zechariah 11:12,13, but more closely to **The Hebrew** version. The Greek NT agrees more closely with **The LXX Version**: "They took" & "They gave" instead of the Hebrew's-"I took" & "I gave". Both **The Peshitta NT** and **The Greek NT** agree with the Hebrew version's "The Potter" rather than **The LXX version's** -"The furnace" , found twice in Zechariah 11:13 . Generally **The Greek NT** agrees better with **The LXX** than with **The Hebrew Bible**, and **The Peshitta NT** agrees better with **The Hebrew Bible** than with **The LXX**. It appears that The Greek texts attribute the quotation to Jeremiah because Jeremiah 18:2 & 3 are the only references to "The Potter's house" in the entire LXX:the phrase is as close to "Potter's field" as The LXX has, certainly better than "the furnace" ! Those verses, however, have nothing to do with this prophecy to which Matthew referred.

11 But Yeshua himself stood before the Governor and the Governor asked him and said to him, "You are The King of the Judeans?", and Yeshua said to him, "You have said."

12 And when the Chief Priests and the Elders accused him, he did not return any answer.

13 Then Pilate said to him, "Have you not heard how much they testify against you?"

14 And he gave him no response, not even a word, and at this he marveled greatly.

15 Now, at every feast, the Governor was accustomed to release one prisoner to the people, whomever they had chosen.

16 But one of their prisoners was a notable prisoner called Barabba.

17 And when they had been assembled, Pilate said to them, "Whom do you wish that I should release to you, Barabba, or Yeshua who is called The Messiah?"

18 For Pilate knew that for jealousy they had delivered him.

19 But when the Governor sat on the judgment seat, his wife sent to him and she said, "Have nothing to do with that Righteous One, for I have suffered greatly in my dream today because of him."

20 But the Chief Priests and the Elders had persuaded the crowds to ask for Barabba, but to destroy Yeshua.

21 And the Governor answered and said to them, "Whom do you want me to release to you of the two?" But they said, "Barabba."

22 Pilate said to them, "And Yeshua, who is called The Messiah, what shall I do to him?" And all of them were saying, "Let him be crucified."

23 The Governor* said to them, "What evil has he done", but increasingly, they cried out and they said, "Let him be crucified!."

• Critical Greek omits "Governor".

24 And when Pilate saw that nothing availed, but that there was an increasing clamor, he took water, washing his hands before the crowds and he said, "I am free from the blood of this righteous man. Know that."

25 And all the people answered, and they said, "His blood be upon us and upon our children."

26 Then he released Barabba to them and scourged Yeshua with whips and delivered him to be crucified.

27 Then the soldiers of the Governor led Yeshua to the Praetorium, and they gathered the whole regiment around him.

28 And they stripped him and they clothed him with a scarlet robe.

29 And they wound a garland of thorns and placed it on his head and a reed in his right hand and they bowed on their knees before him and were mocking him and saying, "Hail, King of the Judeans!"

30 And they spat in his face and they took the reed and they were hitting him on his head.

31 And when they had mocked him, they stripped him of the robe and clothed him in his garments and led him to be crucified.

32 And as they went out, they found a Cyrenian man whose name was Shimeon; they compelled him to carry his cross.

33 And they came to the place that was called "Gagultha", which is interpreted, "a Skull".

34 And they gave him vinegar* to drink that was mixed with gall, and he tasted and he did not want to drink it.

- Most Greek mss. have οξος- "Vinegar"; The Critical Greek (W & H) text has οινος –"Wine". The Peshitta reading did not come from The Critical Greek text here. The Peshitta in verse 2, however, agrees with The Critical Greek text. Does that mean it was translated from that text in verse 2, no Greek text in verse 9, & The Majority Text in v. 23 & 34? That would be very unlikely. This pattern of agreement and disagreement with the Greek text types and with no Greek text at all within a chapter or even a few verses continues throughout <u>The Peshitta NT</u> !

35 And when they had crucified him, they divided his garments by lots.

36 And they were sitting and keeping watch for him there.

37 And they placed over his head the cause of his death in writing: "This is Yeshua the King of the Judeans."

38 And two robbers were crucified with him, one at his right hand and one at his left.

39 But those who were passing by were reviling him and shaking their heads;

40 And they were saying, "The One who destroys The Temple and builds it in three days, save yourself, if you are The Son of God, and come down from the cross."

41 Thus also the Chief Priests were mocking with the Scribes and the Elders and the Pharisees.

* The Majority Greek Text has "και φαρισαιων"- "and the Pharisees", agreeing with The Peshitta; The Critical Greek (א,B) & Alexandrinus (A) omit this phrase.

42 And they were saying, "He saved others, he cannot save himself; if he is The King of Israel, let him descend now from the cross and we will trust in him."

43 "He trusted on God, let him save him now, if he delights in him, for he has said, 'I am The Son of God.' "

44 Thus also those robbers who were crucified with him were taunting him.

45 But from the sixth hour there was darkness over the whole land until the ninth hour.

46 And toward the ninth hour Yeshua cried with a loud voice and he said, "Oh God, oh God! Why have you forsaken me?"

All Greek texts give a <u>transliteration</u> of <u>the Aramaic</u> of Our Lord's cry and then <u>translate the words into Greek</u>. The Peshitta text has no Greek transliteration nor a translation of Greek into Aramaic. The major Greek texts also differ in their versions of the verse: The Majority Greek has ανεβοησεν

("cried aloud") while the Critical Greek has εβοησεν ("cried");

The Majority Greek has "ηλι ηλι λιμα σαβαχθανι";

The Critical Greek has "ελωι ελωι λεμα σαβαχθανι";

The Textus Receptus has "ηλι ηλι λαμα σαβαχθανι"

All are obvious attempts to transliterate Aramaic which , according to The Peshitta, would be "**ειλ ειλ λεμανα σαβαχθανι. "O God, O God, Why have you forsaken Me ?" The Greek versions may represent an attempt to reconstruct the cry in transliterated Hebrew: "Eli Eli lamah azabthani" ,** as it stands in Psalms 22:1. If so, (and this looks quite likely) there was a mixing of the Aramaic verb "Shebaqthani" with the Hebrew words, **"Eli" (My God)** and **"lamah" ("Why ?").**
All Greek texts have the following:
" **τουτ εστιν θεε μου θεε μου ινα τι με εγκατελιπες" ("This is, My God, My God, Why have You forsaken Me ?) The transliterated Semitic words are connected to a Greek translation of the same by the words "τουτ εστιν" – "This is".** Here is a declaration that the original words of Our Lord were not Greek, but Hebrew or Aramaic (Since **the main verb is Aramaic,** I shall assume Aramaic is intended and the scribe involved resorted to another Aramaic source , being unfamiliar with the Palestinian Aramaic word for God- איל ,& substituted the more familiar אלי ("My God") along with the Hebrew (or Aramaic) למה as found in Psalm 22:1).
Here is an ancient Targum (Aramaic translation of the Hebrew) of Psalm 22:1-
מה שבקתני רחיק מן פורקני מילי
אלי. אלהי" מטול
You can see that אלי is an Aramaic form as well as Hebrew, so the Greek ηλι could represent Aramaic. The Greek letters for אלי or אלהי would be the same (ηλι or ελι), since <u>Greek has no letter to represent the Aramaic letter ה –"Het".</u> ελωι- (The Critical Greek reading), could also be an attempt to render אלהי, substituting an "ω" for an Aramaic ה –**"Het".** למה- **"Lamah"** (λαμα in Greek) is also Biblical Aramaic, meaning **"Why ";** so it looks as if the Greek **"Eli,Eli, lama sabachthani"** could be from **<u>an Aramaic Targum of the Hebrew Psalm 22:1</u>.** This seems the most likely explanation for the Greek readings.

The Targum would have looked like this:
אלהי אלהי <u>למה שבקתני</u>
רחיק מן פורקני מילי

<u>למה שבקתני</u> is the quoted section found in Matthew. The Peshitta of Mark 15:34 has :
אלהי אלהי למנא שבקתני as the Syriac interpretation of the Galilean Aramaic of Our Lord, **which is also identical to The Peshitta OT Version of Psalm 22:1.** The exact quote by Mark is exactly the same as Matthew's: איל איל למנא שבקתני
אלהי & איל are both direct address forms of **Alaha (God)** in different dialects, so there is no difference in meaning between them. Matthew wrote to the Jews of Israel and Mark to the Syrians and other Aramaic speaking peoples outside Israel in Asia Minor, hence the translation of the cry from the cross into the Syrian dialect. Most of the written words of different dialects agree, whereas the pronunciations

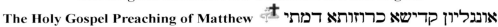
will vary somewhat. **That is why Mark translates from one dialect to another only twice!**
The Greek NT usually quotes from an OT source when recording OT quotations, usually from the Greek LXX. Here, since the writer wants to quote Our Lord's spoken words, he resorts to an Aramaic Targum of Psalm 22 instead of The Peshitta text of Matthew 27:46, as the quote is practically identical to Psalm 22:1.
Neither Matthew's nor Mark's Peshitta text makes sense as a transliteration or translation of the Greek readings. Why would both writers use איל איל ,
an uncommon form of **Alaha**, if the original were ηλι
or ελωι ? This is not **to be expected either as a transliteration or translation of** ηλι or ελωι.
Why does Mark have two dialects of Aramaic in his text, one Palestinian and the other Syrian, if he is translating from Greek ? That makes no sense whatsoever.
The Peshitta text certainly did not come from any Greek transliteration reading ! The facts as they are beg the question, "Why does the Greek give an Aramaic transliteration and then a Greek translation if the original words were Greek ? If the original words were not Greek, why would The Gospels be composed in a Greek translation, (for this is most certainly declared to be a translation) ?
Here and other places make clear that Our Lord and His people of Israel spoke Aramaic. Why in the name of Sam Hill would the original Gospels be written in Greek, which would be only a translation of everything that was said and done ? Again, the Aramaic can very easily make sense of the Greek , but the Greek cannot explain the Aramaic of the Peshitta.
The Greek in Matthew has: περι δε την ενατην ωραν ανεβοησεν ο ιησους φωνη μεγαλη
Aramaic sentence = Greek translation λεγων
ηλι ηλι λιμα σαβαχθανι τουτ εστιν θεε μου θεε μου ινα τι με εγκατελιπες.
Is not this a declaration of an Aramaic original and a Greek translation ? The Greek NT has 7 such transliterations with declared translations of Aramaic into Greek whereas the Peshitta has no example of transliteration and translation of Greek into Aramaic. If Greek were the original and Aramaic the translation, how can these things be ? Me thinks Greek primacists are in denial , which is somewhere in Egypt, I think (Alexandria?).

47 Those people who were standing there, when they had heard, they were saying, "This one has called Elijah."
48 At that moment one of them ran and took a sponge and filled it with vinegar and placed it on a reed and gave a drink to him.
49 But the rest were saying, "Let him alone; we shall see if Elijah comes to save him."

The Critical Greek Text of Westcott & Hort (ℵ,B,C,L) have added: αλλος δε λαβων λογχην ενυξεν αυτου την πλευραν και εξηλθεν υδωρ και αιμα.
"Another took a lance and pierced His side, and water and blood came out." This would mean that Our Lord was killed with a spear, which is ridiculous. He had said, "No man takes My life; I lay it down of My own will." The separation of the blood into red cells and clear serum takes places only after death. But according to the next verse, Our Lord was still alive ! This is a misplaced quote from John

19:34 which refers to what occurred after His death. So much for the reliability of (ℵ,B,C,L) –"the oldest and best manuscripts" !

50 But Yeshua cried again with a loud voice, and his Spirit departed.
51 And at once the curtain entrance of The Temple was ripped in two from top to bottom. The earth was shaken and the rocks were split.
52 Tombs were opened, and many bodies of the Saints who were sleeping arose.
53 And they came out, and after his resurrection, they entered the Holy City, and they appeared to many.
54 And the Centurion and those who were guarding Yeshua, when they saw the quake and those things that happened, they were very afraid, and they said, "Truly, this was The Son of God."
55 But there were also many women there who had seen from a distance, these who had come after Yeshua from Galilee and had ministered to him.
56 One of them was Maryam Magdalitha and Maryam the mother of Yaqob and of Yose and the mother of those sons of Zebedee.
57 When it was evening, a rich man from Ramtha, named Yoseph, came, who also had been a disciple of Yeshua,
58 This one came to Pilate and requested the body of Yeshua, and Pilate commanded that the body would be given to him.
59 And Yoseph took the body and wound it in a sheet of pure linen.
60 And he placed it in a new tomb belonging to him, which was cut in stone, and they rolled a great stone and set it against the doorway of the tomb and they departed.
61 But Maryam Magdalitha and the other Maryam were there, sitting opposite the tomb.
62 And the next day, which is after Friday sunset, the Chief Priests and the Pharisees were gathered together unto Pilate,
63 And they were saying to him, "Our Lord, we recall that the deceiver said while he was alive, 'After three days, I will arise.' "
64 "Command therefore to guard the tomb until the third day, lest his disciples should come and steal it in the night and say to the people that he is risen from the grave, and the last deception be worse than the first."
65 Pilate said to them, "You have guards, go guard it just as you know how."

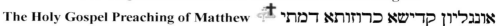
66 But they went to guard the tomb, and they together with the guards sealed the stone.

Chapter 28

1. **But** on the eve of the Sabbath, when the first of the week was dawning, Maryam Magdalitha and the other Maryam came to see the tomb.

2. And behold there was a great earthquake, for The Angel of **THE LORD JEHOVAH** descended from Heaven, and he came, he rolled the stone from the entrance and sat upon it.

3. And his appearance was like lightning and his clothing was white as snow.

4. And from dread of him, those who were keeping watch were shaken, and they became like dead men.

5. But the Angel answered and said to the women, "Do not be afraid, for I know that you are seeking Yeshua, who was crucified."

6. "He is not here, for he is raised just as he said; come see the place in which Our Lord was laid."

• The Critical Greek text omits "Lord" altogether; The Majority Greek has it, although The Peshitta has a much more interesting reading: מרן –"Maran" ("**Our Lord**"). The Peshitta in verse 5 says "the **Angel of Jehovah (The LORD, v. 2)**" & in v. 6 calls Yeshua "Jesus" "**Our Lord**", thus acknowledging **Yeshua as Jehovah, his Lord, THE LORD JEHOVAH of men and angels.**

7 "And go quickly; say to his disciples that he has risen from the grave, and behold, he goes before you to Galilee; there you will see him; behold I have told you."

8 And they went quickly from the tomb with fear and with great joy, and they ran to tell his disciples.

9 And behold, Yeshua met them and he said to them, "Peace to you", but they came and held his feet and they worshiped him.

The Majority Greek text begins v. 9: ως δε επορευοντο απαγγειλαι τοις μαθηταις αυτου –"And as they went to tell his disciples". The Critical Greek text agrees with The Peshitta here, as does The Latin Vulgate. The Majority Greek reading looks like it is based on a repeat reading of the end of v. 8, probably from the Aramaic, translating ורהטין –("& they ran") as אזלין ("they went") or ונפקו ("& they went forth") – the latter is more likely, and the Greek επορευοντο actually does twice parallel נפק in The NT .

10 Then Yeshua said to them, "Do not be afraid, but go tell my brothers to go to Galilee and there they will see me."

11 And as they were going, some of the guards came to the city and they told the Chief Priests everything that had occurred.

12 And they gave not a few silver shekels to the guards and they gathered with the Elders and held a council.

13 And they were saying to them, "Say, 'His disciples came and stole it in the night, while we slept'."

14 "And if this should be reported before the Governor, we will persuade him, and we will relieve your concerns."

15 But when they took the silver coins, they did as they had instructed them, and this story has gone out among the Judeans till this day.

16 But the eleven disciples went to Galilee to the mountain where Yeshua had appointed them.

17 And when they saw him they worshiped him, but some of them doubted.

18 And Yeshua spoke with them and he said to them, "All authority has been given to me in Heaven and in the earth; in the manner in which my Father has sent me, I am sending you."

The major Greek texts and mss. lack "**As My Father has sent Me, so I send you**."There is at least one Western Greek ms. with the sentence, as well as The Diatesseron of Tatian. Rarely does The Peshitta contain a passage that is not found in any major Greek text, which leads me to believe there was only one Greek translation of the Aramaic original and that either the Peshitta ms. used lacked this sentence in v. 18 or the Greek scribe simply missed it. It is surprising that later Greek revisers never caught this.

19 "Therefore go disciple all the nations and baptize them in the name of The Father and The Son and The Spirit of Holiness."

20 "And instruct them to keep everything whatever I have commanded you, and behold, I am with you every day, even unto the end of time. Amen"

• -The Critical Greek has no "**Amen**", whereas the Majority Greek does.
• In Matthew 28 alone , The Peshitta agrees with a major variant of the Majority Greek text in verse 2, then a major variant of The Critical Greek text in v. 9, neither Greek text in v. 18 with a sentence lacking in all major Greek texts, and then again with the Majority Greek text in verse 20. This validates the previous observation in Matthew that The Peshitta follows no known Greek text with any consistency. It does generally agree with The Majority Byzantine Greek text type best, but departs from it with the Critical Greek perhaps 25% of the times those two Greek types differ, and it differs significantly from all Greek readings about as often as it agrees with any major Greek text type! At the same time , The Peshitta

readings can explain a host of Greek variants of both the major text types , whereas the Greek as we know it cannot account for the Peshitta text and the relatively extremely small number of variants found among its 350 manuscripts.

While it is true that any particular Greek ms. will exhibit idiosyncratic readings , even compared to others of the same text type, the Peshitta will exhibit essentially the same readings and departures from Greek mss. regardless the Peshitta manuscript under scrutiny. Practically any Peshitta manuscript will fairly represent the Peshitta family of manuscripts as a whole and produce the same statistics as mentioned above for The Peshitta text in general. Such a claim cannot be made for any Greek ms. My analysis of the variations among Greek mss. compared to those among Peshitta mss. shows that there are approximately 70 times the number of variants among Textus Receptus Greek mss. (and they have the highest ratio of agreement among Greek NT mss.) as among Peshitta NT mss. ! When considering the Critical Greek mss. in their variations from each other and the Majority Greek text (Byzantine) the number jumps by a factor of ten. Two of those mss. have at least 700 times the number of variant readings between them as found among two typical Peshitta mss. !

שלם אונגליון קדישא כרוזותא דמתי

The end of The Holy Gospel preaching of Matthew

The Gospel According To Saint Mark

Chapter 1

1. The beginning of The Gospel of Yeshua The Messiah, The Son of God. (Codex W has "Son of God", unlike Westcott & Hort's Critical Greek edition.)

2. As it is written in Isaiah the Prophet, "Behold, I shall send my messenger before your presence to prepare your way."

(Greek Codex W agrees with **Peshitta & Latin Vulgate** in omitting **"before you"** at the end of the verse ; Disagrees with W&H)

3. "A voice that cries in the wilderness, prepare the way of **THE LORD JEHOVAH** and make level his paths."

4. Yohannan was in the wilderness, baptizing and preaching the baptism of repentance for the release of sins.

5. And all the country of Judea and all the people of Jerusalem were going out to him, and he baptized them in the Jordan when they confessed their sins.
(Greek mss. have "Jordan river"; Codex W agrees with Peshitta reading here.)

6. But the same Yohannan was clothed with clothing of hair of the camel and he was bound with a belt of leather at his waist and his food was locusts and honey of the field.

7. And he was preaching and he said, "Behold, after me shall come he who is mightier than I, the strap of whose sandals I am not worthy to stoop and to loose.

8. I have immersed you in water, but he will immerse you in The Spirit of Holiness.

9. And it was in those days; Yeshua came from Nazareth of Galilee and was immersed in the Jordan by Yohannan.

10. And at once, as he came up from the waters, he saw the heavens being ripped open and The Spirit who was descending upon him as a dove.

11. And there was a voice from the heavens: "You are my Son, The Beloved; with you I am delighted."

12. And at once The Spirit drove him into the wilderness.

13. And he had been there in the wilderness forty days when he was tempted by Satan. And he was with the animals, and Angels were ministering to him.

14. After Yohannan was delivered up, Yeshua came to Galilee and was preaching The Gospel of the Kingdom of God.

15. And he said, "Time is coming to an end. The Kingdom of God has arrived. Repent and believe in The Good News."

16. And as he walked around the Sea of Galilee, he saw Shimeon and his brother Andraeus who were casting a net into the sea, for they were fishermen.

17. And Yeshua said to them, "Come after me, and I will make you fishers of men."

18. And at once they left their nets and went after him.

19. And when he passed by a little he saw Yaqob, son of Zebedee, and Yohannan his brother, and also those in the ship who were setting their nets in order.

20. And he called them and at once* they left their father Zebedee in the boat with the hired servants and they went after him.
(Greek mss. omit "at once" ; Codex W has it.)

21. And when they entered Kapernahum, at once he taught in their synagogue on the Sabbath.

22. And they were dumbfounded at his teaching, for he was teaching them as one having authority and not like their Scribes.

23. And in their synagogue there was a man who had a vile spirit in him, and he cried out,

24. And he said, "What business do we have with you, Yeshua the Nazarene? Have you come to destroy us? I know who you are, The Holy One of God."

25. And Yeshua rebuked him and said, "Shut your mouth and come out of him."

26. And the foul spirit threw him down and he cried out in a loud voice and came out of him.

27. And all of them marveled* and they were inquiring with one another, saying, "What is this?", and "What is this new teaching? For he commands even the foul spirits with authority and they obey him."
*Most Greek mss. have ΕΘΑΜΒΗΘΗΣΑΝ -("were amazed") where W has ΕΘΑΥΜΑΖΟΝ -("marveled"). W matches The **Peshitta** reading here, which has אתדמרו-("marveled"). 42/55 (76%) of the Θαυμαζω ("marvel") root words in The Greek NT are matched with the דמר ("marvel") root in **Peshitta** NT.

28. And at once his fame went out in the whole region of Galilee.

29. And they went out from the synagogue and they came to the house of Shimeon and Andraeus with Yaqob and Yohannan.

30. And the Mother-in-law of Shimeon was lying ill with fever and they told him about her.

31. And he came near and took her by the hand and raised her up and at once her fever left her and she was waiting on them.

32. But in the evening at the going down of the sun they brought to him all of them who had been ill and demon possessed.

33. And the whole city was assembled at the door.

34. And he healed multitudes that had become ill with various diseases and he cast out many evil spirits. He did not allow them to speak because they did know him.

35. And in the very early morning he arose first and went on to a desolate place and there he prayed.

36. And Shimeon and his companions were seeking for him.

37. And when they found him they were all saying to him, "The people are all looking for you."

38. He said to them, "Walk to the villages and the cities near to us, so that I also may preach there, for because of this I have come *."

> *Most Greek mss. have ΕΞΕΛΗΛΥΘΑ –"**I have come out**".Codex W has ΕΛΗΛΥΘΑ –"I have come".(ΕΛΗΛΥΘΑ Agrees with Peshitta and the verse disagrees with ΑΛΛΑΧΟΥ –"from another place", in W&H. Also unique in reading ΚΗΡΥΞΙΝ "**to preach**" which is agreeable with the Peshitta reading- אכרז, translatable as "I shall preach, or "to preach".)

39. And he was preaching in all their synagogues and in all Galilee and he cast out demons.

40. A leper came to him, fell at his feet, and begged him, saying, "If you are willing, you are able to make me clean."

41. Yeshua was moved with compassion* for him. Reaching out his hand he touched him and said, "I am willing; be cleansed."

> * Greek codex D has "οργισθεις"-"**being angered**".The other Greek reading is σπλαγχνισθεις-"moved with compassion", which hardly looks like "οργισθεις"-"**being angered**".
> Here is The Peshitta reading and the "**being angered**" reading in a Dead Sea Scroll script:
> אתרחם -"moved with compassion"
> אתחמת-"being angered"
> My thanks to Paul Younan, web host of Peshitta.org for pointing out this example supporting Peshitta primacy.

42. In that moment his leprosy went from him and he was cleansed.

43. Yeshua reproved him and sent him out.

44. He said to him, "See that you tell no man, but go and show yourself to the priest. Bring gifts for your cleansing, just as Moses commanded for their testimony."

45. But when he went out he began preaching *it* much and he reported the event so that Yeshua was not able to openly enter the cities. He was in deserted places and they were coming to him from every place.

Chapter 2

1. Yeshua again entered Kapernahum for some days. When they heard that he was in the house,

2. So many were assembled that it was not able to hold them before the door. He was speaking the word with them

3. When a paralytic was brought to him, being carried by four men.

4. Because they were not able to be brought near him due to the crowds, they went up to the roof and removed the roof tiles of the place where Yeshua was. They let down the litter in which the paralytic lay.

5. When Yeshua saw their faith, he said to the paralytic, "My son, your sins are forgiven you."

6. But some Scribes and Pharisees sitting there thought in their hearts,

7. "Who is this speaking blasphemy? Who is able to forgive sins except God alone?"

8. Yeshua knew in his Spirit that they were thinking these things in themselves. He said to them, "Why do you reason these things in your hearts?"

9. "What is easier to say to the paralytic: 'Your sins are forgiven you', or to say,'Arise, take your litter, and walk.'" ?

10. "But that you may know The Son of Man is authorized to forgive sins in the earth", he said to the paralytic:

11. "I say to you, get up, pick up your bed and go home."

12. And immediately he stood up, picked up his pallet and went out before the eyes of all of them, so that they were all astonished and they glorified God, as they were saying, "We have never seen such a thing!"

13. And he went out again to the sea and all the crowds were coming to him and he was teaching them.

14. As he passed, he saw Levi, son of Khalphi, sitting down at the place of taxation and he said to him, "Come after me", and rising he went after him.

15. And it was that as he reclined at supper in his house, there were many Tax Collectors

and sinners reclining at supper with Yeshua and with his disciples, for many had come, and they were following him.

16. And when the Scribes and Pharisees saw him eating with Tax Collectors and with sinners, they said to his disciples, "How is it that he eats and drinks with Tax Collectors and sinners?"

17. But when Yeshua heard, he said to them, "The healthy have no need for a physician, but those who have become very ill; I have not come to call the righteous, but sinners."

18. But the disciples of Yohannan and the Pharisees had been practicing fasting, and they came and they were saying to him, "Why do the disciples of Yohannan and of the Pharisees fast and your disciples do not fast?"

19. Yeshua said to them, "Are the children of the bridal chamber able to fast as long as the groom is with them? No!"

* The Peshitta says,"No! The Greek texts have a longer ending: "**As long as they have the bridegroom with them, they cannot fast**."
The two major Greek text types differ in word order, and the clause is a redundant and verbose (**10 Greek words**) Greek elaboration on the Aramaic word for "**No**" – ("**La**"- לא)! If "**brevity be the soul of wit**", the Greek version is much too long winded here to be witty. <u>The Peshitta</u> displays superior wit to the supposed inspired original Greek! The Greek translator was "too smart by half"; Our Lord said, "**Let your word be 'yes ,yes' and 'no ,no'; whatever is more than these comes of evil**."-Matthew 5:37 & see also James 5:12.

20. "But the days will come when the groom will be taken from them; then they will fast in those days."

21. "No man places a new strip of cloth and sews it on an old garment lest the fullness of that new cloth takes from the old, and it rips more."

22. "And no man pours new wine into old wineskins, lest the wine burst the wineskins and the wineskins are destroyed and the wine is spilled; but one pours new wine into new wineskins."

23. And so it was that when Yeshua went out on the Sabbath to a grain field, his disciples were walking and picking the ears of wheat.

24. And the Pharisees were saying to him, "Look, why are they doing something that is illegal on the Sabbath?"

25. Yeshua said to them, "Have you never read what David did when he was in great need and was hungry, he and his companions,

26. As he entered the house of God when Abiathar was Chief Priest, and he ate the bread of the altar of THE LORD

JEHOVAH, which was not legal to eat except for the priests? And he gave also to those who were with him."

27. And he said to them, "The Sabbath was created for the sake of man and not man for the sake of the Sabbath."

28. "Therefore The Son of Man is also master of the Sabbath."

Chapter 3

1. And Yeshua again entered the synagogue and a certain man was there, whose hand was shriveled.

2. And they were watching him, so that if he would heal him on the Sabbath, they might accuse him.

3. And he said to that man whose hand was shriveled, "Stand in the center."

4. But he said also to them, "Is it legal to do what is good on the Sabbath or what is evil; to save life or to destroy?" But they were silent.

5. And he gazed at them in anger as he was grieved for the callousness of their hearts, and he said to that man, "Stretch out your hand.", and he reached out and his hand was restored.

6. And the Pharisees went forth immediately with some of the house of Herodus and took counsel concerning him how they might destroy him. ("of the House of Herodus" is an idiom which indicates "supporters of Herod")

7. And Yeshua with his disciples went to the sea, and many people from Galilee and from Judea had gone out.

8. And great crowds came to him from Jerusalem and from Edom and from the region of Jordan, and from Tyre and from Zidon, because they had heard everything that he had done.

9. And he told his disciples that they should bring him a ship because of the crowds, lest they would throng him.

10. For he was healing many until they would be falling on him so that they might touch him.

11. And those who had plagues from foul spirits, when they saw *him*, they were falling down and they were crying out and they were saying, "You are the Son of God!"

12. And he greatly rebuked them lest they would reveal him.

13. And he went up a mountain and he called those whom he wanted and they came to join him.

14. And he chose twelve to be with him, and to send them to preach

15. And to be authorized to heal the sick and to cast out devils*. (Aramaic has several words referring to demons: the 2 main root words are שדא -"Shada" and דיוא – "Daywa". To distinguish between them, I translate "Shada" as "Demon" & "Daywa" as "devil" (small d) , in the archaic KJV sense of the word. Greek has only one root word for "demon"- "daimon". It is difficult to account for the two Aramaic roots with the theory that The Peshitta was translated from the Greek NT. Mt 12:24 in The Peshitta has both Aramaic words שדא -"Shada" and דיוא –"Daywa", as does Luke 11:14,15. Verse 14 has שדא -"Shada" twice; verse 15 has דיוא –"Daywa" twice.Greek everywhere has the root "daimon". "Shada" occurs 33 times and "Daywa" 30 times in The NT.

16. And he gave Shimeon the name Kaypha,

"Kaypha" does not come from Greek; it is Aramaic; The Greek has "Petros", which in the Greek mss. of John 1:42 is explained as the translation from the Aramaic "Kaypha" into Greek. If Yeshua had called Shimeon- "Peter" & the Aramaic were a translation of a Greek original, as is commonly supposed, the Aramaic could have easily transliterated "Petros" – פטרוס and then included a translation in Aramaic (Kaypha) כאפא. Instead we have the reverse.

17. And to Yaqob, the son of Zebedee and to Yohannan the brother of Yaqob he assigned the name B'nay Regshay*, which is B'nay Rama ("Passionate Sons").

- Greek has "Boanerges", clearly another transliteration of the Aramaic. Greek lexicons plainly state this is an Aramaic name. "Sons of Rage" specifies the meaning of "B'nay Ragshay", which could mean "Sons of rage", "Sons of tumult", "Sons of feeling" or "Sons of thunder", depending on the dialect of Aramaic and context. The Peshitta translates the Northern & Syrian Aramaic dialect- "B'nay Ragshay" into The Southern Palestinian dialect -"B'nay Rama", here. Usually the two dialects are the same in written form; they differ in only a few places in The Peshitta Gospels, which were written for Jewish and Gentile audiences in Israel, Syria, Persia & Asia Minor, who read Aramaic.

Codex W has:

KAIEΠEΘHKENONOMAENWNHTIETPON
KOINWCΔEAYTOYCEKAΛECENΒOANHPΓE
ΓE ΘECTINYIOIΒPONTHC HEANΛEOYTW

ΚΟΙΝΩΣ ΔΕ ΑΥΤΟΥΣ ΕΚΑΛΕΣΕΝ ΒΟΑΝΑΝΗΡΓΕΣ Ο ΕΣΤΙΝ ΥΙΟΙ ΒΡΟΝΤΗΣ

But He commonly called them "Boanan-erge", which is "Sons of Thunder".

All Greek mss. but W have "Boan-erges"- "Sons of Thunder". The Aramaic name in The Peshitta is

בני-רגשי –"Benay Regshayi".

DSS script:

בני-רמא –"Benay Rama" (Sons of Thunder)

בני-רגשי –"Benay Regshay" (Sons of Rage)

בני-רגה –"Benay-Regah" (Sons of Passion)

בני-רגזי –"Benay Ragzi" (Sons of Anger)

Estrangela: ܒܢܝ ܪܡܐ –"Benay Rama" (Sons of Thunder)

ܒܢܝ ܪܓܫܝ –"Benay Regshay" (Sons of Rage)

ܒܢܝ ܪܓܐ –"Benayn-Regah" (Sons of Passion)

ܒܢܝ ܪܓܙܝ –"Benayn Ragzi" (Sons of Anger)

ΒΟΑΝΑΝΗΡΓΕ looks like it represents "Benayn Aragah" (Sons of Passion"), which is a slight misreading of "Benay Regshi" ("Sons of Rage,feeling or perception").The grey shaded words above are the Greek reading of W in Aramaic words; just above them are the words in The Peshitta's Aramaic. Both words have the ideas of "Anger,Excitement,Tumult,Commotion,Uproar,". In DSS script which was used in the first century Aramaic of Israel,

"Regshay-Rage" is רגשי ;

"Regah-Passion" is רגא.

The Greek "υιοι βροντης" –"sons of thunder" is probably taken from the second phrase in the Peshitta describing the sons of Zebedee, which is

בני-רמא –"Benay Rama". This phrase has the same meaning as the first, just in a different Aramaic dialect (Southern Judean, as opposed to Northern Galilean for the first phrase)."Rama" can mean "Thunder,Pity,Rage,Resonance". Obviously, both names in the two dialects necessarily have the same meaning. The one on the two share in common is "Rage". The Greek transliteration in all Greek mss., including W, apparently misinterpreted the second name as "Sons of Thunder" whereas the first was a poor transliteration (in all Greek mss.) of "Benay Regsha", but a transliteration nonetheless. The "Sons of Thunder" reading in Greek is also shown to trace to the Aramaic of The Peshitta, interpreting the **Rama** part with the most common meaning, but a meaning inconsistent with the first name.

18. And Andreas and Philippus and Bar Tolmay* and Mattay and Thoma and Yaqob son of Khalphi and Thadi and Shimeon the Zealot,

* "Bar-Tolmay" , like so many other names with the "Bar" prefix, (meaning "son of") is plainly Aramaic. The Greek NT has over 50 of these Aramaic "Bar" names transliterated throughout The Gospels ,Acts and the Epistles of Paul. This indicates again that the NT books were written about Aramaic speaking people with Aramaic names and culture. A Greek speaking people would have primarily Greek names. This verse in W reveals a very unusual variation on "Bar-Tholomew"; it reads "Mar-Tholomew" here. "Mar" is Aramaic for "Master". In Luke 6:14, we find "Mat-Tholomew"!
Here is Bar-Tholomew in Dead Sea Scroll Aramaic:
ברתולומי
Here is Mar-Tholomew in Dead Sea Scroll Aramaic:
מרתולומי
Here is Mat-Tholomew in Dead Sea Scroll Aramaic:
מתתולומי
You can see how easily **the first century Aramaic script can account for the unique Greek readings in Codex W.** Mem (מ) and Beth (ב) are very similar to each other; Tau and Resh can also be mistaken, especially considering that the Resh is followed by a Tau also, and may have been pushed very close to it, looking like this: רת Here are two Tau's together:
תת
The corresponding Greek letters do not look similar: B – M ; P – T. The Aramaic can account much better for the slip up than Greek can. I have demonstrated this in more than 100 places in my Aramaic-English Interlinear New Testament, and in The Original Aramaic New Testament in Plain English, illustrated in Herodian Aramaic script (Dead Sea Scroll Aramaic) and in Greek script. This is more evidence that Codex W is a 1st century translation of The Peshitta text in a 1st century Dead Sea Scroll Aramaic script.

19. And Yehudah Skariota, he who would betray him, and they came to the house.

20. And crowds assembled again so that they were not going to be able to eat bread.

21. And his relatives heard and they went out to take hold of him, for they were saying, "He has gone out of his mind."

22. And the Scribes who had come down from Jerusalem were saying, "He has Beelzebub in him and by The Ruler of devils he casts out devils."

23. And Yeshua called them, and he said to them in parables, "How is Satan able to cast out Satan?"

24. "For if a kingdom will be divided against itself, that kingdom will not be able to stand."

25. "And if a house will be divided against itself, that house will not be able to stand."

26. "And if Satan were to rise up against himself and be divided, he would not be able to stand, but it would be his end."

27. "A man cannot enter the house of a mighty one and rob his valuables, unless he first binds the mighty one, and then he shall plunder his house."

28. "Truly I say to you, all sins and blasphemies that the sons of men will blaspheme shall be forgiven them,"

29. "But there is never forgiveness to whoever will blaspheme against The Spirit of Holiness, but he is condemned to eternal judgment;"

30. Because they were saying, "He has a foul spirit."

31. And his mother and his brothers came, standing outside, and they sent that they might call him to them.

32. But the crowd was sitting around him, and they said to him, "Behold, your mother and your brothers are outside looking for you."

33. And he answered and said to them, "Who is my mother and who are my brothers?"

34. And he looked on those who were sitting with him and he said, "Here *is* my mother and here *are* my brethren."

35. "For whoever shall do the will of God is my brother and my sister and my mother."

Chapter 4

1. But he began teaching again at the seaside and great crowds were gathered to him, so that he would go up and sit in a boat in the sea and all the crowd was standing on land at the shore.

2. He was teaching them in many parables, and he said in his teaching:

3. "Listen; behold, a sower went out to sow."

4. "And as he sowed, there was some that fell on the side of the road and a bird came and ate it."

5. "But other seed fell on rock where there was not much soil, and immediately it sprouted because there was no depth of soil."

6. "But when the sun arose it was scorched, and because it had no roots, it dried up."

7. "Other fell among the thorns and the thorns came up and choked it, and it yielded no fruit."

8. "But other fell in good ground, and it came up and grew and it yielded fruit, some thirty fold and some sixtyfold and some a hundredfold."

9. And he said, "Whoever has an ear to hear, let him hear."

10. But when they were by themselves, those twelve who were with him inquired of him about that parable.

11. Yeshua said to them, "It has been given to you to know the secrets of the Kingdom of God, but to outsiders, everything has been in parables,"

12. "So that seeing they shall see and not see, and hearing they shall hear and they shall not understand, unless perhaps they shall be converted and their sins shall be forgiven them."

13. He said to them, "Do you not know this parable? How shall you know all the parables?"

14. "The sower, who sowed, sowed the word."

15. "But these upon the side of the road are those who have the word sown in them, and when they have heard, immediately Satan comes and takes the word away that was sown in their hearts."

16. "And those that were sown upon the rock are those who when they have heard the word immediately receive it with joy."

17. "And they have no root in themselves, but they abide for a while, and when there is distress or persecution because of the word, they are soon subverted."

18. "And those sown among the thorns are those who have heard the word,"

19. "And the cares of this world and the seductiveness of wealth and other desires are entering in and choking the word and it becomes unfruitful."

20. "And they that were sown in the good ground are those who hear the word and

receive *it,* and yield fruit, thirtyfold , sixtyfold and a hundredfold."

21. And he said to them, "Does one bring a lamp to be put under a basket or under a bed? Should it not be put on a lampstand?"

22."For there is nothing covered that shall not be revealed, and nothing secret that will not be discovered."

23."If a man has an ear to hear, let him hear."

24.And he said to them, "Take heed what you hear; that measure in which you are measuring is measured to you, and it is increased to you who hear."

25.For whoever has it, it shall be given to him; and whoever does not have it, from him shall be taken even that which he has.

26.And he said, "Thus is the Kingdom of God like a man who cast seed in the ground."

27."And he shall sleep and arise by night and by day and the seed grows and lengthens while he is unaware."

28."For the earth produces fruit itself; first shall be the blade and afterward the ear, then finally the full wheat in the ear."

29."But whenever the fruit ripens, immediately the sickle is brought because the harvest has arrived."

30.And he said, "What shall resemble the Kingdom of God and with what shall a parable compare it?"

31. "It is like a grain of mustard seed, which when it is sown in the ground, is the smallest of all the herb seeds on the earth."

32."And when it is sown it comes up and becomes greater than all the small herbs and produces great branches, so that the birds will be able to perch in its shade."

33.Yeshua was speaking parables like these with them, parables such as they were able to hear.

34.And without parables he was not speaking with them, but he expounded all things to his disciples privately.

35.He said to them that day in the evening, "Let us pass over to the other side."

36.And they left the crowd and brought him as he was in the ship, and there were other boats with them.

37.And there was a great storm and the wind and the waves were beating into the ship and it was close to being filled.

38.But Yeshua was sleeping on a pillow in the stern of the ship and they came and awakened him and they were saying to him,

"Our Master, do you not care that we are perishing?!"

39.And he arose and rebuked the wind and he said to the sea, "Stop! Shut up!", and the wind stopped, and there was a great calm.

40.And he said to them, "Why are you so fearful? Why do you not have faith?"

41. And they were greatly afraid, and they were saying one to another, "Who is this, really, that the wind and sea obey him?"

Chapter 5

1. And he came to the other side of the sea to the region of the Gadarenes.

2. And when he went out from the ship, a man met him from among the tombs that had a foul spirit in him.

3. And he dwelt among the tombs and no one was able to bind him with chains,

4. Because whenever he had been bound in shackles and chains he had broken the chains and cut the shackles apart and no one was able to subdue him.

5. And always at night and in the daytime he was among the tombs and in the mountains and was crying out and cutting himself with stones.

6. But when he saw Yeshua from a distance he ran and prostrated himself.

7. And he cried out in a loud voice and he said, "What do I have to do with you, Yeshua, Son of God Most High? I adjure you by God that you will not torture me!"

8. For he had said to him, "Come out from the man, foul spirit!"

* "Tenapta" ("foul") is usually feminine in gender to agree with "Rokha" ("Spirit"), which is also feminine in gender, regardless of context; here , however, "Tenapa" is masculine, probably indicating that a masculine spirit was the ruling spirit of "The Legion" of spirits.

9. And he had asked him, "What is your name?" He said to him, "Our name* is Legion, for we are many." * Greek has "My name". שמען is "our name" in Aramaic. שמי is "my name" in Aramaic.

10. And he begged of him much that he would not send him out of the region.

11. But there was near the mountain a great herd of swine that were feeding.

12. And those evil spirits were begging of him and they were saying, "Send us unto those swine that we may enter them."

13. And he allowed them, and these foul spirits went out and entered into the swine, and that herd ran to a precipice and fell into

the sea, about two thousand *of them,* and they drowned in the water.

14. And they who were herding them fled and told it in the city, also in the villages, and they went out to see what had happened.

15. And they came to Yeshua and they saw him who had been possessed by the evil spirits with him, clothed and reverent, and he who before had the Legion in him was sitting, and they were afraid.

16. And those who had seen how it had been with him whom the evil spirits had possessed, reported to them, and also about those swine.

17. And they began to ask him to depart from their coast.

18. And after he embarked the ship, he whom the evil spirits had possessed was requesting of him that he might remain with him.

19. And he did not allow him, but he said to him, "Go to your house to your people and relate to them what **THE LORD JEHOVAH** has done for you and that he has had compassion upon you."

20. And he departed and he began preaching in the ten cities what Yeshua had done for him, and they were all astounded.

21. And after Yeshua had crossed in the ship to the other side, great crowds were again assembled unto him while he was on the seaside.

22. And one of The Rulers of the synagogue, whose name was Yorash, came, and when he had seen him, he fell at his feet.

23. And he was begging him greatly and he said to him, "My daughter has become very ill; come lay your hand upon her and she will be healed, and she will live."

24. And Yeshua went on with him and a great crowd was close to him and pressing upon him.

25. But there was a certain woman who had a flow of blood twelve years

26. Who had suffered greatly from many physicians and had spent everything that she had and she had not been helped at all, but she had become even worse.

27. When she heard about Yeshua, she came in the press of the crowd from behind him and she touched his garment,

28. For she said, " If I touch even his garment, I shall be saved."

29. And at once the fount of her blood dried up, and she sensed in her body that she was healed of her plague.

30. But Yeshua knew in himself at once that power had gone out from him and he turned to the crowds and he said, "Who has touched my garment?"

31. And his disciples were saying to him, "You see the crowd pressing against you, and do you say, 'Who has touched me?' "

32. And he was gazing that he might see who had done this.

33. But that woman, being afraid and trembling, for she knew what had happened to her, came and fell down before him and told him all the truth.

34. But he said to her, "My daughter, your faith has saved you; go in peace and be whole from your disease."

35. And while he was speaking, those who were from the house of The Ruler of the synagogue came, and they were saying, "Your daughter has died. Why should you now trouble The Teacher?"

36. But Yeshua heard the words which they spoke and he said to The Ruler of the assembly, "Do not fear; only believe."

37. And he allowed no one to go with him except Shimeon Kaypha and Yaqob and Yohannan, brother of Yaqob.

38. And they came to The Chief of the assembly's house and he saw those who were disturbed and weeping and wailing.

39. And he entered and he said to them, "Why are you disturbed and weeping? The girl is not dead, but she is sleeping."

40.   And they were laughing at him, but he put all of them out and he took the father of the girl and her mother, and those who were with him, and he entered the place where the girl was lying.

41. And he took the girl's hand and he said to her, "Little girl, arise."

42. Immediately the young girl arose, and she was walking, for she was twelve years old, and they were astounded with great astonishment.

43. And he commanded them strictly that they should not relate this to anyone, and he said that they should give her food.

Chapter 6

1. And he went out from there and he came to the city, and his disciples were staying close to him.

2. And when it was The Sabbath, he began to teach in the synagogue and many who

heard were amazed and they were saying, "From where does this man have these things? What is this wisdom given to him that mighty works like these should be done by his hands?"

3. "Is this not the carpenter, son of Maryam and brother of Yaqob, and Yose and Yehudah and Shimeon, and are not his sisters here with us?" And they were suspicious of him.

4. And Yeshua said to them, "There is no Prophet who is despised except in his city and among his kindred and in his house."

5. And he was not able to do even one powerful work there, but only laid his hands upon a few sick folks and healed them.

6. He was astonished at the lack of their faith and he was going around in the villages as he taught.

7. And he called his twelve and he began to send them two by two and he gave them authority over vile spirits to cast them out.

8. And he commanded them that they would not take anything on the road except perhaps a staff, no bag, no bread, no copper in their purses,

9. But that they would wear sandals, and they should not wear two tunics.

10. And he said to them, "Into whatever house you enter, stay there until you depart from there."

11. "And all who will not receive you and will not hear you, when you leave that place, shake off the dust that is on the soles of your feet for their testimony; truly I say to you that it will be tranquil for Sadom and Amorah in the day of judgment compared to that city."

12. And they went out and they preached that they should return *to God*.

13. And they were casting out many evil spirits, and they were anointing the many sick with oil and they were healing *them*.

14. And Herodus The King heard about Yeshua, for his name was known to him and he said, "He is Yohannan The Baptizer; he is raised from the grave, therefore, mighty works are performed by him."

15. Others were saying, "He is Elijah", and others, "He is a Prophet like one of The Prophets."

16. Now when Herodus heard, he said, "Yohannan, whose head I cut off, has arisen from the grave."

17. For Herodus had sent and seized Yohannan and bound him in the prison for the sake of Herodia, whom he had taken, the wife of Phillipus his brother.

18. For Yohannan had said to Herodus, "It is not lawful for you to take the wife of your brother."

19. But Herodia was threatening him and she wanted to kill him and was unable.

20. Herodus had been afraid of Yohannan because he had known that he was a righteous and holy man, and he protected him and he heard many things that he had said and did services *for him* , and he heard him with pleasure.

21. It was a notable day when Herodus made a supper for his nobles and for the Captains and the Leaders of Galilee on his birthday.

22. And the daughter of Herodia came in, and she danced, and she pleased Herodus and those who were reclining with him, and The King said to the girl, "Ask of me anything that you desire, and I shall give it to you."

23. And he swore to her, "Anything that you shall ask, I shall give to you, unto the half of my Kingdom."

24. But she went out and said to her mother, "What shall I ask?" She said to her, "The head of Yohannan The Baptizer."

25. At once she entered with diligence to the King, and she said to him, "I want you to give me on a dish, this hour, the head of Yohannan The Baptizer."

26. And it grieved The King much, but because of the oath and because of the dinner guests, he was unwilling to deny her.

27. The King sent the executioner at once and commanded to bring the head of Yohannan and he went and cut off the head of Yohannan in the prison.

28. And he brought it on a plate and he gave it to the girl and the girl gave it to her mother.

29. His disciples heard and they came and took his corpse and laid it in a tomb.

30. And The Apostles were gathered unto Yeshua and they told him everything that they had done and everything whatever they had taught.

31. And he said to them, "Come, we shall go to the country alone and rest yourselves a little." For there were many going and coming and there was not a place for them even to eat.

32. And they went to a deserted place in a ship by themselves.

33. And many saw them as they were going, and they recognized them and they ran on

land from all the cities before him to that place.

34. And Yeshua went forth, seeing the great crowds, and he was moved with pity on them, for they were like sheep without a shepherd, and he began to teach them many things.

35. And when the time had grown late, his disciples came to him and they were saying to him, "This is a desolate place and the time is late."

36. "Dismiss them that they may go to the market that they may go around to the villages also and buy bread for themselves, for there is nothing for them to eat."

37. He said to them, "You give them food." They said to him, "Shall we go buy 200 denarii of bread and give them to eat?"

38. He said to them, "Go see how many loaves you have here." When they looked, they said to him, "Five loaves and two fish."

39. And he commanded them to seat everyone on the grass.

40. And they were seated by hundreds and by fifties.

41. And he took those five loaves and two fish and gazed into Heaven and he blessed and broke the bread, and he gave to his disciples to set before them and they divided those two fish for all of them.

42. And they all ate and they were filled.

43. And they took up twelve baskets full of the fragments and also of the fish.

44. Now those who ate the bread were five thousand men.

45. And at once he urged his disciples to board the ship and go before him to the other side to Bethsaida while he sent the multitude away.

46. And when he had sent them away he went to a mountain to pray.

47. But when it had become evening, the boat was in the middle of the sea and he was alone on the land.

48. And he saw them laboring as they were rowing, for the wind was against them. And it was, that in the fourth watch of the night, Yeshua came toward them as he was walking on the sea, and he wanted to pass by them.

49. They saw him that he was walking on the water, and they thought to themselves that he was a hallucination and they cried out,

50. For they all saw him and they were afraid and immediately he spoke with them and he said to them, "Take heart, I AM THE LIVING GOD; do not be afraid."

51. And he came up to join them in the ship and the wind ceased, and they were greatly astonished and they wondered in their souls.

52. For they had not learned from the bread, because their heart was stupid.

53. And when they had crossed to the other side, they came to the land of Genesar.

And when they had crossed to the other side, they came to the land of Genesar.
Three Greek versions follow:
(WH) και διαπερασαντες επι την γην ηλθον εις γεννησαρετ και προσωρμισθησαν
And when they had crossed over, they came to the land unto Gennesaret, and drew to the shore.
(BYZ) και διαπερασαντες ηλθον επι την γην γεννησαρετ και προσωρμισθησαν
And when they had crossed over, they came into the land of Gennesaret, and drew to the shore.
(DSS) και τιαπερασαντες ηλθον εις γεννησαρετ και προσωρμισθησαν
And when they had crossed over, they came unto Gennesaret, and drew to the shore.
What is particularly interesting is the third Greek version; it is called **7Q5**, and was found in Cave 7 with other Dead Sea scrolls in Israel. It is dated approx. AD 50. It and the two other versions represent each a valid translation of the Peshitta text, except for the last part **"& they drew to the shore"**, which is not found in The Peshitta. The word "land", or "city" is sometimes not found in Greek where it is found in The Peshitta in conjunction with its name. The same phenomenon occurs in the LXX Greek translation of the OT , where the Hebrew word for "Land"- "eretz" occurs; The Greek drops it about 7% of the time. The Westcott and Hort text apparently drops the word four times of the twenty times it occurs in a place name in the NT. The Peshitta generally agrees more with the majority Byzantine text, but not infrequently sides with the Critical editions. It does not consistently follow any Greek text type , and frequently disagrees with all Greek texts. At the same time, it can usually be shown that the Greek versions are derived as translations from the Aramaic of The Peshitta.
7Q5 seems to have set a precedent for the other Greek texts. It looks as if it read The Peshitta with a different word order, the third ,"**Ebra**" can mean ,"**the other side, the crossing, the region, to pass over, to draw near, to pass away**" and fifth (**"Area"- "land, earth,ground,soil"**-probably the cognate for the English, "Area") words placed at the end of the sentence. They could easily be interpreted as "**drew to the shore**". These are the very two words that seem missing in the text at first; the third ("Ebra" -"other side") seems at first to have been missing in all the Greek texts; the fifth, ("Erea"- "land") seemed missing in 7Q5 and displaced in the other two.
Quite often, we see an apparent change in word order in various Greek versions as compared to The Peshitta. Nevertheless, 7Q5 looks like the first Greek exemplar, on which the other Greek texts built, following the interpretation- "**προσωρμισθησαν**" -"drew to the shore", and yet adding "**επι την γην** " ("to the land") before "Gennesaret" , according to The Peshitta.
The discovery of 7Q5, (See Thiede's "The Dead Sea Scrolls", copyright 2000), means that the NT was translated very early into Greek, probably before AD 50. I have more analysis and comparison of Greek Mark with The Peshitta at my web site: http://aramaicnt.com
Codex W (1st century) has the closest reading of any Greek ms. to The Peshitta here and in the next verse.

54. And when they went out from the boat, immediately the men of the place recognized him.

Codex W

KAI ΔIAΠEPAΣANTEΣ HΛΘAN EΠI THN ΓHN EIΣ
ΓENNHΣAPET - v. 53
KAI EΞEΛΘONTΩN AYTΩN EK TOY ΠΛOIOY
EYΘYΣ EΠIΓNONTEΣ AYTON OI ANΔPEΣ
TOY TOΠOY – v. 54

**"And crossing over they came to the land into Gennesaret.
And when they got out of the boat, immediately the
men of the place knew him."**
This reading of W is amazingly close to The Peshitta reading
and is unlike any other Greek reading.

55. And they ran in all that area, and they
began to bring those who had become sick, as
they were carrying them in litters to the place
where they heard that he was.
56. And wherever he had entered a village or
city, they were laying the sick in the streets,
and they were begging him if they might
touch even the fringe of his garment, and all
those who were touching it were healed.

Chapter 7

1. The Pharisees and the Scribes who had
come from Jerusalem gathered around him.
2. And they saw some of his disciples eating
bread when they had not washed their hands,
and they found fault.

The Greek texts exhibit some interpretation in verse two:
"having **defiled, that is unwashed hands**". The Critical Greek
text of Westcott and Hort has two words not found in the
Majority Greek text, another verb is different in form from the
majority text's participle , and the last verb, "EMEMΨANTO"
(emempsanto –"they found fault"), is missing completely,
making the whole verse a dangling modifier , and not a
sentence at all in Greek! If one were to argue that W&H are
correct, then one must argue for a sentence (v.2-v.5) four
verses long in Mark, which is highly unlikely, since his style is
very terse and plain with simple sentences. The Peshitta has
each verse as a complete sentence.

3. For all the Judeans and the Pharisees do not
eat unless they wash their hands carefully*
because they keep the tradition of the Elders.

*Here Codex W seems more accurate than the other Greek
mss.. They have ΠYΓMA ("fist"), which looks like a
misreading of W's ΠYKNA ("often,diligently").The Old
Syriac lacks anything answering to either word, while The
Peshitta has דבטילאית (D'vetilayth-"carefully,diligently").

4. And *coming* from the marketplace, unless
they bathe, they do not eat. And there are
many other things which they had received to
keep: washings of cups and pots and copper
vessels and of beds.

- The different Greek texts have βαπτισωνται "**baptize**" –
Majority text & , ραντισωνται "**wash**"- Vaticanus and
Sinaiticus (4th cent.).The Aramaic word "עמדין" can mean
"baptize", "wash" or "bathe". Might this account for the
Greek variants? If this were the only such place where this type
of inter-language correlation occurs between Aramaic &
Greek, perhaps not, but this is not the only place. There are
hundreds such occurrences in The NT!

5. And the Scribes and Pharisees asked him,
"Why do your disciples not walk according to
the tradition of the Elders, but eat bread
without having washed their hands?"

Here again, the Greek texts display variation, as in
verse 2. The Majority Greek text has "ανιπτοις
χερσιν"- "**unwashed hands**"; Westcott & Hort's
text has "κοιναις χερσιν" –"**defiled hands**".
Verse 2 in the Greek texts has both , seemingly in an
attempt to **interpret** it correctly! "Unwashed" is the
Peshitta's meaning; "Defiled" is the religious
interpretation the Pharisees put on "Unwashed". The
Greek texts seem to "**interpret**" various Aramaic
words; another word for "interpret" is the Greek word
"**hermayneuo**"- (i.e, "**translate**").The Greek NT uses
that very word six times with literal Aramaic phrases
and words, which it then "**hermayneuo 's**" **into
Greek!**

6. But he said to them, "Isaiah the Prophet
prophesied beautifully of you imposters, just
as it is written: 'This people honors* me with
its lips, but their heart is very far from Me.'
Greek:TIMA ("honors").
AΓAΠA ("loves") -Codex W Greek

(AΓAΠA –Codices W,D,Tertullian) AΓAΠA in
Aramaic can be רחם or חבב .
TIMA is יקר . In Pesher Habakkuk script:
(Aramaic text) or (Aramaic text) -"loves"
& (Aramaic text) - "honors".
Codex D also often follows **Peshitta** readings against all
other Greek readings.

20706

(Aramaic text lines)

Ancient 1st century Aramaic alphabet (Pesher Habakkuk
Dead Sea Scroll script (circa 40 to 1 B.C.) looks like
this: (Aramaic alphabet)
The Essene Dead Sea script of The Great Isaiah
Scroll (100 B.C.) looks like this:
(Aramaic alphabet)

7. 'And in vain they pay reverence to me as
they teach doctrines of commandments of the
sons of men.'
8. "You forsake the commandments of God
and you keep the traditions of the sons of
men: washings of cups and pots and many
such things like these."
9. He said to them, "Well you reject the
commandment of God that you may
establish* your traditions."

*Three very old (1st,5th -6th cent.) Greek mss. agree with
The Peshitta reading "that you may **establish** your
traditions". The other Greek mss. have "that you may
keep your traditions".Greek for keep is THPHΣHTE;
ΣTHΣHTAI is "establish", found in Codex W.
(Aramaic text) OS
(Aramaic text)
(D,W,Θ) agree with **Peshitta** against other Greek mss. & OS.

ܩܡ, ܩܡ fut. ܢܩܘܡ, act. part. ܩܐܡ, ܡܣܚܐ verbal adj. ܩܐܡ, ܡܬܩܡ see above. *a) to rise, arise,* esp. ܩܡ ܡܢ ܫܢܬܐ *from sleep; from death;* ܡܩܝܡܢܐ *pre-existent.* ETHPA. ܐܬܩܝܡ *to be established, strengthened, confirmed, ratified, to come to pass; to be erected; to be appointed; able* as a promise; also *to stand by, keep to one's word, the law, with* ܒ *or* ܥܠ. *g) to*

The Aramaic root word "**Qam**" has both meanings- "**keep**" and "**be established**". Can it be that all of them got their readings from The Peshitta's Aramaic ?

10.For Moses said, "Honor your father and your mother", and "Whoever reviles* father and mother shall die the death."

> *Greek: O <u>KAKOΛOΓΩN</u>-"He who <u>speaks evil</u>"
> **Codex W:** O AΘETΩN-"He who **rejects**"
> AΘETΩN –"rejects", in Aramaic is ܡܣܠܐ. Only Codex W has this reading.
> <u>KAKOΛOΓΩN</u> –"speaks evil", is ܡܨܚܐ . All other Greek mss. have this.
> Both readings seem better explained as translations of Aramaic rather than vice-versa.

11.But you say, "If a man shall say to his father or to his mother, 'My offering is anything that you shall gain from me.'

12.Then you do not allow him to do anything for his father or his mother.

13.And you reject the word of God for the traditions that you deliver, and many things like these you do."

14.And Yeshua called to all the crowds, and he said to them, "Hear me all of you and understand."

15."There is nothing outside of a man that enters into him that can defile him, but the thing that proceeds from him, that is what defiles the man."

16."Whoever has an ear to hear, let him hear."

17.But when Yeshua entered the house from the crowds, his disciples asked him about that parable.

18.He said to them, "Are you also stupid? Do you not know that nothing entering from outside a man can defile him?"

19."Because it does not enter his heart, but his belly, and is discharged by excretion, which purifies all foods."

20."But the thing that proceeds from a man, that defiles the man."

21."For from within the heart of the children of men proceed evil ideas, adultery, fornication, theft, murder."

22."Greed, wickedness, deceit, harlotry, an evil eye, blasphemy, boasting, senselessness."

23."All these evils proceed from within and defile a man."

24.Yeshua arose from there and came to the coast of Tyre and of Sidon, and he entered a certain house and he did not want anyone to know him and he could not be hidden.

25.For immediately a certain woman heard about him, whose daughter had a foul spirit, and she came falling before his feet.

26.But she was a pagan woman from Phoenicia of Syria, and she was begging him to cast out the demon from her daughter.

27.And Yeshua said to her, "Let the children be filled first, for it is not right to take the children's bread and throw it to the dogs."

28.But she answered and said to him, "Yes, my lord, *but* even the dogs from under the table eat the children's crumbs."

29.Yeshua said to her, "Go; because of this saying the demon has gone out from your daughter."

30.And she went to her house and found her daughter lying in bed, and the demon had been cast out of her.

31.Yeshua again went out from the coast of Tyre and Sidon, and he came to the Sea of Galilee at the border of The Ten Cities.

32.And they brought him a certain deaf man who was dumb and they begged him to lay hands upon him.

33.And he took him aside from the crowd alone and put his fingers in his ears and spat and he touched his tongue.

34.And he gazed into Heaven and he groaned and he said to him, "Be opened*."

> * אתפתח –"Ethpathakh", "Be opened", is transliterated in all Greek mss. and then translated into Greek. This is just another of many such cases in all known Greek mss. of The Gospels and Acts. The Peshitta has no cases of transliterating Greek phrases with a translation following.
> <u>What is difficult to account for is that there are any translations of Aramaic into Greek accompanying a transliterated Aramaic word or phrase, **assuming the Greek to be the original.**</u>
> There are many more transliterations which are simply left alone; no translation follows. "Raca","Mammon", "Corban", "Maranatha", "Gehenna", etc.
> The inclusion of those contained in The Greek begs the question: Where is the original Aramaic?
> The many other tell tale Aramaic words have over two hundred total occurrences in the Greek NT, suggesting Aramaic sources which occasionally posed a challenge to a translator, hence the puzzling transliterations : "Beelzebub", "Belial", "Raca", "Maranatha", "Mammon", "Corban", all of which are unexplained and untranslated. They are not Greek words. They are all Aramaic –"Belial" is Hebrew; So also for the Hellenism "Satanas", from the Aramaic, "Satana.". The LXX always translates The Hebrew "Ha Satan" with the Greek "Diabolos", except in *1* Kings 11:14, where it transliterates "Satan" as "Satan"(not " Satana") twice. The Greek NT translates the Aramaic "Satana" with the Greek "Diabolos" about half the time, and the other half uses the Aramaic word "Satana" in Greek letters. The Aramaic "Satana" occurs 36 times in the Majority Greek text in twelve books from Matthew to Revelation!

35. And at that moment his ears were opened and a bond of his tongue was released and he spoke distinctly.

36. And he warned them not to tell anyone, and as much as he warned them, they all the more proclaimed it.

37. And they were greatly astonished, and they were saying, "He has done everything beautifully; he has made the deaf to hear and him who was mute to speak."

Chapter 8

1. But in those days when there was a great crowd and there was nothing for them to eat, he called his disciples and said to them:

2. "I have pity on this crowd, for behold, they have continued with me three days and there is nothing for them to eat."

3. "And if I send them away fasting to their houses they will faint in the road, for some among them have come from far away."

4. His disciples said to him, "From where here in the desert can a man supply enough bread for all of these?"

5. He asked them, "How many loaves do you have?, and they said, "Seven."

6. And he commanded the crowds to recline on the ground and he took those seven loaves and blessed and broke and he gave to his disciples to be set out, and they set them out for the crowd.

7. And there were a few fish, and he blessed them, and he said to set them out.

8. And they ate and were filled and they took up the leftovers of fragments seven baskets.

9. But there were about four thousand men who ate.

10. And he sent them away and came up at once to the ship with his disciples and came to the region of Dalmanutha.

11. And Pharisees came out and they began to inquire with him and they were asking him for a sign from Heaven, while tempting him.

12. And he groaned in his spirit and he said, "Why does this generation seek for a sign? Truly I say to you, a sign shall not be given to this generation."

13. And he left them and boarded the ship and they went to the other side.

14. They had forgotten to take bread, and except for one cake, there was nothing with them in the ship.

15. And he commanded them and he said to them, "Behold, beware of the yeast of the Pharisees and of the yeast of Herodus."

16. And they were reasoning with one another, and they were saying, "It is because we have no bread."

17. But Yeshua knew and he said to them, "Why are you considering that you have no bread? Do you not yet know? Do you not yet understand? Your heart is still hard."

18. "You have eyes and do not see and you have ears and you do not hear, neither do you remember."

19. "When I broke those five loaves for the five thousand, after they were filled, how many baskets of fragments did you take up?" They said to him, "Twelve."

20. He said to them, "And when the seven to the four thousand, after they were filled, how many baskets of fragments did you take up?" They said, "Seven."

21. He said to them, "How is it that you still do not understand?"

22. And he came to Bethsaida, and they brought a blind man to him, and they were begging him to touch him.

23. And he grasped the hand of the blind man and took him outside the town and he spat in his eyes and laid his hand upon him and he asked him what he saw.

24. He gazed and he said, "I see people like trees that are walking."

25. He laid his hand again on his eyes and he was healed, and he saw everything clearly.

26. And he sent him to his house and he said, "Do not enter the town, neither tell anyone in the town."

27. Yeshua and his disciples went out to the villages of Caesarea Philippi, and he was asking his disciples in the road and he said to them, "What is it the people are saying about me as to who I am?"

28. Some said, "Yohannan the Baptizer", and others "Elijah" and others, "One of The Prophets."

29. And Yeshua said to them, "But what is it you are saying about me as to who I am?" Shimeon answered and he said to him, "You are The Messiah, The Son of THE LIVING GOD*."

* Codex W (1ˢᵗ cent.?) alone has the reading, "**The Son of the Living God**", among early Greek mss.. The Farrar group (a collection of 13 late miniscules, 11ᵗʰ-15ᵗʰ century) also have this reading. What is noteworthy of this reading is that The Peshitta has it. W often supports Peshitta readings not found in most Greek mss., as well as often supporting those which are found in most Greek

mss..(See the fascinating book, <u>Kodex W, Old and Holy,</u> by Dr. Lee Woodard.)

30. And he admonished them that they should not speak about him to anyone.

31. And he began to teach them: "The Son of Man is going to suffer many things and to be rejected by the Elders and by the Chief Priests and by the Scribes and he shall be killed, and in three days he shall rise."

32. And he was speaking the word openly and Kaypha took him aside and began to rebuke him.

33. But he turned and gazed at his disciples and rebuked Shimeon and said, "Depart behind me Satan, for you do not reason of God, but of the children of men."

34. And Yeshua called the crowds with his disciples, and he said to them, "Whoever is willing to come after me, let him renounce himself* and take up his cross and let him come after me."

* "Himself" is "Napsha"- נפשא in Aramaic; this Aramaic word occurs five times in verses 34-38 and can mean: "Breath of life, Person, Self, Soul, Life,". It is very similar to the Hebrew word, "Nephesh" נפש. An asterisk marks the places in each of these verses where Napsha occurs. See my interlinear for details.

35. "Whoever desires to save his soul* will lose it. Everyone who will lose his life* for me and for my gospel will save it."

36. "For how is a man benefited if he should gain the whole world and he should lose his soul*?"

37. "Or what payment shall a man give to regain his soul* again?

38. "For everyone who shall be ashamed of me and my words in this sinning and adultery committing generation, of him also shall The Son of Man be ashamed whenever he comes in the glory of his Father with his Holy Angels."

Chapter 9

1. And he said to them, "Amen, I say to you, there are men standing here who shall not taste death until they will behold the Kingdom of God coming with wonders."

2. And after six days Yeshua led Kaypha, Yaqob and Yohannan and took them up to a high mountain by themselves and he was transfigured before their eyes.

3. And his garment was shining and became very white, like snow, in a manner by which men on earth are not able to whiten.

4. And Elijah and Moses appeared to them as they were speaking with Yeshua.

5. And Kaypha said to him, "Rabbi, it is beautiful for us to be here ; let us make three tabernacles, one for you, one for Moses, and one for Elijah."

6. But he did not know what he was saying, for they were in awe.

7. And there was a cloud and it was a shelter about them, and a voice from the cloud which said, "This is my Beloved Son, hear him."

8. And suddenly afterward, the disciples gazed up, and they saw no one except Yeshua alone with them.

9. And when they descended from the mountain, he commanded them that they would tell no one anything that they had seen until after The Son of Man had risen from the dead.

10. And they seized on that statement in their souls and they were inquiring, "What is this statement, 'When he rises from among the dead?"

11. And they asked him and they said, "Why do the Scribes say therefore that Elijah must come first?"

12. He said to them, "Elijah does come first, so that he may prepare all things, and just as it is written about The Son of Man, he will suffer much and be rejected."

13. "But I say to you also that Elijah has come and they did to him everything whatever they wished, just as it is written about him."

14. And when he came to the disciples he saw the great crowds among them and the Scribes debating with them.

15. And immediately all the crowds saw him and they were astonished and ran and greeted him.

16. And he was asking The Scribes, "What are you debating with them?"

17. And one from the crowds answered and said, "Teacher, I brought my son to you, who has a dumb spirit."

18. "And whenever it comes upon him, it throws him and it beats him and he gnashes his teeth and he wastes away, and I spoke to your disciples that they might cast it out, and they were not able."

19. Yeshua answered and said to them, "Oh faithless generation, how long will I be with

you? How long shall I endure you? Bring him to me."

20. And they brought him to him, and when the spirit saw him, immediately he threw him and he fell on the ground and he was convulsed and he foamed.

21. Yeshua asked his father, "How long a time now has he been like this? He said to him, "From his childhood."

22. "And many times it has thrown him into fire and into water to destroy him. But if you can do anything, help me, and have mercy on me!"

23. Yeshua said to him, "If you are able to believe, everything is possible to the one who believes."

24. And immediately the father of the boy cried out weeping and saying, "I believe my lord ; help the lack of my faith."

25. And when Yeshua saw that the people ran and gathered near him, he rebuked that foul spirit and he said to it, "Deaf spirit, that does not speak, I am commanding you, go out from him, and you shall not enter him again."

26. And that demon screamed greatly and pounded him and went out and he was like a dead man, so that many were saying, "He is dead."

27. But Yeshua took him by his hand and raised him up.

28. But when Yeshua had entered the house, his disciples asked him among themselves, "Why were we not able to cast it out?"

29. He said to them, "This sort cannot come out by anything except by fasting and by prayer."

30. And when he went out from there, they were passing through Galilee, and he did not want anyone to recognize him.

31. For he was teaching his disciples and he said to them, "The Son of Man will be delivered into the hands of men and they will kill him, and when he has been killed, on the third day he shall rise."

32. But they did not understand that saying, and they were afraid to ask him.

33. And they came to Kapernahum and when they entered the house, he asked them, "What were you reasoning on the road among yourselves?"

34. But they were silent, for they had been arguing on the road with one another who was the greatest among them.

35. And Yeshua sat down and he called the twelve and he said to them, "He who wants

to be first shall be last, and the servant of every person."

36. And he took a certain boy and stood him in the midst and took him up on his shoulders and he said to them:

37. "Whoever shall receive one boy like this in my name is receiving me, and whoever receives me has not received me, but him who sent me.

38. Yohannan said to him, "Rabbi, we saw a man casting out demons in your name, and we forbade him because he did not go out with us."

39. Yeshua said to them, "Do not forbid him, for there is no man who does a powerful work in my name and can soon speak badly about me."

40. "Whoever therefore is not against you is for you."

41. "But everyone who will give you only a cup of water to drink in the name that you are one who belongs to The Messiah, amen, I say to you, he shall not lose his reward."

42. "And everyone who shall subvert one of these little ones who believe in me, it were better for him if a millstone of a donkey were hung around his neck and he were cast into the sea." ("Millstone of a donkey" is a large, flat, circular, cut stone weighing a 1/2 ton or more. Grain was ground between two millstones while a donkey, tied to a long pole attached to the upper millstone would walk around a circle.)

43. "If your hand subverts you, cut it off, for it is better for you that you enter the Life maimed, than when you have two hands, you would go to Gehenna."

44. "Where their worm does not die and their fire is not quenched."

The literalist insists Gehenna is Hell with a literal worm and a literal fire , yet he keeps both eyes, both hands and both feet, because they are meant figuratively! He believes that it is fanaticism to dismember oneself, as Origen did, for the Kingdom of God. If taking hands and feet literally here is madness, what is it to take Hell fire and worms literally? The former makes a man a self mutilator; **the latter makes God a mass butcher and monster whose "Final Solution" would make Adolph Hitler and Joseph Stalin look like girl scouts !**
Obviously, then, the passage is meant to be spiritually interpreted in its entirety. We cannot make half figurative and the other literal. **If it were wicked to chop off hands, it would be far worse to cast the whole person into a fire for any length of time. What are people thinking? Apparently they are not, which is why many of Our Lord's words are misunderstood and He is blasphemed.**
Which of the disciples mutilated his own body and instructed others to do so ? If they did not do and teach this as a literal practice, they must have understood the passage in a different way. And the word "Gehenna" is not even found in the epistles or Revelation, only in The Gospels of Matthew , Mark and Luke. James in the Greek has it once in error, translating "**Nuhra**"in

Aramaic as "**Gehenna**",which the Greek says ignites the tongue of man! Hardly a literal sense, at that!
   Gehenna was a place in Israel where garbage was always burning and where criminals bodies were thrown. Alas, the fires of Gehenna are no more, but the Lord was teaching us to think about where we are heading in a spiritual sense. "**Hell" has more to do with <u>what is in you</u> than what you are in.**

45. "If your foot causes you to commit an offense, cut it off, for it is better for you to enter the Life crippled than when you have two feet that you should fall into Gehenna."

46. "Where their worm does not die and their fire is not quenched."

47. "And if your eye causes you to commit an offense, pluck it out, for is better for you that you should enter the Kingdom of God with one eye than having two eyes that you should fall into the Gehenna of fire."

48. "Where their worm does not die and their fire is not quenched."

49. "For everything will be seasoned with fire and every sacrifice will be seasoned with salt."

50. "Salt is excellent, but if salt becomes tasteless, with what shall it be seasoned? Have salt in you and be at peace with one another."

Chapter 10

1. And he arose from there and came to the borders of Judea to the crossing of the Jordan, and great crowds went there to join him, and he taught them again as he had been accustomed.

2. And Pharisees approached, tempting him, and asking, "Is it lawful for a man to divorce his wife?"

3. He said to them, "What has Moses commanded you?"

4. But they said, "Moses allowed us to write a letter of divorce and we may get a divorce."

5. Yeshua answered and he said to them, "He wrote you this commandment confronting the callousness of your heart."

6. "But from the beginning, God made them male and female."

7. "Because of this a man shall leave his father and mother and cleave to his wife."

8. "And the two shall be one flesh; after that they are not two, but one flesh."

9. "The things that God unites let not a son of man separate."

10. And his disciples asked him again in the house about this.

11. And he said to them, "Every man who divorces his wife and takes another commits adultery."

12. "And if a woman divorces her husband and another man shall have her, she commits adultery."

13. And they were bringing children to him that he might touch them, but his disciples were rebuking those who brought them.

14. But Yeshua saw and was displeased and he said to them, "Let the children come to me and do not forbid them, for the Kingdom of God belongs to such as these."

15. "Amen, I say to you, no one who will not receive the Kingdom of God like a child will enter it."

16. And he took them up in his arms and he laid his hand upon them and he blessed them.

17. And as he traveled on the road, one came running and fell on his knees and asked him and said, "Good teacher, what shall I do that I may inherit eternal life?"

18. Yeshua said to him, "Why do you call me good? There is no one good but The One God."

19. "You know the commandments: 'You shall not commit adultery', 'You shall not steal', 'You shall not murder', 'You shall not give false testimony', 'You shall not cheat', 'Honor your father and your mother.'"

20. He answered and said to him, "Teacher, I have kept all these things from my childhood."

21. But Yeshua gazed at him and he loved him and he said to him: "You have one thing missing: go sell everything that you have and give to the poor, and you shall have treasure in Heaven, and take the cross and come after me."

22. But he was saddened at this saying and he departed grieving, because he had great wealth.

23. But Yeshua gazed at his disciples and he said to them, "How hard it is for those who have wealth to enter the Kingdom of God!"

24. But the disciples were astonished at his words. And Yeshua answered again and he said to them, "Children, how hard it is for those who rely upon their wealth to enter the Kingdom of God!"

25. "It is easier for a camel to enter into the eye of a needle than for a rich man to enter the Kingdom of God."

26. But they were all the more astonished, and they were saying among themselves, "Who can be saved?"

27. But Yeshua gazed upon them and he said to them, "With the sons of men, this is impossible, but not with God; everything is possible with God."

28. Kaypha began to say, "Behold, we have left everything and have cleaved to you."

29. Yeshua answered and said, "Amen, I say to you, there is no man who has left houses or brothers or sisters or father or mother or wife or children or town for my sake and for my Gospel's sake,

30. Who will not receive each one a hundredfold now in this time, houses and brothers and sisters and mothers and children and towns with persecutions, and in the world that is coming, eternal life.

31. But many are first who shall be last, and the last first."

32. And as they were going up the road to Jerusalem, Yeshua was in front of them, and they were amazed and they were going after him as they were awe-struck, and he took his twelve, and he began to tell them the things that were going to happen to him:

33. "Behold, we are going up to Jerusalem and The Son of Man will be delivered to the Chief Priests and to the Scribes, and they will condemn him to death and they will deliver him to the Gentiles,

34. And they will mock him, and will scourge him, and will spit in his face, and will kill him; and the third day he will arise."

35. And Yaqob and Yohannan, the sons of Zebedee, approached him, and said to him: "Teacher, we desire that you would do for us all that we ask."

36. He said to them: "What do you want me to do for you?"

37. They said to him: "Grant to us, that one may sit at your right hand, and the other on your left, in your glory."

38. But he said to them: "You do not know what you ask. Are you able to drink the cup of which I drink, and to be baptized with the baptism in which I am baptized?"

39. They were saying to him: "We are able." Yeshua said to them: "The cup that I drink, you will drink, and in the baptism in which I am baptized, you will be baptized."

40. "But for you to sit at my right and at my left is not mine to give, except to those for whom it is prepared."

41. When the ten heard, they began complaining greatly about Yaqob and Yohannan.

42. Yeshua called them and he said to them, "You are aware that those who are considered rulers of the Gentiles are their lords and their great ones have authority over them."

43. "But it will not be so among you, but whoever wants to be great among you will be a servant to you."

44. "And he among you who wants to be the first will be a servant to all."

45. "For even The Son of Man came not to be served, but to serve and give his life a ransom in the place of the many."

46. And they came to Jericho, and when Yeshua went out from Jericho, he and his disciples and the many crowds, Timai, son of Timai, a blind man, was sitting on the side of the road begging,

47. And he heard that it was Yeshua the Nazarene, and he began to cry out and to say, "Son of David, have mercy on me!"

48. And many were rebuking him that he would be quiet, but he was crying out all the more and he said, "Son of David, have mercy on me!"

49. And Yeshua stood and commanded that they would call him and they called the blind man and they were saying to him, "Take heart, arise, he is calling for you."

50. But that blind man threw off his garment and arose, coming to Yeshua.

51. And Yeshua said to him, "What do you want me to do for you?" But the blind man said to him, "Rabbi*, that I might see."

* The Greek texts have "**Rabbouni**", an Aramaic term meaning "**our Master**". This blind man spoke Aramaic, according to the Greek NT, as did almost all Judeans. "**Rabbi**" is Aramaic also, of course.

52. And Yeshua said to him, "See*; your faith has saved you.", and immediately he saw, and he was going down the road.

The Greek texts have, "**Go**, your faith has saved you", ... "Go" is "υπαγε" in Greek. "See" is "ιδε". In Aramaic, the word , "Go", is usually " זל " (masculine) or "דזל "(with Dalet proclitic); "See" is "חזי".The two Greek words are not to be easily confused, so if The Peshitta were a translation of Greek, "Go" - "υπαγε" would not be mistaken as "See"- "ιδε". However, "See" - "חזי"could very easily be taken as "Go" - "דזל", especially considering the early script of the first century: " See"- "חזי"is ⅄ח "Go"- "דזל" is ⅃ч I put these two together here for easy comparison of a Dead Sea Scroll (Habbakuk) script from circa 100 B.C. :
   ⅄ח –"See"(Peshitta)
   ⅃ч -"Go".(Greek reading in Aramaic)
Certainly these would be far more easily confused than "ιδε" & "υπαγε ".Considering other Greek variants in this passage and even in this one verse, I would hazard a guess that the original Greek translator was getting pretty bleary eyed at this point in his translation work.

Chapter 11

1. **A**nd when he approached Jerusalem on the side of Bayth Pagey and Bayth Anya to Tura d'Zaytay *, he sent two of his disciples.

    * (Mount of Olives)

2. And he said to them, "Go to that village opposite us, and immediately entering you will find a colt that is tied which no one of the children of men has ridden. Loose him and bring him,"

3. "And if a man says to you, 'Why are you doing this?' , say to him, 'He is needed by Our Lord.' And at once he will send him here."

4. And they went and found a colt that was tied on the gate outside in the street, and as they untied him,

5. Some among those who were standing *there* said to them, "What are you doing that you are untying the colt?"

6. But they said to them according to what Yeshua had commanded them, and they allowed them.

7. And they brought the colt to Yeshua and they threw their garments on it, and Yeshua rode upon him.

8. But many were spreading their coats in the road and others were cutting branches from trees and spreading them in the road.

9. And those who were before him and those who were behind were cheering and they were saying, "Hosanna! Blessed is he who comes in the name of **THE LORD JEHOVAH!**"

10. "Blessed is the Kingdom that comes of our father David! Hosanna in The Highest!"

11. And Yeshua entered Jerusalem *and* into The Temple, and he saw everything, but when it was evening he went out to Bayth-Ania with the twelve.

12. And on the next day when he went out from Bayth-Ania he was hungry.

13. And he saw a fig tree from a distance that had leaves on it and he came to it that perhaps he might find something on it, and when he came, he found nothing on it but leaves, for it was not the season of figs.

14. And he said to it, "From now and forever no man will eat fruit from you!" And his disciples heard *it* and they came to Jerusalem.

15. And Yeshua entered The Temple of God and he began to cast out those who bought and sold in The Temple and he overturned the tables of the money exchangers and the seats of those who were selling doves.

16. And he allowed no one to carry merchandise inside The Temple.

17. And he taught and he said to them, "Is it not written: 'My house shall be called a house of prayer for all the nations?' But you have made it a den of robbers."

18. And the Chief Priests and the Scribes heard and they were seeking how they might destroy him, for they were afraid of him, because all the people were awestruck at his teaching.

19. And when it was evening, they went outside the city.

20. And in the morning when they were passing by, they saw the fig tree after it had dried up from its roots.

21. And Shimeon remembered and he said to him, "Rabbi, look, that fig tree that you cursed has dried up!"

22. Yeshua answered and he said to them, "May the faith of God be in you."

23. "For, amen, I say to you, whoever shall say to this mountain: 'Be lifted up and fall into the sea', and will not doubt in his heart but shall believe that thing which he says, anything that he says shall be done for him."

24. "Therefore I say to you, that everything that you pray and ask, believe that you are receiving it and you shall have it."

25. "And whenever you stand to pray, forgive whatever you have against anyone, so that your Father who is in Heaven may also forgive you your faults."

26. "But if you are not forgiving, neither will your Father in Heaven forgive you your faults."

27. And they came again to Jerusalem and when he was walking in The Temple, the Chief Priests and the Scribes came to him, and the Elders.

28. And they were saying to him, "By what authority are you doing these things? And who gave you this authority to do these things?"

29. But Yeshua said to them, "I will ask you also one matter that you should tell me and I will tell you by what authority I do these things."

30. "From where was the baptism of Yohannan, from Heaven, or from the sons of men? Tell me."

31. And they reasoned in themselves and they said, "If we say to him from Heaven, he will say to us, 'And why did you not believe him?'"

32. "And that we should say, 'From the sons of men', there is the fear of the people, for they all are holding that Yohannan was truly a Prophet."

Codex W has : "If we say, 'from men', we fear the people", whereas all other Greek mss. have, "But should we say, 'from men', they feared the people"- ("crowd"-W&H). Codex W makes much better sense and sounds more original than the other Greek. The Codex W also has "All **knew** (ηδεισαν) that John was a Prophet." The Peshitta has אחדין -"Akhydyn" which can mean "**to hold**" or "**to comprehend**". The mss. **D & Θ** also have (ηδεισαν), indicating again that the Greek texts probably are derived from The Peshitta Aramaic. The other Greek mss. have ειχον-"eixon"-"held".

33. And they answered and they were saying to Yeshua, "We do not know." And he said to them, "Neither am I telling you by what authority I do these things."

Chapter 12

1. And he began to speak with them in a parable: "A certain man planted a vineyard and enclosed it with a hedge and dug a wine press in it and built a tower into it and gave its care to laborers, and he went abroad."

2. "And he sent his servant to the workers in time to receive the fruits of the vineyard."

3. "But they beat him and sent him away empty."

4. "And he sent another servant to them again and they threw rocks at him and cut him, and they sent him away shamefully."

5. "And again he sent another also and they murdered him; he sent many other servants, and some of them they beat and they murdered some of them."

6. "Finally, he had one beloved son, and he sent him to them afterward, for he said, 'Doubtless, they will be ashamed before my son.'"

7. "But those laborers said within themselves, 'This is the heir; come, we will kill him and the inheritance will be ours.'"

8. "And they took and murdered him and cast him outside of the vineyard."

9. "What therefore will the Lord of the vineyard do? He will come destroy those laborers and will give the vineyard to others."

10. "Have you not even read this scripture: 'The stone that the builders rejected has become the head of the corner,' "

11. "'This One was from the presence of **THE LORD JEHOVAH**, and he is wonderful in our eyes.' "?

12. And they were seeking to seize him and they were afraid of the people, for they knew that he had spoken this parable about them and they left him and departed.

13. And they sent men to him from the Scribes and from the followers of Herodus to trap him in his words.

14. But those came and asked him, "Teacher, we know that you are true, and that you are not motivated by care for any man, for you do not regard the person of the sons of men, but you teach the way of God in truth. Is it lawful to give head tax to Caesar or not? Should we give or should we not give?"

15. But he knew their treachery and he said to them, "Why are you testing me? Bring me a penny that I may see it."

16. And they brought it; he said to them: "Whose is this image and writing?" They said, "Caesar's."

17. Yeshua said to them, "Give what is Caesar's to Caesar and what is God's to God." And they marveled at him.

18. And the Sadducees came to him, who say there is no resurrection, and they were asking him and they were saying:

19. "Teacher, Moses wrote to us that if a man's brother dies and he leaves a wife and leaves behind no sons, his brother shall take his wife and raise up seed * for his brother."

* "Zara"-"Seed" is a reference to male offspring. The Law of Moses referred to the need to carry on the family name of a married man through a son. (See Deut. 25:5-10)

20. "There were seven brothers; the first took a wife and he died and left no son behind."

21. "And the second took her and he died, having also not left any son behind, and the third likewise."

22. "And the seven of them took her and they left no seed after any of them, and the woman died also."

23. "Therefore in the resurrection, whose wife among them will she be, for the seven had taken her?"

24. Yeshua said to them, "Do you not therefore err, because you do not know the scriptures, nor the mighty work of God?"

25. For when they have arisen from the dead, they do not take wives, neither do men have wives, but they are like the Angels in Heaven."

Our Lord speaks of past resurrections, not future. Resurrection is not reserved for a future dispensation. The next two verses make this clear. To make this refer to a future dispensation is to ignore and distort the tense of the verb "Qamu"; It is definitely a perfect tense, **indicating past action**. The Greek texts have an "aorist subjunctive" verb –

"**may arise**", very much like a future tense, while The Peshitta has "Qamu"-"**they arose**" past tense.

26. "But concerning the dead, that they rise, have you not read in the scripture of Moses how God said to him from the Bush, 'I AM THE LIVING GOD, The God of Abraham, and the God of Isaaq and the God of Jaqob?'"

27. "He is not the God of the dead, but of the living. You therefore are greatly mistaken."

28. One of the Scribes approached him and he heard them debating and he saw that he had answered them beautifully and he asked him, "Which is the first commandment of all?"

29. Yeshua said to him, "The first of all the commandments: 'Hear Israel, THE LORD JEHOVAH your God, THE LORD JEHOVAH, he is One.'"

30. "'And you shall love THE LORD JEHOVAH your God with your whole heart and with your entire soul and with your entire mind and with all your power.' This is the first commandment"

31. "And the second is like it: 'You shall love your neighbor as yourself.' There is no other commandment greater than these."

32. And that scribe said to him, "Excellent, Rabbi! You have spoken the truth, for he is One, and there is not another outside of him."

33. "And for a man to love him with all the heart and with the entire mind and with all the soul and with all the strength, and to love his neighbor as himself, is more than all burnt offerings and sacrifices."

34. But Yeshua, seeing that he had answered wisely, answered and said to him, "You are not far from the Kingdom of God." And no man again dared to question him.

35. And Yeshua answered and said as he taught in The Temple, "How are the Scribes saying that The Messiah is the son of David?"

36. "For David himself said in The Spirit of Holiness: 'THE LORD JEHOVAH said to my Lord, "Sit at my right until I shall constitute your enemies as a footstool under your feet."'"

37. "David therefore called him, 'My Lord", and how is he his son?" And the whole crowd was listening to him with pleasure.

38. And in his teaching, he said to them, "Beware of the Scribes who like to walk in robes and love greetings in the streets,

39. And the best seats in the synagogue and top rooms at feasts,

40. They who devour widows' houses by an offering for making their long prayers; they shall receive the greater judgment."

41. And when Yeshua sat down near the treasury, he beheld how the crowds cast money into the treasury and many rich men were casting in much.

42. And one poor widow came and cast in two minas that were shemonas *(a quarter penny)*.

43. But Yeshua called his disciples and he said to them, "Amen, I say to you, this poor widow has cast in more than all the people who have cast into the treasury,

44. For they all cast in from the surplus that they had, but this one has cast in from her want, everything that she had; she cast in all her possessions."

Chapter 13

1. And when Yeshua went out from The Temple, one of his disciples said to him, "Teacher, look, see what stones and what buildings!"

2. But Yeshua said to him, "Do you see these great buildings? There is not left here one stone standing upon another that will not be pulled down."

3. And when Yeshua sat down at Tora D' Zaytha* opposite The Temple, Kaypha and Yaqob and Yohannan and Andraeus asked him alone:

(Mount of Olives)

4. "Tell us, when will these things be? What is the sign when all these things are near to being fulfilled?"

5. But Yeshua himself began to say to them, "Take heed lest a man shall lead you astray."

6. "For many will come in my name, and they will say, 'I AM THE LIVING GOD', and they will deceive many."

7. "Whenever you hear war and reports of battles, you should not be afraid; that is going to happen, but it is not yet the end."

8. "For nation shall rise against nation, and kingdom against kingdom. There will be earthquakes in various places, and there will be famines and sedition; these are the beginning of the labor pains."

9. "But take heed to yourselves, for they will deliver you to Judges and you will be scourged in their synagogues and you will stand before Kings and Governors for my sake as a testimony to them."

10. "But first my gospel is going to be preached in all the nations."

11. "Whenever they bring you to deliver you up, you should not be anxious beforehand what you will speak, neither should you consider, but whatever is given to you in that hour, speak, for you will not be speaking, but The Spirit of Holiness."

12. "But brother will deliver his brother to death and a father his son; children will rise up against their parents and put them to death."

13. "And you will be hated by everyone because of my name, but whoever will endure until the end will be saved."

14. "But whenever you see the unclean sign of desolation, which was spoken of by Daniel the Prophet, standing where it ought not (He who reads, let him perceive) then those who are in Judea should flee to the mountains."

15. "Whoever is on the rooftop should not come down and should not enter to take anything from his house."

16. "And whoever is in the field should not turn to go back to take up his garment."

17. "But woe to the pregnant and to those who are nursing in those days."

18. "Pray that your flight will not be in the winter."

19. "For there will be distress in those days, the likes of which has never been since the beginning of the creation which God has created until now, and never will be."

20. "And if **THE LORD JEHOVAH** had not shortened those days, no one would live; but for the sake of the chosen ones whom he has chosen, he has shortened those days."

21. "Then, if a man shall say to you, 'Look, here is The Messiah, and 'Look, he is going there', you should not believe him."

22. "And false Messiahs and lying Prophets will arise, and they will give signs and wonders and they will deceive if possible, even the chosen ones."

23. "But pay attention; behold, I have anticipated *this*; I have told you everything."

24. "But in those days, after that distress, the sun will darken and the moon will not give its light."

25. "And the stars will fall from the heavens and the powers of the heavens will be shaken."

26. "And then they will see The Son of Man when he comes in the clouds with great power and with glory."

27. "Then he will send his Angels and gather his elect ones from the four winds and the bottom of the earth* even unto the top of Heaven."

* "**Min ryshah**" can be used as an idiom meaning, "**upside down**". Since "rysh" normally signifies the head or the top of something, I have translated "**Min ryshah**" as "**the bottom**". This would indicate the sphericity of the earth, as opposed to a flat earth.

28. "But learn an allegory from the fig tree: whenever its branches are tender and its leaves bud, you know that summer* has arrived."

* Summer comes in May in Israel.

29. "Thus also whenever you see these things happen, know that it is near, at the door."

30. "Amen, I say to you, this generation will not pass until all of these things will come to pass."

31. "The heavens and the earth will pass away, and my words will not pass away."

32. But of that day and of that hour no man knows, neither the Angels of Heaven, neither The Son, but The Father only."

33. "Take heed, watch and pray, for you do not know when that time is."

34. "It is like a man who traveled abroad and left his house and gave authority to his servants and to each man his work and he commanded the gatekeeper to be watchful."

35. "Watch therefore, for you do not know when the Master of the house comes, in the evening or at midnight or at cockcrow* or in the morning." * (Lit. "the crowing of the rooster")

36. "Lest suddenly he come and find you sleeping."

37. "But what I say to you, I say the same to you all: 'Be watching.' "

Chapter 14

1. But after two days was the Passover of Unleavened Bread, and the Chief Priests and Scribes were seeking how they would seize him by treachery and kill him.

2. And they were saying, "Not during the feast, lest there be a tumult among the people."

3. And while he was in Bayth-Ania in the House of Shimeon the Potter * , as he was reclining, a woman came who had with her an alabaster vase of ointment of the best

spikenard, very expensive, and she opened it and poured it on Yeshua's head.

* "Garba" is Aramaic for "Leper" .With different (unwritten) vowels, it is "Graba" for "Potter." It seems very unlikely Shimeon was a leper if he were blessed with the acquaintance of Yeshua Meshikha. The Greek texts all have "Leper", which means they most likely mistranslated "Graba" as "Garba" - "Leper", when "Potter" was meant. The two words look identical in ancient Aramaic: ܓܪܒܐ & ܓܪܒܐ

4. But there were some of the disciples who were displeased within themselves and they said, "Why the loss of this ointment?"

5. "It would have been possible to sell this for more than 300 denarii and *for it* to be given to the poor." And they were indignant at her.

6. But Yeshua said, "Let her alone. Why are you troubling her? She has done a beautiful deed for me."

7. "For the poor are always with you, and whenever you wish, you can do good for them, but I am not always with you."

8. "She has done what she could, and she has anticipated anointing my body for burial."

9. And amen, I say to you, that everywhere that this my gospel shall be preached in all the world, this thing that she has done shall also be spoken in her memory."

10. But Yehuda Skariota, one of the twelve, went to the Chief Priests to betray Yeshua to them,

11. But when they heard, they rejoiced, and they promised they would give money to him and he sought an opportunity to betray him.

12. And on the first day of Unleavened Bread, in which the Jews slaughter the Passover lamb, his disciples were saying to him, "Where do you want us to go to prepare for you that you may eat the Passover?"

13. And he sent two of his disciples and said to them, "Go to the city and behold, you will meet a man among you, bearing a vessel of water. Follow him."

14. "And in the place that he enters, say to the owner of the house, "Our Master says, 'Where is the house chamber, where I may eat the Passover with my disciples?' "

15. "And behold, he will show you a great upper room, laid out and prepared; there make ready for us."

16. And his disciples went out and they came to the city, and they found just as he told them, and they prepared the Passover.

17. And when it was evening he came with his twelve.

18. And as they reclined and ate, Yeshua said, "Amen, I say to you, one of you who eats with me will betray me."

19. But they began to lose heart, and they were saying to him, each one, "Is it I?"

20. But he said to them, "One of the twelve who dips with me in the dish."

21. "The Son of Man goes just as it is written about him, but woe to that man by whose hand The Son of Man is betrayed. It were better for that man if he had not been born."

22. And while they were eating, Yeshua took bread, and he blessed and he broke and he gave to them, and he said to them, "Take; this is my body."

23. And he took the cup, and he gave thanks and he blessed; and he gave to them and they all drank from it.

24. And he said to them, "This is my blood of the new covenant, which is shed in exchange for the many."

25. "Amen, I say to you, I shall not drink from the fruit of the vine again until the day in which I shall drink it anew in the Kingdom of God."

26. And they sang praises, and they went out to Tur Zaytay *(the Mount of Olives).*

27. And Yeshua said to them, "All of you will be ashamed of me this night, for it is written: 'I shall strike The Shepherd, and his lambs will be scattered.' "

28. "But when I am risen, I shall go before you to Galilee."

29. And Kaypha said to him, "If all of them will be subverted, yet I shall not."

30. Yeshua said to him, "Amen, I say to you that today, this night, before the rooster will crow two times, you will renounce me three times."

31. But he was saying all the more, "If I am to be put to death with you, I shall not renounce you, my Lord!" And like him also, all of them * spoke.

The Eastern Peshitta has תלמידא - "The disciples", as second to the last word in v. 31. The Western does not; neither does this critical Peshitta edition. The Greek agrees with the Western Peshitta here.

32. And they came to the place which is called Gethsemane*, and he said to his disciples, "Sit here while I pray."

*Codex W has ΓΕϹϹΗΜΑΝΙΝ –"Gessemanin" where most Greek mss. have ΓΕΘΣΗΜΑΝΗ- "Gethsemane". The Peshitta's Aramaic has גדשמן ("Gedsemane"). In Matthew 26:32, W has ΓΕΔΣΗΜΑΝΗ ("Gedsemane"), which is an exact transliteration of the Aramaic name -גדסמן ("Gedsemane") in The Peshitta. Also interesting is the fact that the common Greek spelling ΓΕΘΣΗΜΑΝΗ - "Gethsemane" is a phonetic spelling of the Aramaic גדסמן; the Dalet ד has a soft "th" sound in this word (normally a hard "d" sound), and is represented in Greek by a theta θ ("th" sound), so Codex W represents an exact transliteration of Aramaic in Matthew 26:32, and the other Greek mss. represent a phonetic spelling of Aramaic there and elsewhere, where the Greek word "**Gethsemane**" occurs.

33.And he took Kaypha and Yaqob and Yohannan with him, and he began to be saddened and languid.

34.And he said to them, "My soul is saddened unto death. Stay here and watch."

35.And he approached a little and he fell on the ground, and he prayed that if it were possible, the hour would pass from him.

36.And he said, "Father*, my Father, you can do everything; let this cup pass from me, yet not my own will, but yours."

* All Greek texts have "Abba"- the Aramaic word for "Father", followed by "Pater", the Greek word for "Father." Greek manuscripts have many such Aramaic words and even phrases, testifying to an Aramaic original. (Only Codex W agrees here with The Peshitta reading, "My Father" and ΔΥΝΑΤΑ ΕΣΤΙΝ -"are possible". No other Greek ms. has either of these readings.)

37.And he came and found them while they were sleeping and he said to Kaypha, "Shimeon, are you sleeping? Were you not able to watch one hour?"

38."Watch and pray lest you enter into temptation. The spirit is willing and ready, but the body is weak."

39.And he went again and prayed, and he said the same words.

40.And returning, he came again and found them sleeping because their eyes were heavy, and they did not know what to say to him.

41. And he came the third time and he said to them, "Sleep now and take rest; the end has arrived; the hour has come; behold The Son of Man is betrayed into the hands of sinners."

42."Arise, let us go; behold, he who betrays me is approaching."

43.And while he was speaking, Yehuda Skariota came, one of the twelve, and many men with swords and clubs from the presence of the Chief Priests and the Scribes and the Elders.

44.And the traitor who betrayed *him* had given them a sign and he said, "He whom I shall kiss is the one; seize him securely and bring him."

45.And immediately he approached and he said to him, "Rabbi,* Rabbi", and he kissed him.

* The Greek manuscripts have "Rabbi" also (though only once) which is also Aramaic.

46.But those laid hands upon him and they seized him.

47.One of those who were standing drew a sword and hit the servant of The High Priest and took off his ear.

48.But Yeshua answered and said to them, "Have you gone out as against a band of robbers with swords and with clubs to seize me?"

49."I was with you every day when I taught in The Temple, and you did not seize me. But this has happened that the Scriptures may be fulfilled."

50.Then his disciples forsook him and they fled.

51.And one young man had come after him and was clothed with a cloth. He was naked, and they seized him.

52.But he left the cloth and fled naked.

53.They brought Yeshua to Qaiapha the High Priest, and all the Chief Priests and the Scribes and the Elders gathered to him.

54.But Shimeon was coming from a distance after him until within the courtyard of The High Priests, and he sat down with the servants and warmed himself near the fire.

55.But the Chief Priests and all their assembly were seeking testimony against Yeshua, that they might put him to death, and they were not able.

56.For many were testifying against him, but their testimony was not worthy.

57.But people rose up against him and they were testifying lies, and they said:

58."We have heard him say, 'I shall destroy this temple that is made with hands and in three days I shall build another that is not made with hands.'"

59.But likewise, neither was their testimony worthy.

60.The High Priest stood up in the center and asked Yeshua, and he said, "Do you not answer? Why are these testifying against you?"

61. But he was silent, and he did not answer him anything. And again, The High Priest asked him and said, "Are you The Messiah, The Son of The Blessed One?"

62. But Yeshua said to him, "I AM THE LIVING GOD, and you shall behold The Son of Man sitting at the right hand of Power and coming on the clouds of Heaven."

63. But The High Priest ripped his tunic and he said, "Why now do we need witnesses?"

64. "Behold, you have heard the blasphemy from his own mouth. How does it appear to you?" But they all judged that he deserved death.

65. And the people began spitting in his face and covering his face and hitting him, and they were saying, "Prophesy", and the guards were hitting him on his jaw.

66. And while Shimeon was below in the courtyard, a certain handmaid of The High Priest came.

67. She saw him warming himself and she stared at him and she said to him, "You also were with Yeshua the Nazarene."

68. But he denied it and he said, "I don't know what you are saying,", and he went forth outside to the porch and a rooster crowed.

69. And that handmaid saw him again and she began to say to those who were standing there, "This is also one of them."

70. But he again denied it and after a little while again those who were standing said to Kaypha, "Truly, you are one of them, for you are also a Galilean and your speech is similar."

71. But he had begun cursing and swearing: "I do not know this man of whom you speak."

72. And at that moment, the cock crowed the second time, and Shimeon was reminded of the word of Yeshua, who had said to him, "Before a cock shall crow two times, you will deny me three times", and he began to weep.

Chapter 15

1. And at once in the morning the Chief Priests made a council with the Elders and with the Scribes and with the whole assembly, and they bound Yeshua and brought him and delivered him to Pilate.

2. And Pilate asked him, "You are The King of the Judeans?" But he answered and said to him, "You have said."

3. And the Chief Priests accused him of many things.

4. Then Pilate again asked him and said to him, "Do you not answer? See how many are testifying against you!"

5. But Yeshua gave no answer, to Pilate's amazement.

6. But he had set a time at every feast to release one prisoner to them, whomever they requested.

7. And there was one who was called Barabba, who was bound with those who had made sedition, who had committed murder in the sedition.

8. And the people cried out and they began to ask that he would keep the custom which he had been doing for them.

9. And Pilate answered and said, "Are you willing that I release to you The King of the Judeans?"

10. For Pilate had known that for envy the Chief Priests had delivered him to them.

11. But the Chief Priests urged the crowd all the more that he would release Barabba.

12. But Pilate said to them, "What do you want me to do to this one whom you call The King of the Judeans?"

13. But they again cried out, "Crucify him!"

14. But Pilate said to them, "What evil has he done?" And they were crying out even more, "Crucify him!"

15. But Pilate chose to do the will of the crowds and he released Barabba to them and delivered Yeshua to them, after he had been scourged, to be crucified.

16. But the soldiers led him within the courtyard, which is the Praetorium, and they called the whole company of soldiers.

17. And they clothed him in purple and they wound and placed on him a crown of thorns.

18. And they began to greet him: "Hail, King of the Judeans!"

19. And they were hitting him on his head with a reed and spitting in his face and bowing on their knees and worshiping him.

20. And when they had mocked him, they stripped him of the purple and clothed him in his clothes and led him to crucify him.

21. And they detained one who was passing by, Shimeon, a Cyrenian, who had come from the field, the father of Alexander and Rufus, to take up his cross.

22. And they brought him to the place Gagultha, which is interpreted, "The Skull."

23. And they gave him wine to drink, mixed with myrrh, but he would not take it.

24. And when they crucified him, they divided his garments and cast lots for them, who would take what.

25. But it was the third hour when they crucified him.

26. And the pretext of his death was written in this writing: "This is The King of the Judeans."

27. And they crucified two robbers with him, one at his right, and one at his left.

28. And the scripture was fulfilled that says, "He was numbered with wicked men."

29. But those also who were passing by were blaspheming against him and were shaking their heads and they were saying, "Oh destroyer of The Temple and the one who builds it in three days,"

30. "Save yourself and come down from the cross!"

31. And likewise the Chief Priests were joking with one another and the Scribes and they were saying, "He saved others; he cannot save himself!"

32. "Let The Messiah, The King of Israel, descend now from the cross that we may see and we will believe in him." And those also who were crucified with him were reviling him.

33. And when it was the sixth hour, darkness was over all the earth until the ninth hour.

34. And in the ninth hour Yeshua cried out in a loud voice, and he said: "Eil, Eil, lemana Shabaqthani", which is, "My God, my God, why have you forsaken me?"

35. And the people who heard among those standing there were saying, "He called to Elijah."

36. But one ran and filled a sponge with vinegar and tied it on a reed to give him a drink and they said, "Let him alone. Let us see if Elijah comes to take him down."

37. But Yeshua cried with a loud voice, and he expired.

38. And the curtain of the entrance of The Temple was ripped in two from the top unto the bottom.

39. But when that Centurion who was standing with him saw that he had so cried out and expired, he said, "Truly, this man was the Son of God."

40. But there were also women there from afar off, who were looking: Maryam Magdalitha and Maryam, mother of Yaqob The Small, and of Yose and Shalom.

41. They were those who had joined him when he was in Galilee and ministered to him and many other *women* who had gone up with him to Jerusalem.

42. And when it was Friday evening, which is before the Sabbath,

43. Yoseph came, who was from Ramtha, an honorable counselor who had been waiting for the Kingdom of God, and he ventured and entered to Pilate and requested the body of Yeshua.

44. But Pilate wondered if he had been dead that long, and he called the Centurion and asked him if he had died before the time.

45. And when he learned, he gave his body to Yoseph.

46. And Yoseph had bought linen and he took it down and wrapped it and placed it in a tomb that was hewn out in rock and he rolled a stone at the entrance of the tomb.

47. But Maryam Magdalitha and Maryam, the mother of Yose, saw where he had been laid.

Chapter 16

1. And when the Sabbath had passed, Maryam Magdalitha and Maryam of Yaqob and Shalome bought sweet spices that they might come to anoint him.

2. But in the early morning in the first day of the week they came to the tomb when the sun arose.

3. And they were saying among themselves, "But who will roll the stone away for us from the tomb?"

4. And looking they saw that the stone had been rolled away, for it was very great.

5. And they entered the tomb and saw a young man sitting on the right side. He was wearing a white robe, and they were astonished.

6. But he said to them, "Do not be afraid. You are seeking Yeshua the Nazarene, who was crucified; he has arisen; he is not here. Behold the place where he was laid."

7. "But go say to his disciples and to Kaypha, "Behold, he will go before you to Galilee; you will see him there, just as he said to you."

8. When they heard, they fled and went out from the tomb, for shock and trembling had seized them and they said nothing to anyone, for they were afraid.

9. But at dawn, on the first day of the week, he arose and appeared first to Maryam

Magdalitha, from whom he had cast out seven demons.

10. And she went and proclaimed The Good News to those who had been with him, who were mourning and weeping.

11. And when they heard them saying that he was alive and had appeared to them, they did not believe it.

12. After these things, he appeared before two of them in another form as they walked and they were going to a village.

13. And they went and told the rest; neither did they believe them.

14. But afterward, he appeared to the eleven when they reclined at a meal and he condemned the lack of their faith and the callousness of their heart, because they had not believed them who had seen him before.

15. And he said to them, "Go to the entire world and preach my Good News in all creation."

16. "Whoever believes and is baptized has life, and whoever does not believe is condemned."

17. "But these signs will accompany these who believe: in my name they will cast out demons, and they will speak in new languages."

18. "And they will take up snakes, and if they should drink lethal poison, it will not harm them, and they will place their hands on the sick and they will be healed."

19. But Yeshua Our Lord, after he was speaking with them, ascended into Heaven, and he sat down at the right side of God.

20. But they went forth and they preached in every place, and Our Lord was helping them and confirming their words with the signs that they were doing.

שלם אונגליון קדישא כרוזותא דמרקוס
The end of The Holy Gospel preaching of Mark

The Gospel According To Saint Luke

Chapter 1

1. Because many were willing to write an account of those events of which we are persuaded,

2. Like the things which they delivered to us who from the first were eyewitnesses and servants of The Word*,

* *"The Word" is* מלתא – *"Miltha" . This is the term John uses in his Gospel to designate "Yeshua Meshikha" (Jesus The Messiah).That Luke refers to Him is fairly evident, as he refers to "The eyewitnesses and servants of The Word". The spoken or written word does not have eyewitnesses and servants. Also the Aramaic word "* דילה *" – "Dilah" ("of His") adds personal possession to the relationship of eyewitnesses and servants with the Word. They "belong to Him". This would be out of place with respect to the spoken or written word*

3. He appeared *also to me because I had approached all things carefully, that I would write everything in order to you, excellent Theophila.

* אתחזי – *"He appeared" is the most natural meaning of "Ethkhazay" and would refer to the previous word-* דמלתא *"of the Word". Luke is saying that The Lord Yeshua The Messiah had appeared to him and had authorized and directed his writing of this Gospel. Why would it be received otherwise ? If Luke merely "thought it good to write" , why would the churches have put it on a par with the inspired Gospels, Matthew, Mark and Luke ? He would have been merely rehashing second hand information and serving warmed up leftovers. That is no recommendation worthy of an inspired Gospel of The New Testament. "Theophila", to whom Luke wrote, would have thrown it in the trash if that were Luke's meaning. Verse 2 says the other gospels were written by "eyewitnesses". Verse three says Luke was also an eyewitness of The Messiah. If he were not, then he would be disqualified to write a gospel. It would seem that Western churches , in their misunderstanding of Luke's introduction, have allowed scholarship to supplant Divine inspiration as its authority. This has subtly and slowly supplanted the Spiritual with the intellectual, which Luke the Physician has come to represent. He was not writing a literary composition here; he was writing from God, just as every other God inspired writer of scripture wrote: 1Co 2:13 "Which things we also speak; not in the teaching of the words of man's wisdom, but in the teaching of The Spirit; and we compare spirituals with spirituals." 2Pe 1:21 "For at no time was it by the pleasure of man, that the prophecy came; but holy men of God spoke, as they were moved by the Holy Spirit."* Would an inspired writer say, "I thought I would write a Gospel account because many others were writing accounts like those the apostles were writing" ? That would be the height of presumption. Would he then suppose that he would improve on the inspired accounts ?- " It seemed good to me also, having had perfect understanding of all things from the very first, to write unto thee in order, most excellent Theophilus" – This is the King James translation, which demonstrates here the presumptive attitude attributed to Luke. This is a very poor translation of the Greek of verse 3, but all translations get it wrong in the first word of the verse, which is the most critical. The Greek has the verb "εδοξεν" from "dokeo"-("to seem"). The Aramaic verb "Ethkhazay" -(He appeared) – אתחזי could mean "seemed", but its usual meaning is "appeared" or "was

seen". This passive form of the Aramaic "חזי"- "Khaza" ("to see") occurs 29 times in the Peshitta NT. 18 times Murdock translates it "appeared", 7 times- "seen" , three times "received sight" and once (incorrectly, in my opinion)- "seemed".

The Comprehensive Aramaic Lexicon has: חזי – xzy
Verb
peal_1 ImpArMesop,BibAr,MiddleAr,JLA,Syr,Bab (lit.) to see
__2 BibArDan (metaph. like European langs.) to understand, to realize
__3 JLAGal,Syr to visit
__4 JLATg to see a vision > xzy#2
__5 ImpArEg +%b_% to be victorious over
__6 Syr %)ayk.anA) xAze))an~t nap$Ak% how are you?
pael_1 OAPal to see
(h)afel_1 ImpArEgOst,Palestinian,JBA to show
2 JLAGal %)pyn% to console
[ethpeel 1 OASyr,JLATg,Syr,JBA to be seen
2 Syr %leh% to be able to see
3 Palm,JBA to be fit, to be proper (occurs 1 time out of 50 ?; Luke 1:3 has the only questionable occurrence- comment is mine)
__4 JLAGal to appear in a vision]
ettafal_1 Syr,JBA to be made visible
LS2 224
The Targum of Jonathan has 21 occurrences of the passive verb " Ethkhazay" and " Ethkhaza" in former and latter Prophets ; none has the meaning "seemed", or "it was fit, proper". It would "appear" or "seem" (pun intended) that the latter meaning is a rare one. In Luke 1:3, it also contradicts the intention of Luke to employ that meaning
If I am right about Luke 1:3, Luke's Gospel was probably written after John's Gospel, since Luke refers to The Word as "He" , a Person of Whom the Apostles are "eyewitnesses and servants". He also "appeared" to Luke. This refers plainly to John 1:1& 14. Luke would probably be the last of the four Gospels written, not John.

4. That you may know the truth of the words of which you have been instructed by such.

Verse 4 confirms what I have written for verse three. If Luke were an eyewitness of The LORD Yeshua and His words and deeds, then he could confirm The Gospel accounts as true; if not, all the research and talent in the world would be useless toward composing an accurate account of The Messiah, as the information required exceeds the capacity of man to secure on his own. Only Divine revelation can provide the Truth of Him Whose Name is "The Truth, The Way, The Life", apart from Whom, no one can approach to The Eternal Father.

5. In the days of Herodus, The King of Judea, there was a certain Priest whose name was Zechariah from the Ministry of the house of Abia and his wife was named Elizabeth who was of the daughters of Aaron.

6. Both of them were righteous before God, and they were walking in all the commandments and in the judgments of THE LORD JEHOVAH without reproach.

7. But they did not have a son, because Elizabeth was infertile, and both of them were advanced in their days.

8. And as he was exercising his priestly function in the order of his service before God,

9. In the tradition of the priesthood, it befell him to offer incense, and he entered The Temple of **THE LORD JEHOVAH**.

10. And all the crowds of the people were praying outside at the time of incense.

11. And an Angel of **THE LORD JEHOVAH** appeared to Zechariah who stood at the right side of the altar of incense.

12. And Zechariah was troubled when he saw him and dread fell upon him.

13. And the Angel said to him, "Do not be afraid, Zacharia, because your prayer has been heard and your wife Elizabeth will bear you a son, and you shall call his name, Yohannan."

14. "You will have joy and gladness and many will rejoice at his birth."

15. "He will be great before **THE LORD JEHOVAH**, and he will not drink wine or strong drink, and he will be filled with The Spirit of Holiness while he is in the womb of his mother."

16. "And he will turn many of the children of Israel to **THE LORD JEHOVAH**, their God."

17. "And he will go before him in the spirit and in the power of Elijah The Prophet to turn the heart of The fathers to the children and those who do not have faith to the knowledge of The Just One and he will prepare a perfect people for **THE LORD JEHOVAH**."

18. And Zacharia said to the Angel, "How shall I know this, for I am old and my wife is advanced in her days?"

19. The Angel answered and he said to him, "I am Gabriel who am standing before God, and I am sent to speak with you and to give you these tidings."

20. "Henceforth, you will be dumb, and you will not be able to speak until the day that these things will occur, because you did not believe my words, which will be fulfilled in their time."

21. But the people were standing and waiting for Zacharia, and they were wondering at his tarrying in The Temple.

22. But when Zechariah came out, he was not able to speak with them, and they perceived that he had seen a vision in The Temple and was making signs, gesturing to them, and he still remained mute.

23. And when the days of his service were fulfilled he went to his house.

24. And it happened after those days, Elizabeth his wife conceived and she had secluded herself for five months, and she said:

25. "**THE LORD JEHOVAH** has done these things for me in the days in which he regarded me to take away my reproach among the children of men"

26. But in the six month, Gabriel the Angel was sent from the presence of God to Galilee to the city whose name was Nazareth,

27. To a virgin who was engaged to a man from the house of David, whose name was Yoseph, and the name of the virgin was Maryam.

28. The Angel entered her presence, and he said to her, "Peace to you, full of grace, Our Lord is with you; you are blessed among women."

29. But when she saw him, she was alarmed at his word, and she was wondering, "What is this greeting?"

30. And the Angel said to her, "Do not fear, Maryam, for you have found favor with God,

31. For behold, you shall conceive and you shall give birth to a son, and you shall call his name Yeshua.

32. This One will be great and he will be called The Son of The Highest and **THE LORD JEHOVAH** will give to him the throne of David his father,

33. And he will reign over the house of Jaqob eternally and to his Kingdom there will not be an end."

34. Maryam said to the Angel, "How will this be, for no man has known me?"

35. The Angel answered and said to her, "The Spirit of Holiness shall come and the power of The Highest shall rest upon you, therefore he who shall be begotten in you shall be holy and he shall be called the Son of God."

36. "And behold, Elizabeth your cousin also has conceived a son in her old age, and this is the sixth month for her, who is called barren,"

37. "Because nothing is difficult for God."

38. Maryam said, "Behold, I am the handmaid of **THE LORD JEHOVAH**; let it be done to me according to your word", and the Angel departed from her.

39. But Maryam arose in those days, and she went instantly to the mountains to a city of Judea.

40. And she entered the house of Zechariah, and she invoked the peace of Elizabeth.

41. And it was when Elizabeth heard the greeting of Maryam, the baby in her womb leaped and Elizabeth was filled with The Spirit of Holiness,

42. And she cried with a loud voice and she said to Maryam, "You are blessed among women and blessed is the fruit that is in your womb."

43. "From where is this to me that the mother of my Lord would come to me?"

44. "For behold, when the voice of your greeting fell on my ear, the baby in my womb leaped in great joy."

45. "And blessed is she who believed that there would be a fulfillment to those things that were spoken with her from the presence of THE LORD JEHOVAH."

46. And Maryam said, "My soul exalts THE LORD JEHOVAH"

47. "And my spirit rejoices in God my Savior."

48. "For he has regarded the lowliness of his Maidservant, for behold, from this hour all generations will ascribe blessedness to me."

49. "Because he who is mighty has done unto me great things and holy is his name."

50. "And his mercy for posterity and generations is upon those who revere him."

51. "He has wrought victory with his arm and he has scattered the proud with the opinion of their heart."

52. "He has cast down the mighty from thrones and has raised up the lowly."

53. "He has filled the hungry with good things and the rich he has sent away empty handed."

54. "He has helped Israel his servant and he has remembered his mercy,"

55. "Just as he spoke with our Patriarchs, with Abraham and with his seed eternally."

56. But Maryam stayed with Elizabeth about three months, and she returned to her house.

57. But it came time for Elizabeth to give birth, and she bore a son.

58. And her neighbors heard, and the members of her family, that God had magnified his mercy to her, and they rejoiced with her.

59. And it was the eighth day, and they came to circumcise the boy, and they were calling him by the name of his father Zachariah.

60. And his mother answered, and she said to them, "Not so, but he will be called Yohannan."

61. And they said to her, "There is no man among your generations who is called by this name."

62. And they signed to his father how he wished to name him.

63. He requested a tablet and he wrote and he said, "Yohannan is his name", and everyone was amazed.

64. And at once his mouth was opened, and his tongue, and he spoke and blessed God.

65. And there was awe upon all of their neighbors, and in all the mountains of Judea these things were being spoken.

66. And all those who heard were contemplating in their heart and they were saying, "What indeed will this boy be?" And the hand of THE LORD JEHOVAH was with him.

67. And his father Zechariah was filled with The Spirit of Holiness and he prophesied and he said:

68. "Blessed is THE LORD JEHOVAH, The God of Israel, who has visited his nation, and he has wrought for it redemption."

69. "And he has raised up for us a trumpet of redemption in the house of David his servant,"

70. "Just as he spoke by the mouth of his holy Prophets that which is from eternity,"

71. "That he would save us from our enemies and from the hand of all of them who hate us."

72. "And he has wrought his mercy with our fathers and he has remembered his holy covenants"

73. "And the oath that he swore to Abraham our Patriarch that he would grant us"

74. "That we would be saved from the hands of our enemies, and we would serve before him without fear,"

75. "All of our days with justice and in righteousness."

76. "And you, boy, you will be called the Prophet of The Highest, for you will go before the face of THE LORD JEHOVAH that you may prepare his way,"

77. "That he may give the knowledge of life to his people in forgiveness of their sins,"

78. "In the compassions of the mercy of our God in which The Manifestation from Heaven will visit us,"

79. "To enlighten those who were sitting in darkness and in the shadow of death, that he may direct our feet in the path of peace."

80. But The Boy was growing and being strengthened in spirit, and he dwelt in the wilderness until the day of his manifestation unto Israel.

Chapter 2

1. **B**ut it occurred in those days that a command also went out from Augustus Caesar that every nation* of his empire would be registered.

*All Greek texts have "οικουμενην" (**"the inhabited world"**). This is not an accurate word to use, as Caesar did not register everyone in the world, only those of The Roman Empire, which did not include large sections of the eastern world and the Middle East. "**Every nation of his empire**" makes much better sense and is accurate historically. Thayers Greek English Lexicon says that οικουμενη may refer to the Roman Empire, but it is never translated as such in any NT translation that I can see but for one place in Acts 24:5 by The Bible in Basic English; neither does it have such a meaning in any of the 39 times it occurs in The LXX (certainly, the Roman empire did not even exist when The LXX was translated, but The Greek Empire did.)

2. This census was the first in the government of Quraynus in Syria.

3. And everyone was going to be registered in his own city.

4. But Yoseph had come up from Nazareth, a city of Galilee, to Judea to the city of David called Bethlehem, because he was from the house and from the lineage of David,

5. With Maryam his bride when she was pregnant, that he might be registered there.

6. And it was, that while they were there, the days were completed for her to give birth.

7. And she brought forth her firstborn Son and she wrapped him in swaddling bands, and she laid him in a manger because there was no place for them where they might lodge.

8. But there were some shepherds in the region lodging there and they kept the nightly watch over their flocks;

9. And behold, the Angel of God came to them and the glory of **THE LORD JEHOVAH** shone upon them and they were greatly afraid;

10. And the Angel said to them, "Do not be afraid, for behold, I proclaim to you great joy which will be to the entire universe*,"

עלמא- "EAlma", can refer to all creation- "**The * heavens and the earth**", though sometimes just the earth or the people in it. It can include Heaven and Sheol and all created beings of all time. עלמא –

EAlma" , like its Hebrew cognate, עולם – "**Owlam**" refers to time , space and matter- all the components of the universe, and even "**Eternity**". The word for "**Eternity**" is also עלמא –" EAlma". It truly signifies "all that exists", in its proper sense.

The Greek mss. all have "παντι τω λαω" – "**all the people**". "People" in Aramaic is עמא; Comparing עלמא & עמא makes it easy to see that if עלמא (Universe,World) were to lose its second letter- ל , it becomes עמא (People,Nation).The **Greek** for "World" is Κοσμος- "**Kosmos**" or "οικουμενη" – oikoumenay (inhabited places). λαω (People) could hardly be mistaken for κοσμω (World) , assuming hypothetically an Aramaean were translating Greek to Aramaic. However, it is possible that such an Aramaean scribe might intend to write עמא and add a **Lamed,** writing עלמא,but such an error would be less likely to occur, since it would involve an intention to write עמא ("people") and actually writing another word עלמא ("world") by adding a letter, which would be an error of the hand rather than the eye. He would have been thinking "**People**" and writing "**World**". The reverse scenario is a much more likely one. It is much easier to **misread** the word עלמא as עמא than to **miswrite** עמא as עלמא. **Again, the Peshitta reading can more easily account for the Greek reading than vice versa.**

Mark, Paul and John all wrote of the redemption of the whole creation: See Romans 8:21-23;Mark 16:15,Rev. 5:13.

Two similar and more compelling examples follow:
1 Timothy 6:19

19 (MUR) and that they lay up for themselves a good foundation for that which is future; that they may take hold of real life.

שתאסתא טבתא למדם דעתיד דנדרכון חיא שרירא ונסימון לנפשהון 19 (Peshitta)

19 (BYZ) αποθησαυριζοντας εαυτοις θεμελιον καλον εις το μελλον ινα επιλαβωνται της αιωνιου ζωης

19 (AV) Laying up in store for themselves a good foundation against the time to come, that they may lay hold on eternal life.

19 (WH) αποθησαυριζοντας εαυτοις θεμελιον καλον εις το μελλον ινα επιλαβωνται της οντως ζωης

19 (ASV) laying up in store for themselves a good foundation against the time to come, that they may lay hold on the life which is life indeed.

Old Dead Sea Scroll script

The Peshitta in 1 Tim. 6:19 ends with – חיא שרירא ("True Life").

The Byzantine Greek text has αιωνιου ζωης ("Eternal Life") .

The Critical Greek (Vaticanus) has οντως ζωης ("Really Life")

1. 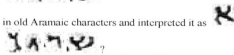 ,= שרירא = "True"

2. ,= שריכא = "Remaining"

Is it likely The Byzantine Greek translator saw

in old Aramaic characters and interpreted it as

?

If so, then αιωνιου (eternal) would approximate

-"Remaining".

The Critical Greek would be closer to the original here, following

"True" with οντως- "Really".

In Rev. 15:3 we have:

אחיד כל כאנין ושרירין עבדיך מלכא דעלמא
דאמרא ואמרין רורבין ותמיהין עבדיך מריא אלהא
תשבוחתא דמושא עבדה דאלהא ותשבוחתא
ומשבחין Re 15:3 Aramaic Crawford ms.

Re 15:3 και αδουσιν την ωδην μωυσεως του
δουλου του θεου και την ωδην του αρνιου
λεγοντες μεγαλα και θαυμαστα τα εργα σου
κυριε ο θεος ο παντοκρατωρ δικαιαι και
αληθιναι αι οδοι σου ο βασιλευς των εθνων –
Byz. Greek

Re 15:3 και αδουσιν την ωδην μωυσεως του
δουλου του θεου και την ωδην του αρνιου
λεγοντες μεγαλα και θαυμαστα τα εργα σου
κυριε ο θεος ο παντοκρατωρ δικαιαι και
αληθιναι αι οδοι σου ο βασιλευς των αιωνων –
Critical Greek

Here is a situation similar to Luke 2:9 .
The Crawford Aramaic mss. has דעלמא, **"D'elama"**
– ("of the world") .
The Majority Greek text has εθνων, "ethnown" –("of nations").
The Critical Greek text has αιωνων ,"aiownown" –
("of ages"). (Mss. P47, ℵ,C)
Here is The Comprehensive Aramaic Lexicon entry for the Aramaic word , עלם, עלמא:

CAL Outline Lexicon: GENERAL עלם –
עלמא , עלם (Noun) .
1 passim **eternity**
2 Palm,Palestinian,Syr,JBA **world**
3 Syr **nation**
LS2 527
LS2 V: (AlmA)
Smiths Compendious Syriac Dictionary has:

ܥܠܡܐ pl. ܢ̈ , ܐ̈ m. 1) constr. st. ܥܠܡ.
*an age, generation, life-time, era; eternity,
ever*; ܥܠܡܐ ܒܝܬ *a tomb*; ܥܠܡܝܢ ܠܥܠܡ

2) const. st. ܥܠܡ a) *the world; temporal
life; worldly* or *lay life* opp. monasticism;
ܐܢܬܘܢ ,ܢܘܗܪܗ ,ܐܝܟ *ye are the light of
the world*; ܟܠܢܫ *every one*; ܐܢܫ̈

So the Greek mss. have two different readings, both in
agreement with the Aramaic
word עלמא , which can mean "ages", "eternity",
"nations" or "world".
**It is stretching credulity beyond the breaking point
to believe** The Peshitta NT **is a translation of** The
Greek NT, **given the fact that so many Greek
variations exist in** The Greek NT **that agree with
different derivations of Aramaic words, which just
so happen to be used at the parallel grammatical
places of those readings in** The Peshitta NT, **and
given that The Peshitta has practically no variant
readings. If The Greek is the original, "How can
these things be ?"** .

11. "For today, The Savior has been born to
you, who is **THE LORD JEHOVAH** The
Messiah*, in the city of David."

*This is one of the most amazing of statements in The
Gospels, and probably the first unequivocal revelation of the
Deity of Yeshua Meshikha. (מריא משיחא -**Marya Meshikha**
means "Yahweh The Messiah"). I have translated "**Marya**" as
"Jehovah" in most places, since it is more familiar than
"**Yahweh**". There are disputes about the Hebrew
pronunciation, but "**Jehovah**" still conveys the sense of
"YHWH", the Hebrew Tetragrammaton (4 letter Name) of
"**The LORD God**" of Israel and all creation. The Aramaic
מריא -"**Marya**" is found over 6000 times in The Peshitta Old
Testament ,translating the Hebrew YHWH-מריא -"**Marya**",
as such, in the singular Name form, can refer only to **The**

LORD God. **This most holy of Names is applied to Yeshua
32 times in The Peshitta NT!** The Greek mss. have no such
unequivocal reference in those 32 places , since the Greek
word used is "**Kurios**", meaning, "**Lord**", or "**Sir**", in a
Divine or human sense.

12. "And this is a sign for you: You will find
The Baby wrapped in swaddling bands and
lying in a manger."

13. And suddenly (Lit. "from the silence"), the
great armies of Heaven appeared with the
Angel, while shouting praises to God, and
they were saying:

14. "Glory to God in Heaven, and upon earth
peace, Good News to the children of men."

15. It was that as the Angels went from them
into Heaven, the shepherds spoke one with
another and they were saying, "Let us go as
far as Bethlehem, and we shall see this event
that has occurred as **THE LORD
JEHOVAH** has revealed to us."

16. And they came quickly and they found
Maryam and Yoseph and The Baby who was
lying in a manger.

17. "And when they had seen, they made
known the words that had been spoken with
them about The Boy."

18. And all who heard marveled concerning
those things that were spoken to them by the
shepherds.

19. But Maryam was keeping all these words
and was pondering in her heart.

20. And the shepherds returned as they
glorified and praised God concerning
everything, because they had seen and heard
just as it had been spoken with them.

21. And when the eight days were complete
that The Boy should be circumcised, his name
was called Yeshua, which he was called by
the Angel before he would have been
conceived in the womb.

22. And when the days were fulfilled that
they should be purified according to the law
of Moses, they carried him to Jerusalem to
present him before **THE LORD
JEHOVAH**,

23. As it is written in the law of **THE LORD
JEHOVAH**, "Every male who opens the
womb will be called a holy one of **THE
LORD JEHOVAH**,"

24. And to offer a sacrifice, just like that
which was said in the law of **THE LORD
JEHOVAH**, "A pair of turtle doves or two
young doves."

25. But one man was there in Jerusalem,
whose name was Shimeon, and this man was
just and righteous and he was waiting for the

consolation of Israel and The Spirit of Holiness was upon him.

26. And it was told him by The Spirit of Holiness that he would not see death until he would see The Messiah of **THE LORD JEHOVAH.**

27. This one had come by The Spirit of Holiness to The Temple, and as his parents brought The Boy Yeshua to do for him just as it was commanded in the law,

28. He took him in his arms and he blessed God and said:

29. "Now send your servant in peace, my Lord, according to your word."

30. "Behold, my eyes have seen your mercy,"

31. "Him whom you have prepared in the sight of all the peoples."

32. "The Light for the revelation of the Gentiles and The Glory to your people Israel."

33. But Yoseph and his mother were marveling at those things which were spoken about him.

34. And Shimeon blessed them and said to Maryam his mother, "Behold, This One is appointed for the fall and the rise of many in Israel and for a sign of contention."

35. "And a lance will pass through into your soul, so that the thoughts of many hearts may be revealed."

36. And Hannah the Prophetess, daughter of Phanuel from the tribe of Asher, she was also in her old age, and had lived with her husband seven years after her virginity.

37. And she had been a widow about 84 years, and she had not departed from The Temple, and with fastings and with prayers she was serving by day and night.

38. She was also standing in it at that hour and she gave thanks to **THE LORD JEHOVAH** and was speaking about him with everyone who was waiting for the redemption of Jerusalem.

39. And when they had finished everything according to that which is in the law of **THE LORD JEHOVAH,** they returned to Galilee to Nazareth their city.

40. But The Boy was growing and being strengthened in spirit and he was filled with wisdom and the grace of God was upon him.

41. And every year his people were going to Jerusalem at the feast of Passover.

42. And when he was twelve years old, they went out to the feast just as they had been accustomed;

The Majority Greek text has "**they went up to Jerusalem**".

The Critical Greek agrees with The Peshitta reading here.

43. And when the days were past, they were returning, but The Boy Yeshua had remained in Jerusalem and Yoseph and his mother did not know it.

Instead of "**Joseph & His mother**", The Critical Greek has "**His parents**". Most Greek mss. agree with The Peshitta here.

44. For they were thinking that he was with the children of their friends, and when they had come a journey of one day, they looked for him among their people and among whoever knew them,

45. And they did not find him, and they returned again to Jerusalem and they were looking for him.

46. After three days, they found him in The Temple as he sat in the midst of the Teachers and he heard from them and he was inquiring of them.

47. And all who were listening to him were astounded at his wisdom and at his discourses.

48. And when they saw him, they marveled, and his mother said to him, "My son, why have you done this to us? Look, your father and I were looking for you with great anxiety."

49. He said to them, "Why were you looking for me? Do you not know that it was fitting for me to be in my Father's house?"

50. But they did not understand the statement that he spoke to them.

51. And he went down with them and he came to Nazareth, and he was submitted to them; but his mother was keeping all these words in her heart.

52. But Yeshua was growing in his stature and in his wisdom and in favor with God and the children of men.

Chapter 3

1. But in the 15th year of the Kingdom of Tiberius Caesar in the government of Pontius Pilate in Judea, when Herodus was the Tetrarch* in Galilee and Philippus his brother *was* Tetrarch in Ituria and in the region of Trakona, and Lusania *was* Tetrarch of Abilina,

* "Tetrarch" is found three times in this verse . The Aramaic term here is two words רשא רביעיא – "**Rasha Rbiaya**" , meaning **"Ruler of a fourth".** A tetrarch ruled a fourth of a country (give or take a little). Four other times another Aramaic word - טטררכא -"**Tetrarka**" occurs in The NT. It looks like a loan word from the Greek which had been

incorporated into Aramaic. There are some loan words in practically every language borrowed from neighboring or conquering countries . The Greek of Alexander The Great was influential even with the Jews of Israel, which never adopted Greek as a national language. What is interesting about verse three is that the Greek texts also have a slightly different form for "Tetrarch" than that used elsewhere in the NT ; it is a verb form, whereas elsewhere a noun is used. It looks like that may be explained on the basis of the Aramaic of The Peshitta, as the Greek verb form occurs nowhere else in The NT but where these three occur in Luke 3:1 – the same applies to the Aramaic word form used here. The Aramaic form used here is a noun, however. It is understandable that a Greek translator could construe "When Ruler of a fourth" as "When he was Ruler of a fourth" , since the Aramaic lacks a verb and uses כד -"Kad" – "When", before the term, which The Greek NT normally mirrors with a participle, which is exactly what the Greek word thrice used here is : "τετραρχουντος" - ("Tetrarchountos") . The Peshitta has no verb at all here, which is not unusual for Aramaic, but if it were a translation of the Greek , it would most likely include at least a verb of being .Essentially, the Greek looks like a simplification of The two word Aramaic term, very much like verse 14, where the Aramaic term- פלחי אסטרטיא –"Plakhay Estratia"("Military workers") is paralleled by the one Greek word "στρατευομενοι"- "strateuomenoi", another Greek participle meaning, "to go to war" ,"to go on a military expedition", "to be a soldier"

2. During The High Priesthood of Khanan and of Qaiapha, the word of God came upon Yohannan, son of Zachariah, in the wilderness.

3. And he came into the whole region which is around the Jordan while he was preaching a baptism of repentance for the forgiveness of sins,

4. Just as it is written in the book of the words of Isaiah the Prophet, which says*, "The voice which cries in the wilderness, 'Prepare the way of THE LORD JEHOVAH and straighten in the plain* a road for our God."

*The reading, "which says", is not found in the Critical Greek text. * All Greek mss. omit "in the plain*

5. "All the valleys will be filled and all the mountains and high places will be leveled and the rugged place will be smooth and the difficult region a plain,"

6. "And everybody will see The Life* of God."

• חיא – "Khaya" usually refers to "Life", though sometimes refers to "Salvation". The words of verses 4-6 are from Isaiah 40:3-5, generally agreeing with **The Peshitta O.T.** (word for word in Luke 3:5) though verse 6 agrees best with **The LXX** reading of Isaiah 40:5 ("**And all flesh shall see the salvation of God**"). All the Greek mss. agree with The Peshitta reading of v. 6.

7. And he said to the crowds who were coming to him to be baptized, "Offspring of

Vipers! Who has instructed you to flee from the wrath that is coming?"

8. "Produce therefore fruits worthy for repentance and do not start to say within yourselves, 'Abraham is our father', for I say to you that God can raise up from these stones children to Abraham."

9. "But behold, the ax is laid on the root of the tree. Every tree therefore, which is not producing good fruit is cut down and falls into the fire."

10. And the crowds were asking him and they were saying, "What, therefore, shall we do?"

11. And he answered and he said to them, "Whoever has two coats, let him give to him who has not, and whoever has food should do likewise."

12. And Tax Collectors came also to be baptized, and they were saying to him, "Teacher, what shall we do?"

13. But he said to them, "Do not require anything on top of whatever is commanded you to require."

14. And soldiers* were asking him and they were saying, "What shall we do* also?" He said to them, "Do harm to no man, do no injustice and let your wages be sufficient for you."

The Aramaic term- פלחי אסטרטיא –"Plakhay * Estratia"("Military workers") is paralleled by the one Greek word "στρατευομενοι"- "strateuomenoi", another Greek participle meaning, "to go to war" ,"to go on a military expedition", "to be a soldier" .The Greek, as usual, looks like a simplification of the Aramaic. This comports with the idea of the Greek being a translation of the Aramaic, since a translation will generally simplify the original text or speech for the target audience. Since The Peshitta is obviously not a simplified version of any Greek text of The NT, it is extremely unlikely to be a translation of The Greek NT.
* (shall do") נעבד- "Nebad" can mean "we shall do" or "we should do". The Greek mss. have both readings: Majority Greek- "ποιησομεν" - "We shall do" (Future) & the Critical Greek –"ποιησωμεν" –"We should do"(Subjunctive mood). Does anyone see a pattern forming?

15. But as the people had been thinking about Yohannan and they were all pondering in their hearts whether he were The Messiah,

16. Yohannan answered and said to them, "Behold, I am baptizing you in water, but he comes after me, who is mightier than I, the straps of whose shoes I am not worthy to loose. He will baptize you in The Spirit of Holiness and in fire,"

17. "He who holds a winnowing fan in his hand and purges his threshing floor; the wheat he gathers into his barns and the chaff he will burn in unquenched fire."

18. Also he taught many other things, and he preached The Good News to the people.

19. But Herodus the Tetrarch, because he had been reproved by Yohannan on the account of Herodia the wife of Philippus, his brother, and for all the evil that he had done,

20. He added this to all these things and shut Yohannan in prison.

21. It happened that when he had baptized all the people, he baptized Yeshua also, and as he prayed, the heavens were opened.

22. And The Spirit of Holiness was descending upon him in the form of a body of a dove, and there was a voice from Heaven, which said, "You are My Son, The Beloved, in whom I am delighted."

23. But Yeshua was about thirty years old, and he was considered the son of Yoseph, son of Heli *,

---

* "**Yoseph Bar Heli** " marks this as Joseph's genealogy, not Mary's. Mary's name is not here; "**Joseph Bar Heli**" is. All argument defending this as Mary's genealogy is mere sophistry. The Aramaic is even more definite than the Greek, since the Aramaic uses the word "**Bar**" – "**Son of** ", 76 times. The Greek uses the words "Son of"-"υιος του"-(huios tou) only once! 75 times it has "**tou**" –"**of**". That is less precise and leaves much more room for mischief in interpretation. The English translations of the Greek should have "**of** ", as does Rotherham in his Emphasized Bible as also does The Diaglot NT. If "son of" is used, "son" should be in italics, as the Greek "**tou**" is simply a definite article "**the**" in the genitive case-usually translated "of".

24. Son of Matthat, son of Levi, son of Melki, son of Yannai, son of Yoseph,

25. Son of Matatha, son of Amots, son of Nahum, son of Hesli, son of Naggai,

26. Son of Maath, son of Matath, son of Shimei, son of Yoseph, son of Yehudah,

27. Son of Yohannan, son of Resa, son of Zorobabel, son of Salathiel, son of Nari,

28. Son of Melki, son of Addi, son of Qosam, son of Elmodad, son of Ayr,

29. Son of Yose, son of Eliezer, son of Joram, son of Mathitha, son of Levi,

30. Son of Shimeon, son of Yehuda, son of Yoseph, son of Yonam, son of Eliakim,

31. Son of Melia, son of a Mainai, son of Matatha, son of Nathan, son of David,

32. Son of Ashai, son of Obed, son of Boaz, son of Salmon, son of Nahshon,

33. Son of Aminadab, son of Aram, son of Hetsron, son of Pharets, son of Yehudah,

34. Son of Jaqob, son of Isaaq, son of Abraham, son of Terah, son of Nahor,

35. Son of Serug, son of Arau, son of Phaleg, son of Eber, son of Shalah,

36. Son of Qainan*, son of Arphakshar, son of Shaym, son of Noah, son of Lamek,

* All Greek texts support "**Qainan**" as father of Shalah, though all Hebrew mss. as well as Aramaic O.T. mss. seem to lack this reading in Genesis 11:12 and in 1 Chronicles 1:18 . Only The LXX has this reading in Gen. 11:12. The LXX is lacking the verse of 1 Chronicles 1:18. The "Arphakshar"reading here agrees with The Peshitta O.T. spelling of this name in every place in which it is found. Hebrew mss. have "**Arphakshad**", as does The LXX and all Greek mss. of Luke 3:36. This is evidence that The Peshitta NT did not follow Hebrew O.T. mss. or The LXX or The Greek NT, but probably followed The Peshitta O.T. text (or vice versa) for these names. See note on this at the end of the chapter.

37. Son of Methuselah, son of Enoch, son of Jared, son of Mehalaleil, son of Qainan,

38. Son of Enosh, son of Shayth, son of Adam, who was from God.

This genealogy is Joseph's, the husband of Mary. Joseph was a descendant of David, as was Mary. The genealogy of Mary is given in Matthew 1:1-16. The two are definitely not the same. Joseph descended from David's son, Nathan. Mary descended from Solomon, son of David.

Luke 3:23 (MUR) And Jesus was about thirty years old. And he was accounted the son of Joseph, the son of Heli.

איך בר שנין תלתין ומסתבר הוא בר יוסף בר הלי
(PESHITTA) 23 הו דין ישוע איתוהי הוא

Blue Aramaic words are "**Yoseph Bar Heli**".
And Jesus himself began to be about thirty years of age, being (as was supposed) the son of Joseph, which was the son of Heli.

και αυτος ην ιησους αρχομενος ωσει ετων τριακοντα ων υιος ως ενομιζετο ιωσηφ του ηλι. Underlined Greek words are, "**Joseph of Heli**". This form is used throughout the Greek genealogy to indicate sonship. **If Joseph were not descended from Heli, they would not both be in the genealogy like this**. The loose Greek construction is construed by some to refer to Jesus, not Joseph, as descended from Heli. Others have it to mean "**Jesus, accounted son of Joseph, who was son-in law to Heli.**" Neither of these is a natural reading of the Greek; they are attempts to reshape this genealogy into Mary's instead of Joseph's. To take the Greek phrase,(**Name "tou" Name**), which occurs 76 times in the Greek text, as "Joseph, son-in-law to Heli", and then reinterpret it 75 times more as "son" is stretching credulity to its limits. It is playing too fast and loose with language and logic to be credible.
The Aramaic reading is much more precise and definite: "**Joseph Bar Heli, Bar Matthat, …**" **Joseph's name is in it, therefore it belongs to him. If it were Mary's , her name would be in the genealogy. It is not. Her name is in Matthew 1:16. That is her genealogy.**
The genealogy is Joseph's line , so don't expect it to match Matthew's.
The Greek of Luke, which omits the word for "**son**" (υιος) 75 times (**Aramaic has "Bar" 75 times**) , instead uses the genitive article tou (του) 75 times between each name. The genitive is usually translated "of .." :"Jacob **of** Isaac of Abraham of Terah…etc.".

That is a strange construction for a genealogy of The Messiah. One would expect precision in such a case. The Greek is imprecise, both in grammar and in its spelling of Hebrew and Aramaic names. We should expect a Semitic genealogy for all those Semitic names, such as would have been kept in the temple at Jerusalem and at the synagogues.

In The Peshitta, we have such a genealogy, fit for a King. Even the numbers of its words and letters point to a Divine author.

Joseph's genealogy in Luke traces back to Adam- 77 generations to The Messiah !
I defy anyone to show that the Peshitta's Hebrew & Aramaic names in Luke's genealogy came from the Greek N.T.! The Greek names are almost identical to The same names in the LXX version, which, of course , is a translation of the Hebrew Old Testament. The Peshitta genealogy as likely came from the Greek NT as The Hebrew O.T. genealogies were translated from The LXX!
Of the total 77, there are 21 names spelled differently in the two major Greek texts (Byzantine and Westcott & Hort Critical). Practically all of these may be explained as different transliterations and interpretations of the Aramaic letters in The Peshitta. There are 12 Names in The Peshitta NT which differ from Hebrew spelling and agree with The Peshitta Old Testament spelling of those names. These are practically all the names that differ in the two languages , Hebrew and Aramaic, for this genealogy. This indicates that Luke relied on The Peshitta Old Testament or an Aramaic Targum of The Old Testament for his genealogy. .All the other names found in The O.T. are the same in both Hebrew and Aramaic.
The Greek readings also indicate that The LXX Greek version was the source for Greek spellings of names in this genealogy. This is apparent by the sometimes patent mis-spellings of Hebrew names in the Greek text which are shared by The LXX Version ("Phalek" for "Peleg", for instance; others are "Ragau"for "Reu" & "Serouck" for " Serug"). There was also some revision of the Greek , apparently using The Peshitta as a reference, some time later.
If The Peshitta NT is the original from which The Greek NT was translated (and I think I have pretty well established that it is) and The genealogies of Matthew and Luke in The Peshitta refer to The Peshitta OT in listing those names, and elsewhere (and that is also fairly easily demonstrated), then The Peshitta Old Testament must be a document at least 2000 years old and was in circulation before A.D. 50. As such, it is an invaluable witness to the text of The Hebrew Old Testament in the first century A.D. and earlier.

Chapter 4

1. But Yeshua, being full of The Spirit of Holiness, returned from the Jordan and The Spirit led him into the wilderness

2. To be tempted by The Devil for forty days, and he ate nothing in those days, and when he had finished them, at the end he was hungry.

3. And The Devil said to him, "If you are the Son of God, tell this stone to become bread."

4. Yeshua answered and said to him, "It is written: a man does not live by bread alone, but by every utterance of God."

5. And Satan took him up to a high mountain, and he showed him all the Kingdoms of the earth in a short time.

6. And The Devil said to him, "I shall give you all this dominion and its glory, for it is delivered to me, and I give it to whomever I want."

7. "If therefore you will worship before me, it will all be yours."

8. Yeshua answered and said to him, "It is written: 'you shall worship THE LORD JEHOVAH your God, and him only you shall serve.'"

9. And he brought him to Jerusalem and he stood him on the pinnacle of The Temple and he said to him, "If you are the Son of God, cast yourself down from here."

10. "For it is written: 'He will command his Angels concerning you that they will protect you,'"

11. 'And they will carry you upon their arms, lest you should strike your foot on a stone.'"

12. But Yeshua answered and he said to him, "It has been said, 'You shall not tempt THE LORD JEHOVAH your God.'"

13. And when The Devil had finished all his temptations, he departed from his presence for a time.

14. And Yeshua returned in the power of The Spirit to Galilee and a report went out about him in every place around them.

15. And he was teaching in their assemblies and he was being praised by every person.

16. And he came to Nazareth where he had been raised, and as he was accustomed, he entered the synagogue on the Sabbath day, and he stood up to read.

17. And the scroll of Isaiah the Prophet was given to him and Yeshua opened the scroll and he found the place where it is written:

18. "The Spirit of THE LORD JEHOVAH is upon me, and because of this he has anointed me to preach The Good News to the poor; he has sent me to heal broken hearts and to proclaim liberty to captives, vision to the blind, and to restore the crushed with forgiveness,"

19. "And to proclaim the acceptable era of THE LORD JEHOVAH."

20. And he rolled up the scroll and he gave it to the minister and he went and sat down, but all who were in the synagogue fixed their eyes upon him.

21. And he began to say to them, "Today this scripture is fulfilled in your ears."

22. And all of them were testifying to it, and they were amazed at the words of grace that came out of his mouth. And they were saying, "Is not this Yoseph's son?"

23. Yeshua said to them, "Doubtless you will say to me this proverb: 'Physician, heal yourself', and 'Everything that we are hearing that you have done in Kapernahum, do also here in your town.'"

24. But he said, "Assuredly, I say to you, there is not a Prophet who is received in his town."

25. "For truly I say to you that many widows were in Israel in the days of Elijah the Prophet, when the heavens were shut for three years and six months, and there was great hunger in all the land."

26. "And Elijah was not sent to one of them except to Tsarepta of Tsidon unto a widow woman."

27. "And there were many lepers among Israel in the days of Elisha the Prophet, and not one of them was purified except Naaman the Syrian*."

*Literally-"Aramaean". An **Aramaean** would be anyone descended from **Aram** , son of Shem , and included the **Syrians**. Naaman was a Syrian. The Aramaic language was spoken by the Aramaeans (Syrians) and the Assyrians, as well as most of the Jews in Israel and the Diaspora of Asia Minor and Europe. The Assyrians imposed the language on all subjects of the Assyrian empire from the ninth century B.C. and it remained the lingua franca of the nations it had conquered for almost two millennia. One can see the hatred the Jews had for Syrians by the reaction recorded in the next two verses. The two nations of Israel and Syria had been mortal enemies for about nine centuries, and they shared borders just at the north of Israel.

28. And when they who were in the synagogue heard these things, they were all filled with rage.

29. And they arose and they thrust him outside of the city and they brought him unto the ridge of the mountain on which the city was built to cast him from the precipice.

30. But he passed through the midst of them and he departed.

31. And he went down to Kapernahum, a city of Galilee, and he was teaching them on the Sabbath.

32. And they were astonished at his teaching for his message was with authority.

33. And there was a man in the synagogue who had the spirit of a filthy demon in him and he cried with a loud voice

34. And he said, "Let me alone! What business do we have with you, Yeshua Nazarene? Have you come to destroy us? I know you, who you are, The Holy One of God!"

35. And Yeshua rebuked it and he said, "Shut your mouth and come out of him!" And the demon threw him in the midst, and it came out from him, while it did him no harm.

36. And great astonishment gripped everyone and they were speaking with one another and they were saying, "What indeed is this message? For with authority and with power

he commands the foul spirits, and they come out."

37. And a report about him went out into the whole region that was around them.

38. And when Yeshua went out from the synagogue, he entered the house of Shimeon, and Shimeon's mother-in-law was afflicted with a great fever and they besought him for her sake.

39. And he stood over her and rebuked her fever and it left her, and at once she arose and she was waiting on them.

40. But the sun was setting and they brought to him all of those who were ill with various diseases, and he laid his hand on each one of them and healed them.

41. And many demons were going out from many as they screamed and they were saying, "You are The Messiah, the Son of God!" And he was rebuking them and he was not allowing them to say that they knew that he was The Messiah.

42. And at daybreak he went out by himself to a deserted place and the crowds were seeking him, and came to his place, and they held to him that he would not depart from them.

43. But Yeshua said to them, "I must proclaim the Kingdom of God to other cities also; it is for this I am sent."

44. And he was preaching in the synagogues of Galilee.

Chapter 5

1. Now it happened that when the crowd gathered around him to hear the word of God, and he was standing on the side of the Lake of Genesar

2. He saw two ships that stood on the shore of the lake and the fishermen who had come down from them and were washing their nets.

3. And one of them belonged to Shimeon Kaypha, and Yeshua went up and sat down in it, and he said to take it out a little from the land into the water, and he sat down and he taught the crowds from the ship.

4. And when he had ceased speaking, he said to Shimeon, "Take to the deep and cast your nets for a catch."

5. Shimeon answered and he said to him, "Rabbi, we worked all night, and we have not caught anything, but at your word, I will cast the net."

Simon (Peter) called Jesus "**Rabbi**". The Greek texts all have "Επιστατα" – "**Master**". The Peshitta would not get "**Rabbi**" from "Epistata". A master was not

necessarily a Rabbi. However, a Rabbi was necessarily a Master, hence one could derive "**Master**" from "**Rabbi**", which it appears is what happened. The Aramaic text gave rise to the Greek reading .
Strongs Greek-English Lexicon has :
   1988 επιστατης epistates ep-is-tat'-ace
   from 1909 and a presumed derivative of 2476;
TDNT-2:622,248; n m
   AV-Master 7; 7

Thayer's Greek - English Lexicon
1) any sort of superintendent or overseer
Compare Luke 8:24 with Mark 4:38 & Matthew 8:25.
Luke 8:24 in Greek has Επιστατα, Επιστατα. In the parallel passage Mark 4:38 it has διδασκαλε (**Teacher**). The Peshitta has "**Rabban**" (**Our Rabbi**) in both verses . "**Our Rabbi**" did not come from "διδασκαλε (**Teacher**)" or from "Επιστατα Επιστατα"-"**Master Master**". Greek has a problem translating "Rabbi", as it has no one word that satisfactorily signifies it. That is probably why the Greek transliterates it instead 18 times in Greek letters: "Ραββι". The Greek Gospel of John states very plainly however that "Rabbi" is translated as διδασκαλε "didaskale" (**Teacher**) in John 1:38 where it is both transliterated from Aramaic with Greek letters and also translated into Greek:
Joh 1:38 στραφεις δε ο ιησους και θεασαμενος αυτους ακολουθουντας λεγει αυτοις τι ζητειτε οι δε ειπον αυτω ραββι ο λεγεται ερμηνευομενον διδασκαλε που μενεις,
Joh 1:38 (ROTHRHAM) But Jesus, turning, and looking at them following, saith unto them—What seek ye? And, they, said unto him—Rabbi! (Aramaic) which meaneth, when translated, **Teacher** (Greek), Where abidest thou?
This is a plain indication that the Greek text is a translation of an Aramaic source. It also indicates that the Greek word διδασκαλε , may indicate "**Rabbi**"-רבי as its source. There are other possibilities in Aramaic – "Mallpana" – מלפנא (Teacher), for example

Another Aramaic word identified in Greek mss. as meaning "**Teacher**" is "**Rabboni**" in John 20:16:
ואמרא לה עבראית רבולי דמתאמר מלפנא
16 (Peshitta) אמר לה ישוע מרים ואתפנית
16 (MUR) Jesus said to her: Mary! And she turned, and said to him in Hebrew: **Rabbuni**; which is interpreted Teacher.
16 (BYZ) λεγει αυτη ο ιησους μαρια στραφεισα εκεινη λεγει αυτω ραββουνι ο λεγεται διδασκαλε
16 (YLT) Jesus saith to her, 'Mary!' having turned, she saith to him, '**Rabbouni**;' that is to say, 'Teacher.'
   Here is my note for John 20:12 from my interlinear: 16 (& she said) ואמרא (& she turned) ואתפנית (Mary) מרים (Yeshua) ישוע (to her) לה (said) אמר (Teacher) מלפנא (which is called) דמתאמר (Rabbuli *) (in Aramaic *) עבראית (to Him) לה רבולי

- עבראית-"**Ebraith**" means "**Hebrew**" and though Aramaic was the language used, the Jewish people referred to it as Hebrew, since Aramaic had been their native tongue (**the tongue of the Hebrew people**) for six centuries and was used in their scriptures. **Aramaic and Hebrew share the same alphabet and both were written with the same script, so their letters looked the same in the first century.**
- רבולי –"**Rabbuli**" is an Aramaic word meaning "**My Master**" and is the same as "**Rabboni**" , which the Greek versions have in Greek letters transliterated Ραββουνι . **Notice that Mary is not presented as speaking Greek; neither is any other person mentioned in the four Gospels. "Ebraith"– "Hebrew" is defined by its Greek equivalent, "Hebrais", as "The Hebrew tongue; not that however in which the OT was written, but the Chaldee."-Thayer's Greek – English Lexicon.** Webster's unabridged 20th century Dictionary defines

"Chaldee" as **The Aramaic language** of the Chaldaeans (Babylonians 600 B.C.)

"**Rabbi**" רבי & "**Rabban**" רבן , occur 36 times as a Title of address in the Peshitta NT. The Greek mss. have διδασκαλος- didaskalos (**Teacher**) for **13** of these , Ραββι "**Rabbi**" 18 times (This is an Aramaic word, not Greek, transliterated in Greek letters) , Επιστατα occurs **7** times matching **Rabbi**- all in Luke.Ραββουνι occurs once matching **Rabbi** and once matching "**Rabbuli**" רבולי . All of these Greek translations and transliterations are evidence supporting an Aramaic original. Greek simply has no word of its own for "Rabbi" and so it used διδασκαλος ,Επιστατα, & 20 **transliterations of** Ραββι & Ραββουνι . The Greek words διδασκαλος ,επιστατα would not translate to "**Rabbi**" -רבי in Aramaic "**Rabbi**" **has all the meanings of "Teacher" & "Master" & "Leader"; no one of them would do justice to the word. It is also a formal title for the clergyman leader of a synagogue.**

6. And when they had done this, they caught very many fish and the net was breaking.

7. And they beckoned to their partners who were in another ship to come help them and when they came they filled those two ships, so that they were almost sinking.

8. And when Shimeon Kaypha saw it, he fell before the feet of Yeshua and he said to him, "I beg you, my Lord, abandon me, for I am a sinner."

9. For awe had seized him and all of them who were with him, due to that catch of fish which they had caught,

10. Likewise also Yaqob and Yohannan, sons of Zebedee, who were partners of Shimeon, but Yeshua said to Shimeon, "Do not be afraid; from now on, you will be catching men for salvation*."

*I love this text in The Peshitta : "**Henceforth you shall catch men for salvation.**" No Greek ms. has this. Greek does have the verb ζωγρεω which can mean "to take alive", "to capture". The Aramaic word חיא can mean "**life, living**" or "**salvation**". The Greek word ζωγρεω **would hardly give rise to the Aramaic** צאד לחיא ("catch for life", "catch for salvation"). צאד לחיא may **easily have given rise to** ζωγρεω , though it would not seem the best choice.

11. And they brought those ships to land, and they left everything and they came after him.

12. And when Yeshua was in one of the cities, a certain man who was full of leprosy came in and saw Yeshua and he fell down on his face and he begged of him and he said to him, "My Lord, if you are willing, you can purify me."

13. And Yeshua reached his hand and he touched him and he said, "I am willing; be purified." And immediately his leprosy went from him and he was purified.

14. And he commanded him: "Tell no man, but go show yourself to the Priest and offer for your cleansing, just as Moses commanded, for their testimony."

Greek mss. have , " **And He charged him to tell no one, 'But, having gone away, shew thyself to the priest, …"** This is rather awkward and clumsy Greek. The Peshitta has , **"And He commanded him: 'You shall tell no man, but go show yourself to the priest.'"** Much better, don't you think?

15.And fame went out about him increasingly, and many people were   gathered to hear from him and to be healed of their sicknesses.

16.But he was departing to the wilderness and praying.

17.And it happened on one of the days when Yeshua was teaching, the Pharisees and The Teachers of The Law were sitting who had come from every village of Galilee, and of Judea, and of Jerusalem, and the power of **THE LORD JEHOVAH** was there to heal them.

18.And men brought a man on a pallet who was paralyzed, and they were seeking to enter to place him in front of him.

19.And when they found no way to bring him in because of the crowd of people, they went up by themselves to the roof and lowered him with the pallet from the tiles into the center, in front of Yeshua.

20.But when Yeshua saw their faith, he said to that paralyzed man: "Man, your sins are forgiven you."

21.And the Scribes and Pharisees began to think, and they were saying, "Who is this who speaks blasphemy? Who is able to forgive sins except God alone?"

22.But Yeshua knew their thoughts; he answered and said to them, "What thoughts are entertained by you in your heart?"

23."Which is easier: to say, 'Your sins are forgiven you', or to say, 'Arise and walk?'

24.But that you may know that The Son of Man is authorized in the earth to forgive sins", he said to the paralyzed man, "I say to you, arise, pick up your pallet and go to your house."

25.And at once he arose before their eyes and took up his pallet and he went on to his house as he praised God.

26.And astonishment seized everyone and they were praising God, and they were filled with awe and they were saying, "We have seen wonders today."

The Greek NT verse can be translated "**We have seen strange things today".** That is not a convincing reading when compared to The Peshitta reading- "**We have seen wonders today.**"

27.After these things Yeshua went out and he saw a Tax Collector whose name was Levi, who sat in The House of Customs, and he said to him, "Come after me."

28.And he left everything, and rising, he went after him.

29.And Levi made a great reception for him in his house and there was a great crowd of Tax Gatherers and of others who were reclining at dinner with them.

30.And the Scribes and the Pharisees were complaining and they were saying to his disciples, "Why do you eat and drink with the Tax Collectors and sinners?"

31.And Yeshua answered and he said to them, "A doctor is not sought for the healthy but for those who become very ill."

32."I have not come that I may call the righteous, but sinners to repentance."

33.But they were saying to him, "Why do the disciples of Yohannan fast faithfully and pray, also the Pharisees, but yours are eating and drinking?"

34.But he said to them, "You cannot make the children of the bridal chamber fast as long as the groom is with them."

35."But the days will come when the groom will be taken from them and then they will fast in those days."

36.And he told them a parable: "No man tears a strip from a new garment and places it on a worn garment, lest also the new tears the worn and it does not resemble the strip from the new piece."

37."And no man places new wine in old wineskins, lest the new wine should burst the skins and the wine is spilled and the skins are ruined."

38."But new wine is placed in new wineskins and both are preserved."

39.And no man drinks old wine* and at once desires the new, for he says, "The old is sweet."

The Greek texts omit "**wine**" altogether . They also disagree with "**sweet**"; Majority Greek has "**better**"; Critical Greek has "**good**". The Peshitta did not get בסים ("**is sweet**") from Χρηστος ("**good**") or from Χρηστοτερος ("**better**"). The Greek could derive from the Aramaic, as "**sweet**" is generally considered "**good**" , but "**good**" does not imply sweetness. "**Sweet**" is more specific than "**good**". Hence, the Greek looks more like a translation here than does The Peshitta.

Chapter 6

1. Now it happened on the Sabbath* when Yeshua was walking among the grain, his disciples were plucking the ears and were rubbing them in their hands and eating them.

* The Majority Greek Text has a strange word δευτεροπρωτω" –"**second first**" after "**Sabbath**". This is the only place where the word is found in any

Greek writing. The Critical Greek (**P**[75],**B**, **א**) does not have it here. All Greek texts lack "**Jesus**" in this verse.- (See note at v. 12.)

2. But some of the Pharisees were saying to them, "Why are you doing what is illegal to do on the Sabbath?"

3. Yeshua answered and said to them, "Have you not read this thing that David did when he was hungry and those who were with him,"

4. "When he entered the house of God and he took and ate the bread* of the table of **THE LORD JEHOVAH** and he gave to those who were with him, which was not legal to eat except for the Priests only?"

Greek texts have τους αρτους της προθεσεως ("**the loaves of the setting forth**") .The Peshitta's "**bread of the table of Jehovah**" is much plainer and sounds original whereas the Greek sounds artificial.

5. And he said to them, "The Son of Man is Master of the sabbath."

6. But it happened on another Sabbath that he entered a synagogue and he was teaching, and a man was there whose right hand was shriveled.

7. And the Scribes and the Pharisees were watching him whether he would heal on the Sabbath, that they might be able to accuse him.

8. But he knew their schemes and he said to that man whose hand was shriveled, "Stand; come to the center of the synagogue", and when he came and stood,

9. Yeshua said to them, "I ask you, what is legal on the Sabbath: to do good or evil? To save life or to destroy?"

10. And he gazed at all of them and he said to him, "Straighten your hand", and he stretched it out and his hand was restored like his other.

Greek mss. seem to have edited out "**and he straightened it**" & replaced it with "**he did**". The Critical Greek further seems to have edited out "**like the other**" at the end of the verse. Interestingly, The Latin Vulgate seems to have been translated from a slightly different Greek ms. which did not edit the first phrase but did omit the latter.

11. But they were filled with envy*, and they were speaking one with another of what they should do to Yeshua.

The Greek has επλησθησαν ανοιας- "**They were filled with madness**".
חסמא is the Aramaic word for "Jealousy" . Here is the Aramaic for "**Rage**" or "**Venom**"-
חמתא . Might this strange similarity explain the Greek reading ? One could probably easily be mistaken for the other. The Greek has two words used

Peshitta were a translation of The Greek NT , ανοιας (**madness**) would have been hypothetically mistaken as ζηλος , ζηλου or φθονον. Another possibility is that an Aramaean translator might have intended to write חמתא & wrote חסמא. That is not a likely event for a sober scribe. It would be much easier to misread such a word than to miswrite it. ανοιας does not look like ζηλος , ζηλου or φθονον, hence the Greek original scenario is not a very likely explanation. חסמא & חמתא are very similar; they could easily be confused one for another, hence The Peshitta primacy theory is a much more likely explanation here for the Greek reading than is Greek primacy for the Aramaic reading.

ﬡ & ﬡ are the **two** Aramaic words in Estrangela script which was used after AD 100. They do not look as similar in that script, but Estrangela did not exist when the NT was composed, so it would not explain the discrepancies since the Greek NT was written in the first century and the Aramaic script used would have been the square Aramaic characters similar to those used in this interlinear. There are many examples like this one which I point out in this interlinear of The Gospels

I will here re-display a thousand words' worth of evidence for Peshitta Primacy and for a Greek NT translated from The Peshitta:

Peshitta reading	Peshitta meaning
ﬡ מ ס ד	"Jealousy"

Greek reading in Aram.	Greek meaning
ﬡ ת מ ד	"Rage"

Square Aramaic :

חמתא   חסמא
"Jealousy"   "Rage"

12. But it occurred in those days that Yeshua went out to a mountain to pray, and there he was waiting for the morning in the prayer of God.

Yeshua) ישוע (went out) נפק (those) הנון (in days))
הוא (but) דין (it occurred) ביומתא
He was) הוא (waiting for morning) אגה (& there))
ותמן (to pray) למצליו (to a mountain) לטורא
of God) דאלהא (in the prayer) בצלותה)

"Jesus" is lacking in the Greek NT of this verse. Indeed the Greek versions of Luke have the Greek form of Our Lord's Name ,"Ιησους", 88 times (W&H) and 98 times (Byzantine). The Peshitta in Luke has **Yeshua**- ישוע 175 times ! This can be explained in one of two ways:

1. If The Peshitta is the original, (which I unabashedly believe) the Greek translator, (possibly Luke himself wrote both the original and the Greek translation, according to Hegesippus in the 2nd century) **dropped 45% - 50%** of the occurrences of "**Yeshua**" in translation, possibly to present a smoother Greek style, substituting personal pronouns & or third person singular Greek verb.

2. If the Greek is original , the Peshitta translator doubled the occurrences of "Jesus" -"Yeshua" from 88 to 176, for whatever reason. That is a **100% increase** , based on the Critical Greek text of Westcott and Hort.

The # Greek/#Aramaic ratios for "Jesus" in The Gospels and Acts are as follows:
Matthew Greek 150; Aramaic 187; 80% (Byz. 171 ; 91.4%
Mark Greek 82; Aramaic 116; 71% (Byz. 93; 80.2%
Luke Greek 88; Aramaic 175; 50% (Byz. 98; 56.0%
John Greek 242; Aramaic 272; 89% (Byz. 253;

(Acts Greek 69; Aramaic 71; 97% (Byz. 66; 93.0%
NT Totals: Greek 913; Aramaic 1116 ; 81.8%
Another statistic to consider is the number of
occurrences of the name per total words of text:
Peshitta **Yeshua**-ישוע   W&H Greek **Jesus**-Ιησους
Byz. Greek
Matthew 187/13980 = 1.3% 150/18287 = 0.82%
171/18580 = 0.92%
Mark 116/8793 = 1.3% 82/11445 = 0.71%
93/11628= 0.80%
Luke 175/15234 = 1.1% 88/19568 = 0.45%
98/19881= 0.49%
John 272/12409= 2.2% 242/15664 =1.54%
253/15914= 1.59%

The Greek version of Luke has a very low number of
the Name Ιησους –Jesus, compared to the other
Gospels, which accounts for the discrepancy between
it and The Peshitta version of Luke. The Peshitta
Gospels seem to be fairly consistent in the usage of the
Name ; the spread from the mean of 1.48% is 0.37 , or
.25% of the mean value
The Greek values have a mean of 0.88 and a spread of
0.33 , or 37.5% of the mean value. That is a rather
radical variation, primarily produced by the Greek
Luke stats. It looks as if The Peshitta book of Luke is
pretty much in line with the other Peshitta Gospels in
numbers of occurrences per text size, so the
implications are that Greek Luke has been altered.
Adding 77 occurrences of Ιησους to the Greek book
of Luke (the difference in the numbers of The Name
between the two versions) would put Greek Luke on a
par with the other Gospels with regard to the Name
frequency- **0.89%**. The average for Matthew, Mark
and John is **1.02%**. On the other hand, to assume an
hypothetical Peshitta translator added Yeshua 77 times
means he should have written only **88 Yeshua's**
instead, which puts Aramaic Luke at **0.55%** frequency
for that name, which is extremely low frequency
compared to the usage of His Name in the other
Peshitta Gospels. The average for the other 3 Gospels
is **1.6%** , which places the edited Luke at **34%** of the
average , or at a **66% reduction of the average**.
The Greek primacy theory would indicate the Luke
had an aversion to the Name of **Ihsous (Jesus)**. The
other Gospel writers used it once for every 102 words.
Luke used it only once in every 222 words ! That is
less than half the frequency of the others. Why would
an original inspired Gospel of Ιησους contain Ιησους
(Jesus) only half as often as the other Gospels and
substitute mere pronouns (He,Him,His) in place of the
other half ? Was Luke ashamed of the Name of His
Lord ? I think not!!
I think the Greek primacy theory fails its proponents
here, whereas Peshitta primacy can explain the facts
much more easily. The Peshitta has statistics which
support its originality; its four Gospels are consistent
with regard to the frequency of the most important
Name and indeed the Subject of their content. **The
Greek Gospels all have reduced numbers of this
Name, apparently like The LXX Greek of Daniel ,
which has four fewer occurrences of Daniel's name
(71) than the Hebrew & Aramaic text of Daniel has
(75)**. Below is a sample verse of the Aramaic text of
Daniel 6:20 with The LXX below it. Notice the name
of **Daniel** in blue in the Aramaic and in the Greek. The
LXX is missing two "**Daniels**" in this verse: The
original Aramaic verse has three occurrences of
Daniel- דניאל , whereas the Greek verse translated
from it has only one δανιηλ.
(ARAMAIC) לדניאל בקל עציב זעק ענה דניאל מלכא
כמקרבה לגבא <6:21> Da 6:20
אנתה פלח-לה בתדירא היכל לשיזבותך מן-אריותא
ואמר לדניאל דניאל עבד אלהא חיא אלהך די
Da 6:20 (AV) And when he came to the den, he cried
with a lamentable voice unto Daniel: and the King
spake and said to Daniel, O Daniel, servant of **the
living God**, is thy God, whom thou servest
continually, able to deliver thee from the lions?

Da 6:20 (LXX Greek) (#6:# 21) και εν τω εγγιζειν
αυτον τω λακκω εβοησεν φωνη ισχυρα δανιηλ ο
δουλος του θεου του ζωντος ο θεος σου ω συ
λατρευεις ενδελεχως ει ηδυνηθη εξελεσθαι σε εκ
στοματος των λεοντων
Da 6:20 (LXX English) And when he drew near to the
den, he cried with a loud voice, Daniel, servant of **the
living God**, has thy God, whom thou servest
continually, been able to deliver thee from the lion's
mouth?
    The Hebrew book of Joshua has **168** occurrences of
the name of Joshua יהושע , which is the Hebrew
cognate of the Aramaic "Yeshua" (or "Jesus") , which
we are studying in Luke 6:12. The LXX version of
Joshua has only **159** occurrences of the Greek forms
for "Jesus": Ιησους, Ιησου, Ιησοι, Ιησουν. These
are the same forms (except Ιησοι) used in the NT for
"Yeshua" in the Greek NT. That is a Greek/Hebrew
ratio of **94.6%** , very close to John's or Acts'
Greek/Aramaic ratio for "Jesus"/"Yeshua" of **93%**.
**This pattern of dropping words in a translation is
typical. The LXX is certainly a translation of The
Hebrew Bible and consistently compares in this
way to The Hebrew Bible; The Greek NT also
compares in the same way to The Peshitta NT. The
Greek NT "behaves" like a translation. The
Peshitta does not; It "behaves like an original
composition.**
    Here is an example from Joshua 8:16 –
(HEBREW) וירדפו אחרי יהושע וינתקו מן-העיר
Jos 8:16 ויזעקו כל-העם אשר בעיר לרדף אחריהם
Jos 8:16 (AV) And all the people that were in Ai were
called together to pursue after them: and they pursued
after **Joshua**, and were drawn away from the city.
Jos 8:16 (LXX Greek) kai katediwxan opisw twn uiwn
israhl kai autoi apesthsan apo thv polewv
Jos 8:16 (LXX English) And they pursued after the
children of Israel, and they themselves went to a
distance   from the city.
And another from Joshua 9:3 –
(HEBREW) שמעו את אשר עשה יהושע לירדחו ולעי
Jos 9:3 וישבי גבעון
Jos 9:3 ¶ (AV) And when the inhabitants of Gibeon
heard what **Joshua** had done unto Jericho and to Ai,
Jos 9:3 (LXX Greek) και οι κατοικουντες γαβαων
ηκουσαν παντα οσα εποιησεν κυριος τη ιεριχω
και   τη γαι
Jos 9:3 ¶ (LXX English) And the inhabitants of
Gabaon heard of all that the Lord did to Jericho and
Gai.
Notice there is no Greek reference to Joshua "Ιησους"
in those verses.
**The above are three of many examples of the LXX
dropping words from the original; the Greek NT
compares to The Peshitta NT in the same way. I
have demonstrated this in a controlled experiment
which I have included in my book, Divine Contact.**

13. And when it was dawn he called his
disciples and he chose twelve of them, whom
he named Apostles:

14. Shimeon, whom he named Kaypha, and
Andraeus his brother, Yaqob and Yohannan
and Phillipus and Bar Tolmay

15. And Mattay and Thoma and Yaqob Bar
Halphai, Shimeon who is called The Zealot,

16. And Yehuda Bar Yaqob and Yehuda
Scariota who was the traitor.

17. And Yeshua descended with them and he
stood in the valley and a great crowd of his
disciples and a multitude of crowds of people
from all of Judea and from Jerusalem and
from the sea coast of Tyre and Sidon

18. Who came to hear his message and to be healed of their sicknesses, and those who were afflicted by foul spirits, and they were healed.

19. And all the crowds were seeking to touch him, for power was proceeding from him and it was healing all of them.

20. And he lifted his eyes upon his disciples and he said, "Blessed are you poor ones, because yours is the Kingdom of God."

21. "Blessed are you who hunger now, for you shall be satisfied. Blessed are you who weep now, for you shall laugh."

22. "Blessed are you, whenever men shall hate you and shall separate you and shall insult you and shall cast out your name as evil for The Son of Man's sake."

23. "Rejoice in that day and leap for joy, for your reward is great in Heaven, for so were their fathers doing to The Prophets."

24. "But woe to you rich men, for you have received your comfort!"

25. "Woe to you satisfied ones, for you shall hunger!" Woe to you who are laughing now, for you shall weep and you shall wail!"

26. "Woe to you when men* shall say wonderful things about you, for so were their fathers doing to the false Prophets!" * **Critical Greek and some Byzantine mss. (Codex W) have "παντες οι ανθρωποι"- "all men"; this probably is a misreading of the Aramaic Peshitta's words –**

"בני אנשא"-"sons of men" ; Look at the same words– "sons of men" in a Dead Sea Scroll Aramaic script, called Pesher Habbakuk: אנשא בני . Compare that to the Aramaic for "everyone": א נש כל

Pesher Habbakuk
אנשא בני –"Sons of men"
כל נש א –"Everyone"

So it may be that a 1st century Greek translator mistook "Benay nasha" –"**Sons of men**" for "Kol nash"-"**Everyone**".

27. "But I say to you who are hearing, Love your enemies and do what is wonderful to those who hate you."

28. "Bless those who curse you, and pray over those who take you away by force."

29. "And to him who strikes you on your cheek, offer the other, and from whoever takes away your cloak, withhold not your coat also."

30. "Give to everyone who asks you and do not demand from him who takes what is yours."

31. "And just as you desire people to do for you, do also for them."

32. "For if you love those who love you, what goodness do you have? Even sinners love those who love them."

33. "And if you are doing good to those who treat you well, what goodness do you have? For even sinners do likewise."

34. "And if you lend to him from whom you expect to be repaid, what goodness do you have? For even sinners lend to sinners to be repaid likewise."

35. "But love your enemies and treat them well and lend and do not cut off* the hope of any person, and your reward shall be great and you shall be the children of The Highest, because he is kind toward the evil and toward the unbelievers."

*

For "**Do not cut off the hope of any person**", the Greek texts have "**hoping for nothing**" or "**never despairing**".
I do not see how The Peshitta got "**Do not cut off the hope of any person**"- from Greek, however I can see how the Aramaic could be chopped down to μηδεν απελπιζοντες -"**hoping for nothing**". According to Thayer's Greek-English Lexicon, that Greek phrase may mean "**causing no one to despair**", though it is ambiguous. The Aramaic is quite clear.
Strong's Lexicon:
560 απελπιζω apelpizo ap-el-pid'-zo from 575 and 1679; TDNT-2:533,229; v
AV-hope for again 1; 1
Thayer's Greek-English Lex.
apelpizw
1) nothing despairing
2) despairing of no one
3) causing no one to despair

36. "Be therefore merciful, just as also your Father is merciful."

37. "Do not judge, and you will not be judged. Do not condemn, and you will not be condemned. Forgive and you will be forgiven."

38. "Give and it will be given to you in good measure, pressed down and overflowing, they shall cast into your lap. For with what measure you measure it will be measured to you."

39. And he told them a parable: "Can a blind man to lead a blind man? Will not both of them fall into a ditch?"

40. "There is no disciple greater than his mentor, for everyone who is perfected shall be like his mentor."

41. "But why do you observe a chip in the eye of your brother, but you do not see the plank that is in your eye?"

42. "Or how can you say to your brother, 'My brother, let me cast the chip out of your eye, when behold, the plank that is in your own eye is not visible to you? Hypocrite! First cast out the plank from your own eye, and then sight will be given to you to pull out the chip from your brother's eye."

43. "There is not a good tree that produces bad fruit, neither a bad tree that produces good fruit,"

44. "For every tree is known by its fruits, for they do not pick figs from thorns, neither do they gather grapes from a bush."

45. "A good man brings forth good from the good treasure that is in his heart and the evil man brings out evil from the evil treasure that is in his heart. For the lips speak from the fullness of the heart."

46. "Why are you calling me, 'My Lord, my Lord", and you are not doing whatever I say?"

47. "Every person who comes to me and has heard my words and does them, I shall show you what he is like":

48. "He is like a man who built a house and he dug and he went deep and laid the foundation on the rock, and when there was a flood, the flood beat on that house and it could not shake it, for its foundation was founded on the rock*."

*The Critical Greek of Westcott & Hort has ,"For it was well built", instead of ,"For its foundation was founded on the rock". The Majority Greek text agrees with the Peshitta here.

49. "And he who heard and did not do it is like the man who built his house on the soil without a foundation, and when the river beat on it, immediately it fell, and the fall of that house was great."

Chapter 7

1. And when he had finished all these words before the audience of the people, Yeshua entered Kapernahum.

כפרנחום -"Kapernakhum" , commonly known as "Capernaum" is an Aramaic or Hebrew name meaning, "The Hamlet of Nahum". It was where Nahum The Prophet had lived centuries before- the one who wrote the Old Testament book of Nahum.

2. But the servant of a certain Centurion who was precious to him had become ill, and he had come near to death.

3. And he had heard about Yeshua, and he sent Elders of the Jews to him and he was begging him to come and save the life of his servant.

4. But when they came to Yeshua, they were seeking from him diligently and they were saying, "He is worthy that you should do this for him."

5. "For he loves our nation and also has built a synagogue for us."

6. And Yeshua was going with them and when he was not very far from the house, the Centurion sent his friends and he said to him, "My Lord, you should not trouble yourself, for I am not worthy that you should enter under my roof."

7. "Therefore, I was not worthy to come to you, but say in a word and my boy will be healed."

8. "For I am also a man who is put under authority, and I have soldiers under my hand and I say to this one, 'Go', and he goes, and to another, 'Come', and he comes, and unto my servant, 'Do this', and he does it."

9. But when Yeshua heard these things, he was amazed at him, and he turned and he said to the crowd that came after him, "I say to you that not even in the house of Israel have I found faith like this."

10. And those who had been sent returned to the house and they found that the servant who had been sick was already well.

11. And it happened the day after, he went to the city whose name was Nain, and his disciples were with him and the crowds.

12. And when he approached the gate of the city, he saw as a dead man was being escorted who had been the only son of his mother, and his mother was a widow, and many of the people of the city had assembled with her.

13. But Yeshua saw her and he was moved with pity for her and he said to her, "Do not weep."

14. And he went and touched the palette, and those who were bearing it stood still and he said, "Young man, I say to you, arise."

15. And he who had died sat up and began to speak, and he gave him to his mother.

16. And awe gripped all the people, and they were glorifying God, and they were saying, "A great Prophet has arisen among us, and God has visited his people."

17. And this word about him went out in all Judea and in all the region that was around them.

18. And his disciples revealed all these things to Yohannan.

19. And Yohannan called two of his disciples, and he sent them to Yeshua and he said, "Are you The One who was coming or are we waiting for another?"

20. And they came to Yeshua and they were saying to him, "Yohannan The Baptizer has sent us to you, and he said, "Are you the one

who was coming or are we waiting for another?"

21. But in that hour, he healed many from diseases and from plagues and of evil spirits, and he gave sight to many blind people.

22. And Yeshua answered and he said to them, "Go tell Yohannan everything that you have seen and that you have heard; that they who were blind are seeing*, and they who were lame are walking, and they who were lepers are cleansed, and they who were deaf are hearing, and they who were dead are raised, and those who were poor are given Good News."

*

The Aramaic participles used by Our Lord are quite versatile , bearing possible past, present or future tenses. The past tense is the best for these people whom He had healed or resurrected: **"they who were blind, they who were lame, they who were deaf"**, etc. It would be an error to say ``the dead rise`` or to say ``the blind see``.

The Greek versions contain those very errors: All the pertinent words for the above groups are Greek nouns, which are completely inflexible: ``Blind men do see again, lame do walk, lepers are cleansed, deaf do hear, dead are raised, poor have good news proclaimed``-Young's Literal Translation (of the Greek).This makes for great drama but very poor logic. Our Lord and The Holy Spirit would not speak so.

And logic also would show that the last category of people – ``those who were poor`` had also been delivered from their condition (**``they who were poor``**).The ``Good News`` makes rich those who believe it. **Blessed are you poor; yours is the Kingdom of God**.(Luke 6:20). מסכין –``M'skayn`` – ``waiting`` (see v. 20) & מסכנא –``Meskanna`` –``poor`` are probably related. The poor are those who are in expectation, waiting for deliverance from calamity. מסתברין – ``M'sethbarayn``,``Given good news`` comes from ``סבר`` – ``S'bar`` – ``to hope, to trust, to expect``. A poor man is one who is waiting for ``his ship to come in``. To be given good news or given hope , in the Biblical sense, is more than adding more hope or expectation. It is giving, or announcing as accomplished, the thing hoped for to those who were hoping. Hope is , in this sense, the accomplishment of our desires, prayers and hopes. To receive The Gospel message is as great a miracle as raising the dead; indeed it combines all the other miracles mentioned here: It gives sight to the blind, hearing to the deaf, walking to the lame, cleanses the leper and is life to the dead. It is the miracle of the ages- the fulfillment of all hope and desire, the redemption of the world from sin & death by Him Whose Name is "Eternal Life". In a word, it is Christ. Luke 6:20 means , "Blessed are you poor, for your ship has come in". That was The Good News. They were henceforth rich men and women.

The following scriptures speak of hope as the very thing hoped for, or as the fulfillment of a Divine promise:
Pr 13:12 Hope deferred maketh the heart sick: but when the desire cometh, it is a tree of life. (Desire coming is the fulfillment of desire & hope.)
Jer 17:7 Blessed is the man that trusteth in the **LORD**, and whose hope the **LORD** is.
Ga 5:5 For we through the Spirit wait for the hope of righteousness by faith. (We don`t wait to hope some more, do we ?)
Col 1:5 For the hope which is laid up for you in heaven, whereof ye heard before in the word of the truth of The Gospel;
Col 1:27 To whom God would make known what is the riches of the glory of this mystery among the Gentiles; which is Christ in you, the hope of glory:(Christ is not a hoping for glory; He is the Glory for which we hoped.)

1Ti 1:1 Paul, an apostle of Jesus Christ by the commandment of God our Saviour, and Lord Jesus Christ, which is our hope;
Tit 2:13 looking for the blessed hope, and the manifestation of the glory of the great God, and our Life-giver, Jesus the Messiah;
Heb 6:18 so that, by two things which change not, and in which God cannot lie, we, who have sought refuge in him, might have great consolation, and might hold fast the hope promised to us;
Heb 6:19 Which hope we have as an anchor of the soul, both sure and stedfast, and which entereth into that within the veil; (Most hopes men hold; this Hope holds men.)
Heb 7:19 For the law perfected nothing; but in the place of it there came in a hope, which is better than it, and by which we draw near to God.

23. "And blessed is he, whoever will not take offense at me."

24. But when the disciples of Yohannan left, he began to say to the crowds about Yohannan, "What did you go out to the wilderness to see? A reed being shaken by the wind?"

25. "But what did you go out to see? A man who is clothed in soft garments? Behold, those who are in glorious clothing and in luxury are in a King's house."

26. "But what did you go out to see? A Prophet? Yes, I say to you, and more than a Prophet."

27. "This is he about whom it is written: 'Behold, I am sending my messenger before your face to prepare the way before you.'"

28. "I say to you, there is not a Prophet among those born of women who was greater than Yohannan The Baptizer, but a little one in the Kingdom of God is greater than he."

29. And all the people who heard and also the Tax Collectors justified God, for they had been baptized by the baptism of Yohannan.

30. But the Pharisees and the Scribes rejected the will of God in their souls, because they were not baptized by him.

31. "To what therefore shall I compare the men of this generation, and what does it resemble?"

32. "It is like boys sitting in the street and calling their friends and saying, 'We sang to you and you did not dance, and we howled to you and you did not cry.'"

33. "For Yohannan The Baptizer came not eating bread neither drinking wine, and you were saying, 'He has a demon.' "

34. "The Son of Man came eating and drinking and you were saying, 'Behold, a man a glutton and a drinker of wine and a friend of Tax Collectors and of sinners.' "

35. "And wisdom is justified by all its works*."

*

The Greek ms. Sinaiticus (4th century) reads "ergwn"-"works". The Majority Greek Text reads "teknown"-"children". בניה-**Benayyah**" could come from one of two roots: -Plural of "**Bra**" –"**Son**", or "**Bna**"-"**to build**"בניה. could be construed as "**Its works**" or "**Its children**". This confirms again that the Greek texts come from the Aramaic **Peshitta**, since both Greek readings, "teknown"-**(children)** & "ergown"-**(works)** are possible translations of the Aramaic בניה.(See Matthew 11:19)

36. But one of the Pharisees came asking him to eat with him and he entered the Pharisee's house and he reclined.

37. And a sinner woman who was in the city, when she knew that he was staying in the Pharisee's house, she took an alabaster vase of ointment.

38. And she stood behind him at his feet, and she was weeping and she began washing his feet with her tears and wiping them with the hair of her head. And she was kissing his feet and anointing them with ointment.

39. But when that Pharisee who had invited him saw, he thought within himself and he said, "If this one were a Prophet, he would have known who she is and what her reputation is, for she is a sinner woman who touched him."

40. But Yeshua answered and he said to him, "Shimeon, I have something to tell you." But he said to him, "Say it, Rabbi."

41. And Yeshua said to him, "One landowner had two debtors; one debtor owed him 500 denarii and the other fifty denarii."

42. "And because they had nothing to pay he forgave both of them. Which of them therefore will love him more?"

43. Shimeon answered and he said, "I suppose that he who was forgiven most." Yeshua said to him, "You have judged correctly."

44. And he turned to that woman and he said to Shimeon, "Do you see this woman? I entered your house, yet you gave no water for my feet and she has washed my feet with her tears and has wiped them with her hair."

45. "You did not kiss me, but look, from when she entered, she has not ceased to kiss my feet."

46. "You did not anoint my head with oil, but this one has anointed my feet with oil of ointment."

47. "On account of this, I say to you, that her many sins are forgiven her because she loved much, but he who is forgiven a little loves a little."

48. And he said to her, "Woman, your sins are forgiven you."

49. But they who were reclining said in their souls, "Who is this that he even forgives sins?"

50. But Yeshua said to that woman, "Your faith has given you life, go in peace."

Chapter 8

1. It happened after these things that Yeshua was traveling a circuit in the cities and villages and preaching and announcing the Kingdom of God and his twelve were with him,

2. And these women who had been healed from sicknesses and from evil spirits: Maryam who is called Magdalitha, she from whom seven demons had gone out

3. And Yohanna the wife of Chuza, the steward of Herodus, and Shushan and many others who were ministering to them of their possessions.

4. And when a great crowd had gathered, and they were coming to him from all the cities, he said in a parable:

5. "A sower went out to sow his seed, and as he sowed, there was that which fell on the side of the road and it was trampled and a bird* ate it.

• All Greek mss. have "**birds of the heaven**", where the Peshitta has merely "**a bird**". This may be due to a perceived את -"**Alep-Tau**"(Alpha- Omega) code on the part of the original Greek translator. I have identified approx. 30 places in the Greek NT where the word "**God**", "**Christ**", or even "**Heaven**" is found and yet does not occur in The Peshitta. What does occur **in 22 places**, very interestingly, is the את "**Alep-Tau**" letter combination in a relevant Aramaic verb or noun , which signifies the Divine Name of Jesus revealed in Revelation 1:8 : "**I AM The Alep & The Tau**". Alep is the first letter of the Aramaic alphabet; Tau is the last. The combination may be reversed in some places, as in the above verse of Luke 8:5 – תא- "**Tau-Alep**" in the word , פרחתא (Parakhta) -"**Bird**". If the Greek translator (whom I shall affectionately call "Zorba") believed **Alep Tau** or **Tau Alep** was a code word for **Deity** or **Heaven**, then he might insert that meaning into the Greek translation where it did not truly exist in the Aramaic of The Peshitta original. "**Birds of Heaven**" is the apparent result here. If פרחתא were seen as the code word, then פרחתא ("**Parakhta**") would conveniently be broken into פרח – "**Parakh**" , which still means "**bird**" or "**birds**" and תא , which in this mystical Kabbalah and esoteric sense would mean "**God**" or "**Heaven**"- ("**Heaven**" is sometimes used synonymously for "**God**" in the NT- See Mat. 4:17 & Mark 1:15). את & תא were not always seen as codes; only in those **22 places** where a **mystery** or special revelation was associated with the text where the potential code existed. Can it be a coincidence that the Aramaic alphabet (**Alep to Tau**) has **22 letters** ? Can it also be a coincidence that the Aramaic word ארזא (Araza) "**Mystery**"(See v. 10) **occurs 22 times** in its emphatic form in The Peshitta NT ? Even The King James Version has the word "**Mystery**" 22 times.

6. And other seed fell on the rock and in an hour it sprang up, and because there was no moisture for it, it dried up.

7. And other seed fell among thorns and the thorns sprang up with it and they choked it.

8. Other seed fell in good and excellent ground, and it sprang up and produced fruit one hundred fold. And when he had said these things, he cried, "He that has an ear to hear, let him hear."

* The verb "to hear" is singular, indicating that אדנא ,"Edna"(Ear) is singular. Most Aramaic nouns have the same form in plural as in singular. The Greek versions have ωτα ,"ota"-"Ears". One hearing ear is sufficient to receive the message.

9. And his disciples asked him, "What is this parable?"

10. But he said to them, "It has been given to you to know the secret of the Kingdom of God, but to those others, it is spoken in an allegory, that while seeing they will not perceive, and when hearing, they will not understand."

11. "But this is the parable: the seed is the word of God."

12. "But those upon the side of the road are they who hear the word, and the enemy comes and takes the word from their heart, lest they should believe and they should live."

13. "But these upon the rock are they, who when they have heard, they receive the word with joy, and there is no root in them, but their faith is temporary and in time of temptation they are subverted."

14. "But these which fell among thorns are those who hear the word and by cares and by riches and the desires of the world, they are choked and they yield no fruit."

15. "But these which are on the good ground are those who hear the word with a pure and good heart, and they hold onto it and they yield fruit with patience."

16. "No man lights a lamp and covers it with a vessel or sets it under a bed, but he sets it upon a lamp stand that everyone who enters may see its light."

17. "For there is nothing covered that will not be revealed, neither hidden that will not be made known and come into the open."

18. "Take heed how you hear. Whoever has it, it will be given to him, and whoever does not have it, also that which he thinks he has will be taken from him."

19. But his mother and his brothers came to him, and they were not able to speak with him, because of the crowd.

20. They said to him, "Your mother and your brothers are standing outside and they desire to see you."

21. But he answered and said to them, "These are my mother and my brothers; those who are hearing the word of God and are practicing it."

22. But it was on one of those days, Yeshua went up and sat down in the boat, he and his disciples, and he told them, "Let us cross to the other side of the lake."

23. And as he journeyed, Yeshua himself was asleep and there was a tempest of wind on the lake and the ship was coming close to sinking.

24. And they came and they awakened him and they were saying to him, "Our Master, our Master, we are being destroyed!" But he arose and rebuked the wind and the waves of the seas, and they ceased and there was calm.

25. And he said to them, "Where is your faith?" But they, being in awe, were marveling, and they were saying one to another, "Who is this, truly, who commands even the wind, the waves and the sea, and they obey him?"

Jeremiah 31:35 says in The Peshitta Version: "He rebukes the sea and stills its waves; **The LORD of Hosts is His Name**." Yeshua stilling the storm at sea was a sign that he is **Jehovah Sabaoth-"The LORD of Hosts"**. The Hebrew text has the same meaning.

26. And they sailed and they came to the region of the Gadarenes which is on the other side next to Galilee.

27. And when he unboarded to land, a man met him from the city who had a demon in him for a long time. He was not wearing clothes, and he was not living in a house but among the tombs.

28. And when he saw Yeshua, he screamed and he fell before him, and with a loud voice, he said, "What business do we have with you Yeshua, the Son of God Most High? I beg of you, do not punish me!"

29. For Yeshua had commanded the vile spirit to go out from the man, as it had possessed him for a long time. And he had been kept bound in chains and in shackles and he would burst his bonds and he would be driven by the demon into the desert.

30.But Yeshua asked him, "What is your name?" But he said to him, "Legion", because many demons had entered him.

31.And they were begging him that he would not command them to enter the abyss.

32.Now a herd of many swine was there grazing on the mountain, and they were begging him to permit them to enter the swine, and he permitted them.

33.And the demons went out from the man and they entered the swine, and the whole herd went straight to the precipice, and they fell into the lake and drowned.

34.But when the herdsmen saw what happened, they fled, and they related it in the city and in the villages.

35.And people went out to see the thing that happened and they came to Yeshua, and they found that man, whose demons had gone out, being clothed, sober and sitting at the feet of Yeshua, and they were in awe.

36.And those who had seen it related to them how the demoniac man had been healed.

37.And the crowds of Gadarenes were all begging him that he would go from them, because great fear had seized them, and he, Yeshua, embarked the ship and returned from among them.

38.But that man from whom the demons had gone out was begging him that he might join him and Yeshua dismissed him and he said to him:

39."Return to your house and relate the thing that God has done for you." And he went on, and he was preaching in the whole city the thing that Yeshua had done for him.

40.But when Yeshua returned, a great crowd received him, for they had all been looking for him.

41.And one man whose name was Yorash, head of the synagogue, fell before the feet of Yeshua and he begged him to enter his house.

42.For he had an only daughter, about twelve years old, and she was about to die, and when Yeshua went with him a great crowd was pressing him.

In the parallel passage of Matthew 9:18, The Greek texts say The Ruler said, "My daughter is already dead, ..."The Peshitta has, "My daughter is dying..",however the Aramaic verb could be construed to mean "is dead" or "is dying". Apparently a Greek translator interpreted the former meaning. The Greek aorist tense verb is not quite as flexible as the Aramaic perfect tense verb. The Aramaic of The Peshitta can explain the Greek reading here as in so many other places. See my book Jegar-Sahadutha- "Heap of Witness" for hundreds of examples demonstrating graphically the case for The Peshitta New Testament as the original behind the Greek New Testament. (See Aramaicnt.com).

43.Now there was certain woman whose blood had flowed twelve years, who spent all her property among physicians, and she could not be healed by anyone.

44.She approached him from behind, and she touched the fringe of his garment and immediately the flow of her blood stopped.

45.And Yeshua said, "Who touched me?" And when everyone denied, Shimeon Kaypha* and those with him said to him, "Our master, the crowds are pressing close to you and they are pushing, and you say, 'Who touched me?' "*All Greek mss. have "Petros" where The Peshitta has "Shimeon Kaypha". According to the Greek of John 1:42, The name "Petros" is a translation of his Aramaic name "Kaypha". This fact implies that "Petros" here and in most places would be a Greek translation of the Aramaic "Kaypha".It also implies that the Greek text generally is a translation, not an original. "Petros" occurs 162 times in The Greek NT

46.But he said, "Someone has touched me, for I know that power has gone out from me."

47.When the woman saw that she had not escaped his notice, she came trembling, and she fell and she worshiped him, and she told before the eyes of all the people for what cause she had touched him, and how she had been healed immediately.

48.But Yeshua said to her, "Take heart, my daughter; your faith has given you life; go in peace."

49.And while he was speaking, the man who was of the house of the leader of the synagogue came and he said to him, "Your daughter has died; do not trouble the teacher."

50.But Yeshua heard and he said to the father of the girl, "Do not be afraid; only have faith, and she will live."

51.But Yeshua came to the house and he did not allow anyone to enter with him except Shimeon, Yaqob, Yohannan, the father of the girl and her mother.

52.And all of them were weeping and wailing over her but Yeshua said, "Stop weeping; for she is not dead, but she is sleeping."

53.And they were laughing at him, for they knew that she had died.

54.But he sent everyone outside and he held her by her hand and he called her, and he said, "Little girl, arise."

55.And her spirit returned, and at once she arose, and he commanded them to give her food.

56.And her parents were staggered, but he warned them not to tell anyone what had happened.

Chapter 9

1. **A**nd Yeshua called the twelve and he gave power to them and authority over all demons and diseases to heal the sick.

2. And he sent them to preach the Kingdom of God and to heal the sick.

3. And he said to them, "You shall take nothing for the road; no staff, neither moneybag, nor bread, nor money, neither two tunics will be with you."

4. "And whatever house you enter, stay there and from there go out."

5. "And whoever does not receive you, whenever you leave that city, shake off even the sand of your feet against them for a testimony."

6. And The Apostles went out and were walking around in the villages and cities and they were preaching The Good News and healing in every place.

7. But Herodus the Tetrarch heard all the things that were being done by his hand and he was amazed because the people were saying, "Yohannan has arisen from among the dead."

8. But others were saying, "Elijah has appeared", and others, "A Prophet among the ancient Prophets has risen."

9. And Herodus said, "I have cut off the head of Yohannan, but who is this about whom I have heard these things?" And he wanted to see him.

10. And when The Apostles returned, they were relating to Yeshua everything that they had done and he took them by themselves to a deserted region of Bethsaida.

11. But when the crowds knew, they went after him and he received them and he was speaking with them about the Kingdom of God, and those who were in need of healing he healed.

12. But when the day began to decline, his disciples came and they were saying to him, "Dismiss the crowds that they go to the surrounding villages and hamlets to lodge in them and to find provisions for themselves, because we are in a deserted place."

13. Yeshua said to them, "You give them food." But they were saying, "We don't have more than five loaves and two fish, unless we go and buy provisions for this entire people."

14. For there remained about five thousand men, and Yeshua said, "Make them recline by groups of fifty men in a group."

15. And the disciples did so and they made them all recline.

16. And Yeshua took those five loaves and two fish, and he gazed into Heaven and he blessed and he broke and he gave to his disciples to set before the crowds.

17. And they all ate and were satisfied, and they took up the fragments that remained, twelve large baskets.

18. And when he was praying alone, and his disciples were with him, he asked them and he said, "What is it the crowds are saying about me, who I am?"

19. They answered and they were saying to him, "Yohannan the Baptizer", and others, "Elijah", and others, "A Prophet, one of the ancient Prophets has risen."

20. But he said to them, "Who is it you are saying that I am?" Shimeon answered and he said, "The Messiah of God."

21. But he admonished them and he warned them that they should not say this to anyone.

22. And he said to them, "The Son of Man is going to suffer many things and to be rejected by the Elders and the Chief Priests and Scribes, and they will murder him, and on the third day he will arise."

23. And he said before everyone, "Whoever is willing to come after me, let him deny himself, let him take up his cross everyday, and let him come after me."

24. "For whoever wills to save his soul, destroys it; but whoever will give up his soul for my sake, this one saves it."

25. "For how would a man benefit to gain the whole world but destroy his soul or lose *it*?"

26. "Whoever will be ashamed of me and of my words, of that one will The Son of Man be ashamed whenever he comes in the glory of his Father with his Holy Angels."

27. "I tell you the truth; there are men who stand here who will not partake of death until they behold the Kingdom of God."

28. But it happened after these words, about eight days later, Yeshua took Shimeon and Yaqob and Yohannan and he went up a mountain to pray.

29. And as he prayed, the appearance of his face was transfigured and his garments became white and they were shining.

30. And behold, two men were speaking with him, who are Moses and Elijah,

31. Who appeared in glory, but they were speaking about his exodus which was going to be fulfilled in Jerusalem.

32. And Shimeon and those with him were groggy with sleep, and they awakened with difficulty, and they saw his glory and those two men who were standing with him.

33. And when they began to part from him, Shimeon said to Yeshua, "Rabbi, it is beautiful for us to be here. Let us make three Tabernacles: one for you, one for Moses, and one for Elijah." And he did not know what he said.

34. And as he said these things, there was a cloud that formed a tabernacle about them and they were afraid when they beheld Moses and Elijah who entered into the cloud.

35. And there was a voice from the cloud that said, "This is my Son, The Beloved; Hear him."

36. And when the voice had occurred, Yeshua was found alone, and they were silent and told no man in those days what they had seen.

37. And it occurred the day after as they descended from the mountain, a great crowd met them.

38. And one man from that crowd called and he said, "Teacher, I beg you, restore my son to me; he is the only child I have."

39. "And a spirit suddenly comes upon him, and suddenly he screams and gnashes his teeth and becomes ill, and it departs from him with difficulty whenever it attacks him."

40. "And I begged of your disciples to cast it out and they could not."

41. Then Yeshua answered and said, "Oh generation without faith and perverse! How long shall I be with you and endure you? Bring your son here."

42. And when he came near to him that demon threw him down and convulsed him. And Yeshua rebuked the foul spirit and he healed the boy and he gave him to his father.

43. And they were all astonished at the majesty of God, and as everyone was marveling at everything that Yeshua did, he said to his disciples:

44. "Put these words in your ears, for The Son of Man is going to be delivered into the hands of men."

45. They did not understand the saying because it was hidden from them lest they

should perceive it, and they were afraid to ask him about this saying. *

46. And deliberation entered among them of who was great among them.

47. But Yeshua knew the thought of their heart, and he took a boy and he stood him by him.

48. And he said to them, "Whoever receives a boy like this one in my name, that one receives me, and whoever receives me receives the one who sent me, for whoever is least among you all, this one will be great."

49. And Yohannan answered and said, "Our master, we saw a man who cast out a demon in your name and we forbade him, for he does not come after you with us."

50. Yeshua said to them, "You shall not forbid, for whoever is not against you* is for you*."

The Majority Greek text has "**who is not against us is for**   *
us", while the Critical Greek agrees with The Peshitta reading here : "**who is not against you is for you**". If The Peshitta were a translation, it followed The Critical Greek text here (or The Western Greek, if such existed) and then ignored it and followed the Majority Greek text in verses 56 & 57, just six verses down from here!

51. And it was that when the days of his ascent were fulfilled, he prepared himself to go to Jerusalem.

52. And he sent messengers before his presence and they went and entered a village of the Samaritans so as to prepare for him.

53. And they did not receive him because his person was determined to go to Jerusalem.

54. And when Yaqob and Yohannan his disciples saw it, they were saying to him, "Our Lord, do you want us to speak and fire will descend from Heaven, and will consume them as Elijah also did?"

55. And he turned and he rebuked them and he said, "You do not know of which Spirit you are."

*Critical Greek mss. lack the last half of this verse and most of the next verse. The Majority Greek text and The Latin Vulgate (translated in 4ᵗʰ century from Greek mss.) contain the Peshitta reading.

56. "For The Son of Man has not come to destroy lives but to give life." And they went to other villages.

57. And as they were going on the road, a man said to him, "I shall come after you to the place that you will go, my lord."

58. Yeshua said to him, "Foxes have dens and birds of the sky have shelters, but The Son of Man does not have a place to lay his head."

59. And he said to another, "Come after me." But he said to him, "My lord, permit me first to go bury my Father."

60. And Yeshua said to him, "Let the dead bury their dead and you go announce the Kingdom of God."

61. And another said to him, "I shall come after you, my lord, but permit me first to say goodbye to my children, and I shall come."

62. Yeshua said to him, "No man lays his hands to the blade of the plow and stares behind him and is fit for the Kingdom of God."

Chapter 10

1. After these things Yeshua appointed another seventy of his disciples and he sent them two by two before his presence to every place and city where he was prepared to go.

2. And he said to them, "The harvest is great and the workers are few; pray therefore the Lord of the harvest to send workers to his harvest."

3. "Go; behold, I am sending you as sheep among wolves."

4. "You shall not take for yourselves moneybags, nor wallets, nor sandals and do not greet a man on the road."

5. "And to whatever house you enter, first say, 'Peace to this house.'"

6. "And if a son of peace is there, your peace shall rest upon it, but if not, it will return to you."

7. "But stay in that house while you are eating and drinking of what is theirs, for the worker is worthy of his fare, and do not move from house to house."

8. "And whatever city you enter, and they receive you, eat anything that is offered to you."

9. And heal those who are sick in it and say to them, "The Kingdom of God has come near to you."

10. "But whichever city you enter and they will not receive you, go out to the street and say":

11. 'Even the sand that cleaves to our feet from your city we wipe off unto you, yet know this, The Kingdom of God has come near to you.'

12. "I say to you that it shall be pleasant for Sadom in that day, compared to that city."

13. "Woe to you Korazin, woe to you Bethsaida, because if the miracles had occurred in Tyre and Tsidon that have occurred in you, they doubtless would have repented in sackcloth and in ashes.

14. "Yet for Tyre and for Tsidon it shall be pleasant in the day of judgment compared to you."

15. "And you Kapernahum, she that was exalted unto Heaven, you shall be debased unto Sheol."

The Aramaic "**Kapernakhum**" (**Capernaum**) means "**Hamlet of Nakhum**". **Nakhum** is Nahum the Prophet, who wrote the book of Nahum. That was their exaltation to Heaven .They rejected The Messiah Yeshua, Who preached and performed miracles in its streets; that is their descent into Hell. Capernaum no longer exists today, in fact, the location of its ruins is in doubt.

16. "Whoever listens to you listens to me, and whoever rejects you, rejects me, and whoever rejects me rejects The One who sent me."

17. And those seventy whom he had sent returned with great joy and they were saying to him, "Our Lord, even the demons are subject to us in your name."

18. But he said to them, "I was beholding Satan himself who fell like lightning from Heaven."

19. "Behold, I have given you authority that you may tread on snakes and scorpions and all the power of the enemy and nothing will harm you."

20. "However, you should not rejoice in this, that the demons are subject to you, but rejoice that your names are written in Heaven."

21. And in that hour Yeshua* triumphed in The Spirit of Holiness* and he said, "I thank you, my Father, Lord of Heaven and earth, that you have hidden these things from the wise and learned and have revealed them to infants; yes, my Father, for thus it was a pleasure before you."

The Critical Greek text agrees with "The Holy Spirit**" reading of **The Peshitta** but lacks the "**Jesus**"(Yeshua) reading. The Majority Greek contains the "**Jesus**" reading but lacks "**Holy**". Did **The Peshitta** combine the Critical and Majority readings here (& in hundreds of other places) to construct the verse, or are the separate Greek texts derived from **The Peshitta** ? The latter is a much more tenable position.

22. And he turned to his disciples and he said to them, "Everything has been delivered to me from my Father, and no man knows who The Son is except The Father only, and who The

Father is except The Son, and he to whom The Son will be pleased to reveal *him.*"

23. And he turned to his disciples by themselves and he said, "Blessed are those eyes that are seeing whatever you are seeing."

24. "For I say to you that many Prophets and Kings have desired to see the things that you are seeing, and they have not seen, and to hear the things that you are hearing and they have not heard."

25. And behold, a scribe arose to test him, and he said, "Teacher, what shall I do to inherit eternal life?"

26. But Yeshua said to him, "How is it written in the law? How do you read it?"

27. He answered and he said to him, "You shall love **THE LORD JEHOVAH** your God from all your heart and from all your soul and from all your strength and from all your mind and your neighbor as yourself."

28. Yeshua said to him, "You have said correctly; do this and you shall live."

29. But as he wanted to justify himself, he said to him, "And who is my neighbor?"

30. Yeshua said to him, "A certain man was going down from Jerusalem to Jericho and robbers fell upon him, and they plundered and beat him and left him when little life remained in him and they departed."

31. "And it happened a certain priest was going down that road and he saw him and passed by."

32. "And so also a Levite coming arrived at that place and he saw him and he passed by."

33. "But a Samaritan man as he traveled came where he was and he saw him and he took pity on him."

34. "And he came and bound his wounds and poured wine and oil on them and set him on his donkey and he took him to an inn and cared for him."

35. "And at the break of day, he produced two denarii and gave them to the innkeeper and he said to him, 'Take care of him and if you spend anything more, whenever I return I will give it to you.'"

36. "Who therefore of these three appears to you to have been a neighbor to him who fell into the hands of the robbers?"

37. But he said, "He who took pity on him." Yeshua said to him, "You go and do likewise."

38. And it was that when they were traveling on a road, he entered a certain village and a woman whose name was Martha received him into her house.

39. And she had a sister, whose name was Maryam, and she came and sat herself at the feet of Our Lord, and she was listening to his words.

40. But Martha was busy with serving many things and she came and said to him, "My lord, does it not concern you that my sister has left me alone to serve? Tell her to help me."

41. But Yeshua answered and said to her, "Martha, Martha, you take pains and are troubled about many things."

42. "But one thing is necessary; Maryam has chosen that good part for herself which will not be taken away from her."

Chapter 11

1. It was that when he was praying in a certain place, when he finished, one of his disciples said to him, "Our Lord*, teach us to pray, just as Yohannan also taught his disciples."

* In 68 of the 299 **Peshitta NT** occurrences of מרן ("**Our Lord**") , "(κυριος ημων"- "**kurios hmwn**" or "**kuriou hmwn , kuriw hmwn, kurie hmwn, kurion hmwn**"-"**Our Lord**") occurs in **The Greek NT**. That is a 23% correlation or a 77 % defection rate. This means that either the Greek drops the personal pronoun "our" 77 % of the time or that The Peshitta adds (construction rate) **340 %** of the number of occurrences in the hypothetical Greek original to the hypothetical Aramaic translation of the Greek NT. Which is more likely ?Consider the following: In **The Hebrew OT**, the Hebrew אדני -"**Adonai**" ("**My Lord**") occurs 625 times; of those 625 places, **The LXX** has "(κυριος μου"- "**kurios mou**" or "**kuriou mou, kuriw mou, kurie mou, kurion mou**"-"**My Lord**"), 144 times. 144/625= 23%. That is a defection rate in **The LXX** (dropping the personal possessive pronoun "my") of 77 % - exactly the same rate for **The Greek NT** as compared to **The Peshitta NT** ! In this and in many other similar comparisons, the Greek NT compares to **The Peshitta NT** just as **The LXX Greek OT** compares to **The Hebrew OT**, which means **The Greek NT** looks statistically very much like a translation of **The Peshitta NT**.

2. Yeshua said to them, "When you pray, you shall say thus: 'Our Father, who are in Heaven'

3. 'Hallowed be your name, let your Kingdom come, let your will be done also in the earth as *it is* in Heaven. Give us our necessary bread every day,'

4. 'And forgive us our sins even as we forgive all who are indebted to us, and do not lead us into temptation, but save us from The Evil One.'"

Here is the Lord's Prayer according to the Critical Greek text in Luke 11:
And he said unto them, When ye pray, say, Father, Hallowed be thy name. Thy Kingdom come.
Give us day by day our daily bread.
And forgive us our sins; for we ourselves also forgive every one that is indebted to us. And bring us not into temptation.

And that's it ! This looks like sabotage to me. Leaves one a bit flat, don't you think ? Even "**Thy will be done**" is missing, as is "**Deliver us from evil**"- a quite pathetic rendering of the world's most beautiful and sublime model prayer.
Thankfully, most Greek mss. preserve it in the fuller version with which most of us are familiar, as also The Peshitta has it.

5. And he said to them, "Who among you has a friend and will go to him at midnight and will say to him, "My friend, lend me three loaves",

6. "For my friend has come to me from the road and I have nothing that I can set before him,"

7. "And his friend from within will answer and will say to him, 'Do not disturb me, for behold, the door is bolted and my children are in bed with me; I cannot rise and give to you?' "

8. "I say to you that if because of friendship he will not give to him, because of his persistence he will arise and he will give him as much as he needs."

9. "I am also saying to you, Ask and it shall be given to you, seek and you shall find, knock and it will be opened to you."

10. "For everyone who asks receives, and whoever seeks finds, and whoever knocks, it is opened to him."

11. Which of you is a father whose son will ask him for bread and would hand him a stone, and if he asks him for a fish will, instead of a fish, hand him a snake,"

12. "And if he would ask of him an egg, would give him a scorpion?"

13. "And if you, who are evil, know to give good gifts to your children, how much more will your Father in Heaven give The Spirit of Holiness to those who ask him?"

14. And when he was casting out a demon that was making *a person* mute, it happened that when that demon went out, the mute spoke, and the crowds were astonished.

15. But men among them said, "This one exorcises devils by Beelzebub the Chief of devils*."

 דיוא –"**Deeva**" or "**Deewa**" may be the etymological original for the English word "**devil**", and therefore I translate it as such, using "**devil**" as the original King

James Version does when it refers to a demon, not Satan . דיוא never refers to "**The Devil**". It is also synonymous with שאדא- "**Sheda**" in Aramaic, which is usually translated "**demon**". The reader then knows that "**devil**" comes from דיוא –"**Deeva**", and "**demon**" normally comes from שאדא- "**Sheda**". Interestingly, "**Sheda**" is phonetically very similar to the English "**Shade**", which can refer to a spirit or ghost. The English "**Diva**" also refers to originally to "**a goddess**" , from the Latin "**Diva**". **The Greek NT** has only one word for "**Demon**" – "δαιμονιον" . On the basis of a Greek original, it is difficult, to say the least, to account for the fact that The Peshitta has two very different root words for "**demon**" while Greek has only one. The Peshitta NT has 40 occurrences of שאדא (Sheda) & 30 of דיוא (Deeva). **Matthew 12:24 has both words in one verse !** Acts 17:18 has "**Alaha**"("**God**") in Aramaic where the Greek has "δαιμονων" –"demons". It is definitely a reference to Jesus, Whom Paul was preaching to the Greeks. Δαιμονων may refer to "**deities**", but this would be the only such reference of the 60 places in the Greek NT where it occurs. All others refer to demons. Notice that verse 14 has "**Sheda**" twice and verse 15 has "**Deeva**" twice; The Greek, of course, has a form of "δαιμονιον"-(daimonion) in every place. Why would a translator (assuming a Greek original) translate **Daimonion** twice as **Sheda** in verse 14 and then change it to **Deeva** twice in the next verse? All four references are in the same context. Luke 8:27 through 8:33 alternates between the two Aramaic words –Deeva-Sheda-Deeva-Sheda for each of the four occurrences of the Greek " **Daimonion**" within a passage of seven verses! A Greek translation of The Peshitta original is an idea that makes a lot more sense here, as in so many other places.

16. But others were testing him, and they were asking him for a sign from Heaven.

17. But because Yeshua knew their thoughts he said to them, "Every realm that is divided against itself will be laid waste, and the home that is divided against its nature falls."

18. And if Satan is divided against himself, how will his Kingdom stand?; for you say that by Beelzebub I cast out devils."

19. "And if I am exorcising devils by Beelzebub, by whom are your children exorcising? Because of this they will be your judges."

20. "But if I cast out devils by the finger of God, the Kingdom of God has come near to you."

21. "Whenever an armed strongman keeps his homestead, his property is at peace."

22. "But if one who is stronger than he will come to overpower him, he takes all his weapons in which he was trusting and he divides his spoil."

23. "Whoever is not with me is against me and whoever does not gather with me is scattering."

24. "Whenever a vile spirit has gone out from a man, it goes traveling around in places where there is no water to seek rest for itself;

Whenever it does not find it, it says, 'I shall return to my house from whence I came.' "

25."And when it has come, it finds it swept and decorated."

26."And it goes bringing seven others spirits which are more evil than itself, and they are entering and dwelling there, and the end of that man will be worse than his beginning."

27.And while he was speaking these things, a woman raised her voice from the crowd and she said to him, "Blessing to the womb that carried you and to the breasts that suckled you."

28.He said to her, "Blessings to those who have heard the word of God and keep it."

29.And when the crowds were assembling he began to say, "This wicked generation seeks for a sign and a sign will not be given to it except the sign of Jonah the Prophet."

30."For just as Jonah was a sign to the Ninevites thus also The Son of Man shall be to this generation."

31.The Queen of The South shall stand in judgment with the people of this generation, and she shall condemn them, for she came from the far side of the land that she might hear the wisdom of Solomon and behold, he who is greater than Solomon is here."

32."The Ninevite men will rise in judgment with this generation and they shall condemn it because they repented at the preaching of Jonah and behold, he who is greater than Jonah is here."

33."No man lights a lamp and sets it in a hidden place or under a bushel but over a lamp stand, that those who enter may see its light."

34."The lamp of the body is your eye; when therefore your eye is clear your whole body shall be illuminated, but if it should be bad, your body also shall be darkened."

35."Take care therefore lest the light that is in you is darkness"

36."But if your whole body is enlightened, and there is no darkened part, it shall be shining entirely like a lamp giving you light by its flame"

37."But while he was speaking, one Pharisee requested of him that he would dine with him, and he entered and reclined."

38.But that Pharisee when he saw him, he was amazed that he did not wash before his dinner.

39.But Yeshua said to him, "Now you Pharisees are cleansing the outside of the cup and of the dish, but the inside of some of you is full of rape and wickedness."

40."Mindless ones! Has not The One who made the outside also made the inside?"

41."However, give whatever you have in charity and behold, everything is pure to you."

It has been said (though the source slips my mind-George Lamsa?) that "the good eye" is an Aramaic idiom signifying a generous person and "the bad eye" is an idiom signifying a stingy person. Verse 41 would seem to validate that view in connection with verses 34-36. I do believe the good eye-evil eye concepts involve much more than generosity and stinginess, however. They describe a person's viewpoint of the world as either positive or negative- good or bad.
Giving away all one's money to charity may be exactly the cure for the eye trouble with which our culture suffers.

42."But woe to you Pharisees, for you tithe mint and dill and every herb and you pass over justice and over the love of God, but these it was necessary for you to do and not that you should forsake the other!"

43."Woe to you Pharisees who love first class seats in the synagogues and greetings in the streets!"

44."Woe to you, Scribes and Pharisees, phonies, who are like tombs that are not known, and the children of men walk over them and do not know."

45.And one of the Scribes answered and he said to him, "Teacher, when you say these things, you insult us also."

46.But he said, "Woe to you also, you Scribes, for you load the children of men with heavy burdens and you will not touch those burdens with one of your fingers."

47."Woe to you who are building the tombs of The Prophets, for your fathers murdered them."

48."You testify therefore and you approve the deeds of your fathers, for they murdered them and you build their tombs."

49."Because of this The Wisdom of God said, "Behold, I am sending Prophets and Apostles to them, and some of them they shall persecute and murder",
(Paul The Apostle declares, "The Messiah is The Power of God and The Wisdom of God." - 1 Cor. 1:24)

50."So that the blood of all The Prophets that was shed from when the world was created shall be required of this generation,"

51. "From the blood of Abel and unto the blood of Zachariah who was killed between The Temple and the altar; Yes, I say to you, that it shall be required of this generation."

Abel was "when the world was created" (v.50) ! Our Lord declares for Creationism and a young earth! Big Bang proponents cannot justify this language from The Son of God with the theory that the world was created billions of years before Abel.

52. "Woe to you Scribes, because you have taken away the keys of knowledge! You have not entered and those who are entering you have hindered."

53. And when he had said these things to them, the Scribes and Pharisees began to be offended at them and they were angered and they disparaged his words.

54. And they acted deceitfully toward him in many things, while they sought to seize on something from his mouth so that they would be able to accuse him.

Chapter 12

1. And when multitudes of great crowds were gathered together so that they would tread on one another, Yeshua began to say to his disciples, "First, beware among yourselves of the yeast of the Pharisees, which is phoniness."

2. "For there is nothing covered that will not be revealed, neither anything secret that will not be known."

3. "For everything that you will say in darkness shall be heard in the light and whatever you whispered in an ear in an inner chamber will be preached on the rooftops."

4. "And I say to you my friends, do not be afraid of those who kill the body and after this there is nothing more for them to do."

5. "But I will show you whom you should fear: that one who after he kills is authorized to cast into Gehenna; yes I say to you, be afraid of this one*."

 * Since Our Lord does not name God as what we should fear , and since God is not authorized by anyone, being all authority Himself, and the pronouns used may refer to an ideal conceptual entity, it is reasonable to posit "yourself" as what is "authorized to cast into Gehenna" after having killed. We should fear **Self**, since it has produced all the evils of this world and of that which is to come. He tells us in verse 7, "**Fear not therefore, you are more valuable than many sparrows.**" He does not want us to fear our Father in Heaven, as He loves us and will take care of us. He **does** want us to fear **ourselves**; we have the power to obey or disobey, to live or to die, to enter Heaven or Hell, to bring a blessing or a curse upon ourselves. The power to commit sin, logically indicates the power to do right, so if we are condemned, we are self condemned. Someone asked Madame Guyon (the 16th century French mystic who had been severely persecuted & put in a dungeon for her faith) about her thoughts on the interpretation of the seven headed beast in **Revelation 13:1**
And I saw a beast of prey come up from the sea, having ten horns, and seven heads; and upon his horns ten diadems, and upon his heads names of blasphemy.
2 And the beast of prey which I saw, was like a leopard; and his feet like those of a wolf, and his mouth like the mouth of lions: and the dragon gave to him his own power and his throne, and great authority.
8 And all that dwell upon the earth shall worship him, whose names are not written in the book of life of the Lamb slain from the foundation of the world.

Her answer was simply, "**It is Self**".

6. "Are not five sparrows sold for two assarii, and not one of them is forgotten before God?"

7. "But every hair of the hairs of your heads is numbered, therefore you shall not be afraid, because you are better than a multitude of sparrows."

8. "And I say to you that everyone who will confess me before the children of men, The Son of Man will also confess him before the Angels of God."

9. "But whoever denies me before the children of men shall himself be denied before the Angels of God."

10. "And everyone who will say a word against The Son of Man shall be forgiven, but whoever blasphemes The Spirit of Holiness, it will not be forgiven to him."

11. "But whenever they bring you to assemblies before rulers and authorities, you shall not be concerned how you will give an answer or what you will say."

12. "For The Spirit of Holiness shall teach you in that hour what it is necessary for you to say."

13. A man from that crowd said to him, "Teacher, tell my brother to divide the inheritance with me."

14. But Yeshua said to him, "Man, who has set me as a judge and a divider over you?"

15. And he said to his disciples, "Beware of all greed, because life is not in the abundance of riches."

16. And he told a parable to them: "A certain rich man's land brought him many crops."

17. "And he thought to himself and said, 'What shall I do, for there is no place for me to gather my crops?'"

18. "And he said, 'I shall do this: I shall pull down my barns, and I shall build and enlarge them, and I shall gather all my produce and my goods.'"

19. "And I shall say to my soul, 'My soul, you have many goods laid up for many years, be contented, eat, drink and be merry.'"

20. "Then God said to him, 'Fool, in this night your soul will be required from you, and whose will these things be which you have prepared?'"

21."Thus is whoever lays down a treasure for himself and is not rich in God."

22.And he said to his disciples, "Because of this, I say to you that you shall not be taking pains for yourselves what you will eat, neither for your bodies, what you will wear."

23."For the soul is more important than food, and the body than clothing."

24."Consider the ravens that they do not sow, neither do they reap; there is no inner chamber or granary for them, and God feeds them; therefore, how much more important are you than the birds?"

25."Which of you by taking pains* can add one cubit to his height?"

*

"Taking care"- יצף (Yatsap) refers to "**taking pains**" or "**being diligent**" to procure something. The lesson is illustrated by the animal world: "**Birds do not sow nor reap**"; "**Ravens do not gather into barns**" . These activities illustrate the care Our Lord says we need not rely on to live. If crows don't need it, why would we?

We must remember that Our Lord's teaching is always radically against the grain and opposed to the ways of the world (& too often, the church) to seem acceptable or even reasonable to us, but then, "**My ways are not your ways, neither are My thoughts your thoughts, saith The LORD.**"-Isaiah 55:8

It is exactly this principle that commends the teaching of The Messiah to me as truth; if it were conventional wisdom, I would not believe it to be the truth of God. What has **He** to do with convention and the ways of the world?

26."But if you cannot do the small thing, why do you take pains* over the rest?"

* This is not about worrying, but about our efforts to sustain ourselves. Our Lord does not challenge us to add a cubit (18 inches) to our stature by worrying, but by any means at our disposal. Who of us can do that by our efforts ? That is a small thing, however, compared to keeping ourselves well fed and clothed, yet we do not see it that way. We believe we can do the great thing but not the small thing. The fact is, we can do **nothing!**

27."Consider the lilies how they grow, that they do not labor neither do they weave, but I say to you that not even Solomon in all his glory was robed like one of these."

28."But if God so clothes the grass that today is in the field and tomorrow will fall into a fire, how much better is he to you, O' small of faith?"

29."You should not seek what you will eat and what you will drink, neither should your mind be distracted by these things."

30."For all the people of the world are seeking these things, for your Father knows that these things are necessary for you."

Are you one of "**all the people of the world**", or do you hail from another realm? The people of the world worship and serve Mammon- i.e. , they "**labor for the**

food that perishes", not for eternal bread which gives eternal life (See John 6:27).The world seeks temporal things by laboring for them. If they would labor for the eternal, they would need not fear for their welfare in the world.

31."However, seek The Kingdom of God, and all these things are added to you."

32."Fear not, little flock, for your Father desires to give you The Kingdom."

33."Sell your possessions and give charity; make for yourselves pouches that do not wear out and treasure that is not diminished in Heaven, where a thief does not come in and a moth does not devour."

34."For wherever your treasure is, there shall your heart be also."

35."Let your waist be girded and your lamps burning."

36."Be like people waiting for their Lord when he will return from the wedding chamber, so that whenever he comes and knocks, they may open to him at once."

37."Blessings to those servants whom, when their Lord will come, he will find while they are watching. Amen, I say to you, that he will gird his waist and he will make them recline and he will go through and wait on them."

38."And if he will come in the second or third watch, and he will find them thus, blessings to those servants."

39."Know this, that if the owner of a house had known in which watch a thief would come, he would have been awakened and would not have allowed his house to be broken into."

40."Be you also ready therefore, for in that hour when you are not expecting, The Son of Man comes."

41.Shimeon Kaypha said to him, "Our Lord, are you saying this parable to us or to everyone also?"

42.Yeshua said to him, "Who is indeed the faithful and wise steward, whom his Lord will appoint over his servants to give a portion in his time?"

43."Blessed is that servant whom, when his Lord will come, he will find doing so."

44."Truly, I say to you, that he will appoint him over all his possessions."

45."But if that servant will say in his heart, 'My Lord delays to come', and he should begin to strike the servants and the maids of his Lord and he should begin to eat and to drink and to get drunk."

46."The Lord of that servant will come in a day when he does not expect and in an hour when he does not know; he shall cut him off* and he shall appoint his portion with those who are unbelievers."*

ונפלגיוהי- "**Pelegaywi**" is an idiom referring to "**cutting off**" a person from society by incarceration or death.

47."The servant who knew the will of his master and did not prepare for him according to his will, he shall be beaten many times."

48.But he who did not know and did something worthy of blows shall be beaten with few blows, for from everyone to whom much is given, much shall be required, and of him to whom they commit much, they shall require more."

49."I have come to set fire to the earth, and I only wish it were already burning."

50."I have a baptism with which to be baptized, and I am much afflicted until it is fulfilled."

51."Do you think that I have come to bring peace to the earth? I say to you, no, but division."

52."From now on there shall be five in one house who are divided, three against two and two against three."

53."For a father will be divided against his son and son against his father, mother against her daughter and daughter against her mother, mother-in-law against her daughter-in-law and daughter-in-law against her mother-in-law."

54.He said to the crowds, "Whenever you see a cloud that rises from the West, and at once you say, 'Rain is coming', it is so."

55."And when a south wind blows, you say, 'It will be hot', and it is."

56."Accepters of faces, you know to discern the face of the earth and sky, how do you not discern this time?" ("Accepters of faces" and "face of the earth and sky" is a play on words in Aramaic. They were superficial (on the surface) people.

57."Why do you not judge the truth from yourselves?"

58."For whenever you go with your plaintiff to the Ruler, while you are on the road, give merchandise and be ransomed from him, lest he bring you to the Judge and the Judge deliver you to the Officer and the Officer should cast you into prison."

59."I say to you, you shall not go out from there until you give the last quarter cent."

Chapter 13

1.At that time some people came and told him about those Galileans whose blood Pilate had mingled with their sacrifices.

2.And Yeshua answered and said to them, "Do you think that these Galileans were sinners moreso than all Galileans because this happened to them?"

3." But I say to you, no, for all of you also shall likewise be destroyed, unless you repent."

4."Or those eighteen upon whom the tower of Shilokha fell and killed them: Do you think that they were sinners moreso than all the children of men who dwell in Jerusalem?"

5." But I say to you, no, for unless you repent, all of you shall be destroyed like they were."

6.And he told this parable: "A man had a fig tree that was planted in his vineyard and he came seeking fruit on it and he found none.

7.And he said to the cultivator, 'Behold, three years I have come seeking fruit in this fig tree, and I find none; cut it down; why is it taking up space?'

8.The cultivator said to him, 'My Lord, leave it also this year, while I shall cultivate it and I shall manure it',

9.And perhaps it will have borne fruit, otherwise next year* you should cut it down."

The Greek texts have "**after that**, you shall cut * it down". The Greek "εις το μελλον" – "**eis to mellon**" literally means "**into the coming**", referring to the future.

למנחי- "**Next year**" looks very like למנחי , which is a compound of למן הי -"**After that**". The letters **Khet** ח & **Het** ה being very similar, are very easily mistaken one for the other, as was למנחי for למנחי by a Greek translator. There is no easy accounting for the reverse scenario. The Greek "εις το μελλον" – "**eis to mellon**" could translate to למנחי -"**After that**" , but the Aramaic has למנחי "**Next year**". The scribe would have had to have meant to write למנחי and written למנחי instead. Such an error is possible, but an error of the hand is much less likely than the error of the eye in the first scenario. The Peshitta has no demonstrable errors of the hand or eye , whereas the Greek has been shown to have a considerable number of such errors, simply by reason of its many thousands of variant readings. Both Eastern & Western Peshittas have the same reading. The Greek mss. all have the phrase "εις το μελλον", though **The Critical Greek text** has:
"If it bears fruit after that, but if not, you shall cut it down." Papyrus 45 & D,Θ & The Majority Byzantine Text have:
"And if it bear fruit: and if not, after that thou shalt cut it down. As you can see, neither Greek text makes good sense.
An interesting possibility in the Peshitta text is that למנחי plus the following letter ת-Tau gives (למנחית) which makes sense as "**Why should it be living ?**" and the remaining word תפסקיה ("**You should cut it down**") would become פסקיה ("**Cut it down**"). However, I can find no evidence of any such reading in any Peshitta manuscript. They all seem to agree with the interlinear text I provide above, including **The Khabouris manuscript**, whose scribe writes that it is

a direct copy of a fourth century (pre A.D. 360) manuscript.[I rely on Paul Younan's expertise in Aramaic and Assyrian history, as he is a native Assyrian, for the date and translation of the scribal notes, which I have not yet seen.]

10. But when Yeshua taught on the Sabbath in one of the synagogues,

11. A woman was there who had a spirit of affliction eighteen years, and she was bent over, and she had not been able to be straightened at all.

12. But Yeshua saw her and he called her and said to her, "Woman, you are released from your affliction."

13. And he laid his hand upon her and at once she was straightened, and she glorified God.

14. But the Leader of the synagogue, being angered, answered, because Yeshua had healed on the Sabbath, and he said to the gathering, "There are six days in which it is legal to work; you may come in them and be healed and not on the Sabbath day."

15. But Yeshua answered and he said to him, "Hypocrite! Does not each one of you on the Sabbath release his ox or his donkey from the stall and go to water it?"

16. "But this is a daughter of Abraham and The Devil has bound her, behold, for eighteen years. Is it illegal that she be released from this bondage on the Sabbath Day?"

The ruler of the synagogue had argued that it was illegal (v. 14) to heal on the Sabbath. This is the word Our Lord uses against him. The primary meaning of the Aramaic word ולא - "Walay", is "It is right". The Jewish leaders regularly insisted that Jesus violated the law of Moses by healing on the Sabbath.

17. And when he had said these things, those who had opposed him were all ashamed, and all the people were rejoicing at all the miracles that were wrought by his hand.

18. But Yeshua said, "What is the Kingdom of God like, and to what shall I compare it?"

19. "It is like a grain of mustard seed, which a man took and cast into his garden, and it grew and became a great tree and a bird of the sky nested in its branches."

20. Again, Yeshua said, "To what shall I compare the Kingdom of God?"

21. "It is like yeast which a woman took and hid in three 3-gallon measures* of flour until all of it was fermented."

* Aramaic סאא "Seah" (3 gallons) is also reflected in the Greek text , which has σατα- "Sata", which Thayer's Greek-English Lexicon has as "σατον" (pronounced "Sahton") , "(Hebr. סאה, Chald. סאתא, Syr. ܣܐܬܐ)". The Greek text uses a Hebrew-Aramaic word which is borrowed from the emphatic form of the Aramaic ܣܐܬܐ or סאתא (Aramaic letters) -pronounced "Satha". We can nail σατον -"Sahton" down as a loan word from the Aramaic סאתא ("Satha") ; in fact

σατα- "Sata" is exactly what a Greek would write if copying the standard lexical form סאתא ("Satha") of the Aramaic word into Greek letters. The Hebrew סאה "Seah" would never have the סאתא -"Satha" form ; the plural סאתים -"Sathim" would be the closest Hebrew form of the word.

22. And he traveled in villages and cities as he taught and he went on to Jerusalem.

23. But a man asked him if there are few who have life.

24. But Yeshua said to them, "Strive hard to enter the narrow gate, for I say to you, many shall seek to enter and they shall not be able."

25. "Then the Lord of the house will rise and shall bolt the gate, and you will be standing outside knocking at the gate, and you will begin to say, 'Our Lord, Our Lord, open to us." And he shall answer and he shall say, 'I say to you that I do not know you. From where are you?' "

26. "And you shall begin to say, 'We ate and we drank before you and you taught in our streets.' "

27. "And he shall say to you, 'I do not know you and from where you are; depart from me, workers of lies.' "

28. "There will be weeping and gnashing teeth when you will behold Abraham and Isaaq and Jaqob and all The Prophets in the Kingdom of God, but you shall be cast out."

29. "And they shall come from The East and from The West and from The South and from The North and they shall recline in the Kingdom of God."

30. "And behold, there are the last who shall be the first and there are the first who shall be the last."

31. That day, some of the Pharisees approached, and they were saying to him, "Depart from here, because Herodus wants to kill you."

32. But Yeshua said to them, "Go tell this Fox, 'Behold, I cast out demons and do cures today and tomorrow and on the third day I shall be perfected.' "

33. "However, it is right for me that today and tomorrow I should work and I should go the following day, because it is not possible that a Prophet shall perish outside of Jerusalem."

34. "Jerusalem, Jerusalem, you have murdered The Prophets and you have stoned those who were sent to her. How many times I have desired to gather your children as a hen that gathers her chicks under her wings, and you were not willing!"

Our Lord's lament for Jerusalem is an astonishing revelation of His psyche; He speaks as the Deity of Israel and His words are reminiscent of the word of God spoken to the Prophets:

Isa 30:15 For thus saith the Lord GOD, The Holy One of Israel; In returning and rest shall ye be saved; in quietness and in confidence shall be your strength: and ye would not.
Jer 6:16 Thus saith the LORD, Stand ye in the ways, and see, and ask for the old paths, where is the good way, and walk therein, and ye shall find rest for your souls. But they said, We will not walk therein.
Jer 44:4 Howbeit I sent unto you all my servants the Prophets, rising early and sending them, saying, Oh, do not this abominable thing that I hate.
Jer 44:5 **But they hearkened not, nor inclined their ear** to turn from their wickedness, to burn no incense unto other gods.
Zec 1:4 Be ye not as your fathers, unto whom the former Prophets have cried, saying, Thus saith the LORD of hosts; Turn ye now from your evil ways, and from your evil doings: but they did not hear, nor hearken unto me, saith the LORD.

In the words of C.S. Lewis, "The idea of a great moral teacher saying what Christ said is out of the question. In my opinion, the only person who can say that sort of thing is either God, or a complete lunatic, suffering from that delusion which undermines the whole mind of man."

35."Behold, your house is left to you desolate, for I say to you, you shall not see me until you will say, 'Blest is he who comes in the name of **THE LORD JEHOVAH!'**"

Chapter 14

1. And it was that when he entered the house of one of the leaders of the Pharisees to eat bread on the Sabbath day, and they were observing him,
2. Behold, one man who was swollen with fluid was there before him.
   (The man had a disease called "Edema")
3. And Yeshua answered and said to the Scribes and to the Pharisees, "Surely it is legal to heal on the Sabbath."
4. But they were silent, and he held him and healed him and he dismissed him.
5. And he said to them, "Who of you, whose son* or ox should fall in a pit on the Sabbath day, would not at once pull and lift him out?"

Only one early Greek ms. (א) has the reading "a donkey or * an ox"; The Majority Greek text, along with Vaticanus (B),Alexandrinus (A) and P45 & P75 (both 2nd or 3rd century mss.) agree with The Peshitta here ("son or ox"). Codex Beza (D) of the 6th cent. has "Sheep or ox", another indication that the Greek is a translation of The Peshitta, since "Barah" can refer to any young animal. Many Greek variants can be so explained. "Barah"- ברה usually means "Son", but can refer to "a young animal". Possibly a translator looked at או תורה ברה -"his son or his ox" and saw ברה המרה - "his young donkey" & then re-read the second Aramaic word תורה "Tora" correctly as "Ox" after writing the Greek ονος - "Onos"- "Donkey".

6. And they could not give him an answer to this.

7. And he told a parable to those who were invited there when he saw those who chose the places of the best seats.
8. "When you are invited by a man to a banquet house, do not go seat yourself at the best seat, lest it may be that he will appoint a man there who is more honorable than you"
9. "And he who invited you and him should come and say to you, 'Give the place to this man', and you will be ashamed when you stand and you take the last place."
10."But whenever you are invited, seat yourself last, that whenever he who invited you should come, he may say to you, 'My friend, come up and be seated', and there shall be glory to you before all* of those who sit with you."

The Majority Greek text omits "**All of them**" while the * Critical Greek text has the phrase. Interesting, isn't it, that in verse 5, The Peshitta agrees with the Majority Greek text, and five verses later, it agrees with The Critical Greek text? Which Greek text would The Peshitta translate, if it is a translation of Greek?

11."Because everyone who will exalt himself shall be humbled and everyone who will humble himself shall be exalted."
12.Then he said also to the one who had invited him, "Whenever you make a banquet or supper, do not call your friends, neither your brothers, nor your relatives, nor your rich neighbors, lest also they should invite you and this would be a reward to you."
13."But whenever you make a reception, invite the poor, the disabled, the maimed and the blind."
14."And you will be blessed, for they have nothing to repay you, for your reward will be in the resurrection of the righteous*."

* The Aramaic זדיקא "**Zaddyka**" can be singular or plural; the singular would refer to the resurrection of The Messiah- "**The Righteous One**". This is the only mention of this particular phrase "**the resurrection of the Righteous**" in the NT. Paul later writes that "**He was delivered up because of our sins, and He arose to justify us.**" Romans 4:25 . " **And ye have been buried with him, by baptism; and by it ye have risen with him; while ye believed in the power of God, who raised him from the dead.**" Col 2:12

15.But when one of those who were sitting there heard these things, he said to him, "Blessing to him who will eat bread* in the Kingdom of God."

The Majority Greek text (including Codex **W**) has ". "**dinner**" where the Critical Greek has "**bread**"

16. Yeshua* said to him, "A certain man made a great supper and he called many." * All Greek mss. lack "**Yeshua**"(Jesus)

17. "He sent his servant at the time of the supper to say to those who were invited, 'Behold, everything* is ready for you; Come.' "

* **"Everything"** is lacking in the Critical Greek mss. P45, P75, א, B,Θ. The Majority Greek (including Codex W) agrees with The Peshitta here. All Greek mss. lack "Behold" & "for you. In verse 15, The Peshitta agrees with the Critical Greek text; in verse 16 it agrees with no Greek text in reading "Yeshua: in v. 17 it agrees with no Greek text in two places & once it agrees with the Majority text. Where is the Greek text that can account for these different readings in three consecutive verses, not to mention verses 5 & 10 ? It is much more reasonable to account for the Greek readings on the basis of omissions & alternate word meanings in translating from a Peshitta original, than vice versa. The Peshitta can in this way account for all Greek texts; No Greek text can reasonably account for the Peshitta.

18. "And they began each and every one of them to make excuses; the first said to him, 'I have bought a field, and I am compelled to go to see it. I beg of you, allow me to be excused.' "

19. "Another said, 'I have bought five yoke of oxen, and I am going to examine them; I beg of you, allow me to be excused.'"

20. "Another said, 'I have taken a wife, and therefore I cannot come.' "

21. "And that servant came and he told his employer these things; and the owner of the house was angry and he said to his servant, 'Go out quickly to the marketplaces and to the streets of the city and bring here the poor and the afflicted and the feeble and the blind.' "

22. "And the servant said, 'My lord, it is as you ordered, and still there is room.' "

23. "And the owner said to his servant, 'Go out to the streets and to the place of hedges and compel them to enter, that my house may be filled.'

24. For I say to you that none of those men who were invited will partake of my supper.' "

25. And as there were great crowds going with him, he turned and he said to them:

26. "Whoever comes to me and does not hate his father and his mother and his brothers and his sisters and his wife and his children and even himself, he cannot be my disciple."

27. "And whoever does not take his cross and come after me, cannot be my disciple."

28. "For who among you, who wants to build a tower, does not first sit down and calculate its cost, if he is able to finish it,"

29. "Lest when he lays the foundation and cannot finish, all who see will mock him,"

30. "And they say, 'This man began to build and could not finish.' ?"

31. "Or who is the King who goes to battle to fight with a neighboring King and does not first consider whether he can with ten thousand confront him who comes against him with twenty thousand?"

32. "And if not, while he is far off from him, he sends envoys and pleads for peace."

33. "So none of you who does not forsake all his possessions can be my disciple."

34. "Salt is excellent, but if even the salt becomes insipid, with what will it be seasoned?"

35. "It is not fit for land nor is it fit for manure, *but* they cast it outside. Whoever has an ear that hears, let him hear."

Chapter 15

1. But Tax Collectors and sinners were approaching to hear him.

2. And the Scribes and Pharisees were complaining and they were saying, "This one receives sinners, and he eats with them."

3. And Yeshua told them this parable:

4. "What man among you has a hundred sheep, and if one of them should be lost, would not leave the ninety-nine in the wilderness and go seek* that one which is lost until he would find it?" *

"Seek" is missing in the Greek NT text except Codex D (6th century).

5. "And whenever he has found it he rejoices and carries it on his shoulder."

6. "And he comes to his house and he calls his friends and his neighbors and he says to them, "Rejoice with me, for I have found my sheep which was lost."

7. "I say to you that there shall be joy like this in Heaven over one sinner who returns home*, more than over ninety-nine righteous ones who do not need a homecoming."

Taav" תאב primarily means "**to return**"; it also means "**to** turn to God". The word "**repent**" conveys an incomplete meaning- the point Our Lord makes in His parables is that the lost are found and come home again where they belong. **God** is our "**Home**" to which we must return. "**Taav**" in the spiritual sense refers to the soul's homecoming.

8. "And who is the woman who has ten quarter shekels* and will lose one of them and does not light a lamp and sweep the house and search for it carefully until she finds it?"

A "Zuza"- זוזא was worth about ten pence , the equivalent of two weeks wages, in the first century. This was one tenth of the woman's dowry. The Greek mss. have "Drachma", which is "**a Greek silver coin about the same weight as a Roman Denarius**". What business had the Jews of Israel with Greek drachmas ? This is simply the Greek monetary exchange for the "**Zuza**". The Romans occupied Israel at this time, and that is reflected in **The Peshitta**'s use of the Latinism "Denari"elsewhere for the common coin used in commerce, based on the "coin of the realm", the Roman "Denarius".A Jewish woman's dowry would be worn around her head, like a crown. It would contain the Jewish coins of the time, **not the pagan currency of Greeks**. Hence, the Greek book of Luke reveals that the three uses of the Greek " **Drachma**" are not original, but a Hellenization (Greek conversion) of **The Peshitta**'s Aramaic term.

9. "When she has found it, she calls her friends and her neighbors, and she says to them, 'Rejoice with me, for I found my quarter shekel that was lost.' "

10. "I say to you that there will be joy like this before the Angels of God over one sinner who returns home."

11. And Yeshua said to them again, "One man had two sons."

Jesus (Yeshua) is missing in all Greek texts

12. "And his younger son said to him, 'My father, give me the portion that befalls me from your estate.' Then he divided to them his wealth."

13. "And after a few days his younger son gathered everything that was coming to him and he went to a distant country, and there he squandered his wealth while living wastefully."

14. "And when he had spent everything that he had, there was a great famine in that country and he began to be wanting."

15. And he joined himself to one of the citizens of that country, and he sent him to a field to herd pigs.

16. And he longed to fill his belly from the carob pods that the pigs were eating, and no man was giving anything to him.

Greek texts have two readings meaning "to fill": Critical Greek -χορτασθηναι (**chortasthaynai**) & Majority Greek - γεμισαι (**gemisai**).I explain this as two different translations of the same Aramaic word מלא-"**Mala**" (to fill). This I call a split Greek translation. See verse 23 for the next example of this.

17. And when he came to himself, he said, 'Now, how many hired servants are in my father's house who have plenteous bread for themselves, and here I am dying with hunger!'

18. 'I shall arise and go to my father and say to him, "My father, I have sinned toward Heaven, and before you.'

19. "Now I am not worthy to be called your son. Make me as one of your hired servants."

20. "And rising, he came to his father, and while he was still distant, his father saw him and he was moved with compassion for him and he ran and fell on his neck and he kissed him."

21. And his son said to him, "My father, I have sinned toward Heaven and before you, and I am not worthy that I should be called your son."

22. But his father said to his servants, 'Bring the best robe and clothe him and put a ring on his hand and put shoes on him.'

23. 'Bring and kill the fattened ox; let us eat and celebrate.'

Greek mss. have two different readings meaning . "**Bring**": Majority Greek-ενεγκαντες & Critical Greek-φερετε

24. 'Because this, my son, was dead, and he is alive; he was lost, and now he is found.' And they began to celebrate.

25. But his older son was in the field and as he came, he approached the house and he heard the sound of many people singing*.

דסגיאא -"**of many**" may have been read as רקדא- "**dancing**"; Greek mss. have "music and dancing". דסגיא with one Alep still has the same meaning: דסניא. ד & ר are practically identical. ק & ס could be confused with a smudged **Semqat**- ס . ני , if pressed together or smudged (apparently some smudging occurred at the last word in the verse) may appear ד , & both words end with א. דסניא becomes רקדא . This is quite a feasible explanation for the Greek reading "**Dancing**". Another, and perhaps more likely, possibility is that the Greek translator skipped "**many**" and read the first word of the next sentence "וקרא"(and called) & read it as רקדא -"**dancing**", and then , after translating it as χορων -"**dancing**", looked back and read it a second time, "only correctly the second time as "**called**".

I would like to hear someone who believes The Peshitta came from the Greek explain how The Peshitta got its reading of דסגיאא (d' sagaya) "**many**" from the Greek word χορων (chorone)-"**dancing**". All Peshitta mss. have the same reading : דסניאא-"**of many**". I show again the two Aramaic words for "& he called" and "Dancing" in a Dead Sea Scroll script for comparison:

"ܘܩܪܐ"(& he called)

"ܪܩܕܐ"(Dancing)

It is easy to see how the eye could have skipped ܐܐܝܓܣܕ to the next word ܐܪܩܘ and read it as ܐܕܩܪ .This phenomenon is not unusual in the Greek New Testament, in the author's opinion, verifying the theory that the Greek text is derived from The Aramaic Peshitta text.

26. He called one of the boys and he asked him, "What is this?"

27. And he said to him, "Your brother has come, and your father has killed the fattened ox, because he has received him well."

28. And he was angry and he did not want to enter and his father went out pleading with him.

29. But he said to his father, "Behold, I have served you for many years of servitude, and I have never transgressed your command, and

you never gave a goat to me that I may celebrate with my friends."

30. "But when this your son, who had wasted your money with whores, has come back, you killed for him the fattened ox."

31. His father said to him, "My son, you are always with me and everything that I have is yours."

32. "But it is right for us to celebrate and to rejoice, for this your brother was dead, and he is alive; he was lost, and is found."

Chapter 16

1. And he told a parable to his disciples: "There was a certain rich man who had a steward, and they were accusing him that he was squandering his wealth."

2. And his Lord summoned him and said to him, "What is this I have heard about you? Give me an inventory of your stewardship, for you cannot be a steward for me any longer."

3. That steward said to himself, "What shall I do? My Lord has taken the stewardship from me; I cannot dig, and I am ashamed to beg."

4. "I know what I shall do, that when I am put out from the stewardship, they may receive me into their houses."

5. "And he called each one who was indebted to his lord and he said to the first, 'How much do you owe to my lord?'"

6. "And he said to him, 'A hundred baths of oil', and he said to him, 'Take your book, sit quickly and write fifty baths.'"

A "Bath" was a Hebrew liquid measure of about 10 ＊ gallons. The Aramaic word is מתרין , from מתריא "Metraya" . The Greek texts in this verse have Βατους , from "Batos", which is of Hebrew origin – "Bath". The **Peshitta O.T.** sometimes translates the Hebrew "Bath" with "Metraya". It is interesting that **The LXX** has no occurrences of the Greek form Βατος -"Batos" , nor does it occur anywhere in Greek literature or elsewhere in **The Greek NT**. The only other place it occurs is in **Josephus' Antiquities** where he , **translating his original Aramaic text into Greek**, explains what a "Bath" measure is. All Greek texts have "Batos" just once in this verse (& in the NT), whereas **The Peshitta** has the equivalent "Metraya" twice here. It is more likely the Greek was translated from the Aramaic than vice versa; it is not very likely, generally, that a translator will add words not in the original, especially when the text is the Bible; it is more likely that he or she will omit a word, inadvertently. Since the translator knew this word was of Hebrew origin, he probably simply gave the Hebrew term in Greek form- "Batos", rather than translate the Aramaic word "Metraya"(which would be "metron" in Greek).

7. "And he said to another, 'And what do you owe to my lord?', and he said to him, 'A hundred cors of wheat.' He said to him, 'Take your book and sit and write eighty cors.' "

＊ A "Cor" is another Hebrew term (Aramaic has "Korine" from the singular form "Kore"). Greek texts have "Korous", which is from the Hebrew "Cor". A Cor was equivalent to ten "Baths" in volume, or about 100 gallons. Thayers' Greek-English Lexicon lists both "Koros" and "Batos" as Hebrew in origin. The OT **Greek LXX** translates the Hebrew word "Cor" with the Greek form "Koros" twice and three times it is translated from the Hebrew "homer" , which was about the same size as a "Cor". **Korous** (from **Koros**) is found only once in **The Greek NT**, like "Batos". The Aramaic word כורין "Korine" occurs twice in this verse, as does מתרין -"Metraya" in verse six.

8. And Our Lord praised the evil steward, because he acted wisely, for "The children of this world in this their generation are wiser than the children of light."

9. "Also, I say to you, make for yourselves friends of this money* of evil, that whenever it has been spent, they may receive you into their eternal dwellings."

● ממונא "Mammone" (Mammon=Money) occurs three times in this passage and only one other time in the NT (Matthew 6:24). In every place, the Greek has the Aramaic word μαμωνα ("mammona") in Greek letters, which shows an Aramaic original behind the Greek text. The LXX Greek never uses this word anywhere in the Old Testament, nor is it found anywhere in Greek literature, according to Thayer's Greek Lexicon. Grey shaded words are not found in most or any Greek mss. The Majority Greek text has "When you fail" instead of "When it has been spent". The Critical Greek (P[75], B, ℵ, D, Θ,) plus all Syriac versions, agree with The Peshitta. Two late Greek mss. have "their dwellings" whereas all others lack "their". No Greek ms. has all The Peshitta readings in this verse.

● We see in the Greek Gospel of Luke (even in chapters 15 & 16) that the currency, standards of measure and language of the Israeli people of the 1st century were not Greek, but Hebrew & Aramaic, and that the Greek version is a translation, often transliterating Aramaic and Hebrew terms. The Jewish people had repudiated Greek culture altogether, as Josephus also testified. It is ludicrous to assume the original Gospels, all of which would have been first circulated among the first Christians who lived in Judea, were written in Greek! They would not have been able to read them and it would have been an insult to their conscience to learn Greek.

10. "Whoever is faithful with little is faithful with much also, and whoever does evil with a little also does evil with much."

11. "If therefore you are not faithful with the wealth of evil, who will commit to you the reality?"

12. "And if you are not found faithful with what is not yours, who will give you what is yours?"

13. "There is no servant who can serve two masters, for either he will hate the one and

love the other, or he will honor the one and he will neglect the other. You cannot serve God and money."

14. But when the Pharisees heard all these things, they were mocking him because they loved money.

15. But Yeshua said to them: "You are those who justify themselves before men, but God knows your hearts, for the thing that is exalted among men is disgusting before God."

16. "The Law and The Prophets were until Yohannan; from then, the Kingdom of God is announced, and everyone is pushing to enter it."

17. "But it is easier for Heaven and earth to pass away than for one symbol* of The Law to pass away."

אתותא – "**Atwatha**" may refer to a "**letter, sign or character**". All of these are **symbols**, so I chose that to translate this word. In Matthew 5:18, The Peshitta records Our Lord as saying "**not one Yodh or one Taag will pass from the Law, till everything will come to pass**". A "Yodh" is the smallest letter; a "Taag" is a crownlet symbol used by the Scribes in their Massorah to designate certain letters of certain significant words , their usages and number of occurrences in the scriptures. It was an apparent reference to the Massoretic scribal tradition of precision in copying scripture going back to the first century and before, which accounts for the extreme accuracy and uniformity among manuscripts of The Hebrew Bible. "Atwatha"would include **letters** and **signs**, essentially restating Matthew 5:18. **The Greek NT** has the word κεραιαν ("a little horn, point"); the same is used in Matthew 5:18, and confirms the Aramaic sense of "Taag" or "Symbol". Our Lord held a very high view of **The Hebrew Bible.** It was for Him Divinely inspired , letter by letter, and preserved also letter by letter. It would be easier to destroy Heaven and earth than to destroy one letter from The Law (The Law sometimes refers to the entire Hebrew Bible-See John 10:34, 15:25).It is safe to say that Our Lord Yeshua held to the infallibility of scripture and understood that to include the idea that even in His time, 1500 years after Moses received the Law on Mt Sinai, every letter of the original text had been Divinely preserved and would be preserved until the end of time and beyond into eternity. He saw the Word of God as more sacred than all creation, and completely unshakeable. We can place all confidence in it; We have **His Word** on it.

Notwithstanding, He seems to indicate a change in dispensation from "**The Law & Prophets**" to "**The Kingdom of God**" in verses 16 - 18. This does not mean He "came to destroy the Law or The Prophets", but "to fulfill them"(Matthew 5:17). It does mean that "**Heaven & earth would pass away**" and all things would become new in a new creation. The primary instruments in effecting that great transformation would be a cross and a tomb: a cross upon which would hang and die The Creator of heaven and earth, and The Life thereof; a tomb, in which He Who suffered and died on that cross would be buried and rise again the third day. Paul The Apostle explains this all later in his great epistles. They were to be universal and eternal events, starting at the Top of all things with The Godhead and including all creation in its activities, thus transforming all things in a complete redemption.

To verify that He moved from "**Law & Prophets**" to a new order, He lays down a new law, unwritten in The Law of Moses. That law follows in verse 18.

18. "Whoever divorces his wife and takes another commits adultery, and everyone who takes her who is divorced commits adultery."

19. "There was a certain rich man, and he wore fine white linen and purple and everyday he celebrated luxuriously."

20. "And there was a certain poor man whose name was Lazar and he lay at the gate of that rich man, being stricken with abscesses."

21. "And he longed to fill his belly with the fragments that fell from the rich man's table, but also the dogs would come licking his abscesses."

22. "But that poor man died and Angels brought him to The Bosom of Abraham. And the rich man also died and he was buried."

23. "And suffering in Sheol, he lifted up his eyes from afar off and he saw Abraham, and Lazar in his bosom."

24. "And he called in a loud voice* and he said, 'My father, Abraham, have pity on me and send Lazar to dip the tip of his finger in water and moisten my tongue for me; behold, I am suffering in this flame.' "

*

All Greek mss. lack "**in a loud voice**".

25. "Abraham said to him, 'My son, remember that you have received your good things in your life and Lazar, his evil things, and now, behold, he is comforted here and you are suffering.' "

26. 'And along with all these things, there stands a great abyss between us and you, so that those who would pass from here to you are not able, neither is whoever is there able to pass over to us.'

27. "He said to him, 'Therefore, I beg of you, my father, to send him to my father's house.' "

28. 'For I have five brothers; he should go testify to them so that they would not come to this place of torment also.'

29. "Abraham said to him, 'They have Moses and The Prophets, let them hear them.' "

30. "But he said to him, 'No, my father Abraham, but if a man will go to them from the dead, they will be converted.' "

31. "Abraham said to him, 'If they will not hear Moses and The Prophets, they will not believe him, even though a man would rise from the dead.' "

The Greek texts have "**They will not be persuaded**"; No Greek text has "**They would not believe him**", as The Peshitta does; Codex W and Codex D have: "**They would not believe** .″

Chapter 17

1. **A**nd Yeshua said to his disciples, "It is not possible that offenses shall not come, but woe to him by whose hand they shall come."

2. "It were better for him if the millstone of a donkey were hung on his neck and he were cast into the sea than that he would stumble one of these little ones."

3. "Guard your souls. If your brother should sin, rebuke him, and if he repents, forgive him."

4. "And if he sins against you seven times in a day and seven times in the day returns to you and says, 'I am sorry', forgive him."

5. And The Apostles said to Our Lord, "Increase our faith."

6. He said to them, "If you have faith like a grain of mustard seed, you may say to this sycamore tree, 'Be uprooted and be planted in the sea', and it would obey you."

7. "But who among you has a servant who drives a plow or who tends to sheep, and if he would come from the field, would say to him at once, 'Go on; recline for supper"'?

8. "But he says to him, 'Prepare for me something to eat and put on your apron to serve me until I shall have eaten and have drunk; after this you also will eat and drink.'"

9. "Does that servant receive his thanks because he did the thing that he was commanded? I think not."

10. "So also you, whenever you have done all those things that were commanded you, you should say, 'We are unprofitable servants, because we have done that which we were obligated to do.'"

11. And it was that as Yeshua went to Jerusalem, he passed through among Samaritans to Galilee.

12. And when he approached to enter a certain village, ten men who were lepers met him, and they stood afar off.

13. And they lifted up their voices and they were saying, "Our Rabbi*, Yeshua, have mercy on us!" *

*See notes at Luke 5:5 on רבן - "**Rabban**" & the Greek reading ΕΠΙΣΤΑΤΑ - "epistata" – "Master*

14. And when he saw them, he said to them, "Go show yourselves to the priests", and as they were going, they were purified.

15. But one of them, when he saw that he was purified, he returned to him and he was praising God with a loud voice.

16. And he fell on his face before the feet of Yeshua as he gave thanks to him, and this one was a Samaritan.

17. But Yeshua answered and he said, "Were there not ten who were purified? Where are the nine?"

18. "Have they neglected to come give glory to God, except this one who is from a foreign people?"

19. And he said to him, "Arise; go. Your faith has saved you."

20. And when some of the Pharisees asked Yeshua, "When is the Kingdom of God coming", he answered and he said to them, "The Kingdom of God does not come with what is observed."

21. "Neither do they say, 'Behold, here it is!' and, 'Behold, it is *from* here to there!', for behold, the Kingdom of God is within some of you."

*

The Kingdom of God is within <u>some of you</u>", makes good sense theologically and grammatically in the Aramaic. Only **The Peshitta** has this reading, however. מנכון has this meaning in several other places in **The Peshitta NT** and the word מן (used in the compound word מנכון) has the partitive sense ("some", "some of you", "some of them") in many places in **The Peshitta OT** as well as in **The Peshitta NT**. 1 Cor. 10:7-10 has four examples of this sense of the word ("some of them"). Luke 11:49 and Rev. 2:10 also use מנכון in the partitive sense ("some of you").

22. And he said to his disciples, "The days will come when you shall long to see one of the days of The Son of Man, and you shall not see."

23. "And if they will say to you, 'Behold, he is here.' and 'Behold he is there', do not go."

24. "For just as lightning flashes from the sky and lights up all beneath the sky, thus shall The Son of Man be in his day."

25. "But first, he is going to suffer many things and he shall be rejected by this generation."

26. "And as it was in the days of Noah, thus shall it be the days of The Son of Man."

27. "For they were eating and drinking and taking wives and giving *them* to men until the day that Noah entered the ark and the flood came and destroyed everyone."

28. "And again, just as it was in the days of Lot, they were eating and drinking and buying and selling and planting and building."

29. "But in the day that Lot went out from Sadom, **THE LORD JEHOVAH** caused it

to rain fire and brimstone from the sky and destroyed all of them."

30. "Thus shall it be in the day when The Son of Man is revealed."

31. "In that day, whoever is on the roof, and his stuff in the house, let him not come down to take them. And whoever is in the field, let him not turn back."

32. "Remember Lot's wife."

33. "Whoever chooses to save his life shall lose it, and whoever will lose his life shall find it."

34. "I say to you, in that night, two shall be in one bed; one shall be taken captive and the other shall be left."

35. "Two women shall be grinding meal together; one shall be led away captive and the other shall be left."

.Codex ℵ (4ᵗʰ Cent. Greek) omits verse 35

36. "Two shall be in a field; one shall be taken captive and the other shall be left."

Most Greek mss. lack v. 36 ; Only Codex D and about 40 late miniscules and lectionaries contain it. The Latin Vulgate contains it in verse 35.

37. And they answered and they were saying to him, "To where, Our Lord?" He said to them, "Wherever the bodies are, there the eagles shall be gathered."

Chapter 18

1. He told them also a parable that they should pray at all times and they should not grow weary:

2. "There was in one city a certain judge who did not worship God and did not honor the children of men."

3. "There was a certain widow in that city, and she was coming to him and saying, 'Vindicate me of my legal adversary.' "

4. "And he would not for long time, but after this, he said to himself, 'Although I do not worship God neither honor people'

5. 'Nevertheless, because this widow wearies me, I shall avenge her, lest she be constantly coming and annoying me.' "

6. And Our Lord said, "Hear what the evil judge said."

7. "Shall not God all the more perform vindication for his Elect, who cry to him by day and by night, and he delays his Spirit concerning them?"

8. "I say to you that he shall perform their vindication quickly. However, The Son of Man shall come, and will he then find faith on the earth?"

9. And he told this parable against those men who trusted in themselves that they were righteous, and they held contempt for everyone:

10. "Two men went up to The Temple to pray: one a Pharisee and the other a Tax Collector."

11. The Pharisee was standing alone by himself and he was praying these things: "God, I thank you that I am not like other men: extortioners, oppressors, adulterers, and not like this Tax Collector."

12. "But I fast twice in a week and I tithe everything that I possess."

13. "But that Tax Collector was standing from a distance and he would not even lift his eyes up to Heaven, but he was smiting on his chest and he said, 'God, have pity on me, a sinner.' "

14. "I say to you that this one went down to his house justified rather than that Pharisee, for every man who exalts himself shall be humbled, and everyone who humbles himself shall be exalted."

15. But they brought him also infants that he might touch them, and his disciples saw them, and they rebuked them.

16. But Yeshua himself called them and he said to them, "Let the children come to me and do not refuse them, because the Kingdom of Heaven belongs to those who are like these."

17. "Amen, I say to you, whoever does not receive the Kingdom of God as a little boy shall not enter it."

18. And one who was a nobleman asked him and said to him, "Good teacher, what shall I do to inherit eternal life?"

19. Yeshua said to him, "Why do you call me good? There is no one good except the one God."

20. "You know the commandments: You shall not murder, You shall not commit adultery, You shall not steal, You shall not testify a false testimony, Honor your father and your mother.' "

The Greek texts have different word order: "You shall not commit adultery, you shall not murder."
The Latin Vulgate agrees with The Peshitta: "You shall not murder, you shall not commit adultery."

21. He said to him, "I have kept all these things from my childhood."

22. But when Yeshua heard these things, he said to him, "You lack one thing: Go sell everything that you have and give to the poor, and you shall have a treasure in Heaven, and come after me."

23. But when he heard these things, it grieved him, for he was very rich.

24. And when Yeshua saw that it grieved him, he said, "How hard it is for those who have wealth to enter the Kingdom of God."

The Critical Greek lacks "**that it grieved him**". All other Greek and Latin texts have it.

25. "It is easier for a camel* to enter the eye of a needle than for a rich man *to enter* the Kingdom of God."

It is easier for a camel to enter into the eye of a *needle than for a rich man the Kingdom of God. I have read and rejected the translation, "**It is easier for a rope…**", for these reasons: "**Rope**" is an obscure sense for "Gamla"; "**Great beam that supports rafters**" is a more common sense than "a rope", yet that is not chosen as an alternative reading with any merit. "**Camel driver**" or "**Giraffe**" are also possible, but no one chooses either of them as the meaning. The verb נעול "**nawal**" is active in all translations "**to enter**", yet what rope can actively "enter" or do anything? If "**a rope**" were the meaning, the verb would be the Aphel form (causative sense "**to bring**") and would apply also to the rich man, since one verb serves for both objects. If "**a rope**" were the sense, the sentence would most likely read: "**It is easier to insert a rope into the eye of a needle than a rich man into the Kingdom of God.**" The problem is that we must picture both the rope and the rich man as objects rather than subjects. The real subject or subjects in that scenario is unnamed and unknown and is seen as pushing a rope and then a man through a very small opening. The idea of needing someone to push a man into the Kingdom of God is unnatural and ridiculous. Either he fits and can make it on his own or he does not belong there. A camel can move under its own power, yet it cannot fit itself into the eye of a needle. A camel and a rich man are both living active agents capable of initiating and performing action. A rope is inanimate and cannot "enter" anything. The fact of the unnamed subjects is the real problem in the "rope" scenario. **A camel driver may be seen as pushing his camel to try squeezing him through the eye of a needle; Who is the subject pushing the rich man into the Kingdom of God ? Surely if it were God, there would be no problem, but there is obviously quite a big problem, so who is it trying this unlikely and silly feat ?** No one was pushing the rich nobleman who came to Jesus; He asked of his own initiative and was told what he must do, and he decided it was asking too much. Our Lord used the same verb in the previous verse- "**to enter**" the Kingdom; Did he mean, "**to be pushed**"? I think not.
Another problem with the "**rope**" hypothesis is a theological and psychological one: **No one is going to try getting a camel to go through the eye of a needle to prove a rich man might get into the Kingdom of God; however, a man might try getting a rope through the eye of a needle; it sounds like a challenge worthy of ingenuity that just might pay off and yield hope that it is possible to do the other also.** Is it Our Lord's intention to challenge us to try getting rich men into the Kingdom, or to cause us to

see the futility of trying it? **The rope hypothesis only encourages rebellion , not faith.**

26. Those who heard were saying to him, "And who can have life?"

27. But Yeshua said, "Those things which are impossible with men can happen with God."

28. Shimeon Kaypha* said to him, "Behold, we have left everything and we have come after you."

• All Greek texts have Πετρος –"**Petros**" – ("**Peter**") where The Peshitta has "Shimeon Kaypha". In John 1:42, the Greek mss. all read: συ κληθηση κηφας ο ερμηνευεται πετρος- "**you shall be called Kayphas, which is translated Peter.**" There the Greek text states that Petros is a translation of **Kayphas** –(Greek form of **Kaypha**). "Kaypha", the Aramaic word, is the original behind "**Petros**". Must we not then understand that **the 160 some occurrences of "Petros" , referring to the Apostle Peter, are all translations of the Aramaic "Kaypha**"?Is not John 1:42 a declaration (like at least five other similar statements in the NT) that the Greek text is a translation of an Aramaic original? John 1:41 has another such statement : ευρηκαμεν τον μεσσιαν ο εστιν μεθερμηνευομενον ο χριστος –" **We have found the Messiah (which is, being translated, Christ").** The Peshitta lacks the underlined portions of the two verses, because it is not translating a Greek text or the Greek language at all. But the Greek mss. declare in John 1:41 that they are translating the Aramaic "Meshikha" (It comes out "**Messias**" in Greek letters). Is this not a key to understanding that the **571 occurrences of the Greek word** "**Christos**" in The Greek NT are translations of the Aramaic original "Meshikha" ? Does not Greek John 1:41 declare itself and The Gospel to be a translation – "**which is being translated, Christ**"- of an Aramaic original ? Shimeon's name was not "**Petros**"; "**Petros**" s Greek. "Shimeon" was not Greek and did not speak Greek; He was an Israeli Jew who spoke Aramaic and had an Aramaic name. **Yeshua Meshikha** was not a Greek and did not have a Greek name. He was and is an Israeli Jew (not to mention being **Jehovah** God) with an Aramaic Name and spoke Aramaic. He was never called "**Christos**" by His disciples nor "**Iaysous**" by those who knew Him, neither did He ever call Himself by those names. He is and was "**Yeshua Meshikha**" and spoke His native language to His countrymen and disciples, all of whom spoke and understood Aramaic and not Greek. **He also spoke Aramaic from Heaven to Saul of Tarsus** on the road to Damascus. (See Acts 26:14 in Greek & look up Ηεβραις-"**Hebrais**" (translated "Hebrew") in a Greek lexicon. (Or see my note at John 20:16) Here is an excerpt:
• "**Hebrais**", as "**The Hebrew tongue; not that however in which the OT was written, but the Chaldee.**"-Thayer's Greek – English Lexicon. Webster's unabridged 20th century Dictionary defines "Chaldee" as **The Aramaic language** of the Chaldaeans (Babylonians 600 B.C.) .

29. Yeshua said to him, "Truly, I say to you, there is no man who has left house or parents or brother or wife or children for the sake of the Kingdom of God,"

30. "Who shall not receive in great multiples in this time, and in the coming world, eternal life."

31. And Yeshua led his twelve and he said to them, "Behold, we are going up to Jerusalem and all that is written in The Prophets about The Son of Man shall be fulfilled."

According to this statement of Our Lord Yeshua, **all Old Testament prophecies concerning Him** would be fulfilled in Jerusalem during His last day and the days following. That fact should give us serious pause and cause some serious contemplation of the immensity of His suffering and death on the cross and His resurrection. Interestingly, this would also include Daniel's prophecy of the "**coming of The Son of Man in the clouds of Heaven**" (Dan. 7:13).But He told Caiaphas the High Priest ,"**You shall see The Son of Man coming in the clouds of Heaven**". It did not take long to occur. Many need to rethink their Eschatology and interpretation of prophecy.

32. "For he shall be delivered to Gentiles, and they shall mock him and they shall spit in his face."

Greek texts have "**He shall be mocked & abused & spit upon**" . The Peshitta has "**they shall abuse Him**" in the next verse where the Greek does not.

33. "They shall scourge him, they shall abuse him and they shall kill him, and on the third day he shall rise."

34. But they understood none of these things and this saying was hidden from them and they did not know these things that were spoken with them.

35. And when they came near to Jericho, a certain blind man was sitting on the side of the road and begging.

36. And he heard the sound of the crowd that passed by and he was asking, "Who is this?"

37. They were saying to him, "Yeshua the Nazarene passes by."

38. And he cried out and he said, "Yeshua, Son of David, have mercy on me!"

39. And those who were going in front of Yeshua were rebuking him that he should be quiet, but he was crying out even more, "Son of David, have mercy on me!"

40. And Yeshua stood still, and he commanded to bring him to him, and when he came near to him, he asked him,

41. And he said to him, "What do you want me to do for you?" But he said, "My Lord, that I may see."

42. And Yeshua said to him, "See; your faith has saved you."

43. And immediately he saw, and he was coming after him and he was praising God, and all the people who saw were giving glory to God.

Chapter 19

1. And when Yeshua entered and passed through Jericho,

2. A certain man was there whose name was Zakkai; he was a rich man and Chief of Tax Collectors,

3. And he wanted to see who Yeshua was and he was not able to from the crowd because Zakkai was small in stature.

4. And he ran before it to Yeshua and he climbed up a bare fig tree to see him because he was going to pass by there.

5. And when he came to that place, Yeshua saw him and said to him, "Hasten, come down, Zakkai, for today I must stay at your house."

6. And he made haste and he came down and received him rejoicing.

7. But when all of them saw *it,* they were all complaining and they were saying, "He entered and lodged with a man that is a sinner."

8. Then Zakkai arose and he said to Yeshua, "Behold, my Lord, I give half my wealth to the poor, and anything that I have seized I repay fourfold to every man."

9. Yeshua said to him, "Today, The Life has come to this house, because This One also is The Son of Abraham."

Consider that **Our Lord speaks of Himself** to Zakkai as "**The Life**" and also **The Son (The Promised Seed) of Abraham.** He is declaring Himself to be **God and Man, i.e.**, **The Messiah.**

10. "For The Son of Man has come to seek and to save that which was lost."

11. And as they heard these things, he added to speak a parable because he was nearing Jerusalem, and they were expecting in that same hour that the Kingdom of God was going to be revealed.

12. And he said, "A certain man, a son of great descent, went to a distant region to receive a Kingdom and to return."

13. And he called his ten servants and he gave them ten minas* and he said to them, "Invest in trading until I come."

A "**Mina**", in the first century would have be **✱** the equivalent of a modern British pound (£), or an average four months' wages for a laborer. The Greek texts have the word μνας – "**mnas**", from μνα – "**mna**" , which Thayer's Greek-English Lexicon describes as "of Eastern origin" , displaying the -Arabic pronounced "**Mahn**" , Šyriac- ܡܢܝܐ "**Manya**" , & , من Hebrew מנה "**Maneh**".The Greeks had no such word for their coins. Μνα is found in The LXX **several times to translate the Hebrew** מנה - "Maneh", which is the same unit of weight and money as the Aramaic word ܡܢܝܐ "Manya" .Here is the entry for the Aramaic word from Smith's Compendious : Syriac Dictionary

ܡܢܐ pl. ܡܢ̈ܐ, ܡܢܬܐ, ܡܢܝܐ m. a measure of weight and of value ; *a mina, a pound.*

Here is the Hebrew word definition from Strong's Hebrew Lexicon: 04488 מנה manch maw-neh'
from 04487; TWOT-1213b; n m
AV-pound 4, manch 1; 5
1) manch, mina, pound
1a) 60 shekels and 1/50 talent (of silver)
1a1) 1/60 talent in early Babylonian standard
1b) 100 shekels and 1/100 talent (of gold)

The Greek transliteration of the Hebrew-Aramaic words "μνα" only occurs in scripture (The LXX & The Greek NT) . No Greek literature has it. That is because "μνα" is not Greek. Here is the Aramaic word entry from Strong's Hebrew-Aramaic Lexicon :
04484 מנא mene' (Aramaic) men-ay'
pass. participle of 04483; TWOT-2835a; n m
AV-MENE 3; 3
1) (P'al) mina, maneh
1a) a weight or measurement; usually 50 shekels but maybe 60 shekels

Remember "**Mene mene tekel upharsin**" in Daniel 5, the story of the handwriting on the wall ? That was the Aramaic language. The Greek μνα , which is an exact transliteration of מנא -"**mene**" , is not as close to the Hebrew מנה -"**Maneh**" .**Can Greek primacists (those who believe in a Greek original NT) read the handwriting on the wall ? Not unless they can read ! Aramaic. I have read it, and it isn't Greek** An apparent conflict exists in the value of a Mina in Mark 12:42, the account of the widow's mites. There the two mites are said to be "a **Shimona**", which is worth only ¼ cent. There were three different standards of currency however: There was the **gold** standard, the **silver** and the **copper**. A gold talent was much more valuable than the silver , and the silver than the copper; the same for the shekel, which was about 65 cents in silver and 10 dollars in gold. **A silver mina was 60 shekels, and the copper coins were much lower in value than the silver, which probably accounts for the difference in the values noted**. A table of weights and values is presented for comparisons:

gerahs = **1 shekel** =65 cents silver; 10 dollars 20 gold
shekels= **1 maneh**=1 pound=100 drachmas=16 60 dollars silver; 490 dollars gold; 1/8 cent copper
manehs=**1 talent**= 1960 dollars silver; 29,374 60 dollars gold

14. But the citizens of the city hated him and they sent envoys after him and they were saying, "We do not want this man to reign over us."

15. And when he had received the Kingdom and returned, he said to summon to him his servants to whom he had given money that he may know what everyone of them had traded.

16. The first came and he said, "My Lord, your mina has gained ten minas."

17. He said to him, "Excellent, good servant! Because you are found faithful with a little, you shall be a ruler over ten fortress cities."

18. The second came and he said, "My Lord, your mina has gained five minas."

19. He said also to this one, "You also shall be ruler over five fortress cities."

20. Another came and he said, "My lord, behold, that mina, which I had is now laid in fine linen."

21. "For I was afraid of you, for you are a hard man, for you take up that which you have not laid down and you reap the thing which you have not sown."

22. He said to him, "I will judge you from your own mouth, you evil servant, for you had known me that I am a hard man, and I take up the thing that I have not laid down, and I reap the thing that I have not sown.

23. Why did you not put my money upon the exchange and I would have come to seek it with its interest?"

24. And he said to those who stood before him, "Take from him the mina and give to him who has ten minas with him."

25. And they were saying to him, "Our Lord, he has ten minas."

26. He said to them, "I tell you that everyone who has it, it shall be given him, and from him who does not have it, even that which he has shall be taken from him."

27. "However, those my enemies, who did not want me to reign over them, bring them and kill them in front of me."

28. And when Yeshua had said these things, he went out to those before him to go to Jerusalem.

29. And when he arrived at Bethphage and Bayth-Ania on the side of the Mount which is called 'Bayth Zaytha', he sent two of his disciples.

Bayth Zaytha" means "**The place of Olives**" and is ". known as "**The Mt. of Olives.**

30. He said to them, "Go to the village which is opposite us, and when you enter, behold, you shall find a colt tied on which a man has never ridden; loose and bring him."

31. "If a man asks you why you are loosing him, say thus to him: 'He is needed for Our Lord.' "

32. And they who were sent went and found just as he had said to them.

33. And as they loosed the colt, its owners were saying to them, "Why are you loosing that colt?"

34. And they said to them, "He is needed for Our Lord."

35. And they brought him to Yeshua and they cast their garments on the colt and set Yeshua upon him.

36. As he went they were spreading their garments in the road.

37. When he approached the descent of the Mount of Bayth Zaytha, all the crowds of disciples began rejoicing and praising God with loud voices for all the mighty works that they had seen.

38. And they were saying, "Blessed is The King who comes in the name of **THE LORD JEHOVAH**; peace in Heaven and glory in The Highest."

39. But some of the Pharisees from among the crowds were saying to him, "Rabbi, rebuke your disciples."

40. He said to them, "I say to you that if these would be silent, the stones would be crying out loud."

41. And when he came near and he saw the city he wept over it.

42. And he said, "If only now you had known those things that are of your peace, if even in this your day! But now these things are hidden from your eyes."

43. "The days shall come to you when your enemies shall surround you and they shall press you in from every side."

44. "And they shall destroy you and your children within you and they shall not leave you one stone standing on another, because you did not know the time of your visitation."

45. And when he entered The Temple he began to cast out those who bought and sold in it.

46. And he said to them, "It is written: 'My house is the house of prayer', but you have made it a den of robbers.'"

47. He was teaching everyday in The Temple, but the Chief Priests and the Scribes and the Elders of the people were seeking to destroy him.

48. And they could not find what they might do to him, for all the people were hanging on him to hear him.

Chapter 20

1. And it happened on one of the days while he was teaching the people in The Temple and evangelizing, there stood about him Chief Priests and Scribes with Elders.

The Majority Greek text has "the priests" whereas the Critical Greek has "The Chief Priests", like The Peshitta

2. They were saying to him, "Tell us by what authority do you do these things, and who is he who has given you this authority?"

3. Yeshua* answered and he said to them, "I shall also ask you a question and you answer me."

Greek lacks "**Jesus**

4. "Was the baptism of Yohannan from Heaven, or from men?"

5. But they were counseling among themselves and they were saying, "If we say, 'From Heaven', he will say to us, 'And why did you not believe him?'"

6. "But if we say, 'From men', all the people will stone us, for they are convinced that Yohannan is a Prophet."

7. And they said to him, "We do not know from where it was."

The Greek has literally: "**And they answered not to know from where**"; The Peshitta has, "**And they said to Him, 'We do not know from where it was**'". The Greek is rather awkward ("They answered not to know") and The Peshitta has three more bits of information than the Greek, underlined in the previous sentence. Translations delete information from the original; they do not create it, generally, and The Greek NT throughout contains thousands fewer bits of data than The Peshitta NT.

8. Yeshua said to them, "Neither do I say to you by what authority I do these things."

9. And he began to tell the people this parable: "A certain man planted a vineyard and handed it over to laborers and he went abroad for a long time."

10. And at the season he sent his servant to the workers to give him some of the fruits of the vineyard, but the workers beat him and they sent him away stripped.

11. And he added and sent another servant, but they beat that one also and they abused him and they sent him away naked.

12. But he added and sent a third, but they also wounded that one and cast him out.

13. The owner of the vineyard said, 'What shall I do? I shall send my beloved son. Doubtless they will see him and they will be ashamed.'

14. "But when the workers saw him, they were counseling among themselves and they were saying, 'This is the heir; come let us kill him, and the inheritance shall be ours.'"

15. "And they cast him out of the vineyard and murdered him. What therefore will the owner of the vineyard do to them?"

16. "He shall come and destroy those workers, and he shall give the vineyard to others"; but when they heard, they said, "May this not be!"

17. But he gazed upon them and he said, "And what is this that is written: 'The stone which the builders rejected has become the head of the corner'"?

18. "And everything that falls on that stone shall be broken, and it will scatter everything whatsoever upon which it will fall."

19. But the Chief Priests and the Scribes were seeking to lay hands upon him at that hour, and they were afraid of the people, for they knew that he had spoken this parable against them.

20. And they sent spies who imitated righteous men to catch him in discourse and to deliver him to the Judge and to the authority of the Governor.

21. And they asked him, and they were saying to him, "Teacher, we know that you are speaking and teaching correctly, and you do not show favoritism, but you teach the way of God in truth."

22. "Is it legal for us to give poll tax* to Caesar or not?"

*

The Greek has "φορος"("Foros"), which apparently was the wrong word, as it was a tax paid in produce, not with money.
See the following definitions of the various Greek words for taxes:
φορος ("Foros") indicates a direct tax which was levied annually on houses, lands, and persons, and paid usually in produce.
Τελος ("Telos") is an indirect tax on merchandise, which was collected at piers, harbors, and gates of cities. It was similar to modern import duties.
κηνσος,("Kaynsos") originally an enrollment of property and persons, came to
  mean a poll-tax, levied annually on individuals by the Roman government.
διδραχμον ("Didrachmon") was the coin used to pay an annual tax levied by the
religious leaders of Israel for the purpose of defraying the general expenses of the Temple.
As The Peshitta has "a head tax" which was also called a "poll tax" , the Greek word φορος does not match it, meaning The Peshitta is not a translation of φορος , which does not fit the tax being described. The Greek word which fits is κηνσος ("Kaynsos") , but **no Greek manuscript known has** κηνσος; **All have** φορος **("Foros")** , which was normally paid in barter, not coins.
Therefore, the Greek is plainly a mistranslation of the Peshitta's poll tax (כסף רישא) "kespa resha" . The Greek is incorrect here and the Aramaic is flawless.

23. "But he perceived their cunning and he said, "Why are you testing me?"

24. "Show me a denarius. Whose image and inscription is on it?" They said, "Caesar's."

A **denarius** was a silver Roman coin worth 8 ½ cents

25. Yeshua* said to them, "Give therefore to Caesar what is Caesar's, and to God what is God's."

Greek omits Yeshua -"**Jesus**"

26. And they could not lay hold of any word from him before the people, and they were amazed at his answer, and they kept silent.

27. But some of the Sadducees came, those who say that there is no resurrection, and they asked him,

28. And they were saying to him, "Teacher, Moses wrote to us that if a man dies and his brother has a wife without sons*, his brother shall take his wife, and he shall raise up a son* to his brother."

זרעא- "**Zrea**" – "**Seed**" refers normally to male offspring; the Law of Moses (Deut. 25:5-10) required that a son be raised to keep the family name alive. The Majority Greek text has the verb "**dies**" twice; The Critical Greek text has it just once, like **The Peshitta NT.**

29. "But there were seven brothers and the first took a wife and he died without sons."

30. "And the second took her for his wife, and he died without sons."

31. "And the third again took her and thus also the seven of them, and they died and left no sons."

32. "And finally the woman died also."

The Critical Greek agrees more closely with with The Peshitta here; The Majority Greek has "**last of all, the woman died also**"; The Critical Greek has "**afterward, the woman died also.**" Both, however are reasonable translations of the Aramaic of The Peshitta.

33. In the resurrection therefore, whose wife will she be, for the seven of them married her?

34. Yeshua said to them, "The sons of this world take women and women are given to men.

All Greek mss. have "**The sons of this age marry and are given in marriage**". The Greek word υιος ("hweeos"), is the word "**son**". In what first century culture were sons given in marriage ? If the meaning were simply "**children**", the word "**teknon**" would be used, referring to males and females. No Greek text has "**Women are given to men**", as does The Peshitta. Of which Greek text or manuscript is The Peshitta a translation ? Again, the Greek is incorrect and The Peshitta is flawless.

35. But those who are worthy for that world and for the resurrection from among the dead are not taking women, neither are women taking men.

The Aramaic here mentions "**Men**" & "**Women**". The Greek mss. have neither. Some have concluded from the Greek that people are gender neutral in the glorified state in Heaven. The Peshitta nowhere suggests that. (neither does the Greek, in my opinion)

36. For neither can they die again, for they are like The Angels, and they are the children of God because they are the children of the resurrection.

37. But that the dead rise, Moses also declared, for he recounts at the bush, when THE LORD JEHOVAH said, "The God of Abraham and the God of Isaaq and the God of Jaqob.

38. But he was not the God of the dead, but of the living, for all of them were alive to him."

39. And some of the Scribes answered, and they were saying to him, "Teacher, you have spoken beautifully."

40. And they dared not ask him about anything again.

41. He said to them, "How do the Scribes* say about The Messiah that he is the son of David?

*

The Greek mss. do not have "**The Scribes**". Where did The Peshitta get this , if it is a translation of Greek ? The Greek has "**How do they say The Christ is the Son of David?**"

42. And David said in the book of Psalms, THE LORD JEHOVAH said to my Lord, "Seat yourself at my right hand,

43. Until I put your enemies under your feet.'

The Greek has , "**Until I set your enemies your footstool.** "The Peshitta and one Greek ms. (D) have "**Until I set your enemies under your feet.** " This verse (Psalms 110:1) is quoted seven times in The NT. The following are all seven quotations in Aramaic and Greek

לך מן ימיני עדמא דאסים בעלדבביך תחת רגליך דאמר מריא למרי תב Mt 22:44 Peshitta

'THE LORD JEHOVAH said to my Lord, "Seat yourself at my right hand,
    until I place your enemies under your feet.'

Mt 22:44 ειπεν κυριος τω κυριω μου καθου εκ δεξιων μου εως αν θω τους εχθρους σου υποκατω των ποδων σου –WH   "The LORD said to my Lord, 'Sit at My right hand,
    till I place Your enemies under Your feet'."

Μτ 22:44 ειπεν ο κυριος τω κυριω μου καθου εκ δεξιων μου εως αν θω τους εχθρους σου υποποδιον των ποδων σου –BYZ agrees with LXX -"The Lord said to my Lord, 'Sit at My right hand,
    till I place Your enemies a footstool of Your feet'."

ימיני עדמא דאסים בעלדבביך כובשא תחת רגליך אמר ברוחא דקודשא דאמר מריא למרי תב לך מן הו גיר דויד Mr 12:36 Peshitta

'THE LORD JEHOVAH said to my Lord, "Seat yourself at my right hand,
    until I place your enemies under your feet.'

Mr 12:36 αυτος δαυιδ ειπεν εν τω πνευματι τω αγιω ειπε κυριος τω κυριω μου καθου εκ δεξιων μου εως αν θω τους εχθρους σου υποκατω των ποδων σου * -WH
    -David said in The Holy Spirit, "The Lord said to my Lord, 'Sit at My right hand,

till I place Your enemies under Your feet'."

Mr 12:36 αυτος γαρ δαυιδ ειπεν εν πνευματι αγιω λεγει ο κυριος τω κυριω μου καθου εκ δεξιων μου εως αν θω τους εχθρους σου υποποδιον των ποδων σου * (BYZ) agrees with LXX
    -David said in The Holy Spirit, "The Lord said to my Lord, 'Sit at My right hand,

till I place Your enemies a footstool of Your feet'."

עדמא דאסים בעלדבביך תחת רגליך Lu 20:43 Peshitta

"until I place your enemies under your feet.'

Lu 20:43 εως αν θω τους εχθρους σου υποποδιον των ποδων σου –WH agrees with LXX
    "till I place Your enemies a footstool of Your feet."

Lu 20:43 εως αν θω τους εχθρους σου υποποδιον των ποδων σου (BYZ) agrees with LXX
    "till I place Your enemies a footstool of Your feet'."

Lu 20:43 εως αν θω τους εχθρους σου υποκατω των ποδων σου –Codex D. *
    "till I place Your enemies under Your feet."

עדמא דרגליך כובשא לרגליך Ac 2:35 agrees with Hebrew OT, Pesh. OT & LXX
    "until I place your enemies a stool for your feet.'

Ac 2:35 εως αν θω τους εχθρους σου υποποδιον των ποδων σου * -WH agrees with Hebrew OT, Pesh. OT & LXX "till I place Your enemies a footstool of Your feet'."

Ac 2:35 εως αν θω τους εχθρους σου υποποδιον των ποδων σου * (BYZ) agrees with Hebrew OT, Pesh. OT & LXX "till I place Your enemies a footstool of Your feet'."

ימיני עדמא דאסים בעלדבביך כובשא תחת רגליך Heb 1:13 למן דין מן מלאכא ממתום אמר דתב מן Peshitta   To which of the angels did he ever say, "Seat yourself at my right hand, until I place your enemies a footstool under your feet?

Heb 1:13 προς τινα δε των αγγελων ειρηκεν ποτε καθου εκ δεξιων μου εως αν θω τους εχθρους σου υποποδιον των ποδων σου * -WH agrees with LXX - "To which of the angels did he ever say, "Seat yourself at my right hand, until I place your enemies a footstool of your feet?"

Heb 1:13 προς τινα δε των αγγελων ειρηκεν ποτε καθου εκ δεξιων μου εως αν θω τους εχθρους σου υποποδιον των ποδων σου * (BYZ) agrees with LXX -"To which of the angels did he ever say, "Seat yourself at my right hand, until I place your enemies a footstool of your feet?"

1Co 15:25 (MUR) For he is to reign, until he shall place all his enemies under his feet. תחת רגלוהי הו גיר דנמלך עדמא דנסים בעלדבבוהי כלהון עתיד 1Co 15:25 (Peshitta)

1Co 15:25 (BYZ) δει γαρ αυτον βασιλευειν αχρις ου αν θη παντας τους εχθρους υπο τους ποδας αυτου * -"For He must reign until He places all enemies under His feet?"

1Co 15:25 (WH) δει γαρ αυτον βασιλευειν αχρις ου θη παντας τους εχθρους υπο τους ποδας αυτου *
* -"For He must reign until He places all enemies under His feet?"

Heb 10:13 (MUR) and thenceforth waited, until his foes should be placed as a footstool under his feet. עדמא דנתתסימון בעלדבבוהי כובשא תחת רגלוהי ומקוא מכיל Heb 10:13 (Peshitta)

Heb 10:13 (BYZ) το λοιπον εκδεχομενος εως τεθωσιν οι εχθροι αυτου υποποδιον των ποδων αυτου* agrees with LXX "as to the rest, expecting till He may place his enemies *as* his footstool of His feet."

Heb 10:13 (WH) το λοιπον εκδεχομενος εως τεθωσιν οι εχθροι αυτου υποποδιον των ποδων αυτου * agrees with LXX -"as to the rest, expecting till He may place his enemies *as* his footstool of His feet."

Of the seven quotes of Psalm 110:1 , The Peshitta disagrees with all the major Greek readings in four (Shaded grey) and agrees with them in 3 cases.. It also agrees with The Peshitta OT and The Hebrew OT in one of the cases and also with The LXX in that same place where The LXX and The Hebrew OT & Peshitta OT all agree. (Acts 2:35).

The Greek texts agree with The LXX in ten out of 15 (2 Greek texts) places.

This shows four things:

1. The Peshitta does not translate the Greek readings . In several cases, The Peshitta contains "**footstool under your feet**" where the Greek has a subset – "**footstool**" or "**under your feet**". In Mark 12:36 , The Critical Greek has "**under your feet**" and The Majority Greek has "**your footstool of your feet**". The Peshitta has "**your footstool under your feet.**"

2. The Greek conforms generally to The LXX (67% correlation).

3. The Peshitta NT quotes do not conform to any particular established OT text. It does not agree with The Hebrew OT or The Peshitta OT more than twice of the seven times Psalm 110:1 is quoted. That is only 28 % correlation.

4. The Greek readings are subsets of The Peshitta readings in 12/15- (80%) of the cases. In the other 20%, the Greek text conforms to The LXX. That means the Greek readings may be derived from The Aramaic , but not vice versa. For the Peshitta to have come from Greek, there would have had to be selective conflation (pasteing two different readings together to form a longer one), and editing among different Greek text types, with no particular rhyme or reason behind it; Often the Peshitta follows no particular Greek reading whatsoever (56% of the time). This is not a reasonable scenario for an Aramaic translation from Greek. All the data support a Greek translation from a Peshitta base.

44. If, therefore, David called him, 'my Lord', how is he his son?"

The following is a photo of the ancient Khabouris Peshitta Manuscript, which was copied from a fourth century manuscript no later than AD 360, according to the scribe 's notes.

I show this because the word order is different here from the 1905 edition used in this interlinear, and may explain the difference in the Greek readings of the verse. **The Khabouris (& the Eastern Peshitta) has** the word order:

If therefore David called Him my Lord, how his son is He?

The Western Peshitta mss. have, If therefore David my Lord called Him, how his son is He

The 4th century Greek ms. Vaticanus has "David therefore Him Lord calls, and how his son is He?" This is closer to the Eastern Peshitta than to the Western.

All other Greek mss. have: "David therefore Lord Him calls, and how son his is He?"

This is closer to the Western word order than to the Eastern. These facts lead me to believe that the Vaticanus manuscript is a translation of the Aramaic text according to the Eastern Peshitta and that the Majority Greek text is translated from the Western Peshitta text. There are very few differences between the two Peshittas, however, by which to compare the Greek texts, but the available data seem to support this conclusion.

Matthew 22 says twice that "David called Him (The Messiah) מריא –**Jehovah** " ; Luke and Mark say "David called Him , מרי – my Lord ". There is one letter difference between "**Jehovah** " & "my Lord " in

Aramaic: מריא & מרי . This may seem to be a contradiction in The Peshitta NT, however, the text of Matthew says that Our Lord was addressing the Pharisees directly and asking them for their views of The Messiah. Mark and Luke (in The Peshitta) have , "How do the Scribes say that The Messiah is David 's son ? The circumstances were different from the account of Matthew, and the approach with the Pharisees in Matthew was deeper and more expository and theological than with the common folk. With the Pharisees, He said twice that David calls The Messiah "**Jehovah**" – מריא (MarYah) , which is not based on His quotation of Psalm 110:1, but rather on a further examination of Psalm 110:5 in the first century text of the verse which was later revised by the Massoretes from **Jehovah** (or YAHWEH) in Hebrew to "Adonai" – "my Lord ". Why did the Massoretes do this ? Beats me, but they did this in 134 places in the Hebrew Bible and kept notes of the changes for every one of them in their Massorah (Scribal notes and alternate readings in the margins of manuscripts). The Peshitta Old Testament also retains the correct reading in this and all the other places where the reading was later changed in Hebrew mss. Psalm 110:5 says: "**Jehovah at Your right hand** shall defeat Kings in the day of His wrath. " If **Jehovah** is at the right hand of **Jehovah** then there are two **Jehovah** 's mentioned in this Psalm: God The Father and God The Son Messiah. If The Son is at the right hand of The Father, as verse one teaches, then The Father cannot be the One to Whom verse 5 refers as "YAHWEH" at your right hand". If The Son is at the right hand of The Father, The Father cannot be at the right hand of The Son; otherwise , we make nonsense of language and reason. My understanding of Hebrew exposition is that the first verse of a Psalm signifies the whole Psalm, when quoted. Quite often, the first verse of a Psalm is quoted in The NT, but the first verse is a title for entire Psalm, often as a song begins with the title words by which the song is known.

The Greek text of Matthew 22: 43-46 says basically the same as the Greek of Mark 12 & Luke concerning Psalm 110, because Greek usually uses the same word (Kurios-"Lord ") for the Aramaic MarYah (LORD JEHOVAH) as for the Aramaic Mari (Lord). **The Peshitta of Matthew 22:43-46 says twice that The Messiah is Jehovah (The Lord God) of The Hebrew people and of the whole creation.** This Aramaic Name "MarYah" occurs 239 times in The Peshitta NT. The Greek rarely makes a distinction between "Lord"(which may refer to God or man) and Jehovah "(which always refers to God).

45. And while all the people heard, he said to his disciples:

46. "Beware the Scribes who like to walk in robes and love greetings in the markets and first class seats in the synagogues and first class rooms at banquets.

47. They who consume widows houses for an offering* of making their long prayers; those shall receive an extreme judgment."

עלתא – "Elltha" can mean "pretext", "cause", "article", or "offering", "sacrifice". "Pretext" is not convincing, as most translations have it. Surely the Scribes would pray at the widows' homes and pray long prayers. It was not pretending that was the problem, it was charging widows for their prayers that was the problem. Are we to believe that it would have been acceptable if they had actually prayed long prayers in exchange for "**devouring widows' houses** " ?

Chapter 21

The Holy Gospel Preaching of Luke ✝ אונגליון קדישא כרוזותא דלוקא

1. **But** Yeshua gazed at the rich who were casting in their offerings to the treasury.
The Greek mss. lack the name "**Jesus**" in verse 1. **Old Syriac** agrees with Greek in the first verb "**looked up**" and having no "**Yeshua**"-"**Jesus**".

2. And he saw also a certain poor widow who cast in two shemonas.
שמונא (Shemona) is a **farthing** , which was a small copper coin worth 1/4th cent

3. And he said, "I tell you the reality, that this poor widow has cast in more than anyone.

4. For all of these have cast in whatever abundance they had into the place of God's offerings, but this one from her want has cast in everything that she owned."
The Critical Greek text lacks "**of God**" in v. 4, as does **Old Syria**.

5. And as people were talking about The Temple, that it was adorned with beautiful stones and with gifts, Yeshua* said to them:
            * "Jesus" is not in the Greek mss.

6. "Do you see these things? The days will come in which not one stone will be left standing upon another stone that shall not be pulled down."

7. And they were asking him and they were saying, "Teacher, when will these things occur, and what is the sign that these things are close to occurring?"

8. But he said to them, "Beware that you be not deceived, for many shall come in my name, and they shall say, 'I am God*, The Messiah', and the time is near, but do not go after them.

אנא אנא - "Ena na" is an Aramaic idiom used in The Old Testament Peshitta to translate Divine utterances: "I AM The LORD"; "I AM God"; "I AM the first and the last", etc. . 97% of the 146 occurrences of this expression I have examined in the OT refer to God; a few times it may refer to a mere human saying "I am...". I here translate it in the Divine sense, as it amounts to a claim of false Prophets to be The Messiah, Who is certainly Divine. The Greek mss. never convey this sense in the 46 places where it occurs in The Peshitta NT, as the Greek "ego eimi" never was an idiom meaning "I AM God". The Greek mss. also lack "The Messiah" in this verse, leaving merely the inane statement, "**Many shall come in My Name saying, I am.**" This they repeat in some other places in The Gospels, making a claim to Deity into a vague and meaningless statement in Greek. This is surely a defect in the Greek NT in several places such as : "**If you believe not that I am, you shall die in your sins.**"-Jn. 8:24. It is a deficiency in those 24 other "**I AM**" statements of Our Lord in John, such as "**I am the bread of life.**" The Peshitta has "Ena na" in those places, meaning "I AM the Living God". John 6:51 then reads: "**I am The Living God, the bread of life**, who have come down from heaven: and if a man shall eat of this bread, he will live for ever. And the bread which I shall give, is my body, which I give for the life of the world.**"

9. And whenever you hear wars and commotions, do not be afraid, for these things are going to happen first, but the end will not have yet arrived.

10. For nation shall arise against nation and Kingdom against Kingdom.

11. Great earthquakes shall be in various places, and there shall be famines and plagues and panics and terror, and great signs from the sky shall appear and there shall be great storms.
"**And there shall be great storms**" is entirely missing from all Greek texts (except one very late miniscule ms. that has "**and storms**".
   Did an Aramaean translator invent this phrase and add it to a translation of Greek , or did a Greek translator simply miss it in his translation from The   Peshitta? Reason will dictate that the latter is far more likely than the former.

12. But before all these things they will lay hands on you and they shall persecute you and they shall deliver you to councils and prisons, and they shall bring you before Kings and Governors because of my name*.

מטל שמי -"**Metul Shemi**" ("**because of My Name**") is * such an important phrase, repeated in v. 17 & elsewhere as the cause of all the controversy and persecution against the church. What is His Name and why all the persecution ? His Name, according to The Peshitta, which every believer must confess and to Which each was baptized is, מריא ישוע משיחא " (**MarYah Yeshua Meshikha**) -"**The LORD God Yeshua The Messiah**" . Paul would later write: "**No one can say Yeshua is Jehovah (LORD God) except by the Holy Spirit.**" Whoever does not believe He is **Jehovah** God does not believe in Him. Whoever has not confessed with his mouth "**The LORD God Yeshua**" should do so. The Holy Spirit alone can bring this home to the heart and soul and compel the mouth to confess it, as He did to Peter. Some day. "**Every knee shall bow and every tongue shall confess** that **Yeshua Meshikha is MarYah (The LORD GOD)** , to the glory of God The Father.**" –Phillip. 2:11

13. But it will happen to you for a testimony.

14. But settle in your hearts that you will not be taught to give an answer.

15. For I will give you a mouth and wisdom which all your enemies will not be able to withstand.

*The majority of Greek mss. have "**all your opposers shall not be able to refute nor resist**". The Critical Greek text has "**all your opposers shall not be able to resist nor refute**", with the last two verbs switched. In all major Greek texts, two verbs are used instead of the Peshitta's one. See how The Peshitta text accounts for this: למקם - l'maqum" can mean "**to stand**" or "**to oppose**" ; the next Aramaic word לקובלה -"l'qublah", means "**against it**", however it looks very much like לקבולה "l'qabulah", which means "**to impeach it**" or "**to accuse it**". The Greek translator appears to have mistaken the Aramaic לקבולה for לקובלה. The fact that למקם - "l'maqum" can mean "**to stand**" or "**to oppose**" doubles the likelihood that the Greek readings with these two verbs — "**to refute or resist**" are based on the Aramaic Peshitta text. The Critical Greek agrees better with The Peshitta word order, given the error in translation. למקם - "l'maqum"-(to oppose) would answer to the Greek word, "αντιστηναι" "antistaynai" -(to resist) and לקבולה "l'qabulah", which*

means "*to impeach it*", answers to the Greek "αντειπειν" - "*anteipein*", which means "*to refute*". One Greek ms. (*D*) 6th century has only the verb αντιστηναι – "*to resist*", which agrees well with The Peshitta. **Codex D** often does agree more closely (though by no means consistently) with *The Peshitta* than do the major Greek texts. *D* also has numerous strange, independent and unique readings. All these Greek texts are thus demonstrated to be probable translations of *The Peshitta* in this verse. *Old Syriac* agrees with The Peshitta reading
לקובלה – "*l'qublah*", means "*against it*"
לקבולה "*l'qabulah*", means "*to accuse it*"

16. But your parents and your brothers and your relatives and your friends shall deliver you over, and they shall put some of you to death.

The Majority Greek text has a different word order than The Peshitta: "**your parents, relatives friends & brothers.** The Critical Greek text agrees with The Peshitta. **Old Syriac** has "**your brothers, your parents, your relatives, your friends**".

17. And you shall be hated by every man, because of my name.
18. A hair of your heads shall not be lost.
19. But by your perseverance you shall possess your souls.
20. But whenever you will see Jerusalem being surrounded by armies, know then that its destruction has come near to it.
21. And let those who are in Judea flee to the mountains, and those who are within it escape, and those in the villages, let them not enter into it.
22. These are the days of vengeance, to fulfill everything whatsoever that has been written.
23. But woe to those who are pregnant and those who nurse in those days, for there shall be great suffering in the land and wrath upon this people.
24. And they shall fall by the mouth of the sword and they shall be led captive to every region, and Jerusalem shall be trodden down by the Gentiles until the time of the Gentiles will be finished.

"The mouth of the sword" is a Semitic idiom found in Hebrew and Aramaic, referring to "The edge of the sword".

25. And there shall be signs in the sun and in the moon and in the stars and in the earth, suffering of nations and clasping of hands*, from the alarm of the sound of the sea,

The Greek is quite different; I cannot see how The Peshitta obtained the phrase "**clasping of hands**" from Greek mss. No Greek ms. has the phrase ; Greek has the word "**aporia**" – "**perplexity**". Why in the name of Sam Hill would a translator add such a phrase ? The Aramaic phrase פושך אידיא "clasping of hands" is doubtless an idiom referring to perplexity. If the Greek were to be translated into Aramaic, the word פושך would do it. Of course, I do not accept the notion that The Peshitta writers were translating anything; The Greek text is translated from The Peshitta. An original text should

have more such idioms than a translation would. The translator would tend to simplify them and render a text that is simpler than the base text and simpler than an original text in the translation language. The Greek NT has all the earmarks of a **translation Greek** contained in The LXX translation of **The Hebrew Bible**. It employs Semitic word order of **Verb-Subject-Object** far more often than Greek normally does. I owe this observation to native Aramaean , Paul Younan, web host of Peshitta.org, and others who have posted this with many examples on their web sites.

26. And an earthquake* which drives out the souls of the children of men by the terror of whatever is going to come on the earth, and the hosts of the Heavens shall be shaken.
An earthquake " is wanting in Greek mss. " Would a translator add this to the text? I think not; That a Greek translator simply dropped it is much easier to believe and support.

27. And then they shall see The Son of Man, who comes in clouds with many mighty works and great praises.
I love the Aramaic language! "עננא – "Enanna" (Clouds) , חילא – "Khayla"- (strength,power,miracle,army,mighty works, host,possibility) & שובחא – "Shoobkha " (glory,praise,honor,hymn,tenet,opinion) have such rich possibilities of meaning and application. **Clouds** often signify trouble and turbulence, confusion and despair. "Khayla " is strength and the miraculous we find all around us every day if we look and consider; "Shoobkha " is the highest and noblest, most sublime reality and concept conceivable to the mind, whether to man , angel or God Himself. The Deity would comprise that glory. Wherever there is despair or sorrow, strength or possibility, honor or praise, The Son of Man is revealed and present, for these all come from Him and bring us eventually to Him.
He sends "Enanna" – (Clouds) to teach us to pray and look up in hope for the Sun
then he gives us of His "Khayla"(Strength & Miracle) in answer to our prayer
and in response, we give Him "Shoobkha" (Glory and Praise) for all His mighty works and blessings to us
: And with each of these three gifts
Enana, Khayla & Shoobkha
The Son of Man comes to us
It has always been so, and shall be so always
. He never changes
"Behold, I come quickly"

28. But whenever these things begin to happen, take heart and lift up your heads, because your salvation draws near."
29. And he told them the parable: "Behold the fig tree and all of the trees.
30. When they bud, at once you understand by them that summer approaches.
31. Thus also whenever you see these things occurring, know that the Kingdom of God is near.
32. Amen, I say to you, this generation shall not pass until all of these things shall come to pass.

"**Generation**" means "**generation**"; "**This**" means "**this**". Our Lord was not speaking of a future generation. Futurists need to go back to the words of The Son of God and rethink their prophecy schemes. His words in Luke 21 and Matthew 24 have been fulfilled through The Holy Spirit , The Gospel proclamation and advent of Messiah to every heart and land where he was received, and judgment to those who rejected Him.

33. Heaven and Earth shall pass away and my words shall not pass away.

34. But beware in your souls that your hearts never grow cold with gluttony and with drunkenness and with the cares of the world, and suddenly that day shall come upon you.

35. For it shall spring like a trap upon all of those who dwell upon the face of all the earth.

36. Be watching at all times, therefore, and praying that you will be worthy to escape from these things which are going to occur, and to stand before The Son of Man."

37. And by day he was teaching in The Temple and by night he went out, spending the night in the mount which is called 'Bayth Zaytha'. (Bayth Zaytha means, "Place of Olives")

38. And all the people were coming early to him to The Temple to hear his word.

Chapter 22

1. Now The Feast of Unleavened Bread was nearing, which is called Passover.

The Greek mss. for "**Passover**" have "**Pascha**"(See v. 13 also). Here is Strong's Dictionary entry for the Greek word: 3957 πασχα pascha pas'-khah : of **Aramaic** origin, cf 06453 פסח; TDNT-5:896,797; n n
AV-Passover 28, Easter 1; 29 .
This Aramaic word occurs 29 times in the Greek NT, in The Gospels, Acts, I Corinthians and Hebrews. The Greek πασχα-"Pascha" is an exact transliteration , letter for letter, of the Aramaic word פצחא - "Pascha".

2. And the Chief Priests and Scribes were seeking how they would kill him, but they were afraid of the people.

3. But Satan had entered Yehuda, who is called Skariota, he who had been of the number of the twelve.

The English word "**Satan**" comes from **Aramaic-** סטנא - "Satana" , as does the Greek word σατανας "Satanas".**Strong's Greek –English Dictionary** has : 4567 σατανας , Satanas, sat-an-as' of **Aramaic** origin corresponding to 4566 (with the definite affix); TDNT-7:151,1007; n pr m
AV-Satan 36; 36
1) **adversary** (one who opposes another in purpose or act), the name given to
1a) **the prince of evil spirits**, the inveterate adversary of God and Christ
1b) a Satan-like man
Again, the Greek testifies to an Aramaic original. Σατανας-"Satanas" , was not used in Greek writing anywhere but in The Greek NT. & Σαταν – "Satan" in one verse of The LXX

(1 Kings 11:14), which is translated from the Hebrew שטן "Satan".

4. And he went and spoke with the Chief Priests and the Scribes and the Commanders of the forces of The Temple so as to deliver him to them.

All major Greek texts lack "**& The Scribes**", & "**of the temple**". Codex C (5th century) & Codex N (6th cent.) have και γραμματευσιν -"**kai grammateusin**"-(**& Scribes**). Codex D (6th cent.) lacks "στρατηγοις"-"**Military commanders**".

5. And they rejoiced and they promised to give him money.

6. And he made an agreement with them and he was seeking occasion to deliver him to them apart from a gathering.

7. The Day of Unleavened Bread arrived in which it was the custom for the Passover lamb to be slain.

8. And Yeshua sent Yohannan and Kaypha and he said to them, "Go prepare for us to eat the Passover."

Greek mss. have "Πετρος"- "**Petros**"(Peter) where The Peshitta has "**Kaypha**". According to the Greek mss. of John 1:42, Πετρος ("Peter") is a Greek translation of "Kaypha": κηφας ο ερμηνευεται πετρος-"Cephas -(Aramaic) , which is to be translated, Peter- (Greek)". So it is then in the some 162 places where Πετρος occurs in The Greek NT. And if the name is a translation in those 162 places, is not the rest of the text also a translation of an Aramaic original? How about the name of **The Messiah**, as written in Greek mss. of John 1:41: τον μεσσιαν (Aramaic) ο εστιν μεθερμηνευομενον ο χριστος (Greek) - "the Messias (Aramaic), which is, being translated, the Christ (Greek)". "Christos" is here declared to be a translation of the Aramaic word "Messiah". Cephas called Yeshua "The Messiah", not "Christos". The original is "Messiah"; "Christos" is the Greek translation , and it occurs 569 times in the NT. Is this not tantamount to declaring 569 times that the Greek NT is a translation of an Aramaic original? 569 + 162 = 731 times, for Peter + Christ. That should tip off the reader that The Greek NT is a translation, not the original.

9. But they said to him, "Where do you want us to prepare it?"

10. He said to them, "Behold, when you enter the city, you shall meet a man who bears a jug of water; go after him.

11. And wherever he enters, say to the owner of the house, "Our Rabbi says, 'Is there a place of dwelling where I may eat Passover with my disciples?'

12. And behold, he shall show you a great furnished upper room; prepare there."

13. And they went and found as he had told them, and they prepared the Passover.

14. And when it was time, Yeshua came and reclined and the twelve Apostles with him.

15. And he said to them, "I have greatly desired to eat this Passover with you before I suffer.

16. For I say to you, from now on, I shall not eat it until it shall be fulfilled in the Kingdom of God."

17. And he took a cup, and he gave thanks and he said, "Take this and divide it among yourselves.

Verses 17 and 18 are not found in The Peshitta manuscripts but in some other 5th century Aramaic manuscripts called "The Palestinian Syriac". All Greek mss. and other ancient versions have these verses.

18. I say to you that I shall not drink from the fruit of the vine until the Kingdom of God shall come."

19. He took bread and he gave thanks, he broke and he gave to them and he said, "This is my body, which shall be given for the sake of your persons. You shall be doing this to commemorate me."

20. And thus also concerning the cup after they had dined, he said, "This cup is the new covenant in my blood, which shall be shed in your stead.

21. However, behold; the hand of him who shall betray me is on the table.

22. The Son of Man goes just as it was appointed, yet woe to that man by whose hand he shall be betrayed!"

23. And they began to inquire among themselves which one of them it was indeed who was going to commit this.

24. But there was also a dispute among them, of who among them was great.

25. Then Yeshua said to them, "The Kings of the nations are their lords and they who rule over them are called Benefactors.

26. But you are not so, for whoever is great among you shall be as the little man, and whoever is chief shall be like a waiter.

27. For who is greater: he who sits or he who is a waiter? Is it not he who sits? But I am among you as he who is a waiter.

28. But you are those who have remained with me in my trials.

29. And I am promising you a Kingdom as my Father promised me.

30. For you shall eat and you shall drink at the table of my Kingdom, and you shall sit on thrones, and you shall judge the twelve tribes of Israel."

31. And Yeshua said to Shimeon, "Shimeon, behold, Satan has requested that he may sift you all like wheat,"

32. And I have prayed for you that your faith will not fail, and when you are restored, confirm your brothers."

33. But Shimeon said to him, "My Lord, I am ready for prison and for death with you."

34. Yeshua said to him, "I say to you, Shimeon, that a rooster shall not crow today until you shall deny three times that you know me."

35. And he said to them, "When I sent you without a money bag and without wallet and shoes, did you lack anything? And they were saying to him, "Nothing!"

36. He said to them, "From this hour, whoever has a money bag should take it and thus also a wallet, and whoever lacks a sword, let him sell his tunic and buy a sword for himself.

37. For I say to you, that this also that is written must be fulfilled in me, 'He was numbered with the evil doers', for all that concerns me shall be fulfilled."

38. And they were saying to him, 'Our Lord, behold, here are two swords.' He said to them, 'They are enough.'

39. And he went out, and he went on as he was accustomed to the Mount Bayth Zaytha, and his disciples also went after him.

Bayth-Zytha" is usually paralleled in Greek by "ελαιων" " – "elaiown" ("Olives), which is a partial translation of the Aramaic name, which means, "Place of Olives ". In John 5:2, The Critical Westcott & Hort text has βηθζαθα, "Baythzatha " which is a transliteration of the same Aramaic name "Bayth-Zytha". Whoever wrote The Peshitta knew the Aramaic names of the villages (& hills) in first century Israel. The Greek sometimes translates names, giving their meanings, which is evidence that the Greek not only is not original, but the writer may not have been familiar with those places. It would be akin to writing "Teaching of Peace" for "Jerusalem ". No one living in Israel would call **Jerusalem** , "Teaching of Peace", even in a translation. <u>An original text in the original language of the country would have the original names of the towns and people of that country in the same language and forms familiar to the people who lived there. These The Greek NT does not have; The Peshitta NT does.</u> If the Peshitta were translated centuries later in Syria or a country other than Israel, as is commonly supposed, how would the translator have gotten all the Semitic names of villages , coins and people in first century Israel where the Greek did not have them?

The Greek coins λεπτον ("Leptov") & κοδραντης ("Kodrantays") are Greek equivalent names, not the Jewish terms for the Roman coins, "Mina" & "Shimona ". In fact, The Greek NT has two different translations for the Jewish "Mina": λεπτον ("Leptov") & Μνα ("Mna"), the latter being a transliterated form of the Aramaic word מנא , " Mina ", while the former is a translation equivalent in Greek currency.

40. And when he arrived at the place, he said to them, "Pray, lest you enter temptation."

41. And he withdrew from them about a stone's throw and he bowed his knees and he prayed.

42. And he said, "Father, if you are willing, let this cup pass from me; however not my will, but yours be done."

43. And an Angel appeared to him from Heaven, who strengthened him.

44. And as he was in fear, he prayed urgently, and his sweat was like drops of blood, and he fell upon the ground.

Several old Greek mss. omit verses 43 & 44, including (A,B 4th cent.), P75- (3rd cent.) and also **The Sinaitic Old Syriac ms.** (5th cent.). Several old Greek mss. and Versions contain them, as well as church fathers: (ℵ,D, **Itala 4th cent, Vulgate 4th cent, Old Syriac Curetonian (5th cent.), Armenian 5th cent. , Justin & Irenaeus (both 2nd cent.), Hippolytus & Dionysius (Both 3rd cent.).**

45. And he arose from his prayer and he came to his disciples and found them sleeping from the anguish.

46. And he said to them, "Why are you sleeping? Arise; pray, lest you enter temptation."

47. And while he was speaking, behold, a crowd and he who is called Yehuda, one of the twelve, came. He went before them, and he came to Yeshua and he kissed him, for he had given a sign to them: "Whomever I kiss is the one."

48. Yeshua said to him, "Yehuda, do you betray The Son of Man with a kiss?"

49. But when those who were with him saw what happened, they were saying to him, "Our Lord, shall we strike them with swords?"

50. And one of them struck the servant of The High Priest and took off his right ear.

51. Then Yeshua answered and he said, "Enough for now." And he touched the ear of him who was wounded, and he healed him.

52. And Yeshua said to those Chief Priests and Elders and Commanders of the army of The Temple, who had come upon him, "Have you come out for me as for a robber, with swords and with clubs to seize me?

53. I was with you every day in The Temple and you did not stretch forth your hands against me, but this is your hour and of the Prince of Darkness."

54. And they seized him and brought him to the house of The High Priest, and Shimeon was coming after him from a distance.

55. But they kindled a fire in the midst of the courtyard and they were sitting around it and Shimeon was also sitting among them.

56. And a certain Maidservant saw him as he sat at the fire and she stared at him and she said, "This man also was with him."

57. But he denied it and he said, "Woman, I do not know him."

58. After a little while another saw him and he said to him, "You also are one of them." ,but Kaypha said, "I am not."

59. And after an hour another was disputing and he said, "Surely this man also was with him, for he is also a Galilean."

60. Kaypha said, "Man, I do not know what you are saying", and at once, while he was speaking, a rooster crowed.

61. And Yeshua turned and he gazed at Kaypha, and Shimeon remembered the saying of Our Lord that he had told him: "Before a rooster shall crow, you shall deny me three times."

62. And Shimeon went outside and wept bitterly.

63. And the men who were holding Yeshua were mocking him, and they were covering him

64. And striking him on his face, and they were saying, "Prophesy, who is hitting you?"

65. And they were uttering many other blasphemies and they were speaking against him.

66. And when day had dawned, the Elders and the Chief Priests and the Scribes were gathered together and they brought him to the place of their assembly.

67. And they were saying to him, "If you are The Messiah, tell us." He said to them, "If I tell you, you will not believe me.

68. And if I will ask you, you will not give me an answer, neither will you release me.

69. Henceforth The Son of Man will be sitting at the right hand of the power of God."

70. But all of them were saying, "You are therefore the Son of God?" Yeshua said to them, "You are saying that I AM THE LIVING GOD."

71. And they were saying, "Why do we need witnesses again, for we hear from his *own* mouth?"

Chapter 23

1. And their whole gathering arose and brought him to Pilate.

2. And they began slandering him and they were saying, "We found this one seducing our people and he forbids giving head tax to Caesar, and he has said about himself that he is The King Messiah."

3. Then Pilate asked him and he said to him, "You are The King of the Judeans?" He said to him, "You have said."

4. And Pilate said to the Chief Priests and to the crowd, "I find no fault concerning this man."

5. But they were shouting and saying, "He has stirred up our people and he taught in all Judea and began from Galilee even unto here."

6. But when Pilate heard the name of Galilee, he asked if the man were a Galilean.

7. And when he knew that he was under the authority of Herodus, he sent him to the presence of Herodus, because he was in Jerusalem in those days.

8. Now when Herodus saw Yeshua, he was very glad, for he had wanted to see him for a long time, because he had heard many things about him and he had hoped to see some sign from him.

9. And he was asking him of many matters but Yeshua gave him no answer.

"Yeshua" – "Jesus" absent in Greek mss

10. But the Chief Priests and the Scribes were standing and were vehemently accusing him.

11. But Herodus and his servants mocked him, and when he had insulted him, he clothed him with a purple robe and he sent him to Pilate.

12. And on that day, Pilate and Herodus became friends with each other, because there had been hostility between them before that.

13. Then Pilate called the Chief Priests and the Rulers of the people,

14. And he said to them, "You brought me this man as subverting your people, and behold I have examined him in your sight, and I find no fault in this man in anything of which you are accusing him;

15. Neither has Herodus, for I sent him to him, and nothing worthy of death has been committed by him.

The Majority Greek has "**for I sent you to him**". The Critical Greek has "**for he sent him to us**". How did the Peshitta get "**for I sent Him to him**" from either Greek reading? But I will show how the Greek texts may have gotten their readings from the Aramaic:

שדרתכון גיר לותה is "For I sent you to him."

שדרתה גיר לותה is " I sent Him to him"(Actual Peshitta reading)

שדרה גיר לותן is "For he sent Him to us". Compare גיר; שדרתכון & שדרתגיר & שדרתה; the first (black letters) is the Peshitta reading , "for I sent Him"; the second is the same with one letter missing and the next word (Gir) pushed into the first; The third reading is "I sent you". This misreading of "Gir" as "Kown" is a hypothetical explanation for the Greek readings. **In the square Aramaic of Dead Sea Scroll script, a - Yodh and Waw can be easily confused** Yodh and Waw. In regular Hebrew-Aramaic they are י ,ו . - ^ , ן .Waw is simply longer on the down stroke גיר "Gir"- "For") & כון- ("-kown"- "you") are composed of letters which differ basically in the length of their respective strokes , and could be misconstrued if carelessly read or written. That is what I believe happened with the Majority Greek translation. The Critical Greek can be more easily explained:

שדרתה גיר לותה became שדרה גיר לותן by dropping a letter (ת) & misreading another letter ה for ן. ן is called a final Nun, the form of Nun (נ) at the end of a word. **The difference between the two Greek readings is twenty one Greek letters; the difference between those two readings in the Aramaic language would be six Aramaic letters;(These 1 highlight in red below).** So it would be much easier to account for both Greek readings on the basis of an Aramaic base, than vice-versa. Besides, the Peshitta reading cannot have come from Greek; **no Greek text has the Peshitta reading!**

I	sent	for	you	to	him

Majority Greek: ανεπεμψα γαρ υμας προς αυτον

He	sent	for	him	to	us

Critical Greek: ανεπεμψεν γαρ αυτον προς ημας

Aramaic Base Readings:

Original Peshitta	Majority Greek reading	Critical Greek
to him for I sent Him	to him for I sent you:	to us for he sent Him

שדרה גיר לותן : שדרתכון גיר לותה :שדרתה גיר לותה

The Greek readings in Aramaic have 58% and 78% letter correlation with the Peshitta Aramaic reading of one or two pertinent words. The Critical and Peshitta readings in Greek have 0% & 0% correlation with the Majority Greek reading of the two pertinent words involved. That means it is highly unlikely any Greek reading was translated into the Peshitta reading; rather it is much more likely the reverse happened.

Dead Sea Scroll Aramaic Script

"You"– Heb.-כון-DSS- גןכ "For"–Heb.-גיר– DSS-ריג"

If it be objected that The Peshitta was compiled by editing and translating both major Greek traditions, I respond that over 50% of the time it differs from one Greek text, it differs from both of them with readings unique and unknown even among The Latin Vulgate mss.. Besides, what translator would be editing and collating mss. on the fly as he is translating those mss.? He wants a single straightforward document in front of him to translate- not that I would grant for a minute that The Peshitta is a translation of Greek, or of anything else, for that matter. It is too plain a document and uncluttered with variant readings , too full of Aramaic idioms , Aramaic syntax and sentence structure for that to be the case. Greek mss. on the other hand, are too full of variant readings, alternate synonyms of corresponding Aramaic words, transliterations of Aramaic in hundreds of places, translational statements declared as such from Aramaic, Aramaic sentence structure as opposed to Greek (very similar to The LXX) and very low lexical density as compared to original Greek compositions (Greek NT compares very well to LXX LD), for the Greek to be anything but a translation of an Aramaic document. The Peshitta has a Lexical Density (ratio of vocab. words to total word number) almost identical to The Hebrew Old Testament / See my articles titled

"**Computerized Primacy Test**" and "**Wisdom of Solomon**" for detailed computer analysis of these data I have compiled.

16. Therefore I shall discipline him and release him."

17. For it was a custom to release them one prisoner at the feast.

18. But the entire mob shouted, and they were saying, "Take this one away and release us Barabba",

19. Who, because of a sedition and murder that had occurred in that city, had been cast into prison.

20. Pilate spoke with them again as he wanted to release Yeshua.

21. They were shouting and saying, "Crucify him! Crucify him!"

22. The third time, he said to them, "What evil has this one done? I have not found any fault in him that deserves death. I shall chastise him, therefore, and I shall release him."

23. But they were urging him in a loud voice and demanding that they would crucify him, and their voice prevailed, and that of the Chief Priests.

The Critical Greek & Latin Vulgate omit "**& that of the Chief Priests**". The Majority Greek text contains it. The **Old Syriac** also contains the phrase.

24. And Pilate commanded that their demand should be performed.

25. And he released to them him who had been cast into prison for sedition and murder, whom they had demanded, but he delivered Yeshua to their pleasure.

26. And as they brought him, they seized Shimeon a Cyrenian who came from a village and they laid upon him the cross to carry after Yeshua.

27. And a multitude of people came after him and those women who were lamenting and howling over him.

28. And Yeshua turned to them, and he said, "Daughters of Jerusalem, do not weep for me, but weep for yourselves and for your children.

29. For the days are coming in which they shall say, 'Blessed are the barren and the wombs that have not borne, and the breasts that did not nurse.'

30. And you shall begin to say to the mountains, 'Fall upon us', and to the hills, 'Cover us.'

31. For if they are doing these things with green wood, what will happen with the dried?"

32. And there were two others coming with him, evildoers to be killed.

The Majority Greek: ηγοντο δε και ετεροι δυο κακουργοι συν αυτω αναιρεθηναι –" **And there were also others—two evil-doers—with him, to be put to death**".- **(Young's Literal Translation)**.

The Critical Greek : ηγοντο δε και ετεροι κακουργοι δυο συν αυτω αναιρεθηναι– " **And there were being led, two other evil-doers also, to be lifted up.** "- (Rotherham)

The Latin Vulgate : ducebantur autem et alii duo nequam cum eo ut interficerentur. "**And there were also two other malefactors led with him to be put to death.**" (Douay)

Old Syriac : "And there were coming with Him two evil doers to be killed". Hello ? According to the Critical Greek Text and The Latin Vulgate, The Messiah was an evil doer like the two robbers crucified with Him! How can anyone who has sincere faith in Messiah countenance such blasphemies in supposedly

inspired Bible texts?
The Peshitta and the Majority Greek agree here in the general wording that " **there were with Him two others- evil doers** ", not "**two other evil doers**". There is a world of difference, an infinite and eternal difference between those two statements.

33. And when they came to a certain place called Qarqpatha (The Skull), they crucified him there and those evildoers, one at his right, and one at his left.

34. But Yeshua was saying, "Father, forgive them, for they know not what they do." And they divided his garments, and they cast lots for them.

Greek mss. (**P75, B, D, W, Θ**) & Old Syriac Sinaiticus <u>omit</u> "**Father forgive them, for they know not what they do.** " I ask the reader: Can such witnesses as these be trusted to testify truly to the very words of God Himself when they omit and distort the plainly inspired utterances of our Savior and **LORD** such as this one? If these words be not inspired of The Holy Spirit, what is? Fortunately, most manuscripts and versions contain this most holy and sublime utterance of Our Lord from the cross. **May God forgive textual critics who edit the words of God, for they know not what they do!**

35. But the people were standing and watching and the leaders were mocking him and they were saying, "He gave life to others; let him save himself if he is The Messiah, The Chosen One of God."

36. And the soldiers were also scoffing at him as they came near to him and they were offering him vinegar.

37. And they were saying to him, "If you are The King of the Judeans, save yourself."

Old Syriac adds , "**And they placed a crown of thorns on His head**"!!!???

38. And there was an inscription that was written over him in Greek and in Latin and in Aramaic: "This is The King of the Judeans."

Vaticanus and other Alexandrian Greek mss. omit "**written in Greek , Latin and Aramaic**".

39. But one of those evildoers who were crucified with him was blaspheming him and

he said, "If you are The Messiah, save yourself and save us also."

40.   And his companion rebuked him and he said to him, "Are you not even afraid of God? For you also are in condemnation with him.

41. And we justly so, because we are worthy, for we are repaid according to what we have done, but nothing evil has been done by this one."

42. And he said to Yeshua, "My Lord, remember me when you come into your Kingdom."

The Critical Greek omits "**My Lord**". The Majority Greek has, "**Lord**.

43. But Yeshua said to him, "Amen, I say to you that today you shall be with me in Paradise."

44.   But it was about the sixth hour and there was darkness upon all the earth until the ninth hour.

45. And the sun grew dark, and the curtain of The Temple was ripped apart from its middle.

46.   And Yeshua called out in a loud voice and he said, "My Father, into your hands I lay down my spirit." He said this and he expired.

47. When the Centurion saw what had happened, he glorified God and he said, "Truly this man was The Righteous One."

48. And all the crowds which had gathered for this spectacle, when they saw what had happened, returned while smiting on their chests.

49. And all the acquaintances of Yeshua and those women who had come with him from Galilee were standing afar off and they were beholding these things.

50. A certain man whose name was Yoseph, a Sanhedrin member from Ramtha, a city of Judea, was a good man and just.

4. And it happened that while these wondered at this, behold, two men stood above them and their clothing was shining.

5. And they were in fear and they bowed their faces to the ground, and they were saying to them, "Why are you seeking The Life among the dead?

6. He is not here; he is risen. Remember when he spoke with you as he was in Galilee,

7. And he said, 'The Son of Man is going to be delivered into the hands of sinful men, and he shall be crucified, and the third day he shall arise?'"

8. And these remembered his words.

The Greek texts put "**from Ramatha a city of Judea**" in the next verse.

51. This one had not consented to their decision and to their action, and he was waiting for the Kingdom of God.

Greek has "**(The same had not consented to their counsel and doings), from Arimathaea, a city of the Jews, & he waited for the Kingdom of God**", which is a bit awkward, to say the least.
Old Syriac adds, "**This man was one who did not take part with the mind of The Devil.**"

52. This man came to Pilate, and he asked for the body of Yeshua.

53. And he took it down and wrapped it in a winding sheet of linen, and he placed it in a cut out tomb in which no one had yet been placed.

54. The day was Friday and the Sabbath was beginning.

55. But these women who came with him from Galilee were approaching and they saw the tomb and how his body had been laid.

56. And they returned, and prepared sweet spices and ointment, and on the Sabbath they rested according to that which had been commanded.

Chapter 24

1. But on Sunday morning, while it was dark, they came to the tomb and they brought the spices that they had prepared, and there were other women with them.

The Critical Greek text lacks "**& there were other women with them**"; The Majority Greek has "**& some with them**".

2. And they found the stone which had been rolled from the tomb.

3. And they entered and they did not find the body of Yeshua.

9. And they returned from the tomb and they were telling all these things to the eleven and to the rest.

10. And they were Maryam Magdalitha and Johanna and Maryam the mother of Yaqob, and the rest who were with them, who told these things to the Apostles.

11. And these words appeared as insanity in their eyes and they did not believe them.

12. But Shimeon arose and he ran to the tomb, and beholding, he saw the linen that was placed by itself and he left wondering in his soul over what had happened.

Greek mss. have "**Petros**"-"Peter" for "**Shimeon**"; but we know from Greek mss. of John 1:42 that "**Petros**" is a translation of the apostle's Aramaic name "**Shimeon Kaypha**" (See Matthew 4:18 & 10:2, Jn. 1:44) ; "**Petros**" is not his name; it is a translation of his name. "The Greek, "**Christos**"-("**Christ**") also is a translation of "**Meshikha**", according to the Greek mss. of John 1:41. Does that not support the premise that the Greek text is a translation and that the original was Aramaic ? The Greek NT does not support the idea that the Jews of Israel were bilingual in Aramaic and Greek. John uses the phrase several times: **(Aramaic term)** " is translated " as **(Greek term)**. It does not say, "**You shall be called Kaypha and Petros**". If they were bilingual in Aramaic and Greek, everyone would have had an Aramaic name and a Greek name. It says, "**You shall be called, Kaypha, <u>which is translated</u> Petros**." This formula , used several times in John, gives away the Greek text as a translation of an Aramaic original. Our Lord was not named "Ιησους"-"**Iaysous**"- translated "**Jesus**". His name was not Greek, it was the Aramaic ישוע-"**Yeshua**"(Perhaps pronounced "**Yayshu**" in first century Israel). Practically no one had a Greek name in Israel, according to the Greek NT. That would not be so if Greek were a second language there.

13. And behold, two of them that day were going to the village whose name is Emmaus, and it is sixty furlongs from Jerusalem.

A furlong is 1/8th mile. Emmaus was 7.5 miles from Jerusalem.

14. And they were speaking with one another about all these things that had occurred.
15. And while they were talking and inquiring one with another, Yeshua came and he met them and he was walking with them.
16. And their eyes had been held shut lest they would recognize him.
17. And he said to them, "What are these matters of which you speak, one with another, as you are walking and are gloomy?"
18. One of them answered, whose name was Cleopa, and he said to him, "Are you indeed a foreigner by yourself in Jerusalem that you do not know the thing that has occurred in it in these days?"
19. He said to them, "What thing?" They were saying to him, "Concerning Yeshua, who was from Nazareth, a man who was The Prophet mighty in word and in deed before God, and before the whole nation.
20. And the Chief Priests and the Elders delivered him to the sentence of death, and they crucified him.

ܥܩܝܕ - "**iqid**" instead of ܝܩܝܪ - "**yaqqir**", (assuming the later Estrangela script used in the second century and onward) , though it is much less likely than an error in reading the square Aramaic יקיר as יקיד -(ד & ר are easily confused one for another , whereas the Estrangela **Dalet** - ܕ & **Resh**-ܪ are carefully distinguished by their dots within or above) , or a scribe may have mistaken ܥܩܝܕ - "**iqid**" in an original Peshitta translation manuscript of Luke and have written ܝܩܝܪ - "**yaqqir**", and no one after him copied the original , only the

21. But we had been hoping that he was going to deliver Israel and behold, it is the third day now, since all these things occurred.
22. But also women among us stupefied us, for they had gone first to the tomb.
23. And when they did not find his body, they came and they were telling us, 'We saw Angels there', and they were saying of him, 'He is alive.'
24. Also, some from us went to the tomb and they found according to what the women said, but they did not see him."
25. Then Yeshua said to them, "Oh deficient of mind and slow of heart to believe in all the things that The Prophets have spoken!
26. Was it not necessary for The Messiah to endure these things and to enter into his glory?"
27. And he began from Moses and from all The Prophets and he expounded to them about himself from all of the scriptures.
28. And they arrived at that village to which they were going, and he was announcing to them how he was going to a distant place.
29. And they constrained him and they were saying to him, "Stay with us, because the day is declining *and* it is becoming dark", and he entered to stay with them.
30. And it happened that when he reclined with them, he took bread and he blessed, and he broke and he gave to them.
31. At once their eyes were opened and they recognized him and he ascended from them.
32. And they were saying one to another, "Was not our heart dull* within us when he was speaking with us on the road and expounding to us the scriptures?"
*

All Greek manuscripts have, "Did not our hearts **burn** within us?"
  Here is "dull" in Aramaic: יקיר
  Here is "**burn**" in Aramaic:יקיד . Hard to tell the difference, isn't it?
  Perhaps Zorba the Greek mistook יקיר as יקיד.
  Greek for "burn" here is καιομενη.
  Greek for "dull": βαρεως or νωθρος.
So which explains which ? I will grant that an Aramaean translator might see καιομενη and miswrite his translation as

second generation copy with the error in it. That seems highly unlikely, however, given that the original would have been copied more than once, and most copies would have the correct reading if the original were correct. **As it stands, no Peshitta manuscript of the 16 mss. collated by Gwilliam in this passage of Luke agrees with the Greek reading. Thus it is very difficult to support that The Greek was original and a hypothetical Peshitta translator miswrote his translation as** ܥܩܝܕ **instead of** ܝܩܝܪ **,and that no second or third translator did** another translation or checked the first one against the Greek original. The Peshitta was copied by scribes trained in their art in Monasteries to be exact and to uphold the Massoretic tradition of verifying and making notes of all variants and spelling irregularities observed. The Greek tradition was not nearly as rigorous and precise, as can be easily observed in the Greek mss. themselves.

Internal evidence also supports the Peshitta reading. Our Lord said the two disciples had "stupid hearts" in v. 25. The Greek has the word "Βραδεις" – "Bradeis", meaning "stupid". He did not say they had "burning hearts". The Peshitta has the same word there that it has here in v. 32- ܝܩܝܪ

"Yaqqir"(Dull,stupid).

One Old Latin ms. has "optusum" (dull) & the famous Greek Uncial , Codex D (6ᵗʰ century) has κεκαλυμμενη Kekalummenay – "covered".

The clincher in this kind of Aramaic-Greek variation is that we do not find that the Aramaic can be explained by a possible slight difference between two Greek words which differ significantly in meaning /i.e. , επελαθομην –epelathomayn ("forgot") & επελαβομην -epelabomayn, ("took") or spilas ("ledge") & spilos ("spot")/. We find the converse; we find in many cases that we can explain the Greek reading(s) on the basis of an Aramaic word which may have been misinterpreted or read differently by a translator and which accounts for the Greek text or more than one Greek text.

The data support the concept that The Greek text is a translation of The Aramaic , and not versa-vice.

33. And they arose in that hour, and they returned to Jerusalem, and they found the eleven assembled and those who were with them,

34. As they were saying, "Truly Our Lord has risen and he has appeared to Shimeon!"

35. They also related those things that had occurred on the road and how he was known to them when he broke the bread.

36. And when they were speaking these things, Yeshua stood in their midst and he said to them, "Peace be with you; I AM THE LIVING GOD, be not afraid."

Most Greek mss. lack the last part which I have translated, "I AM The Living God; be not afraid." A fifth century Greek ms. (W) has the phrase "Εγω ειμι, μη φοβεισθε" – ("Ego eimi, may fobeisthe") . "It is I, be not afraid." A couple other Greek mss. and The Latin Vulgate (4ᵗʰ century) also have the phrase.

37. And they were alarmed and were in terror, for they thought that they were seeing a ghost.

38. And Yeshua said to them, "Why are you shaken, and why do imaginations arise in your hearts?"

39. "See my hands and my feet, that it is I; touch me and know that a ghost does not have flesh and bones, as you see that I have."

40. And when he had said these things, he showed them his hands and his feet.

Codex D and The two "Old Syriac" mss. omit verse 40, therefore Nestle 's Greek NT (25ᵗʰ ed.) omits the verse and relegates it to the footnote apparatus at the bottom of the page!

41. Even until this moment they did not believe because of their joy, and they were awe-stricken. He said to them, "Do you have anything here to eat?"

42. So they gave him a piece of roasted fish and some honeycomb.

A few Greek mss.& one Old Syriac ms. (Sin.) lack " & a piece of honeycomb". Most Greek mss. and eight Church fathers before A.D. 400 have this phrase. Who in the world would invent & add such a reading? Textual Criticism seems to have run amuck and to be without accountability toward rhyme or reason.

43. And he took and he ate in their sight.

44. And he said to them, "These are the words that I spoke with you when I was with you, that everything that is written about me in The Law of Moses and in The Prophets and in The Psalms must be fulfilled."

45. Then he opened their mind to understand the scriptures.

46. And he said to them, "Thus it is written: and thus it was right for The Messiah to suffer and to arise from the grave the third day,

47. And that conversion to the forgiveness of sins would be proclaimed in his name in all the nations, and the beginning would be at Jerusalem.

48. And you are witnesses of these things.

49. And I shall send upon you The Promise of my Father; but you stay in the city of Jerusalem until you shall be clothed in power from on high."

50. And he brought them unto Bayth-Ania and he lifted his hands and he blessed them.

51. And it was that as he blessed them, he was separated from them, and he ascended to Heaven.

Two Greek mss. (א (4ᵗʰ cent.), D) & one "Old Syriac" ms.(Old Syriac is not Peshitta) omit "& He ascended to Heaven", therefore Nestle 's Greek NT omits it from the text, yet Vaticanus (B) 4ᵗʰ century and P⁷⁵ (3ʳᵈ century) have the phrase! Almost all Greek mss. of Luke have it and all Latin mss.

52. But they worshiped him and they returned to Jerusalem in great joy.

One Greek ms. (D) & one "Old Syriac" ms.(Old Syriac is not Peshitta) omit "They worshiped Him", therefore Nestle 's Greek NT omits it from the text, yet Vaticanus (B) 4ᵗʰ century and P⁷⁵ (3ʳᵈ century) have the phrase! Almost all Greek mss. of Luke have it and all Latin mss.

53. And they were in The Temple at all times, praising and blessing God. Amen.

God has given us The Gospel message of Luke in its original form. If we read and believe, we can share in the communion of joy and praise the apostles and disciples experienced and felt. That is the proper effect of The Messiah and His word upon the human spirit.

שלם אונגליון קדישא כרוזותא דלוקא
The end of The Holy Gospel preaching of Luke

We have every cause to rejoice.
He Who walked with the two on the road
to Emmaus walks with us.
Let us not walk in unbelief and sadness
as they did.
He is risen and returned victorious from
the greatest war ever waged
-   The war against sin, death and hell.
-   He has won that war for all time and
eternity.
We must celebrate and worship Him
Whose Name is above every name.
In The Name of Yeshua, every knee shall
bow
Every knee in Heaven & Earth
And under the Earth
And every tongue shall confess ,
That THE LORD JEHOVAH is Yeshua
The Messiah
To the glory of God His Father.
(Thus teaches The Peshitta)
Amen.

The Gospel according to The Apostle John

Chapter 1

1 In the origin The Word had been existing and That Word had been existing with God and That Word was himself God.

2 This One himself was at the origin with God.

3 Everything was in his hand, and without him not even one thing existed of the things that existed.

4 In him was The Life and The Life is The Light of men.

5 And The Light is shining in the darkness, and the darkness did not overtake it.

6 There was a man sent from God; his name was Yohannan.

7 He came for a witness, to testify about The Light, that everyone by him would believe.

8 He was not The Light, but was sent to bear witness of that Light.

9 For That One was The Light of Truth, which enlightens every person that comes into the world.

10 He was in the world, and the world existed by his hand, and the world knew him not.

11 He came unto his own, and his own received him not.

12 But those that received him, to them he gave authority to become the sons of God, even to them that believe on his Name,

13. Those who had not been born of blood, nor of the desire of the flesh, nor of the desire of a man, but of God.

14. And The Word became flesh and dwelt among us, and we beheld his glory, the glory as of The Only Begotten of The Father, full of grace and truth.

15 Yohannan testified concerning him and cried, saying, "This was he of whom I spoke: 'He that comes after me is preferred in honor before me, for he had priority over me.'

16 And of his fulness we have all received, and grace for grace.

17 For The Law was given by Moses, but grace and truth came by Yeshua The Messiah.

18 No man has seen God at any time; The Only Begotten God Who is in the bosom of The Father, he has declared him."

19 And this is the testimony of Yohannan when the Judaeans sent Levites and priests to him from Jerusalem in order to ask him: "Who are you?"

20 And he confessed and did not deny and confessed: "I am not The Messiah."

21 And they asked him again, "What, therefore? Are you Elijah?" And he said, "No." "Are you a Prophet", and he said "No."

22 And they said to him, "And who are you? Tell us that we may give a statement to those who sent us. What do you say about yourself?"

23 He said: "I am the voice that cries in the wilderness: 'Prepare the way of THE LORD JEHOVAH', just as that which Isaiah the Prophet said."

24 And they that were sent were of the Pharisees.

25 And they asked him and said to him, "Why therefore are you baptizing, if you are not The Messiah, nor Elijah, nor The Prophet?"

26 Yohannan answered and said to them, "I am baptizing in water; but he is standing in your midst whom you do not know."

27 "This is he who comes after me and he was preferred in honor before me, he whose sandal strap I am unworthy to loose."

28 These were in Bayth-Ania at the crossing of the Jordan where Yohannan was baptizing.

This study uncovers possible evidence supporting a very early Greek translation of The Peshitta (1st Century A.D.)

John 1:28

הלין (these) בביתעניא (in Bayth-Ania) * הוי (were)
בעברא (in the crossing) דיורדנן (of Jordan)
איכא (where) דמעמד (baptizing) הוא (was) יוחנן (John)

* [Some Greek mss. have "Bethabara" for Bethany. "Bethabara" is probably a misreading of the Aramaic text ביתעניא, where the Greek translator copied בית from Bethany (the blue word meaning "house" in the blue and red Aramaic word above, and then his eye went to עברא ("Abara") ,which is colored red in the Aramaic text, since עברא & עניא both start with the same letter , have four letters and end with the same letter – Alap, and can look very similar in the square Aramaic characters. The second and third letters in עברא ("abara") are essentially extended forms of the second and third letters of עניא ("anya") .
These are the Aramaic words עניא ("anya") & עברא ("abara") from Dead Sea Scroll photos of Aramaic characters in The Great Isaiah Scroll :.עברא ‏עניא‏

This is strong evidence that the Received Greek mss. were originally translations from Aramaic mss. written in early 1st century Aramaic. The Estrangela script was developed later (circa A.D. 100) and the characters in question do not look as similar: ܥܢܝܐ & ܥܒܪܐ .

This is support for a first century Aramaic New Testament written in the square Aramaic script like that of The Dead Sea Scrolls, and also a first century Greek translation of that Aramaic NT text, represented by the type of Greek manuscripts which the King James Bible translators used for their NT translation. There are other like examples I have cited elsewhere, supporting the very same conclusion.]

29 And the day after, Yohannan saw Yeshua Who came to him and Yohannan said : "Behold , The Lamb of God who takes away the sins of the world!"

30 "This is The One of whom I said: 'After me a man is coming and he was himself before me because he had priority over me.'"

31 "And I did not know him, but so that he should be made known to Israel, therefore I have come to baptize in water."

32 And Yohannan testified and said: "I saw The Spirit who was descending from Heaven like a dove and remaining upon him."

33."And I did not know him, but he who sent me to baptize in water, he said to me: "The One on whom you see The Spirit descending and remaining, This is The One who baptizes in The Spirit of Holiness."

34."And I have seen and have testified that This One is The Son of God."

35.And another day Yohannan was standing and two of his disciples;

36.And he gazed upon Yeshua as he was walking and said: "Behold: The Lamb of God."

37.And the two of his disciples heard as he spoke and they went after Yeshua.

38.And Yeshua turned and he saw them coming after him and he said: "What are you seeking?", and they said, "Our Master*, where are you staying?"

*רבן (our Master) : The Greek texts have a transliteration of רבן - ραββι -("Rabbi") , an Aramaic word, with a following translation of the same : ο λεγεται ερμηνευομενον διδασκαλε ("which is translated ,"Teacher").

John has six instances of this, each of which is evidence that the original was Aramaic and the Greek is a translation (ερμηνευομενον) of Aramaic. The Peshitta, of course, has no such translation in any of these six places in John.

39 He said to them: "Come and see." And they came and saw where he lived and stayed with him that day, and it was about the tenth hour.

40 One of those* who heard Yohannan and followed Yeshua himself was Andrew, Shimeon's brother.

* The Peshitta has הנון – "Those" where all the Greek texts have δυο - "Two".
In Aramaic - תרין is "Two". The "He"- ה and "Tau"- ת in Aramaic script are easily mistaken one for the other, as are "Yodh" & ' and "Waw" ו (See photo samples from Dead Sea Scrolls for these letters below).
DSS script: הנון "Those"
ונרין "Two"
The Resh and Nun are not as easily mistaken, however they are not very unlike each other, the Resh having two of the three strokes of the Nun. This similarity could easily account for the Greek reading - δυο -"Two " in all the Greek texts. The Great Isaiah Scroll shows that early Aramaean copyists would interchange Waw 's and Yodh 's between consonants without changing word meaning. The Great Isaiah Scroll widely

employed Aramaic orthography and spelling throughout the scroll.
If this explanation is valid, it is evidence that a Greek translation was made from an early Aramaic script of square characters like those I have printed above. This script was not used by Aramaean scribes after the first century A.D. .
To argue the reverse scenario (Greek affected the Peshitta reading) one would no doubt need to make the case for a late Aramaic square character in use, when Estrangela was the current script , and a mistranslation of "δυο" Two ,to הנון – "Those " – an explanation that is no explanation at all ! No Peshitta (or **Old Syriac** ms.) has תרין at John 1:40. **All have** הנון . The Peshitta can account for the Greek reading. The Greek cannot account for The Peshitta reading.

41 This one first saw Shimeon his brother and he said to him: "We have found The Messiah."

The Greek text of the ending of this verse says this: "ευρηκαμεν τον μεσιαν ο εστιν μεθερμηνευομενον χριστος " – (ASV) **"We have found the Messiah (which is, being interpreted, Christ)**. The Greek word "μεσιαν" (Majority) or "μεσσιαν" (Westcott & Hort) is a transliteration of the Aramaic speech of Andrew and of 1st century Palestine : משיחא ("Meshikha " or "Meshiha "). The Hebrew word משיח ("Meshiach ") is almost identical, though we know Aramaic was the native tongue of Palestine at the time. The Greek text follows this word **"Messian" (Messiah)** with a translation ("which being translated is Christ ".) The Greek word "χριστος " is declared here to be a translation of the original Aramaic word (transliterated in Greek letters as "μεσιαν "). But "χριστος " is the source behind the English word "Christ". "χριστος " occurs 565 times throughout the Greek NT in every book except 3 John!
Logically, we would have to conclude that Greek John 's writer is telling us that wherever "χριστος " occurs, we are reading a translation of Our Lord 's original title (משיחא- "Meshikha "). His disciples did not speak Greek; neither did the people of Israel. By the way, Greek John 4:25 has the same formula as this verse: **"the Messiah (which is, being interpreted, Christ")**. The Peshitta text has no such translation in either reference !
The Greek NT has , in "Christos", at least 565 witnesses to the Greek NT as a translation !

42 And he brought him to Yeshua and Yeshua gazed at him and he said: "You are Shimeon, son of Yona; you shall be called Kaypha." ("A Stone ")

* שמעון - "Shimeon " occurs 165 times in the Peshitta NT. The Greek equivalents "Σιμων "& " Σιμεων " ("Simon " & " Shimeon ") occur only 82 times . Often the Greek Name. "Πετρος "- "Petros " is used instead. The Greek of this verse , however, retains the Aramaic "Shimeon" and "Kaypha", which it then explains with the words : "κηφας ο ερμηνευεται πετρος" – "Cephas , which is translated Petros." Here the Greek text declares that the name "Petros" is a translation of the Aramaic name "Kaypha ". We here find hard evidence, and in 160 other places where this Greek name occurs, that the Greek NT is translated from Aramaic! Naturally, the Peshitta has no similar translation from Greek to Aramaic, here or anywhere else. Repeat the above statement several times and ponder it: The Greek text declares itself to be translated from Aramaic !

43.And the next day Yeshua wanted to depart to Galilee and he met Phillipus and he said to him: "Follow me."

44.Phillipus himself was from Bethsaida, the city of Andrew and Shimeon.

45.Phillipus found Nathaniel and said to him: "We have found him of whom Moses wrote in The Written Law and in The Prophets; he is Yeshua Bar Yoseph from Nazareth."

46.Nathaniel said to him: "Can anything good come from Nazareth?" Phillipus said to him, "Come and see".

47.Yeshua saw Nathaniel when he came to him and said about him: "Behold, truly a son of Israel in whom is no deceit."

48.Nathaniel said to him: "From where do you know me?" Yeshua said to him: "Before Phillipus called you, when you were under the fig tree, I saw you."

49.Nathaniel answered and said to him: "Rabbi, you are The Son of God; you are The King of Israel."

50.Yeshua said to him: "Do you believe because I said to you, 'I saw you under the fig tree.'? You shall see greater things than these."

51.He said to him: "Timeless truth I speak to you all: From this hour you shall see Heaven being opened and the Angels of God as they ascend and descend unto The Son of Man."

[Note: "Amen" in Aramaic has two basic meanings: "Eternal" and "True". This double use is unique to John's Gospel and is used only by Our Lord, indicating a very important revelation of eternal doctrine from The Eternal LORD Yeshua. It occurs 25 times in John's Gospel.]

He said to him: **"Timeless truth I speak to you all: From this hour you shall see Heaven being opened and the angels of God as they ascend and descend unto The Son of Man."**

This Man called Jesus The Messiah is the most astonishing Being ever encountered, and the most mysterious. If we think we know Him well, we are surely deceived. " No man has ever seen God", wrote John. I believe he speaks of understanding God, or properly knowing Him. We are finite beings; even angels desired to "look into" the things concerning Christ's suffering , death and resurrection glory. We shall never fathom Him.
Here in the last section he astonishes Nathaniel with prophecy; Nathaniel confesses that Jesus is The Son of God, and Jesus says that Phillip hasn't seen anything yet.
It is not enough to know Jesus as The Son of God; He is more than that! How can that be ? , you might say. I believe Jesus is The Son of God, born of a virgin, anointed of The Holy Spirit, etc. , etc. That is not Who He is. That is a theological statement.
John presents the transcendent Christ; a Christ Who is so large , so great, so infinite, that glimpses of His true identity are blinding bursts of supernova like light. **25 times John records Jesus saying "Amen, Amen, I speak to you."** No other gospel or book has this statement; no other Person utters it but The Christ. It means "Eternal Truth I tell you". It is a statement of absolute authority. "No man ever spoke like this Man", said one of the Temple priests. "He speaks with authority, not as the scribes", said the common people. "Where does this authority come from", the Jews asked.
More importantly, John also records another unique phrase 25 times in His Gospel : The Aramaic has it "Ena Na". It means, "I AM", literally. It is an Aramaic phrase from The Old Testament, which 97% of the time, refers to the name of God and comes from the mouth of God Himself: "I AM The LORD." ; "I AM The **LORD** your God", etc.. In John, Jesus

alone utters this phrase, usually followed by a description or definition of His Person:
"I AM THE LIGHT of the world"; "I AM THE BREAD of LIFE." "I AM THE GOOD SHEPHERD", etc..
Here in verse 51, Jesus says something that should confuse and astound the most devout believer. "You will see Heaven is being opened" …the angels of God Ascending and descending unto the Son of Man."
What He has said is : I am on earth and I am in Heaven- omnipresent God and a limited man. I am a man here on earth and I am **Jehovah** The Eternal in Heaven at all times. I don't understand how this can be , but He describes the angels coming to Him on earth and also coming to Him in Heaven, all apparently simultaneously !
And so, He has got my attention. I want to know Him better, and I will. When I do, I will discover another mystery (something that is unknown).
Think about it; it is not what you know that piques your curiosity; it is the thing you don't know. We should be discovering that we don't know something. That will draw us to seek Him out :
"Our Master, where do you live?" They said.
The answer will be the same for you as it was for those first disciples:

"**Come and see.**"

Chapter 2

1.And on the third day there was a wedding feast in Qatna, a city of Galilee, and the mother of Yeshua was there.

2.And also Yeshua himself and his disciples were invited to the wedding banquet,

3.And it was lacking wine, and his mother said to Yeshua, "There is no wine for them."

4.Yeshua said to her, "What do we have in common, woman? My hour has not quite yet come."

* "What to me & to you ?" is an Aramaic idiom meaning: "**What do we have in common?**"- clearly a bit of humor from Jesus toward his mother. Notice that He did respond to her request by performing His first miracle.
Jesus said to her, "What do we have in common, woman ? My hour has not quite come yet."
Remember that for thirty years, Our Lord had performed no miracle; He was an obscure and humble Person
Who patiently waited for His appointed time to serve publicly in Israel. Those thirty years of silence and obscurity are in a very real sense more miraculous than the last three years of His earthly Life, considering Who He was and is. "**Verily thou art a God that hidest thyself, O God of Israel, the Saviour**". (Isaiah 45:15). The patience and humility of God are far more surprising and unbelievable to men than His miracles, and these are stumbling blocks to the faith of many, if not all of us. Consider how many would have believed in Him had He never performed a miracle; consider also the grief of His heart, knowing that so many , if not all, of those who professed faith, believed only in the outward signs, but did not know Him. Our Lord knew that to begin performing miracles would be to come out of hiding, (out of character for God) and that would also make Him susceptible to misunderstanding and false devotion, when His usual design is to make men seek after Him Who hides, and recognize Him in His disguises.

5.His mother said to the servants, "Whatever he says to you, do."

6.But there were there six watercasks of stone, set for the purifying of the Judeans, which held two or three nine-gallon-measures each.

7.Yeshua said to them: "Fill the watercasks with water." And they filled them up to the brim.

8.He said to them: "Draw out now and take to The Master of Ceremonies."

9.And when The Master of Ceremonies tasted that water that had become wine, and did not know from where it was, (but the servants knew) The Master of Ceremonies called the bridegroom,

10.And he said to him: "Every man first calls for the good wine, and when they are drunk, then that which is inferior, but you have kept the good wine until now."

11.This first miracle Yeshua did in Qatna of Galilee and he manifested his glory, and his disciples believed in him.

This is the first miracle Jesus did in Qatna of Galilee and He manifested His glory; and His disciples believed in Him.

Every miracle of Jesus is called "Atha"- אתא - "A Sign". As such, we are to look for a valuable lesson being taught in the "Sign". Water being turned to wine is a creative act, certainly pointing to God's presence and power as Creator. Water is common and cheap; wine is rare and expensive; water is a necessity of life; wine is a luxury that signifies joy and celebration. God delights in our joy and happiness, more than we can know, and begrudges us no joy. Notice that Jesus made over 100 gallons of wine, possibly 160 gallons of the very best wine possible (The MC noticed it was better than the best, which he thought had already been served, and undoubtedly it had). That is a lot of wine! God is no tee-totaler! He is almost mad with joy and abandon, not a Stoic or Ascetic, as some imagine. Jesus would become known as a wine drinker and a glutton to the Pharisees and Scribes!

The water of purification would be externally used in a ritual ceremony ; Wine is applied internally. Our Lord was always more interested in man's inner life and what is inside a man than in externals. True religion is concerned with the state of the soul , spirit and mind, whereas much of what is religious is concerned with everything but the internal life. There is nothing wrong with ceremony, as long as we don't lose the realities they signify: The Spirit, The Truth, Love, Joy, Righteousness, Peace, Heaven and God Himself.

Do not be afraid of joy , laughter and life. These are God's lavish gifts He pours out to overflowing upon us and wants us to enjoy. Have you ever considered that men might be judged , not for enjoying life too much, **but not enough**?

12.After this he went down to Capernaum, he, his mother, his brothers and his disciples, and they were there a few days.

13.And the Passover of the Jews was drawing near, and Yeshua went up to Jerusalem.

14.And he found in The Temple those that were selling lambs, sheep and doves, and there were money exchangers sitting.

15.And he made for himself a whip from rope and cast all of them out of The Temple, and the sheep, the lambs, and money exchangers, and he poured out their money and overturned their tables.

16.And to those who had been selling doves he said: "Take these things out of here, and

do not make my Father's house a house of trade."

17.And his disciples called to mind that which is written: "The zeal of your house has consumed Me."

Jesus had no patience for self serving religion and irreverence toward God. The glory of His Father and His goodness and love were everything to The Son of God, and He was always grieved how little men knew of it and believed in it. He also knew how much His Father would sacrifice for the salvation of the world, and could not tolerate shallowness and spiritual stupidity in those who were supposed to be teaching the people and leading them closer to God.

18.But the Judeans answered and said to him: "What sign are you showing us that you are doing these things?"

19.Yeshua answered and said to them: "Tear down this temple, and in three days I will raise it up."

20 The Jews were saying to him: "For forty six years this temple has been being built, and will you raise it in three days?"

21 But he said this concerning the temple of his body.

22 But when he had risen from the grave, his disciples were reminded that he had said this, and they believed the scriptures and the word that Yeshua had spoken.

23 But when Yeshua was staying in Jerusalem at Passover during the feast, many trusted in him because they saw the miracles that he performed.

24 But Yeshua did not entrust himself to them, because he knew all men,

25 And he did not need a man to testify to him about anyone, for he himself knew what was in a man.

Chapter 3

1 One man of the Pharisees was living there; his name was Nicodemus. He was a leader of the Judeans.

2. This man came to Yeshua at night and said to him: "Rabbi, we know that you are a teacher sent from God, for no man is able to do these miracles that you are doing unless God were with him."

3.Yeshua answered and said to him: "Timeless truth I am telling you: If a person is not born again*, it is impossible for that one to see the Kingdom of God."

* ["Again"- מן דריש - "Min d'reesh" literally means "From the top".]

A person has no control or decision concerning his or her conception and birth. Birth is a result of a former act of the parents and of God. **The verb "Metilled"("Born") is passive , indicating that birth , whether physical or spiritual, is an action performed upon the subject, not by him.** Our Lord never intended to instruct or exhort Nicodemus to be born again. Jesus was telling him that Nicodemus was spiritually dead and knew nothing about God and His Kingdom. No one knows God by instruction and education; One obtains this by a new birth from The Holy Spirit, straight from God Himself, according to His choice and purpose.

4.Nicodemus said to him: "How can an old man be born? Is it not impossible for him again to enter his mother's womb a second time and be born?"

5.Yeshua answered and said to him: "Timeless truth I am telling you: "If a person is not born from water and The Spirit, it is impossible that he shall enter the Kingdom of God.

6.That which is born from flesh is flesh, and that which is born from The Spirit is spirit.

7.Do not be surprised that I said to you that all of you must be born again.

8.The Spirit breathes where he will, and you hear his voice, but you do not know from where he comes and where he goes; thus is everyone who is born from The Spirit."

Our Lord used three words with double meanings: **Rukha** (Spirit or Wind) ,**Nshaba** (Breathe or Blow) and **Qala** (Voice or Sound). The verse could be translated ,"The wind blows where it will and you hear its sound…", but He obviously speaks in spiritual terms here, using "**Rukha**" twice; the second reference is obviously "Spirit" and it seems inconsistent to use it in two different ways in the same sentence. Nevertheless, it is understandable that Nicodemus was confused by this statement in Aramaic.

9 Nicodemus answered and said to him, "How can these things be?"

10 Yeshua answered and said to him: "You are the Teacher of Israel and you do not know these things?

11 Timeless truth I speak to you: The things that We know We are speaking and the things that We see We are testifying, and Our testimony *all of* you do not accept.

12 If I have told all of you that which is in the earth and you are not believing, how shall you believe me if I tell you that which is in Heaven?

13 And no man has gone up to Heaven except he who went down from Heaven: The Son of Man- he who is in Heaven.

14 And just as Moses lifted up the serpent in the wilderness, thus The Son of Man is going to be lifted up,

15. So that every person who believes in him shall not be lost, but shall have eternal life.

16. For God loved the world in this way: so much that he would give up his Son, The Only One, so that everyone who trusts in him shall not be lost, but he shall have eternal life.

17 For God did not send his Son into the world that he would condemn the world, but that he would give life to the world by him.

18 Whoever believes in him is not judged, and whoever does not believe is judged already, because he does not believe in The Name of The Only Begotten Son of God.

19 This is the judgment: The Light has come into the world and the children of men loved the darkness more than The Light, because their works were evil.

20 For everyone who does what is hateful, hates The Light and does not come to The Light, lest his works should be convicted.

21 But he who does The Truth comes to The Light, so that his works may be revealed, that they are performed by God."

22 After these things, Yeshua and his disciples came to the land of Judea, and he was employed there with them and he baptized.

23 But Yohannan was also baptizing in Ainyon next to Shalim, because there was water there, and many were coming and were baptized.

24.For Yohannan had not yet gone to prison.

25.But there was a dispute between one of Yohannan's disciples and a certain Judeaen about purification.

26.And they came to Yohannan and said to him: "Our Rabbi, he who was with you at the crossing of Jordan, about whom you testified, Behold, he is baptizing and many are coming to him."

27.Yohannan answered and said to them: "A man cannot receive anything of his own will unless it is given to him from Heaven.

28.You are bearing me witness that I said I am not The Messiah, but I am the one sent before him.

29.He who has the bride is the bridegroom, but the friend of the bridegroom who stands and listens for him rejoices with great joy because of the voice of the bridegroom. Therefore this, my joy, behold, it is full.

30.It is necessary for him to increase and for me to decrease.

31. For he who came from above is higher than all, and he who is from Earth is from the ground, and speaks from the earth. He who has come from Heaven is higher than all.

32. And whatever he has seen and heard he testifies, and no one is receiving his testimony.

33. But he who receives his testimony attests that God is true.

34. For he whom God has sent speaks the words of God, for it was not in a measure that God has given The Spirit.

35. The Father loves The Son and he has given all things into his hands.

36. Whoever is trusting in The Son, has The Eternal Life, and whoever disobeys The Son shall not see The Life, but the anger of God shall abide upon him."

Chapter 4

1 But Yeshua knew that the Pharisees had heard that he was making many disciples and was baptizing more than Yohannan,

2 When it was not Yeshua himself baptizing, but his disciples.

3 And he left Judea, and went on again to Galilee.

4 But it was necessary for him to come and pass through Samaria.

5 And he came to a Samaritan city called Shikar, beside the village that Jaqob had given to his son Joseph.

6 And Jaqob's spring of water was there, and Yeshua, weary from walking, sat down by himself at the spring at the sixth hour (around noon).

7 And a woman from Samaria came to draw water and Yeshua said to her, "Give me water to drink."

8 For his disciples had entered the city to buy provisions for themselves.

9 And the Samaritan woman said to him, "How is it that you, a Jew, would ask me, a Samaritan woman, for a drink?" For the Jews do not associate with the Samaritans.

10 Yeshua answered and said to her, "If only you knew what the gift of God is, and who this is who says to you, 'Give me to drink', you would have asked for what he has, and he would have given you living waters."

11. This woman said to him, "My Lord, you have no bucket and the well is deep. From where do you have living waters?"

12 Are you greater than our forefather Jaqob, he who gave us this well, and he drank from it, also his children and his flock? "

13 Yeshua answered and said to her, "Everyone who shall drink from these waters shall thirst again;

14 But everyone who shall drink of the waters that I will give him shall not thirst for eternity, but those waters that I give him shall be springs of waters in him that shall spring up into eternal life."

15 This woman said to him, "My lord, give me from these waters that I shall not thirst again, and so I am not coming to draw from here."

16 Yeshua said to her, "Go call your husband and come here."

17 She said to him, "I have no husband." Yeshua said to her, "You have said correctly, "I have no husband.

18 For you have had five husbands, and this man that is with you now is not your husband; this you have spoken truly."

19 The woman said to him, "My lord, I perceive that you are a Prophet.

20 Our forefathers worshiped in this mountain, and you say that in Jerusalem is the place where it is necessary to worship."

21 Yeshua said to her, "Woman, believe me that the hour is coming in which neither in this mountain nor in Jerusalem will you worship The Father.

22 You are worshiping what you do not know. We know what we are worshiping, for The Life is of the Jews.

23 But the hour is coming and now is, when the true worshippers will worship The Father in The Spirit and in The Truth, for The Father also is seeking such worshippers as these.

24 For The Spirit is God, and it is fitting that those who worship him worship in The Spirit and in The Truth."

25 The woman said to him, "I know that The Messiah is coming, and when he comes, he will teach us all things."

26 Yeshua said to her, "I AM THE LIVING GOD *, I who am speaking with you."

---

*["Ena Na" in Aramaic is almost always a reference to The Name of God and is used to indicate direct discourse from the mouth of God himself: "I AM THAT I AM" Exodus 3:14, where God reveals his Name as "I AM" "Ahiah", in Hebrew and Aramaic. John 's Gospel contains 25 instances of this phrase- 23 from the lips of Our Lord himself. In one instance, His utterance of this Name is so powerful that it knocks down a band of soldiers backward to the ground, which had come to

arrest God. (See 18:6) Our Lord also responded with this Name to The High Priest Qaiapha, when put under oath to testify as to His identity. The Peshitta OT in Ezekiel has "Ena Na" seventy times; Nine other OT books contain 67; All but three of the 147 (98%) total occurrences are from the mouth of God himself :"I AM Jehovah", "I AM **Jehovah** of Lords", "I AM **Jehovah**, "I AM God Almighty", "I AM The God of Abraham…"; one is the discourse of Joseph: "I am Joseph." There are exceptions in The NT Peshitta as well, but it appears that Yohannan's record is unanimous in testimony to the Divine reference in these words, all from Yeshua' lips. I have chosen George Lamsa's rendering of "Ahiah Asher High" from Exodus 3:14: "**I AM THE LIVING GOD**", for "Ena Na." These words are implied but not unequivocal, since the literal sense may be taken as the pronoun and verb pair "I am." Most often, the hearer took the latter meaning from these words; sometimes the Divine meaning. I have no doubt Our Lord used them intentionally in the Divine sense in almost every, if not in every case, as a test of faith and understanding for his audience. I would therefore be remiss to omit the Divine sense from a translation, while also including the mundane meaning. This does illuminate some obscure passages, especially where the statement stands alone : "**So you may know that I am**", does not make good sense. "So you may know that **I AM THE LIVING GOD**", makes excellent sense. This stand alone statement occurs five times in Yohannan: (8:24,28; 13:19, 18:6,8).

27 And while he was speaking, his disciples came and they were amazed that he was speaking with the woman, but no man said, "What are you seeking?, or, "Why are you speaking with her?"

28 And the woman left her cruse and went to the city and said to the men:

29 "Come see a man who told me everything that I have done. Is he The Messiah?"

30 And the men departed from the city and they came to him.

31 And in the midst of these things his disciples were begging him and were saying to him, "Our Master, eat."

32 But he said to them, "I have food to eat of which you do not know."

33 The disciples were saying among themselves, "Did someone bring him something to eat?"

34 Yeshua said to them, "My personal food is that I do the will of him who has sent me and finish His work.

35 Do you not say, 'After four months the harvest comes?' Behold, I say to you, lift up your eyes and behold the fields that are white and are ready to harvest even now.

36 And whoever reaps receives wages and he gathers fruit for life eternal and the sower and reaper shall rejoice together.

37 For in this is a word of truth, that 'One sows and another reaps.'

38 I sent you to harvest something in which you were not laboring, for another labored and you have entered upon their labors."

39 Many Samaritans from that city believed in him because of the woman's saying which

she testified: "He told me everything that I have done."

40 And when those Samaritans came to him, they requested of him that he would stay with them, and he was with them for two days.

41 And many believed in him because of his word.

42 And they were saying to that woman, "Now it is not because of your word that we believe in him, for we have heard and we know that This One is truly The Messiah, The Lifegiver of the world."

The Critical Greek text omits "The Messiah" in this verse. Here are three different possible scripts for the Aramaic text of "**Messiah Savior**":

ܡܫܝܚܐ ܡܚܝܢܐ – Estrangela Aramaic script (AD 100-600)

משיחא מחינה – Massoretic Square Aramaic script (BHS)
מחינה אחישמ – Pre- Massoretic Square Aramaic script (400 BC- AD 100).
In the Aramaic Peshitta , the two words occur together as above .
All that is needed to account for the Greek reading of the Critical text is homoteleuton ("same ending") of the two words in the third script, as represented by The Great Isaiah Dead Sea Scroll (Letters are pasted from a photocopy of the scroll). Both words have five letters and the first and last letters of each look the same (Alep 𐤀 and He 𐤄 look almost identical in this ancient script, unlike the more modern fonts). Each also has a middle Yod and initial Mem. It would appear, then, that a Greek translator ,of the first century AD, saw שריראית ("truly") and translated it , then his eye went to

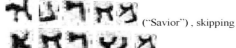 ("Savior") , skipping

("Messiah"), due to the similarities noted. Another Greek translator may have done the same (Byzantine) and then caught his error, tacking on "Messiah: at the very end (ο χριστος), thus changing the word order as found in the Aramaic original.
The words in Estrangela script are not as similar in appearance as they are in the older square Aramaic characters. That does not mean they could not account for such a mistake, simply that the older script is more likely to do so. This is consistent with other variations in the Greek text of John , presented previously.

43 And after two days, Yeshua went out from there and left for Galilee.

44 For Yeshua had been testifying that a Prophet is not honored in his city.

45 But when he came to Galilee, the Galileans received him because they saw all the miracles that he did in Jerusalem at the feast, for they had also gone to the feast.

46 But Yeshua came again to Qatna of Galilee, where he had made the water wine, and a servant of a certain King was staying in Kapernahum, whose son was ill.

47 This man had heard that Yeshua came from Judea to Galilee and he went to him and

was imploring him to come down and heal his son, for he was coming close to dying.

48 Yeshua said to him, "If you will not see signs and wonders, you will not believe."

49 That servant of The King said to him, "My lord, come down or else the boy will die."

50 Yeshua said to him, "Go; your son is saved." And that man believed in the word that Yeshua spoke to him, and he went on.

51 But when he was going down, his servants met him and they announced good news to him and were saying to him, "Your son is saved."

52 And he asked them at what time he was cured; they were saying to him, "Yesterday, in the seventh hour, the fever left him."

53 And his father knew that in that same hour Yeshua said to him, "Your son is saved." And he believed and his whole household.

54 This is again the second miracle Yeshua did, when he came from Judea to Galilee.

Chapter 5

1 After these things there was a feast of the Judeans, and Yeshua went up to Jerusalem.

2 But there was a certain baptismal place in Jerusalem called in Aramaic, Bayth Khesda*, and there were in it five porches.

*Thayer's Greek Lexicon has for the word "Bethesda": 964 βηθεσδα Bethesda bay-thes-dah`
of **Aramaic origin**, cf 01004 and 02617 בית-חסדא; ; n pr loc
AV-Bethesda 1; 1
Bethesda =" house of mercy" or "flowing water"
1) the name of a pool near the sheep-gate at Jerusalem, whose waters had curative powers

3 And in these many people were lying who were ill, blind, crippled, cancerous, and they were awaiting the moving of the water;

4 For an Angel descended from time to time to the baptismal and moved the water for them; whoever first descended after the moving of the water was cured of all sickness whatever he had.

5 But a certain man was there who had been diseased for thirty eight years.

6 Yeshua saw this man lying, and he knew that he had been so for a long time, and he said to him: "Do you want to be cured?"

7 The sick man answered and said : "Oh, my lord, there is no one to put me in the baptismal when the waters are moved, but while I am coming, another goes down before me."

8 Yeshua said to him: "Get up! Pick up your bed and walk."

9 And immediately that man was healed, and he stood up, took his bed, and he walked, and it was the Sabbath day.

10 And the Jews were saying to him who was healed: "It is the Sabbath. You are not permitted to carry your bed."

11 But he answered and said to them: "He who made me well, he said to me, 'Take up your bed and walk.' "

12 And they asked him: "Who is this man who said to you, 'Take up your bed and walk?' "

13 But he that had been healed did not know who Yeshua was, for he had withdrawn himself in the great crowd that was in that place.

14 After a time Yeshua found him in The Temple and said to him: "Behold, you are well again; do not sin, lest something worse than before should happen to you."

15 And that man departed and said to the Jews that Yeshua was the one who had healed him.

16 And because of this, the Jews were persecuting Yeshua and were seeking to kill him, because he did these things on the Sabbath.

17 But Yeshua himself said to them: "My Father is working until this hour, and I am also working."

18 And because of this, the Jews were especially seeking to kill him, not only because he broke the Sabbath, but also because he said that God was his Father, and was making himself equal with God.
Yeshua said His Father and He were working together; a mere human's work could not be compared to God's works nor be worthy of mention in conjunction with God's power.

19 But Yeshua answered and said to them: "Timeless truth I tell you: The Son cannot do anything of his own will, but the thing that he sees The Father is doing; for those things that The Father does, these also The Son does like him.

20 For The Father loves his Son and he shows him everything he does; greater deeds than these He will show him, that you may be astonished.

21 For just as The Father raises the dead and gives them life, thus also The Son gives life to them whom he will.

22 For it is not The Father who judges a man, but he has given all judgment to The Son.

23 That everyone should honor The Son as one honors The Father. He who does not honor The Son is not honoring The Father who sent him.

24. Timeless truth I speak to you: "Whoever hears my word and trusts in him who has sent me has the eternal Life, and he comes not into judgment, but he moves from death into Life.

25 Timeless truth I speak to you: The hour is coming, it is even now, when the dead shall hear the voice of The Son of God, and they who hear shall live.

26 For just as The Father has The Life in himself, so he has given also to The Son to have The Life in himself.

27. And he has given him authority to also do judgment, because he is The Son of Man.

28. Do not be astonished at this, for the hour is coming when all who are in the graves shall hear his voice,

29. And they shall come out: those who have done good things, to the resurrection of life, and those who have done evil deeds, to the resurrection of judgment.

30. I cannot do anything of my own will, but according to that which I have heard, I judge, and my judgment is just, for I am not seeking my will, but the will of him who has sent Me.

31. And if I testify about myself, my testimony is not true.

32 There is another who testifies about me, and I know that his testimony, which he testifies of me, is true.

33 You sent to Yohannan and he testified concerning the truth.

34 But I was not receiving the testimony of a man, but I say these things that you may live.

35 He was a blazing and shining lamp, and you were willing to boast about the time in his light.

36 But my testimony *which is borne* to me is greater than Yohannan's, for the works that my Father gave me to finish, those works which I have done testify for me that The Father has sent Me.

37 And The Father who has sent me, he testifies of me. You have never heard his voice and you have not seen his appearance,

38 And his word is not abiding in you, because you are not trusting in him whom he has sent.

39. Search the scriptures, for in them you hope that you have eternal life, and they testify concerning Me,

40 And you are not willing to come to me that eternal life may be yours.

41 I do not receive glory from the children of men.

42 But I know you, that the love of God is not in you.

43 I have come in The Name of my Father and you do not receive me, and if another shall come in his own name, you will receive him.

44 How can you believe, who are accepting glory one from another, and you are not seeking the glory of The One God?

45 Do you think that I am accusing you before The Father? There is one who accuses you: Moses, the one in whom you hope.

46 For if you had trusted Moses, you would also trust me, for he wrote about Me.

47 And if you do not believe his writings, how will you believe my words?"

Chapter 6

1 After these things, Yeshua went to the other side of the Sea of Galilee -'*The Sea* of Tiberias'.

2 And great crowds were going after him, because they saw the miracles he did for the sick.

3 And Yeshua went up to a mountain and sat down there with his disciples.

4 But the feast of The Passover of the Jews was drawing near.

5 And Yeshua lifted up his eyes and saw great crowds coming to him, and he said to Phillipus: "Where shall we buy bread that these may eat?"

6 But he said this as a test for him, for he knew what he was going to do.

7 Phillipus said to him: "Two hundred denarii worth of bread is not enough, even if each of them takes a very little."

8 One of his disciples, Andraus, Shimeon Kaypha's brother, said to him:

9 "There is a boy here who has five loaves of barley bread and two fish with him; but what are they to all of these?"

10 Yeshua said to them: "Have all the people be seated." And there was much grass in that place and they were seated, the number of men being five thousand.

11 And Yeshua took the bread and blessed and distributed to them who were seated, and thus also from the fish, as much as they wanted.

12 And when they were full, he said to his disciples, "Gather the leftover fragments, that nothing be lost." (This statement of Yeshua has more significance than the miracle itself, in the translator's opinion.)

13 And they gathered and filled twelve large baskets with fragments left over to them who ate from the five loaves of barley bread.

14 But those people who saw the miracle that Yeshua did were saying, "Truly, This is The Prophet who is coming to the world."

15 But Yeshua knew they were prepared to come seize him and make him King, and he withdrew to that mountain alone.

16 And when it was evening, his disciples went down to the sea.

17 And they sat in the boat and were coming to the coast to Kapernahum and it was growing dark and Yeshua had not come to them.

18 But the sea rose up against them because a great wind was blowing.

19.And they drove about twenty five or thirty furlongs and they saw Yeshua as he was walking on the lake, and when he drew near to the ship, they were afraid. (1 furlong = 1/8ᵗʰ mile)

20 But Yeshua said to them, "I AM THE LIVING GOD, do not be afraid."

21 And they wanted to receive him into the boat, and immediately the boat was at that land to which they were going.

22 And the day after, the crowd that had stood at the shore of the sea saw that no other boat was there except that one on which the disciples had embarked, and that Yeshua had not entered with his disciples into the boat.

23 But other ships had come from Tiberias, next to that place at which they had eaten the bread which Yeshua blessed.

24 And when that crowd saw that Yeshua was not there, neither his disciples, they embarked these ships and came to Kapernahum and they were looking for Yeshua.

25 And when they found him at the other side of the sea, they were saying to him, "Our Master, when did you come here?"

26 Yeshua answered and said to them, "Timeless truth I speak to you: you seek me, not because you saw the signs but because you ate the bread and were filled."

27 "Do not work for food that perishes, but for food that endures for the eternal life that The Son of Man will give you, for This One has The Father sealed as God with his seal of approval."

28 And they were saying to him, "What shall we do to work the service of God?"

29 Yeshua answered and said to them: "This is the service of God, that you trust in him whom he has sent."

30 They were saying to him, "What sign will you do, that we may see and believe in you? What sign will you perform?

31 Our forefathers ate manna in the wilderness, just as it is written 'He gave them bread from Heaven to eat.' "

32 Yeshua said to them, "Timeless truth I speak to you: It was not Moses who gave you bread from Heaven, but my Father gave you The True Bread from Heaven."

33 "For The Bread of God is he who has descended from Heaven and gives life to the world."

34 They were saying to him, "Our Lord, always give us this bread."

35 Yeshua said to them, "I AM THE LIVING GOD, The Bread of Life; whoever comes to me shall not hunger, and whoever trusts in me shall never thirst."

36 "But I said to you that you have seen me and you do not believe."

37 "Everyone whom my Father has given me shall come to me, and whoever will come to me I shall not cast out."

38 "For I came down from Heaven, not to do my will, but to do the will of him who has sent me."

39 "But this is the will of him who has sent me: I shall not destroy anyone from him whom he has given to me, but I shall raise him in the last day."

40 "For this is the will of my Father: Everyone who sees The Son and trusts in him shall have eternal life, and I shall raise him in the last day."

41 But the Judeans were murmuring about him for saying : "I AM THE LIVING GOD, The Bread, which has descended from Heaven."

42 And they were saying, "Is not this Yoseph's son, whose father and mother we know? How does this man say, 'I have come down from Heaven?' "

43 Yeshua answered and said to them, "Do not mutter one with another."

44 "No man can come to me, unless The Father who has sent me will draw him, and I shall raise him in the last day."

45 "For it is written in The Prophets, 'All of them will be taught of God.' Everyone, therefore, who has heard from The Father and has learned from him, comes to me."

46 "No man has seen The Father, except he who is from God; he himself sees The Father."

47 "Timeless truth I speak to you: 'Whoever trusts in me has eternal life.'"

48 "I AM THE LIVING GOD, The Bread of Life."

49 "Your forefathers ate manna in the wilderness and they died."

50 "This is The Bread that came down from Heaven, that a man may eat of it and he shall not die."

51 "I AM THE LIVING GOD, The Living Bread, who have come down from Heaven, and if a man will eat of this bread, he will live for eternity,   and the bread that I shall give is my body that I give for the sake of the   life of the world."

52 But the Jews were arguing with one another and saying, "How can this man give us his body to eat?"

53 And Yeshua said to them, "Timeless truth I speak to you: Unless you eat the body of The Son of Man and drink his blood, you have no life in yourselves."

54 "But whoever eats of my body and drinks of my blood has eternal life, and I shall raise him in the last day."

55 "For my body truly is food, and my blood truly is drink."

56 "Whoever eats my body and drinks my blood abides in me and I in him."

57 "Just as The Living Father has sent me, and I am living because of The Father, whoever will eat me, he also will live because of Me."

58 "This is the bread that came down from Heaven. It is not as your forefathers who ate manna and have died; whoever eats this bread shall live for eternity."

59 These things he said in the synagogue when he taught in Kapernahum.

60 And many of his disciples who heard were saying, "This saying is hard. Who is able to hear it?"

61 But Yeshua knew in his soul that his disciples were murmuring about this, and he said to them, "Does this subvert you?"

62 "Truly you will see therefore The Son of Man ascending to the place where he was from the first."

63 "The Spirit is The Life Giver; the body does not benefit anything. The words that I speak with you are spirit and life."

64 "But there are men among you who do not believe", for Yeshua himself knew from the first who they were who were not believing and who he was who would betray him.

65 And he said to them, "Because of this, I said to you that no man can come to me unless it has been given to him from my Father."

66 Because of this saying, many of his disciples went back and were not walking with him.

67 And Yeshua said to the twelve, "Do you also wish to leave?"

68 Shimeon Kaypha answered and said, "My Lord, to whom shall we go? You have the words of eternal life."

69 "And we believe and know that you are The Messiah, The Son of THE LIVING GOD."

70 Yeshua said to them, "Have I not chosen you twelve, and one of you is a Satan?"

71 But he said this about Yehudah, son of Shimeon Scariota, for he was going to be the one to betray him, being one of the twelve.

Chapter 7

1 After these things, Yeshua was walking in Galilee, for he did not want to walk in Judea, because the Judeans were seeking to kill him.

2 And the Jewish Feast of Tabernacles was near.

3 And his brothers said to Yeshua :"Remove yourself from here and go to Judea, that your disciples may see the works that you do."

4 "For no man does anything in secret and wants it done openly. If you are doing these things, show yourself to the world."

5 For his brothers also did not believe in Yeshua.

6 Yeshua said to them: "My time has not yet come, but your time is always ready."

7 "The world cannot hate you, but it hates me because I am testifying about it, that its servants are evil."

8 "You go up to this feast; I am not going up to this feast, because my time is not yet finished."

9 He said these things and he remained in Galilee.

10 But when his brothers went up to the feast, then he also went up, not openly, but as secretly.

11 But the Judeans were seeking him in the feast and they were saying, "Where is he?"

12 And there was much murmuring in the crowd because of him, for there were those who said, "He is good", and others were saying, "No, but he deceives the people."

13 But no man spoke openly about him, for fear of the Judeans.

14 But when the midpoint of the feast had arrived, Yeshua came up to The Temple and he taught.

15 And the Judeans were astonished and were saying, "How does this man know the scrolls, having not learned?"

16 Yeshua answered and said: "My teaching is not Mine, but from him who sent Me."

17 "Whoever is willing to do his will understands my teaching, whether it is from God or whether I speak for my own pleasure."

18 "Whoever speaks for the pleasure of his own mind is seeking glory for himself, but he who seeks glory for the one who sent him is faithful and there is no evil in his heart."

19 "Was it not Moses who gave you The Written Law? Yet no one among you keeps The Written Law."

20 "Why are you seeking to kill me?" The crowds answered and were saying, "A demon is in you. Who is seeking to kill you?"

21 Yeshua answered and said to them, "I have done one work, and all of you are astonished."

22 "For this reason Moses gave you circumcision, not that it is from Moses but because it is from the forefathers, and you circumcise a son on the Sabbath."

23 "And if a son is circumcised on the Sabbath day because The Written Law of Moses should not be broken, do you complain about me because I have completely healed a man on the Sabbath day?"

24 "Do not judge with partiality, but judge just judgment."

25 And the men from Jerusalem were saying, "Is This not he whom they seek to kill?"

26 "And behold, he speaks openly and they say nothing to him. Is it possible the Elders know that This truly is The Messiah?"

27 "But we know from where This One is. When The Messiah comes, no one will know from where he is."

28 And Yeshua lifted up his voice as he taught in The Temple and he said, "You know me and from where I am, and I have not come of my own pleasure, but he who has sent me is true, whom you do not know."

29 "But I do know him, because I am from unity with him, and he has sent Me."

30 And they sought to seize him, and no man laid hands on him, because his hour had not yet come.

31 But many from the crowds trusted in him and they were saying, "When The Messiah comes, will he do more miracles than these which This One has done?"

32 And the Pharisees heard the crowds speaking these things about him and they and the Chief Priests sent guards to seize him.

33 And Yeshua said, "A little longer I am with you, and I will go join him who has sent Me."

34 "And you will seek me and you will not find me, and wherever I am, you cannot come."

35 The Judeans were saying among themselves, "Where is This Man prepared to go that we cannot be? Is He indeed prepared to go to a region of the Gentiles and teach the pagans?"

36 "What is this statement that he spoke? : 'You will seek me and will not find me, and wherever I am, you are not able to come?' "

37 But at the great day, which is the last of the feast, Yeshua stood and he proclaimed and said : "If a man is thirsty, let him come to me and drink."

38 "Everyone who trusts in me, just as the scriptures have said, rivers of living water shall flow from within him."

39 But this he spoke about The Spirit, Whom those who were trusting in him were being prepared to receive; for The Spirit had not yet been given, because Yeshua had not yet been glorified.

40 But many from the crowds who heard his words were saying, "This is truly The Prophet."

41 Others were saying, "This One is The Messiah." Others were saying, "Can The Messiah come from Galilee?"

42 "Has not the scripture said that The Messiah is coming from the seed of David and from Bethlehem, the village of David?"

43 And there was division among the crowd because of him.

44 And there were people among them who wanted to seize him, but no man put hands on him.

45 And those guards came to the Chief Priests, and the Pharisees and the Priests said to them, "Why have you not brought him?"

46 The guards were saying to them, "Never in this way has a man spoken as This Man speaks."

47 The Pharisees were saying to them, "Have you also been deceived?"

48 "Have men of the leaders or of the Pharisees trusted in him?"

49 "However, this people who do not know The Written Law are damned."

50 Nicodemus said to them (he is one of them who had come to Yeshua at night):

51 "Does our Written Law condemn a man unless one shall hear him first and know what he has done?"

52 They answered and said to him, "Are you also from Galilee? Search and see that a Prophet will not arise from Galilee."

[The Peshitta mss. do not contain this following passage 7:53 - 8:11. It is found in The Palestinian Syriac (5ᵗʰ cent. AD) and in most Greek mss, as well as in most ancient versions of John. A translation of the ancient Palestinian Aramaic text follows, from John Gwynn's edition, a collation of eight Syriac mss. :]
(Please refer to **Appendix –Pericope de Adultera**.)

53 Then everyone went to his house.

Chapter 8

1. But Yeshua went to Tura d'Zaytay, and in the morning he came again to The Temple.

Tura d'Zaytay is traditionally known as "The Mount of Olives".

2 And all the people came to him, and when he sat, he taught them.

3 But the Scribes and the Pharisees brought a women who had been seized in adultery, and when they stood her in the midst,

4 They were saying to him, "Teacher, this woman was taken openly in the act of adultery."

5 "But in The Written Law of Moses, he commanded that we shall stone such as these."

Verse 5 has נרגום **"Nargum"** , **("we shall stone")**. Byzantine has λιθοβολεισθαι ("to be stoned").

רלדאך occurs only here in the Peshitta NT , meaning , "the one such", or "they that are such". It is literally rendered in Greek as "τας τοιαυτας" –"they that are such". Apparently some Greek scribes read- פקד דלדאך ("commanded that such") as פקדן לדאך ("commanded us such"), seeing ד as ן attached to פקד –(פקדן , which means "commanded us".) The Textus Receptus and The Critical Greek text (W&H) have ημιν μωσης ενετειλατο- "**Moses commanded us**". The Aramaic explains the Greek readings; The Greek readings cannot explain The Aramaic of The Peshitta. All the Greek texts have either ημιν "us" or, ημων "our". The Peshitta has no personal pronoun with פקד-" commanded " . **This explanation would presume a very early Aramaic text with square Aramaic script in the first century**; this explanation does not work with Estrangela script : ܦܩܕܠܕܐܟ .

ܦܩܕܠܕܐܟ

Here is the text again in Aramaic characters:
פקדלדאך & פקדולדאך. How the words are separated changes the meaning of the text, especially with the confusion of the letter Dalet for a final Nun.
The second example in each pair represents what a Greek translator may have misconstrued from the actual reading shown first.

6 "What therefore do you say?" This they said, as they were tempting him, so that they might have something for which to accuse him, but Yeshua, stooping down, was writing upon the ground.

Verse 6 has several signal markers indicating the Greek came from Aramaic and that the Aramaic came not from the Greek texts. Ελεγον ("they were saying") –Critical text & TR, ειπον ("they said") – Byzantine & Orthodox ,are both good translations of the Aramaic אמרו. κατηγοριαν κατ αυτου ("an accusation against him") – Byzantine & Orthodox vs. κατηγορειν αυτου ("to accuse him") - W&H, shows two variations on the Aramaic verb – דנקטרגוניהי - "that they should accuse Him". דתהוא להון ("for them- that it may be") is an Aramaic idiom preceding the above verb, making it awkward for a Greek translator to translate: Normally it means "They have" , so , what is the object ? Did they have "an accusation" (a noun) or did they have "to accuse him" (a verb) ? One Greek said the former and another the latter, both understandable translations. It seems unlikely that it went from Greek to Aramaic here: The Aramaic uses neither an infinitive verb ("to accuse him"), as Westcott & Hort's Greek text does, nor a noun ("an accusation against him") , as The Byzantine Greek text does.

7 But as they persisted asking him, he stood up and he said to them, "He among you who is without sin, let him first cast a stone upon her."

8 And stooping down again, he wrote on the ground.

9 But when these heard, they were exiting, one by one, beginning from the Elders, and the woman who had been in the midst was left alone.

10 But when he stood up, Yeshua said to the woman, "Where are they? Has no man condemned you?"

11 But she said, "Not even one, LORD GOD"; and Yeshua said, "Neither do I condemn you. Go, and from now on, sin no more."

This text reveals a very powerful testimony from the woman taken in adultery. She addressed Jesus with the Divine Name

The Original Aramaic New Testament in Plain English

The Holy Gospel Preaching of John ✝ אונגליון קדישא כרוזותא דיוחנן

"**MarYah**", which is "**Yahweh**", The most holy Name of The God of the Hebrews ,in Aramaic! "**MarYah**" means "**LORD JEHOVAH**". This would indicate that THE Holy Spirit had revealed Our Lord's identity to her, and that her soul was saved on the spot, according to the scripture, "No one can say Jesus is "**MarYah**"(THE LORD JEHOVAH) except by **The Holy Spirit**."-1 Cor. 12:3. The Greek texts are ambiguous , using the phrase "**Kurios Ihsous**"- "**Lord Jesus**". "**Kurios**" can refer to Deity or to a mere human King or landowner. The Aramaic is unequivocal in its reference to The Deity revealed to Moses and the Prophets.

12 And Yeshua spoke again with them and he said: "I AM THE LIVING GOD, The Light of the world. Whoever follows me shall not walk in darkness but shall find* the light of life."

The Greek texts have εξει ("shall have") where the Peshitta has נשכה ("shall find"). Here is a possible explanation: "Shall find" in three scripts- (BHS, Estrangela, DSS) :

נשכה , ܢܫܟܚ , 𐤍𐤔𐤊𐤇

"Shall have" in three scripts- (BHS, Estrangela, DSS) :

נהוה , ܢܗܘܐ , 𐤍𐤄𐤅𐤄

("**Have**" does not really exist in Aramaic ; נהוה לה ("**Nehweh lah**") really means "**It shall be to him**".) It appears again that a Greek translator in the first century (reading old Aramaic script) mistook that script , reading "**Nishkakh**"("**Shall find**") as "**Nehweh**" ("**Shall be**"), thereby translating it into the Greek equivalent, εξει ("**shall have**"). The Old Aramaic script represented above from the Dead Sea Isaiah Scroll illustrates how easy it would have been to confuse the two words, thereby giving the different Greek reading. The Greek εξει ("**shall have**") would be unlikely to give rise to the Aramaic reading ("shall find") נשכה. Again, the Aramaic characters of the two Aramaic words look far more similar than do the Estrangela letters, supporting a first century Greek translation of the Aramaic text, since Estrangela replaced square Aramaic characters after A.D. 100.

13 The Pharisees were saying to him: "You are testifying about yourself; your testimony is not true."
14 Yeshua answered and said to them, "Even if I testify about myself, my testimony is true, because I know from where I have come and where I am going, but you do not know from where I have come and where I am going."
15 "You are judging carnally; I am judging no one."
16 "But even if I do judge, my judgment is true, because I am not alone, but I and my Father who has sent Me."
17 "And in your Written Law it is written: 'The testimony of two men is true.' "
18 "I AM THE LIVING GOD, I who testify about myself, and my Father who has sent me has testified about Me."
19 They were saying to him, "Where is your Father?" Yeshua answered and said to them, "You know neither me nor my Father. If you had known me, you would have known my Father also."
20 He spoke these words in the treasury as he taught in The Temple, and no man seized him, for his hour had not yet come.
21 Yeshua spoke again to them: "I am moving on and you will seek me and you will die in your sins, and where I am going, you cannot come."
22 The Judeans were saying, "Will he now kill himself?", because he had said, "Where I am going, you cannot come."
23 And he said to them, "You are from below and I am from above. You are from this world; I am not from this world."
24 "I said to you that you shall die in your sins, for unless you shall believe that I AM THE LIVING GOD, you shall die in your sins."
25 The Judeans were saying, "Who are you?" Yeshua said to them, "Even though I have begun to talk with you,
26 There are many things for me to say and judge concerning you, but he who has sent me is true, and those things that I have heard from him, these things I am speaking in the world."
27 And they did not know that he spoke to them about The Father.
28 Yeshua spoke again to them : "When you have lifted up The Son of Man, then you shall know that I AM THE LIVING GOD, and I do nothing for my own pleasure, but just as my Father has taught me, so I am speaking.
29 And he who has sent me is with me, and my Father has not left me alone, because I am doing always what is beautiful to him."
30 When he was speaking these things, many trusted in him.
31 And Yeshua said to those Judeans who trusted in him, "If you will continue in my word, you are truly my disciples."
32 "And you will know the truth, and that truth will set you free."
33 And they were saying to him, "We are the seed of Abraham, and never have we served in bondage to a man; how do you say, "You shall be children of liberty"?
34 Yeshua said to them: "Timeless truth I speak to you: Whoever commits sin is a servant of sin."
35 "And a servant does not always remain in the house, but a son always remains."

36 "If The Son therefore will set you free, you will truly be the children of liberty."

37 "I know you are the seed of Abraham, but you seek to kill me because you cannot comprehend my word."

38 "I am speaking the thing I have seen with my Father; you are doing the thing that you have seen with your father."

39 They answered and were saying to him, "Abraham is our father." Yeshua said to them, "If you were children of Abraham, you would have been doing the works of Abraham."

40 "But now, behold, you are seeking to kill me; I am a man who have spoken the truth with you, which I have heard from God; this Abraham did not do."

41 "But you are doing the deeds of your father." They were saying to him, "We are not from fornication; we have one father, God."

42 Yeshua said unto them, "If God were your father, you would have loved me, for I have proceeded from God and have not come of my own pleasure, but he has sent Me."

43 "And why do you not understand my word? *It is* because you cannot hear my word."

44 "You are from your father The Devil, and the desire of your father you are willing to do ; from the beginning he has been murdering men and does not stand in the truth because there is no truth in him; whenever he speaks a lie, he speaks from what is his, because he is of falsehood and *is* also its father."

45 "But you are not believing in me, I who am speaking the truth."

46 "Who among you is convicting me of sin? And if I speak the truth, why do you not believe me?"

47 "Whoever is from God hears God's words; therefore you are not hearing, because you are not from God."

48 The Jews answered and they were saying to him, "Are we not saying correctly that you are a Samaritan and have a demon in you?"

49 Yeshua said to them, "A demon is not in me, but I honor my Father and you dishonor Me."

50 "But I am not seeking my glory ; There is One who seeks and judges."

51 "Timeless truth I speak to you: whoever keeps my word shall never see death."

52 The Jews were saying to him, "Now we know that a demon is in you. Abraham is

dead and The Prophets, and you are saying, 'Whoever keeps my words shall never taste death .' "

53 "Are you greater than our father Abraham who died and The Prophets who have died? Who are you making yourself?"

54 Yeshua said to them, "If I glorify Myself, My glory is nothing; it is my Father who glorifies me, he of whom you say, 'He is our God.' "

55 "And you do not know him, but I know him, and if I had said that I did not know him, I Myself would have been a liar like you, but I do know him and I keep his word."

56 "Abraham your father desired to see my day, and he saw *it* and rejoiced."

57 The Jews were saying to him, "You are not yet fifty years old, and you have seen Abraham?"

58 Yeshua said to them: "Timeless truth I speak to you: Before Abraham would exist, I AM THE LIVING GOD."

59 And they picked up stones to stone him, and Yeshua hid himself and went out from The Temple and passed through their midst and moved on.

Chapter 9

1 And as he passed, he saw a man blind from his mother's womb.

2 And his disciples asked him and they were saying, "Our Master, who is it that has sinned, this one or his parents, that he would be born blind?"

3 Yeshua said to them, "He had not sinned nor his parents, but that the works of God may appear in him."

4 "It is fitting that I do the works of him who has sent me while it is day; the night is coming in which a man cannot work."

5 "As long as I am in the world, I am The Light of the world."

6 And when he had said these things, he spat on the ground and formed clay from his spittle and he smeared it on the eyes of him who was blind.

7 And he said to him, "Go wash in the baptismal pool of Shilokha", and he went on, he washed, and as he was coming, he saw.

8 But his neighbors and those who had seen him begging before were saying: "Was this not he who sat and begged?"

9 Some were saying, "This is he", and some were saying, "No, but he is someone like him", but he said, "I am he."

10 They were saying to him, "How were your eyes opened?"

11 He answered and said to them, "A man by the name 'Yeshua' made clay and anointed me on my eyes and said to me, 'Go wash in the water of Shilokha', and I went, I washed and I saw."

12 They were saying to him, "Where is he?" He said to them, "I do not know."

13 And they brought him, who before had been blind, to the Pharisees.

14 But it was the Sabbath when Yeshua made clay and opened his eyes for him.

15 And the Pharisees asked him again, "How did sight come to you?" He said to them, "He put clay on my eyes and I washed and sight came to me."

16 And some of the Pharisees were saying, "This man is not from God because he does not keep the Sabbath"; but others were saying, "How is it possible for a man who is a sinner to do these miracles?" And there was a division among them.

17 Again they were saying to him who had been blind, "What do you say about him who opened your eyes for you?" He said to them, "I say he is a Prophet."

18 But the Judeans did not believe concerning him that he had been blind and was seeing, until they called the parents of the man who was seeing.

19 And they asked them: "Is this your son, the same whom you were saying that was born blind? How does he now see?"

20 But his parents answered and said, "We know that this is our son and that he was born blind;"

21 "But how he sees now or who he is that opened his eyes for him we do not know. He has come of age, ask him, for he shall speak for himself."

22 His parents said these things because they were afraid of the Judeans, for the Judeans had decided that if a man would confess him to be The Messiah, they would cast him out of the synagogue.

23 Therefore his parents said, "He has come of age; ask him."

24 And they called the man a second time who had been blind and they were saying to him, "Glorify God, for we know that this man is a sinner."

25 He answered and said to them, "If he is a sinner, I do not know, but one thing I do know: I was blind and behold, now I see."

26 They were saying to him again, "What did he do to you? How did he open your eyes for you?"

27 He said to them, "I told you and you were not listening. Why do you want to hear again? Do you also want to become his disciples?"

28 But they were insulting him and were saying to him, "You are his disciple; we are the disciples of Moses."

29 "And we know that God spoke with Moses, but we do not know from where this man is."

30 That man answered and said, "This is therefore to be marveled at, that you do not know from where he is and he opened my eyes."

31 "But we know that God does not listen to the voice of a sinner, but listens to whoever worships him and does his will."

32 "It has never been heard that a man has opened the eyes of one who was born blind."

33 "If this one were not from God, he would not have been able to do this."

34 They answered and were saying to him, "You were born entirely in sins, and are you teaching us?" And they cast him out.

35 And Yeshua heard that they had cast him out, and he found him and said to him, "Do you believe in the Son of God?" *

* Greek Codex W agrees with the Critical Greek text in reading : "In the Son of Man".
אלהא דברה - "InThe Son of God" according to The Peshitta's Aramaic.
דאנשא דברה - "In The Son of Man" in Aramaic, according to Codex W's reading.
In Aramaic, the two readings are practically identical.
In Greek, ΘΕΟΥ (of God) & ΑΝΘΡΩΠΟΥ (of man) are not similar.
Greek Uncial abbreviations : ΘΥ (of God) & ΑΝΟΥ (of man) are not similar.

36 He who had been healed answered and said, "Who is He, my lord, that I may trust in him?"

37 Yeshua said to him, "You have seen him, and he is The One who is speaking with you."

38 But he said, "I believe, my Lord", and falling down, he worshiped him.

39 And Yeshua said, "For the judgment of this world I have come, that those who do not

see may see, and that those who see may become blind."

40 And those of the Pharisees who had been with him heard these things and they said to him, "Are we also blind?"

41 Yeshua said to them, "If you were blind, you would not have sin, but now you say, 'We see.' Because of this, your sin stands."

Chapter 10

1 "Timeless truth I speak with you: whoever enters not by the gate to the sheepfold, but comes up from another place, is a thief and a robber."

2 "But he who enters by the gate is the shepherd of the flock;"

3 "To this one the gate keeper opens the gate and the flock hears his voice; he calls his sheep by their names and leads them out.

4 And when he has brought forth his flock, he goes before it and his own sheep go after him, because they know his voice.

5 But the flock goes not after a stranger, but flees from him, for it does not know a stranger's voice."

6 Yeshua spoke this allegory to them, but they did not know what he was speaking with them.

7 But again Yeshua said to them, "Timeless truth I speak to you; I AM THE LIVING GOD, The Gate of the flock."

8 "And all who had come were thieves and robbers, but the flock did not hear them."

9 "I AM THE LIVING GOD, The Gate; if anyone will enter by me, he shall live and shall go in and out and shall find the pasture."

10 "But a thief does not come except to steal, kill and destroy; I have come that they may have life and have whatever is abundant."

11 "I AM THE LIVING GOD, The Good Shepherd. The Good Shepherd lays down his life for his flock."

12 "But a hired man who is not a shepherd and does not own the sheep, whenever he may see a wolf coming, leaves the flock and runs."

13 "But a hired man runs because he is a hired man, and cares not about the flock, and a wolf comes snatching at and scattering the flock."

14 "I AM THE LIVING GOD, The Good Shepherd. I know mine and am known by mine."

15 "Just as my Father knows me and I know my Father, and I lay down my life for the flock's sake."

16 "But I have other sheep which were not from this fold; I must also bring them. They also will hear my voice, and the entire fold shall be one, and One Shepherd."

17 "Because of this my Father delights in me, because I am laying down my life that I may receive it again."

18 "No man takes it from me; I am laying it down of my own will, for I am authorized to lay it down, and I am authorized to receive it again; this commandment I have received from my Father."

19 And again there was a division among the Judeans because of these words.

20 And many among them were saying, "There is a demon in him and he is raving mad, why are you listening to him?"

21 But the others were saying, "These are not the words of one who is possessed. Can a demon open the eyes of the blind?"

22 But it was the Feast of Dedication in Jerusalem and it was winter.

23 And Yeshua was walking in The Temple on the porch of Solomon.

24 And the Judeans surrounded him and were saying, "How long will you keep our souls *in suspense?* If you are The Messiah, tell us plainly."

25 Yeshua answered and said to them, "I have told you, and you do not believe, and the works that I do in the Name of my Father, they testify of Me."

26 "But you do not believe, because you are not of my sheep, just as I said to you."

27 "My sheep hear my voice and I know them and they follow Me."

28 "And I am giving them eternal life, and they shall never perish, and no one shall snatch them from my hand."

29 "For my Father who gave them to me is greater than all, and no one is able to snatch anything from my Father's hand."

30 "I and my Father, We are One."

31 And the Judeans picked up stones again to stone him.

32 And Yeshua said to them, "Many excellent works from the presence of my Father I have shown you. For which of those works are you stoning me?"

33 The Judeans were saying to him, "It is not for excellent works that we are stoning you, but because you blaspheme, and as you are a man, you make yourself God."

34 Yeshua said to them, "Is it not written in your law, 'I have said, "You are gods"'?"

35 "If he called those men gods because The Word of God was with them and the scripture cannot be destroyed",

36 "Are you saying to The One whom The Father sanctified and sent into the world, "You blaspheme", because I said to you, 'I am The Son of God.'?"

37 "If I am not doing the works of my Father, you should not believe me",

38 "But if I am doing *them*, even though you do not believe me, believe those deeds, so that you may know and that you may believe that my Father is in me and I in my Father."

39 And they again sought to seize him, and he escaped from their hands.

40 And he went on to the crossing of The Jordan, to the place where Yohannan had been before when he was baptizing, and there he stayed.

41 And many people came to him and were saying, "Yohannan did not perform even one miracle, but everything that Yohannan had said about This Man is true."

42 And many believed in him.

Chapter 11

1. And a certain man was sick, Lazar of the town of Bayth-Ania, the brother of Maryam and of Martha.

The Greek has :ην δε τις ασθενων λαζαρος απο βηθανιας εκ της κωμης μαριας και μαρθας της αδελφης αυτης

1 ¶ (AV) Now a certain man was sick, named Lazarus, of Bethany, the town of Mary and her sister Martha.

The Peshitta has : מן בית-עניא קריתא אחוה דמרים ודמרתא
אית הוא דין חד דכריה לעזר

1 ¶ (MUR) And a certain man was sick, Lazarus of the town of Bethany, the brother of Mary and Martha.

Her Brother: (Aramaic) אחוה -

Her Sister: (Aramaic) דחתה-

Her Sister: (Hebrew) אחתה -

It also looks like a Greek translator had a problem with the Semitic form of naming a town (בית-עניא קריתא) , "Bethany Town" and the spelling of "

("Achuah"-"Brother"), which apparently was mistaken for

("D'Khatha"-"Sister"). The Greek has "the town of Mary and her sister Martha"; The Peshitta's Aramaic has "the brother of Mary and Martha".

"Town" should not be connected with any word following it, only with "Bethany".

A very literal reading, disregarding the Semitic use of town as part of the name of Bethany would lead to something like the following sense: " And a certain man was sick, Lazarus of Bethany, the town of the brother of Mary and Martha." That would have been OK, but apparently, the Greek translator misread "Brother" as "Sister", thereby throwing a monkey wrench into the meaning of the verse: "The sister of Mary and Martha" does not work, so "sister" must be moved in the Greek text to follow "Martha":

Hence, "the town of Mary and her sister Martha".

Please note that the Greek does not really make good sense here: "Lazarus was <u>from the town</u> of Mary and her sister" ? So what ? He was their brother ! The next verse alludes to that, but The Peshitta makes it plain in verse 1.

The Hebrew spelling of the word "Her sister" is even closer to the Aramaic spelling of "Her brother" than the old Aramaic script spelling:

Compare "Her Brother": (Aramaic) אחוה -

and "Her Sister": (Hebrew) אחתה -

For "la piece de la resistance", here is <u>Jastrow</u>'s Aramaic – Hebrew entry from the Targums on the Aramaic word "Akhatha"(Same as the Hebrew spelling above):

אֲחָת (אֲחַת), אַחֲתָא f. ch.=h. אָחוֹת. Targ. Jer. XXII, 18; a. fr.—Pes. 4ª; a. fr.—*Pl.* אֲחָוָתָא. Targ. Job. I, 4 (ed. אֲחָיָת); a. e.—Yeb. 32ᵇ. Sabb. 13ª. Yeb. 66ª top (*twin sisters*).

Apparently the older Aramaic retained the Hebrew form and was used as in The Aramaic Targum in Jeremiah 22:18, meaning "Sisters": אחות .

Here is The Peshitta reading ,"her brother" - אחוה .

Whether the translator thought he saw

or

either is close enough to

or אחוה to account for a possible error in translation and produce the Greek reading from the Aramaic of The Peshitta.

It would be a very difficult case to make to say the Aramaic came from the Greek, even if "sister" were to be misread as "brother", which are very similar in Greek; there would have been more than reconstructive surgery going on here. To get "Lazarus of the town of Bethany, the brother of Mary and Martha" from "Lazarus, of Bethany, the town of Mary and her sister Martha" would be progressive evolution! **The translator would have misread the definite article "της" as well as "αδελφης"("Sister") and dropped "αυτης"("her"), all three of which are feminine,** and made a masculine noun "brother" out of them. It is triply unlikely that three words would be misread, as opposed to one, as in the other scenario discussed above.

One would also be arguing that the Peshitta translation made much better sense than the original in such a case (and The Peshitta does make much better sense than the Greek text). That also seems extremely unlikely and counter productive to NT Theology.

2. This Maryam was the one who had anointed the feet of Yeshua with ointment and wiped them with her hair, whose brother Lazar was sick.

3. And his two sisters sent to Yeshua and they were saying, "Our Lord, behold, he whom you love is sick."

4. Yeshua said, "This sickness is not of death, but for the glory of God, that the Son of God may be glorified because of it."

5. Now Yeshua did love Martha and Maryam and Lazar.

6.And after he heard that he was sick, he remained in the place where he was for two days.

7.After this he said to his disciples, "Come, we shall go again to Judea."

8.His disciples were saying to him, "Our Rabbi, the Judeans had been just now seeking to stone you, and are you going there again?"

9.Yeshua said to them, "Are there not twelve hours in the day? If a man walks in the daylight he does not stumble, because he sees the light of this world."

10."And if a man walks in the night he stumbles, because there is no light with him."

11.These things Yeshua said and afterwards he said to them, "Lazar our friend is resting; I am going that I may awaken him."

12.His disciples were saying to him, "Our Lord, if he is sleeping, he is recovering health."

13.But Yeshua spoke about his death, and they had thought that he had been talking about lying down, taking sleep.

14.Then Yeshua said to them plainly, "Lazar has died."

15."And I am glad that I was not there for your sakes, that you may believe, but you should go there."

16.Thomas, who is called the Twin, said to his fellow disciples, "Let us go also and die with him."

17.Yeshua came to Bayth-Ania, and he found that he had been four days in the tomb.

18.But Bayth-Ania was beside Jerusalem, separated from it by about fifteen furlongs. (1 furlong = 1/8th mile)

19.And many of the Judeans were coming to Martha and Maryam to comfort their hearts concerning their brother.

20.But when Martha heard that Yeshua had come, she went out to meet him; but Maryam was sitting in the house.

21.And Martha said to Yeshua, "My Lord, if you had been here, my brother would not have died."

22."But even now I know that as much as you ask God, he gives to you."

23.Yeshua said to her, "Your brother shall arise."

24.Martha said to him, "I know that he shall rise in the resurrection in the last day."

25.Yeshua said to her, "I AM THE LIVING GOD, The Resurrection and The Life; whoever trusts in me, even if he dies, he shall live."

26.And everyone who lives and believes in me shall never die. Do you believe this?"

27.And she said to him, "Yes, my Lord, I do believe that you are The Messiah, The Son of God, who has come into the world."

28.And when she had said these things, she went and called Maryam her sister, secretly, and she said to her, "Our Rabbi has come and has called for you."

29.And when Maryam heard, she arose quickly and came to him.

30.But Yeshua had not yet come to the village, but he was in that place in which he met Martha.

31.But the Judeans also, who were with her in the house, who were comforting her, seeing Maryam rise quickly and go out, went after her, for they thought she went to the tomb to weep.

32.But Maryam, when she came where Yeshua was and saw him, she fell before his feet and she said to him, "My Lord, if only you would have been here, my brother would not have died!"

33.But when Yeshua saw that she wept and those Jews who had come with her weeping, he was powerfully moved in his spirit and his soul was moved.

34.And he said, "Where have you laid him?" And they were saying to him, "Come see, Our Lord."

35.And the tears of Yeshua were coming.

36.And the Judeans were saying, "See how much he loved him!"

37.But some of them said, "Was not this one who had opened the eyes of the blind man able to cause that even this one would not have died?"

38.But Yeshua, being powerfully moved within himself, came to the tomb, and the tomb was a cave and a stone had been placed over its doorway.

39.And Yeshua said, "Take away this stone." Martha, the sister of him who had died, said to him, "My Lord, by now it is putrid, for it has been four days."

40.Yeshua said to her, "Did I not tell you that if you would believe you would see the glory of God?"

41.And they took away that stone and Yeshua himself lifted his eyes above, and he said, "Father, I thank you that you have heard me."

42."And I know that you always hear me, but for the sake of this crowd that is standing here I said these things, that they may believe that you have sent me."

43. And when he had said these things, he cried in a loud voice, "Lazar, come out!"

44. And he who had died came out, while his hands and his feet were bound in swathing bands, and his face was bound in a turban. Yeshua said to them, "Unbind him and let him go."

45. And many of the Judeans that had come to Maryam, when they saw the thing that Yeshua did, believed in him.

46. And some of them went to the Pharisees, and they told them the thing which Yeshua did.

47. And the Chief Priests and the Pharisees were gathered, and they were saying, "What shall we do? This man is doing great miracles."

48. "And if we allow him *to do* so, all the people will believe in him and the Romans will come and take away our position and our nation."

49. But one of them, whose name was Qaipha, was The High Priest that year, and he said to them, "You know nothing,"

50. "And you do not consider that is profitable for us that one man should die instead of the nation, and not that the whole nation perish."

51. But this he said not of his own accord, but because he was The High Priest that year, he prophesied that Yeshua was going to die for the nation.

52. And not only in place of the nation, but so that also the children of God who had scattered, he would gather together into one.

53. And from that day they planned to kill him.

54. But Yeshua was not walking openly among the Judeans, but he went from there to the region near Arabah, to a fortress city, which is called Ephraim, and there he was employed with his disciples.

55. But the Passover of the Jews was drawing near. Many came out from the villages to Jerusalem before the feast to purify their souls.

56. And they were seeking for Yeshua, and they were saying to one another in The Temple, "What do you think? Will he come to the feast?"

57. But the Chief Priests and the Pharisees ordered that if anyone knew where he was, he

would show them so that they might seize him.

Chapter 12

1. But Yeshua came to Bayth-Ania before the six days of the Passover, where Lazar was, whom Yeshua had raised from the grave.

2. And they made a supper for him there and Martha was serving and Lazar was one of the guests with him.

3. But Maryam took an alabaster vase of ointment of the best Indian spikenard, very expensive, and she anointed the feet of Yeshua and wiped his feet with her hair and the house was filled with the fragrance of the ointment.

4. And Yehudah Scariota, one of the disciples, who was about to betray him, said:

5. "Why was not this oil sold for three hundred denarii and given to the poor?"

6. He said this, not because he was concerned about the poor, but because he was a thief and he had the money box and anything which fell into it he carried.

7. But Yeshua said, "Let her alone, for she has kept it for the day of my burial."

8. "For you have the poor with you always, but you do not have me with you always."

9. And great crowds of the Judeans heard that Yeshua was there and they came, not because of Yeshua only, but also that they might see Lazar, him whom he had raised from the grave.

10. And the Chief Priests had deliberated that they would also kill Lazar,

11. Because many of the Judeans were leaving because of him and believing in Yeshua.

12. And the next day a great crowd which had come to the feast, when they heard that Yeshua had come to Jerusalem,

13. Took branches of palm trees and went out to meet him, and they were shouting and saying, "Hosanna! Blessed is he that comes in the name of **THE LORD JEHOVAH**, The King of Israel!"

14. But Yeshua found a donkey and sat down upon it just as it is written:

15. "Fear not, daughter of Zion, behold your King comes to you and rides on a foal, a colt of a donkey."

16. But his disciples did not understand these things at that time, but when Yeshua was glorified, his disciples were reminded that

these things were written about him and that they had done these things to him.

17.And the crowd testified that they were with him when he called Lazar from the tomb and raised him from the dead.

18.And because of this, great crowds went in front of him who heard that he had done this miracle.

19.And the Pharisees were saying to one another, "Do you see that you are not gaining anything? Behold, the whole world is going after him."

20.But there were also some of them from among the Gentiles who came up to worship at the feast.

21.These came and approached Philippus, who was from Bethsaida of Galilee, and they asked him and were saying to him, "My lord, we wish to see Yeshua."

22.And Philippus himself came and told Andreas, and Andreas and Philippus told Yeshua.

23.But Yeshua answered and said to them, "The hour has come for The Son of Man to be glorified."

24."Timeless truth I speak to you: Unless a grain of wheat falls and dies in the ground, it remains alone, but if it dies, it yields much fruit."

25."Whoever loves his life shall destroy it and whoever hates his life in this world shall keep it for eternal life."

26."If a man serves me, he shall come after me, and where I am there shall also my servant be. Whoever ministers to me, The Father shall honor."

27."Behold, now my soul is troubled, and what shall I say: My Father, deliver me from this hour? But for this I have come to this hour."

28."Father, glorify your name." And a voice was heard from Heaven: "I have glorified and I am glorifying it again."

29.And the crowd that was standing there heard, and they were saying, "It was thunder", and others were saying "An Angel spoke with him."

30.Yeshua answered and said to them, "This voice was not for my benefit, but for your benefit."

31."Now is the judgment of this world; now The Ruler of this world is hurled outside."

32."And when I am lifted up from the earth, I will draw everyone to myself."

33.He said this that he might show by what death he would die.

34.The crowds were saying to him, "We have heard from The Law that The Messiah abides forever. How do you say that The Son of Man is going to be lifted up? Who is this Son of Man?"

35.Yeshua said to them, "The Light is with you a little time longer. Walk while The Light is with you, lest the darkness overtakes you. Whoever walks in darkness does not know where he is going."

36."While The Light is with you, believe in The Light, that you might be the children of The Light." These things spoke Yeshua, and departing, he hid himself from them.

37.And whereas he did all these miracles before them, they did not trust in him,

38.That the word of Isaiah the Prophet might be fulfilled, which says, "My Lord, who is believing our report and to whom is the arm of THE LORD JEHOVAH revealed?"

39.Therefore they were not able to believe, because again Isaiah had said:

40."They have put out their eyes and darkened their hearts lest they shall see with their eyes and understand in their hearts and should be converted and I would heal them."

41.Isaiah said these things when he saw his glory and spoke about him.

42.Many also among the Leaders believed in him, but they were not confessing him because of the Pharisees, lest they would end up outside of the synagogue.

43.For they loved the praise of men more than the praise of God.

44.But Yeshua cried and said, "Whoever trusts in me, trusts not in me, but in him who sent me."

45."And whoever sees me sees him who has sent me."

46."I, The Light, have come to the world, that no one who believes in me shall abide in darkness."

47."And whoever hears my words and does not keep them, I am not judging him, for I have come, not to judge the world, but to give life to the world."

48."Whoever rejects me and does not receive my words has one that judges him: the word that I have spoken, that shall judge him in the last day."

49."For I have not spoken from myself, but The Father who sent me, he gave me commandments, what I will say and what I will utter."

50."I know that his commandments are eternal life, therefore, these things which I am speaking, just as The Father tells me, thus I speak."

Chapter 13

1.**B**ut before the feast of the Passover, Yeshua had known that the hour had arrived that he would depart from this world to his Father, and he loved his own who were in this world and until the end he loved them.

2.And when it was supper he cast Satan into the heart of Yehuda son of Shimeon Scariota, so that he would betray him.

The most natural Aramaic grammar would have Satan as the direct object and Our Lord as the subject: **"He cast Satan into Judah's heart"**. It is only theological shock that would decree that the traditional translation is correct. We should allow the word to dictate theology, not vice versa. Our Lord certainly has all sovereign power over Satan.

3.And because Yeshua himself knew The Father had given everything into his hands and that he had gone out from God and he would go to God,

4.He arose from supper and put off his robe and took a towel and tied it around his waist.

5.He took water in a wash basin and began to wash the feet of his disciples and he wiped them with a towel which he had tied around his waist.

6.But when he came to Shimeon Kaypha, Shimeon said to him, "Are you washing my feet for me, my Lord?"

7.Yeshua answered and said to him, "What I am doing now you do not understand, but after this you will know."

8.Shimeon Kaypha said to him, "You will never wash my feet." Yeshua said to him, "If I do not wash you, you do not have any part with me."

9.Shimeon Kaypha said to him, "Therefore, my Lord, do not wash my feet only, but also my hands and my head."

10.Yeshua said to him, "He who is bathed does not need to wash except his feet only, for he is wholly clean. You are also entirely clean, but not all of you."

11.Yeshua had known who would betray him, therefore, he said, "Not all of you are clean."

12.But when he had washed their feet, he took up his robe and reclined at the table and he said to them, "Do you know what I have done to you?"

13.You call me, 'our Rabbi' and 'Our Lord', and you say rightly, for I am."

14.If I therefore, your Lord and your Rabbi, have washed your feet for you, how much more ought you to wash one another's feet?"

15.For I have given you this example, that you also should do in the same way as I have done to you."

16."Timeless truth I speak to you: there is no servant greater than his master and no apostle is greater than he who sent him."

17."If you know these things, blessed are you if you do them."

18."I have not spoken about all of you, for I know those whom I have chosen, but that the scripture may be fulfilled, 'He who eats bread with me has lifted up his heel against me.' ",

19."Now I am telling you before it happens, that when it has occurred, you shall believe that I AM THE LIVING GOD."

* Several times Our Lord tells the disciples that they shall believe "**Ena na**" (**I AM**). They apparently had not yet believed in His absolute Deity until after His death and resurrection. So sublime and deep is the significance of these words, that they were seldom understood or even heard by those to whom He spoke them. I have counted 150 occurrences of this term in 10 books of The Peshitta OT, 147 of which are utterances of The Deity – (**98 %**).
No other text beside The Peshitta properly sets forth this claim of Our Lord Yeshua Meshikha as plainly. Along with the 32 times the title "**MarYah**"-("**Jehovah**") is applied to Yeshua Meshikha,there are, counting the 25 " **Ena na**" statements in John, 57 very powerful testimonies to the absolute Deity of The Messiah Yeshua in The Peshitta New Testament not found in other Bible texts.

20."Timeless truth, I speak to you: whoever receives him whom I send receives me and whoever receives me receives him who sent me."

21.Yeshua said these things and was powerfully moved in his spirit and he testified and said, "An eternal reality I tell you: 'One of you will betray me.' "

22.But the disciples observed one another because they did not know about whom he spoke.

23.But there was one of his disciples who was supported in his bosom, for whom Yeshua had great affection.

24.Shimeon Kaypha gestured to him to ask him, "Who is it of whom he spoke?"

25.And that disciple fell on the breast of Yeshua and said to him, "My Lord, who is it?"

26.Yeshua answered and said, "It is he for whom I dip the bread and give it to him." And

Yeshua dipped the bread and gave to Yehuda Bar Shimeon Scariota.

(Here we see, as in 6:71 and 13:2 that Judas Iscariot was so named because he was **Yehuda son of Shimeon Scariota**, which the Greek texts seem to confuse here and elsewhere. The Majority Greek text has "**Judas Iscariot of Simon**," while the Critical Greek has "**Judas, of Simon Iscariot**", which is more in agreement with The Peshitta here. If the Peshitta were a translation of Greek, it would have been a translation of a Critical Alexandrian type Greek ms. here, of a Majority Byzantine type Greek ms. in John 13:2, and again of an Alexandrian type Greek ms. in John 6:71. This seems very unlikely, and when combined with all the variations and alternations found between Greek texts, this hypothesis would have The Peshitta translated from three or four Greek text types in alternation several times in every few verses, sometimes from several Greek versions in each verse! The other model is much more feasible: The Greek text types are simply various translations of The Peshitta. The principle of "Occam's Razor" applies beautifully here. The correct explanation is usually the simplest one. See the author's **Aramaic-English Interlinear New Testament** for in-depth discussion and comparisons of Greek and Aramaic readings.

27.And after the bread, then Satan was brought into him, and Yeshua said to him, "What you are doing, do quickly."

28.But no man among those reclining knew why he spoke to him.

29.For the men thought that because Yehuda had the money box that he had commanded him to buy something needed for the feast or that he would give something to the poor.

30.But Yehuda took the bread immediately and he went outside, and it was night when he left.

31.Yeshua said, "Now The Son of Man is glorified and God is glorified in him."

32."And if God is glorified in him, God also glorifies him in himself and at once glorifies him."

33."My children, a little longer I am with you, and you will seek me, and just as I said to the Judeans, 'The place to which I am departing, you cannot come', also I say to you now."

34."I give a new commandment to you: 'Love one another; just as I have loved you, you should also love one another.'"

35."Every person will know by this that you are my disciples, if you shall have love one to the other."

36.Shimeon Kaypha said to him, "Our Lord, where are you going?" Yeshua answered and said to him, "Where I go, you cannot now come after me, but at the end you shall come."

37.Shimeon Kaypha said to him, "My Lord, why cannot I come after you now? I will lay down my life for you."

38.* And Yeshua said to him, "Will you lay down your life for my sake? Amen, amen, I say to you: 'A rooster will not crow until you deny me three times.'"

Chapter 14

1."Let not your heart be troubled. Believe in God and believe in me." (Greek is ambiguous here: "Believe in God and believe in Me" or "You believe in God, you believe also in Me", or any combination of the two meanings. The Aramaic is clearly imperative both times: "Believe in God and believe in Me".)

2."There are many lodgings in my Father's house, and if not, I would have told you, because I go to prepare a place for you."

3."And if I go prepare a place for you, I shall come again and bring you to join me, that where I am you shall be also."

4."And where I am going, you know, and you know the way."

5.Thoma said to him, "Our Lord , we do not know where you are going and how can we know the way?"

6.Yeshua said to him, "I AM THE LIVING GOD, The Way and The Truth and The Life; no man comes to my Father but by me alone."

7."If you had known me, you also would have known my Father, and from this hour you do know him and you have seen him."

8.Philippus said to him, "Our Lord, show us The Father, and it is sufficient for us."

9.Yeshua said to him, "All this time I am with you and you have not known me Phillip? Whoever has seen me has seen The Father, and how do you say, 'Show us The Father'?"

10.* "Do you not believe that I am in my Father and my Father in me? The words which I am speaking, I am not speaking from myself, but my Father who dwells within me, he does these works."

11."Believe that I am in my Father and my Father in me, otherwise believe because of the works."

12."Timeless truth, I tell you: 'whoever believes in me, those works which I have done he will also do, and he will do greater works than these, because I am going to the presence of my Father.'"

13."And anything that you will ask in my name I shall do for you, that The Father may be glorified in his Son."

14."And if you will ask me in my name, I shall do this."

15."If you love me, keep my commandments."

16."And I shall request from my Father and he will give you another Redeemer of the accursed*, that he will be with you for eternity."

* According to the lexicons, "Parqlayta" (without yod) could be a contraction of Paraq + Qlayta (Redeemer –Protector), or it could be Paraq + Lyta ("Redeemer of the accursed"). The latter would seem to be the more accurate etymology. "Another Redeemer" implies a former Redeemer, which was Yeshua himself. The Greek word "Parakletos" (Advocate, Comforter, Intercessor) is never applied in The Gospels to Our Lord. The disciples did know him as the "Paroqa" & "Makhyana" (Redeemer, Lifegiver, Savior).

17."He is The Spirit of Truth, whom the world cannot receive, because it has neither seen him nor known him; but you know him, for he dwells with you and he is in you."

18."I shall not leave you as orphans, for I shall come to you in a little while."

19."And the world will not see me, but you shall see me; because I live, you also shall live."

20.At that day, you will know that I am in my Father and you are in me and I am in you."

21."Whoever has my commands and keeps them, he does love me, but he who loves me shall be loved from my Father and I shall love him, and I shall show myself to him."

22.Yehuda said to him (he was not Scariota), "My Lord, how is it you are going to show yourself to us and not the same to the world?"

23.Yeshua answered and said to him, "Whoever loves me keeps my word, and my Father will love him, and we will come to him, and we will make our lodging with him."

24."But he who does not love me does not keep my word, and this word which you are hearing is not mine, but The Father's who has sent me."

25."I have spoken these things with you while I am with you."

26."But he, The Redeemer of the accursed, The Spirit of Holiness, whom my Father sends in my name, he will teach you all things and he will remind you of everything whatsoever I have told you."

27."Peace I leave with you; my peace I give to you. It is not as the world gives that I give to you. Do not let your heart be troubled, and do not let it be afraid."

28."You have heard that I said to you, 'I am going away, and I am coming to you'; if you had loved me, you would have rejoiced that I am going to join my Father, for my Father is greater than I."

29."And now, behold, I have told you before it happens, that when it has happened, you may believe."

30."After this I will not be speaking much with you, for The Prince of the world is coming and he has nothing to use against me*.

* "W'bai layt lah meddem" is an idiomatic expression meaning : "He has nothing against me." Today, we might say: "He has nothing on me", meaning, "he cannot rightfully accuse me of anything and he has no damaging information he can use against me".

31.But that the world may know that I love my Father, and just as my Father has taught me, so I have done. Rise up, let us depart from here."

Chapter 15

1."I AM THE LIVING GOD, The True Vine, and my Father is the vine dresser."

2."Every branch on me not yielding fruit he takes away, and that which yields fruit he purges that it may bring forth much fruit."

3."From now on you are purged because of the word which I have spoken with you."

4."Stay with me, and I am in you. Just as the branch cannot yield fruit by itself unless it remains on the vine, so neither do you unless you stay with me."

5."I AM THE LIVING GOD, The Vine, and you are the branches; whoever abides with me and I in him, this one brings forth much fruit, because without me, you can do nothing."

6."If a man does not abide with me, he is thrown away like a shriveled up branch, and they gather it, throwing it into the fire to burn."

7."But if you are abiding in me and my words will abide in you, everything whatsoever you desire to ask, it shall be done for you."

8."In this The Father is glorified, that you will bring forth much fruit and that you will be my disciples."

9."Just as my Father has loved me, even so I have loved you; continue in my friendship."

10."If you keep my commands, you will remain in my love, just as I have kept my Father's commands and I abide in his love."

11."I have spoken these things with you that my joy may be in you and that your joy may be perfect."

12."This is my commandment, that you love one another, just as I have loved you."

13."There is no greater love than this: that a person would lay down his life for the sake of his friends."

The Greek texts have a different reading:
"Greater love has no man than this, that a man lay down his life for his friends".

I have little doubt that a Greek translator mistook דאנש -"that a man" as לאנש -"to a man". לית לאנש, the misread text with a Lamed ל where there was a Dalet ד, means, "No man has". In so reading it, the translator would have created the Aramaic idiom לית לאנש , meaning , "No man has".

The actual reading cannot mean that; it is an absolute statement of truth: "There is no greater love than this, that a man will lay down his life for his friends."

(Blue words represent the two Aramaic words לית דאנש. The Greek reading : "Greater love has no man than this, that a man lay down his life for his friends"(blue words represent לית לאנש).

It is easy, once again, to see how the Aramaic could give rise to the Greek ,especially from a square Aramaic script (used until the first century in Aramaic mss.), as is used here. I believe it would be very difficult to account for the Aramaic reading of the Peshitta as a translation of the Greek text. The Greek would not translate into the Aramaic of The Peshitta. The Peshitta simply does not look like a translation of the Greek, here & in many other places.

Just a graphic recap. illustrating the Aramaic basis for the Greek reading :

Peshitta reading	Greek reading in Aramaic
לית דאנש	–"there is not, that a man":
לית לאנש	–"no man has"

DSS Aramaic

–"there is not, that a man":
–" no man has"

The Greek verse does not compare to the implications of The Peshitta reading.

This Peshitta verse is probably one of the most important in all of scripture, theologically. It not only sets the standard and definition for the greatest love possible, but for The greatest possible God. Think about this statement with reference to Him, and you have something to think about and contemplate for an eternity.

14."You are my friends if you will do all that I command you."

15."No longer do I call you servants, because a servant does not know what his master does, but I have called you my friends, because all that I have heard from my Father, I have taught you."

16."You have not chosen me, but I have chosen you and I have appointed you so that you also will go bring forth fruit and your fruit will remain, so that all you will ask my Father in my name, he will give to you."

17."These things I command you that you will love one another."

18."And if the world hates you, know that it hated me before you."

19. "And if you had been from the world, the world would have loved its own; but you are not from the world, but I have chosen you from the world; because of this the world hates you."

20."Remember the word that I have spoken to you, that there is no servant greater than his master. If they have persecuted me, they will persecute you also; if they have kept my word, they will also keep yours."

21."They will do all these things among you because of my name, because they do not know him who has sent me."

22."If I did not come speaking with them, they would have no sin, but now there is no excuse for their sin."

23."Whoever hates me hates my Father also."

24."If I had not done the works in their sight which no other man had done, they would not have sin,

25.That the word which is written in their law may be fulfilled: 'They hated me for nothing.' But now they have seen and hated me and my Father also."

26."But when The Redeemer of the accursed comes, him whom I shall send to you from the presence of my Father, The Spirit of Truth, he who proceeds from the presence of my Father, he shall testify concerning me."

27."You also are testifying, who are with me from the beginning."

Chapter 16

1."I have spoken these things with you that you would not be subverted."

2."For they shall put you out from their assemblies, and the hour will come when everyone who would kill you will think that he presents an offering to God."

3."And they shall do these things because they do not know either my Father or me."

4."I have spoken these things with you that when their time comes, you will remember them; I did not tell you these things before, because I was with you."

5."But now I am going to join him who sent me, and no man among you asks me, 'Where are you going?'"

6."For I said these things to you and sadness has come and has filled your hearts."

7."I tell you the truth: it is beneficial for you that I go away, for if I do not go away, the Redeemer of the accursed will not come to you, but if I depart I shall send him to you."

8."And when he comes, he will correct the world concerning sin and concerning righteousness and concerning judgment;"

9."Concerning sin, because they do not trust me;"

10."Concerning righteousness, because I will go to my Father's presence and you will not see me again;"

11."Concerning judgment, because The Prince of this world is judged."

12."I have much to say to you, but you are not able to grasp it now."

13."But whenever The Spirit of The Truth comes, he will lead you into the whole truth, for he will not speak of his own will, but he shall speak whatever he shall hear and he shall reveal the future to you."

14."And he shall glorify me, because he shall take that which is mine and shall show you."

15."Everything that my Father has is mine, therefore I said to you that he shall take that which is mine and he shall show you."

16."A little while and you will not see me; again a little while and you will see me because I am going to the presence of The Father."

17.And his disciples were saying to one another, "What is this that he said to us: 'A little while and you will not see me and again a little while and you shall see me', and, 'I am going to join my Father.'"?

18.And they were saying, "What is this, 'A little while', that he says? We do know not what he is uttering."

19.But Yeshua knew that they wanted to ask him and he said to them, "Are you inquiring about this with each other, because I said to you, 'A little while and you will not see me and again, a little while, and you will see me'"?

20. "Timeless truth, I speak to you: you shall weep and mourn and the world will rejoice, and you will have sorrow, but your sorrow will be turned into joy."

21."When a woman is giving birth, she has sorrow because the day for her delivery has arrived, but when she has delivered a son, she does not remember the distress for the joy that a son has been born into the world."

22."You also now have sorrow, but I shall see you again, and your heart shall rejoice, and your joy no man shall take from you."

23."And in that day you will not ask me anything. Timeless truth I speak to you: Everything that you shall ask my Father in my name, he shall give to you."

24."Until now you have not asked anything in my name. Ask and you will receive, that your joy may be perfect."

25."I have spoken these things in parables with you, but the hour is coming when I shall speak with you, not in parables, but I shall declare to you about The Father plainly."

26."In that day, you will ask in my name, and I do not say to you that I shall request from The Father for you."

27."For The Father himself loves you because you have loved me and have believed that I have come forth from union with God *." *
(Eastern Peshitta mss. have ,"**The Father**", as do the Alexandrian Greek mss. . The Western Peshitto, The Majority Greek and Latin Vulgate have, "**God**".)

28.For I have proceeded from union with The Father and I have come into the world, and again I leave the world, and I am going to join The Father."

29.His disciples were saying to him, "Behold, now you are speaking plainly and you are not speaking any parable."

30."Now we know that you know everything and that you do not need that anyone should ask you; in this we believe that you have proceeded from God."

31.Yeshua said to them, "Believe it."

32."Behold the hour comes and now it has come, when you will be scattered everyone to his place and you will leave me alone, and I shall not be alone because The Father is with me."

33."I have spoken these things to you so that you shall have peace in me. You shall have suffering in the world, but take heart, I have overcome the world."

Chapter 17

1.These things spoke Yeshua and lifted his eyes unto Heaven and he said: "My Father, the hour has come; Glorify your Son, that your Son may glorify you."

2."Just as you have given him authority over all flesh*, he will give eternal life to them, because you have given all things* whatsoever unto him."

* "**All flesh**"- "**Kol basar**" is singular in number grammatically , though certainly plural in meaning. "He will give **to it**"- " **Natal lah**" grammatically refers "it" to "**all flesh**" quite well. A similar construction occurs in the Peshitta version of Genesis 6:17.
See Luke 3:6 and Acts 2:17. It has always been God's promise to save all people. There are many promises of salvation to "**all flesh**" in The Hebrew Bible. That salvation is called the **Will of God** in 1Timothy 2:3,4 and **The Promise of The Gospel** to Abraham in Galatians 3:8. It is also called **The New Covenant** in Jeremiah 31:31-34 and Hebrews 8:8-13. There are too many references to list here, but certainly Our Lord God Yeshua Meshikha said: "**I came not to judge the world, but to save the world**."(John 12:47) Shall we trust and follow a liar or a failure? God forbid!

* כל מא - "Koll ma" means "**everything**" , never "everyone" (See v. 7, as well as Mt 7:12 Mt 13:46 Mt 17:12

Mt 18:18 Mt 23:20 Mt 28:20 Mr 6:30 Mr 9:13 Lu 21:22 Joh 14:26 Joh 15:7 Joh 17:2 Ac 3:22 Ac 4:23 Ac 4:28 Ac 10:33 Ac 10:39 Ac 15:4 Ac 15:12 Ac 17:24 Ac 21:19 Ac 26:2 Re 1:2. All other translations of this verse are confused and unfaithful to both the Greek and Aramaic texts (though the Aramaic is more accurate) in a blatant attempt to circumvent the universalism in Our Lord's prayer.

3."But these things are eternal life: They shall know you, for you alone are The God of Truth, and Yeshua The Messiah whom you have sent.' "

4."I have glorified you in the earth; I have accomplished the work that you have given me to do."

5."Now, glorify me, my Father, in union with yourself, in that glory which I had in union with you before the universe was."

6."I have revealed your Name to the children of men, those whom you have given me from the world; yours they were, and you have given them to me, and they have kept your word."

7."Now I * know that everything * whatsoever you have given me is from your Presence." (* Most Greek mss. have "They know"; Codex W has "εγνωκα"-"I have known"; * כל מא - "Koll ma" means "everything".)

8."For the words that you gave me I have given them, and they have received them and known truly that I have proceeded from unity with you."

9."I pray over them; I was not praying over the world, but I was praying for those whom you have given me, for they are yours, and they have believed that you have sent me."

10."And everything that is mine is yours, and yours is mine, and I am glorified in them."

11."From now on, I do not dwell in the world, but these are in the world, and I am coming to join you. Holy Father, keep them in your Name - that Name which you have given me, so that they shall be one, just as we are."

12."When I was with them in the world, I kept them in your Name; I have kept those whom you gave me, and no man among them has perished, except The Son of Destruction, that the scripture should be fulfilled."

13."But now I come to you, and I am speaking these things in the world, that my joy shall be complete in them."

14."And I have given them your word, and the world has hated them, because they are not from the world, even as I am not from the world."

15."It is not that I am praying you would take them from the world, but that you would preserve them from The Evil One."

16."For they are not from the world, even as I am not from the world."

17."Father, sanctify them by your truth, because your word is truth."

18."Just as you have sent me into the world, I also have sent them into the world."

19."And I sanctify myself for them, that they also shall be sanctified in the truth."

20."Neither do I pray only for them, but also for these who are trusting in me by their word,"

21."That they all shall be one, just as you, my Father, are in me, and I am in you, so that they also shall be one in us. "

22."And I have given them the glory that you have given me, so that they shall be one, just as we are one, so that the world shall believe that you have sent me. "

23."I in them and you in me, so that they shall be perfected as one, and so that the world shall know that you have sent me, and that you have loved them just as you have also loved Me. "

24."Father, I will that these whom you have given me shall also be with me where I am, that they shall see my glory which you have given me, because you have loved me from before the foundation of the world. "

25."My Righteous Father, although the world has not known you, I have known you, and these have known that you have sent Me."

26."And I have revealed to them your Name, and I am revealing it, so that the love with which you have loved me shall be in them, and I shall be in them."

Chapter 18

1.Yeshua said these things and went forth with his disciples to the crossing of the torrent of Qedrown; The place was a garden, where he and his disciples entered.

2.But Yehuda the traitor had also known that place, because Yeshua had met there many times with his disciples.

3.Therefore Yehuda led a company* also from the presence of the Chief Priests and the Pharisees. He led the guards and came there with torches and lamps and weapons. * (A company consisted of 500 to 1000 soldiers.)

4.But Yeshua, because he knew all these things had come upon him, went out and said to them, "Whom are you seeking?"

5.They were saying to him, "Yeshua the Nazarene." Yeshua said to them, "I AM THE LIVING GOD." But Yehuda the traitor was also standing with them.

6.And when Yeshua said to them, "I AM THE LIVING GOD", they went backward and fell to the ground.

7.Yeshua said again, "Whom are you seeking?" But they said, "Yeshua the Nazarene."

8.Yeshua said to them, "I have told you that I AM THE LIVING GOD, and if you are seeking me, let these men go",

9.So that the saying might be fulfilled: "Of Those whom you have given me, I have not lost one." (Referring to John 17:12)

10.But Shimeon Kaypha had a sword on him and he drew it and struck the servant of The High Priest and took off his right ear, and the name of the servant was Malka.

11.Yeshua said, "Kaypha, put the sword in its sheath. The cup that The Father has given me, shall I not drink it?"

12.Then the company and a Captain of a thousand, and guards of the Judeans, seized Yeshua and bound him.

13.And they brought him to the presence of Hannan first, because he was Father-in-law of Qaypha, who was The High Priest that year.

14.But it was Qaypha who counseled the Jews that it was better that one man should die for the sake of the nation.

15.But Shimeon Kaypha and one of the other disciples were coming after Yeshua, and that disciple had known The High Priest and he entered with Yeshua to the courtyard.

16.But Shimeon was standing outside near the gate and that other disciple who knew The High Priest went out and spoke to her who kept the gate and he brought in Shimeon.

17.But the maiden gatekeeper said to Shimeon, "Are you also one of this man's disciples?" He said to her, "No."

18.And the servants and the guards were standing and they were setting a fire to warm themselves because it was cold, but Shimeon was also standing with them and warming himself.

19.And The High Priest asked Yeshua about his disciples and about his teaching.

20.And Yeshua said to him, "I have spoken openly with the people, and at all times I have taught in the synagogue and in The Temple, where all of the Judeans assemble and I have spoken nothing in secret."

21."Why do you ask me? Ask those who heard what I spoke with them, behold, they know what I have said."

22.And when he had said these things, one of the guards who was standing *there* struck Yeshua on the cheek and said to him, "Do you answer thus to The High Priest?"

23.Yeshua answered and said to him, "If I have spoken evil, testify of the evil, but if I have spoken correctly, why do you strike me?"

24.But Hannan sent Yeshua, being bound, to the presence of Qaypha the High Priest.

25.And Shimeon Kaypha was standing and warming himself and they were saying to him, "Are you also one of his disciples?" And he denied and said, "I am not."

26.And one of the servants of The High Priest, near kin of him whose ear Shimeon had cut off, said, "Did I not see you with him in the garden?"

27.And Shimeon denied again, and in that hour a rooster crowed.

28.They brought Yeshua from the presence of Qaypha to the Praetorium, and it was dawn, and they did not enter the Praetorium, lest they would be defiled, until they had eaten the Passover.

29.But Pilate went outside to their presence and he said to them, "What accusation do you have against this man?"

30.And they answered, and they were saying to him, "If he were not an evildoer, we would not have delivered him to you."

31.Pilate said to them, "Take him and judge him according to your law." The Judeans were saying to him, "It is not permitted for us to kill a man",

32.So that the saying may be fulfilled that Yeshua spoke when he revealed by what death he was going to die.

33.But Pilate entered the Praetorium and he called for Yeshua and said to him, "Are you The King of the Judeans?"

34.Yeshua said to him, "Have you said this of yourself, or have others spoken to you about me?"

35.Pilate said to him, "Am I a Judean? The people of your nation and The High Priests have delivered you to me. What have you done?"

36.Yeshua said to him, "My Kingdom is not from this world; if my Kingdom were of this world, my servants would be fighting that I would not have been delivered up to the Judeans, but now my Kingdom is not from here."

37.Pilate said to him, "You are a King then?" Yeshua said to him, "You have said that I am a King. For this I was born and for this I have come into the world: to testify of the truth. Everyone who is of the truth hears my voice."

38.Pilate said to him, "What is the truth?" And when he had said this he went out again to the Judeans and he said to them, "I find not even one fault in him."

39."But you have a custom that I should release to you one prisoner at Passover. Do you wish therefore that I release you this man, The King of the Judeans?"

40.And they all cried out when they were saying, "Not this one, but Barabba." But this Barabba was a robber.

Chapter 19

1.Then Pilate scourged Yeshua.

2.And the soldiers wound a crown from thorns and they placed it on his head and clothed him with a purple robe.

3.And they were saying, "Hail to you, King of the Judeans", and they were hitting him on his cheeks.

4.And Pilate went outside again and he said to them, "Behold, I bring him forth to you outside that you may know that I find no occasion for complaint in him, not even one cause."

5.And Yeshua went forth outside with the crown of thorns upon him and the purple robe, and Pilate said to them, "Behold, here is the man."

6.But when the Chief Priests and the guards saw him, they cried out and they were saying, "Crucify him! Crucify him!" Pilate said to them, "Take him and crucify him, for I do not find any fault in him."

7.The Judeans were saying to him, "We have a law and according to that in our Written Law he is condemned to death because he made himself the Son of God."

8.But when Pilate heard this statement he was even more afraid.

9.And he entered the Praetorium again and he said to Yeshua, "Where are you from?" But Yeshua gave him no answer.

10.Pilate said to him, "Are you not speaking with me? Do you not know that I have power

to release you and I have power to crucify you?"

11.Yeshua said to him, "You have no power at all over me unless it has been given to you from above; therefore, whoever has delivered me to you has greater sin than yours."

12.Because of this Pilate wanted to release him, but the Judeans were crying out, "If you release this man, you are not Caesar's friend, for everyone who makes himself King is an adversary of Caesar."

13.But when Pilate heard this statement he brought Yeshua outside and sat down on the judgment seat and the place that was called R'tsiftha d'Kaypha, but in Hebrew* it is called Gpiptha.

---

* "R'Tsiftha d'Kaypha" & "Gpiptha" are in Northern (Galilean) and Southern (Judean) dialects of Palestinian Aramaic. Both names mean "**The Pavement**." The Greek has "Gabbatha" (Γαββαθα), another obvious transliteration of the Aramaic ("Gpiptha") גפיפתא, in which the letter "Pe" פ was mistaken for a "Beth" ב , easily done with square Aramaic script. This does not work in a Greek to Aramaic translation scenario. "**Gabbatha**" (ΓΑΒΒΑΘΑ in Greek) would not be mistaken for ("Gpiptha") גפיפתא ("ΓΑΦΙΦΘΑ" or ΓΑΠΙΠΘΑ in Greek).

The Judean Aramaic dialect is here called "**Hebrew**" because both Aramaic & Hebrew shared Hebrew alphabet & characters, and Aramaic was spoken by the Hebrew people. The following are excerpts from Jastrow's Hebrew Aramaic Dictionary on the word "Ebraith (Hebrew)":

עִבְרִי m., עִבְרִיָּה, עִבְרִית f. (b.h.) Hebrew; '> (לשון) Hebrew language; '> (כתב) Hebrew character, type. Kidd. I, 2 עבד '> a Hebrew slave; אמה הע' a Hebrew hand-maid. Gen. R. s. 42 '> ומשיח בלשון, v. עֲבַר II. Gitt. IX, 6 עברית לע' an Aramaic translation read before Aramæan Jews. Ex. R. s. 3 למה קורא אותם ע' על שם שעברי ים why does he call them 'Ibriim (Ex.III,18)? Because they passed the sea (on going to Egypt). Ib. s.1. Pesik. R. s. 23; a. fr.

According to ancient word usage, "Ebraith" –"Hebrew", can refer to Aramaic, & always does so in the NT.

14.And it was the eve of the Passover, and it was about the sixth hour, and he said to the Judeans, "Behold, here is your King!"

15.But they were crying out, "Take him away! Take him away! Crucify him! Crucify him!" Pilate said to them, "Shall I crucify your King?" The Chief Priests were saying, "We have no King but Caesar!"

16.Then he delivered him to them that they would crucify him, and they led Yeshua and brought him out.

17.Then he took up his cross to the place called Qaraqpatha, but in Hebrew * it is called Gagultha, * See note at v. 13

18.Where they crucified him and two others with him, one on one side and one on the other side, and Yeshua in the center.

19.And Pilate wrote a title and placed it on his cross, but it was written thus: "This is

Yeshua the Nazarene, The King of the Judeans."

20. And many of the Judeans read this tablet, because the place in which Yeshua was crucified was near the city, and it was written in Aramaic and in Greek and in Latin.

21. And the Chief Priests said to Pilate, "Do not write, 'He is The King of the Judeans', but, "He said, 'I am The King of the Judeans.'"

22. Pilate said, "What I have written, I have written."

23. But the soldiers, when they had crucified Yeshua, took his garments, and they made four parts, a part to each of the soldiers; but his tunic was without a seam: it was woven entirely from the top.

24. And they said to one another, "Let us not tear it, but let us cast lots for it, who will be allowed to have it." And the scripture was fulfilled that says, "They divided my garment among them and for my clothing they cast lots." The soldiers therefore did these things.

25. But his mother and the sister of his mother, and Mary, who was of Cleopa, and Maryam Magdalitha, were standing at the cross of Yeshua.

26. But Yeshua saw his mother and the disciple whom he loved standing and he said to his mother, "Woman, behold, your son."

27. He said to that disciple, "Behold, your mother." And from that hour that disciple received her to himself.

28. After these things Yeshua knew that everything had been finished, and that the scripture may be fulfilled, he said, "I thirst."

29. And a vessel had been set full of vinegar, but they filled a sponge from the vinegar and placed it on hyssop and they put it near to his mouth.

30. When he took the vinegar, Yeshua said, "Behold, it is finished." And he bowed his head and gave up his Spirit.

31. But the Judeans, because it was evening, they were saying, "These bodies will not pass the night on their crosses, because the Sabbath day is approaching", for it was a great Sabbath day. And they sought from Pilate to break the legs of those who had been crucified, and they would be taken away.

32. And the soldiers came and they broke the legs of the first and of the other who was crucified with him.

33. When they came to Yeshua, they saw that he had died already and they did not break his legs.

34. But one of the soldiers struck him on his side with his spear, and at once blood and water issued forth.

35. And he who saw testified and his testimony is true and he knows that he spoke the truth so that you also may believe.

36. For these things happened that the scripture should be fulfilled that says, "Not a bone of him will be broken",

37. And another scripture again, that says, "They shall gaze at him whom they pierced through."

38. After these things, Yoseph, who was from Ramtha, sought from Pilate because he was a disciple of Yeshua, (and it was secretly from fear of the Judeans), that he might take the body of Yeshua; and Pilate gave him permission and he came and took away his body.

39. And Nicodemus also came, who had come before to Yeshua by night, and he brought with him spices of myrrh for Yeshua and of aloes about a hundred pounds.

40. And they took away the body of Yeshua and wrapped it in linen and in sweet spices, just as the custom of the Judeans is for burying.

41. And there was in that place where Yeshua had been crucified a garden, and in the garden a new tomb in which a man had not yet been laid.

42. And they laid Yeshua there because the Sabbath was approaching and because the tomb was nearby.

Chapter 20

1. But on the first day of the week, in the very early morning while it was dark, Maryam Magdalitha came to the tomb and she saw the stone that had been removed from the tomb.

2. And she ran and came to Shimeon Kaypha and to that other disciple whom Yeshua had loved, and she said to them, "They have taken away Our Lord from the tomb, and I don't know where they have laid him."

3. Shimeon went out and that other disciple, and they came to the tomb.

4. And they were both running together, but that disciple ran in front of Shimeon and he came first to the tomb.

5. And he looked, gazing at the linens where they were lying, but he did not enter.

6. Then Shimeon came after him and entered the tomb, gazing at the linens where they were lying,

7. And a grave cloth, which had been bound about his head, not with the linens, but as it was wrapped and set on the side in one place.

8. Then that other disciple entered, who came first to the tomb, and he stared and he believed.

9. But they had not yet known from the scriptures that he was going to rise from the dead.

10. And those disciples departed again to their place.

11. But Maryam was standing at the tomb and was weeping, and while weeping she looked inside the tomb.

12. And she saw two Angels in white sitting, one at his pillow, and one at the foot, where the body of Yeshua had been laid.

13. And they were saying to her, "Woman, why are you weeping?" She said to them, "They have taken away my Lord, and I don't know where they have laid him."

14. She said this and turned around and saw Yeshua standing and she did not know that he was Yeshua.

15. Yeshua said to her, "Woman, why are you weeping, and whom are you seeking?" But she thought he was the Gardener, and she said to him, "Sir, if you have taken him, tell me where you have laid him; I will go take him away."

16. Yeshua said to her, "Maryam." And she turned and said to him in Hebrew * , "Rabbuli", which is to say "Teacher."

* עבראית "Ebraith" means "Hebrew" and though Aramaic was the language used, the Jewish people referred to Judean Aramaic as Hebrew, since it had been their native tongue (the tongue of the Hebrew people) for six centuries and was used in their scriptures. Aramaic and Hebrew share the same alphabet and both were written with the same script, so their letters looked the same in the first century. Southern Judean Aramaic is probably referred to as "Hebrew". Northern Aramaic would have differed slightly in a few places in written form.
רבולי –"Rabbuli" is an Aramaic word meaning "My Master" and is the same as "Rabboni", which the Greek versions have in Greek letters transliterated "Rabbouni". Notice that Maryam is not presented as speaking Greek; neither is any other person mentioned in the four Gospels. "Ebraith" – "Hebrew" is **defined by its Greek equivalent, "Hebrais", as "The Hebrew tongue; not that however in which the OT was written, but the Chaldee."** Thayer's Greek – English Lexicon. Webster's unabridged 20th century Dictionary defines "Chaldee" as **The Aramaic language of the Chaldaeans (Babylonians 600 B.C.)**

17. Yeshua said to her. "Don't cling to me, for I have not yet ascended to join my Father, and go join my brothers and say to them that I ascend to join my Father and your Father, my God, and your God."

18. And Maryam Magdalitha came and announced to the disciples, "I have seen Our Lord", and that he had said these things to her.

19. But when it was evening of the first day of the week and the doors were barred where the disciples were staying, because of fear for the Judeans, Yeshua came and stood in their midst and he said to them, "Peace be with you."

20. He said this and he showed them his hands and his side and the disciples rejoiced because they saw Our Lord.

21. But Yeshua said to them again, "Peace be with you. Just as my Father has sent me, I also am sending you."

22. When he had said these things, he breathed upon them and he said to them, "Receive The Spirit of Holiness."

23. "If you will forgive a man's sins, they will be forgiven him, and if you hold a man's, they will be held."

24. But Thoma, one of the twelve, who is called The Twin, he was not there when Yeshua had come.

25. And the disciples were saying to him, "We have seen Our Lord", but he said to them, "Unless I see in his hands the places of the nails and I shall put my fingers in them, and reach my hand into his side, I will not believe."

26. And after eight days, again the disciples were inside and Thoma was with them and Yeshua came when the doors were barred; he stood in the center and he said to them, "Peace be with you."

27. And he said to Thoma, "Put your finger here and behold my hands and put your hand and reach into my side and do not be an unbeliever, but a believer."

28. And Thomas answered and said to him, "My Lord, and my God."

29. Yeshua said to him, "Now that you have seen me, you have believed. Blessed are those who have not seen me and have believed."

30. But Yeshua did many other signs before his disciples, which are not written in this scripture.

31. But these things are also written that you may believe that Yeshua is The Messiah, the Son of God, and when you believe, you shall have eternal life in his name.

This verse is much more pointed and specific in Aramaic than in the Greek versions: "And when you believe, you shall have eternal life in his Name." The Greek versions are rendered: "And that believing ye may have life in his name." The Greek is unclear about the "When" and the "Eternal", because those words are not found in the Greek versions of this verse. The Aramaic also uses the future tense -"Shall have", where the Greek uses the subjunctive mood : "May have", "Should have", which is a less certain prospect than the future tense.

Chapter 21

1.After these things Yeshua again showed himself to his disciples by the Sea of Tiberius, and he appeared thus:

2.There were together Shimeon Kaypha and Thoma, who is called The Twin, and Nathaniel who was from Qatna of Galilee and the sons of Zebedee and two others of the disciples.

3.Shimeon Kaypha said to them, "I am going to catch fish." They were saying to him, "We are also coming with you." And they went out and embarked the ship, and that night they caught nothing.

4.But when it was dawn, Yeshua stood on the side of the sea and the disciples did not know that it was Yeshua.

5.And Yeshua said to them, "Lads, do you have anything to eat?" They said to him, "No."

6.He said to them, "Throw your net on the right side of the ship, and you will find." And they cast and they could not haul in the net from the multitude of the fish it had caught.

7.And that disciple for whom Yeshua had great affection said to Kaypha, "This is Our Lord." But Shimeon, when he heard that he was Our Lord, he took his tunic, girding his loins because he was naked, and he threw himself into the sea to come to Yeshua.

8.But the other disciples came in the boat, for they were not very far from the land, but about two hundred cubits, and they were dragging the net with the fish.

9.But when they came up to the land they saw burning coals, which had been set, and fish were lying on them, and bread.

10.And Yeshua said to them, "Bring some of those fish that you have caught just now."

11.And Shimeon Kaypha came up and dragged the net to the land as it was filled with 153 great fish, and with all this weight, the net was not ripped.

12.And Yeshua said to them, "Come have breakfast", but none of the disciples dared ask him who he was, for they knew that he was Our Lord.

13.But Yeshua came near and took the bread and the fish and gave to them.

14.This was the third time Yeshua appeared to his disciples after he had risen from the tomb.

15.And after they had breakfast, Yeshua said to Shimeon Kaypha, "Shimeon, Bar Yonah, do you love me more than these things?" He said to him, "Yes, my Lord, you know that I love you." He said to him, "Shepherd my lambs for me."

16.He said to him again a second time, "Shimeon Bar Yonah, do you love me?" He said to him, "Yes, my Lord. You know that I love you." Yeshua said to him, "Shepherd my sheep for me."

17.He said a third time, "Shimeon Bar Yonah, do you love me?" And Kaypha was saddened that he said to him the third time, "Do you love me?" And he said to him, "My lord, you discern everything; you know that I love you." Yeshua said to him, "Shepherd my ewes for me."

18."Amen, amen, I tell you, that when you were young, you were girding your loins and you were walking where you wanted, but when you are old, you shall reach out your hands and others shall gird your loins for you and shall escort you to where you do not want."

19.But he said this to show by what death he was going to glorify God. And after he had said these things, he said to him, "Come after me."

20.And Shimeon Kaypha turned around and saw that disciple whom Yeshua had loved, who had come after him, who had lain at supper on the breast of Yeshua and had said, "My Lord, who is he that shall betray you?"

21.When Kaypha saw this one, he said to Yeshua, "And what of this man, my Lord?"

22.Yeshua said to him, "If I want this one to remain until I come to you, what is it to you? You come after me."

23.And this saying went forth among the brethren that this disciple would not die. But Yeshua had not said that he would not die, but, "If I want this one to remain until I come to you, what is it to you?"

24.This is the disciple who testified about all these things, and he also wrote them, and we know that his testimony is true.

25.There are also many other things that Yeshua did, which if they were to be written, each one, I suppose even the world would be insufficient for the books that would be written.

שלם אונגליון קדישא כרוזותא דיוחנן
The end of The Holy Gospel preaching of
Yohannan

שלם
למכתב בכתבא הנא טטראונגליון קדישא
The end of the writing in this book of the four
Holy Gospels

שובחא לאבא ולברא ולרוחא
דקודשא השא וכלזבן ולעלם אלמין אמין
Glory to The Father and to The Son and to
The Holy Spirit, now, always
and for the eternity of eternities, amen !

The Acts of The Apostles

Chapter 1

1. I wrote the former book, Oh Theophila, about all those things that Our Lord Yeshua The Messiah * began to do and to teach *

This is the first occurrence of the full title, "**Our Lord Yeshua The Messiah**" –"**Maran Yeshua Meshikha**", which occurs 110 times in The Peshitta. The Greek equivalent occurs only 88 times in the Majority Greek text and Textus Receptus (KJV Greek text). The Latin Vulgate has it 98 times. The Critical Greek text has the title only 64 times!

2. Until the day in which he was taken up, after he had commanded the Apostles whom he had chosen by The Spirit of Holiness,

3. Those to whom also he showed himself alive, after he had suffered, by many signs for forty days when he was appearing to them, and he spoke about The Kingdom of God.

4. And as he ate bread with them, he commanded them not to depart from Jerusalem, but to wait for The Promise of The Father, "Which", he said, "you have heard from me."

(Three versions of this verse follow:)

4 (Peshitta) **And when He had eaten bread with them**, he commanded them not to depart from Jerusalem, but to wait for the promise of the Father, which (said he) you have heard from Me.

4 (MKJV) **And, being assembled with** *them*, commanded them that they should not depart from Jerusalem, but wait for the promise of the Father, which, *saith he*, ye have heard from me.

4 (DOUAY) And eating together with them, he commanded them, that they should not depart from Jerusalem, but should wait for the promise of the Father, which you have heard (saith he) **by my mouth**.

*In the above verse, **The Peshitta** text differs significantly from all the Greek texts and Jerome's **Latin Vulgate** (from a Western Greek text). If **The Peshitta** is a translation of Greek, from **which Greek text** was it translated?*

5. "For Yohannan baptized in water, and you shall be baptized in The Spirit of Holiness, after not many days".

6. But when they were assembled, they asked him and said to him, "Our Lord, are you at this time restoring The Kingdom to Israel?"

7. He said to them, "It is not yours to know the times or seasons which The Father has placed in his authority."

8. "But when The Spirit of Holiness will come upon you, you shall receive power. You shall be witnesses to me in Jerusalem and in all Judea, and also among the Samaritans, and unto the borders of The Earth."

9. And when he had said these things, as they saw him, he was taken up and a cloud received him and he was hidden from their eyes.

10. And as they were gazing into the sky, as he was going, two men were present standing with them in white clothing.

11. And they were saying to them, "Galilean men, why are you standing and gazing into the sky? This Yeshua, who was taken up from you into Heaven shall come in this way, as when you saw him going up into Heaven."

12. And after this, they returned to Jerusalem from the Mount which is called Bayth Zaytha, which is beside Jerusalem and separated from it by about seven furlongs. (1 furlong = 1/8th mile)

Two translations- one from Aramaic & one from Greek, follow:
(Murdock) And afterwards they returned to Jerusalem from the mount called Bayth-Zaytha, which was next to Jerusalem, and distant from it **about seven furlongs.**

KJV) Then they returned to Jerusalem from the mount called Olivet, which is from Jerusalem **a Sabbath day's journey.**

** How plainly the Greek declares itself to be a translation may be seen in the word ελαιωνος ("Olive grove"). "**Bayth Zaytha**" was called "**Bayth Zaytha**" because that was its name, just as "**Jerusalem**" was called "**Oreshlem**" in Eastern Aramaic;it was not called "**Teaching of Peace**"(the meaning of "**Jerusalem**") διδαχη ειρηνης –"**Teaching of Peace**" in Greek. No one called Jerusalem "**Teaching of Peace**" or "**Didachay Eiraynays**". "**Philadelphia**" means "**Brotherly love**", but that city is called "**Philadelphia**", not "**Brotherly Love**". The fact that the Greek gives the definition of **Bayth Zaytha** instead of the name itself is a dead giveaway that the Greek ελαιωνος ("Olive grove") is a translation. Essentially the same Greek translation is used in Luke 19:29 & Luke 21:37.*

*"**Seven**" in Aramaic is שבעא "Shaba"; "Sabbath" has several forms, one of which is שבא "Shaba".Obviously the Greek translator mistook שבא-"Shba" from שבעא-"Shaba" and omitted the last word "אסטדון" – "Estadown" (Stadia, Furlongs).It is easy to see how this happened. The reverse scenario is a very hard sell: "σαββατου εχον οδον" – "Sabbath days journey" in Greek, does not become אסטדון שבעא -"Seven furlongs" in Aramaic. σαββατου εχον οδον" – "Sabbath days journey" is a very strange phrase in Greek, literally, "of a Sabbath having way", found nowhere in The LXX or elsewhere in The Greek NT or any Greek literature. The two words after "Sabbath" – εχον οδον" are pronounced "ekon hodon"; Compare the Aramaic word for "Furlongs"- "Estadwan".The Greek looks almost like a transliteration of the Aramaic; This writer thinks the Greek is a forced translation attempt at some Aramaic the translator seemed to have difficulty reading, for whatever reason. A Greek audience may very well have scratched their heads upon reading this phrase, especially due to their unfamiliarity with Jewish law and custom.*

שבעא- "**Seven**"(Peshitta)
שבתא- "**Sabbath**"(Greek reading in Aramaic)

13. And after they entered, they came up to an upper room in which were staying Petraus *, Yohannan, Yaqob, Andraeas, Philippus, Thoma, Mattai , Bar Tolmay, Yaqob Bar Halphai, Shimeon The Zealot and Yehuda Bar Yaqob. ("Petraus" is Simon Peter's Latin name, used here because he was the first to preach to a Roman household and open the door of evangelism to the Gentiles.)

14. These all were continuing together in prayer with one soul with the women and with Maryam, Mother of Yeshua, and with his brothers.

15. And in those days, Shimeon Kaypha stood among them in the midst of the disciples, and there were assembled there about one hundred and twenty men, and he said:

16. "Men, brethren, it was right that the Scripture should be fulfilled which The Spirit of Holiness before spoke by the mouth of David about Yehuda, he who was the guide to those who seized Yeshua,"

17. "Because he was numbered with us, and he had a part in this ministry."

18. "This is the one who purchased a field for himself with the reward of sin and he fell on his face on the ground, and all his insides burst from within him and gushed out."

19. "And this is known to all those who live in Jerusalem, and so that field is called in the language of the region, 'Haqel Dama' *, which is, in its translation, 'Field of Blood'."

* This verse in Greek has the Aramaic name "Ακελδαμα", "**Akeldama**" transliterated, and says that "In their language was called ακελδαμα , which is "Field of blood". Thayer's Greek English Lexicon has this entry for ακελδαμα :
184 Ακελδαμα Akeldama ak-el-dam-ah' of Aramaic origin, corresponding to 02506 and 01818 חקל דמא;
n pr loc AV-Aceldama 1; 1
Aceldama =" Field of Blood"
So The Greek NT declares the language of the Jews in Jerusalem to have been Aramaic. Notice it says "Their **language**", not "Their **languages**". Only one language is mentioned as belonging to the region, and ακελδαμα, "**Akeldama**", is plainly an Aramaic name of two words : חקל –"Haqel"-**Field**" & דמא-"Dama"- "**Blood**". <u>So here the Greek NT says that the Jews of Jerusalem spoke Aramaic and contradicts the notion that they also spoke Greek</u>; it also <u>transliterates Aramaic here and elsewhere and then translates its meaning into Greek for a Greek audience</u>. Luke came from Syria and probably wrote in his native Syrian Aramaic, which explains the translation of the Aramaic of Israel into Syrian Aramaic in this verse ("**Field of Blood**") and in Acts 4:36, where BarNaba' name (Israeli Aramaic) is defined in a Syrian Aramaic dialect.

20. "For it is written in the book of Psalms, 'His dwelling shall be desolate, and there will be no inhabitant in it, and another will take his ministry.' "

21. "Therefore it is right that one of these who have been with us all this time in which Our Lord Yeshua went in and out among us",

*"Our Lord Yeshua" in Aramaic is "The Lord Yeshua" in Greek. This is a common difference. **Either Zorba The Greek(s) ignored or missed the pronoun "our"** about 50% of the time (318 out of 646 times) **in The NT overall, in translating Aramaic to Greek, or an Aramean translator deliberately added 318 of the pronoun "our" (97%) to the 328 Greek occurrences, effectively doubling the Greek number in The hypothetical Peshitta "translation"! What are the odds of the latter scenario compared to the former?***

22. "Beginning with his baptism by Yohannan, until the day that he was taken up

from our presence, would be a witness with us of his Resurrection."

23. And they presented two, Yoseph, who was called Bar-Shaba, who is named Justus, and Matthaya.

24. And when they prayed, they said, "You, LORD JEHOVAH, know what is in the heart of everyone; show the one which you have chosen of these two,"

*– How would an hypothetical Aramaean translator decide when to translate the Greek κυριε ("**Lord**") as מריא ("Maryah"- "**Lord JAH**")? There are 239 of מריא in The Peshitta N.T. Κυριε, κυριος, κυριου, κυριον, etc., occurs 751 times in The Greek NT.*
*239/751=32%. **32% of the Greek "κυριος" is matched by** מריא in The Peshitta overall.*
The stats. (# Kurios,# Maryah),ratio Maryah/Kurios %) for individual books are:
*Mt.:76,21,**28%**; Mk.:18,9,**50%**;Luke:97,40,**41%**;Yokhanan: 51,9,**18%**;Acts:104,51,**49%**;Romans:39,10,**26%**;1 Cor.:60,18,**26%**;2 Cor.:27,8,**30%**;Gal.- Philemon:128,14,**9%**;Hebrews:15,11,**73%**;Yaqob- Jude:42,19,**45%**;Rev.:21,14,**66%**.*
If an Aramaean translator were to simply pick a percentage of the Greek "κυριος" as מריא, why the radical change from Matthew to Mark of 28% to 50% conversion rate? Why such a change from Luke-41% to Yokhanan's 18% (less than half of Luke's)?
Then from Yokhanan's 18% to Acts' 49%? The very next book, Romans, drops to 26%. This remains fairly level then up to 2 Corinthians, then abruptly drops again to its lowest level at 9% in the rest of Paul's epistles! Then the next book, Hebrews has the highest level in the NT – 73%! A radical drop again to 45% for General Epistles and a big jump again in Revelation's 66%! None of this is consistent with the Greek primacy theory and The Peshitta being translated from Greek. There would be more consistency in the ratios from one book to another.

*Looking at this from another perspective, I see Luke and Acts have similar absolute numbers and percentages; Romans, 1 & 2 Cor. have 26%, 26% & 30%. These facts fit with the idea of Peshitta primacy, since Kurios occurrences and the ratios would reflect total number of Aramaic words with the מר –"**Mar**", root (**Lord**) behind Greek "κυριος".*
*Those numbers should be similar in books written by the same author, as Luke and Acts are written by Luke; Romans,1 Cor. & 2 Cor. were written by Paul.The fact that the rest of the smaller epistles of Paulus do not reflect the same ratio as the major epistles is probably due to the relative lack of Old Testament quotations in those smaller books; in the major epistles, half of the מריא references are "**saith The LORD**"(Jehovah) OT quotes. There are none such in the smaller epistles of Paul.*
*Hebrews has five such quotes of its own, accounting for the 73% ratio of "**Maryah**" to "Kurios".None of these occurrences is explainable on the basis of a Greek original. **Maryah** is a Semitic Name, referring to The Hebrew "**Yahweh**" with no Greek equivalent. A translation from Greek should produce מרא (**Mara**-"**Lord**) or מרן (**Maran**-"our Lord") – not מריא.*

25. "That he would receive a part of the ministry and Apostleship from which Yehuda withdrew, that he should go to his place."

26. And they cast lots, and it came up to Matthaya, and he was numbered with the eleven Apostles.

Chapter 2

1. And when the days of Pentecost were fulfilled, as all of them were assembled together,

2. Suddenly there was from Heaven a sound like a mighty wind and the whole place in which they were sitting was filled with it.

3. And tongues like fire that were divided appeared to them, and they sat * on each one of them.

* *Greek mss. & editions have εκαθισεν – "It sat", which disagrees with the plural subject – "tongues". Only two Greek mss. agree with The Peshitta – "They sat"; they are Codex D (6th century), which appears to be a later translation of The Peshitta, very commonly agreeing with it when other Greek mss. depart from it, and Codex ℵ*. The other Greek mss. have incorrect grammar here.("as fire" does not qualify as the subject of the sentence-it is merely a simile describing the*   the   *subject, "tongues").*

4. And all of them were filled with The Spirit of Holiness, and they were going out speaking in various languages, according to whatever The Spirit was giving them to speak.

5. But there were men dwelling in Jerusalem who were worshipers of God, Jews from every nation under Heaven.

6. And when that noise occurred, the entire populace gathered and was agitated, because each one of them heard that they were speaking in their dialects.

7. And they were all marveling and were amazed as they were saying, each to the other, "Are not all these who are speaking Galileans?"(How did these people know the disciples were Galilean? Was it not because they were familiar with the Galilean dialect of Aramaic?)

8. "How are we hearing, everyone, his own dialect in which we were born?"

9. "Parthians and Medes and Elanites, and those who dwell in Bayth- Nahrayn, Judeans and Qapodoqians and those who are from the regions of Pontus and of Asia,"

* *"Bayth-Nahrayn" means "Between the rivers"; Greek has* μεσοποταμιαν - *"Mesopotamia", which is the Greek translation of the actual Aramaic name of this Aramaean place. "Mesopotamia" also means "Between the rivers".See The Hebrew OT -0763* ארם נהרים *'Aram Naharayim ar-am' nah-har-ah'- yim from* 0758 *and the dual of* 05104*;; n pr loc AV-Mesopotamia 5, Aramnaharaim 1; 6 Aram-naharaim =" Aram of the two rivers"*
1   *1) Mesopotamia This Hebrew name occurs inThe HebrewBible six times and in The Peshitta OT is* ארם נהרין *—Aram Nahrayn.The LXX Greek OT has* μεσοποταμιαν - *"Mesopotamia"in those places.Mesopotamia is a translation of the name, much as "Teaching of Peace" is a translation of "Jerusalem" and "Brotherly love" is a translation of "Philadelphia".Names are normally transliterated,not translated.A translation of a name in scripture would usually be an indication that the translation language was not the origin language of that name.*

10. "And from the regions of Phrygia and of Pamphylia and of Egypt and of the countries of Libya which are near to Cyrene and those who came from Rome, Jews and proselytes",

11. "And who are from Crete, and Arabians, behold, we are hearing from those who are speaking in our own dialects, the wonders of God." (Dialects can refer to different regional accents and pronunciation in the common lingua franca of Aramaic among the Jews of the different nations.)

12. And they were all astonished and bewildered. They were saying one to another, "What is this phenomenon?"

13. But others were mocking them as they said, "These have drunk new wine and have become drunk."

14. After this, Shimeon Kaypha arose with the eleven Apostles and he lifted up his voice and he said to them, "Men, Jews, and all who dwell in Jerusalem, let this be known to you and give attention to my words." (How did Peter preach to all the people at the same time and make himself understood? He did not speak in dozens of languages at once. If he had, all the Jews in Jerusalem at Pentecost would have been converted. That did not happen. They all understood Aramaic, though many spoke different dialects of it. Not even a majority of pilgrim Jews were converted, considering that millions of Jews would have been in Jerusalem for the annual feasts of Passover and Pentecost. The gift of tongues (different dialects) was primarily to get the people's attention so that the Apostle Peter could address them in their common Aramaic language, which was fairly well understood, one dialect to the next, especially the Judean and Galilean dialects, to Jews familiar with the country and people of Israel.)

15. "These are not drunk as you are thinking, for behold, it is now the third hour." (9 A.M.)

16. "But this is what was spoken by Joel, The Prophet:"

17. "It shall be done in the last days, says God,' I shall pour out my Spirit on everybody, and your sons and your daughters shall prophesy, and your young men shall see visions and your Elders shall dream dreams."

18. "And I shall pour out my Spirit upon my Servants and upon my handmaids and in those days they shall prophesy."

19. "And I shall give signs in the Heavens and miracles in The Earth, blood, fire and plumes of smoke."

20. "The sun shall be turned into darkness and the moon into blood until the great and awesome day of THE LORD JEHOVAH will come."

The Greek mss. have επιφανη – *"notable", "manifest" where* The Peshitta *has* ℵ... -*"D'khyla"- "Awesome". "Notable" would be* ℵ... or ℵ... *in Aramaic.These are very similar; not so in Greek:* επιφανη – *"notable";* Φοβερον –*"fearful" Can we really believe The great day of Jehovah would be merely "notable"? I cannot. "Awesome" it will be; "Notable" is a flimsy and lame substitute which grossly misses the point.*

21. "And it shall be that everyone who calls on the name of **THE LORD JEHOVAH** shall receive life.' " (See verses 36 & 38.)

22. "Men, sons of Israel, hear these words: Yeshua The Nazarene, The Man who appeared to you from God with mighty works and with signs and with miracles, which God did among you by his hand, as you know,"

23. "This one, who was separated to him for this, in the foreknowledge and will of God, you have betrayed into the hands of the wicked, and you have crucified and murdered."

24. "But God raised him and he destroyed the destructions of Sheol because it was not possible for him to be held captive in Sheol."

- "He destroyed the destructions of Sheol" is one possible translation; others are "He loosed the cords of Sheol", "He destroyed the pains of Sheol", "He loosed the cords of the grave", "He has loosed the travail of Sheol."
I have chosen the first as it presents the poetic paradox which is so powerfully employed in Scripture to highlight the power of God: He leads captivity captive, tells the poor they are rich, the rich are poor, the high are low and the lowly exalted, and finally kills death, casting death and Sheol into a Lake of Fire. Whichever translation is preferred, the Apostle Peter is declaring that Sheol has been defanged- neutralized & rendered impotent by The Messiah's death and resurrection. All Greek mss but codex D have – "Λυσας τας ωδινας του θανατου" – "He loosed the pains of death". Codex D , which usually seems to follow The Peshitta more closely, has "Λυσας τας ωδινας του αδου" – "He loosed the pains of Hades". "Hades" is the Greek cognate for the Hebrew-Aramaic "Sheol". The Greeks sometimes translated the Hebrew "Sheol" with "Θανατος"- "Death". (See 2 Sam. 22:6 Greek LXX and Hebrew, Prov. 23:14) . Both Greek readings (Hades & Death) represent The LXX translation words used for The Hebrew "Sheol", which is almost identical to the Aramaic spelling of "Sheol".The Hebrew of that verse has the phrase חבלי שאול –"Khebli Sheol" , where The Peshitta OT has the same phrase found here in Acts 2:24- חבליה שיול , translated, "The pangs of Sheol" by George Lamsa. דמותא חבליה is also found in that version of 2 Sam. 22:5 , which he translated "Pangs of death". The same text is repeated in Psalms 18:4,5 & 116:3 (115:3 in Peshitta) using the same Aramaic words in The Peshitta and the same translation in Lamsa.

25. For David said about him: "I foresaw my Lord always who was upon my right hand that I should not be disquieted."

26. "Therefore, my heart is delighted and my glory celebrates; also my body shall rest upon hope."

27. "Because you did not leave my Soul in Sheol and you did not give your Pure One to see destruction."

28. "You have shown to me the way of life. You shall fill me, O' Sweetness, with your presence!"

29. "Men, brothers, it is permitted me to speak openly to you about the Chief Father, David, who died and also was buried, and his tomb is with us until today."

30. "For he was a Prophet, and he knew that God had sworn to him in an oath: "One from the fruit of your body I shall seat upon your throne."

31. And he saw and spoke before about the resurrection of The Messiah, that he would not be left in Sheol, neither would his body see corruption."

32. "God has raised up this Yeshua, and we are all his witnesses."

33. "He is The One who is exalted at the right hand of God and he has received from The Father The Promise which is concerning The Spirit of Holiness, and he has poured out this gift, which, behold, you are seeing and hearing."

34. "For David had not ascended to Heaven, because he said, "**THE LORD JEHOVAH** said to my Lord, 'Sit at my right hand' ",

35. "Until I make your enemies a footstool for your feet."

36. "Let therefore the whole house of Israel know truly, God has made this Yeshua, **LORD JEHOVAH** * and The Messiah, whom you had crucified."

*No Greek text can account for this reading. The Greek - κυριον αυτον και χριστον εποιησεν ο θεος τουτον τον ιησουν *simply says: "that both Lord and Christ, God made this Yeshua, whom you crucified".* κυριον -"Lord" *is not necessarily a Divine Title. The Peshitta records an unabashed declaration of the absolute Deity of Yeshua. If any object that* "**God made him Jehovah**" *means Yeshua was given a title that He had not previously, I respond that this is a setting forth of the fact that Yeshua,* **THE LORD JEHOVAH and Messiah** *(See Luke 2:11) really and truly died to all that He was on the cross, and all that He was- died. In the resurrection, all that He was came back again to Life out of the oblivion of His Spiritual death on the cross (not His physical death and resurrection) from His Father God. Thus He became again "**Jehovah and The Messiah** "from the dead - The LORD of a new creation- a New Heaven and a New Earth.For as "**One died for all, all died with Him**", and we are now risen with Him in His resurrection- (2 Cor. 5:14 & Ephesians 2:4-6). **Hallelujah!**

37. And when they heard these things. They were stricken in their hearts, and they said to Shimeon and to the rest of the Apostles, "What should we do, brothers?"

38. And Shimeon said to them, "Return to God and be immersed everyone of you, in the name of **THE LORD JEHOVAH** Yeshua, for release from sin, so that you may receive the gift of The Spirit of Holiness."

39. "For The Promise is to you and to your children and to all those who are afar off, those whom God shall call."

40. And with many other words he was testifying to them and beseeching them as he said, "Be saved from this perverse generation."

41. And people among them readily received his word, and they believed and were immersed, and there were added that day about three thousand souls.

42. And they were continuing in the teaching of the Apostles, and they became partakers in prayer and in breaking of the Eucharist.

"Eucharist"- אוכרסטיא (Eukhristya) is supposed to be a Greek word in Aramaic letters, however, the Greek mss. do not have **"Eucharist"** here or in the two other places where אוכרסטיא occurs. How did the Peshitta reading אוכרסטיא get here and in those two other places without any such word in the Greek texts? "Eucharist" occurs nowhere in The Greek NT! I submit that this word "Eucharist" came from the original early first century Peshitta NT, not from Greek.

43. And there was fear in every soul, and many signs and miracles were occurring by the hand of the Apostles in Jerusalem.

44. And all those who believed were together and everything they had was communal.

45. And those who had a possession were selling it and distributing to each man according to whatever was needed.

46. And every day they were continuing in The Temple with one soul, and in the houses they were breaking loaves of bread, and they were receiving food as they celebrated, and in the simplicity of their hearts

47. They were praising God as they were given affection before all the people*, and Our Lord was adding unto the church everyday those who were coming to life.

* Greek Codex D- a 6th century uncial, has κοσμον - "Kosmon"-"World".
Compare the Peshitta reading עמא- "Amma" – "People" to עלמא –"Alama"-"World,age,eternity"- just one letter difference! Practically all other Greek mss. have λαον –"People" which scarcely resembles κοσμον -"Kosmon"-"World"; it is easy to account for the Greek variant reading on the basis of The Peshitta reading. There are so many examples of this in The NT that it would be ludicrous to maintain a Greek original and a Peshitta version translated from Greek when practically all the evidence paints another picture- the negative image of the conventional western model. "The church" – עדתא (Edta) means "An assembly", from the Aramaic verb עד "Ad", "Aoed"–**To set a meeting**", "To assemble". If we split the word in half, we have עד תא – **"Meet, Come"** , which sounds like an invitation to gather together as a body to worship. It may also be construed as a compound of the two words עד אתא – "Until he comes", which is reminiscent of the Apostle's words: "As oft as you eat this bread and drink this cup, you do show the Lord's death till He come." That is also the function of the church. The Greek word "Εκκλησια"- "Ekklaysia" for "Church" , used in this and other places means ,literally, "Called out", which gives essentially a negative connotation to the meaning of the church. But the purpose of calling the assembly is far from a negative separating people out from the world, but a gathering of them unto him Who loved us all, and gave

Himself for us, that we may meet with him and fellowship with him and his Father in The Holy Spirit, and also with one another on a spiritual level in The Kingdom of Heaven on Earth. It is a call into the very Presence of God and glory in Heaven- fairly positive, on balance!

Do not the church and the world today need to see and hear this positive invitation and call to celebrate and experience the Presence of **THE LIVING GOD** that constitutes all the joy of Heaven itself ?

"And he said unto me, Write, Blessed are they which are called unto the marriage supper of the Lamb. And he said unto me, These are the true sayings of God. And The Spirit and the bride say, "Come". And let him that hears, say, "Come". And he that is thirsty, let him come and take the water of Life freely."
– (Rev. 22:17 translated from The Crawford Aramaic manuscript.)

Chapter 3

1. And it was that when Shimeon Kaypha and Yohannan went up together to The Temple at the time of prayer, which was the ninth hour,

2. Behold , men who were keeping an appointment were carrying one man crippled from his mother's womb, bringing and placing him at the gate of The Temple, which is called Shappira, to be asking charity from those entering The Temple. (Shappira" means "Beautiful")

3. This one, when he saw Shimeon and Yohannan entering The Temple, was begging them to give him charity.

4. And Shimeon and Yohannan gazed at him and they said to him, "Look at us."

5. And he gazed at them, as he had hoped to receive something from them.

6. Shimeon said to him, "I have no gold or silver, but what I do have, I give to you: In the name of Yeshua The Messiah, the Nazarene, stand up and walk."

7. And he seized his right hand and raised him up, and in that moment, his legs and his feet were restored.

8. And he jumped, stood and walked and entered with them into The Temple as he was walking and jumping and praising God.

9. And all the people saw as he was walking and praising God.

10. And they knew that he was that beggar who sat every day and asked for charity at the gate, which is called Shappira, and they were filled with astonishment and wonder concerning what had happened.

11. And as he was holding to Shimeon and Yohannan, all the people, while marveling, ran to them at the porch which is called Solomon's.

12. And when Shimeon saw it, he answered and said to them, "Men, children of Israel: why do you wonder at this, or why do you gaze at us as if it was by our own power or by our authority that we have done this, that this man would walk?

13. "The God of Abraham and Isaac and Jacob, The God of our fathers, has glorified his Son Yeshua, him whom you handed over and rejected in the presence of Pilatus, when he had rightly judged to release him."

14. "But you rejected The Holy One and The Righteous One and you demanded a man who was a murderer to be given to you."

15. "And you killed him, The Ruler of Life, whom God raised from among the dead, and we are all his witnesses."

16. "And by the faith of his Name, this one whom you see and know, he has restored and healed, and faith in him has given him this health before you all."

17. "But now my brothers, I know that because of deception you did this as your Rulers did."

18. "And God has thus fulfilled the thing which before was preached by the mouth of all The Prophets, that his Messiah would suffer."

19. "Repent therefore and be converted, so that your sins will be blotted out, and the times of rest from before the face of THE LORD JEHOVAH will come to you."

20. "And he shall send to you The One who was prepared * for you, Yeshua The Messiah."

* The Textus Receptus Greek (KJV Greek) text has "Who was preached"; coincidentally , the Aramaic דמטיב –"Who was prepared,appointed" is very similar to דמטב ("Who informed") & דטביב ("Who was made known") . All other Greek mss. agree with The Peshitta reading. It looks here like The Textus Receptus represents an alternate Greek translation of The Peshitta Aramaic , which appears also to be the case in other places of The NT.

21. "Whom Heaven must receive until the end times of all those things which God has spoken by the mouth of all his Holy Prophets, who were from ancient times."

22. "Moses said , THE LORD JEHOVAH shall raise up to you a Prophet like me from your brothers. Hear him in everything that he will speak with you."

23. "It shall be that every soul who will not hear that Prophet, that soul shall perish from among his people."

24. "And all The Prophets from Samuel and those who were after him have spoken and preached of these days."

25. "You are the children of The Prophets and of the covenant which God appointed to our fathers, when he said to Abraham, 'By your Seed all the families of The Earth shall be blessed.' "

26. "God appointed to you from the first and sent his Son to bless you, if you are converted, and you return from your evils."

Chapter 4

1. And when they were speaking these words to the people, The Priests and The Sadducees and the Rulers of The Temple rose up against them,

2. As they were angered with them that they taught the people in their preaching about the resurrection from among the dead by The Messiah.

3. And they laid hands upon them and kept them to the next day, because evening was approaching.

4. And many who heard the word believed, and they were in number about five thousand men.

5. And the next day the Rulers and the Elders and The Scribes assembled,

6. And also Hannan The High Priest, Kaypha, Yohannan, Alexandrus and those who were from the family of The Chief Priests.

7. And when they set them in the midst, they were asking them, "By what power or in what name do you do this?"

8. Then Shimeon Kaypha was filled by The Spirit of Holiness, and he said to them, "Rulers of the people and Elders of the house of Israel, listen."

9. "If we today are judged by you for the beautiful thing which happened to an ill man, by what means this man was healed",

10. "Let this be known to you and to all the people of Israel, that in the name of Yeshua The Messiah, the Nazarene, him whom you have crucified, whom God has raised from among the dead, behold, in it and by him this man stands before you whole."

11. "This is the stone which you builders have rejected, and he is The Head of the corner."

12. "And there is no salvation in any other man, for there is no other name under Heaven given to the children of men by which it is necessary to receive life."

13. And when they had heard the discourse of Shimeon and of Yohannan, that they spoke it openly, they perceived that they did not know

the scrolls and that they were uneducated, and they were amazed at them and recognized them that they had lived with Yeshua.

14.And they saw him who had been crippled, who had been healed, standing with them, and were unable to say anything against them.

15.Then they ordered to remove them from their assembly, and they were saying one to another:

16."What shall we do to these men? For behold, a public sign that has occurred by their hands is known to all the inhabitants of Jerusalem and we cannot deny it."

17."But lest this report proceed more among the people, let us threaten that they do not speak again in this name to anyone of the people."

18.And they called them and ordered them that they should not speak at all neither teach in the name of Yeshua.

19.Shimeon Kaypha and Yohannan answered and they said to them, "If it is right before God that one should listen to you rather than to God, you judge."

20."For we are unable not to speak whatever we see and hear."

21.And they threatened them and released them, for they had not found a cause to pursue their lives, because of the people, because everyone was praising God for what had happened.

22.For the man in whom this sign of healing had occurred was more than forty years old.

23.And when they were dismissed, they came to their brethren, and they related to them everything whatever The Priests and the Elders had said.

24.And when they had heard, they raised their voice as one to God, and they said, "LORD JEHOVAH, you are God, who made the Heavens and The Earth and the seas and all that is in them."

25.And you are he who spoke by The Spirit of Holiness in the mouth of David, your Servant: "Why have the nations raged and the peoples devised nothingness?"

26."The Kings of The Earth stood up and the Rulers held counsel together against THE LORD JEHOVAH and against his Messiah."

27.For truly, Herodus and Pilatus, with the Gentiles and the mobs of Israel gathered in this city against The Holy One, your Son Yeshua, The One whom you anointed,"

28."To do all whatsoever your hand and your will had ordained beforehand to happen."

29."Also now LORD JEHOVAH, behold and see their threats, and grant to your Servants that they would be preaching your word openly."

30."And stretch your hand for healing and for mighty acts and for signs to occur in the name of your Holy Son* Yeshua."

* All Greek texts have "Paidos"- usually meaning "a Servant" and sometimes "a child".

31.And when they had prayed and made supplication, the place was shaken in which they were assembled, and they were all filled with The Spirit of Holiness, and they were speaking the word of God openly.

32.But the crowds of people who believed had one soul and one mind and none of them was saying that the wealth which he possessed was his own, but they had all things common.

33. And those Apostles were testifying with great power to the resurrection of Yeshua The Messiah, and there was great grace with all of them.

34.And there was none among them who was needy, for those who possessed fields and houses were selling them and bringing the proceeds of those things that were sold.

35.And they were laying them at the feet of the Apostles, and it was given to anyone according to whatever was needed.

36.But Yoseph, named BarNaba by the Apostles, which is translated, "Son of comfort", a Levite from the country of Cyprus,

37.Had a field, and he sold it and brought its price and laid it before the Apostles' feet.

Chapter 5

1.One man whose name was Khanan-Yah, with his wife, whose name was Shappira, had sold his field.

2.And he took some of its price and concealed it while his wife was aware of it, and he brought some of the money and placed it before the Apostles' feet.

3.And Shimeon said to Khanan-Yah, "Why has Satan filled your heart to cheat The Spirit of Holiness and to hide some money of the proceeds of the field?"

4.Was it not yours until it was sold? And after it was sold, again you had power over its proceeds. Why have you set your heart to do this thing? You have not cheated men but God."

5.And when Khanan-Yah heard these words, he dropped dead and great fear came upon all those who heard.

6.And young men among them arose and gathered him up, and they took him out and buried him.

7.And after three hours had passed, his wife also entered, not knowing what had happened.

8.Shimeon said to her, "Tell me if for these proceeds you sold the field." But she said, "Yes, for these proceeds."

9.Shimeon said to her, "Because you have agreed to tempt The Spirit of THE LORD JEHOVAH, behold the feet of those who buried your husband are at the door and they will take you out."

10.And at that moment she fell before their feet and died, and those young men came in and found her dead. And they took her up and brought her out and buried her beside her husband.

11.And there was great fear upon the entire church among all those who heard.

12.And there were occurring by the hands of the Apostles signs and many mighty acts among the people and they were all assembled together at the porch of Solomon.

13.And none of the other people dared to come near them, but the people were magnifying them.

14.And those who were believing in THE LORD JEHOVAH were added all the more, multitudes of men and women,

15.So that they were bringing the sick out into the streets lying in litters, that when Shimeon would come, at least his shadow might overshadow them.

16.And many were coming to them from the other cities which were around Jerusalem, as they were bringing the sick and those who had foul spirits, and they were all being healed.

17.And The High Priest and all who were with him, who were of the doctrine of the Sadducees, were filled with jealousy.

18.And they laid hands on the Apostles and seized and bound them in prison.

19.Then in the night The Angel of THE LORD JEHOVAH opened the door of the prison and brought them out, and he said to them:

20."Go stand in The Temple and speak to the people all these words of life."

21.And they went out at dawn and entered The Temple and they were teaching; but The High Priest, and those with him, called their associates and the Elders of Israel and they sent to the prison to bring the Apostles.

22.And when those who were sent went from them, they did not find them in prison and they returned and came,

23.And they were saying, "We found the prison locked securely by the guards who were standing at the door, and we opened it and we found no one there."

24.And when The Chief Priests and the Leaders of The Temple heard these words, they were astonished at them and they were considering what this was.

25.And a man came informing them: "The same men whom you shut up in the prison, behold, they are standing in The Temple teaching the people."

26.And the Leaders went with the attendants to bring them, not with force, for they were afraid lest the people would stone them.

27.And when they brought them, they stood them before the whole Council and The High Priest began to say to them:

28."Have we not emphatically commanded you that you teach no one in this name? But behold, you have filled Jerusalem with your teaching and you wish to bring the blood of this man upon us."

29.Shimeon answered with the Apostles and said to them, "God ought to be obeyed more than men."

30."The God of our forefathers raised up Yeshua, The One whom you murdered, when you hanged him on a tree."

31."God has appointed This One The Head and The Life Giver and he has exalted him to his right hand, so as to give repentance and forgiveness of sins to Israel."

32."And we are witnesses of these accounts, and so is The Spirit of Holiness, whom God gives to those who believe in him."

33.And when they heard these words, they were enraged with a passion, and they were considering killing them.

34.And one of The Pharisees there stood up whose name was Gamaliel. He taught The Law, and he was honored by all the people, and he commanded to take the Apostles out for a short time.

35.And he said to them, "Men, sons of Israel, take heed to yourselves and see what is right for you to do concerning these men."

36."Before this time Theuda arose and said that he was something great and about four hundred men went after him; he was killed and those who were going after him were scattered and they became as nothing."

37."And Yehudah the Galilean arose after him in the days when the people were registered for the head tax and he seduced many people after him and he died and all those who were following him were scattered."

38."And I say to you, separate yourselves from these men and leave them, for if this counsel and work is from men, they will dissolve and pass away."

39."But if it is from God, you have no power to destroy it, lest you be found opposing God."

40.And they were persuaded by him and called the Apostles and scourged them and commanded them not to speak in the name of Yeshua, and they dismissed them.

41.And they departed from before them, rejoicing that they were worthy to be disgraced for The Name.

42.And they did not cease to teach every day in The Temple and in houses, and to evangelize about Our Lord Yeshua The Messiah.

Chapter 6

1.And in those days when the disciples had multiplied, the Hellenist disciples complained against the Hebrews*, that their widows were disregarded in the daily ministry.

---

* "Hebrews" comes from עבריא –"Ebraya" Below is the extract from **Jastrow's Aramaic-Hebrew Dictionary** :

עִבְרִי m., עֶבְרִית, עִבְרִיָּה f. (b. h.) Hebrew; '(לשון) Hebrew language; '(כתב) Hebrew character, type. Kidd. I, 2 עבד '(ע a Hebrew slave; '(אמה ה'(ע a Hebrew hand-maid. Gen. R. s. 42 '(ע ומשרת בלשון, v. עָבַר II. Gitt. IX, 6

'(וב אחד עברי כד if one witness signed in Hebrew type, and the other in Greek, and again one in Hebrew &c. Ib. 8 '(וב עברית שכתבו גט if a letter of divorce was written in Hebrew, and its witnesses signed in Greek. Y. Meg.1, 71[b] bot.; Esth.R.to I, 22, a.e. '(ע לדיבור the Hebrew language is adapted for oratory; a. fr.—Meg. 18[a] קראה עברית... if he read the Megillah in a trans-Euphratean (Aramaic) translation.—Pl. עְבְרִיִּים, עִבְרִיּוֹת; f. עִבְרִיּוֹת. Ib. '(לע עברית an Aramaic translation read before Aramean Jews. Ex. R. s. 3 שעברו ק' כל שם קרא אותם '(ק לבה why does he call them'(Ibriim (Ex.III,18)? Because they passed the sea (on going to Egypt). Ib. s. 1. Pesik. R. s. 23; a. fr.

According to Jastrow's, The Aramaic form עבריא used here has the same meaning as the Hebrew word עברי; it can mean "Hebrew" or "Aramaean". A **Hellenist** was a Greek speaking

Jew; this term indicates that Israel's national tongue was <u>not</u> Greek and that Greek was as peripheral as Hellenists were to Israel; Hellenists were a small minority in Israel. Josephus and The New Testament attest to the fact that Greek was not <u>the</u> language (and there was only one prominent language) of Israel. It has been commonly assumed that all Jews in Israel were Hellenists, as it is commonly taught that they all spoke Greek! That is sheer nonsense! (See the note at Acts 1:19)

2.And the twelve Apostles called the whole assembly of the disciples and they said to them, "It is not acceptable for us to forsake the word of God and to serve tables."

3."Search therefore, my brothers, and choose seven men among you upon whom is the testimony and who are full of The Spirit of **THE LORD JEHOVAH** and wisdom, and we shall appoint them over this matter."

4."And we shall continue in prayer, and in the Ministry of the word."

5.And this statement was pleasing before all the people, and they chose Estephanos, a man who was full of faith and of The Spirit of Holiness, and Philippus, Procuros, Nicanor, Timon, Parmena and Nicholas, an Antiochene proselyte.

6.They presented these before the Apostles, and when they had prayed, they placed hands on them.

7.And the word of God was magnified and the number of the disciples was multiplied greatly in Jerusalem, and many people of the Judeans were obeying the faith.

8.But Estephanos was full of grace and power and was doing signs and wonders among the people.

9.And there arose men from the synagogue which was called the Libertine, and Cyrenians and Alexandrians, and from Qiliqia and from Asia, disputing with Estephanos.

10.And they were not able to withstand the wisdom and The Spirit who was speaking in him.

11.And they sent men and instructed them to say, "We have heard him speak words of blasphemy against Moses and against God."

12.They stirred up the people and the Elders and the Scribes and they came and they stood around him and they seized and brought him to the center of The Council.

13.And they appointed false witnesses who said, "This man does not cease speaking words against The Written Law and against this holy place."

14."We have heard him say that Yeshua the Nazarene will destroy this place and will change the customs that Moses delivered to you."

15. And all of them who were sitting in the assembly stared at him, and they saw his face as the face of an Angel.

Chapter 7

1. And The High Priest asked him, "Are these things so?"

2. But he said, "Men, brothers and fathers, listen; The God of glory appeared to our father Abraham when he was in Bayth-Nahrayn, when he had not come to dwell in Haran,

> * "Bayth Nahrayn" means "Between the rivers" (Tigris and Euphrates) ; Greek has "Mesopotamia", which has the same meaning and is a compound   word formed from "Meso"-"between" and "Potamoi"-"Rivers". "Bayth Nahrayn" was never a Greek speaking region and hence, "Mesopotamia" is not the name of the region (also formerly known as the "Fertile Crescent"), but "Mesopotamia" is the Greek translation of the meaning of the Aramaic name.

3. And he said to him, 'Depart from your land and from the presence of the people of your relatives and come to the land which I shall show you.'

4. And then Abraham went out from the land of the Chaldeans and came and dwelt in Haran, and from there, when his father had died, God removed him to this land in which you dwell today.

5. And he gave him no inheritance in it, not even a footprint, and he promised to give it to him to inherit for himself and for his seed when he had no son.

6. And God was speaking with him when he said to him, 'Your seed will be a stranger in a foreign land, and they will enslave him and will afflict him four hundred years;'

7. 'And that people whom they serve in slavery, I will judge.' God said, 'After these things, they will go out and they will serve me in this place.'

8. And he gave him the covenant of circumcision, and then he begot Isaac and circumcised him on the eighth day and Isaac begot Jacob and Jacob begot our 12 fathers.

9. And our fathers were jealous of Joseph and they sold him into Egypt and God was with him.

10. And he saved him from all his sufferings and he gave him grace and wisdom before Pharaoh The King of Egypt and he appointed him Ruler over Egypt and over his whole house.

11. And there was a famine and great distress in all of Egypt and in the land of Canaan, and there was nothing to satisfy our fathers.

12. When Jacob heard that there was produce in Egypt, he sent our fathers first.

13. And when they went the second time, Joseph made himself known to his brothers and the family of Joseph was made known to Pharaoh.

14. Joseph sent and brought his father Jacob and all his family, and they were seventy five souls in number,

15. (And Jacob went down to Egypt and died there, he and our fathers,)

16. And he was moved to Shechem and was placed in a tomb, which Abraham had bought with silver from the sons of Hamor. ("He was moved & placed in a tomb" is "They were moved & placed in a tomb" in all Greek mss, which is clearly an error. Only Jacob was buried in the tomb Abraham had bought in Hebron, according to Genesis 50:1-14. Joseph was later buried in a plot Jacob had bought much later in Shechem for 100 silver pieces; See Genesis 33:18-20 & Joshua 24:32. Jacob actually bought the tomb in Shechem mentioned here, in which Joseph was buried. The only sense in which Abraham may be said to have bought it, is as the Head Patriarch of Isaac and Jacob and unity by Divine covenant of inheritance with all his seed through Isaac and Jacob. "In thee (Abraham) shall all nations be blessed", and "the blessing of Abraham may come upon you by the faith of Jesus The Christ."- is the model from which we may derive this principle. Abraham is the head of the race of believers. All that they do is seen as his action. Abraham, Isaac & Jacob are treated as one. So "he" in verse 16 is Joseph. The Aramaic verbs for "he was moved" & "he was placed" may have been interpreted as 3rd person feminine plural "they were moved" & they were placed" , which is grammatically incorrect as the subject is masculine and must match the verb gender. Apparently the Greek translation of Aramaic mistook the singular masculine forms as feminine plural, which are identical in appearance. Josephus of the 1st century says the other sons of Jacob were buried in Hebron in the cave Abraham bought. Shechem is 40 miles north of Hebron.

17. And when the time had arrived which God had promised with an oath to Abraham, the people had multiplied and had grown strong in Egypt,

18. Until another King arose over Egypt who did not know Joseph.

19. He was deceptive toward our race and did evil to our fathers and commanded to cast out their male infants that they would not live.

20. At that time Moses was born, and was dear to God and was raised three months in his father's house.

21. When he was cast out by his mother, the daughter of Pharaoh found him and she raised him as her son.

22. And Moses was instructed in all the wisdom of the Egyptians, and was prepared in his words and in his deeds also.

23. When he was forty years old, it came upon his heart to visit his brethren and the children of Israel.

24. And he saw one of the sons of his tribe being compelled by violence and he avenged

him and executed justice for him and killed the Egyptian who had wronged him.

25. And he hoped that his brethren, the sons of Israel, would have understood that God would give them deliverance by his hand, and they did not understand.

26. And the next day he appeared to them when they contended with one another and he appealed to them to be reconciled when he said: "Men, brothers, why are you doing wrong to one another?"

27. But he who was doing wrong to his fellow thrust him away from him and said to him, "Who appointed you the Ruler and Judge over us?"

28. "Do you want to kill me as you killed the Egyptian yesterday?"

29. And Moses fled at this saying and he became a nomad in the land of Midian and he had two sons.

30. And when forty years were fulfilled to him, The Messenger of **THE LORD JEHOVAH** appeared to him in the wilderness of Mount Sinai in the fire which burned in a bush.

31. And when Moses saw it, he marveled at the vision, and when he approached to see, **THE LORD JEHOVAH** said to him in a voice:

32. 'I AM THE LIVING GOD*, The God of your fathers, The God of Abraham and Isaac and Jacob', and as Moses was trembling, he did not dare to gaze at the vision.

---

* אנא אנא –"**Ena na**" is an Aramaic idiom signifying Divine speech in **98%** of its 221 occurrences in The Peshitta Old Testament. The literal meaning is "**I am**", but as an idiom is not normally to be taken literally, but with the meaning the idiom conveys. I have chosen to translate this phrase in accordance with Lamsa's translation of Exodus 3:14 where the Aramaic "**Ahiah Ashur High**" ("**I AM Who I AM**") occurs. Our Lord Yeshua used this phrase as recorded in John's Gospel 25 times , declaring Himself to be The Eternal Deity with each of those twenty five utterances; even a regiment of Jewish soldiers (**200-600** men) fell backward to the ground when Our Lord uttered this phrase in the Garden of Gethsemane. John 8:24 records that Our Lord made this point critical to our salvation: **I said to you, That you will die in your sins; for if ye believe not that ("Ena Na")** <u>I Am The Living God</u> **, you will die in your sins.**

---

33. And **THE LORD JEHOVAH** said to him, 'Loose your shoes from your feet, for the ground on which you stand is holy.'

34. 'I have looked and have seen the suffering of my people who are in Egypt and I have heard its groans and I have come down to save them; and now come, I shall send you to Egypt.'

35. This Moses, whom they rejected when they were saying, 'Who appointed you the Ruler and Judge over us?', this one God sent as the Ruler and Deliverer to them by the hand of The Messenger who appeared to him at the bush.

36. This is he who sent them out when he did signs and wonders and mighty works in the land of Egypt and at The Sea of Reeds* and in the wilderness forty years.

* ("The Sea of Reeds" is "Yamma D` Suph" or "Yamma Suph" in Aramaic, very similar to the Hebrew of Exodus "Yam Suph". "The Red Sea" is a mistranslation in Greek taken from the LXX which has it wrong consistently in the Old Testament. The Hebrew Bible never mentions a "**Red Sea**", only **The Sea of Reeds**". See Hebrews 11:29) This verse and Hebrews 11:29is strong support for Peshitta primacy and Divine inspiration and opposition to Greek primacy and inspiration. The Peshitta did not get this reading from Greek, though the Greek LXX consistently translated "Yam Suph"-("Sea of Reeds") as ερυθρα θαλασση-(**eruthros Thalassay-Red Sea),** and the Greek NT seems to have followed suit here and in Heb. 11:29.

37. This is Moses who said to the children of Israel, '**THE LORD JEHOVAH** God shall appoint you a Prophet like me from your brethren. You shall listen to him.'

38. This is he who was in the assembly in the wilderness with The Messenger who had spoken with him and with our fathers at the mountain of Sinai, and he was receiving the living words which he would give to us.

39. And our fathers chose not to obey him, but they forsook him and in their hearts they returned to Egypt,

40. As they said to Aaron, 'Make gods for us to go before us, because we do not know what has become of this Moses who brought us out from the land of Egypt.'

41. And they made a calf for themselves in those days, and they sacrificed sacrifices to the idol and they were delighting in the work of their hands.

42. And God turned and handed them over to become worshipers of the hosts of the Heavens, just as it is written in the Scriptures of The Prophets, 'Why have you brought animals or sacrifices to me for forty years in the wilderness, sons of Israel?'

43. 'But you carry the tabernacle of Malcom and the star of The God Rephan, which images which you have made to worship. I shall remove you farther than Babel.'

44. Behold, the tabernacle of the testimony of our fathers was in the wilderness according to what he who spoke with Moses commanded to make it, with the likeness which he showed him.

45. And our fathers brought the same tabernacle and carried it with Joshua* to the land that God had given them as an inheritance from the nations which he had driven out from before them, and it was carried until the days of David,

* Joshua refers to Joshua, son of Nun, of The Old Testament Book of Joshua. The Aramaic spelling is the same for "**Yeshua**" The Messiah.

46. He who found affection before him who is God, and he requested to find a tabernacle for The God of Jacob.

47. But Solomon built a house for him.

48. And The Exalted One does not dwell in the product of hands as The Prophet says:

49. 'Heaven is my throne and The Earth is the stool which is under my feet. Where is the house that you will build for me?, says **THE LORD JEHOVAH**, or where is the place of my rest?'

50. 'Behold, has not my hand made all these things?'

51. Oh, stiff necks, who are uncircumcised in their hearts and in their hearing, you always are opposing The Spirit of Holiness, as your fathers did, so do you!

52. Which of The Prophets have not your fathers persecuted and murdered, who before had searched out concerning the coming of The Righteous One, him whom you have betrayed and killed?

53. You have received The Law by the visitation of Angels and have not kept it."

54. And when they heard these things, they were filled with rage in their souls and they were gnashing on him with their teeth.

55. And he, being filled with faith and The Spirit of Holiness, gazed into Heaven and he saw the glory of God, and Yeshua as he stood at the right side of God.

56. And he said, "Behold, I see the Heavens opening and The Son of Man standing at the right hand of God."

57. And they yelled with a loud voice and stopped up their ears, and they all rushed upon him.

58. And they seized and brought him outside the city, and they were stoning him, and those who testified against him placed their robes at the feet of a young man, one who is called Shaul.

59. And they were stoning Estephanos as he prayed and said, "Our Lord Yeshua, accept my spirit!"

60. And when he knelt down, he cried out in a loud voice and he said, "Our Lord, do not let this sin stand against them!" When he had said this, he fell asleep.

Chapter 8

1. But Shaul was consenting and participating in his murder, and in that day there was great persecution toward the church which was in Jerusalem, and they were all scattered into the villages of Judea, and among the Samaritans, except for the Apostles.

2. And believing men gathered up and buried Estephanos, and they grieved over him greatly.

3. But Shaul was persecuting the Church of God, as he was entering houses and dragging men and women and delivering them to prison.

4. Those who were scattered were traveling and preaching the word of God.

5. But Philippus went down to the city of the Samaritans and he was preaching to them about The Messiah.

6. And as they were listening to his message, the people who were listening were persuaded by all that he had said, for they saw the signs that he did.

7. For many who had been seized by foul spirits were screaming with a loud voice, and they were coming out from them, and others who were paralytic and crippled were healed.

8. And there was great joy in that city.

9. But there was a man there whose name was Simon who had dwelt there in that city for a long time. By his sorcery he deceived the people of the Samaritans as he was magnifying himself and saying, "I am the great God."

10. And they were all praying to him, noble and common, and they were saying, "This is the great power of God."

11. And they were all persuaded by him, because many times he had astonished them by his sorceries.

12. When they believed Philippus, who was proclaiming The Kingdom of God in the name of Our Lord Yeshua The Messiah, they were being baptized, men and women.

13. Simon also believed and was baptized and was joined to Philippus, and when he saw the signs and the great miracles that were done by his hand, he marveled and was astonished.

14. And when the Apostles of Jerusalem heard that the people of the Samaritans had received the word of God, they sent Shimeon Kaypha and Yohannan to them.

15. And they went down and prayed over them so that they would receive The Spirit of Holiness.

16. For he was upon none of them yet, but they had only been baptized in the name of Our Lord Yeshua.

17. And they were laying hands upon them, and they were receiving The Spirit of Holiness.

18. And when Simon saw that by laying on of the hands of the Apostles The Spirit of Holiness was given, he brought silver to them,

19. As he said, "Give me also this authority that he on whomever I place a hand will receive The Spirit of Holiness."

20. Shimeon Kaypha said to him, "Your silver will go with you to destruction, because you thought that the gift of God is acquired by the possessions of the world."

21. "You have no part or allotment in this faith, because your heart is not upright before God.

22. But turn from this your evil and request from God that perhaps the treachery of your heart may be forgiven you.

23. For I see that you are in the wrath of bitterness and in a knot of evil."

24. Simon answered, and he said, "Ask God for my sake, that none of these things which you have said may come upon me."

25. But Shimeon and Yohannan, when they had testified and taught the word of God, returned to Jerusalem. And they preached The Gospel in many villages of the Samaritans.

26. And The Angel of THE LORD JEHOVAH spoke with Philippus and he said to him, "Arise, go to the south by the desert road that goes down from Jerusalem to Gaza."

27. And he arose to go and met a certain Eunuch who had come from Kush, an official of Qandiqe, Queen of the Kushites, and he was authorized over all her treasury and had come to worship in Jerusalem.

28. As he turned to go, he sat down on the chariot and was reading in Isaiah The Prophet.

29. And The Spirit said to Philippus, "Approach and join the chariot."

30. And as he approached, he heard what he read in Isaiah The Prophet and he said to him, "Do you understand what you are reading?"

31. And he said, "How can I understand unless a man will instruct me?" And he asked Philippus to come up and sit with him.

32. But the section of Scripture he read had this in it: "He was led as a lamb for sacrifice and as a ewe before its shearer is silent, also in this way he opened not his mouth."

33. "He was led in his humility from imprisonment and from judgment and who will narrate his time? For his life is taken from The Earth."

34. And that Eunuch said to Philippus, "I beg of you, about whom did The Prophet say this, about himself or about another man?"

35. Then Philippus opened his mouth and began from this Scripture to preach about Our Lord Yeshua to him.

36. And as they were going on the road, they were arriving at one place that had water in it, and that Eunuch said, "Behold, water! What is the hindrance to me being baptized?"

37. And Philippus said, "If you believe with all the heart, it is authorized." And he answered and said, "I do believe that Yeshua The Messiah is The Son of God."

• This verse is absent in The Peshitta mss. , however, the Aramaic Scriptures Research Society 1986 edition of The Aramaic Peshitta Text (an edition of The Eastern text) contains it [in brackets] and The 1979 Syriac NT critical edition of The Peshitta also has it at the bottom of the page with a note which states that no Syriac manuscript contains it and that "it was first supplied in Hutter's edition of 1599-1600".The Harklean Syriac version does have this verse, being revised from Greek in AD 616; one Greek uncial E (8th cent.) has it, The Textus Receptus Greek editions have it as do some Latin Vulgate mss. and The Old Itala Version (2nd cent.). Obviously, the 1905 Peshitta edition I translated does have it.
The ending of verse 36 is- כליתא דאעמד ; In DSS : נעחוא דאתעבד.
The ending of verse 37 is : ברה דאלהא הו ; In DSS : הו ברה דאלהא. Possibly a copyist copied verse 36 and was confused by the similar endings of 37 and 36 and instead of going on to v. 37, he skipped it, assuming he had just copied it and went on to v. 38.
The beginning of verse 37 is ואמר.
The beginning of verse 38 is ופקד. It is more likely a copyist had finished v. 36 and was glancing ahead at 37 in the original ms. and noted visually ואמר but actually proceeded with v. 38 ופקד instead, due to the similarities in the respective first words of each verse. It is certainly easier to account for the omission of this verse than for its fabrication as Scripture.

38. And he commanded to stop the chariot and the two of them went down to the water and Philippus baptized that Eunuch.

39. And when they had come up from the water, The Spirit of THE LORD JEHOVAH took Philippus up and the Eunuch did not see him again, but he went on the road rejoicing.

40. But Philippus was found in Azotus and from there he was traveling and preaching in all the cities until he came to Qesarea.

Chapter 9

1. But Shaul was full of menace and the fury of murder against the disciples of Our Lord.
2. And he requested a letter for himself from The High Priest and to give it for Darmsuq for the synagogues, that if he were to find those following in this way, men or women, he may bind and bring them to Jerusalem.
3. And as he was going, he began to approach Darmsuq; suddenly there was light from the Heavens shining upon him,
4. And he fell upon the ground and he heard a voice which said to him: "Shaul, Shaul, why do you persecute me? It is hard for you to kick against the goads."
5. He answered and said, "Who are you my lord?" And Our Lord said, "I AM THE LIVING GOD, Yeshua the Nazarene, He whom you are persecuting."
6. "But arise and enter the city, and there it will be told you what you must do."
7. And the men who were traveling with him on the road were standing amazed because they were hearing the sound only, but The Man was not visible to them.
8. And Shaul got up off the ground and could not see anything, while his eyes were open. And while they held his hands they brought him to Darmsuq.
9. And he could see nothing for three days, and he did not eat or drink.
10. But there was a disciple in Darmsuq and his name was Khanan-Yah and THE LORD JEHOVAH had said to him in a vision, "Khanan-Yah", and he said, "Behold, it is I, my Lord."
11. And Our Lord said to him, "Arise, go to the street which is called Straight and inquire at the house of Yehuda for Shaul, who is from the city Tarsus, for behold, he is praying."
12. "He sees in a vision a man whose name is Khanan-Yah entering and laying a hand upon him so that his eyes will be opened."
13. And Khanan-Yah said, "My Lord, I have heard from many about this man, how much evil he has inflicted on the Saints in Jerusalem."
14. "And behold, he also has authority here from The Chief Priests to imprison all those who call upon your name."

15. And THE LORD JEHOVAH said to him, "Arise, go, because he is a chosen vessel to me to take my name to the Gentiles and Kings and among the children of Israel."
(Notice that here Yeshua Our Lord is named as "THE LORD JEHOVAH". This is one of at least 32 such places in The Peshitta NT, including The Four Gospels, Acts, four Epistles and Revelation)
16. "For I shall show him how much he is going to suffer for my name."
17. Then Khanan-Yah went to the house to him and laid a hand upon him and said to him, "Shaul, my brother, Our Lord Yeshua who appeared to you on the road, when you came, has sent me so that your eyes would be opened and you would be filled with The Spirit of Holiness." (Ananias here identifies THE LORD JEHOVAH of verse 15 as Our Lord Yeshua.)
18. And immediately, some things that were like scales fell from his eyes and his eyes were opened, and he arose and he was baptized.
19. And he received food and was strengthened and he was with those disciples who were in Darmsuq for *some* days.
20. And within an hour he was preaching in the synagogue of the Jews about Yeshua, that he is The Son of God.
21. And all those who heard him were astounded and they were saying, "Was this not he who was persecuting all those who are calling on this Name in Jerusalem? And he was even sent here to bind them to convey them to The Chief Priests!"
22. But Shaul was strengthened even more and was agitating those Jews who were dwelling in Darmsuq as he was showing that This One is The Messiah.
23. And as the days progressed, the Jews produced a plot against him to kill him.
24. But the plot was shown to Shaul, what they were seeking to do to him. And they were watching the gates of the city day and night that they might kill him.
25. Then the disciples put him in a basket and let him down from the wall by night.
26. And he went on to Jerusalem, and he wanted to join the disciples and they were all afraid of him and they did not believe that he was a disciple.
27. But BarNaba took him and brought him to the Apostles and he related to them just how he had seen THE LORD JEHOVAH on the road and that he had spoken with him on the road, and how in Darmsuq he had spoken openly in the name of Yeshua.

28. And he was entering and exiting with them in Jerusalem.

29. And he was speaking in the name of Yeshua openly and disputing with the Jews who knew Greek, but they were seeking to kill him.

• According to this verse, in Greek and in Aramaic, there were some Hellenist –"Greek speaking" Jews in Jerusalem; not all were Hellenists, of course.

30. And when the brethren knew, they brought him by night to Qesaria, and from there they sent him to Tarsus.

31. However, the church that was in all Judea and in Galilee and in Samaria had peace, and it was built up and was proceeding in the worship of God and was growing in the comfort of The Spirit of Holiness.

32. And it happened that when Shimeon was traveling among the cities, he came down also to The Holy Ones who dwelt in the city Lud .

33. And he found one man whose name was Annis who was lying in bed and had been paralyzed for eight years.

34. And Shimeon said to him, "Annis, Yeshua The Messiah is healing you. Stand and make your bed", and at that moment he got up."

35. And all of those who dwelt in Lud and in Sarona saw and they were converted to God.

36. There was a female disciple whose name was Tabitha, in the city Joppa. She was rich in good works and in the charity which she was doing.

* Greek has "ταβιθα η διερμηνευομενη λεγεται δορκας"- "Tabitha, which, being translated, means Dorcas (a gazelle)." δορκας -"Dorkas" occurs twice in this chapter in the Greek texts, which according to the Greek of this verse, is a Greek translation of an Aramaic word: 5000 Ταβιθα Tabitha tab-ee-thah' of Aramaic origin, cf 06646 טבירא; ; n pr f AV-Tabitha 2; 2 Tabitha =" female gazelle" - (1) the name of the woman that Peter raised from the dead . - (Thayers Greek-English Lexicon). Is it not strange that the Greek text has the Aramaic "Tabitha " transliterated in Greek letters and then states "which being translated means Dorcas " ? We do not find this phenomenon in The Peshitta, that is, we do not find Greek words transliterated into Aramaic letters and then translated into Aramaic words. The Greek NT has this phenomenon recorded at least six times in The Gospels and in Acts. Why in the name of Sam Hill would Luke have written this in Greek originally if the persons , language and culture involved were Aramaean ? And why would we have a Greek translation of a name if the original was Greek ? And why would we have a Greek translation of a person's name at all , unless it were a highly significant name with a highly significant meaning, like that of **Meshikha-**"Christ" or "**Kaypha**" – "**Peter**" ?
The fact that the Greek texts have both "**Tabitha**" and "**Dorcas**" in this passage with the statement , "**this is translated into [Greek] Dorcas**" is a giveaway of the fact that the Greek text is not the original language but a translation

language of a Semitic original (probably Aramaic). This writer believes the Greek translation of "Tabitha" was a faux pas; names are hardly ever to be translated into the target language, but simply transliterated in their original form. The fact that this one was **transliterated and translated into Greek** twice in this chapter testifies powerfully to the Greek as a translation of an Aramaic original. See v. 39 also.

37. But she was sick in those days, and she died. They washed her and placed her in an upper room.

38. And the disciples heard that Shimeon was in Lud, that city which is beside Joppa, and they sent two men to request of him, "Do not neglect to come with them."

39. And Shimeon arose and went with them, and when he came they took him up to the upper room and all the widows were gathered standing around him, weeping and showing him the coats and cloaks which Tabitha had given them when she was alive.
* Greek has "δορκας"- **Dorkas** ", which is the Greek translation of The Aramaic name "Tabitha"; Both mean "**Gazelle**". Even the Greek has "Tabitha" in v. 36 and in the next verse!

40. But Shimeon sent all of the people outside and bowed on his knees and prayed, and he turned to the corpse and said, "Tabitha, get up", but she opened her eyes, and when she saw Shimeon, she sat up.

41. And he reached his hand toward her and raised her up, and he called the Saints and the widows and he gave her to them alive.

42. And this was made known in the whole city, and many believed in Our Lord.

43. But he was in Joppa not a few days while he dwelt in the house of Shimeon a Tanner.

Chapter 10

1. But in Qesaria was a certain man, a Centurion whose name was Cornelius, from the regiment which is called Italiqa.

2. And he was righteous and was a worshiper of God, he and his whole house, and he did great charitable work among the people and always prayed to God.

3. This man saw an Angel of God in a vision plainly before his face at the ninth hour of the day, who entered his presence and said to him, "Cornelia."

4. And he gazed at him and was afraid and said, "What, my lord?" And The Angel said to him, "Your prayer and your charity have gone up for a remembrance before God.

5. "And now send a man to the city Joppa and bring Shimeon who is called Kaypha.

6. Behold, he dwells in the house of Shimeon a Tanner which is on the seaside."

7. When The Angel went who had spoken with him, he called two of the men of his household and one Servant who worshiped God, who was agreeable to him,

8. And he related to them everything that he had seen and he sent them to Joppa.

9. And the next day, when they were traveling on the road and came near to the city, Shimeon went up to the roof to pray at the sixth hour.

10. And he was hungry and he wanted to eat, and as things were being gotten for him, he fell into a trance,

11. And he saw Heaven as it was opened, and a garment which was tied at the four corners like a great linen, and it was descending from Heaven to The Earth,

12. And there were in it all *kinds* of four footed animals and creeping things of The Earth and birds of the sky;

13. And a voice came to him saying, "Shimeon, arise, slay and eat."

14. And Shimeon said, "Never, my Lord, because I have never eaten anything defiled or polluted."

15. And a voice came again a second time to him: "Those things which God has purified you shall not make impure."

16. This happened three times and the garment was taken up to Heaven.

17. And as Shimeon wondered in himself what this vision was that he had seen, those men arrived who were sent from Cornelius, and they asked for the house in which Shimeon dwelt and they came and stood at the gate of the courtyard.

18. And they were calling there asking, "Is Shimeon who is called Kaypha lodging here?"

19. And as Shimeon was pondering the vision, The Spirit said to him, "Behold, three men are seeking you.

20. Arise, go down and go with them, doubting nothing in your mind, because I am he who has sent them."

21. Then Shimeon went down to those men and said to them, "I am he whom you seek. What is the reason for which you have come?"

22. They said to him, "A certain man whose name is Cornelius, a good Centurion and worshiper of God, for whom all the people of the Jews vouch, was told in a vision by a holy Angel to send and bring you to his house and hear a message from you."

23. And Shimeon brought them in and received them where he was lodging, and the day after he arose and went out with them, and some men of the brethren of Joppa went with him.

24. And the next day he entered Qesaria, but Cornelius had been waiting for them while all of his relatives and close friends whom he had were gathered to him.

25. And when Shimeon entered, Cornelius met him and fell worshiping at his feet.

26. And Shimeon raised him up and said to him, "Stand up; even I am human."

27. And as he spoke with him, he entered and found many who had come there.

28. And he said to them, "You know that a man who is of the Jews is not allowed to join a foreign person, who is not one of his race. God has shown me that I should not say that a man is unclean or defiled."

29. "Because of this, I have readily come when you sent after me. However, I ask you why you have sent after me."

30. Cornelius said to him, "It has been four days now since I was fasting, and at the ninth hour, while I was praying in my house, a certain man stood in front of me, being clothed in white."

31. He said to me, 'Cornelius, your prayer is heard and your charity is a memorial before God.

32. However, send to the city Joppa and bring Shimeon who is called Kaypha. Behold, he dwells in the house of Shimeon, a Tanner, upon the seaside, and he will come speak with you.'

33. And immediately I sent to you and you have done well to come, and behold, we are all before you and wish to hear everything whatever is commanded you from the presence of God."

34. But Shimeon opened his mouth and he said, "In truth, I understand that God is no respecter of persons.

35. But among all nations, whoever worships him and works righteousness is acceptable to him.

36. For the word which he sent to the children of Israel and announced good news of peace and tranquility to them by Yeshua The Messiah, (This One is **LORD JEHOVAH** of all),

37. You also are aware of the word that has come to all Judea, which went out from

Galilee after the baptism that Yohannan preached,

38. About Yeshua who was from Nazareth, whom God anointed with The Spirit of Holiness and with power, and he was traveling and healing those injured by The Evil One, because God was with him.

39. And we witnessed him concerning all whatsoever he did in all the land of Judea and of Jerusalem. The Judeans hanged him on a tree and murdered him.

40. And God raised him up the third day and granted him to appear publicly.

41. But not to all the people, but to us who were chosen by God to be witnesses for him, we who ate and drank with him after his resurrection from the grave.

42. And he commanded us to preach and to testify to the people that This is He who was appointed by God to be The Judge of the living and of the dead.

43. And all The Prophets have borne him witness, that everyone who believes in his Name will receive forgiveness of sins."

44. And when Shimeon was speaking these words, The Spirit of Holiness rested on all of those who were hearing the word.

45. And circumcised brethren who had come with him were stupefied and astonished that the gift of The Spirit of Holiness was poured forth also upon Gentiles,

46. For they heard them speaking in various languages and magnifying God, and Shimeon was saying:

47. "Can anyone refuse water that they should not be baptized? For, behold, they have received The Spirit of Holiness, as when we did."

48. Then he commanded them to be baptized in the name of Our Lord Yeshua The Messiah, and they begged him to stay with them for some days.

Chapter 11

1. And it was heard by the Apostles and by the brethren who were in Judea that Gentiles had also received the word of God.

2. And when Shimeon came up to Jerusalem, those who were of the circumcision were contending with him,

3. As they were saying that he had entered into the presence of the uncircumcised and had eaten with them.

4. And Shimeon interjected, in order to say to them:

5. "When I was praying at Joppa, I saw in a vision a garment descending which was like a linen and was tied at the four corners, and it was coming down from the sky and it came unto me.

6. I stared at it and I saw beasts in it, four footed animals and creeping things of The Earth and birds of the sky.

7. And I heard a voice that said to me, 'Shimeon, arise, slay and eat.'

8. And I said, 'Never, my Lord, because what is polluted or defiled has never entered my mouth.'

9. And again a voice said to me from Heaven: 'Whatever God has purified, you shall not make defiled.'

10. This happened three times, and everything was taken up to Heaven.

11. At that moment, three men who were sent to me from Cornelius of Qesaria came and stood at the gate of the courtyard where I was dwelling.

12. And The Spirit said to me, 'Go with them without doubting.' And these six brothers also came with me and we entered the man's house.

13. He related to us how he had seen an Angel in his house, who stood and said to him, 'Send to Joppa the city and bring Shimeon who is called Kaypha,

14. And he will speak with you words by which you will receive life, you and all your household.'

15. And as I was continuing to speak there, The Spirit of Holiness rested upon them as when upon us from the first."

16. And I was reminded of the word of Our Lord, which he had said: 'Yohannan baptized in water, but you shall be baptized in The Spirit of Holiness.'

17. If God therefore has equally given The Gift to those Gentiles who have believed in Our Lord Yeshua The Messiah, as also to us, who am I that I would be qualified to forbid God?"

18. And when they heard these words, they were silent; and then they praised God and they were saying, "Perhaps God has given a restoration to life to the Gentiles also."

19. But those who were scattered by the suffering which occurred concerning Estephanos had reached Phoenicia and the region of Cyprus and unto Antiakia, when they were speaking the word with no one but the Jews.

20. Some of them there were from Cyprus and from Qorina who went in to the Antiochenes, and they were speaking with the Hellenists and preaching concerning Our Lord Yeshua.

21. And the hand of THE LORD JEHOVAH was with them, and many believed and were turned to THE LORD JEHOVAH.

22. And this was heard by the ears of the members of the Church of Jerusalem and they sent BarNaba to the Antiochenes.

23. And when he had come there and had seen the grace of God, he rejoiced and he was exhorting them that with all their heart they would cleave to Our Lord.

24. For he was a good man, and he was filled with The Spirit of Holiness and with faith, and many people were added to Our Lord.

25. And he was going to Tarsus to seek Shaul;

26. And when he found him, he brought him with him to Antiakia, and they were assembling together for a full year with the church and they taught many people. From that time, the disciples were first called Christians by the Antiochenes.

27. And in those days Prophets came there from Jerusalem.

28. And one of them stood up whose name was Agabus and instructed them by The Spirit that a great famine would occur in the whole land and that this famine would be in the days of Claudius Caesar.

29. But the disciples set aside, according to what each one of them had, to send for the service of the brethren who dwelt in Judea;

30. They sent by the hand of BarNaba and Shaul to the Elders who were there.

Chapter 12

1. But at that time, King Herodus, who was surnamed Agrippa, was laying hands on the people who were in the churches, to do evil to them.

2. And he murdered Yaqob the brother of Yohannan with the sword.

3. And when he saw this pleased the Judeans, he proceeded to seize also Shimeon Kaypha, and they were the days of Unleavened Bread.

4. And he arrested him and cast him into prison and delivered him unto sixteen Soldiers to guard him so that after Passover he would deliver him to the people of Judea,

5. And while Shimeon was guarded in prison, continual prayer was offered by the church for him to God,

6. And that night toward dawn, he was preparing to hand him over while Shimeon was asleep between two Soldiers and was bound with two chains, and the others were keeping the gate of the prison.

7. The Angel of THE LORD JEHOVAH stood over him, and the light shone in the entire place and he jabbed him in the side and raised him up and said to him, "Arise quickly." And the chains fell from his hands.

8. And the Angel said to him, "Wrap your garment around your waist and put on your sandals", and he did so; again, he said to him, "Wrap your cloak and follow me."

9. And he went out and followed him while he did not know that this was real which was happening by the hand of The Angel, for he thought that he was seeing a vision.

10. And as they passed the first guard and the second they came to an iron gate, and it opened to them of its own accord, and when they went forth past one street, The Angel departed from him.

11. And Shimeon realized and said, "Now I know in truth that THE LORD JEHOVAH has sent his Angel to save me from the hand of Herodus The King and from that which the Judeans were plotting against me."

12. And as he pondered this, he came to the house of Maryam, the mother of Yohannan who was surnamed Marqus, because many brethren were gathered there and praying.

13. And he knocked at the door of the courtyard and a girl went out to answer it whose name was Rhoda.

14. She recognized the voice of Shimeon and in her joy she did not open the door to him, as she went back running and saying to them, "Shimeon, behold, is standing at the door of the courtyard!"

15. They were saying to her, "You are crazy.", and she was protesting, "It is true." They said to her, "Perhaps it is his messenger."

16. And Shimeon was knocking at the gate and they went out and saw him and they marveled among themselves.

17. And he was gesturing to them with his hands so as to silence them, and he entered and related to them how THE LORD JEHOVAH had brought him out from the

prison. And he said to them, "Tell these things to Yaqob and to the brethren." And he went out to another place.

18. When it was morning, there was a great uproar among the Soldiers about Shimeon: "What happened to him?"

19. But when Herodus had searched for him and did not find him, he condemned the guards and ordered to execute them, and he went out from Judea and was staying in Qesarea.

20. And because he was at enmity with the Tyrians and against the Sidonians, they gathered and came together to him and persuaded Blastus the Chamberlain of The King and asked him that they might have a peace treaty, because the sustenance of their countries was from The Kingdom of Herodus.

21. But on a notable day, Herodus was wearing the royal garments and sat down on the judgment seat and was speaking with the multitude.

22. All the people were crying out and saying, "These are the sayings of God and not of men."

23. And because he did not give the glory to God, immediately The Angel of THE LORD JEHOVAH struck him and he was infested with worms and he died.

24. And The Gospel of God was proclaimed and it grew.

25. Then BarNaba and Shaul returned from Jerusalem to Antiakia after they had finished their service and they took Yohannan with them, who was surnamed Marqus.

Chapter 13

1. But there were Prophets in the Church of Antiakia and Teachers: BarNaba and Shimeon who is called Niger, Luqius, who is from the city Qorina, Manael, son of the rearers of Herodus the Tetrarch, and Shaul.

2. And as they were fasting and beseeching God, The Spirit of Holiness said to them, "Separate to me Shaul and BarNaba for the work to which I have called them."

3. And after they had fasted and prayed, they placed hands upon them and they sent them.

4. When they were sent by The Spirit of Holiness, they went down to those in Seluqia and from there they journeyed by sea unto Quprus.

5. And when they entered the city Salamna, they were preaching the word of Our Lord in the synagogues of the Jews, and Yohannan was ministering to them.

6. And as they traveled the whole island to the city of Paphos, they found a Jewish man, a Sorcerer who was a false Prophet, whose name was Bar Shuma.

7. This man adhered to a wise man who was the Proconsul and he was called Sergius Paulus; the Proconsul called Shaul and BarNaba and he was requesting to hear from them the word of God.

8. But the Sorcerer Bar Shuma, whose name is translated Alumas, withstood them because he wanted to turn aside the Proconsul from the faith. ("Alumas" is Arabic for "Sorcerer".)

9. But Shaul, who was called Paulus, was filled with The Spirit of Holiness, and he stared at him.

10. And he said, "Oh, full of all treacheries and all evils! Son of The Devil and enemy of all righteousness! You do not cease to twist the straight ways of THE LORD JEHOVAH!

11. Now the hand of THE LORD JEHOVAH is upon you and you will be blind, and you will not see the sun for a time." At that moment a blackness and darkness fell upon him and he was going around and seeking someone to take his hand.

12. And when the Proconsul saw what happened, he was amazed and he believed in the teaching of THE LORD JEHOVAH.

13. But Paulus and BarNaba journeyed by sea from Paphos, the city, and they came to the city Perga of Pamphylia and Yohannan separated from them and went on to Jerusalem.

14. But they went forth from Perga and came to Antiakia, a city of Pisidia, and they entered a synagogue and sat down on the Sabbath day.

15. And when The Law and The Prophets were read, the Elders of the synagogue sent to them and said, "Men, brothers, if you have a word of comfort, speak with the people."

16. And Paulus stood and lifted his hand and said, "Men, Sons of Israel and those who are worshipers of God, listen.

17. The God of this people chose our fathers and raised up and multiplied them when they were foreigners in the land of Egypt and with a high arm he brought them forth from it.

18. And he sustained them in the wilderness forty years.

19. And he destroyed seven nations in the land of Canaan, and he gave them their land for an inheritance.

20. For four hundred and fifty years he gave them Judges until Samuel The Prophet.

21. And then they asked for themselves a King, and God gave them Shaul, son of Qish, a man from the tribe of Benjamin, for forty years.

22. And he removed him and raised up for them David The King and testified of him and said, 'I have found David the son of Jesse, a man according to my heart. He shall do all my pleasure.'

23. From the seed of this man God raised up to Israel, according to what was promised, Yeshua The Savior.

24. And he sent Yohannan to preach the baptism of repentance before his coming to all the people of Israel.

25. And when he had finished his ministry, Yohannan was saying, 'I am not who you think I am. Behold, he comes after me, the strap of whose sandals I am not worthy to loose.'

26. Men, brothers and children of the lineage of Abraham, and those who worship God with you: To you He has been sent: The Word of Life.

* This reference to "**The Word**" is a reference to Our Lord, as the next verse confirms: "They did not perceive **Him**", referring back to this verse. Luke used this title in his Gospel at the very beginning in his prologue of verses 1:1-3. Please see that passage and my notes at Luke 1:3.

27. And these inhabitants of Jerusalem and their Leaders did not understand him nor the Scriptures of The Prophets which are read on every Sabbath, but they judged him and they fulfilled these things which are written.

28. And when they found no cause of death, they asked Pilatus to kill him.

29. And when they had fulfilled everything that was written about him, they took him down from the cross and laid him in a tomb.

30. But God raised him from among the dead.

31. He appeared for many days to those who came up with him from Galilee to Jerusalem, and they are now his witnesses to the people.

32. We also, behold, we preach good news to you, that The Promise which was to our fathers,

33. Behold, God has fulfilled it to us their children, because he raised Yeshua, as it is written in the second Psalm: 'You are my Son; today I have begotten you.'

34. And so God raised him from among the dead that he will not return again to see destruction, as it says: 'I shall give you the favor of faithful David.'

35. Again, it says in another place: 'You have not given your Pure One to see corruption.'

36. For David served the will of God in his generation and he fell asleep and was added to his fathers and he saw corruption.

37. But This One whom God raised did not see corruption.

38. Therefore, know brothers, that by This One, the forgiveness of sins is preached to you.

39. And all who believe in This One are justified of all things from which you cannot be justified by the law of Moses.

40. Beware therefore, lest that which is written in The Prophets come upon you:

41. 'Behold, scorners, and marvel and be destroyed, for I will do a work in your days, which you will not believe even if a man reports it to you.' "

42. And as they were going out from their presence, they asked of them that they would speak these words with them on another Sabbath.

43. And when the synagogue was dismissed, many Jews followed them, even foreigners who were worshipers of God, and they were speaking and persuading them to be joined to the grace of God.

44. And on another Sabbath, the whole city gathered to hear the word of God.

45. And when the Jews saw the great crowds, they were filled with anger, and they were opposing the words which Paulus was speaking and they were blaspheming.

46. But Paulus and BarNaba said: "It was necessary that the word of God be spoken to you publicly first, but because you drive it away from you and you determine against yourselves that you are unworthy of eternal life, behold, we turn to the Gentiles."

47. "For so Our Lord commanded us just as it is written: 'I have set you *as* a light to the Gentiles to be life unto the ends of The Earth.'"

48. And as the Gentiles were hearing, they were rejoicing and glorifying God, and they that were appointed to eternal life believed.

(Or, "They believed that they were appointed to eternal life")

49. And of the word of **THE LORD JEHOVAH** was spoken in that whole region.

50. But the Jews stirred up the Leaders of the city and those honorable women who were worshiping God with them and they raised persecutions against Paulus and against BarNaba and expelled them from their borders.

51. When they went forth, they shook the dust of their feet off against them and they came to the city Iqonion.

52. And the disciples were filled with joy and The Spirit of Holiness.

Chapter 14

1. **A**nd they came and entered the synagogue of the Jews, and thus they spoke with them, so many of the Jews and of the Greeks believed.

2. But the Jews who were unconvinced stirred up the Gentiles to harm the brethren.

3. And they were there for a long time publicly speaking about **THE LORD JEHOVAH**, and He was testifying concerning the word of his grace by signs and wonders that He was doing by their hands.

4. And the whole multitude of the city was divided; some of them were with the Jews and some of them were joined to the Apostles.

5. But there was a decree against them by the Gentiles and by the Jews and their Leaders, to abuse them and to stone them with stones.

6. And when they knew it, they departed and took refuge in the cities of Lyconia, Lystra and Derby and the villages around them.

7. And they were there preaching The Good News.

8. And a certain man was sitting in the city of Lystra who was lame in his feet, crippled from his mother's womb, who had never walked.

9. This one heard Paulus speaking and when Paulus saw him, and it was known that he had faith to receive salvation,

10. He said in a loud voice, "I say to you in the name of Our Lord Yeshua The Messiah, stand on your feet!" And he jumped, stood and walked.

11. When the crowds of people had seen this thing that Paulus had done, they raised their voices in the language of the country*, and they were saying, "The gods have become like men and have come down to us."

    * Etruscan inscriptions have been found in Lyconia; Etruscan is essentially Latin.

12. And they were naming BarNaba, The Lord of the gods, * and Paulus, Hermes, because he had been introducing the message.

    *(Zeus was the Chief deity of the Greek gods; Hermes was The Messenger of the gods. Lyconia was a Roman colony of which Lystra was part.)

13. And The Priest of The Lord of the gods, who was outside the city, brought bulls and garlands to the gates of the courtyard where they were staying and he wanted to sacrifice to them.

14. BarNaba and Paulus, when they heard, they tore their robes and leaped and went out to them among the mob and were crying out,

15. And they were saying, "Men, what are you doing? We are also men of passions like you, we who preach to you that you should turn from these worthless things to **THE LIVING GOD** who made The Heavens and The Earth and The Sea and all that is in them,

16. He who in the former ages was allowing all nations to go in their own way,

17. While he did not leave himself without a testimony, as he was giving them precious things from the Heavens and sending rain down to them, multiplying their fruits in their times and was satisfying their hearts with food and gladness."

18. And as they were saying these things, with difficulty they restrained the people that no one would sacrifice to them.

19. But there came Jews from Iqonion and from Antiakia and stirred up the people against them and they stoned Paulus and dragged him outside of the city, because they thought that he was dead.

20. And the disciples gathered around him, and he stood up and entered the city, and the next day he went out from there with BarNaba, and they came to the city Derbe.

21. While they were preaching to the people of that city, they discipled many and they returned and came to Lystra and to Iqonion and to Antiakia,

22. While they were confirming the souls of the disciples and seeking that they would continue in the faith; and they were saying to

them that it is necessary to enter The Kingdom of God by much suffering.

23. And they appointed them Elders in every church while they were fasting with them and praying, committing them to Our Lord in whom they had believed.

24. And when they had traveled in the region of Pisidia, they came to Pamphylia.

25. And as they spoke the word of THE LORD JEHOVAH in the city of Perga, they came down to Italia. (Italia is Italy)

26. And from there they journeyed by sea and came to Antiakia, because from there they were commending the work which they had finished to the grace of THE LORD JEHOVAH.

27. And when the whole church had gathered together, they were relating everything that God had done with them and that he had opened the door of the faith to the Gentiles.

28. And they spent much time there with the disciples.

Chapter 15

1. But men had come down from Judea and were teaching the brethren: "If you are not circumcised in the custom of The Law, you cannot have life."

2. There was great tumult and debate with them for Paulus and BarNaba, and it happened that Paulus and BarNaba and another with them would go up to the Apostles and the Elders who were in Jerusalem because of this dispute.

3. And the church accompanied and sent them and they were traveling in all Phoenicia and also among the Samaritans, as they were recounting the conversion of the Gentiles, and they were creating great joy to all the brethren.

4. And when they came to Jerusalem, they were received by the church and by the Apostles and by the Elders and they recounted to them everything that God had done with them.

5. But some of the school of The Pharisees who had believed stood up, and they were saying, "It is necessary for you to circumcise them and to command them to keep The Law of Moses."

6. But the Apostles and the Elders assembled to look into this matter.

7. And as there was a great dispute, Shimeon arose and he said to them, "Men,

brothers, you are aware that from the first days God chose the Gentiles to hear the word of The Gospel from my mouth and to believe."

8. "And God, who knows what is in the hearts, testified to them and gave them The Spirit of Holiness as to us."

9. "And he made no distinction between us and them, because he purified their hearts by faith."

10. "And now, why are you tempting God, so as to put a yoke on the necks of the disciples, which not even our fathers nor we were able to bear?"

11. But by the grace of Our Lord Yeshua The Messiah, we believe in order to receive life, as they *do*".

12. And all the crowds were silent, and they were listening to Paulus and to BarNaba, who related everything whatever God had done by their hands: signs and mighty deeds among the Gentiles.

13. And after they had ceased, Yaqob arose and he said, "Men, brothers, hear me."

14. "Shimeon has related to you how God began to choose from the Gentiles a people for his name."

15. "And the words of The Prophets agree with this, just as that which is written:"

16. 'After these things I shall return and I shall raise the tabernacle of David, which had fallen. And I shall build that which had fallen from it and I shall raise it up,

17. So that the rest of the children of men may seek THE LORD JEHOVAH, and all the nations upon which my name is called, says THE LORD JEHOVAH, who does all of these things.'

18. Known from eternity are the works of God."

19. "Therefore I say, let us not trouble those who are being turned to God from the Gentiles."

20. "But let it be sent to them that they separate from the defilement of sacrifices and from fornication and from what is strangled and from blood."

21. "For from the first ages there have been preachers for Moses who read him on every Sabbath in every town* in the synagogues."*
Jewish synagogues were in every town, giving Paul a platform and foundation for New Testament evangelism and church planting.

22. Then the Apostles and the Elders, with the whole church, chose men from among them and they sent Yehuda, who is called

Bar-Shaba, and Shila, to Antiakia with Paulus and BarNaba, men who were Leaders among the brethren."

23. And they wrote an epistle by their hands thus: "The Apostles and Elders and the brethren, to those who are in Antiakia and in Syria and in Qiliqia, brethren who are of the Gentiles, peace."

24. "We hear that men among us went out and have alarmed you with words and have subverted your souls, as they were saying, 'Be circumcised and keep The Law', which we have not commanded them."

25. "Therefore we counseled when we all assembled and we chose men and sent them to you with our beloved friends, Paulus and BarNaba,"

26. "Men who have surrendered themselves for the name of Our Lord Yeshua The Messiah."

27. "And we sent Yehuda with them and Shila, for they shall tell you the same things by speech."

28. "For it was the will of The Spirit of Holiness and also of us that we would not put upon you a burden greater than those things which are necessary:"

29. "Abstain from what is sacrificed, from blood, from what is strangled, and from fornication, for when you keep yourselves from these things, you will be well. Be faithful in Our Lord."

30. But those who were sent came to Antiakia, and they gathered all the people and gave them the letter.

31. And when they read it, they rejoiced and were comforted.

32. And with a bountiful message they strengthened the brethren and established them who were followers of Yehuda and Shila because they also were Prophets.

33. And after they were there awhile, they released the brethren to the Apostles in peace.

34. However, it was Shila's will to remain there.

(Many Greek mss. omit this verse, as does The Eastern Peshitta; many Greek mss. also contain it. According to verse 40, Shila-"Silas" did remain behind with Paul. Codices D & C include it (5th and 6th century) as well as The AD 616 Harklean Syriac Version, some Latin Vulgate mss, The Sahidic Version (2nd-3rd cent.) and St. Ephraim of Syria in the 4th century.)

35. But Paulus and BarNaba did remain in Antiakia and they were teaching and preaching the word of God with many others.

36. And after some days, Paulus said to BarNaba, "Let us return and visit the brethren who are in every city in which we preached the word of God and see how they are doing."

37. But BarNaba had wanted to take Yohannan, who was surnamed Marqus.

38. But Paulus did not want to take him with them, because he had left them when they were in Pamphylia and did not go with them.

39. Because of this dispute, they separated one from another. BarNaba took Marqus and traveled by sea and went to Cyprus.

40. But Paulus chose Shila, and he went out when he was commended by the brethren to the grace of God.

41. And he was traveling in Syria and in Qiliqia, and he was confirming the churches.

Chapter 16

1. And he arrived at the city Derby and at Lystra, but a disciple was there whose name was Timotheus, son of a certain Jewess believer, and his father was an Aramaean*. -*
(Or "Syrian"; All Greek mss. have "Greek" here and in verse 3, and everywhere else in The 20 places in the NT where The Peshitta has "Aramaean" or "Aramaic"! I discuss this at length in my Aramaic-English Interlinear New Testament and in my book, Divine Contact. See especially Interlinear notes at Romans. 1:16, Galatians 3:28 and Revelation 9:11.) An Aramaean was a Gentile who spoke Aramaic. A non-Aramaic speaking Gentile was called "Bar-Amma"; The plural is "Ammay"- "Gentiles". Jews and Aramaeans spoke Aramaic and the Aramaic language was quite prominent in the area of the world where Paul traveled in the Middle East, Asia Minor and even in Europe where The Jews had migrated due to many persecutions. There were Jewish settlements in Italy and in Spain for several centuries since The Babylonian conquest of Israel and deportation of thousands of Jews. The "Sephardim" are Jews who were emigrated from Judea to Spain and Portugal in the 6th century BC or possibly even earlier, according to tradition. The Hebrew word "Sepharad" occurs in Obadiah verse 20 and means "separated". Strong's Hebrew dictionary describes it as "a place to which Israelites were exiled, site unknown." Very interestingly, the ancient Peshitta translation of The Hebrew Tanach reads "Espania" (Spain) for "Sepharad" in Obadiah, verse 20. Large colonies of Jews have lived in Spain and Portugal from ancient times and are testament to their widespread settlements in Europe and Asia from times immemorial. It was to the Jews first that Paul brought The Gospel, wherever he went, and established Christian churches among them.

2. And all the disciples who were from Lystra and from Iqonion were testifying about him.

3. Paul wanted to take this man with him and he took and circumcised him, because all the Jews in that place knew that his father was an Aramaean.

4. As they were going among the cities preaching, they were also teaching them to keep those commandments that the Apostles and Elders who were in Jerusalem had written;

5. Yet the churches were established in the faith and growing in numbers everyday.

6. But they walked in the regions among Phrygia and Galatia, and The Spirit of Holiness forbade them to speak the word of God in Asia.

7. When they came to the region Musia, they desired to go from there to Bithunia and The Spirit of Yeshua* did not permit them.

*Most Greek mss. lack "Ἰησοῦ" (**Jesus**) here.

8. And when they went forth from Musia, they went down to the region Troas.

9. And in a vision of the night, a man appeared to Paulus from Macedonia who stood and begged of him as he said, "Come to Macedonia and help me."

10. But when Paulus saw this vision, we desired at once to proceed to Macedonia, because we understood that Our Lord was calling us to evangelize them.

11. And we traveled from Troas and went straight to Samothracia, and from there, the day after, we came to the city Neapolis,

12. And from there to Philippus, which is the capital of Macedonia, and it is a colony, but we were in this city for notable days.

13. And we departed on the Sabbath day outside the gate of the city on the riverside, because there was seen there a house of prayer, and when we sat, we were speaking with the women who had gathered there.

14. And one woman, a merchant of purple who was a worshiper of God, whose name was Lydia, from the city Thayatira, whose heart Our Lord had opened, was listening to what Paulus said.

15. And she was immersed and the children of her house, and she was begging of us and saying: "If you are truly confident that I have believed in Our Lord, come lodge yourselves at my house", and she urged us much.

16. And it was that as we were going to the house of prayer, there met with us one girl who had a spirit of divination upon her and she was making a great business for her masters in the divination that she had been practicing.

17. She was coming after Paulus and after us, crying and saying, "These men are Servants of the highest God, and they are evangelizing to you the way of life."

18. And thus she was doing for many days, and Paulus was angered and he said to that spirit, "I command you in the name of Yeshua The Messiah to come out of her", and at that moment, it came out.

19. When her masters saw that the hope of their business had departed from her, they seized Paulus and Shila, and they dragged and brought them to the marketplace.

20. And they presented them to the Magistrate and to the Leaders of the city and they were saying, "These men are troubling our city because they are Jews."

21. "And they are preaching to us customs which are not allowable for us to receive and do, because we are Romans."

22. And great crowds were gathered against them and then the Magistrates tore their garments and commanded to scourge them.

23. And when they had scourged them much, they cast them into the prison and commanded the Keeper of the prison to keep them securely.

24. But when he had received this order, he brought them and shut them up in the inner room of the prison and bound their feet in the stocks.

25. In the middle of the night, Paulus and Shila were praying and singing to God and the prisoners were listening to them.

26. And suddenly there was a great earthquake and the foundation of the prison was shaken, and immediately all the doors were opened and their chains were all released.

27. And when the Keeper of the prison was awakened and he saw that the doors of the prison were open, he took a sword and sought to kill himself because he thought that the prisoners had escaped.

28. And Paulus called him in a loud voice and he said to him, "Do no harm to yourself, because we are all here."

29. And he lit a lamp and he leaped and entered, trembling, and he fell before the feet of Paulus and of Shila,

30. And he brought them outside and he said to them, "Sirs, what must I do so that I may live?"

31. And they said to him, "Trust in Our Lord Yeshua The Messiah, and you shall live, you and your household."

32. And they spoke with him the word of **THE LORD JEHOVAH**, and with all the people of his household.

33. And at that hour of the night, he took and washed them of their wounds and

immediately he was immersed and all the people of his household.

34. And he led and brought them to his house and he set a table for them, and he rejoiced and the people of his house in the faith of God.

35. And when it was dawn, the Magistrates sent the Rod Bearers to say to The Warden of the prison, "Release these men."

36. And when The Warden of the prison heard, he entered and he spoke this message to Paulus: "The Magistrates have sent so that you should be released, and now depart; go in peace."

37. Paulus said to him, "They scourged us without an offense, publicly before the world, all of us being Roman men, and they cast us into prison, and now they are releasing us secretly? No, but those men should come and release us."

38. And the Rod Bearers went and they told the Magistrates these words that were spoken to them, and when they heard that they were Romans, they were afraid.

39. And they came to them and they begged them to go out and depart from the city.

40. And when they went out from the prison they returned to Lydia, and there they saw the brethren and comforted them, and they left.

Chapter 17

1. They passed unto the cities Amphipolis and Apollonia and they came to Thessaloniqa where there was a synagogue of the Jews.

2. And Paulus entered as he was accustomed with them, and on the third Sabbath he spoke with them from the Scripture,

3. As he was expounding and showing: "The Messiah was going to suffer and rise from the grave, and he is Yeshua The Messiah, this one whom I proclaim to you."

4. And some of them believed and joined Paulus and Shila, and many of those Greeks who were worshipers of God, even notable women, not a few.

5. And the Jews were envious and drew evil men to themselves from the streets of the city and formed a great mob; they were terrorizing the city and they came and raised them against the house of Jason and were seeking to bring them out from there to hand them over to the mob.

6. And when they did not find them there, they dragged Jason and the brethren who were there and they brought them to The Governor of the city as they were crying out, "These have terrorized the whole area and behold, they have come here again!"

7. "And this is their host, Jason, and these all oppose the commands of Caesar, while they are saying that there is another King, Yeshua."

8. But the Governor of the city and all the people were alarmed when they heard these things.

9. And they took bail from Jason and also from the brethren and then they released them.

10. But the brethren immediately that night sent Paulus and Shila to the city Berea. And when they came there, they were entering a synagogue of the Jews.

11. For those Jews who were there were nobler than those Jews who were in Thessaloniqa, and they were hearing gladly from the word every day while they were distinguishing from Scripture whether these things were so.

12. And many of them believed, and so also of the Greeks, many men and notable women.

13. And when those Jews who were from Thessaloniqa knew that the word of God was preached by Paulus in the city Berea, they came there and did not cease to stir up and to alarm the populace.

14. And Paulus sent the brethren to go down to the sea and Shila and Timotheos remained in the city.

15. And those who accompanied Paulus came with him to Athens the city and when they left his presence, they took a letter from him to Shila and Timotheos that they should go quickly to him.

16. But while Paulus remained in Athens, he was provoked in his spirit when he saw that the whole city was full of idols.

17. And he was speaking in a synagogue with the Jews and with those who were worshipers of God and in the market place with those who gathered everyday.

18. Also philosophers from the school of Epicurus and others who are called Stoics were debating with him and some of them were saying, "What does this collector of words want?" And others were saying, "He is proclaiming foreign gods", because he was

proclaiming Yeshua and his resurrection to them.

19. And they took him and brought him to the place of judgment, which is called Arios-Pagos, while they were saying to him, "Can we know what this new teaching is that you proclaim?"

20. "For you have sown strange words in our hearing and we wish to know what these things are."

21. But all the Athenians and those foreigners who come there are concerned about nothing except to tell and to hear something new.

22. And when Paulus arose in Arios-Pagos, he said, "Men, Athenians, I see that in all things you excel in the worship of daemons."
(Greek has an absurdly long compound word found nowhere else in Greek: δεισιδαιμονεστερους – transliterated as deisidaimonesterouv (adjective, **"fearing the gods"**).Greeks did not think of Demons as evil, but as lesser deities.

23. "For as I was going around and beholding your temples, I found one altar on which it was written: "The Unknown God"; him therefore whom you do not know and yet worship, I proclaim to you."

24. "For The God who made the world, and everything whatsoever is in it, and is the Lord of the Heavens and of The Earth, does not dwell in temples made with hands."

25. "And he is not served by the hands of men, and he has no need of anything, because he gives every person life and a soul."

26. "And from one blood he made the whole world of humanity to be dwelling on the whole surface of The Earth and he marked out the times in his decrees and set the coasts of the dwelling places of humanity,"

27. "So that they would be seeking and inquiring* after God; and they may find him by his creation, because also he is not far from everyone of us."

* Greek mss. have, "To seek the Lord, if they may feel him and find though, indeed, He is not far from each one of us."
Here is "**to inquire**" in DSS Aramaic: מֶעְקִיּ.
Here is "**to feel**","touch" in DSS Aramaic: מֶקְיּ.
I estimate **75%** letter correlation between these two Aramaic words, with 4 of 6 corresponding letters identical and the other pairs (עק, קק) sharing a ק-(Qop) & other certain dyslexic similarities.
Greek for "they may inquire" is ακριβησειαν or εξεζητησουσιν or εξερευνησειαν. None of these is close to ψηλαφησειαν –" they may feel".I suppose the 1st is the more similar of the three, with about **54%** letter correlation between the two Greek words.

28. "For it is by him that we have life and we move and exist; so also some of the wise men among you have said: "Our lineage is from him."

29. "Men, therefore, because our lineage is from God, we ought not to think that gold or silver or stone carved by the skill and knowledge of a man is like The Godhead."

30. "For God has banished the times of deception, and at this time he commands all the children of men: 'Everyone in every place shall return to God.'"

31. "Because he has appointed the day in which he is going to judge the whole Earth in righteousness by the man whom he has designated and he has turned everyone to his faith in that he has raised him from among the dead."

32. And when they heard of the resurrection from among the dead, some of them were mocking and some were saying, "We shall hear you another time about this."

33. And so Paulus went out from among them.

34. And some of them joined him and believed, but one of them was Dionysius of the Judges of Areos-Pagos, and one woman whose name was Damaris, and others with them.

Chapter 18

1.And when Paulus went out from Athens, he came to Corinthus.

2.And there he found one man, who was a Jew, whose name was Aqilaus, who was from Pontus, who at that time had come from the country of Italia, he and Priscilla his wife, because Claudius Caesar had ordered all the Jews to leave Rome, and he came to them.

3.And because he was a member of their craft, he stayed with them, and he was working with them in their craft, for they were Tentmakers.

4.And he was speaking in the synagogue on every Sabbath and was persuading the Jews and the Pagans.

5.And when Shila and Timotheos had come from Macedonia, Paulus was constrained in the word* because the Jews were opposing him and blaspheming as he was testifying to them that Yeshua is The Messiah.

● *Majority Greek & TR Greek has "in his spirit".
Critical Greek agrees with The Peshitta reading.Following are the two readings in Pesher Habakkuk Dead Sea Scroll script:
בֶּמֶלְתָא-"in the word"
בֶּרוּחָא-"in the spirit"
I see **80%** correlation between the letters of each (4/5). The two readings in Greek are: λογω & πνευματι.They have **0%** correlation. How about in Greek uncial (capital letters) script? ΛΟΓΩ & ΠΝΕΥΜΑΤΙ - 0% still! The Greek primacy theory just keeps taking a beating, for almost every example of Greek variant readings I can find!

6.And he shook his clothes and he said to them, "From now on I am clean; I myself go to the Gentiles."

The Greek mss. have, "**He said unto them, 'Your blood is upon your head—I am clean; henceforth to the nations I will go on.'**" Just a thought: One does not cleanse oneself of blood by shaking his clothes. The action does not fit the metaphor. Now look at the following two Aramaic phrases in Ashuri script an attempt to explain the Greek reading:

דמך ועל לרישך –"Your blood also *is* upon your head"
תמן ועל לביתה – "there & unto his house" (phrase in verse 7)

<u>In Dead Sea Scroll Script:</u>

–"Your blood also *is* upon your head"
– "there & unto his house" (phrase in verse 7)

<u>Estrangela script:</u>

–"Your blood also *is* upon your head"

– "there & unto his house" (phrase in verse 7)

The two phrases in Dead Sea Scroll script (also called Herodian) show high correlation between letters of about **82%**. Ashuri and Estrangela scripts show about **73%** letter correlations.

The Aramaic of the first phrase above is in the singular. A Greek translator would most likely correct this to read the plural "your"- υμων instead of the singular "your" - σου, since Paul was addressing a large group in verse 6. In this scenario, it looks like the Greek translator's eye went inadvertently from verse 6 to verse 7 before he had finished translating, translated the 3 word phrase above and misread it as shown in DSS script, and then went back again to finish verse 6. The translator strangely would have then correctly translated the same Aramaic phrase as – "There & unto the house", when translating v. 7.

Of course, according to Greek primacy theory, it is possible that an Aramaean translator of the Greek text may have simply neglected to translate the Greek phrase in question. One example by itself would not prove anything. Several hundred would.

7.And he left there and entered the house of a man whose name was Titus, one who was a worshiper of God, and his house was joined to the synagogue.

8.And Krispus, The Leader of the synagogue was trusting in Our Lord, he and all the children of his household, and many Corinthians were listening and were trusting in God and being baptized.

9.And **THE LORD JEHOVAH** said in a vision to Paulus, "Do not be afraid, but speak and do not be silent,

10.Because I am with you, and no man can harm you, and I have many people in the city."

11.And he remained one year and six months in Corinthus and was teaching them the word of God.

12.And when Galion The Proconsul of Akaia was there, the Jews gathered together as one against Paulus, and they brought him before the judgment seat,

13.While they were saying, "This one persuades people to be worshiping God outside of The Law."

14.And when Paulus had requested to open his mouth and speak, Galion said to the Jews, "If you are accusing about a matter of wickedness or fraud or what is hateful, Oh Jews, I would receive you on the merits.

15.But if the charges are about a discourse or about names or about your law, you know among yourselves that I do not want to be judge of these matters."

16.And he expelled them from his judgment seat.

17.And all the Pagans were seizing Sosthenes, the Elder of the synagogue, and they were beating him before the judgment seat and Galion was disregarding these things.

18.And when Paulus had been there for many days, he bade farewell to the brethren and he journeyed by sea to go to Syria, and Priscilla and Aqilaus came with him when he shaved his head in Qenkreos, because he had vowed a vow for himself.

19.And he arrived at Ephesaus and Paulus entered the synagogue and he was speaking with the Jews.

20.And they were asking him to tarry with them, and he did not consent,

21.As he said, "I must always observe the coming feast in Jerusalem, and if God wills, I shall return again to you." And he left Aqilaus and Priscilla in Ephesaus.

22.He traveled by sea and came to Qesaria, and he came up and invoked the peace of the members of the church and he went on to Antiakia.

23.And when he was there for notable days, he went out and traveled in the countries, one after the other, of Galatia and Phrygia, establishing all of the disciples.

24.One man, a Jew whose name was Apollo, a native of Alexandria and instructed in the word, was familiar with the Scriptures and he came to Ephesaus.

25.This man had been taught the way of **THE LORD JEHOVAH** and he was fervent in spirit, speaking and teaching thoroughly about Yeshua, yet not knowing anything except the baptism of Yohannan.

26.And he began publicly speaking in the synagogue, and when Aqilaus and Priscilla heard him, they brought him unto them, and thoroughly showed him the way of THE LORD JEHOVAH.

27.As he wanted to go to Akaia, they exhorted the brethren and wrote to the disciples to receive him and when he went, he helped all the believers greatly by grace.

28.He was powerfully instructing contrary to the Jews before the crowds while showing from the Scripture concerning Yeshua, that he is The Messiah.

Chapter 19

1. And when Apollo was in Corinthus, Paulus went about in the upper countries and came to Ephesaus, and was questioning those disciples whom he had found there:

2. "Have you received The Spirit of Holiness since you have believed?" They answered, and were saying to him, "We have not even heard if there is a Spirit of Holiness."

3. And he said to them, "Unto what were you baptized?" They were saying, "Unto the baptism of Yohannan".

4. Paulus said to them, "Yohannan baptized the people in the baptism of repentance while he was telling them to believe in that One who would come after him, who is Yeshua The Messiah."

5. And when they heard these things, they were baptized in the name of Our Lord Yeshua The Messiah.

6. And Paulus laid a hand on them and The Spirit of Holiness came upon them, and they were speaking in various languages and were prophesying.

7. But they were all of twelve men.

8. And Paulus was entering the synagogue and he was speaking publicly three months and persuading concerning The Kingdom of God.

9. Some of them were hardened and were disputing and reviling the way of God before the assembly of the Gentiles; then Paulus left and he separated the disciples from them and was speaking every day with them in the school of a man whose name was Turanos.

10. And this continued for two years until all who dwelt in Asia heard the word of THE LORD JEHOVAH, Jews and Aramaeans.

11.And God was doing great miracles by the hand of Paulus.

12. So also napkins or rags which were placed upon his robe or his body were brought and placed on the sick, and the diseases were departing from them; even demons were going out.

13. But there were also some Jewish men who were going around and were exorcists of demons, exorcising in the name of Our Lord Yeshua over those who had a foul spirit in them while saying, "We exorcise you in the name of Yeshua whom Paulus preaches."

14. But there were seven sons of a man who was a Jew, a Chief Priest, whose name was Sqewa, who were doing this,

15. And that evil spirit answered and said to them, "I know Yeshua, and I know Paulus, but who are you?"

16. And that man who had the evil spirit in him jumped upon them and overpowered them and threw them down, and when they were stripped and wounded, they fled from the house.

17. And this became known to all the Jews and Aramaeans dwelling in Ephesaus and great fear fell upon all of them, and the name of Our Lord Yeshua The Messiah was exalted.

18. Many of those who believed were coming and relating their wrongdoing, and they were confessing the things that they were doing.

19. Many sorcerers also gathered their books and brought and burned them before everyone and they calculated their price, and it came up to fifty thousand silver pieces.

20. And thus with great power the faith of God was increasing in strength and growing.

(Greek mss. have, του κυριου ο λογος ηυξανεν -"The word of the Lord increased".) Here are both readings in Pesher DSS Aramaic:

אלהא דיהות- "the Faith of God"

דיהוד1א אלהא- "it is of The LORD the word" ("It is" has been pushed into "The LORD" without spacing.)

There is direct correlation in 7 out of 11 letters in DSS Aramaic between the two readings. The Greek for "Faith of God" is πιστις του θεου or του θεου η πιστις; Compare that to του κυριου ο λογος-"The word of the Lord". Only 3 letters out of twelve look similar in the Greek readings. This does not bode well for the Greek primacy position.

21. But when these things were done, Paulus set in his mind to journey in all Macedonia and in Akaia and to go to Jerusalem, and he said, "When I have gone there, I must also see Rome."

22. And he sent two men of those who were ministering to him to Macedonia: Timotheos and Erastus, but he stayed for a time in Asia.

23. But there was a great commotion at that time about the way of God.

24. And a certain Silversmith was there whose name was Demetrius, who was making silver shrines for Artemis, and he was

enriching the members of his craft with great profits.

25. This man gathered all members of his craft together and those who worked with them, and he said to them, "Men, you know that all of our profit is from this work."

26. "You also hear and see that this Paulus has persuaded and turned away, not only the citizens of Ephesaus, but also the multitudes of all Asia, when he said, "Those are not gods which are made by the hands of men."

27. "Neither is this matter only exposed and finished, but so also is The Temple of Artemis, the great goddess, reckoned as nothing. And even this goddess, whom all Asia and all nations worship, is despised."

28. And when they heard these things, they were filled with rage and were crying out and saying, "Great is Artemis of the Ephesians!"

29. And the entire city was stirred up and ran as one and went to the theater, and they took by force and brought with them Gaius and Aristarkus, Macedonian men and companions of Paulus.

30. And Paulus had wanted to enter the theater and the disciples restrained him.

31. Even the Rulers of Asia, because they loved him, sent and begged him not to offer himself to enter the theater.

32. But the crowds that were in the theater were very chaotic and they were shouting to each other, but many of them did not know why they had assembled.

33. But the people of the Judeans who were there put forth a man of them, a Jew whose name was Alexandrus, and as he arose, he beckoned with his hand and wanted to put forth a defense to the people.

34. And when they knew that he was a Jew, they all shouted with one voice for about two hours: "Great is Artemis of the Ephesians!"

35. And the Governor of the city pacified them and he said, "Men, Ephesians! Who of the children of men does not know of the city of the Ephesians and of the temple worship of the great Artemis and the image that descended from Heaven?"

36. "Because therefore no one can speak against this, you must be quiet and not do anything hasty."

37. "For you have brought these men, although they have not robbed temples neither have reviled our goddess."

38. "But if this Demetrius and the fellows of his trade have a judgment with any, behold, the Proconsuls of the city are skilled; let them approach and dispute one with another."

39. "And if you seek anything other than what is granted by the law, the assembly will be dismissed."

40. "For even now we are in danger of being accused as seditious, so that we will not be able to offer a defense for the crowd today, because we have assembled needlessly and we are in an uproar without a cause."

41. And when he has said these things, he dismissed the multitude.

Chapter 20

1. And after the uproar had ceased, Paulus called the disciples and comforted them and kissed them, and he departed and went to Macedonia.

2. And when he traveled those regions and comforted them with many words, he came to the country of Greece.

3. And he was there three months, but the Jews made a plot against him when he was going to leave for Syria and planned to return to Macedonia.

4. And Supatros went out with him to Asia, who was from the city Berea, and Aristarkus and Sequndus, who were from Thessaloniqa, and Gaius, who was from the city Derby, and Timotheos, who was from Lystra, and Tykiqos and Trophimos from Asia.

5. These went before us and waited for us in Troas.

6. But we departed from Philippus, the city of Macedonia, after the days of unleavened bread, and we went by sea and came to Troas in five days and remained there seven days.

7. In the first day of the week, when we assembled to break the Eucharist, Paulus was speaking with them, because the next day he was going to go out by himself and he prolonged speaking until midnight.

8. And there were many fire lamps there in an upper room in which we were gathered.

9. And there was a young man whose name was Eutikus, sitting there in a window, and he listened and he sank into a deep sleep, and as Paulus had prolonged the message, in his sleep he fell from the third story, and he was taken up as dead.

10. And Paulus came down and fell upon him and embraced him and he said, "Do not be troubled, because his life is in him."

11. But when he got up, he broke bread and ate, and he spoke until sunrise, and then he went out to depart by land.

12. And they brought the youth alive, and they rejoiced over him greatly.

13. But we went into the ship and we sailed to the port of Thesos, because from there we prepared to receive Paulus, for thus he had commanded us when he had gone on by land.

14. And when we had received him from Thesos, we took him into the ship and came to Mitolina.

15. And from there the next day we sailed next to Kios the island, and again the next day we came to Samos and we stayed in Trogulion and the next day we came to Miletus,

16. For Paulus was determined to pass by it to Ephesaus, lest he be delayed there because he was hurrying, that if he were able, he would keep the day of Pentecost in Jerusalem.

17. And from Miletus he sent and brought the Elders of the Church of Ephesaus.

18. And when they came to him, he said to them, "You are aware that from the first day that I entered Asia, how I have been with you all the time,"

19. "As I served God in much humility and in tears, and in those trials that have come upon me by the treachery of the Jews."

20. "And I have neglected nothing that was useful for your souls, to preach and to teach in the marketplace and in houses,"

21. "While I was testifying to the Jews and to the Aramaeans about returning home to the Presence of God and the faith in Our Lord Yeshua The Messiah."

22. "And now I am shackled by The Spirit, and I go on to Jerusalem, and I do not know what will meet me there."

23. "However, The Spirit of Holiness testifies in every city to me and he says, 'Chains and afflictions are prepared for you.'"

24. "But my life is esteemed nothing to me, so that I may finish my race course and the ministry which I have received from Our Lord Yeshua, to testify of The Gospel of the grace of God."

25. "And now I know that none of you will see my face again, all of you among whom I have gone and preached to you The Kingdom."

26. "And because of this, I testify to you today that I am pure from the blood of all of you."

27. "For I have not declined to show you the whole will of God."

28. "Pay attention to yourselves therefore, and to the whole flock in which The Spirit of Holiness has appointed you overseers, to shepherd the Church of God* which he has purchased with his blood." *

The Eastern Peshitta has :
משיחא דעדתה -"the church of The Messiah"
Compare to The Western Peshitta:
דאלהא דעדתה -"the church of God"
דמריא דעדתה - "the church of The Lord Yahweh"
The third reading is a hypothetical misreading of the true reading.
The top two shaded words correlate between corresponding letters with approximately **70%** similarity.
Add to this the fact that practically all Greek mss. have Κυριου και Θεου -"**Lord & God**" or Κυριου του Θεου -"**Lord God**" ; Codex B & Codex ℵ have του Θεος -"**God**" and that no Greek ms. has ο Χριστος –"**The Christ**", and it becomes clear that the original reading was not "The Messsiah". Four old Greek mss. (P[74],A,C,D) have **Kuriou** -"**The Lord**". The Greek readings may all be traceable to a misreading of the Aramaic, דאלהא (of God) which could have been mistaken for דמריא (of The Lord Yahweh).

Those two words also are very similar to each other, with about 80% letter correlation. דמריא -"**d'MarYah**" could also explain the Greek readings Κυριου και Θεου -"**Lord & God**" or Κυριου του Θεου -"**of Lord God**", as "MarYah" literally means "**Lord Yahweh**" and is matched by itself with Κυριος ο Θεος -"**Lord God**" in Acts 3:22 , 1 Peter 3:15 & Rev. 18:8. Most often, however, "**MarYah**" is matched in Greek simply with "Κυριος"-"**Lord**", which would also explain the reading of the four old Greek mss. (P[74],A,C,D), which have Κυριου -"**of The Lord**".
Both the Eastern Peshitta reading "**of The Messiah**"-משיחא & the four Greek readings are easily explained on the basis of the Western Peshitta reading, "**of God**"-דאלהא . The Eastern Peshitta reading does not explain how it is that **no Greek manuscript among the many hundreds of The Book of Acts extant has the reading "του Χριστου" - "of The Christ"**.
Some of these mss. date to the 3rd century AD and 99% of them contain Θεου -"**God**", in agreement with The Western Peshitta. The evidence is decidedly in favor of The Western Peshitta reading and against The Eastern reading.
Here is the phrase of Acts 20:28 in three of the oldest Greek Uncials:
Codex B (Vaticatus-4th century):
ΘΕΤΟΕΠΙCΚΟΠΟΥCΠΟΙ
ΜΑΙΝΕΙΝΤΗΝΕΚΚΛΗCΙ
ΑΝΤΟΥΟΥΗΝΠΕΡΙΕΠΟΙ
ΗCΑΤΟΔΙΑΤΟΥΑΙΜΑΤΟC
ΤΟΥΙΔΙΟΥΟΤΙΕΓΩΟΙΔΑ
Codex ℵ (Sinaiticus-4th century)
ΝΟΕΠΙCΚΟΠΟΥΙΗ
ΜΕΝΙΝΤΗΝΕΚΚΛΙ
CΙΑΝΤΟΥΟΥΗΝΠ·
ΡΙΕΠΟΙΗCΑΤΟΔΙΑ
ΤΟΥΑΙΜΑΤΟCΤΟΥΙ
ΔΙΟΥ
Codex D (Bezae-5th century)
ΠΟΙΜΕΝΕΙΝΤΗΝΕΚΚΛΗCΙΑΝΗCΤΟΕΠΙCΚ
ΗΝΠΕΡΙΕΠΟΙΗCΑΤΟCΑΥΤΟΥ
ΔΙΑΤΟΥΑΙΜΑΤΟCΤΟΥΙΔΙΟΥ

The Greek uncial mss. use abbreviations for the words, "God,Lord,Christ" in many places, and here the above mss. all use them, so there is only one letter difference between "God" –

a two letter abbreviation. The Western Peshitta reading can account for all four Greek readings as well as for the Eastern Peshitta reading.

29. "For I know that after I go, powerful wolves will enter with you that will not spare the flock."

30. "And even some of you and your own men will arise, speaking perversions so as to turn the disciples to go after them."

31. "Therefore be vigilant, and remember that for three years I have not been silent by night and by day, while with tears I was warning each one of you."

32. "And now I commit you to God and to the word of his grace, which is able to build you up, and to give you an inheritance with all of The Holy Ones."

33. "I have not coveted silver, gold, or apparel."

34. "And you know that these my hands have ministered to my needs and to those who were with me."

35. "And I have shown you everything, that thus it is necessary to labor and to take care of those who are weak and to remember the words of Our Lord Yeshua, who said, 'He who gives is more blessed than he who receives.'"

36. And when he had said these things, he knelt on his knees and he prayed, and all the men with him.

37. And there was great weeping among all of them, and they were embracing him and kissing him.

38. But they were all the more pained about that statement which he said, that they were not going to see his face again; and they accompanied him to the ship.

Chapter 21

1. And we departed from them and we traveled straight to the Isle Qo*, and the next day we came to Rhodus, and from there to Patara. * (Critical Greek mss. and Latin Vulgate have "Ko"; the Majority Greek mss. have "Kon".)

2. And we found a ship there going to Phoenicia and we boarded it and sailed.

3. We came as far as to The Island Cyprus, and we passed it to the left and we came to Syria, and from there we arrived at Tyre, for the ship was to unload its cargo there.

4. And when we found disciples there, we stayed with them seven days, and they were saying to Paulus everyday by The Spirit not to go to Jerusalem.

5. And after these days we went out to go by road, and they were all following us with their wives and their children to the outside of the city. And they knelt on their knees by the seaside, and they prayed.

6. And we kissed one another, and we boarded the ship, and they returned to their homes.

7. And we journeyed from Tyre and we came to the city Akko*, and we gave greeting to the brethren there and we lodged with them one day. * (Greek has "Ptolemais" for the old name of the Sea port "Akko". It was named "Ptolemais" after Ptolemy the King of Egypt rebuilt it in 103 BC. The Hebrew OT has the same name and spelling as The Peshitta has here; See Judges 1:31. The Peshitta did not get this from Greek. The name was changed again by Claudius Caesar to "Colonia Claudii Caesaris", who reigned AD 41-54. The Greek version of Acts was probably written before Caesar renamed it. Akko would have been the name the Jews of Israel used, since it was part of Galilee, and not a Greek city.)

8. And the next day we departed and came to Caesarea, and we entered and lodged in the house of Philippus The Evangelist, he who was of the seven.

9. And he had four virgin daughters who did prophesy.

10. And when we were there many days, a certain Prophet had come down from Judea, whose name was Agabus.

11. And he came to us and took off the leather belt on the waist of Paulus and he tied his own feet and his hands and he said, "Thus says The Spirit of Holiness: 'The Jews in Jerusalem will bind and deliver the man who owns this leather belt into the hands of the Gentiles.'"

12. And when we heard these words we begged of him, we and the people of that place, that he would not go to Jerusalem.

13. Then Paulus answered and said, "What are you doing that you are weeping and breaking my heart? For I am ready not only to be bound, but also to die in Jerusalem for the name of Our Lord Yeshua."

14. And when he was not persuaded by us, we ceased, and we said, "The will of Our Lord be done."

15. After these days, we prepared and we ourselves went up to Jerusalem.

16. And men who were disciples from Caesarea came with us as they took with them a brother to receive us into his house, one of the first disciples, whose name was Mnason, and he was from Cyprus.

17. And when we came to Jerusalem, the brethren received us gladly.

18. And the next day we entered with Paulus unto Yaqob, while all the Elders were there with him.

19. And we gave them greeting and Paulus was reporting in order to them everything that God had done among the Gentiles by his ministry,

20. And when they had heard, they praised God and said to him: "You see our brother, how many tens of thousands are in Judea who have believed, and they are all zealous of The Law."

21. "But it has been told them that you teach all the Jews who are among the Gentiles to separate from Moses while you say that they should not circumcise their sons and that they should not walk by the custom of The Law."

22. "Therefore, because this has been heard by them, they have come here."

23. "Do what we tell you; we have four men who have vowed to purify themselves."

24. "Take them and go be purified with them and pay the cost with them to shave their heads, and it will be known to everyone that whatever was spoken about you is false, and that you fulfill and keep The Law."

25. "But concerning those who believe among the Gentiles, we have written that they would keep themselves from what is sacrificed, from fornication, from strangled things and from blood."

26. Then Paulus took those men and the next day was purified with them and they entered and went to The Temple, showing them the fulfillment of the days of purification until an offering was offered by each one of them.

27. And when the seventh day arrived, the Jews of Asia saw him in The Temple, and they incited all the people against him and they laid hands upon him,

28. As they appealed and they were saying, "Men, sons of Israel, help! This is the man who opposes our people, teaching in every place against the law and against this place, and he also has brought an Aramaean into The Temple and has defiled this holy place." (Notice that the Jews of Asia spoke the same language as did the Jews of Jerusalem, which we know from Acts 1:19 and other sources, was Aramaic. This confirms that The Jews who were scattered to other places took their Aramaic language with them wherever they settled.)

29. For they had seen Trophimos the Ephesian with him before in the city and they were assuming that he had entered The Temple with Paulus.

30. And the whole city was stirred up and all the people assembled and they seized Paulus and they dragged him outside of The Temple and immediately the gates were shut.

31. And while the crowd was seeking to kill him, it was heard by the Chiliarch of the regiment that the whole city had been stirred up.

32. And immediately he took a Centurion and many Soldiers and ran unto them, and when they had seen the Chiliarch and the Soldiers, they ceased beating Paulus.

33. And the Chiliarch called him and took him and commanded to bind him with two chains, and he was asking about him, who he was and what he had done.

34. And men from the mob were shouting this and that about him, and because of their shouting, he was unable to know what the truth was, and commanded to bring him to the encampment.

35. And when Paulus came to the stairs, the Soldiers carried him because of the violence of the people;

36. For many people were coming after him and shouting, and they were saying, "Hang him*!" * (The Aramaic word here, "Shaqulayhi" is the same used in Luke 23:18 and John 19:15 by Christ's enemies when they cried out, "Crucify Him!")

37. And when he approached to enter the encampment, Paulus said to the Chiliarch, "If you allow me, I shall speak with you", but he said to him, "Do you know Greek?" (Notice the Roman Chiliarch's surprise that Paul in Jerusalem knew Greek; this indicates that Greek was uncommon in Jerusalem.)

38. "Are you not that Egyptian who before these days made a disturbance and led four thousand criminal men to the wilderness?" (He assumed he was an Egyptian, where Greek was more common.)

39. Paulus said to him, "I am a man, a Jew from Tarsus, the notable city of Qiliqia in which I was born. I beg of you, let me speak to the people."

40. And when he allowed him, Paulus stood on the stairs and was motioning to them with his hand, and when they were quiet he spoke with them in Judean Aramaic*, and said to them: Jastrow's Aramaic-Hebrew Dictionary has the following entry for עברית "Ebrayth" (Translated "Aramaic"): language is adapted for oratory; a. fr.—Meg. 18ᵃ קראה עברית... if he read the Megillah in a trans-Euphratean (Aramaic) translation.—Pl. עבריים, עבריות; f. עבריות. Ib. לפי עברית an Aramaic translation read before Aramæan Jews. Ex. R. s. 3 יּם לפה קורא אותם ע' כל שם שיִּבברו why The Hebrew word עברית – "Ibrayth" and the Aramaic word עברית "Ebrayith" can each refer to the Hebrew language or the Aramaic language. We know from history and other Biblical evidence that Aramaic was the common tongue of first century Israel.

The Greek text uses the word Εβραις –"Hebrais". Thayer's Greek-English Lexicon has this definition for the word:
1446 εβραις Hebrais heb-rah-is' from 1443; TDNT-3:356,372; n f AV-Hebrew 3; 3
1) Hebrew, the Hebrew language, not that however in which the OT was written but the Chaldee, which at the time of Jesus and the Apostles had long superseded it in Palestine . Webster's unabridged 20th century Dictionary defines "Chaldee" as The Aramaic language of the Chaldeans (Babylonians
600 B.C.).The Greek Εβραις –"Hebrais" refers only to Aramaic according to Thayer, and he is the standard Greek authority
for Koine Greek. This Greek word occurs three times in The Greek NT- all in Acts (this is the first reference). The word Εβραιστι is also used in The Greek NT and in The Apocrypha. It is the same word, only in a different case, called the dative
case; it means "In Aramaic" ; Here is Thayer's again; 1447 εβραιστι Hebraisti heb-rah-is-tee' from 1446; TDNT-3:356,372;
adv ;AV-in the Hebrew tongue 3, in the Hebrew 2, in Hebrew 1; 6
1) in Hebrew, i.e. in Chaldee .
Both Greek forms occur a total of nine times in The Greek NT: four times in John, three in Acts and two in Revelation. They also occur in the LXX apocrypha of Sirach one time and 4th Maccabees twice. All refer to the Aramaic language.
Here is The American Heritage Dictionary entry for "Aramaic":
Ar·a·ma·ic n. A Semitic language, comprising several dialects, originally of the ancient Arameans but widely used by non-Aramean peoples throughout southwest Asia from the seventh century B.C. to the seventh century A.D. Also called Aramean, Chaldean. --Ar"a·ma"ic adj.

So The Greek NT testifies unequivocally that the language of Israel in the first century was Aramaic.
Please note well that Paul did not address the Jews in Greek.

Chapter 22

1. "Brothers and fathers, hear my defense unto you."
2. And when they heard that he was speaking Judean Aramaic with them, they were all the more quiet, and he said to them:
   John's Peshitta Gospel distinguishes the southern Aramaic dialect from the northern dialect of Galilee with the word used here-"Ebraith" (lit. "Hebrew"), as   the speech of the Judean people, even though they were both dialects of the same Aramaic language.
3. "I was raised in this city at the feet of Gamaliel, and I was instructed perfectly in the tradition of our fathers, and I am zealous for God, as also are all of you."
4. "And I persecuted this way unto death, as I would bind and deliver men and women into prison."
5. "And according to what The High Priest witnessed of me, and all the Elders from whom I received warrants to go to the brethren who are in Darmsuq, so I also brought those who were there to Jerusalem as prisoners and they would receive capital punishment."
6. "And as I was going and began to approach Darmsuq at midday, under a quiet sky, a great light burst upon me."

7. And I fell to the ground, and I heard a voice saying to me, "Shaul, Shaul, why do you persecute me?"
8. "But I answered, and I said, "Who are you, my lord?" And he said to me, "I am Yeshua the Nazarene, whom you are persecuting."
9. "And the men who were with me saw the light, but they did not hear the voice which was speaking to me."
10. And I said, "What shall I do, my lord?" And Our Lord said to me, "Rise, go to Darmsuq, and there will be spoken with you concerning everything that you will be commanded to do."
11. "And when I could see nothing because of the glory of that light, they who were with me held me by the hands, and I went to Darmsuq."
12. "And one man, Khanan-Yah, righteous in The Law, as all the Jews were testifying there about him",
13. "Came to me and said to me, 'Shaul, my brother,open your eyes', and at that moment my eyes were opened and I saw."
14. And he said to me, "The God of our fathers has appointed you to know his will and to see The Righteous One and hear the voice of his mouth."
15. "And you shall be a witness for him to all people about everything whatsoever you have seen and heard."
16. "And now why do you wait? Arise, be baptized, and be cleansed from your sins while you call upon his name."
17. "And I returned and came here to Jerusalem, and I prayed in The Temple."
18. "And I saw in a vision as he said to me, 'Hurry and depart from Jerusalem, because they do not receive your testimony about me.' "
19. And I said, "My Lord, they also know that I have delivered to prison and beaten in all our synagogues those who have believed in you."
20. "And when the blood of your witness Estephanos was shed, I also was standing with them and consenting to the will of those who killed him, and I was holding the garments of those who were stoning him."
21. And he said to me, "Go, for I am sending you far away to preach to the Gentiles."
22. And when they had heard Paulus up until this statement, they raised their voice and shouted, "Hang such a person above The Earth, for it is not right for him to live!"

23. And as they were yelling and throwing off their garments and were casting up dust toward the sky,

24. The Chiliarch commanded to take him to the encampment and ordered that he be questioned by scourging, so as to know for what cause they were crying out against him.

25. And when they stretched him with leather straps, Paulus said to the Centurion who was standing over him, "Are you allowed to scourge a Roman who has not been condemned?"

26. And when the Centurion heard this, he called to the Chiliarch and he said to him, "What have you done? This man is a Roman!"

27. And the Chiliarch came to him and he said to him, "Tell me", are you a Roman?" And he said to him, "Yes."

28. And the Chiliarch answered and said, "I bought Roman citizenship with much money." Paulus said to him, "But I was born with it."

29. And at once those who were seeking to scourge him withdrew from him, and the Chiliarch was afraid when he learned that he was a Roman, for he had bound him.

30. And the next day, he had wanted to really know what the accusation was that the Jews had brought against him, and he released him and he had commanded The Chief Priests and all The Council of their Rulers to come, and he led Paulus and brought him down and stood him in the midst of them.

Chapter 23

1. And Paulus gazed at The Assembly and he said, "Men, brothers: in all good conscience I have lived before God, until today."

2. And Khanan-Yah The Priest commanded those who stood on the side to hit Paulus on his mouth.

3. And Paulus said to him, "God is going to strike you, you whitened wall, and are you sitting to judge me according to the law, when you violate the law and command to strike me?

4. And those who stood there said to him, "You accuse God's Priest?"

5. Paulus said to them, "I was not aware, brothers, that he is The Priest, for it is written: 'Do not curse The Ruler of your people.' "

6. And when Paulus knew that some of the people were Sadducees and some Pharisees, he was shouting in The Council, "Men, brothers; I am a Pharisee, son of a Pharisee, and for the hope of the resurrection of the dead I am being judged."

7. When he had said this, The Pharisees and The Sadducees fell one upon the other, and the group was divided.

8. For The Sadducees were saying there is no resurrection, neither Angel, nor spirit, but The Pharisees confess all of these*.

*(Greek texts. all have "The Pharisees confess both", but there were three things the Sadducees denied; "Both" indicates only two. The Peshitta text is   correct. The Greek statement is incorrect.)

9. And there was a great noise. Some of the Scribes stood on the side of The Pharisees and were contending with them and they were saying, "We find no evil in this man, but if a spirit or an Angel has spoken with him, what is there in that?"

* The Majority Greek text and TR (KJV Greek) has μη θεομαχωμεν -"Let us not fight God". The Following are the actual Peshitta reading with the 2nd & 3rd words combined (אבתה)) and the majority Greek reading in Aramaic below it, both in **Dead Sea Scroll Aramaic script**:
Peshitta reading in DSS Aramaic:אבו אתגבה פברדא – "What is there in that ?"
Maj. Greek reading in DSS. : אלא הורין קום עברא-"Let us not resist The Lord"
  The two readings are very similar looking in the DSS Aramaic script, leading me to believe that a Greek translator mistook the one for the other and gave us the Majority Greek reading as found in The King James Version of this verse. The Critical Greek has neither the Majority Greek reading or Peshitta reading. It merely trails off at the end with: **"But if an spirit or a angel has spoken with him."** That is a very poor and defective reading; it is not even a sentence.

10. And when there was a great uproar among them, the Chiliarch was afraid lest they would tear Paulus apart, and he sent Romans to go snatch him from their midst and bring him to the encampment.

11. When it was night, Our Lord appeared to Paulus and said to him, "Be strong, because as you testified of me in Jerusalem, thus you are going also to testify in Rome."

12. And when it was dawn, some of the Jews gathered together and put a curse upon themselves that they would neither eat nor drink until they would kill Paulus.

13. But those who established this covenant with an oath were more than forty men.

14. And they came to The Priests and to the Elders and were saying, "We have put a curse upon ourselves that we shall not taste anything until we shall kill Paulus."

15."And now you and the Rulers of The Council, ask the Chiliarch to bring him to you as if you seek to examine his conduct properly, and we are ready to kill him before he arrives to you."

16.And the son of Paulus' sister heard this plot, and he entered the encampment and informed Paulus.

17.And Paulus sent and called one of the Centurions and said to him, "Escort this young man to the Chiliarch, for he has something to tell him."

18.And the Centurion led the youth and brought him to the Chiliarch and said, "Paulus the prisoner called me and begged me to bring this young man to you, who has something to say to you."

19.And the Chiliarch took the youth by the hand and drew him to one side and was asking him, "What do you have to say to me?"

20.And the youth said to him, "The Judeans have planned to ask you to send Paulus down tomorrow to their Council as if they want to learn something more from him;"

21."Therefore you should not believe them, for behold, there are more than forty men of them who are watching for him in ambush and they have put a curse upon themselves that they will not eat or drink until they kill him. And behold, they are ready and waiting for your promise."

22.And the Chiliarch dismissed the youth as he commanded him: "Let no one know that you have shown me these things."

23.And he called two Centurions and said to them, "Go prepare two hundred Romans to go to Caesarea and seventy horsemen and two hundred right-handed spearmen to go out from the third hour in the night."

24."But prepare also beasts of burden so that they may mount Paulus and let him escape to Felix, the Governor."

25. And he wrote a letter and he gave it to those who were with him thus:

26."Qlaudias Lucius to Felix the Governor, the Excellent: Greeting;"

27."The Judeans seized this man so as to kill him, and I helped with the Romans and saved him when I learned that he is a Roman."

28."And when I sought to know the cause for which they were accusing him, I brought him down to their Council."

29."And I found that they were accusing him about charges of their law, and there was no

cause worthy for imprisonment or death against him."

30."And when it was shown me that the Judeans made a plot by ambush against him, I sent him at once to you and ordered his accusers to go and speak with him before you. Farewell."

31.Then the Romans brought Paulus in the night, as they were ordered, and brought him to the city AntiPatris.

32.And the next day the horsemen dismissed the Foot Soldiers, their comrades, to return to camp.

33.And they brought him to Caesarea and gave the letter to the Governor and presented Paulus before him.

34.And when he read the letter, he was asking him from which province he was, and when he learned that he was from Qiliqia,

35.He said to him, "I shall hear you whenever your accusers have come." And he commanded to keep him in the Praetorium of Herodus.

Chapter 24

1.After five days Khanan-Yah The High Priest came down with the Elders and Tertullos the orator and they informed the Governor concerning Paulus.

2.And when he was called, Tertullos began to accuse him and said, "With the abundance of tranquility we dwell because of you, and this people have much excellent stability in receiving your care."

3."And we all in every place receive your grace, excellent Felix."

4."But that we may not weary you with many things, I beg of you to hear our lowliness briefly."

5."We have found this man, who is a corruptor and agitator of tumult to all the Jews who are in every land, for he is the leader of the doctrine of The Nazarene."

6."And he wanted to defile our Temple, and when we seized him, we sought to judge him according to what is in our law."

7."But Lucius the Chiliarch came and with great violence snatched him from our hands and sent him to you."

8."And he commanded his accusers to come to you, and when you question him you can learn from him concerning all these things of which we accuse him."

9.But those Jews were crying out concerning him, as they were saying, "These things are so!"

10.And the Governor beckoned to Paulus to speak, and Paulus answered and said: "I know that you are the Judge of this nation for many years; because of this, I gladly render a defense for myself."

11."As you may know, it is not more than twelve days since I came up to Jerusalem to worship,

12.Neither did they find me speaking with any man in The Temple nor a crowd that I had gathered, either in their synagogues, nor in the city;"

13."Neither can they demonstrate concerning anything of which they accuse me now."

14."And yet I confess this, that in the same doctrine of which they speak, I serve The God of my fathers, as I believe all things which are written in The Written Law and in The Prophets."

15."And while I have hope in God, which they also do, they preach these things: There is going to be a resurrection from the dead, of the righteous and of the evil."

16."Because of this, I also labor that my conscience may always be pure before God and before all people."

17."But for many years I have come before my people to give charity and to offer gifts."

18."And these men found me in The Temple when I had been purified, not with the crowds, neither with a tumult."

19."But the Jews who came up from Asia, who stirred up the people, ought to be standing with me before you to bring whatever charge they have,"

20."Or let them say what offense they have found in me when I stood before their Council,"

21."Except for this statement, which I cried when I stood in their midst: 'For the resurrection of the dead I am judged today before you.'"

22.But because Felix knew this way fully, he deferred them when he said, "When the Chiliarch comes, I shall hear between you."

23.And the Centurion ordered to guard Paulus at ease and that no one of his acquaintances would be forbidden to minister to him.

24.And after a few days, Felix, and Dursilla his Jewish wife, sent and called Paulus and heard from him concerning the faith of The Messiah,

25.And as he was speaking with them of righteousness, of holiness and of the judgment that was to come, Felix was afraid and he said, "Go now, and when I have a space I will send for you."

26.For he had hoped that a bribe would have been given to him by Paulus, because of this, also, he was continually sending to bring him and speaking with him.

27.And when two years were completed, the next Governor had come in his place, who is called Porqius-Festus, but Felix, in order to do a favor for the Jews, left Paulus as a prisoner.

Chapter 25

1. And when Festus came to Caesarea, after three days he came up to Jerusalem.

2. And The Chief Priests and the Rulers of the Jews informed him concerning Paulus and they were inquiring of him,

3. When they asked him this favor: to send to bring him to Jerusalem, as they were making an ambush by the road to kill him.

4. And Festus returned the answer: "Paulus is kept in Caesarea, and I am in a hurry to travel."

5. "Those therefore among you who are able and have the accusations with them, let them go down with us; let them accuse the man."

6. And when he was there eight or 10 days, he went down to Caesarea and the next day he sat on the judgment seat and commanded to bring Paulus.

7. And when he came, the Jews that descended from Jerusalem surrounded him and many Leaders had brought hard things against him, things that they were unable to demonstrate.

8. And when Paulus rendered a defense that he had not violated anything, not the law of the Jews, neither of The Temple, neither Caesar,

9. Festus, because he wanted to confer a favor on the Jews, said to Paulus, "Will you go up to Jerusalem and be judged there of these things before me?"

10. Paulus answered and said, "I stand at the judgment seat of Caesar. It is right for me to be judged here. I have not sinned against the Jews, as you also know."

11. "If any offense was done by me or anything worthy of death, I do not excuse

myself from death, but if there is nothing to these things of which they accuse me, no man may give me to them as a gift. I call for an appeal to Caesar."

12. And Festus spoke with his Counselors and he said, "You have called for an appeal to Caesar; to Caesar you will go."

13. And when some days passed, Agrippa The King and Bernice came down to Caesarea to inquire the welfare of Festus.

14. And when they were with him some days, Festus related to The King the case of Paulus, when he said, "One man is a prisoner left from the hands of Felix."

15. "When I was in Jerusalem, The Chief Priests and Elders of the Jews informed me of him and requested that I make a judgment of him for them."

16. "And I said to them, 'It is not the custom of the Romans to give a man for slaughter as a favor until his adversary at law shall come and blame him to his face and he shall be given an opportunity to render a defense concerning that of which he is accused."

17. "And when I had come here, without delay the next day I sat on the judgment seat and I ordered them to bring the man to me."

18. "And his accusers stood with him and they could not demonstrate any evil indictment against him like that which I had supposed."

19. "But they had inquiries of one thing or another about their religion and about Yeshua, a man who had died, who Paulus was saying is alive."

20. Because I was not certain about such inquiries, I said to Paulus, "Do you wish to go to Jerusalem, and be judged on these things there?"

21. "But he requested to be kept for the judgment of Caesar, and I ordered that he be kept until I send him to Caesar."

22. And Agrippa said, "I would like to hear this man." And Festus said, "You will hear him tomorrow."

23. And the next day Agrippa came and Bernice, and they entered the court with great pomp with the Chiliarch and the Leaders of the city, and Festus commanded, and Paulus came.

24. And Festus said, "King Agrippa, and all of you men who are with us concerning this man, whom you see: all the people of the Jews complained to me in Jerusalem and here,

while shouting that this man ought not to live any longer,

25. And I have found nothing worthy of death that has been done by him, and because he has asked to be kept for the judgment of Caesar, I have commanded that he be sent."

26. "And I do not know what to write to Caesar about him, therefore I decided to bring him before you, and especially before you, King Agrippa, that when his case is examined, I may find what to write*."

* Critical Greek mss. have γραψω -"**I shall write**"; The Majority Greek Text has γραψαι- "**To write**". It just so happens that the Aramaic verb אכתוב – "**Ektoov**" is the imperfect tense, which **has the <u>future</u> sense or can function as an <u>infinitive</u>**- "To write". Both Greek readings seem to reflect the Aramaic grammar behind אכתוב –" **Ektoov**". This sort of scenario is common in the NT.

27. For it is not right that when we send a man as a prisoner that we do not write his offense.

Chapter 26

1. And Agrippa said to Paulus, "You are permitted to speak for yourself." And Paulus stretched out his hand and offered a defense and said:

2. "Concerning everything of which I am accused by the Jews, King Agrippa, I consider myself blessed, because before you today I bring a defense."

3. "I especially know that you are capable in all inquiries of The Law of the Jews; I therefore ask of you that you will hear me patiently."

4. "For those Jews are also aware, if they wish to testify, of my way of life from my youth from the beginning, in my nation and in Jerusalem,"

5. "Because for a long time they have been persuaded concerning me, for they know that I was living in the official doctrine of the Pharisees."

6. "Now for the hope of The Promise which our fathers had from God, I stand and I am judged."

7. "For to this hope our twelve tribes hope to arrive by diligent prayer by day and night. It is for this hope I am accused by the agency of the Jews, King Agrippa."

8. "How do you judge? Ought we not believe that God raises the dead?"

9. "For I had previously set my mind that I would commit many things contrary to the name of Yeshua the Nazarene."

10."This I did also in Jerusalem, and I cast many Saints into prison by the authority I received from The Chief Priests, and as they were being killed by them, I took part with those who condemned them."

11."And I was torturing them in every Synagogue as I was pressing them to blaspheme the name of Yeshua, and I was filled with great rage against them. I was also going out to other cities to persecute them."

12."And while I was going for this cause to Darmsuq with the authority and approval of The Chief Priests,"

13."At noonday, Oh, King, while on the road, I saw a light from the heavens greater than that of the sun, which burst upon me, and upon all who were with me."

14.And we all fell upon the ground, and I heard a voice, which said to me in Judean Aramaic, "Shaul, Shaul, why do you persecute me? It is hard for you to kick the goads."

15."And I said, "Who are you, my Lord?" And Our Lord said to me, 'I am Yeshua the Nazarene, whom you are persecuting.' "

16."And he said to me, 'Rise to your feet; for this cause I have appeared to you, to appoint you a minister and a witness that you have seen me and are going to see me."

17."But I shall save you from the people of the Judeans and from the other nations to which I am sending you,"

18."That you will open their eyes, so that they will turn from the darkness to the light and from the authority of Satan to God; and they shall receive release from sins and a portion with The Holy Ones by the faith which is in me."

19."Because of this, King Agrippa, I did not stand in dispute against the Heavenly vision."

20."But from the first I preached to those in Darmsuq, and to those in Jerusalem and those in all the villages of Judea, and I preached also to the Gentiles that they repent and be converted to God and to do deeds worthy of a return *to God*."

21."And because of these things, the Jews seized me in The Temple and wanted to kill me."

22."But God has helped me until this day and behold, I stand and testify to small and to great, while I have not said anything outside The Law of Moses and The

Prophets; only those things which they have said were going to happen:"

23."That The Messiah would suffer and that he would be The Origin of the Resurrection from among the dead and would preach light to the nation and to the Gentiles."

24."When Paulus had thus rendered a defense, Festus cried out with a loud voice, "You are insane, Paul! Much study has made you insane!"

25. Paulus said, "I am not insane, excellent Festus, but I am speaking words of truth and integrity."

26. "Also King Agrippa especially knows of such things as these, therefore I speak openly before him, because I do not think one of these matters has escaped him, for they were not done in secret."

27. "Do you believe The Prophets, King Agrippa? I know that you do believe."

28. Agrippa said to him, "In a little bit you will persuade me to become a Christian."

29. Paulus said, "I have desired from God in a little and in much, not for you only, but also for all those who are hearing me now to be like me, except for these chains."

30."And The King stood for him, and the Governor and Berniqa and those who were sitting with them."

31."And when they withdrew from there, they were speaking one with another and were saying, "This man has not done any thing worthy of death or imprisonment."

32.And Agrippa said to Festus, "This man could have been released if he had not appealed to Caesar."

Chapter 27

1. And Festus commanded concerning him to be sent to Caesar to Italia and he delivered Paulus and the other prisoners with him to a certain Centurion from the regiment, Sebasta, whose name was Julius.

2. And when it was time for us to journey, we boarded a ship, which was from the city Adramantius and it was going to the region of Asia, and Aristarkus, a Macedonian, entered the ship with us who was from the city Thessaloniqa.

3. The next day we came to Sidon and the Centurion treated Paulus with compassion and allowed him to go to his friends and be refreshed.

4. And from there we sailed, and because the wind was against us, we went around unto Cyprus.

5. And we passed through The Sea of Qiliqia and of Pamphylia, and we arrived at Mura, a city of Luqia.

6. And the Centurion found a ship there from Alexandria that was going to Italia and he put us on it.

7. And because it was hardly moving for many days, laboring we came next to the island Qnidus, and because the wind would not permit us to go straight, we went around to Crete, opposite the city Salmona.

8. And we labored as we sailed around it and we came to a place called Lemana-Shappira (Beautiful Harbor) and it was near a city whose name was Lasea.

9. We were there for a long time until the day of the fast of the Jews had passed, and it was fearful for a man to travel by sea, and Paulus was counseling them,

10. And he said, "Men, I have seen that our voyage will be with calamity and great loss, not only of the cargo of our ship, but also of ourselves."

11. But the Centurion was listening to the Helmsman and the Shipmaster rather than to the words of Paulus.

12. And because it was not suitable to winter in that port, many of us wanted to journey from there, and if it was possible for us, to arrive and to winter in a certain port which was in Crete, called Phoenix; and it faces toward the south.

13. And when the south wind blew and they hoped to arrive according to their desire, they went around Crete.

14. And after a little while, the wind of a hurricane came upon us called "Typhoniqos Euroqlydon".

15. And the ship was carried by force and could not stand against the wind and we surrendered to its power.

16. And when we passed an island called Qeuda, we were scarcely able to hold the lifeboat.

17. And when we took it up, we girded it and retained it to the ship, because we were afraid lest it fall in a declivity of the sea, and we took down the sail, and so we moved on.

18. And when the storm arose upon us, it was severe; the next day we threw goods into the sea.

19. And the third day, we cast away the implements of the ship with our hands.

20. And as the storm held it for many days and the sun had not appeared, neither the moon nor the stars, all hope for our lives was entirely cut off.

21. And when no one was able to endure* the situation, then Paulus arose in their midst and said, "If you men had believed me, we would not have sailed from Crete, and we would have been spared this loss and this suffering."

* מסתיבר can mean "**to be able to endure**" or "**to be sustained**" –"**to eat**". The Greek text has "**asitias**" (fasting) and is an apparent misunderstanding of the Aramaic word מסתיבר. At this point in the typhoon, eating was not the primary concern. Fourteen days into it, it would be. See verse 33. What the men needed was hope and encouragement, which was what Paul provided; See the next five verses.

22. "And now I counsel that we shall be without harm, for the life of none of you will be lost, but only the ship."

23. "For tonight, an Angel of The God whose I am and whom I serve, appeared to me",

24. "And he said to me, 'Do not fear, Paul, for you will stand before Caesar and, behold, God has given to you as a gift all who travel with you.'"

25. "Therefore, take heart, men, for I believe God, that it is so according to what was spoken to me."

26. "However, we must be cast upon a certain island."

27. And after fourteen days, we wandered and we were buffeted in the Hadrian Sea; at midnight, the Sailors thought that they were approaching land.

28. And they cast an anchor and they found twenty fathoms and they journeyed again a little more and they found fifteen fathoms.

29. And we were afraid lest we would be found in places that have rocks in them; we cast four anchors from the prow of the ship, and we were praying that day would come.

30. But the Sailors sought to flee the ship and lowered the lifeboat from it to the sea, in the pretense that they would go in it and tie the ship to land.

31. And when Paul saw it, he told the Centurion and the Soldiers: "If these do not stay in the ship, you cannot survive."

32. And the Soldiers cut the ropes of the lifeboat from the ship, and they left it adrift.

33. And while it was yet morning, Paulus persuaded all of them to take food, as he said to them, "Behold, today it is the 14th day of peril and you have eaten nothing."

34. "Therefore, I beg you to take food for the sustenance of your lives, for not a hair of any one of your heads will perish."

35. And when he said these things, he took bread and praised God before all of them, and he broke it and began to eat.

36. And they were all comforted and received nourishment.

37. And we in the ship were two hundred and seventy six souls.

38. And when they were filled with food, they lightened the ship, and they took wheat and threw it into the sea.

39. And when it was day, the Mariners did not know what land it was, but they saw beside the dry land a certain bay of the sea where they were wondering if it were possible to drive the ship.

40. And they cut the anchors from the ship and left them in the sea and loosed the rudder bands of the rudder, lifted the small top sail to capture the wind, and they were sailing toward dry land.

41. "And the ship touched a prominence between two deep channels of the sea, and it was stuck in it and stopped upon its front end, and the end of it did not move, but the stern was destroyed by the force of the waves.

42. The Soldiers had wanted to kill the prisoners, lest they would take to swimming and escape from them.

43. And the Centurion denied them this because he wanted to save Paulus, and those who were able to take to swimming he commanded first to swim and to pass on to land.

44. And they sent the rest of them on boards and on other wood of the ship, and thus all of them escaped to land.

Chapter 28

1. And after this we learned that this island was called Melita.

2. And the Barbarians who were dwelling in it showed us great kindness and kindled a fire and called us all to warm ourselves, because there was much cold rain.

3. And Paulus took a bunch of sticks and set them on the fire and a viper came out of them from the heat of the fire, and it bit his hand.

4. And when the Barbarians saw it hanging on his hand, they were saying, "Perhaps this man is a murderer who, while he has escaped from the sea, justice would not let live."

(Josephus wrote his original history in Aramaic & sent it to "the Barbarians of the upper countries." Apparently Luke understood these men, as he wrote down what they said. Luke, from Antioch, Syria, would have known Aramaic & Greek, so it is logical to conclude that these Barbarians spoke Aramaic.)

5. Then Paulus shook his hand and threw the viper into the fire, and nothing bad happened to him.

6. But the Barbarians were thinking that he would immediately swell up and drop dead on the ground. When they had waited for a long time and saw that no evil effect had occurred to him, they changed their talk and they said, "He is a god."

7. But there was in that place a village belonging to a man whose name was Puplios, who was the Chief of the island, and he joyfully received us into his house for three days.

8. The father of Puplios had a fever and was ill with a disease of the intestines and Paulus entered his presence and prayed and laid his hand upon him and healed him.

9. And when this happened, the rest of those who were sick in the island were coming to him, and they were healed.

10. And they honored us greatly, and when we were leaving from there, they loaded us with provisions.

11. But we went out after three months and journeyed on an Alexandrian ship which had harbored at that island, and it had on it the sign of The Twins.

12. And we came to the city Syracuse and remained there for three days.

13. And from there, we traveled around and came to the city, Rhegion; after one day, the wind blew for us from the south and in two days we came to Putielos, a city of Italia.

14. And we found brethren there and they begged of us and we stayed there seven days and then we went on to Rome.

15. And when the brethren there heard, they came forth to meet us at the Forum, which is called Appius-Forus, and unto The Three Taverns, and when Paulus saw them, he praised God and he was encouraged.

16. And we entered Rome and the Centurion allowed Paulus to dwell where he wanted with the Soldier who was guarding him.

17. And after three days, Paulus sent to call the Rulers of the Jews. When they assembled, he said to them, "Men, brothers, while in nothing have I opposed the people or the law of my fathers, I was handed over in

chains from Jerusalem into the hands of the Romans."

18. "And when they had examined me, they wished to release me, because the Rulers found nothing in me deserving death."

19. "And as the Jews were opposing me, I was compelled to call for an appeal to Caesar, not as if I had any accusation against the children of my people."

20. "Therefore, I begged of you to come and to see you and relate to you these things, because for the hope of Israel I am bound in this chain."

21. And they said to him, "We have not received a letter about you from Judea, neither has anyone of the brethren who came from Jerusalem told us anything evil about you."

22. "But we desire to hear from you what you think, because we know this teaching is not accepted by anyone."

23. And they appointed a day for him, and they gathered and many came to him where he was dwelling. And he revealed to them concerning The Kingdom of God as he testified and persuaded them concerning Yeshua from The Law of Moses and from The Prophets, from morning until evening.

24. And some of them were persuaded by his words and others were not persuaded.

25. And they were dismissed from his presence, not agreeing with one another, and Paulus spoke this word to them: "Well spoke The Spirit of Holiness, by the mouth of Isaiah The Prophet against your fathers,

26. Saying, 'Go to this people and say to them, "Hearing, you will hear and you will not understand, and you will see and you will not observe.

27. The heart of this people has become hard, their hearing they have dulled and their eyes they have shut, lest they shall see with their eyes and hear with their ears and understand in their hearts and turn to me and I would forgive them.'"

28. "Know this, therefore: This salvation of God is sent to the Gentiles, for they are listening to it."

29. And when he had said these things, the Jews went forth and many were debating among themselves.

30. And Paulus himself lived in his own hired house and was in it for two years; and he was receiving there all of those who were coming to him.

31. And he was preaching about The Kingdom of God, and teaching publicly about Our Lord Yeshua The Messiah without hindrance.

The Epistle of The Apostle Paul
to the Romans

Chapter 1

1. Paulus, a Servant of Yeshua The Messiah, a called one, and an Apostle, who was separated to The Gospel of God,

2. Which from the first he had promised by his Prophets in the Holy Scriptures,

3. About his Son, who is begotten in the flesh from the seed of the house of David,

4. And was revealed The Son of God in power and by the Holy Spirit, who arose from the place of the dead, Yeshua The Messiah, Our Lord.

5. For in him we have received grace and Apostleship among all the nations, so that they would obey the faith of his name.

6. For you also are of them, called by Yeshua The Messiah.

7. To all who are in Rome, beloved of God, called and holy: Peace and grace be with you from God Our Father and from Our Lord, Yeshua The Messiah.

8. First, I thank my God in Yeshua The Messiah for all of you because your faith is heard* in the whole world. * (Greek mss. have "καταγγελλεται- "It is announced" instead of "It is heard".)

9. For God is calling me to testify, whom I serve by The Spirit in The Gospel of his Son, that without ceasing, I am always reminded of you in my prayers,

10. And I seek favor, that from now on, a way may be opened to me in the will of God that I may come to you,

11. Because I have greatly desired to see you and to give you a gift of The Spirit that you may be confirmed in him.

12. And we will be comforted together in your faith and mine.

13. But I want you to know*, my brethren, that many times I have wanted to come to you and I was prohibited until now, that I also may have fruit in you like that in others of the Gentiles,

*"I want you to know" becomes "I don't want you to be ignorant" in Greek. **Brevity, the soul of wit**, is wanting in the Greek versions. This is also a feature found in The Greek Gospels.

14. Greeks and Barbarians, wise and ignorant, for I owe a debt to preach* to every person.

* "I owe a debt to preach" is simply, "I am a debtor" in Greek. The Greek is fairly vague, a feature uncharacteristic of Paul.

15. And so I take pains that also I may preach The Good News to you who are in Rome.

16. For I am not ashamed of The Gospel, because it is the power of God for the life of all who believe in it, whether of The Judeans first, or of the Aramaeans *.

The Critical Greek and Latin Vulgate agree with the Peshitta reading here: "**I am not ashamed of The Gospel, for it is …**' The Majority Greek has "**I am not ashamed of The Gospel of Christ, for it is …**'
* "**Whether of Judeans first or of Aramaeans**" is highly significant. The Peshitta has the word, ("Aramaeans") ארמיא twenty two times in Matthew,Luke,Acts and Paul's epistles. ("Aramaic")- ארמאית, occurs twice – once in Gal. 2:14 and once in Rev. 9:11. What is really interesting is that almost all The Greek mss. use the word ελλην ("Helleine") or ελληνιστι (Hellenisti) in all but one of the above places . Here is the Strong's entry for the word: 1672 ελλην Hellen hel'-lane from 1671; TDNT-2:504,227; n m ;AV-Greek 20, Gentile 7; 27
1) a **Greek** either by nationality, whether a native of the main land or of the Greek islands or colonies
2) in a wider sense the name embraces all nations not Jews that made the language, customs, and learning of the Greeks their own; the primary reference is to a difference of religion and worship .

The Greek NT has no reference whatever to **Aramaeans** or **Aramaic**. It does have the word , "Syros" –("Syrian") once in Luke 4:27, "Naaman the **Syrian**". The Greek has apparently de-Aramaized The NT! The Peshitta has eight references to Greeks as well as four to the Greek language in Luke,John,Acts, Romans and Colossians. **According to The Greek NT, Aramaic and Aramaeans might as well not have existed!** There is no mention of them anywhere. This makes the Greek highly suspect as a candidate for an original. It appears to have been culturally purged of all Aramaean references and thoroughly Hellenized or reculturated to suit a Greek audience. This is a literary genocide I had not encountered prior to this discovery. I am amazed that it occurs in the Greek New Testament , the supposed original Gospels and New Covenant for all peoples. The Aramaean people and the Aramaic language were almost universal in Asia Minor and The Middle East and The Holy Land of Israel , and had been for many centuries.
The proper order of The Gospel testimony would have been to **The Jews of Israel first, then the Syrians and Assyrians in Syria, Mesopotamia, Persia, Asia Minor** (called Asia then) – **all of whom spoke Aramaic** and whose written Aramaic was the same though not spoken the same, since dialects did not affect Aramaic writing significantly. Later, the books were translated into Greek for Greek speaking peoples of The Roman Empire.

That **The Peshitta** would be a translation of Greek makes no sense here, or in the 21 other references to Aramaeans & Aramaic in the Peshitta. There are too many references to Greek in The Peshitta for there to have been a replacing of "Greek" with "Aramaean" . The Peshitta in Luke and John mentions The Greek inscription on the cross; six references to the Greeks and Hellenists exist in Acts , who heard and accepted The Gospel which Paul preached to them in Greek. There is no anti-Greek bias in The Peshitta NT. There is a very obvious anti- Aramaean bias in The Greek NT.

Please see my book, **Divine Contact** , in which I discuss the possible reasons for this literary genocide of Aramaeans. My web site : aramaicnt.com also has a study of all the references where "Aramaean" & "Aramaic" occur in The Peshitta NT.

17. For the justice of God is revealed in it from faith to faith, according to that which is written: "The just one shall live by faith."
18. For the wrath of God is revealed from Heaven against all the evils and the wickedness of the children of men, those who are holding the truth in evil.
19. Because a knowledge of God is revealed to them, for God has revealed it to them.
20. For the secrets of God from the foundation of the world are appearing to his creatures through intelligence, even his power and his eternal Godhead, that they will be without a defense,
21. Because they knew God, and they did not glorify him as God, nor did they give him thanks, but they became destitute in their reasoning and became dull in their heart without understanding.
22. And when they thought in themselves that they were wise, they became insane.
23. And they changed the glory of God, who is indestructible, into the likeness of the image of man, which is destructible, and into the likeness of birds and of four footed animals and of creeping things of The Earth.
24. Because of this, God handed them over to the vile desires of their heart to disgrace their bodies among themselves.
25. And they exchanged the truth of God for lies, and they revered and served created things more than their Creator, to whom belong praises and blessings to the eternity of eternities*, amen.

* "How can there be more than one eternity ", one may ask. Each of us will have his or her own unique experience in eternity, thus the eternal realm consists of many eternities-as many as there are souls.

26. Therefore God handed them over to disgraceful diseases*, and their females changed their natural need and became accustomed to that which is unnatural.

* "**God handed them over to disgraceful diseases**…" This sounds like prophecy in these days of HIV and AIDS. The gay activists can whistle in the dark and deny that AIDS is primarily a homosexual disease and a judgment from God, but they cannot fool the believer of God's word; nor can they fool God. Disgraceful behavior-v.24, leads to " **disgraceful diseases**". "Shame" and "disgrace" have all but disappeared from the modern Western vocabulary, but only as "**disgraceful**" practices abound more and more.

27. And again also their males in this way abandoned the natural need for females, and they were ravished with desire one for another, even male for male, and committed disgrace and received a right reward in their persons for their error.
28. And because they decided in themselves not to know God, God handed them over to a worthless mind so that they would be doing whatever is inappropriate,
29. As they are filled with every injustice and fornication, bitterness, wickedness, greed, envy, murder, contention, treachery and wicked reasoning,
30. Murmuring, slander, and they are detestable to God, *being* insolent, proud, boasters, inventors of evil, lacking reason, who do not obey their parents,
31. Because they have no stability, neither love, nor peace, nor compassion in them,
32. Who, while knowing the judgment of God, that those who commit such things are condemned to death, were not only doing these things, but also were attached to those who were doing these things.

Chapter 2

1. Therefore, you have no defense, Oh man, *who* judges his neighbor, for that in which you judge your neighbor, of that you are guilty yourself, for you also who are judging are engaged in those things.
2. And we know that the judgment of God is in truth against those who are engaged in these things.

The Eastern Peshitta has the personal pronoun חנן –"**we**" as the second word in the verse; the Western text does not have it. This does not change the meaning at all, as the verb itself is a participle with 1st person plural enclitic attached –"**We know**". This is a typical difference between the two Peshittas.

3. But why are you thinking, Oh son of man, who are judging those who are occupied in these things, that you will escape from the judgment of God, when you also are engaged in them?
4. Or do you presume upon the wealth of his sweetness and upon his patience and upon the place that he gave to you, and do not know that the sweetness of God brings conversion to you? (See Acts 11:18)
5. But because of the callousness of your heart which does not repent, you lay up for yourself the treasure of wrath for the day of wrath and the revelation of the just judgment of God,
6. He who pays every person according to his works:
7. To those who in the patience of good works are seeking glory, honor and indestructibility, he gives eternal life,
8. But those who resist and do not obey the truth, but obey evil, he will pay anger and fury,

9. Suffering and trouble, to every person who cultivates wickedness, to the Jews first and to the Aramaeans*,

* **"Aramaeans"**. Greek mss. all have "**to the Greeks**"; interesting, no? In fact, ארמיא - "**Armaya**"-"**Aramaean(s)**" occurs 20 times in The Peshitta, and in 19 of those places, the Greek mss. all have "ελλην-" –"**Greek**". See note at 1:16

10. But glory, honor and peace to everyone who cultivates good, to the Jews first, and to the Aramaeans.

11. For there is no partiality with God.

12. For those who have sinned without The Written Law are also destroyed without The Written Law, and those who sinned with The Written Law will be judged by The Written Law.

13. The hearers of The Written Law are not righteous ones before God, but the doers of The Written Law are justified.

14. For if the Gentiles who have not The Written Law would perform those things of The Written Law by their nature, while they have not The Written Law, they would be The Written Law to themselves.

15. And they show the work of The Written Law written on their heart and their conscience testifies to them, while their reasoning rebukes or defends each one,

16. In the day when God judges the secrets of the children of men according to my Gospel, by Yeshua The Messiah.

17. But if you are called from the Jews and are comforted by The Written Law and are boasting in God,

18. You who know his will and discern what is right, you who are taught from The Written Law,

19. And you are confident yourself that you are a leader of the blind and a light of those who are in darkness,

20. And an instructor of those lacking understanding and a teacher of children, and you have a model of knowledge and of the truth in The Written Law,

21. You therefore who are teaching others, you do not teach yourself. You who are preaching that people should not steal, you are stealing!

22. You who say that people should not commit adultery, you commit adultery, and you who despise idols plunder the holy place!

23. And you who are boasting in The Written Law, you violate The Written Law, and you insult God himself!

24. For the name of God is blasphemed among the Gentiles because of you, according to what has been written. (Isaiah 52:5;Ezekiel 36:20-23)

25. For circumcision is beneficial, if you will perfectly observe The Written Law, but if you depart from The Written Law, your circumcision becomes uncircumcision.

26. But if he of the uncircumcision will observe the commandments of The Written Law, behold, is not the uncircumcision accounted for circumcision?

27. And uncircumcision which by its nature perfectly observes The Written Law will judge you, who with the Scripture and with circumcision, violate The Written Law.

28. For he is not a Jew who is one outwardly, neither is that which is seen in the flesh circumcision.

29. But he is a Jew who is in secret, and circumcision is that which is of the heart, in The Spirit and not by the Scriptures, whose glory is not from the children of men, but from God.

Chapter 3

1. **W**hat therefore is the excellence of the Jews, or what is the advantage of circumcision?

2. Much in everything; first, that they were entrusted with the words of God.

3. For if some of them did not believe, did they nullify the faith of God by not believing?

4. God forbid! For God is true, and every person lies, just as that which is written: "**Y**ou will be upright in your words and you will be victorious when they judge you."

5. But if our evil establishes the justice of God, what shall we say? Is God doing evil by bringing forth his wrath? I am speaking as a man.

6. God forbid! Otherwise, how will God judge the universe?

7. For if the truth of God is made to superabound for his glory by my lies, why therefore am I judged as a sinner?

8. Or is it as those, whose judgment is reserved for justice*, slander us and report that we say, "Let us practice evil that good may come?

* Greek mss. have "**whose judgment is just**".

9. What, then? Are we held to be greater because we have precedence? We have determined about the Jews and about the Aramaeans that they are all under sin,

10.As it is written: "There is not a just person, not even one,"

11."Neither is there one who understands, nor one who seeks God."

12."They have all turned away together, and they have been rejected*, and there is not one who does good, not even one."

* Greek has "**unprofitable**". אסתליו is the true reading-"**they have been rejected**". "**They are unprofitable**" is אסתרקו or סריקן or בטילין ; This last one is very similar to The Peshitta reading . That correlates very closely to the actual "**they are rejected**" reading - **(80% correlation)**.The Greek word is ηχρειωθησαν - "**they are unprofitable**"; "**They are Rejected**" would most likely be αδοκιμοι .These Greek words are not at all alike. The Aramaic אסתליו seems to account for the Greek; the Greek ηχρειωθησαν - "**they are unprofitable**" seems an unlikely source for the Aramaic reading.
I show the two Aramaic words here in DSS script:
אסתליו - "**They have been rejected**"
אסתרקו - "**They are unprofitable**"
(80% correlation)

13."Their throats are opened tombs, their tongues are deceitful, and the venom of asps is under their lips."

14."Their mouth is full of curses and bitterness,"

15."And their feet are swift to shed blood."

16."Adversity and wretchedness are in their way,"

17."The way of peace they have not known,"

18."And the awesomeness of God is not before their eyes."

19.But we know that whatever things The Written Law has said, it has said to those who are into The Written Law, that every mouth may be shut and the whole universe may be guilty before God,

20.Because by works of The Written Law no one is justified before him, for by The Written Law sin has been made known.

21.But now the justice of God has been revealed without The Written Law and The Written Law and The Prophets testify of it.

22.But the righteousness of God is by the faith of Yeshua The Messiah unto every person, also upon every person* who believes in him, for there is no distinction,

* The Majority Greek agrees with the Peshitta reading in this verse, whereas the Critical Greek omits "**upon every person**" . Romans 1:16 however is clearly favored by the Critical Greek text; so which Greek text did the supposed Peshitta translator use for his translation ? But there are so many examples of this alternation between Greek texts that the Greek primacy theory cannot be maintained against the entire array of NT data. The Peshitta primacy theory can easily account for the Greek readings as alternate and sometimes heavily edited and paraphrased translations of The Aramaic Peshitta original.

23.Because all of them have sinned and are deprived of the glory of God,

24.And are made right by grace without charge and by the redemption that exists in Yeshua The Messiah,

25.This One whom God preordained as the atonement, by the faith of his blood, for the sake of our sins which we had formerly sinned,

26. In the space that God in his patience has given to us, for the demonstration of his justice which is in this time, that he would be The Just One and would by justice declare righteous the one who is in the faith of Our Lord Yeshua The Messiah.

27.Where is pride, therefore? It has been eliminated with him. By what law? Of works? No, but by the law of faith.

28.We determine therefore that by faith a man is made righteous and not by the works of The Written Law.

29.Is he The God of the Jews only? Is he not also of the Gentiles? Yes, of the Gentiles also.

30.Because God is One, who declares the circumcision righteous by faith and also the uncircumcision by faith.

31.Are we therefore eliminating The Written Law by faith? God forbid, but we are establishing The Written Law!

Chapter 4

1. What therefore do we say about Abraham, the chief of our forefathers, that he found in the flesh?

* The Critical Greek text has προπατορα – a word that is found nowhere in Greek literature or **The LXX** , nowhere but here. It is supposed to mean "**forefather**".

2. For if Abraham were declared righteous by works, he would have had pride; but not in the presence of God.

3. For what do the Scriptures say? "Abraham believed God, and it was accounted to him for righteousness."

4. But the wages of one who labors are not accounted to him as a favor, but as that which is owed to him.

5. But to the one who does not labor, but believes only in The One who justifies sinners, is his faith accounted for righteousness.

6. Just as David also said about the blessedness of a man to whom God accounts righteousness without works, as he said:

7. "Blessed are those whose evils are forgiven them and whose sins are covered."

8. "And blessed is the man to whom God will not reckon his sins."

9. Is this blessing therefore on the circumcision or on the uncircumcision? For we say "His faith was accounted to Abraham for righteousness."

10. How therefore was it accounted to him, in circumcision or in uncircumcision? It was not in circumcision, but in uncircumcision.

11. For he received circumcision as a sign and the seal of the righteousness of his faith, when in uncircumcision, that he would be the father to all those who believe among the uncircumcision, that it would be reckoned to them also for righteousness.

12. And he is the father to the circumcision, but not only to those who are from the circumcision, but also to those who follow the steps of faith of the uncircumcision of our father Abraham.

13. For it was not by The Written Law that The Promise came to Abraham and his seed, that he would be the heir to the universe, but by the righteousness of his faith.

14. For if these who are of The Written Law were the heirs, faith would have been worthless and The Promise would have been void.

15. For The Written Law is the worker of wrath, for where there is no Written Law, neither is there a violation of The Written Law.

16. Because of this, he would be justified by faith, which is by grace, and The Promise would be sure to all his seed, not to the one who is of The Written Law only, but also to the one who is of the faith of Abraham, who is the father of us all,

17. According to what is written: "I have appointed you a father to the multitude of the nations, before God, in whom you believed, who gives life to the dead, and he calls those who are not as though they are."

18. And without hope he believed in hope that he would be the father to the multitude of the nations according to what is written: "Thus shall your seed be."

19. And he did not fail in his faith when he considered his body dead, (for he was one hundred years old), and the dead womb of Sarah.

20. And he did not doubt The Promise of God as if his faith were lacking, but he was strengthened in faith and he gave praise to God.

21. And he affirmed that whatever God promised him, He was able to perform.

22. Therefore, it was accounted to him for righteousness.

23. And this was not written for his sake alone that his faith was accounted for righteousness,

24. But also for our sake, for he is going to reckon it to us also, we who believe in The One who raised Our Lord Yeshua The Messiah from the grave,

25. And who was handed over because of our sins; and he arose to justify us.

Chapter 5

1. **B**ecause we have been declared righteous, therefore, by faith, we shall have peace with God in Our Lord Yeshua The Messiah,

2. For in him we have been brought close by faith to this grace in which we stand, and we boast in the hope of the glory of God.

3. And not only in this way, but we boast also in afflictions, for we know that affliction perfects patience in us,

4. And patience, experience and experience, hope,

5. But hope does not disappoint, because the love of God has come in, overflowing our hearts by The Spirit of Holiness who has been given to us.

6. But surely because of our weakness, at this time The Messiah has died for the sake of the wicked.

7. For a man will hardly die for the sake of the wicked*, however a man perhaps may dare to die for the sake of the good.

---

* רשיעא "**Rashyaa**"- means "**Wicked**" .Here is the word in old Aramaic as found in the Dead Sea Scrolls: רישיעא Compare this to the Aramaic word "**Zaddiqa**", which means "**Righteous**", in the same script: זדיקא
Might this explain the Greek reading, "**Hardly for a <u>righteous man</u> would someone die, yet peradventure for a good man some would even dare to die**, whereas the Peshitta has "**Hardly for a <u>wicked man</u> would someone die**." ? Lest someone think the Peshitta got its reading from the Greek, I present the four possible Greek words for "**Wicked**" and the Greek word for "**Righteous**" in Greek script in their proper grammatical forms for this sentence ,in order:
"**Wicked**"- ανομου, κακου,πονηρου, αθεσμου &
"**Righteous**"- δικαιου. Does any of the red underlined Greek words look like the word δικαιου ? I didn't think so. The Greek cannot give an accounting for the Aramaic reading , at least, not a very credible one, when compared to the Aramaic Peshitta words in old Aramaic above. I have not even mentioned the fact that the Greek reading of this verse doesn't make much sense, whereas the Peshitta does. Why would it be hard to die for the righteous and easier to die for the good ?

רישיעא –"Wicked"
זדיקא –"Righteous"
75% correlation

8. Here God demonstrates his love for us, because if when we were sinners, The Messiah died in our place,

9. How much more therefore, would we all the more be justified now by his blood and be saved from wrath by him?

10. For if when we were enemies, God was reconciled with us in the death of his Son, how much more therefore, in his reconciliation, shall we live all the more by his life?

11. And not in this way only, but also we glory in God by Our Lord Yeshua The Messiah, by whom we have now received the reconciliation.

12. For just as by the agency of one man, sin entered the universe, and by means of sin, death, in this way death passed by this *sin* unto all the children of men, because all of them have sinned. ("Death passed by this sin to all" is not in the Greek texts. In Aramaic "this" is grammatically connected to "sin" and not with death. The Greek is ambiguous.)

13. For until The Written Law, sin was in the universe, but it was not accounted as sin, because there was no written law.

14. But death reigned from Adam and until Moses, even over those who had not sinned in the likeness of Adam's violation of the law, who was the image of him who was to come.

15. But the fall was unlike the gift in this way: for if because of the fall of one the many died, much more, therefore, the grace of God and the gift by The One Man Yeshua The Messiah shall superabound to the many.

16. And the gift is not the same as the offense of the one, for the judgment was from the one to pronouncing guilty verdicts, but the gift was from many sins to righteousness.

17. For if because of the offense of one, death reigned, all the more, those who receive an abundance of favor and the gift of righteousness shall reign in life by the agency of The One, Yeshua The Messiah.

18. In like manner therefore, because of the offense of the one there was a guilty verdict to all the children of men, in the same way, because of the righteousness of The One there shall be the victory for Life to all the children of men.

19. For just as because of the disobedience of one man the many became sinners, so also because of the obedience of The One the many become righteous.

20. But there was the introduction to The Written Law that sin would increase, and wherever sin increased, there grace superabounded.

21. That as sin reigned by death, in this way grace shall reign by righteousness to eternal life by Our Lord Yeshua The Messiah.

Chapter 6

1. What shall we say, therefore? Shall we remain in sin that grace may abound?

2. God forbid! For those of us who have died to sin, how shall we live in it again?

3. Or do you not know that those of us who were baptized into Yeshua The Messiah were baptized into his death?

4. We were buried with him in baptism into death, for as Yeshua The Messiah arose from among the dead in the glory of his Father, in this way also we shall walk in a new life.

5. For if we have been planted as one with him in the likeness of his death, in this way also we shall be in his resurrection.

6. For we know that our old person was crucified with him, that the body of sin would be destroyed, that we shall not again serve sin.

7. For whoever is dead has been freed from sin.

8. If therefore we are dead with The Messiah, let us believe that we shall live with The Messiah.

* Greek mss. have - "We shall live **with Him**". The Latin Vulgate agrees with The Peshitta reading, "**with Christ**". The Peshitta contains both readings, as an emphatic Aramaic idiom. This sort is not uncommon in Aramaic and Hebrew. The Peshitta can account for both the Greek and Latin readings, but they cannot account for the Peshitta.

9. For we know that The Messiah arose from the place of the dead and he shall not die again, and death has no authority over him.

10. For he who died to sin, died one time, and because he lives, he is living to God.

11. In this way also consider yourselves that you are dead to sin and that you are living to God in Our Lord Yeshua The Messiah.

12. Sin shall not therefore reign in your dead body so that you shall obey its desires,

13. Neither shall you present your members as weapons of evil for sin, but present yourselves to God as people who are alive from the dead and your members shall be weapons for the righteousness of God.

14. And sin has no authority over you, for you are not under The Written Law, but under grace.

אגרתא קדישתא דפולוס שליחא דלות רהומיא

15. What, therefore? Shall we sin because we are not under *The Written Law* but under grace? God forbid!

16. Do you not know, that to whomever you give yourselves up to serve in bondage, his Servants you are, whom you obey, whether you listen* to sin or to righteousness?

• "The hearing ear" is an Aramaic idiom meaning, "One who listens". The Greek mss. have "sin <u>unto death</u>"; The Latin Vulgate agrees with the Peshitta. The Aramaic idiom ,"The hearing ear", is not a very likely translation of the Greek word , "υπακοης"-"obedience". The word for "ear" is not found in the Greek texts. Following are the Peshitta reading and the Greek reading in a Dead Sea Scroll Aramaic script, found in The Pesher Habakkuk scroll:

עלמדע -"for hearing"
למותא -"unto death"

Possibly a translator misread "for hearing" as "unto death", since 4 of the 5 letters in each look similar in this script.

17. But thank God that you were Servants of sin and you obeyed from the heart that form of the teaching to which you are devoted.

18. And when you were freed from sin you became Servants to righteousness.

19. As a fellow man, I say to you because of the weakness of your flesh, that as you presented your members to the servitude of defilement and of evil, so also now present your members to the servitude of righteousness and of holiness.

20. For when you became Servants of sin, you became free from righteousness.

21. And what fruit did you have then, of which today you are ashamed? For its result is death.

22. And now because you have been freed from sin and you are Servants to God, your fruit is holy, for the result of those things is eternal life.

23. But the product of sin is death and the gift of God is eternal life in Our Lord Yeshua The Messiah.

Chapter 7

1. Or do you not know, my brethren, for I speak to those who know *The Written Law*, that *The Written Law* has authority over a man as long as he lives,

2. As a woman is bound by the law to her lord as long as he lives? But if her husband is dead, she has been freed from *The Written Law* of her husband.

3. But if while her lord lives, she shall leave for another man, she becomes an adulteress to him, but if her lord should die, she has been freed from *The Written Law*, and she is not an adulteress if another man should have her.

4. And now, my brethren, you also have died to *The Written Law* with the body of *The Messiah* that you would be for another, *The One* who arose from the dead, that you would yield fruit to God.

5. When we were in the flesh, the diseases of sin, which are by *The Written Law*, worked diligently in the members that we might yield fruit to death.

6. But now we have been exempted from *The Written Law*, and we are dead to that which had controlled us, so that we shall serve from now on in the newness of *The Spirit* and not in the Old Order Scriptures.* *(Old Testament Scriptures)

7. What therefore shall we say? Is *The Written Law* sin? God forbid! But I would not have learned sin except by *The Written Law*, for I would not have known lust, if *The Written Law* had not said, "Do not lust."

8. In this commandment sin found for itself an occasion and developed in me every lust, for without *The Written Law*, sin was dead.

9. But I was alive without *The Written Law* at first, but when the commandment came, sin lived, and I died.

10. And I found that commandment of life *to be* for death.

11. For sin, in the occasion that it found for itself, seduced me by the commandment, and killed me with it.

12. *The Written Law* therefore is holy and the commandment is holy, just and good.

13. Was the good therefore death to me? God forbid! But sin, that it might appear to be sin, perfected death in me by the means of the good, that sin would be all the more condemned *by the commandment.

Greek has "αμαρτολος" – "Sinful". "Sinful" in Aramaic could be any number of forms of the word "Sin" – חטא. Since the Peshitta reading – "condemned" is a verb, I looked for a feminine verb form of "sin" to see what looked like תתחיב- "Would be condemned" –using Dead Sea Scroll Aramaic. Here is my finding:
"Would be Condemned" is תתחיב
"Would sin" is ------------ תתחטב - Amazing, isn't it ? I see an **70% correlation** between the two words in this script.
The Greek "αμαρτολος" – "Sinful" literally means, "sinner" which would be a verb in Aramaic , hence my finding of a future verb is validated as what a Greek translator probably interpreted The Peshitta reading to be.
I don't see that The Aramaic verb "condemned" would have come from the Greek "αμαρτολος" – "Sinful". "**It would be Condemned**" in Greek is "καταδικασθηση" –"katadikasythaysay" , which is nothing like αμαρτολος -"**Amartolos**" (**0% correlation.**)
This is more strong support for Peshitta primacy and evidence against Greek primacy.
תתחיב - "Would be condemned"

תאסוב -"Would sin"

The above is one of hundreds of examples in my Aramaic-English Interlinear NT showing how the Greek texts were translated from The Aramaic of The Peshitta NT.

14. For we know that The Written Law is spiritual but I am carnal and I am sold to sin.

15. For that which I committed I did not understand, neither was it anything that I chose, but I was doing what I hated.

16. And if I did what I did not choose, I testify of The Written Law that it is excellent.

17. But now it is not I who am committing this, but sin that dwells within me.

18. For I know that good does not dwell within me, (but this is in my flesh), for it is easy for me to delight in the good, but I am unable to perform it.

19. It was not the good that I wanted that I did, but the evil that I did not want to do, that I did.

20. And if I did the thing that I did not want, it was not I doing it, but sin that dwelt within me.

21. I find, therefore, a law agreeing with my conscience which wants to do good, because evil is near me.

22. For I rejoice in the law of God in the inner person.

23. But I saw another law in my members that makes war against the law of my conscience and takes me captive to the law of sin that is in my members.

24. I am a wretched man. Who will deliver me from this body of death?

25. I thank God by Our Lord Yeshua The Messiah. Now therefore, I am a Servant of The Law of God in my conscience, but in my flesh, I am a Servant of the law of sin.

Chapter 8

1. There is therefore no condemnation to those in Yeshua The Messiah who do not walk in the flesh.

 * The Critical Greek has no reference to "who are not walking in the flesh". The Majority Greek has it, plus "who walk in The Spirit". The Latin Vulgate has the Peshitta reading, as do other ancient versions (Itala,Gothic,Armenian) and several early church fathers (4th cent.).

2. For The Law of The Spirit of Life which is in Yeshua The Messiah has freed you* from the law of sin and of death.

 * Most Greek mss have "me"; The 4th century Greek mss. א ,B & The Itala Version (2nd cent.) have "you"(singular), in agreement with The Peshitta.

3. For because The Written Law was weak through the sickliness of the flesh, God sent his Son in the form of sinful flesh, because of sin, to condemn sin in his flesh,

4. That the righteousness of The Written Law would be fulfilled in us, that we would not walk in the flesh but in The Spirit.

5. For those who are in the flesh are governed by the flesh, and those who are of The Spirit are governed by The Spirit.

6. For the mind of the flesh is death, and the mind of The Spirit is life and peace,

7. Because the mind of the flesh is hatred toward God, for it is not subject to the law of God because it cannot be.

8. And those who are in the flesh cannot please God.

9. But you are not in the flesh, but in The Spirit, if truly The Spirit of God dwells within you, but if a man does not have The Spirit of The Messiah in him, this one does not belong to Him.

10. But if The Messiah is in you, the body is dead for the cause of sin, but The Spirit is alive for the cause of righteousness.

11. And if The Spirit of him who raised Our Lord Yeshua The Messiah from among the dead dwells within you, he who raised Yeshua The Messiah from among the dead also will give life to your dying bodies, because of his Spirit who dwells within you.

12. Now my brethren, we are indebted, not to the flesh that we should walk in the flesh,

13. For if you are living in the flesh, you are going to die, and if you are putting to death the practices of the body, you are living.

14. For those who are led by The Spirit of God, these are the sons of God.

15. For you have not received The Spirit of bondage again to fear, but you have received The Spirit of the adoption of children by whom we cry, "Father*, our Father."

 * Greek has "Αββα" (Abba) which is not a Greek word, nor even a loan word, but an Aramaic word transliterated into Greek letters. Why in the name of Sam Hill would Paul be writing Aramaic words to Greek speaking people in Rome (not that I grant his audience spoke Greek) ? And why would he report that the cry of The Spirit of adoption (The Holy Spirit) would cause us to cry "Abba", unless he were translating from an Aramaic original ? This word "Abba" occurs in the Greek NT in Mark 14:36, here and in Galatians 4:6. Why this occurs in The Greek is not seriously dealt with by Greek primacists; one writer cites such Aramaic transliterations in Greek as proof of a Greek original! He seemed to think that if the original were Aramaic, every word would be transliterated and then translated into Greek!

 The Greek NT has numerous examples of this phenomenon of transliteration of Aramaic words into Greek; The Peshitta has no such examples of Greek words transliterated into Aramaic (apart from a few (.proper Greek names

16. And that Spirit testifies to our spirit that we are sons of God;

17. And if sons, then also heirs; heirs of God and co-heirs with Yeshua The Messiah, for if we suffer with him, we shall also be glorified with him.

* Greek has "**if we suffer together**" and "**we shall be glorified together**", which is ambiguous at best- together **with whom ?** The Peshitta is clear: "**with Him**".

18. For I give counsel that the sufferings of this time are not comparable to the glory which is going to be revealed in us.

19. For the whole creation hopes for and expects the revelation of the sons of God.

20. For the creation has been subjected to futility, not by its choice, but because of him who subjected it upon hope.

21. For the creation shall also be freed from the bondage of destruction into the liberty of the glory of the sons of God.

22. For we know that all created things groan and are in labor until today.

23. And not only so, but we also who have in us the first fruits of The Spirit; we groan in ourselves and we look for the adoption of sons and the redemption of our bodies,

24. Because we live in that hope; but hope that is seen is not hope, for if we see* hope, why do we* look for it?

     * Greek has "**whoever sees**" and "**he looks for**".

25. But if we hope for what is not seen, we wait patiently for it.

26. In this way also The Spirit helps our weakness*. We do not know what we should pray for, whenever it is necessary, but that Spirit prays in our place with groaning which is unspoken.

* Greek has two readings: ασθενεια -"**our weakness**" & ασθενειαις -"**our weaknesses**". The Aramaic word כריהותן –"**Karihothan**" can be interpreted either way. I submit that this explains the Greek readings.

27. But he who searches the hearts knows what the mind of The Spirit is, for he is praying according to the will of God in the place of the Saints.

28. But we know that he helps those who love God in everything for good, those whom he preordained to be called.

29. And those whom he foreknew, he also fashioned in the likeness of the image of his Son, that he would be The Firstborn of many brethren.

30. And those whom he pre-fashioned, he called, and those whom he called, he made righteous, and those whom he made righteous, he glorified.

31. What therefore shall we say about these things? If God is for us, who is against us?

32. And if he did not show pity upon his Son, but he handed him over for the sake of us all, how shall he not give us everything with him?

33. Who shall accuse The Elect of God? God is He Who declares righteous.

34. Who is condemning? The Messiah has died and he is risen, and he is at the right hand of God and he prays for us.

35. What will separate me* from the love of The Messiah: Suffering, or imprisonment, or persecution, or famine, or nakedness, or peril, or sword?

* Greek has "**will separate us**". The difference between the two in Aramaic is one letter at the end of נפרשני – "**will sever me**". In DSS script the word is נפרשני ; "**will sever us**" is נפרשן . The Greek for "**us**" is ημας ; "**me**" is με or εμε . These pronouns are not similar in Greek as they are in Aramaic, therefore the evidence supports the theory that the Greek is translated from The Peshitta rather than vice versa. The Greek ημας "**Us**" would not likely give rise to "**Me**" in Aramaic.

Greek Uncial script:
ΗΜΑΣ –"**Us**"
ΕΜΕ -"**Me**"

Ashuri Aramaic script:
נפרשני-"**will separate me**"
נפרשן-"**will separate us**"

Dead Sea Scroll Aramaic script:
-"**will separate me**"
-"**will separate us**"

Estrangela Aramaic script:
-"**will separate me**"
-"**will separate us**"

The Greek word pair have a **25%** letter correlation between them; The Aramaic pair, in each of the three scripts, have **66% to 83%** letter correlations (**Dead Sea Scroll 83%**; the other two -66%). This shows that the Greek reading was much more likely to come from the Aramaic than vice versa.

36. As it is written: "For your sake we are killed every day, and we are accounted as sheep for slaughter."

37. But in all these things we are victorious by him who has loved us.

38. For I am convinced that neither death, nor life, nor Angels, nor Authorities, nor Powers, nor things present, nor things future,

39. Nor height, nor depth, neither any other created thing, shall be able to sever me* from the love of God, which is in Our Lord Yeshua The Messiah.

* Greek has "**to separate us**". The Eastern Peshitta also has "**to separate us**". See v. 35 note. The Eastern Peshitta has "What shall separate **me**?" in verse 35.

Chapter 9

1. I speak the truth in The Messiah, and I do not lie; my conscience bears witness to me in The Spirit of Holiness,

2. That I have great unceasing sorrow and affliction from my heart,

3. For I have been praying that I myself might be destroyed from The Messiah, for the sake of my brethren and my kinsman, who are in the flesh,

4. Who are the children of Israel, whose was the adoption of children, the glory, The Covenant, The Written Law, the ministry which is in it, The Promises,

5. And the Patriarchs; and from them The Messiah appeared in the flesh, who is The God Who is over all, to Whom are praises and blessings to the eternity of eternities, amen.

This is a very important doctrinal statement of the Deity of The Christ. Paul wants it understood that Yeshua is not merely an addition to a pagan pantheon of deities; He is The Supreme God over all the universe.

The Greek mss. have-" ο ων επι παντων θεος ευλογητος εις τους αιωνας αμην": "Who is over all, God blessed to the ages. Amen." This looks like a paraphrase of The Peshitta, substituting "blessed to the ages" for-" to Whom are praises and blessings for the eternity of eternities." The Peshitta did not get that reading from a Greek manuscript.

6. But it was not that the word of God had failed, for they were not all of Israel, who are Israel;

7. Neither because they are of his seed are they all children of Abraham, because it was said, "In Isaac your seed shall be called."

8. But this is not because the children of the flesh are the children of God, but the children of The Promise are accounted for the seed.

9. For The Promise is this word: "At this time, I will come and Sarah will have a son."

10. And not only this, but Rebecca also, when she had a conjugal relation with our father Isaac,

11. Before her children were to be born or would do good or evil, the choice of God was revealed beforehand that this would stand not by works, but by him who called.

12. For it was said, "The elder shall be a Servant to the younger",

13. As it is written: "I have loved Jacob and I have hated Esau."

14. What shall we say, therefore? Is there evil with God? God forbid!

15. Behold, he said also to Moses, "I shall show love on whomever I love, and I shall take pity on whomever I pity."

16. Therefore it is not by means of him who wills, neither by means of him who runs, but in the hand of God, the merciful.

17. For he said in the Scriptures to Pharaoh, "For this I have raised you up, that I may show my power with you, and that my name may be declared in the whole Earth."

18. So then, he shows compassion on whomever he will, and whomever he will, he hardens.

19. Doubtless you will say, "Why does he find fault, for who stands against his will?"

20. Therefore, who are you, oh son of man, that you give a rebuttal to God? Does the thing formed say to the one who formed it, "Why have you made me this way?"

21. Or is not a potter authorized over the clay to make some formed things from it, one vessel for honor and one for dishonor?

22. But if God was willing to show his wrath and reveal his power, bringing wrath with a multitude of patience against vessels of wrath that were perfected for destruction,

23. And his love overflowed on the vessels of compassion that were prepared by God for glory;

24. For we are called, not only from the Jews but also from the Gentiles.

25. Just as it says also in Hosea: "I shall call those who were not my people, 'My people', and you who were not beloved, 'Beloved'.

26. For it shall be in the place where they were called, "Not my people", there they shall be called children of THE LIVING GOD."

27. But Isaiah preached against the children of Israel: "If the number of the children of Israel is as the sand of the sea, a remnant of them shall be saved."

28. He has cut the matter short and has cut *it* off; THE LORD JEHOVAH shall do it upon The Earth.

29. And as that which Isaiah said before: "If THE LORD JEHOVAH of Hosts* had not left survivors*, we would have been like Sadom and we would have been like Amorah.

* "of hosts" – צבאות "Tsabaoth" is a Hebrew word found hundreds of times in The Hebrew OT, usually in conjunction with The Name of "Yahweh". It occurs twice in The Peshitta, here and in James 5:4. מריא "Marya" is the Aramaic cognate for "Yahweh" , the Hebrew Name for God usually translated in English Bibles as LORD in The OT; sometimes translated "Jehovah" , with which I translate מריא "Marya" in The Peshitta Interlinear. The fact that this word σαβαωθ –"Sabaoth" occurs in the Greek mss. and that the Hebrew form occurs in the Aramaic Targum of Jeremiah 5:14 indicates a Hebrew or Aramaic source for the Greek term –

"κυριος σαβαωθ" (Lord Sabaoth) here and in James 5:4 where it also occurs. In The LXX OT, κυριος σαβαωθ always translates the Hebrew יהוה צבאות (Yehovah Tsabaoth) "**Jehovah of Hosts**", which in Aramaic is מריא צבאות (MarYah Tsabaoth) "**LORD JEHOVAH of Hosts**", as found in this verse of The Peshitta. The Greek reading σαβαωθ is not a Greek word; it is not even a loan word from Hebrew or Aramaic; it is a transliteration of Hebrew or Aramaic צבאות (Tsabaoth) "of hosts".

• Four things are certain: 1) "Sabaoth" is not Greek. 2) The Greek reading "Sabaoth" came from a Semitic source (Hebrew or Aramaic in this case). 3) A Gentile audience unfamiliar with The Old Testament would not have understood the term. 4) The Peshitta text is not a translation of the Greek version of this verse. (See "Seed" & "Survivors" note below.)

<u>Comparison of OT Hebrew with Peshitta NT quotation: (Read left to right)</u>

of hosts Yahweh Unless
לולי יהוה צבאוה
Sodom as small remnant us had left
הותירלנו שריך כמעט כסדם
Like Amorah we had been
היינו לעמרה דמינו – Isaiah 1:9 Hebrew

of hosts MarYah Unless
דאלו לא מריא צבאות
Sodom as remnant us had left
אותר לן שריכא איך סדום
we had been like & Amorah we had been
הוין הוין ולעמורא מתדמין הוין
- Romans 9:29 in Aramaic **Peshitta**

I have displayed the Hebrew verse of Isaiah and The Peshitta below it to show the reader how the Aramaic quotations are written in the same letters and have the same structure as the Hebrew Bible they quote. Cognate words are highlighted in the same color, so the reader may see how many cognate words in Hebrew are similar to the Aramaic words. An Aramaic quote like this from The Peshitta would be a much more precise representation of the state of the first century Hebrew Bible which was available to the Jews of Israel at the time, than a Greek translation could be. Greek and Hebrew are very different languages in many ways. Hebrew and Aramaic are very similar in grammar, syntax, spelling, vocabulary and appearance, both Semitic, and using the same alphabet and first century script in Palestine. Notice also that Aramaic has the sacred Tetragrammaton Name "MRYA" which parallels The Hebrew "YHWH" and is used only to designate "**Yahweh**", **The LORD GOD** of Israel. Greek does not have this Name, substituting "**Kurios**" – "Lord", which can often refer to a mere human master or King. The Peshitta NT designates Yeshua (Jesus) as "MRYA"(**The LORD GOD of Israel**") over 30 times ! The Greek NT does not do so, as it adheres to "**Kurios**" only in most of those places.

* Greek has "**a seed**" where The Peshitta has "**a remnant**", "**survivors**". Below are the two readings in Aramaic, one atop the other, first in DSS script:

Dead Sea Scroll | **Ashuri Aramaic**
שׂרֹיכֵֿא שריכא –"Remnant"
זֹרֹעֵֿיתֿא זרעיתא –"Descendants"

Looking at the Dead Sea Script, I see similarity between ˥ & ⅄ simply by rotating either one about 20 degrees; that, along with the two other identical letters gives **66% correlation**.

Here are the two readings in Greek Uncial script:
ΥΠΟΛΕΙΜΜΑ–"Remnant"
ΣΠΕΡΜΑ–"Seed"

I leave it for the reader to decide which pair looks most alike, the Greek or the Aramaic.

30. What shall we say, therefore? The Gentiles, who did not run after righteousness have obtained righteousness, even the righteousness which is from faith,

31. But Israel that had run after The Written Law of righteousness did not obtain the Law of righteousness?
  * The Critical Greek text omits the second "**righteousness**"; The Majority Greek includes it.

32. Why? Because it was not from faith, but from the works of The Written Law, for they were stumbled at the stumbling stone,

33. As it is written: "Behold. I have laid down in Zion a stumbling stone and a stone of offense and whoever will believe in him will not be disappointed."

Chapter 10

1. My brethren, the desire of my heart and my petition before God is on their behalf that they would have life.

2. For I bear witness to them, that they do have zeal for God, but not by knowledge.

3. For they have not known the righteousness of God, but they have sought to establish their own righteousness*, and therefore they have not submitted to the righteousness of God.
  * The Critical Greek text omits the second "**righteousness**"; The Majority Greek includes it.

4. For The Messiah is the consummation of The Written Law for righteousness to everyone who believes.

5. For Moses wrote in this way of the righteousness which is in The Written Law: "Whoever shall do these things shall live in them."

6. But the righteousness which is in faith says thus: "You shall not say in your heart, 'Who ascended to Heaven and sent down The Messiah?',

7. 'And who went down to The Abyss of Sheol and brought up The Messiah from among the dead?'"
  * Greek omits "**Sheol**" (which is usually translated αδης-"Hades").

8. But what does it say? "The answer is near your mouth and your heart." This is the word of the faith that we preach.

9. And if you will confess with your mouth Our Lord Yeshua, and you will believe in your heart that God has raised him from the dead, you shall have life.

10. For the heart that believes in him is made right, and the mouth that confesses him has life.

11. For the Scriptures say, "Everyone who believes in him will be unashamed."

12. And he makes no distinction in this, not for the Jews, neither for the Aramaeans, for he is The One **LORD JEHOVAH** to all of them, who is rich with everyone who calls to him.

13. "For everyone who will call the name of **THE LORD JEHOVAH** shall be saved."
(See Joel 2:32)

14. Therefore, how would they call to This One unless they believed in him, or how would they believe him unless they heard him, or how would they hear without a preacher?

15. Or how will they preach, unless they will be sent, as it is written: "How beautiful are the feet of The Messengers of peace and of The Messengers of good things!"

16. But not all have submitted to the message of The Gospel, as Isaiah said, "My Lord, who believes our report?"

17. Therefore faith is from the hearing ear, and the hearing ear is from the word of God.

18. But I say, "Have they not heard?", and, "Behold, their report has gone out into all The Earth and their words to the ends of the world.'"

19. But I say, "Did not Israel know beforehand?" Moses spoke thus: "I shall make you jealous by a people that is not a people and by a people that is disobedient I shall anger you."

20. But Isaiah was bold and he said, "I appeared to those who did not seek me and I was found by those who did not ask for me."

21. But to Israel he said, "I reached my hands out all day to a contentious and disobedient people."

Chapter 11

1. But I say, "Has God thrust away his people?" God forbid! I am also from Israel, from the seed of Abraham, from the tribe of Benjamin.

2. God has not thrust away his people, who were known to him from the first, or do you not know the Scriptures in which Elijah spoke when he complained to God about Israel and he said:

3. "My Lord, they have murdered your Prophets and they have toppled your altars, and I am left alone, and they seek my life"?

4. It was said to him by revelation*, "Behold, I have left for myself seven thousand men who have not bowed their knees and worshiped Baal."

* Greek has "χρηματισμος" – "**The Divine response**", "**oracle**"; The Aramaic אתאמר -"**It was said**" - may have been seen as a code word to a Greek translator meaning – "**God spoke**". The Greek uses an active verb "λεγει" – "**says**" with χρηματισμος as the subject . This occurs in quite a few places in The NT where a word with **Alap-Tau** - אֵת at the start or end occurs and Greek supplies a Divine title or Name where it does not exist in The Peshitta . **Alap-Tau** is found in Rev. 1:8 and other places as a Divine title for The Messiah. (See note at 1 Timothy 3:16). I have an article on this at my web site – http://aramaicnt.com called "**The Alap Tau Code**".

5. In the same way also at this time there is a remnant left in The Election of grace.

6. But if it is by grace, it is not from works, or else grace is not grace. But if it is by works, it is not from grace, or else work is not work.

7. Why therefore has not Israel found that which it was seeking, but The Election has found it and the rest of them were blinded in their hearts,

8. According to what is written: "God gave them a spirit of frustration, and eyes that will not observe and ears that will not hear", even until today? (Here the quote does not agree with the Hebrew of Isaiah 29:10, neither with The Peshitta text of that verse, nor The LXX nor even with the Greek NT quote, which has "slumber" instead of "frustration". As in so many places, the Peshitta NT quotation is unique, seemingly from a unique OT text used at that time in Israel.

9. And again David said, "Their table shall be a trap before them and their reward, a stumbling block.

10. Let their eyes be darkened, lest they see, and may their back always be bent over." (Here and in the previous verse, the quote agrees exactly with The Peshitta O.T. reading of Psalm 69:22, except for one letter!)

11. But I say, "Did they stumble so that they would fall? God forbid! But by their offense, life came to the Gentiles, to their envy.

12. And if their offense was wealth to the world, and their condemnation *is* wealth to the Gentiles, how much more therefore, their fullness?"

13. But I say to you Gentiles, I who am an Apostle of the Gentiles, I honor my ministry.

14. Perhaps I may make my kindred jealous, and I may save some of them.

15. For if their rejection was the reconciliation for the world, how much greater therefore is their return, if not life from the dead?

16. But if the first fruits are holy, so is the substance. And if the root is holy, so are the branches.

17. And if some of the branches were cut off and you, a wild olive tree, were grafted in their place, and you have become a partaker of the roots and of the fat of the olive tree,

18. Do not boast against the branches; but if you boast, were you not supported by the roots, rather than the root being supported by you?

19. Doubtless you will say, "The branches were cut off that I might be grafted in their place."

20. Fine, these were cut off because they did not believe, but you have stood by faith. Do not be lifted up in your mind, but stand in awe.

21. For if God did not show pity upon the natural branches, surely he will not show pity upon you.

22. Behold therefore, the sweetness and the hardness of God; on those who fell, hardness, and on you, sweetness, if you abide in his sweetness, but if not, you will also be cut off.

23. And if they do not continue in their utter lack of faith, they will also be grafted in, for God is able to graft them in again.

24. For if you who are from a wild olive tree, which is your natural condition, were cut off and are grafted into the good olive tree apart from your natural condition, how much more will those surely be grafted into the olive tree of their own nature?

25. I want you to know my brethren, this mystery, lest you would be wise in your own opinion, that blindness of heart has for a little time come to Israel until the fullness of the Gentiles will come in.

26. And then all Israel shall have life, according to what is written: "The Savior shall come from Zion and he shall turn away evil from Jacob,

27. And then they shall have the covenant which comes from my presence, whenever I shall have forgiven* their sins."

(No currently known version of Isaiah 59:20,21 is followed here in verse 27. Even the Greek of v. 27 is unlike any version of Isaiah 59:21. Verse 26 is much closer to Is. 59:20 in all O.T. versions. Here is Fred Miller's translation of The Great Isaiah scroll (about 100 BC) in the pertinent verses:
(20.) "And the Redeemer shall come to Zion, and to those who repent of transgression in Jacob, says YHWH. (21.)And I, [m..As for me] this is my covenant with them, says YHWH; My spirit that is upon you, and my words which I have put in your mouth, shall not depart out of your mouth, nor out of the mouth of your seed, nor out of the mouth of your seed's seed, from now and for ever." This agrees with The Massoretic Hebrew and with The Peshitta OT version.
* Greek has "I shall take away". שקלת is the most common verb form for "I shall take away"; compare to the reading here – "I shall forgive" שבקת ; In **Dead Sea Scroll** Aramaic script , they are שɔקɔת - שɔɔɔɔ. With the Dalet proclitic added, we have דשקלת ; דשבקת   there is **60-80% correlation** between the two words, depending on how you analyze them. In **DSS**, the letters Lamed ל and Bet

ב are similar enough to mistake one for another, even though they have slightly different positions in their respective words; all the other letters are each in both words, so it is very easy to believe they could be confused, each for the other. The human eye is the best judge of this. Here are the two words, one atop the other:**Ashuri Aramaic script:**

דשקלת -"I shall take away"
דשבקת -"I shall forgive"

Dead Sea Scroll Aramaic script:

ת𝓁ɔ𝓌ɔד-"I shall take away"
ת𝓀ɔ𝓌ɔד-"I shall forgive"

80% correlation for both Aramaic pairs, though the Ashuri Aramaic words look a bit more similar here.

Here are the Greek words for "**I shall take away**" & "**I shall forgive**" : ΑΦΕΛΩΜΑΙ
ΑΦΗΣΩ.

They show **36%** correlation.

28. But they are enemies in The Gospel for your sake, and in The Election they are beloved because of The Patriarchs.

29. For God does not change in his gifts and in his callings.

30. Just as you also were not obeying God from the first and now you have been favored because of their disobedience,

31. So also these have not obeyed, now mercy is upon you so that there shall be mercy upon them also.

32. For God has shut every person into disobedience so that he shall have mercy upon every person.

33. Oh, the depth of the wealth, the wisdom and the knowledge of God, for man has not searched his judgment and his ways are not traced!

34. For who has known the mind of **THE LORD JEHOVAH**, or who has been a counselor to him?

35. And who has first given to him and then has received from him?

36. Because all is from him, and all is by him, and all is in his hand, that to him would be praises and blessings to the eternity of eternities. Amen.

Chapter 12

1. I beg you therefore, my brethren, by the mercies of God, that you present your bodies living sacrifices, holy and acceptable to God by a logical service.

2. And do not imitate this world, but be transformed by the renovation of your minds, and you shall distinguish what is the good, acceptable and perfect will of God.

3.I say to all of you by the grace that is given to me, that you should not have self-esteem beyond what is necessary to have self-esteem, but you should have self-esteem and modesty as God distributes faith to every person by a measure.

4.For just as we have many members in one body, and all those members do not have one function,

5.So also, we who are many, are one body in The Messiah, and each one of us is a member of the other.

6.But we have a variety of gifts, according to the grace that is given us; one has prophecy according to the measure of his faith,

7.And one has ministry in his service, and one has that of a teacher in his instruction.

8.One has that of a comforter, which is in his comforting, and a giver in generosity, and a top leader with diligence, and that of caregiver with cheerfulness.

9.And be not deceitful in your love, but hate evil and cleave to the good.

10.Be affectionate to your brethren and love one another; be preferring and honoring one another.

11.Be diligent and do not be lazy; be enthusiastic in spirit; be working for your Lord.

12.Be rejoicing in your hope. Bear your afflictions bravely. Be persistent in prayer.

13.Be partakers with the needs of the holy; befriend strangers.

14.Bless your persecutors; bless and do not curse.

15.Rejoice with those who rejoice and weep with those who weep.

16.And whatever you esteem about yourselves do also about your brethren. Do not esteem high opinions, but go out to those who are humble, and do not be wise in your opinions of yourselves.

17.Repay no person evil for evil, but be concerned with doing good before all people.

18.And if it is possible, according to what is within you, make peace with every person.

19.Do not avenge yourselves, beloved, but give place to rage, for it is written: "If you will not execute judgment for yourself, I shall execute your judgment, says God."

The quotation is quite different in The Peshitta from that of the Greek and Latin versions. The Greek is a quote from Deut. 32:35 (not LXX, but Hebrew or Peshitta).The Peshitta text of this verse cannot have come from the Greek of this verse; it is not like any OT text that I can find in Hebrew, Greek or Aramaic.

It may be a quote from The Apocrypha or Pseudepigrapha.

20."And if your enemy hungers, feed him, and if he thirsts, give him a drink, and if you do these things to him you will heap coals of fire on his skull." (Proverbs 25:21, generally according to Peshitta OT and LXX texts.)

21.Do not be overcome by evil, but overcome evil by good.

Chapter 13

1. Let every soul be subject to the authority of the great, for there is no authority that is not from the same God, and those authorities who are from God are under orders.

2. Whoever therefore stands against the authority stands against the decrees of God, and these who stand against them shall receive judgment.

3. For judges are not a fear to the good doer*, but to the wicked*. Do you wish, therefore, to be unafraid of the authority? Do good, and you shall have praise from him.

* Greek has two readings: Critical Greek has "αγαθω εργω" -"to a good deed" ; The Majority Greek has "αγαθων εργων" -"to good deeds". The Aramaic of The Peshitta can have either meaning. It can also mean what I have translated -"the doer of good". The Greek has also two readings for בישא – "Beesha" : "κακω" –"Evil" & "κακων" –"Evils". The Aramaic can explain all four Greek readings in this verse without changing one letter of Aramaic.

4. For he is the Minister of God to you for good. But if you have done evil, be afraid, for he does not wear the sword for nothing, for he is the Minister of God and a furious avenger to those who do evil.

5. Therefore it is urgent for us to be subject, not for the sake of wrath only, but also for the sake of conscience.

6. For this cause, also, you pay the head tax, for they are the Ministers of God who are appointed for these things.

7. Therefore pay every person what is owed to him: to whomever head tax, pay head tax, and to whomever a tribute tax, a tribute tax, and to whomever reverence, reverence, and to whomever honor, honor.

8. Owe no person anything but to love one another, for whoever loves his neighbor fulfills The Written Law.

9. For this also that says, "You shall not commit adultery", "You shall not murder", "You shall not steal, "You shall not covet", or if there is any other commandment, it is summed up in the saying: "You shall love your neighbor as yourself."

10. Love does not commit evil against its neighbor, because love is the fulfillment of The Written Law.

11. I know this: Now is the time and the hour to awake from our sleep, for now our life has drawn closer to us than when we believed.

12. The night has now passed and the day has arrived, therefore let us strip off the works of darkness from us, and let us put on the armor of light.

13. And let us walk in a right manner as those in the daytime, not in partying, not in drunkenness, not in orgies, not in envy or in fighting,

14. But put on Our Lord Yeshua The Messiah and do not be concerned for the desires of your flesh.

Chapter 14

1. But offer a hand to the one who is weak in faith and do not be divided by your disputes.

2. For there is one who believes that he may eat everything, and he who is weak eats vegetables.

3. But let not him who eats despise him who does not eat, and let not him who does not eat judge him who eats, for God has accepted him.

4. Who are you to judge a Servant who is not yours*? For if he stands, he stands to his Master, and if he falls, he falls to his Master, for it is appointed to his Master to be able to establish him.

דלא דילך -d'la dilak – "not yours" is matched with the Greek word αλλοτριον – "allotrion"- "strange, foreign" in three places in the NT: Luke 16:12 , Here (Romans 14:4) & Hebrews 9:25.If the Peshitta were a translation of Greek, this Aramaic phrase would not exist in those places. Other words would be much more suitable – נוכריתא ,נוכריא , דאחרנא-"Foreign", "Another's", "Strange" ;
In DSS script:נוכריא , דאחרנא -"Foreign", "Other", "Strange". דלא דילך & in DSS: "not yours" is not a translation of the Greek αλλοτριον – "strange, foreign" .
Notice the two grey shaded phrases. There is 5/8ᵗʰ'ˢ letter correlation (63%) between the two readings, "Another's" & "not yours" in Aramaic.
Most Greek mss. also have θεος – "God" where The Peshitta has מרה "his master".
The Aramaic מרה - "his master" is no translation of θεος – "God"; θεος - "God" is an interpretation of מרה - "his master".

5. There is one who distinguishes one day from another and there is another who judges all days the same, but let every person be certain in his own mind.

6. Whoever esteems whatever day, he esteems it for his Lord, and everyone who does not esteem whatever day, for his Lord he does not esteem it. He who eats, eats for his

Lord and he gives thanks to God, and he who does not eat, for his Lord he does not eat, and he gives thanks to God. * The grey shaded words are omitted by the Critical Greek text.

7. For none of us lives for himself and no man dies for himself.

8. For if we live, we live for Our Lord, and if we die, we die for Our Lord; whether we live, therefore, or we die, we belong to Our Lord. *

* In 68 of the 299 **Peshitta NT** occurrences of מרן ("**Our Lord**") , "(κυριος ημων- "**kurios hmwn**" or "**kuriou hmwn , kuriw hmwn, kurie hmwn, kurion hmwn**"-"**Our Lord**") occurs in **The Greek NT**. That is a 23% correlation or a 77 % defection rate. This means that either the Greek drops the personal pronoun "our" 77 % of the time or that The Peshitta adds (construction rate) **340 %** of the number of occurrences in the hypothetical Greek original to the hypothetical Aramaic translation of the Greek NT. Which is more likely? Consider the following:
In **The Hebrew OT**, the Hebrew אדני -"**Adonai**" ("**My Lord**") occurs 625 times; of those 625 places, **The LXX** has "(κυριος μου"- "**kurios mou**" or "**kuriou mou, kuriw mou, kurie mou, kurion mou**"-"**My Lord**"), 144 times. 144/625= 23%. That is a defection rate in **The LXX** (dropping the personal possessive pronoun "my") of 77 % - exactly the same rate for **The Greek NT** as compared to **The Peshitta NT**! In this and in many other similar comparisons, the Greek NT compares to **The Peshitta NT** just as **The LXX Greek OT** compares to **The Hebrew OT**, which means **The Greek NT** looks statistically very much like a translation of **The Peshitta NT**.

9. For this purpose also The Messiah died and lived and arose, that he would be **THE LORD JEHOVAH** to the dead and to the living.
* The Messiah is "**Jehovah**" according to The Peshitta, which so names Our Lord thirty times or more! See Luke 2:9-11 for the first time He was so named before witnesses on Earth.

10. But why are you judging your brother, or why do you even despise your brother? For all of us are going to stand before the judgment seat of The Messiah*,
* The Critical Greek has **Theou** - "of God" for "of The Messiah".

11. According to what is written: "As I live, says **THE LORD JEHOVAH**, every knee shall bow to me and to me every tongue shall swear."
* Greek adds, "**to God**", following The LXX version of Isaiah 45:23, however, The Hebrew and Peshitta OT agree with the Peshitta reading. Even the Dead Sea Great Isaiah Scroll (100 B.C.) agrees with the Peshitta reading, and with The Massoretic text of Isaiah generally throughout its 66 chapters.(The reader can obtain the entire scroll photocopied on CD Rom with textual notes and translation from Fred Miller's web site on The Great Isaiah Scroll. Simply google search "The Great Isaiah Scroll - Fred Miller".

12. So then, every person among us gives an account of himself to God.

13. From now on let us not judge one another, but determine this rather: "You shall not lay a stumbling block for your brother."

14. For I know and I am persuaded by **THE LORD JEHOVAH** Yeshua that there is

nothing that is defiled in his presence. But to the one who regards anything impure, it is impure to him alone.

See how The Peshitta Names **Jesus (Yeshua)** as **Jehovah**. The Greek NT does not have this, as Greek has no equivalent for **YAHWEH** as Aramaic does – (מריא-**"MarYah"**). The Greek has **"Kurios"** , which means, **"Lord"**, **"Master"**, or **"Sir"**.

15.   But if you grieve your brother because of food, you are not walking in love. You shall not destroy, by your food, one for whose sake The Messiah died.

16.   And let not our good be blasphemed.

17.   For The Kingdom of God is not eating and drinking, but the righteousness and the peace and the joy in The Spirit of Holiness.

18.   For whoever serves The Messiah in these things is beautiful to God and is approved before the children of men.

19.   And now, let us run after peace and after building one another up.

20.   And let us not destroy a Servant of God because of food, for everything is pure, but it is evil to a man who eats with offense.

21.   For it is good that we do not eat flesh, neither drink wine, neither anything by which our brother is subverted.

22.   You who have faith in your soul, hold it before God. Whoever does not judge his soul in the thing which he designates is blessed.

23.   For whoever is doubtful and eats is condemned because it is not in faith, for everything that is not from faith is sin.

Chapter 15

1.   Therefore, we who are strong are indebted to bear the infirmities of the weak and not to please ourselves.

2.   But let each of us please his neighbor with good as for edification,

3.   Because even The Messiah did not please himself, but according to what is written: "The reproach of those reviling you fell upon me."

4.   For everything* that is written from ancient times is written* for our teaching, that by patience and by comfort of the Scriptures we should have hope.

* The Critical Greek agrees here in two places with The Peshitta where The Majority Greek differs: "παντα" – "**All things**" and "**was written**" – second verb in Greek; The Majority has omitted "παντα"and has προεγραφη –"**written before**" as the second Greek verb (προεγραφη is also the first verb). Notice that The Critical Greek agrees in 8:2 with The Peshitta, disagrees in 14:10 and agrees here in 15:4.

5.   But The God of patience and comfort grant you that you may value one another with equality in Yeshua The Messiah, (Slavery

as we in the West experienced it may never have taken hold if this verse had been received from the Peshitta, instead of the Greek text.)

6.   That you may with one mind and one mouth glorify God The Father of Our Lord Yeshua The Messiah.

7.   Because of this, you shall accept and bear with one another, just as also The Messiah has accepted you* for the glory of God.

* The Majority Greek text agrees with The Peshitta reading-"**accepted you**"(2nd p. plural); The Critical Greek has "**accepted us**".

8.   But I say that Yeshua The Messiah ministered to the circumcision for the sake of the truth of God, so as to confirm The Promise of the fathers.

9.   And the Gentiles shall glorify God for the sake of the mercies which have been upon them, as it is written: "I shall give thanks to you with the Gentiles and I shall sing praise to your name."

10. And again it says, "Be delighted, you Gentiles, with his people."

11. And again it says, "Praise **THE LORD JEHOVAH**, all you nations; praise him all peoples."

12.   And again, Isaiah said, "There shall be a root of Jesse and he who shall rise shall be The Ruler of the nations, and upon him the nations shall hope."

13.   But The God of hope shall fill you with all joy and peace by faith, that you shall superabound in his hope by the power of The Spirit of Holiness.

14.   I am also convinced concerning you, my brethren, that you also are filled with goodness and you are filled with all knowledge and you are able also to instruct others.

15.   But I have boldly written a few things to you, my brethren, so as to remind you by the grace that is given to me from God,

16.   That I may be a minister to Yeshua The Messiah among the Gentiles and that I may labor* for The Gospel of God, that the offering of the Gentiles may be accepted and sanctified by The Spirit of Holiness.

* Greek has "ιερουργουντα" – "**perform Priestly function**" where The Peshitta has "**& I may labor**"; A very similar Greek verb ιερατευειν occurs in one other place – Luke 1:8 , matching the Aramaic מכהן .Another form is אכהן ; "**& I may function as Priest**" would be "ואכהון".Let's compare the Peshitta reading with this in DSS script: ואכהון : אכן ואכהון The **Kap - **כ and פ -(**Pe**) could be easily confused, as **Kap** in Ashuri script is כ . The ה – **He** and וו Lamedh-Waw could easily be confused by pushing the latter two together more; the same applies to ח –Khet & וו Waw-Nun . Here they are again without color coding :

Ashuri Aramaic:

The Holy Epistle of Paul The Apostle to The Romans אגרתא קדישתא דפולוס שליחא דלות רהומיא

ואפלוח-**& I may labor**
ואכהן-**& I may serve as a Priest**
DSS Aramaic:
‪–"& I may labor"(Peshitta)
‪–"& I may serve as a
Priest"(Greek reading in Aramaic)

Notice how the last three letters of The Peshitta reading can be matched with the last three Aramaic letters of the hypothetical Aramaic reading behind the Greek.

split vertically through the middle would be - ; could be fused together to form . DSS (Pe) is very similar to an Ashuri (Kap), which is (Kap) in DSS script. These considerations give almost **100% correlation** for the two words in DSS Aramaic script.
Starting to get the picture ?

17. I have pride therefore in Yeshua The Messiah in the presence of God.

18. I dare not speak of anything to the audience of the Gentiles that The Messiah has not done through me by word and by works,

19. By the power of signs and wonders and by the power of The Spirit of God, just as I have gone around from Jerusalem unto Eluriqone and I have fulfilled The Gospel of The Messiah,

20. While I take pains to preach The Good News, not where the name of The Messiah is invoked, lest I build on an unusual foundation.

21. But just as it is written: "Those who had not been told about him shall see him, and those who have not heard shall be convinced."

22. Because of this I was hindered many times when I would have come to you.

23. But now because I have no place in these regions, and I have desired for many years to come to you,

24. When I go to España, I hope to come see you, and when a few of you would accompany me there, I shall be delighted to see you.

25. But now I go to Jerusalem to minister to the Saints.

26. But these who are in Macedonia and in Akaia were willing to share with the poor Saints who are in Jerusalem.

27. They were willing because they also are indebted to them, for if they have been made partners with them in the spiritual, the Gentiles are also indebted to serve them in the physical.

28. When therefore I have finished and have ratified this fruit to them, I am going to pass by you to Espania.

29. But I know that when I come to you, I shall come to you in the fullness of the blessing of The Gospel of The Messiah.
* Critical Greek lacks "of The Gospel".

30. But I beg of you my brethren, by Our Lord Yeshua The Messiah and by the love of The Spirit, that you labor with me in prayer to God for me,

31. That I would be delivered from those who are disobedient who are in Judea, and that the ministry I bring to the Saints in Jerusalem would be well received.

32. And I shall come to you in joy by the will of God, and I shall be refreshed with you.

33. Now may The God of Peace be with all of you. Amen.

Chapter 16

1. I entrust Phoebe our sister to you, who is a Servant of the church of Qenkraus,

2. That you would accept her in Our Lord, as that is right for Saints, and in any matter that she seeks of you, that you would help her, because she is also a helper to many and also to me.

3. Invoke the peace of Priscilla and of Aqilaus, laborers who are with me in Yeshua The Messiah;

4. And they have yielded their necks for my sake, and I do not thank them only, but also all the churches of the Gentiles.

5. And give greetings to the church that is in their house. Invoke the peace of Epentos my beloved, who is the first fruits of Akaia* in The Messiah.

*Critical Greek (see NIV) has "of Asia". "Of Asia" in Aramaic is : is "of Akaia". Here are the words in DSS script: : . It appears that the (Kap) was confused for (Simkat) & the middle (Alap) skipped , making "Akaia" into "Asia". Let's see the words one atop the other :
DSS Aramaic script
‪ - "of Akaia"
‪– "of Asia"
Ashuri Aramaic script
‪- "of Akaia"
‪– "of Asia"

Delete the middle Alap in "Akaia" and you practically have "Asia"!

6. Invoke the peace of Maria, who has labored much among you.

7. Invoke the peace of Andronicus and of Junia, my relatives who were captives with me and were known by The Apostles and they were in The Messiah before me.

8. Invoke the peace of Amphilius, beloved in Our Lord.

אגרתא קדישתא דפולוס שליחא דלות רהומיא

9. Invoke the peace of Eurbanus, who is with us in The Messiah, and Estakus my beloved.

10. Invoke the peace of Appela, chosen in Our Lord. Invoke the peace of the members in the house of Aristobulus.

11. Invoke the peace of Herodion, my relative. Invoke the peace of the members of the house of Narqissus, those who are in our Lord.

12. Invoke the peace of Trupana and Trupsa who labored in Our Lord; invoke the peace of Persis my beloved, who labored much in Our Lord.

13. Invoke the peace of Rufus, chosen in Our Lord, and of his mother and mine.

14. Invoke the peace of Asunqritus and of Plagon and of the brethren who are with them, and of Harma and of Petroba and of Harme.

15. Invoke the peace of Pillagus and of Julia, of Nereus, of his sister and of Alumpa and of all The Holy Ones with them.

16. Invoke the peace of one another with a holy kiss. All the churches of The Messiah invoke your peace.

17. But I beg of you my brethren, beware of those who are causing division and subversion outside of the doctrine which you have learned, that you should stay away from them.

18. For those who are such are not serving Our Lord Yeshua The Messiah, but their own belly, and with sweet words and with blessings they deceive the hearts of the pure.

19. But your obedience has been made known to everyone. I rejoice therefore in you and desire that you would be wise to what is good and innocent to what is evil.

20. But The God of peace shall soon crush Satan under your feet. May the grace of Our Lord Yeshua The Messiah be with you.

21. Timotheus, a worker with me invokes your peace, and Luqios, and Aison and Sosipatros, my brothers.

22. I, Tertius, invoke your peace, who have written the epistle by Our Lord. (Divine inspiration of scripture, & Romans in particular, is here asserted.)

23. Gaius, who receives me and the whole church, invokes your peace. Aristus, steward of the city, and Quertus a brother, invokes your peace.

24. But unto God who is able to confirm you by my Gospel, which has been preached concerning Yeshua The Messiah, by the revelation of the mystery, which from the times of the world has been hidden,

25. But has been revealed in this time by the Scriptures of The Prophets, and has been taught to all the nations by the commandment of The Eternal God for the hearing sense of faith,

26. Unto him Who alone is wise belongs The glory, by Yeshua The Messiah, for the eternity of eternities. Amen.

27. The grace of Our Lord Yeshua The Messiah be with all of you. Amen.

The First Epistle of The Apostle Paul to the Corinthians

Chapter 1

1. Paulus, a called one, and an Apostle of Yeshua The Messiah in the will of God, and brother Sosthenes,

2. To the Church of God which is in Qorinthus, called and holy, which is in Yeshua The Messiah, sanctified, and all those who in every place call on the name of Our Lord Yeshua The Messiah, theirs and ours.

3. Grace be with you and peace from God our Father and from Our Lord Yeshua The Messiah.

4. I give thanks to my God * always on your behalf concerning the grace of God which is given to you by Yeshua The Messiah.

* Greek mss. Vaticanus (B) and Sinaiticus (א) (both 4th century) have Θεω-"God" without the personal possessive pronoun μου-"my". The difference between these two readings in Aramaic would be (not that the Aramaic has two readings): לאלהי & לאלהא. In Dead Sea Scroll Aramaic script, these look like this:

        ᴧ⊓ⶅᴧⶅ   -to my God
        ⶉ⊓ⶅᴧⶅ   - to God-

Might this explain the Greek readings? There is only one letter distinguishing the two in Aramaic. Perhaps a Greek translator mistook the first one for the second word and translated it as Θεω-"God", whereas most Greek mss. have Θεω μου-"my God". The two major Greek texts (Critical Alexandrian and Byzantine) would be the result of separate translations of The Aramaic of The Peshitta; the Alexandrian appears to have been done a bit later as a revision, not a completely new translation, using the Byzantine text as a base.

5. For you are enriched in everything by him, in every utterance and in all knowledge,

6. As the testimony of The Messiah has been verified in you,

7. Because you have not been deprived of any gift, but you are expecting the revelation of Our Lord Yeshua The Messiah.

8. For he will confirm you until, at last, you will be without blame in the day of Our Lord Yeshua The Messiah.

9. God is faithful, for by him you were called into the fellowship of his Son, Yeshua The Messiah Our Lord.

10. But I request of you, my brethren, in the name of Our Lord Yeshua The Messiah, that all of you would have one speech, and that there would be no divisions among you, that you would be perfected in one mind and in one conscience.

11. For brethren from the house of Kloe sent to me about you, that there is contention among you.

12. But I say this: there is one of you who says, "I am of Paulus", and one who says, "I am of Apollo", and one who says, "I am of Kaypha", and one who says, "I am of The Messiah."

13. Has The Messiah been divided, or was Paulus crucified for your sakes, or were you baptized in the name of Paulus?

14. I thank my God that I baptized * none of you except Crispus and Gaius,

15. Lest anyone would say that I have baptized in my name.

* Greek mss. P46,B and א (The major reps. of Alexandrian text) have εβαπτισθητε – "you were baptized". The Peshitta has אעמדת –"I have baptized". "You were baptized" could be one of a few forms; the most likely candidate for explaining the Greek variant reading is עמדתון , which has simply two letters added onto the end and one at the beginning of the actual reading. Here are the two in DSS script:

      ᴧ⊓ⶉⶌⶉⴹ –"I have baptized"
      ⶄ⊓ⶌⶉⴹ –"You were baptized
      Estrangela script

      ܐܬܡܪܬ –"I have baptized"

      ܥܡܕܬܘܢ –"You were baptized

If a Greek translator skipped a letter (א) and read ⶉⶌⶉⴹ , he would still have interpreted "I have baptized"; the next letter is an Alap א in verse 16 (another אעמדת "I baptized" follows), in which the Alap (א) could be dropped and still the word would make sense. Suppose that the Alap - א were seen as part of the previous word ᴧ⊓ⶉⴹ (v. 15) as the last letter - ⶉⶌⶉⴹ but somewhat distorted - ᴨ or ⊓ or ⶄⶄ. If this last ⶄⶄ were what he saw (actually the two letters –Waw,Nun) then we can understand how the Greek variation ⶄ⊓ⶌⶉⴹ –"You were baptized" originated. Here are the actual words in The Peshitta verses compared to the hypothetical Aramaic behind the Greek variant:
ᴧ⊓ⶉⴹⶉⶌⶉⴹⶄⶉ–"in my name I baptized;I baptized.."(Actual Peshitta reading)
ᴧ⊓ⶉⴹⶄ⊓ⶌⶉⴹⶄⶉ--"in my name you were baptized;I baptized.."(Hypothetical Aramaic base of Greek)
The difference in the two readings is two letters in Aramaic or four letters in Greek. The Aramaic readings differ by two letters affecting two words (10 letters), or 80% letter correlation.
The two readings rendered in Greek are: εβαπτισα & εβαπτισθητε;
In ancient uncial script: ΕΒΑΠΤΙΣΑ & ΕΒΑΠΤΙΣΘΗΤΕ. The Greek for both readings differ in four letters out of 11 letters in one word, which is 63% correlation. All else being equal, it is half as likely one would mistake four letters as to mistake two letters.
It appears the Aramaic forms can explain the Greek readings but not vice versa. Alexandrian Greek has 4 letters more than the Majority Greek reading, which is not a likely cause for mistaking ΕΒΑΠΤΙΣΑ for ΕΒΑΠΤΙΣΘΗΤΕ   or vice versa.

16. But I baptized also the household of Estephana, but otherwise I do not know if I baptized any others.

17. For The Messiah sent me not to baptize, but to preach The Good News, not in wisdom of words, lest the crucifixion of The Messiah would be rejected.

18. The message of the crucifixion is insanity to the lost, but to those of us who have life it is the power of God.

19. For it is written: "I shall destroy the wisdom of the wise, and I shall take away the opinions of the intelligent."

20. Where is the wise or where is the Scribe or where is the debater of this world? Behold, has not God shown the wisdom of this world to be insane?

21. And because, in the wisdom of God, the world did not know God by wisdom, God was willing that by the insanity of preaching he would give life to those who believe.

22. Because the Jews ask for signs and the Aramaeans* seek philosophy.

*Syria, Persia, Mesopotamia and Asia Minor had been infiltrated by Babylonian (in Mesopotamia) and Greek culture, language, philosophy and religion through Alexander's conquests, though the Aramaic language continued as the international language of commerce in the Middle Eastern region in spite of the strong Greek influence.

23. But we preach The Messiah as crucified- a scandal to the Judeans and madness to the Aramaeans.

24. But to those who are called, Jews and Aramaeans, The Messiah is the power of God and the wisdom of God.

25. Because the madness of God is wiser than humans and the weakness of God is stronger than humans.

26. For you see also your calling my brethren, that not many among you are wise in the flesh, neither are many among you mighty, neither are many among you children of a great family line.

27. For God has chosen the foolish of the world to shame the wise, and he has chosen the weak of the world to shame the mighty.

28. And he has chosen those of low descent in the world and the rejects and those who are nothing, to nullify those who are,

29. That no one will boast before him.

30. But you also are from him in Yeshua The Messiah, he who has become for us the wisdom of God and the righteousness and the holiness and the redemption,

31. According to what is written: "Whoever boasts, let him boast of THE LORD JEHOVAH."

Chapter 2

1. But when I came to you, my brethren, I did not proclaim to you by magnificent speech, neither by scholarship, The Gospel of the mystery of God.

2. Neither did I judge myself as knowing anything among you, except Yeshua The Messiah, even him as he was crucified.

3. And I was with you in much fear and in trembling.

4. And my message and my preaching were not in the persuasiveness of the words of philosophy*, but in the demonstration of The Spirit and power,

* The Majority Greek has ανθρωπινης σοφιας λογοις–"**human words of wisdom**". The Critical Greek does not have this word. The Aramaic word חכמתא‎ can mean "**wisdom**", "**philosophy**" or "**science**". The Greek translator (Majority text) apparently did not want to convey the sense that Paul had something against wisdom (which the Critical Greek implies), so he added "ανθρωπινης"- **anthropinays**- "**Human**" to clarify the meaning of the Aramaic word from which he translated (In the author's humble opinion).

5. That your faith would not be in the wisdom of men, but in the power of God.

6. But we speak wisdom with the perfect; wisdom, not of this world, neither of the authorities of this world, who are brought to nothing.

7. But we speak the wisdom of God in a mystery, that which was kept secret and God had consecrated before the world for our glory.

8. That which none of the Rulers of this world knew, for if they had known it, they would not have crucified The Lord of Glory.

9. But as it is written: "Eye has not seen, ear has not heard, and upon the heart of man has not come up that which God has prepared for those who love him."

10. But God has revealed *it* to us by his Spirit, for The Spirit searches into everything, even the depths of God.

11. And who is the man who knows what is in a man except only the spirit of the man that is in him? So also a man does not know what is in God, only The Spirit of God *knows*.

12. But we have not received The Spirit of the world, but The Spirit that is from God, that we may know the gift that has been given to us from God.

13. But those things we speak are not in the teaching of the words of the wisdom of men, but in the teaching of The Spirit, and we compare spiritual things to the spiritual.

14. For a selfish* man does not receive spiritual things, for they are madness to him, and he is not able to know, for they are known by The Spirit. * ("d'vanphesh" comes from Napsha –

"soul", "self", "animal life", and can mean, "soulish", "selfish", "brutish".)

15. But a spiritual man judges everything and he is not judged by any man.

16. For who has known the mind of **THE LORD JEHOVAH** that he may teach him? But we do have the mind of The Messiah.

Chapter 3

1. And I, my brethren, have not been able to speak with you as with spiritual ones but as with the carnal and as to babies in The Messiah.

2. I gave you milk to drink and I did not give you solid food, for you have not been able to bear it until now, neither now are you able.

3. For you are still in the flesh, and wherever there is among you envy, contention and division, behold, are you not carnal? You are walking in the flesh.

4. For whenever each of you says, "I am of Paulus", and another says, "I am of Apollo", behold, are you not carnal?

5. For who is Paulus or who is Apollo, but Ministers by whom you have believed? And each man *is* according to what **THE LORD JEHOVAH** has given him.

6. I planted and Apollo watered but God made it grow.

7. Therefore he who plants is nothing, neither is he who waters anything, but God who gives growth.

8. But whoever plants and whoever waters, they are one; and a man receives wages according to his labor.

9. For we labor with God and you are the crop and the building of God.

10. And according to the grace of God given to me, I laid the foundation as a wise architect and another built upon it, and every person should pay attention to how he builds upon it.

11. For no man can lay another foundation than that which has been laid, which is Yeshua The Messiah.

12. And if a man builds on this foundation, gold or silver or precious stones, or wood, hay or stubble,

13. The work of every person is revealed, for that day reveals it, because the work of every person is revealed by fire, what sort it is; the fire will test it.

14. And whosoever work shall remain shall receive his reward from The Builder.

15. And whosoever work will burn up will suffer loss, but he shall escape, but as if by fire.

16. Do you not know that you are the Temple of God, and that The Spirit of God dwells within you?

17. Whoever destroys the Temple of God, God destroys; for the Temple of God is holy, which you are.

18. Let no man deceive himself; whoever among you thinks that he is wise in this world, let him become a fool that he may be wise.

19. For the wisdom of this world is nonsense to God, for it is written: "He has seized the wise in their craftiness."

20. And again, "**THE LORD JEHOVAH** knows the reasonings of the wise that they are worthless."

21. Therefore, let no man glory in the children of men, for everything is yours,

22. Whether Paul, or Apollo, or Kaypha, or the world, or life, or death, or things present, or things future; everything is yours.

23. And you are The Messiah's and The Messiah is God's.

Chapter 4

1. In this way, let us be esteemed by you as Ministers of The Messiah and the stewards of the mysteries of God.

2. Now, henceforth, it is required in stewards that a man should be found being faithful.

3. But to me this is a slight matter that I am judged by you or by any man. I do not even judge myself.

4. For I am not troubled over anything in myself, but I am not justified by this, for my judge is **THE LORD JEHOVAH**.

5. Therefore you should judge nothing before the time until **THE LORD JEHOVAH** will come, who shall illuminate the secrets of darkness and reveal the imaginations of the hearts, and then there shall be praise to each one from God.

6. But I have established these things, my brethren, for your sakes concerning my person and that of Apollo, that you may learn by us not to suppose more than whatever is written and that a man should not be lifted up against his fellow man because of anyone.

7. For who is investigating you, and what do you have that you have not received? And if you have received, why are you boasting as if it is what you have not received?

8. Now you have become full of yourselves and you are made rich and you have reigned without us. But oh, that you had reigned also, that we might reign with you!

9. For I suppose that God has appointed us Apostles at last, as for death, that we would be a stage play for the universe, for Angels and for men.

10. We are insane because of The Messiah, but you are sensible in The Messiah. We are weak and you are mighty; you are praised and we are despised.

11. Until this hour we are hungry and we are thirsty, we are naked, we are abused, and we have no dwelling place,

12. And we toil as we labor with our hands. They dishonor us and we bless; they persecute us and we endure.

13. They accuse us and we beg them. We are as the scum of the world and the offscouring of every person until now.

14. I do not write these things to shame you, but I give admonition as to dear children.

15. For if you should have ten thousand instructors in The Messiah, however, there are not many fathers, for in Yeshua The Messiah I have begotten you by The Gospel.

16. Therefore, I beg of you that you would imitate me.

17. Because of this, I have sent Timotheus to you, who is my beloved son and faithful in THE LORD JEHOVAH, that he may relate my ways to you that are in The Messiah, such things as I teach in all the assemblies.

18. But some of you are boisterous as if I am not coming to you,

19. But if THE LORD JEHOVAH is willing, soon I shall come to you and I shall know, not the words of those whose souls are lifted up, but their power.

20. For The Kingdom of God is not in word, but in power.

21. How do you want it? Shall I come to you with a rod, or in affection and in a spirit of meekness?

Chapter 5

1. In short, it is reported that there is fornication among you; fornication such as this which is not even named among the pagans: As far as a son that would take his father's wife.

2. And you are inflated and have not rather sat in mourning, that whoever has committed

this crime would be taken out from your midst.

3. For while I am distant from you in body, I am near to you in spirit. And now I have judged as being present with whoever has committed this:

4. In the name of Our Lord Yeshua The Messiah, all of you shall assemble and I with you in The Spirit, with the power of Our Lord Yeshua The Messiah,

5. And you shall deliver this one to Satan for the destruction of his body, that he may live in The Spirit in the day of Our Lord Yeshua The Messiah.

6. Your boasting is not good. Do you not know that a little yeast ferments the whole lump?

7. Purge out the old yeast from you that you would be a new lump, just as you are unleavened bread. Our Passover is The Messiah, who was slain for our sake.

8. Therefore let us make a feast, not with the old leaven, neither with the yeast which is in wickedness or of bitterness, but with the leaven* of purity and of holiness.

* * Greek has αζυμοις ειλικρινειας και αληθειας - "unleavened -[ ] of sincerity and truth". It appears to me that the Aramaic phrase בחמירא– (b'khamira) "with the leaven" was read as בפטירא– (b'patira) "with the unleavened";
    Let's look at these two in DSS script:
ܐ݇ܪܝܡܚܒ -"with the leaven"
ܐ݇ܪܝܛܦܒ -"with the unleavened".
 In Ashuri:בחמירא "with the leaven"
            בפטירא "with the unleavened".
   The DSS pair have at least 66% letter correlation (4 of 6 letters are identical) ; In Ashuri, they are even more similar- 82%.
•   The last word in Aramaic is קדישותא – "Holiness" . Compare this with קושתא – "Truth" (Greek has "Truth ").
•   Let's compare these two side by side in DSS Aramaic script: ܐܬܘܫܝܕܩܘ   – "And of Holiness" . Take out the two shaded letters ܝ & ܕ and you are essentially left with- ܐܬܘܫܩܘ – "And of truth". The Yodh of the first word (ܝ) and the Waw # 2 (ܘ) of the second word are easily confused or interchanged in The Great Isaiah Scroll without changing meaning- it is a spelling variation. There is 77% letter correlation in the two Aramaic words.

Here is the actual Aramaic word with the two letters removed: ܐܬܘܫܩܘ .
Here is the Aramaic word for "& of Truth " ----------- ܐܬܘܫܩܘ .
It appears that 1 Corinthians was written in Aramaic and in a Dead Sea Scroll script resembling the Pesher Habakkuk scroll (circa 4 BC) ; more data will be needed to verify or refute the particular script, but Aramaic certainly is the better candidate for the original language in Corinthians than Greek. Greek for "holiness " is αγιωσυνης , αγιασμου , οσιοτης or αγιοτης. Which of these looks like αληθειας (truth)? At best, αγιωσυνης & αληθειας have 22% letter correlation.

9. I have written to you in a letter not to mix with fornicators.

10. But I am not talking about the fornicators who are in this world, or about the greedy, or about extortioners, or about idol worshipers; otherwise you would be obligated to depart from the world.

11. I have written this to you, not to mix, if there is one who is called a brother, and he is a fornicator, or a greedy man, or an idol worshiper, or an abuser, or drunkard, or a robber, with whom you are not even to eat bread.

12. For what business have I to judge outsiders? Judge the insiders.

All Greek mss. but one have: ουχι τους εσω υμεις κρινετε - "Do you not judge them that are within?" Have a look at the Peshitta reading & a possible misreading of it:

ܠܒܪ ܕܝܢܘ ܐܢܬܘܢ -"Judge the insiders"
ܠܒܪ ܐܢ ܠܐ ܕܝܢܝܢ -"Do you not judge within?"
But P46 (2nd century Greek papyrus) has τους εσωθεν υμεις κρινατε – "Judge them that are within", which is the same as the Peshitta reading.

13. But God judges the outsiders; remove the evil one from your midst.

Chapter 6

1. Dare any of you, when he has a dispute with his brother, to judge before the evil and not before the holy?

2. Or do you not know that the Saints shall judge the universe? And if the universe is judged by you, are you not worthy to judge small disputes?

3. Do you not know that we judge the Angels? How much rather those who are of this world?

4. But if you have a judgment concerning a worldly matter, seat those for you in judgment who are neglected in the assembly.

5. But I say to you now: Is there not with you even one wise person who will be able to reconcile between a brother and his brother?

6. A brother disputes with his brother, even before those who are unbelievers.

7. Now therefore you have condemned yourselves, because you have lawsuits with one another; for why are you not rather wronged, and why are you not rather cheated?

8. But you are doing wrong and you are cheating even your brothers.

9. Or do you not know that evil men do not inherit The Kingdom of God? Do not be deceived; no fornicators, neither worshipers of idols, neither adulterers, neither sexual

molesters, neither males lying down with males,

10. Neither frauds, nor thieves, neither drunkards, nor the insolent, neither extortioners; these do not inherit The Kingdom of God.

11. And these things had been in each one of you but you are washed, you are sanctified and you are made righteous in the name of Our Lord Yeshua The Messiah and by The Spirit of our God.

12. Everything is legal for me, but not everything is useful for me. Everything is legal for me, but no man will have dominion over me.

13. Food for the belly and the belly for food, but God brings both of them to nothing; but the body is not for fornication but for Our Lord, and Our Lord for the body.

14. But God has raised even Our Lord and raises us by his power.

15. Do you not know that your bodies are members of The Messiah? Shall we take the member of The Messiah to make it the member of a harlot? God forbid!

16. Do you not know that whoever cleaves to a harlot is one body, for it is said, "They will both be one body."

17. But whoever cleaves to Our Lord becomes one spirit with him.

18. Flee from fornication. Every sin that a man will do is apart from his body, but whoever fornicates sins with his body.

19. Do you not know that your body is the temple of The Spirit of Holiness who dwells within you, whom you have received from God, and you are not your own?

20. For you have been bought with a price; therefore be glorifying God with your body and with your spirit, which are God's.

Chapter 7

1. But concerning those things of which you wrote to me, it is good for a man not to touch a woman,

2. But because of fornication, let a man take a wife and a woman take her husband.

3. Let a man bestow to his wife the love * that is owed; in this way also, the woman to her husband.

* Most Greek mss. have "ευνοια"-"**eunoia**" is "**Good will**" or "**benevolence**"; a few old mss. have simply , οφειλην –"**ofeilayn**"- "**what is owed**". The Aramaic "**khuuba**"(love,charity,affection) comes from "**Akhkhev**", which refers to the burning passion of love. The same written word form with different unwritten vowels -"**khawva**", refers to "**a debt**", which would explain the old greek mss. which read οφειλην –"**ofeilayn**"- "**what is owed**".

4. A wife is not authorized over her body, but her husband *is*. In this way also a man is not authorized over his body, but his wife *is*.

5. Therefore do not deprive one another except when you both agree on a time which you devote to fasting and prayer, and you shall again return to pleasure *, lest Satan tempt you because of the desire * of your bodies.

> * No **pleasure** in the Greek mss.! * No **desire of your bodies** in the Greek, either. Greek has, "ακρασιαν", which is **lack of self control**. The Greek is so discrete that one unfamiliar with Christian doctrine and The New Testament, who was reading this for the first time, would scarcely guess that the whole discussion is about sex!

6. I say this as to the weak, not by commandment.

7. For I wish that all people might be like I am in purity, but every person is given a gift from God, one in this way and one in that way.

8. But I say to those who do not have a wife and to widows, that it benefits them if they should remain as I am.

9. But if they do not endure, let them marry. It is beneficial for them to take a wife rather than to burn with lust.

10. But those who have wives, I command, not I but my Lord: A wife should not depart from her husband.

11. And if she does depart, let her remain without a husband or let her be reconciled to her husband and let not a man forsake his wife.

12. But to others I am saying, not my Lord, if there is a brother who has a wife who is an unbeliever and she is willing to stay with him, let him not leave her.

13. And whichever wife has a husband who is not a believer, and he is willing to stay with her, let her not leave her husband.

14. That man who is an unbeliever is sanctified by the wife who believes, and that woman who is not a believer is sanctified by the husband who believes, otherwise their children are defiled, but now they are pure.

15. But if he who does not believe separates, let him separate. A brother or sister is not in bondage in such cases. God has called us to peace.

16. For what do you know, woman, if you will save your husband, or you, man, if you will save your wife?

17. But as THE LORD JEHOVAH distributes to each man, however God calls him, let each man walk; and so I command all the churches.

18. And if a man was called when circumcised, let him not return to uncircumcision. And if he was called in uncircumcision, let him not be circumcised.

19. For circumcision is not anything, neither uncircumcision, but the keeping of the commandments of God.

20. Let every person continue in the calling in which he was called.

21. If you have been called as a Servant, let it not concern you, but if you can be freed, choose for yourself to do service.

22. For whoever is called *as* a Servant is God's Freeman in Our Lord. So also whoever is called *as* a Freeman is a Servant of The Messiah.

23. You have been bought with a price; you should not be Servants of people.

24. Let every person continue with God in that in which he is called, brethren.

25. Concerning virginity, I do not have a commandment from God, but I give my advice as a man who has received favor from God to be faithful.

26. And I think that this is fair because of the distress of the time, that it is useful for a man to be so.

27. Are you bound with a wife? Do not seek a divorce. Are you divorced from a wife? Do not seek a wife.

28. And if you take a wife, you will not have sinned, and if a man shall keep a virgin, she will not be sinning, but there has been physical suffering for those who are so, and I have pity for you.

29. And I say this brethren: the time now is short, for those who have wives shall be as if they were without them,

30. And those who weep, as if they did not weep, and those who rejoice, as if they did not rejoice, and those who buy, as if they did not acquire.

31. And those who use this world, not apart from the right usage, for the form of this world is passing away.

32. Because of this, I want you to be without care, for whoever does not have a wife thinks upon what is of his Lord and how he may please his Lord.

33. Whoever has a wife cares for what is of the world, how he may please his wife.

34. But there is a distinction between a wife and a virgin. She who has not ever had a

husband thinks upon Our Lord that she may be holy in her body and her spirit, and whoever has a husband thinks of the world so that she may please her husband.

35. But I say this for your benefit, not that I may cast a noose onto you, but that you would be faithful to your Lord in a beautiful way, while you are not attending to the world.

36. But if a man thinks he is disgraced by his virgin who is past her time and he has not given her to a man, and it is fitting to give her as he chooses to do, he does not sin; she may be married.

37. But he who truly determines in his mind and is not pressured to pleasure and has power over his will, judging in this way in his heart to keep his virgin, he does well.

38. And he therefore who gives his virgin does well, and he whoever does not give his virgin girl does all the better.

39. A wife is bound by The Written Law to her husband as long as he lives, but if her husband should fall asleep, she is free to be whoever she will, only in Our Lord.

40. But she is blessed if she remains in this way, according to my mind, but I think also that The Spirit of God is in me.

Chapter 8

1.But concerning sacrifices to idols, we know that knowledge is in all of us, and knowledge puffs up, but love builds up.

2.But if a man thinks that he knows something, he does not yet know anything as he ought to know.

3.But if a man loves God, this one is known by him.

4.Therefore, concerning food sacrifices to idols, we know that the idol is nothing in the universe and that there is no other God but One.

5.For even though there are what are called gods, whether in the Heavens or in The Earth, as there are many gods and many lords,

6.To us, ours is one God The Father, for all things are from him and we are in him, and The One **LORD JEHOVAH** Yeshua The Messiah, for all things are by him, and we are also in his hand.

7.But that knowledge has not been in every person, for there are some people even until now in whose conscience eat what is sacrificed to idols, and because their conscience is weak, it is defiled.

8.But food does not bring us to God, for if we eat, we gain nothing, and if we do not eat, we lose nothing.

9.But take heed, lest this your power shall be a stumbling block to the weak.

10.For if a man should see you who have knowledge in you, reclining in the house of idols, behold, will he not be encouraged to eat what is sacrificed because his conscience is weak?

11.And he* who is sickly, for whose sake The Messiah has died, is destroyed by your knowledge. *(Majority Greek has αδελφος –"a brother"; Critical Greek has "he who". Here are the two readings in a Dead Sea Scroll script:

אחיא -"He who"
אחא - "Brother"

If the middle letters, חי –(Yodh and Nun, right. to left) were pushed a bit closer together, they could easily be mistaken for ח – "Khet".

Estrangela Script:

ܐܝܢܐ -"He who"
ܐܚܐ - "Brother"

12.And if in this way you subvert your brethren and tread on the conscience of the sickly, you commit an offense against The Messiah.

13.Therefore, if food brings down my brother, I shall never eat flesh, lest I cause my brother to sin.

Chapter 9

1.Am I not a son of freedom? (Freeman) Am I not an Apostle? Have I not seen Yeshua The Messiah Our Lord? Are you not my work in my Lord?

2.And if, on one hand, I have not been an Apostle to others, on the other hand I am to you, and you are the seal of my Apostleship.

3.And I give my answer to those who judge me; it is this:

4.Why is it illegal for us to eat and to drink?

5.And why is it illegal for us to travel with a sister-wife as other Apostles and as the brothers of Our Lord and as Kaypha?

6.Or is it only BarNaba and I who have no authority not to labor?

7.Who fights in a war at his own expense, or who plants a vineyard and does not eat from its fruits, or who herds sheep and does not consume the milk of his flock?

8.I say these things as a man. Behold, The Written Law also says these things.

9.For it is written in The Law of Moses, "Do not muzzle the ox that treads." Does God concern himself with oxen?

10. But it is understood that he said it for our sake and for our sake it was written, because it is incumbent upon the plower to plow for hope, and whoever threshes, for the hope of a crop.

11. If we have sown in you from The Spirit, is it a great thing if we shall reap of you from the body?

12. And if others have authority over you, is it not all the more fitting for us? But we have not used this authority, but we have endured all things, that we may not impede The Gospel of The Messiah in anything.

13. Do you not know that those who labor in the Temple are provided for from the Temple, and those who serve the altar share in the altar?

14. In this way also Our Lord commands that those who preach his Gospel shall live from his Gospel.

15. But I have not been accustomed to any of these things, neither have I written this that thus it should be done to me, for it would be better for me to die than that someone would nullify my glory.

16. For also, I have no pride as I preach The Good News, for necessity is laid upon me, but woe to me, unless I shall preach The Good News!

17. For if I do this with my pleasure, I have a reward, but if without my pleasure, I am entrusted with a stewardship.

18. What therefore is my reward? When I evangelize, I may make The Gospel of The Messiah without expense and I do not use the authority that he gives to me in The Gospel.

19. For as I am free from all these things, I have subjected myself to every person that I may gain the many.

20. And I was with the Judeans as a Judean that I may gain the Judeans and I was with those who are under The Written Law like those who are under The Written Law that I might gain those who are under The Written Law.

21. And to those who do not have The Written Law, I was as without The Law, while I am not without law to God, but in the law of The Messiah, that I may win those who are without The Written Law.

22. I was with the weak as weak that I might gain the weak. I was everything to every person that I might give life to every person.

* "That I may give life to everyone" is not found in Greek except for 2 mss (Codex **D** -6th cent. & Codex **G**- 9th cent.) Greek mss. have -ινα παντως τινας σωσω , "**that by all means I may save some**". The Latin Vulgate has: **omnes facerem salvos**- "**That I may save everyone**". John The Baptist had the same mission statement for Israel (See John 1:7).Remember the Great Commission ? "**Go ye, therefore, and instruct all nations; and baptize them in the name of the Father, and of the Son, and of the Holy Spirit.**" Instructing involved more than evangelizing; it involved **baptizing them** and "**teaching them to observe all that I have commanded you**". This is a command to make everyone a believer and disciple of The Lord Jesus Christ. Paul's heart was fully committed to Our Lord's command and purpose. In Colossians 1:23 he writes: (MUR) "**provided ye continue in your faith, your foundation being firm, and ye be not removed from the hope of The Gospel; of which ye have heard, that it is proclaimed in all the creation beneath Heaven; of which gospel I Paul am a minister**". The world was evangelized in one generation by Paul's efforts and those of his converts. Paul wrote: " **the preaching of the cross is the power of God** " (Coloss. 1:18).

23. I have done this so that I might be a partaker of The Gospel.

24. Do you not know that those who run in the stadium all run, but there is one who takes the victory? Run in this way so that you may obtain.

25. But every man who does competition restrains his mind from everything, and these run to receive a destructible crown, but we, what is indestructible.

26. I run therefore in this way, not as if for something unknown, and so I contend, not as one who fights the air,

27. But I subdue my body and I enslave it, lest I who have preached to others would be disqualified myself.

Chapter 10

1. **But** I want you to know, my brethren, that all of our fathers were under a cloud and all of them passed through the sea. ("Our fathers" is a reference identifying Paul's audience as Jewish. Not that all in the church were Jews; many were Gentiles, but here he focuses on the Jews who believed. They were probably the founding members of the church, as was the case in most churches. He also assumes that they know the OT scriptures, which Gentiles would not have known. There were no Christian and Jewish bookstores selling Bibles in those days. Only those who attended synagogue would have known the scriptures.)

2. And they all were baptized by Moses in the cloud and in the sea.

3. And they all ate one food of The Spirit.

4. And they all drank of the one drink of The Spirit, for they were drinking from The Rock of The Spirit, which was with them, but that Rock was The Messiah.

5. But God was not pleased with the multitude of them, for they fell in the wilderness.

6. But these things are an example for us that we would not be lusting for evil, just as they lusted.

7. Neither should we be Servants of idols, even as also some of them served, according to what is written: "The people sat down to eat and to drink and they arose to play games."

8. And neither should we commit fornication as some of them fornicated and twenty three thousand fell in one day.

9. Neither should we tempt The Messiah as some of them tempted and serpents destroyed them.

10. Neither should we complain as some of them complained and they were destroyed by the destroyer.

11. But all these things that occurred to them were for our example and it was written for our admonition, for their end of the world has come upon us. (I believe Paul was writing of the destruction of the nation of Israel. He was writing specifically to the Jewish believers, according to verse 1. Even as the Israelites were destroyed in the wilderness of Sin, so the nation under Rome would be destroyed because of sin. He was not speaking of the absolute end of the world for all people.)

12. From now on, whoever thinks that he stands, let him beware lest he fall.

13. No temptation has come upon you except that of the children of men, but God is faithful, who shall not allow you to be tempted more than whatever you are able, but shall make an exit for your temptation, so that you can endure.

14. Because of this, my beloved, flee from the service of idols.

15. I speak as to the wise. Judge whatever I say.

16. The cup of thanksgiving that we bless, is it not the partaking of The Presence of the blood of The Messiah? And is not our breaking of bread the sharing in The Presence of the body of The Messiah?

"The Presence", as used here twice, it seems to me, explains the meaning of The Lord's Supper to be spiritual, not a physical partaking of the Body and the Blood of Our Lord." "The flesh profits nothing", He said. "The words I speak to you are The Spirit and The Life." John 6:63. Verses 3 & 4 intimate the idea of a Spiritual presence with the physical food and drink Israel partook in the wilderness, as well.

17. Just as that is one bread, and thus we are all one body, for we all receive from that which is one bread.

18. Behold Israel in the flesh. Have not those who eat sacrifices been partakers of the altar?

19. What therefore do I say? Is an idol anything, or is the sacrifice of an idol anything? No!

20. But that which the pagans sacrifice, they sacrifice to demons, and not to God; but I do not want you to be partakers with demons.

21. You cannot drink the cup of Our Lord and of the cup of demons, and you cannot share in the table of Our Lord and in the table of demons.

22. Or do we make Our Lord envious? Are we stronger than he?

23. Everything is legal to me, but not everything is advantageous. Everything is legal to me, but not everything edifies.

24. No man should seek what is selfish, but every person also what is for his neighbor.

25. Everything that is sold in the butcher's shop you may eat without inquiry because of conscience.

26. For The Earth is **THE LORD JEHOVAH**'s with its fullness.

27. But if a man who is a pagan invites you and you wish to go, eat everything set before you without inquiry for the sake of conscience.

28. But if a man should say to you, "This has been sacrificed", you should not eat because of that which he said to you and because of conscience.

29. But conscience, I say, not your own, but his who told you; for, why is my liberty judged by the conscience of others?

30. If I behave with grace, why am I blasphemed because of that for which I give thanks?

31. Whether you eat therefore or drink, or if you do anything, you shall do everything for the glory of God.

32. Be without violation to the Jews and to the Aramaeans and to the Church of God,

33. As I also please everyone in everything and seek not my own advantage, but whatever is advantageous for the many, that they may have life.

Chapter 11

1. Imitate me just as I also do The Messiah.

2. I praise you my brethren, that in everything you remember me, and just as I have delivered you commandments, you are keeping them.

3. But I want you to know that the head of every man is The Messiah, and the head of the woman is the man, and the head of The Messiah is God.

4. And every man who prays or prophesies while covering his head disgraces his head.

5. And every woman praying or prophesying, while revealing her head, disgraces her head, for she is equal with her whose head is shaven.

6. For if a woman is not covered, she should also be sheared, but if it is a disgrace for a woman to be sheared or shaven, let her be covered.

7. For a man ought not to cover his head, because he is the image and the glory of God, but a woman is the glory of Man.

8. For Man is not from Woman, but Woman is from Man.

9. For neither was Man created for the sake of Woman, but Woman for the sake of Man.

10. Because of this, a woman is obligated to have authority over her head, for the sake of the Angels.

11. However, a man is not without a woman, neither a woman without a man, in Our Lord.

12. For just as Woman is from Man, in this way also, a man is by a woman, but everything is from God.

13. Judge among yourselves; is it right for a woman to pray to God while revealing her head?

14. Does not even nature teach you that when a man has grown his hair, it is a disgrace to him?

15. And whenever a woman grows her hair, it is a glory to her, because her hair is given to her in place of a covering.

16. But if a man disputes against these things, we have no such custom, neither does the church of God.

17. But I command you this, not as if I praise you, because it is not to your advantage that you assemble, but you have descended to degradation.

18. For whenever you gather with the assembly, I have heard that there is division among you, and certain things I believe.

19. There are going to be contentions among you, that those who are approved among you may be known.

20. When therefore you assemble, it is not according to what is appropriate for the day of Our Lord that you eat and drink.

First century Aramaic verse:

therefore   when
ﬥﭏﭏﻻ   ﺏﺍ
what is right acc. to   not *you*   assemble
ﺭﺗﻳﭏ   ﻻﺍﺍ ﻝﺍ ﺍﻻﺍﺗﺍﻻﺍ ﻝﺍﻻﺗﻻﻻﺍﻻﻻﺍﻻﭠ
& drink   *you*   eat   of Our Lord for the day
ﻝﺍﺗﻻﺍ ﺍﻻﺍﺗﺍﻻﺍ ﺍﻻﻻﺍﺍﺍ ﻝﻻﺭﺍﺍ ﺍﺍﺭﺍﺩﺍ
Misreading: DSS script:

---

is right   as   one   as
ﺭﺗﻳﭏ ﻻﺍﺍ as ﺍﻻﺍﺍ ﻝﺍﺍ = Greek "επι το αυτο"
= "together" or "into one place".
Apparently , because the writing was difficult to read, the Greek translator saw the two green words (in the color edition)
ﺭﺗﻳﭏ ﻝﺍﺍ -"**According to what is right** as ﺍﻻﺍﺍ ﻝﺍﺍ -"**together**", picked up at ﻝﺭﻣﻻ - ("**of Our Lord**") and so on to "**You eat & drink**". Since "of Our Lord"- ﺩﻣﺭﻥ is without the normally preceding noun to modify, it was taken as modifying the phrase after it, which unfortunately is a verb phrase ("**You eat and drink**"). This phrase was changed into a Greek noun δειπνον ,**deipnon**- "**supper**", and the awkward stand alone genitive construct without an accompanying preceding noun was made into an adjective in Greek – κυριακον , **kuriakon** - "**belonging to the Lord**". Then ﻝﻻﺍﺍ ﺍﺍﻻ ﻝﺭﻣﻻ – ("**the eating of Our Lord**") became κυριακον δειπνον – "**Lord's supper**".
The verb ﻝﻻﺍﺍ was probably read twice , the second time as "**eating**", the first as "**supper**".
Κυριακον - kuriakon occurs only in the New Testament and later Christian writings (here and in Rev. 1:10) and seems to have been invented for this particular verse. Interestingly, the verse in the Aramaic Crawford ms. of Revelation has ביומא דחדבשבא – "**the first day of the week**", which is the Aramaic term for "**Sunday**", which is the term to which "**the day of Our Lord**" in this verse refers. The LXX has no use of this word among its 475,000 words; Josephus' Greek translation of 329,000 words has no such word, nor any Greek writing before the first century.

Hypothetical pre-Greek Aramaic text :

therefore   when
ﬥﭏﭏﻻ   ﺏﺍ
one   as   not   *you*   assemble
ﺍﻻﺍﺍ ﻝﺍﺍ ﻝﺍ ﺍﻻﺍﺗﺍﻻﺍ ﻝﺍﻻﺗﻻﻻﺍﻻﻻﺍﻻﭠ
& drink   *you*   eat   supping of Our Lord
ﻝﺍﺗﻻﺍ ﺍﻻﺍﺗﺍﻻﺍ ﺍﻻﻻﺍﺍﺍ ﻝﻻﺭﺍﺍ ﺍﺍﺭﺍﺩﺍ

One thing seems clear: The Aramaic of this Peshitta verse did not come from the Greek text. The words "ﺯﺩﻕ-**Zadek** (it is right)" and "יומה – **Yoma**"" **(day)** do not appear in any Greek manuscript.

21. But one or another eats his supper beforehand by himself and one has been hungry and one has been drunk!

   Corinthians were actually getting drunk in church!

22. Do you not have houses in which to eat and drink or do you despise the Church of God and shame those who have not? What shall I say to you? Shall I praise you in this? I do not praise you!

23. For I have received from Our Lord that thing which I handed to you, that Our Lord Yeshua, in that night in which he was betrayed, took bread,

24. And he blessed and he broke and he said, "Take eat; this is my body, which is broken for your persons; thus you shall do for my Memorial.

Critical Greek mss. lack "**broken**". Luke's Gospel records the verb ﻣﺗﻻﺩﺍ –"**given**"; Most Greek mss. have "**broken**". I explain this discrepancy by appealing to the image of Our Lord breaking the bread; the action of breaking it was communication as much as His spoken words; He spoke by demonstration as well as by voice, so the disciples saw the word as well as heard it. This may explain many apparent discrepancies in Scripture. Our Lord communicates to us via five spiritual senses as well as five physical senses: "Oh **taste** and **see** that The **LORD** is good…". "All thy garments **smell** of myrrh and cassia out of the ivory palaces…" "How **sweet** are Thy words to my **lips**, sweeter than honey…". "**Kiss** The Son…"."**Hear** the word of the Lord and live"; "**Look** unto Me and be saved, all the ends of The Earth."

25. So after they had dined, he also gave the cup, and he said, "This cup is The New Covenant in my blood. You shall be so doing every time that you drink for my Memorial."

26. For every time that you eat this bread and you drink this cup, you commemorate the death of Our Lord, until his coming.

27. Whoever therefore eats from the bread of **THE LORD JEHOVAH** and drinks from his cup and is unworthy of it, is guilty for the blood of **THE LORD JEHOVAH** and for his body.

No Greek ms. has or can have "**The blood of Jehovah**" or "**The body of Jehovah**", as Greek has no word for the Sacred Name God revealed to Moses. **The Peshitta** has this Name מריא –"**MarYah**"- "**Lord Yahweh**" or "**Lord God**". Greek has "**Kurios**", which means, "**Lord**", whether of God or a human King , landowner or dignitary. No text , whether Old or New Testament, that has not The Sacred Name God revealed to Abraham, Isaac and Jacob, can hold any claim to being original or inspired. **Greek cannot be the language of the original, much less the text of the original. Consider that as The Greek LXX cannot rightly record one word as it was originally given to the Hebrew Prophets, so The Greek NT cannot properly contain one word as it was given to the Aramaic speaking Jews and Aramaeans who wrote the NT. There is absolutely no evidence that God ever spoke any word of Scripture in any languages other than Hebrew and Aramaic. (See Acts 26:14 for NT evidence of the** Deity speaking Aramaic, remembering to look up the Greek definition for εβραις-"**Hebrais**", translated "Hebrew" in KJV.**).**

28. Because of this, let a man search his soul, and then eat of this bread and drink from this cup.

29. For whoever eats and drinks from it being unworthy, eats and drinks a guilty verdict into his soul for not distinguishing the body of **THE LORD JEHOVAH.**

* Is there any question that **The Peshitta NT** names Jesus The Messiah as "Jehovah" –(or "**Yahweh**" , if you prefer) ? The point is that He is named as **The Deity** of the Hebrew people and of the whole world, Who revealed Himself to Moses and the Prophets. **The Peshitta NT** names **Jesus (Yeshua d' Natsari)** as מריא -"**Mar-Yah**" -"**Yahweh**", at least **thirty times. Greek cannot do this**, for it is a **non- Semitic** tongue which never developed a word equivalent for "Yahweh".

30. Because of this, many among you are ill and sickly and many are asleep.

31. For if we would judge ourselves we would not be judged.

32. But when we are judged by Our Lord, we are chastised so that we would not be condemned with the world.

Verse 32 has a doubled verb in Aramaic – an infinitive and participle of the verb רדא –"**Reda**"- "travel,proceed,teach,chastise". This is typical usage in Hebrew and Aramaic used for emphasis; it did not come from Greek, which has no double verb here and does not employ such except in translating Hebrew or Aramaic, and then very rarely.

33. From now on, my brethren, whenever you assemble to eat, you shall wait one for another.

34. But whoever is hungry, let him eat in his house, lest you will be assembling for condemnation; but concerning the rest, when I come, I shall give you orders.

Chapter 12

1. But about spiritual things my brethren, I want you to know,

2. That you were pagans and you were being led without discrimination to those idols which have no voice.

3. Because I inform you of this: there is no man who speaks by The Spirit of God and says, "Yeshua is damned", neither can a man say, "Yeshua is THE LORD JEHOVAH", except by The Spirit of Holiness.

4. But there are diversities of gifts, however The Spirit is One.

5. And there are diversities of ministries, however, **THE LORD JEHOVAH** is One.

6. And there is a diversity of miracles, but God is One who works all in every person.

(Verses 4-6 set forth The Tri-unity of The Godhead "Three are One; One is Three- **God, Lord Jah and The Spirit**".)

7. But the revelation of The Spirit is given to each man as He helps him.

8. There is given to him by The Spirit a word of wisdom, but to another the word of knowledge by The Spirit;

9. To another faith by The Spirit; to another the gift of healing by The Spirit;

10. But to another, miracles and to another, prophecy; to another discernment of spirits; to another, kinds of languages; to another, translation of languages;

11. But all these things, that One Spirit does and distributes to every person as he pleases.

12. For in like manner, because the body is one and there are many members in it, while all of them are many members, they are one body; thus also is The Messiah.

13. For we also are baptized by The One Spirit into one body, whether Jews or Aramaeans or Servants or free men, and we are all made to drink The One Spirit.

14. For also the body is not one member, but many.

15. For if a foot should say, "Because I am not a hand, I am not of the body", is it therefore not of the body?

16. And if an ear should say, "Because I am not an eye, I am not of the body", is it therefore not of the body?

17. For if all the body were an eye, where would the hearing be? And if it all were hearing, how would there be smell?

18. But now God has set everyone of the members in the body just as he has chosen.

19. But if they were all one member, where is the body?

20. But now there are many members, but the body is one.

21. The eye cannot say to the hand, "I do not need you"; neither can the head say to the feet, "I do not need you."

22. But all the more, those members that are considered weak, on the contrary are needful.

23. And those which we think are shameful in the body, we increase greater honor to these and for those that are contemptible we make greater attire.

24. But those members which we honor do not need honor, for God unites the body and he has given greater honor to the small members,

25. Lest there would be divisions in the body; but all the members should be caring equally one for another.

26. So now, when one member shall suffer, all of them shall share the pain. And if one member rejoices, all the members shall rejoice.

27. But you are the body of The Messiah and members in your places.

28. For God has set first in his church, Apostles; after them Prophets; after them, Teachers; after them, miracle workers; after them, gifts of healing, helpers, leaders, different languages.

29. Are they all Apostles? Are they all Prophets? Are they all Teachers? Are they all miracle workers?

30. Do all have gifts of healing? Do all of them speak with languages, or do all of them translate?

31. But if you are zealous for great gifts, I again shall show you a better way.

Chapter 13

1. If I shall speak with every human and Angelic language and have no love in me, I shall be clanging brass or a noise-making cymbal.

2. And if I have prophecy, and I know all mysteries and all knowledge and if I have all faith so that I may remove mountains, and I have no love in me, I would be nothing.

3. And if I should feed everything that I have to the poor, and if I hand over my body to be burned up and I have no love in me, I gain nothing.

4. Love is patient and sweet; love does not envy; love is not upset neither puffed up.

5. Love does not commit what is shameful, neither does it seek its own; it is not provoked, neither does it entertain evil thoughts,

6. Rejoices not in evil, but rejoices in the truth,

7. Endures all things, believes all things, hopes all, bears all.

8. Love never fails; for prophecies shall cease, tongues shall be silenced and knowledge will be nothing;

9. For we know partially and we prophesy partially,

10. But when perfection shall come, then that which is partial shall be nothing.

11. When I was a child, I was speaking as a child, I was led as a child, I was thinking as a child, but when I became a man, I ceased these childish things.

12. Now we see as in a mirror, in an allegory, but then face-to-face. Now I know partially, but then I shall know as I am known.

13. For there are these three things that endure: Faith, Hope and Love, but the greatest of these is Love.

Chapter 14

1. Run after love and be zealous for the gifts of The Spirit, but especially that you may prophesy.

2. For whoever speaks in languages does not speak to men, but he is speaking to God, for no man understands what he speaks, but by The Spirit he speaks mysteries.

3. But he who prophesies speaks edification, encouragement and comfort to children of men.

4. He who speaks in languages builds himself up, and he who prophesies builds the church up.

5. I wish that all of you might speak in languages, but all the more that you may prophesy, for he who prophesies is greater than he who speaks in languages, unless he translates; but if he translates, he edifies the church.

6. And now my brethren, if I come to you and speak languages with you, what do I benefit you, unless I shall speak with you either by revelation or knowledge or by prophecy or by teaching?

7. For even inanimate things which give sound, whether a flute or harp, if they make no distinction between one tone and another, how will anything that is played or anything that is harped be known?

8. For if a trumpet make a sound which is not distinct, who will be prepared for battle?

9. So you also, if you will say words in languages and you will not translate, how will anything be known that you say, for you yourselves will be as one who is speaking to the air.

10. For behold, there are many kinds of languages in the world, and there is not one of them without sound.

N * *Greek has "Φωνων" – "Phonone" – "Sounds" where The Peshitta has "languages".The Aramaic for "Sounds" would be "קלא", "קלני", "קלין". In DSS script:. קٍٍٍٍ, קٍٍٍٍ. "Languages" in DSS is קٍٍٍٍٍٍ. I do think the Aramaic קٍٍٍٍٍٍ -"D'leshana" was misread as קٍٍٍٍ –"Qalanaya". The fact is that the Greek word - "Φωνων" – "Phonone" – "Sounds" can also mean "voices" or "languages"; It refers to "language" in 2 Maccabees in The LXX several times. I have highlighted the above two grey shaded words simply to illustrate that even the two most similar do not reach the level of correlation needed to support a relationship and basis for explaining a Greek reading as a translation of a misread Aramaic word. There is at least 60% letter correlation (3 out of 5) between the two Aramaic words. That is not too low a score to support that קٍٍٍٍٍٍ was read as קٍٍٍٍ. What I do affirm of the Greek of this verse is that it is very awkward and that it does not explain the distinct Aramaic words – "Leshana" – לשנא – "Languages" and קלא – "Qala" – "Sound" at the end. The Greek has in the place of each Aramaic word- "φωνων" – "Phonone" & αφωνος – "Aphonos". "Aphonos" is a negative of "Phonos". It means "Noiseless", "Dumb", "Voiceless". Both Greek words have the same root – "φωνη"- "Phone". It does not make good sense to say, "There are many phonics in the world, and not one of them is without phonics"- but this is what the Greek says. If "phonics" refers to language, then "a-phonics" refers to "no language"; if it is "sound", then "a-phonics" refers to "no sound". The Greek is unclear and confused; The Aramaic is quite clear, using two distinct words: "Leshana"- "Language" and "D'la Qala"- "without sound". I reject the notion that The Peshitta is clear because it "fixes" the confusing or unclear readings of the original Greek. The original New Testament would not be ridiculous or absurd; the Greek NT is just that in some places. The errors cannot be evaded or erased. Some are in every known Greek witness to a particular text.*

11. And if I do not know the import of the sound, I am a foreigner to him who speaks, and also he who speaks is a foreigner to me.

12. So also you, because you are zealous of the gifts of The Spirit, seek to excel for the edification of the church.

13. And he who speaks in languages, let him pray to translate.

14. For if I should pray in languages, my spirit is praying, but my understanding is unfruitful.

15. What therefore shall I do? I shall pray with my spirit, and I shall pray also with my understanding. I shall sing with my spirit, and I shall sing also with my understanding.

16. Otherwise, if you say a blessing in The Spirit, how will he who fills the place of the unlearned say amen for your giving of thanks, because he does not know what you said?

17. For you bless well, but your neighbor is not edified.

18. I thank God that I am speaking in languages more than all of you,

19. But in the church I would rather speak five words with my understanding, that I may instruct others also, than ten thousand words in languages.

20. My brethren, do not be children in your intellects, but be infants in evil and be fully mature in your intellects.

21. It is written in the law, "With foreign speech and with another language I shall speak with this people, and not even in this way will they hear me, says THE LORD JEHOVAH."

22. So then languages are established for a sign, not for believers, but for unbelievers, but prophecy is not for unbelievers, but for those who believe.

23. If therefore it should happen that the whole church assembles and everyone would speak in languages, and the uninitiated or those who are unbelievers should enter, would they not say that such have gone insane?

24. But if all of you would prophesy and the unlearned or an unbeliever should enter, he is searched out by all of you and he is reproved by all of you.

25. And the secrets of his heart are revealed and then he will fall on his face and worship God and he will say, "Truly, God is in you."

26. I say therefore, my brethren, that whenever you gather, whoever among you has a Psalm, let him speak, or whoever has a teaching, or whoever has a revelation, or whoever has a language, or whoever has a

translation, let all things be done for edification.

27. And if any speak in languages, let two speak, or as many as three, and let each one speak and let one translate.

28. And if there is no translator, let him who speaks in a language be silent in the church and let him speak to himself and to God.

29. But let two or three Prophets speak and the others discern.

30. And if something is revealed to another while the first is sitting, let him be quiet.

31. For you can all prophesy one by one, that each person may teach and everyone may be comforted.

32. For the spirit of the Prophet is subject to the Prophet,

33. Because God is not chaotic, but peaceful, as in all the assemblies of The Holy Ones.

34. Let your women be silent in the assemblies, for they are not allowed to speak, but to be in subjection, just as The Written Law also says.

35. And if they wish to learn anything, let them ask their husbands in their homes, for it is a shame for women to speak in the assembly.

36. Or did the word of God come forth from you, or does it come unto you alone?

37. But if any of you thinks that he is a Prophet or spiritual, let him know that these things I write to you are the commandments of Our Lord.

38. But if a man is ignorant, let him be ignorant.

39. Be zealous therefore, my brethren, to prophesy, and do not forbid to speak in languages.

40. But let everything be done with decorum and with order.

Chapter 15

1. I teach you, my brethren, The Gospel that I preached to you, and you received it and you stand in it,

2. And by it you have life in that message which I preached to you, if you remember *, unless you have believed worthlessly.

---

* Greek mss. all have "**if ye hold fast**" "ει κατεχετε" , where **The Peshitta** has "**If you remember**". Here is the Aramaic for "**hold**" in the plural: אחידין , אחידין .Compare these with עהדין –"**remember**", **The Peshitta** reading above.
Ashuri Aramaic:
אחדין –"Hold"
עהדין – "Remember"
Dead Sea Scroll script:

אאזזש –"**Hold**"
עזזש –"**Remember**"
Either script displays very close resemblance between the two words. One extra small downward stroke on the **Ayin** of the DSS script - ש would make it an **Alap** -א ; Everything else is essentially the same in both words. This illustrates plainly how the Greek reading was derived from The Peshitta's Aramaic. The Greek word for "**You remember**" is μνημονευετε . Does that resemble "κατεχετε" –"you hold" ? Hardly ! The Greek cannot credibly account for **the Peshitta** reading here.
A good injunction for all who seek the truth: "**Remember**" this evidence and all the rest I have presented and that yet to come.

3. For I have declared to you from the first, according to that which I have received: The Messiah died for the sake of our sins, just as it is written;

4. And he was buried, and he arose on the third day, according to what is written;

5. And he appeared to Kaypha, and after him, to the twelve.

6. And after that, he appeared to more than five hundred brethren together, many of whom remain until now, and some of them have fallen asleep.

7. And after these things, he appeared to Yaqob, and after him, to all the Apostles,

8. But to the last of all of them, as if to an aborted baby, he appeared also to me.

9. For I am the least of the Apostles and I am not worthy to be called an Apostle, because I persecuted the church of God.

10. But by the grace of God I am whatever I am, and his grace which is in me has not been worthless, but I have labored more than all of them; not I, but his grace that is with me.

11. Whether I, therefore, or they, in this way we preach, and in this way you have believed.

12. But if The Messiah who arose from among the dead is preached, how are there some among you who say there is no life for the dead?

---

* חית מיתא –"**Khayth mitha**"-"**life of the dead**" -See Matthew 22:23; this phrase has to do with the afterlife, not bodily resurrection. The same phrase was used by the Sadducees who denied the afterlife. Our Lord quoted the Written Law (the only books Sadducees accepted) to show Abraham,Isaac and Jacob were alive after death. He did not refer to their physical resurrection, as their dead bodies had never been raised from their graves. So this passage in Cor. refers to spiritual life after physical death; it also would apply to salvation for the lost. The word "**Khaya**" very often refers to **salvation**; a high percentage of occurrences are paralleled by the Greek root , "σωζω"- (Sozo)-"**To save**". When The Holy Spirit uses the words – "**Living**"& "**Life**"(חיא & חית) , He does not refer to those who are half dead or completely dead. He refers to those who have eternal life. "**Life from the dead**" or "**Life of the dead**" is the salvation of those who are lost, not a mere bodily resurrection of spiritually dead people.

13. And if there is no life for the dead, even The Messiah has not risen.

14. And if The Messiah is not risen, our preaching is worthless and your faith is also worthless.

15. But we are also found to be lying witnesses of God, for we testified of God that he raised The Messiah, when he did not raise him.

16. For if those who have died do not live again, not even The Messiah is alive.

קם –"Quum" and קימין –"Quumine" can mean , "rise,stand, **be alive**,abide,exist". Here is the entry for קים from Smith's Compendious Syriac Dictionary :

ܩܳܐܶܡ, ܩܳܡܐ rt. ܩܘܡ. in being, existing, still alive; continuing, lasting; ܩܳܐܶܡ ܝܰܘܡܐ it is yet high day; ܐܢ ܩܳܝܡܝܢ ܫܢ̈ܝܐ ܣܓ̈ܝܐܬܐ if there be yet many years; ܐܢ ܩܰܝܳܡ ܐܰܒܘܗܝ if his father be yet alive; ܩܳܐܶܡ ܠܥܳܠܰܡ abiding for ever; ܒܶܝܬ ܡܳܐܶܬ ܠܒܶܝܬ ܩܳܐܶܡ half-alive;

Since the same root word is used both of those who died and The Messiah, I have used the same translation here to illustrate the drama of Paul's argument for the universal results of the resurrection of The Messiah Yeshua, in which he uses reverse logic to illustrate the absurdity of denying universalism: **"If those who have died do not live again, then The Messiah is dead."**

17. And if The Messiah is not alive, your faith is empty and you are yet in your sins;

18. Doubtless also those who fell asleep in The Messiah have themselves perished.

19. And if in this life only we hope in The Messiah, so it is that we are more wretched than all people.

20. But now The Messiah is risen from among the dead and is the first fruits of those who sleep.

21. Just as by a man death came, in this way also by a man the dead come to life .

22. For just as by Adam all people die, in this way also by The Messiah they all live;

23. Each person in his order; The Messiah was the first fruits; after this, those who are The Messiah's at his arrival.

24. And then the end will come, when he will deliver The Kingdom to God The Father, when he will destroy every Ruler and every Authority and all Powers.

25. For he is going to reign until all his enemies will be set under his feet,

26. And the last enemy death shall be destroyed.

27. For he brought all things to submission under his feet. But when it says, "All things are subjected to him", it is understood that it excludes him who subjected all things to him.

28. And when all is subjected to him, then the Son shall be subject to him who subjected all things to him, that God might be all in all.

29. Otherwise, what shall those do who are baptized for the sake of the dead, if the dead do not live again? Why are they baptized for the sake of the dead?

30. And why are we living in peril every hour?

31. I swear by your pride, my brethren, which I have in Our Lord Yeshua The Messiah, that I die every day.

32. And if, as a citizen of the people, I was cast to wild beasts in Ephesaus, what have I gained if the dead do not rise? Let us eat and drink, for tomorrow we die.

* Greek has εθηριομαχησα -"**I beast fought**" (word not found anywhere else in Greek ?) **The Peshitta** says – "אשתדית לחיותא"- "**I was cast to wild beasts**";
The verbs in Ashuri script are:
אשתדית -"**I was cast**"
אצתנית is -"**I have fought**";
Let's see them in the old DSS script:

אשתרית -"**I was cast**";
אצ֗תנית -"**I have fought**"

Estrangela script:

ܐܫܬܕܝܬ -"**I was cast**";

ܐܨܛܢܝܬ -"**I have fought**"

I see at least **66% correlation** here. Ashuri & DSS has perhaps **75%**.
Greek for "**I was cast to beasts**" is: θηριοις εβληθην or θηριοις επερριφην.These look little like εθηριομαχησα. (5 of 14 letters are the same-**36% correlation** at best).

33. Be not deceived, evil discourse* corrupts pleasant minds.

* Greek mss. have "ομιλια"-"**companionship**" (found once in **The Greek NT**) . The Aramaic שועיתא – "**Shawaytha**","talking,discourse", is very similar to שויתא –"**Shawytha**", "**agreement, fellowship,equality**". The Aramaic שועיתא – "**Shawaytha**","talking,discourse"occurs four times apart from this verse. In those places the Greek has μυθος, "**Mythos**"-"speech,saying, story,fable". If the Aramaic were translated from Greek, it is unlikely "ομιλια" would be translated שועיתא-"**Shawaytha**" .It would most likely be translated שויתא – "**Shawytha**". The adding of the third letter ע (Ayin) to form שועיתא-"**Shawaytha**" by accident would be too fortuitous and unlikely an event to account for **the Peshitta** reading. Scribal errors are far more likely to involve omissions than additions; Nor would "ομιλια"**(Homilia)** be mistaken for "μυθος" or the plural "μυθοι". It is far more likely שועיתא – "**Shawaytha**"was misread as שויתא –"**Shawytha**" by a Greek translator, who wrote "ομιλια" where he should have written "μυθοι"-**(fables,stories)**. The two Aramaic words have **an 84% correlation.**

A graphic review & illustration:
Ashuri script :
שועיתא – "**Shawaytha**"-"talking,discourse ".
שויתא – "**Shawytha**"- "agreement, fellowship,equality ".
Dead Sea Scroll:
שועיתא– "**Shawaytha**"-"talking,discourse ".
שויתא–"**Shawytha**"-"agreement, fellowship, equality ".
Estrangela script:

ܫܘܬܐ -"Shawaytha"-"talking, discourse".

ܫܘܬܐ -"Shawytha"- "agreement, fellowship, equality

34. Righteously awaken your hearts and do not sin, for there are some in whom the knowledge of God does not exist. I say that to your shame.

35. Someone among you will say, "How do the dead rise? With what body do they come?"

36. Fool! The seed that you plant will not live unless it dies.

37. And the thing which you sow is not that body which is going to be, for you sow a naked grain of wheat or barley or of other grain.

38. But God gives it a body just as he chooses and to each one of the grains a body of its nature.

39. But not every body is equal to another, for there is the body of a man and another of an ox and another of a bird and another of a fish.

40. And there is a Heavenly body and there is an Earthly body, but there is one glory of the Heavenly and another of the Earthly.

41. And there is one glory of the sun and another glory of the moon and another glory of a star, and one star is greater than another star in glory.

42. Thus also is the life for those who die. It is sown with corruption, it rises without corruption. ("It is sown" refers to "life"-"Khaytha" which is always plural grammatically and takes plural verbs, though translated as singular. The Greek also translates this as singular.)

43. It is sown with disgrace, it rises with glory; it is sown in weakness, it rises in power.

44. It is sown an animal body; a spiritual body rises, for there is an animal body, and there is a spiritual body.

45. Thus also it is written: "Adam the first man was a living soul; the last Adam - The Life Giver Spirit.

46. But the first was not spiritual, but the animal, and then the spiritual.

47. The first man was dust from the ground; The second man, THE LORD JEHOVAH from Heaven.

48. Just as he who was a being of dust, so also is that which is of the dust, and just as he who is The Being from Heaven, so also is the Heavenly.

49. And as we have worn the image of him who is from the dust, so we shall wear the image of him who is from Heaven.

50. But this I say my brethren: flesh and blood cannot inherit The Kingdom of Heaven, neither does corruption inherit indestructibility.

51. Behold, I tell you a mystery: we shall not all sleep, but we shall all be transformed,

52. Suddenly, like the blink of an eye, at the last trumpet, when it shall sound, and the dead shall rise without corruption, and we shall be transformed.

53. For this destructible is going to wear indestructibility and this mortal shall wear immortality.

54. Whenever this destructible puts on indestructibility and this mortal, immortality, then that word which is written shall come to pass, "Death is swallowed up by victory."

55. Where is your sting, oh death? Where is your victory, oh, Sheol?

56. But the sting of death is sin and the power of sin is The Written Law.

57. But thank God who gives us the victory by Our Lord Yeshua The Messiah.

58. From now on, my brethren and beloved, be steadfast; do not be shaken, but be abounding at all times in the work of THE LORD JEHOVAH, as you know that your toil has not been worthless in THE LORD JEHOVAH.

Chapter 16

1. But concerning that which has been collected for the Saints, just as I have commanded the church of Galatia, do so also.

2. On every Sunday, let each person of you lay aside in his house and keep that which he can, so that when I come there will be no collections.

3. And when I shall come, those whom you elect I shall send with a letter to carry your gift to Jerusalem.

4. But if it is appropriate for me to visit, when I depart, they shall depart with me.

5. But I will come to you when I have passed from Macedonia, for I shall pass through Macedonia.

6. And perhaps I shall remain with you or winter with you, that you may accompany me wherever I go.

7. I do not wish to see you now as I pass by the way, for I hope to tarry for a time with you, if my Lord allows me,

8. But I am staying in Ephesaus until Pentecost.

9. For a great door is opened to me, filled with opportunities and many opponents.

10. But if Timotheus comes to you, see that he will not be intimidated by you, for he cultivates the works of THE LORD JEHOVAH, as do I,

11. Lest therefore any should despise him; but accompany him in peace, that he may come join me, for I wait for him with the brethren.

12. And I have wanted Apollo to come to you very much, my brethren, with the brethren, but doubtless he did not wish to come to you, but when he has time he will come to you.

13. Be alert and stand in the faith; be valiant; be strong.

14. And let all your dealings be with love.

15. But I request of you, my brethren, concerning the house of Estephana, because you know that they are the first generation of Akaia, and they put themselves into the service of The Holy Ones,

16. That you also will listen to those who are such and to every person who toils and helps with us.

17. But I rejoice at the arrival of Estephana, of Fortunatus and Akayqus, for they have supplied things to me which you lacked.

18. For they have refreshed my spirit and yours; do therefore recognize those who are such.

19. All the assemblies in Asia invoke your peace; Aqelaus and Priscilla invoke your peace much in Our Lord, with the assembly that is in their house.

20. All the brethren invoke your peace. Invoke the peace one of another with a holy kiss.

21. Salutations in my own handwriting, (Paulus').

22. Whoever does not love Our Lord Yeshua The Messiah, let him be damned. Our Lord has come.

I think I understand why Paul wrote, "**let him be damned**". Jesus The Messiah is so precious to those who know Him and they love Him so much that the thought and feeling toward a professing Christian who does not love Him is, "**to hell with him**". I do not believe this verse consigns the unbeliever to eternal damnation, though it is a very tempting concept for believers; our love to God can blind us at times to His love for His enemies. We must remember that all of us were enemies toward God at one time. If we love Him now, it is because He first loved us and sacrificed Himself to save us. It is by sheer mercy and grace that we are saved; that same grace and mercy is to be extended to all who are lost. They are dead in sins and the emptiness of the world system.
This verse refers to those in the church body, not those outside. "**What have I to do to judge those outside** ",

wrote Paul. All false brethren deserve to be excommunicated and ostracized from all Christian fellowship. They belong to Satan, and should be delivered over to him fully, so that they either repent or die and suffer the eternal torments, "**that their spirits may be saved in the Day of Our Lord The Messiah**". **Eternal** torment is not "**everlasting torment** "; we must distinguish the two. "**D'lama** " is "**that which is timeless**", according to Paul. "**Everlasting** " defines an infinite time. Infinite time cannot be timeless. Here I leave the matter for the reader to decide what "**eternal torment** " means.

* Greek mss. have μαραν αθα -"**Maran atha**" or μαρανα θα -"**Marana tha**". This two word phrase is two Aramaic words, not Greek at all, not even loan words from Aramaic; these are two Aramaic words in Greek letters. The Majority Greek text has μαραν αθα , -"**Maran atha**" from מרן אתא meaning "**Our Lord has come**" or "**Our Lord is coming**". The Critical Greek has μαρανα θα -"**Marana tha**", which comes from מרנא תא ? – "**Come, Our Lord**".

What business had Paul writing an Aramaic phrase to Greek speakers in Corinth ? The only reasonable explanation is that this is evidence of an Aramaic original (**The Peshitta** has מרן אתא - "**Maran atha**" -"**Our Lord has come**").For some reason, the Greek translator avoided translating this phrase into Greek and transliterated it instead. I surmise that it was thought incriminating to write in Greek that "**Our Lord had come**" in the Roman Empire where Greek was known and where Christian loyalty to The Christ was considered subversive and treasonous toward Caesar. To write that "**He was present**" in The Roman Empire might aggravate Caesar (especially Nero) as Christ's birth did Herod the Tetrarch and he was moved to kill all male children two years old and under in Bethlehem. **The Greek NT** was intended for all Greek-speaking peoples in The Empire of the first century. The Aramaic original was sent to all the churches addressed in the Epistles, as those congregations were founded and largely peopled by Aramaic speaking Jews of the diasporas of Babylon and afterward.

This "**Maran atha**" transliteration supports an Aramaic original and a Greek translation of that Aramaic original.

23. The grace of Our Lord Yeshua The Messiah is with you,

24. And my love is with all of you in The Messiah Yeshua.

The Original Aramaic New Testament in Plain English

The Second Epistle of The Apostle Paul to the Corinthians

Chapter 1

1. Paul an Apostle of Yeshua The Messiah by the will of God, and brother Timotheus, to the assembly of God that is in Qorinthus and to all the Holy who are in all Akaia.

2. Grace be with you and peace from God our Father and from Our Lord Yeshua The Messiah.

3. Blessed is God The Father of Our Lord Yeshua The Messiah, The Father of mercy and The God of all comfort,

4. He who comforts us in all our afflictions that we also can comfort those who are in all our afflictions, with that comfort by which we are comforted from God.

5. For just as the sufferings of The Messiah abound in us, in this way our comforts also abound by The Messiah.

6. But if we are afflicted, it is for the sake of your comfort and for the sake of your life that we are afflicted. And if we are comforted, it is so that you may be comforted, and that there may be discipline in you to endure those sufferings that we also suffer.

7. And our hope for you is sure, for we know that if you are partners in suffering, you are also partners in comfort.

8. But we want you to know, brethren, concerning the affliction that we had in Asia, that we were afflicted greatly beyond our power, until we were close to losing our lives.

9. We passed a sentence of death upon ourselves, that we would not trust upon ourselves, but upon God who raises the dead,

10. He who has delivered us from violent deaths * , and again we hope that he will deliver us,

* Greek mss. have- "**delivered us from death, delivers, and we hope that He will deliver us**". חסינא – "**powerful, violent**" was apparently misread by the original Greek translator as the verb חסא – "**spares**", "**pardons**".Here are the two words side by side in **DSS** script:

חסאנא – "**violent, powerful**"
חסא – "**spares**", "**pardons**"

This is strong support for a Peshitta Aramaic original and a Greek translation version of that Peshitta Aramaic original for **2 Corinthians**, as in the case of **1 Corinthians** and in **Romans** as well. This kind of evidence exists through all of Paul's Epistles , even in the one page Epistle of **Philemon!**

11. By the help of your prayers for our persons, that his gift * to us may be a favor done for the sake of the many, that the many may confess him because of us.

* "**His gift**" is not in the Greek; nor is "**may confess Him**"; Greek has "**for the gift bestowed upon us by means of many, thanks may be given by many persons on our behalf**." God seems to have been displaced in the Greek text by humans.

12. For our pride is this testimony of our conscience, that in generosity and in purity* and in the grace of God we have been employed in the world, and not in the wisdom of the flesh, and all the more with you and yours.

* Greek has "**sincerity of God**"- ειλικρινεια θεου where The Aramaic verse has only ובדכיותא "**& in purity**". A similar phenomenon occurs in about 30 verses in the NT where Greek has "God" or "Christ" and The Peshitta does not, or does it ? A careful scrutiny of such verses shows that in about 22 of those verses, Aramaic has a noun or verb connected to the Deity in which the first two letters or the last two letters of that word are Alap-Tau or Tau-Alap – the first and last letters of the Aramaic alphabet, which are named in Revelation 1:8 as The Name of The **LORD** God and Messiah; they are so used three times in Revelation. It so happens that the word "**Purity**" in this verse has **Tau-Alap** at the end of it: ובדכיותא ; It also so happens that the noun ובדכיות without those last two letters has exactly the same meaning it has with them- "**Purity**". This seems to be the trend in those 22 verses; the "**code word**" with Alap-Tau has essentially the same meaning even without those two letters , which two letters are then apparently translated as **Theos** (God) or **Christos** (Christ) or even a word associated with Deity: χρειματιζομαι –"**Divinely revealed**" or ευσεβεια –"**Divine virtue**". **See my book , Divine Contact** for the complete list and discussion of this **Alap-Tau Code** in **The Greek NT**, available at http://aramaicnt.com

13. We write nothing else to you but those things that you know and you acknowledge, but I trust that you will acknowledge them until the end;

14. Just as you also have acknowledged a few things, that we are your pride as you are also ours, in the day of Our Lord Yeshua The Messiah.

15. With this trust I was willing from the first to come to you that you might receive double grace.

16. And I shall pass by you to Macedonia and again from Macedonia I shall come to you and you will accompany me to Judea.

17. This that I purposed, did I purpose it suddenly? Or perhaps those things that I plan are of the flesh, so that it was necessary for there to be in them, "Yes, yes." and, "No, no."?

18. God is trustworthy, so that our word to you was not "Yes" and "No".
19. For The Son of God, Yeshua The Messiah, who was preached by us to you (by me, by Sylvanus and by Timotheus), was not "Yes" and "No', but in him was, "Yes"!
20. For all The Promises of God in him, (that is in The Messiah), were "Yes"; because of this we give the "Amen" by him to the glory of God.
21. But it is God who establishes us with you in The Messiah, he who has anointed us.
22. And he has sealed us and he has given the down payment of his Spirit into our hearts.
23. But I am testifying to God concerning myself: Because I had pity for you, I did not come to Qorinthus,
24. Not because we are lords of your faith, but we are helpers of your joy, for it is by faith that you stand.

Chapter 2

1. But I decided this in myself that I would not come again in sorrow to you.
2. For if I sadden you, who will gladden me, if not the one whom I sadden?
3. And what I wrote to you is this: that those who ought to give me joy would not make me sad when I come; but I do trust in all of you that my joy but I do trust in all of you that my joy is all yours.
4. And I wrote to you these things in many tears from great suffering and anguish of heart, not so that you would grieve, but so that you would know the abundant love that I have for you.
5. But if a man grieves me, it is not me he grieves, but in a small fashion all of you, so that this statement should not weigh upon you.
6. But this rebuke that is from the many is sufficient for him.
7. And now on the other hand, it is necessary to forgive him and comfort him, lest he who is such be swallowed up in excessive grief.
8. Therefore I beseech you to confirm your love to him.
9. For this cause I have written also to know by a test if you are obedient in everything.
10. But the one whom you forgive, I forgive also; for anything that I forgave him, that which I forgave in the presence of The Messiah I forgave for your sakes,
11. Lest Satan would overtake us, for we know * his devices.

*Greek mss. all have "**We are not ignorant of his devices**".

12. But when I came to Troas with The Gospel of The Messiah and a door was opened to me by **THE LORD JEHOVAH**,
13. I had no rest in my spirit, for I did not find Titus, my brother, but I left them and went out to Macedonia.
14. But I thank God, who at all times makes us a vision in The Messiah and reveals the fragrance of his knowledge by us in every place.

* For "**a spectacle**" - חזתא ; In Pesher Habakkuk DSS: חזות .Greek mss. have "θριαμβευοντι" –"**to triumph**". The Aramaic for "**to triumph**" is נזכא - זכתא -זנותא or דכיא - זנותא or זכיא - זנותא ; "**Victory**" is זכותא - זנותא . Here is the actual Peshitta reading "**Vision**" and the Aramaic for "**Victory**" one under the other in Dead Sea Scroll Aramaic script: חזות -"**Vision**"
זנותא -"**Victory**"

How uncanny is that! If the first two letters of the second word were closer together, the words would be almost identical! It is possible to misconstrue the first word for the second. If the original Aramaic manuscript being translated had a slight break at the top of the first letter- ח –**Khet** , it might have looked like the two letters זנ –**Zayin , Kap**; indeed the Khet does look like two letters put together: ח and the alternate letter reading in small fonts looks like this: זנ .
Here again are the two –the actual and the hypothetical as it may have been interpreted by a Greek translator:

Actual Peshitta Aramaic reading: חזות
= "**Vision, Spectacle**"
Hypothetical Greek translation Aramaic base זנותא
= "**Victory**"
The Comprehensive Aramaic Lexicon (Online) has the following entry for the Peshitta's reading- חזתא - "**Khzatha**"
hzt (ḥzāṭā) n.f. sight

1 the faculty of sight Syr.
2 aspect, appearance Syr.
3 spectacle, wondrous appearance Syr.
4 visitation Syr.
5 spectacle, theatrical performance Syr.
The Greek for "**vision**" is θεωρια or οραμα or οπτασια or ορασις - Which of these looks like θριαμβευοντι – "**to triumph**" ? It would seem that the Aramaic did not come from the Greek reading, but rather the Greek reading came from the Aramaic of the Peshitta.

15. For we are a sweet fragrance to God in The Messiah among those who have life and among those who perish;
16. To the latter, the stench of death for death, and to the former, the fragrance of The Life for life. And who shall be worthy for these things?
17. For we are not like others who blend the words of God, but according to that which is in the truth and according to that which is

from God, before God in The Messiah we speak.

* שרכא- "**Others**" is in **P⁴⁶**, **D** and most Greek mss.. "**Many**" is found in a few mss.- (**א, B , TR**). "**Many**" in Aramaic is סניאא (mis-spelled) or סגיאא. **In DSS** (one Ashuri letter) **script**:

שׁרכא- "**Others**"

סגיאא- "**Many**"

I estimate **73% correlation** in the above pair (8 strokes out of 11)
It could have happened, especially in DSS script. Rotate the second and third letters in שׁרכא counterclockwise 35 degrees and you have something that could be construed as ס⅄⅄א. The Shin שׁ may have been more like the Ashuri Shin שׁ , which is closer to a Semkat - ס : שׁ ⅄ א -"**Others**" with two rotated letters (-35 degrees).The Shin שׁ is a bit smaller to show how it could be misread as ס ⅄⅄א -"**Many**". Greek for "**Others**" is λοιποι; "**Many**" is πολλοι. These in Greek Uncial script are ΛΟΙΠΟΙ :
ΠΟΛΛΟΙ
The Greek pair has **50% correlation**

Chapter 3

1. Do we introduce ourselves again from the beginning to show you what we are, or do we need, as others, letters of commandments to be written to you about us, or for you to write to give decrees concerning us?

2. But you are our letter written in our heart and known and read by everyone.

3. For you know that you are a letter of The Messiah that is ministered by us, written not in ink, but by The Spirit of **THE LIVING GOD**, not in tablets of stone, but in tablets of hearts of flesh.

4.But in this way we have trust in The Messiah toward God,

5. Not that we are sufficient to think anything as from ourselves, but our power is from God,

6. He who made us worthy to be Ministers of The New Covenant, not in The Scripture, but in The Spirit, for The Scripture kills, but The Spirit gives life.

7. But if the ministry of death in The Scripture carved in stone was with glory, so that the children of Israel were not able to gaze at the face of Moses because of the glory of his face (that which has been canceled),

8. How shall therefore the ministry of The Spirit not be all the more with glory?

9. For if the administration of a guilty verdict was certain glory, how much more shall the administration of righteousness superabound in glory?

10. For that which was glorified was not even glorious by comparison to that excellent glory.

11. For if that which has been eliminated was with glory, all the more that which remains shall be with glory.

12. Therefore, because we have this hope, we conduct ourselves publicly all the more.

13. And not as Moses who had laid a veil over his face, so that the children of Israel would not gaze at the termination of that which was ceasing.

14. But they were blinded * in their understanding; for until today whenever the Old Testament is read, that veil remains over them, and it is not revealed that it is being abolished by The Messiah.

* **The Greek NT** has επωρωθη –"**were hardened**"; **The Peshitta** Aramaic word here is אתעורו –"**were blinded**".Here is the Aramaic word for "**Were hardened**" is אתעביו . Let's line up the two Aramaic words side by side in three Aramaic scripts:

English	Ashuri	DSS	Estrangela
"blinded"	אתעורו	אתעורו	ܐܬܥܘܪܘ
"hardened"	אתעביו	אתעביו	ܐܬܥܒܝܘ

Again, the DSS script reveals the closest resemblance between the actual Peshitta reading and the hypothetical Aramaic base for **The Greek NT** translation. There is **83% letter to letter correlation in the two DSS words**. The underlined letters are Resh and Yodh, respectively, which are practically identical but are oriented a bit differently. I suspect that the Resh ר would have been rotated about 35 degrees counterclockwise - ⅂ and the Waw ו to its right had been written hastily with an extra and inadvertent leftward bottom stroke after the down stroke- ⅃ The result would be something like ו ⅂ ⅃ אתע , which might well pass as אתעבי⅄. The Estrangela pair is second with **65%** correlation. The Greek word for "**were blinded**" would be "ετυφλωθη".Compare "επωρωθη" –"**were hardened**" , the actual Greek reading. In uncial Greek, these words are:

ΕΤΥΦΛΩΘΗ - : ΕΠΩΡΩΘΗ (uncial script was used in most ancient Greek mss.).This is **63% correlation**. The root words of each of these Greek words are what differ here, "ΤΥΦΛ"- ("**Blind**") and "ΠΩΡ"- ("**Hard**"), which makes unlikely the prospect that the one was mistaken for the other . The similar letters are the grammatical verb endings that define person, number and mood of the verbs; The first letter E helps define tense – all these letters are the same in hundreds of different Greek verbs. No matter how one analyzes this, Peshitta primacy finds support here while Greek primacy suffers another setback.

15. And until today, whenever Moses is read, the veil is laid over their heart,

16. And whenever anyone of them will be turned to **THE LORD JEHOVAH**, the veil is taken away from him.

* Greek has "**when he (it) turns to The Lord**…"; "**Anyone of them**" is not there in Greek, making the subject very difficult to determine: "**Moses**" , "**the veil**", "**their heart**" ?

17. But The Spirit is **THE LORD JEHOVAH**, and wherever The Spirit of **THE LORD JEHOVAH** is, there is freedom.

18. But we all see the glory of **THE LORD JEHOVAH** with unveiled faces, as in a mirror, and we are changed into the image from glory to glory, as from **THE LORD JEHOVAH, THE SPIRIT.**

Chapter 4

1. **B**ecause of this, it has not been tiresome to us in this ministry which we hold, as mercy has been upon us.

2. But we reject shameful cover-ups and we do not walk in craftiness, neither do we deny the word of God, but we display our souls in the revelation of the truth to all the minds of the children of men before God.

3. But if our gospel is covered up, it is covered up to those who are lost,

4. Those whose intellects The God of this world has blinded, because they do not believe, lest the light of The Gospel of the glory of The Messiah, who is the image of God, should dawn upon them.

5. For we have not been preaching ourselves, but The Messiah Yeshua, Our Lord; but we ourselves are your Servants for Yeshua's sake.

6. For God', who spoke that light would shine out of the darkness, has dawned in our hearts that we would be enlightened with the knowledge of the glory of God in the face of Yeshua The Messiah.

7. But we have this treasure in Earthen vessels, that the greatness of the power would be from God and not from us.

8. For we are squeezed in all things, but we are not strangled; we are harassed, but we are not condemned.

9. We are persecuted, but we are not forsaken; We are cast down, but we are not defeated.

10. We bear at all times in our bodies the dying of Yeshua, that the life also of Yeshua may be revealed in our bodies.

11. For if we, the living, are delivered to death for the sake of Yeshua, so also the life of Yeshua will be revealed in this, our mortal body.

12. Now death labors in us and life in you.

13. Therefore, we also in whom is that one spirit of faith, as it is written: "I have

believed; because of this I also have spoken", we believe; because of this we also speak.

14. And we know that he who raised Our Lord Yeshua shall also raise us up by Yeshua and shall bring us with you to him.

15. For everything is for your sakes, and when grace abounds, thanksgiving will abound by the many to the glory of God.

16. Because of this, it is not tiresome to us, for even if our external person is being destroyed, on the other hand, that which is from within is renewed day by day.

17. For the suffering of this time, while very small and swift, prepares us great glory without limits for the eternity of eternities.

18. For we do not rejoice * in those things that are seen, but in these things that are unseen. For things seen are time related, but those things that are unseen are eternal.

 * Greek has "**We do not look upon things seen**" .
Peshitta has , לא חדינן -"We do not rejoice".
 A possibility for the Greek reading in Aramaic is -
לא חרינן -"We do not look"
Ashuri Aramaic script above shows **88%** letter correlation between the two underlined verbs.

Let's see them both in Dead Sea Scroll script:
ﬤﬤ ﬡﬡ -"We do not rejoice".
ﬤﬤ ﬡﬡ -"We do not look"
Dead Sea Scroll script verbs in the two readings above have **88%** letter correlation.

The Greek reading is ΜΗ ΣΚΟΠΟΥΝΤΩΝ ΗΜΩΝ -"we are not looking"
 ΜΗ ΧΑΙΡΟΝΤΩΝ ΗΜΩΝ –"we are not rejoicing"
The Greek verbs underlined above show **50%** letter correlation at best.
The Peshitta much better explains the Greek reading than vice versa.

Chapter 5

1. **F**or we know that surely this our bodily house * that is in The Earth will be destroyed; but there is a building for us that is from God, a house which is not by the work of hands, in Heaven for eternity.

 * Greek has **σκηνους** –"Tent".

2. For concerning this also we are made to groan, and we long to wear our house that is from Heaven,

3. If also whenever we are clothed we shall not be found naked.

4. For as we are now in this house, we are made to groan by its weight, and we do not want to strip it off, but to put on over it, that its mortality may be swallowed up by life.

5. And he who prepares us for this is God; he it is who gives us the down payment of his Spirit.

* Greek has αρραβονα – arrabon "earnest money" ; **Thayer's Greek Lexicon** has the Hebrew word ערבון –"**Arbown**"; **Aramaic in The Peshitta has** רהבונא – "**Rahabona**" , which is found twice in The Targum (Aramaic) of Esther . The Targums were Aramaic translations of Hebrew Scripture read in synagogues in Israel from the fifth century BC until at least the third century AD. This "Greek" word αρραβονα comes from Hebrew, as probably does the Aramaic word רהבונא –"**Rahabona**". ערבון –"**Arbown**" is "pledge money".

6. Because we know therefore and we are convinced that as long as we dwell in the body, we are absent from Our Lord;

7. For it is by faith that we walk and not by sight.

8. Because of this we trust and we long to depart from the body and to be with Our Lord.

9. We are diligent that, whether away from home or an inhabitant, we may be pleasing to him.

10. For we are all going to stand before the judgment seat of The Messiah, that each man will be paid in his body anything that was done by him, whether of good or of evil.

11. Therefore, because we know the awesomeness of Our Lord, we persuade the children of men, but we are revealed to God, and I hope also that we are revealed to your understanding.

12. We do not praise ourselves again before you, but we give you an occasion that you may boast of us in the presence of those who are boasting in appearance and not in the heart.

13. For if we are insane, it is for God, and if we are conventional, it is for you.

14. For the love of The Messiah compels us to reason this: The One died in the place of every person; so then every person died with him.

15. And he died in the place of every person, that those who live would not live for themselves, but for The One who died for their persons and arose.

16. Now therefore, we do not know a person by the body, and if we have known The Messiah in the body, from now on we do not even know him so.

17. All that is in The Messiah is therefore The New Creation; the old order has passed away to such.

18. And everything has become new from God – he who reconciled us to himself in The Messiah, and he has given us the Ministry of the reconciliation.

19. For God was in The Messiah- he who reconciled the universe with his Majesty, and he has not accounted their sins to them and has placed in us our own message of the reconciliation.

20. We are Ambassadors therefore in the place of The Messiah, and as if he who is God requested of you by us in the place of The Messiah, we beseech *you* therefore: "**Be reconciled to God.**"

21. For he who had not known sin made himself to become sin in your place, that we would become the righteousness of God in him.

Chapter 6

1. **A**nd as helpers we beg of you that the grace of God that you received would not be wasted on you.

2. For he said, "I have answered you in an acceptable time and in the day of salvation I have helped you." Behold, now is the acceptable time, and behold, now is the day of salvation. (Isaiah 49:8)

3. Why should you give any person an occasion of stumbling in anything? Otherwise it would be a defect in our ministry.

4. But in everything we shall show ourselves to be Ministers of God: by much patience, by sufferings, by distresses, by imprisonments,

5. In scourgings, in chains, in seditions, in toil, in vigils, in fasts,

6. By purity, by knowledge, by endurance, by kindness, by The Spirit of Holiness, by love without deceit,

7. By the message of the truth, by the power of God, by the armor of righteousness that is on the right and on the left,

8. By glory and by disgrace, by praise and by reproach, as if deceivers and true,

9. As if unknown and we are known, as if we are dying, and behold, we live, as if we are punished and we are not dying,

10. As if we sorrow and we always rejoice, as if poor and we make many rich, as if we have nothing and yet we possess everything.

11. Our mouth is opened to you, Corinthians, and our heart is enlarged.

12. You are not restricted by us, but you are restricted in your affections.

13. But I speak as to children: "Pay me my remuneration which is with you, and enlarge your love to me."

Greek has , "Howbeit, by way of the like recompense—as, unto children, I speak, be enlarged, even, ye." (Rotherham)
Where did The Peshitta get its reading? Certainly not from Greek!

14. Do not be associates with those who are unbelievers; for what partnership has righteousness with evil, or what intimacy has light with darkness?

15. What harmony has The Messiah with Satan, or what lot has a believer with an unbeliever?

* For "Satan" , Greek mss. have "βελιαρ" –"Beliar" "a name of Satan"- of <u>Syriac</u> (Aramaic) origin according to <u>Thayer's Greek English Lexicon</u>. What business had Greek speaking Corinthians with an Aramaic name for Satan- especially one as obscure as "Beliar"? The fact is that the Corinthians were Aramaic speakers, as this and other Aramaic words in the Greek translation show. See "**Maranatha**" and "**Satan**"(both found in Corinthians) in <u>Strong's Concordance</u>. I challenge anyone to find this Greek transliteration "βελιαρ" -"**Beliar**" anywhere else in any Greek literature in the world. בליעל –"**Belial**" is found in <u>The Hebrew Bible</u> 27 times; once <u>The Greek LXX</u> translates this as βελιαλ- "**Belial**", only one letter off from Beliar! **Latin Vulgate** mss. have "**Belial**". The Greek testifies for an Aramaic original.

בליער – "Beliar" in Aramaic
בליעל– "Belial" in Aramaic

16. And what agreement does the Temple of God have with demons? But you are the Temple of **THE LIVING GOD**, just as it is said, "I shall dwell in them and I shall walk in them, and I shall be their God, and they shall be a people to me."

* For שאדא "**Demons**" , Greek mss. have "ειδωλων" –"**idols**". It seems the Greek translator had a problem translating "**Satan**" and "**Demons**" in this passage. Perhaps this was due to the cultural gap separating the Greek culture of the readers of The Greek NT from the Semitic Eastern culture of The Jews who received the Peshitta original. Greeks did not esteem demons as evil spirits, but as benign and desireable deities, such as the Muses. The famous philosopher Socrates had spoken of "his **Daemon**"- (demon, deity) which inspired him to speak wisdom. The Jewish culture did not seek to be possessed by spirits; All such spirits were unclean to them and the thought of being possessed was repulsive to them. Greeks also were not familiar with the concept of "**Satan**", as that was also a Jewish doctrine and belief. The Greek NT is inconsistent in this regard, which does transliterate "**Satana**" 37 times out of the 49 times this Aramaic name occurs in The Peshitta.

* There is an important clue in discerning which of two versions is the original and which the translation, when it is known that this relationship exists between them, as in the case of The Peshitta NT and The Greek NT. Let's use "**Satan**" as a model case: The Aramaic word for "**Satan**" – סטנא occurs in the Peshitta NT **49 times** . The Greek transliteration "σατανα"- "**Satana**" occurs **37 times**. When I look (using Online Bible, with dozens of Bible versions, including The Peshitta, Greek NT's, Latin, KJV, Murdock,etc.) at the parallel versions of The Greek and Aramaic verses after searching for all the verses with the Greek word σατανας –"**Satanas**"(all forms of the word are

searched), I find that <u>everyone of these is matched by</u> <u>**The Aramaic word** סטנא</u> –"**Satana**". When I do the search for the Aramaic סטנא –"**Satana**", I find that it occurs a total of 49 times and that the Greek word σατανας (in all its forms) is found to match it only 37 times. **The version that is matched with the greater percentage of the cognate language word occurrences is the translation ; the other version is its original!** This method is consistent with the LXX-Hebrew Bible model in a study of matching cognate words in each. The Peshitta NT comes out consistently as the original behind The two Greek NT's I compared with it, even as The Hebrew Bible is shown to be the original behind **The LXX** Greek text. This method is consistent for the many thousands of data I have tested and accumulated thus far for The Old Testament and The New Testament. The reader may read the data and results of this experiment in my book, <u>**Divine Contact**</u>, available at http://aramaicnt.com

17. "Because of this, come out from among them and be separated from them, says **THE LORD JEHOVAH**, and you shall not touch the impure thing, and I shall receive you,"

18. "And I shall be a Father to you, and you will be sons and daughters to me, says **THE LORD JEHOVAH**, The Almighty."

Chapter 7

1. Therefore, because we have these promises, beloved, let us purify ourselves from all impurity of the flesh and spirit and let us cultivate holiness in the awe of God.

2. Bear with us brethren. We have not done evil to anyone; we have not corrupted anyone; we have not cheated anyone.

3. It was not to condemn you that I spoke previously, for I said that you are in our heart to die and to live as one.

4. I have great frankness toward you and much pride in you and I am filled with comfort and I have a great abundance of joy in all my afflictions.

* פרהסיא –(Parehesya) "**Frankness**" has a cognate in Hebrew –"פרהסיא (identical) ; this is possibly a loan word from the Greek word παρρησια (**Parraysia**), in which case, the Hebrew is also borrowed from Greek, or else the Greek borrowed this from Aramaic or Hebrew. There are many such words in Greek which may be borrowed from Aramaic. Please know that Greek borrowed the **Semitic Phoenician alphabet** for its own Greek alphabet. Aramaic is very similar to Phoenician , from which the written form was derived around 1100 BC.
* "**My afflictions**" is "**Our afflictions**" in all Greek mss. apparently. This same phenomenon occurs in Mark 9:22,Romans 8:35 & 39, Galatians 2:4, 1 Thess. 2:18 & [2 Tim. 1:18]. The suffix י (Yodh),meaning "**My**" was mistaken or not seen after the נ (**Nun**) . A final Nun often means "**Us**" or "**Our**". "**Us**" in Greek is "ημας"; "**our**" is "ημων" "**My**" is "μου" . In uncials (capital letters) they are **HMωN & or EMOY or MOU**. "**Us**" and "**Me**" are – **HMAΣ & EME or ME**.
אולצני looks much more like אולצן than **EMOY**

looks like **HMωN**. This supports Aramaic primacy here and in those other references where these pronouns differ. The Greek primacy position is weak here and in those places. The Greek words have **25%** correlation.

Ashuri Aramaic script:
אולצני -"My afflictions"(Peshitta)
אולצנן -"Our afflictions"(Greek reading in Aramaic)

DSS Aramaic script:
ﬡﬡ -"My afflictions"(Peshitta)
ﬡﬡ -"Our afflictions"(Greek reading in Aramaic)

Both Aramaic scripts shown have 84% correlation.

5. For from the time that we came to Macedonia, we had no relief for our body, but we were tormented in all things: combat from without and fear from within.

6. But God, he who comforts the lowly, comforted us with the coming of Titus,

7. And not only with his coming but also with that relief with which he was relieved by you, for he proclaimed to us concerning your love for us and concerning your grief and your zeal for our sakes, and when I heard, I had great joy.

※ "For us" & "for our sake" is "for me" in the Greek mss. This is the reverse phenomenon of what I present above in verse 4.
דלותן -"for us" was probably read as דלותי -"for me". Here are the Greek phrases for each: **HMⲰN & EMOY**. Only one letter in each word is the same-**M (called "Mu")**. That is **25% correlation**.
Here are those words in Dead Sea Scroll Aramaic script:

ﬡﬡ -"for us"
ﬡﬡ -"for me"

Every word pair comparison in Aramaic is a powerful exhibition for Peshitta primacy !

Four of the five letters in each are identical. That is **80% correlation !** It is far more likely Aramaic was the original and a Greek translator mistook the Aramaic word ﬡﬡ for ﬡﬡ than the reverse scenario of a Greek original where **HMⲰN** is mistaken for **EMOY**.

8. For although I grieved you by an epistle, I have no regret, even though I was sorry, for I saw that the same epistle, though it grieved you for an hour,

9. On the other hand gave me great joy, not because you grieved for yourselves but because your grief brought you conversion*, for you grieved for yourselves by that which is from God, so that you would not be harmed by us in anything.

   * תיבותא -"Taybutha" can mean "a return to God", "conversion", "repentance", "return".

10. For grief that is for God's sake produces a remorse of the soul which does not reverse itself and restores to life, but the grief of the world produces death.

11. For behold, this has happened because you were distressed for God's sake. How much more have I effected diligence in you, and apology, anger, fear, love, zeal and vengeance? And you revealed yourselves in all things that you are pure in this matter.

12. But this that I wrote to you will be, not because of the wrong, neither because of him who did wrong, but so that your diligence toward us might be made known in the presence of God.
   * The Majority Greek text has "**our diligence toward you**" instead of "**your diligence toward us**".

13. Because of this we are comforted, and with our* comfort we rejoice all the more in the joy of Titus, whose spirit was refreshed with all of you.
   * The Majority Greek text has "**your comfort**".

14. I am not ashamed in whatever I have boasted to him concerning your persons, but as we have spoken the truth in everything with you, so also our boasting to Titus was found to be in truth.

15. Also his affections are increased all the more for you as he remembers the obedience of you all, that you received him with awe and trembling.

16. I rejoice that in everything I trust in you.

Chapter 8

1. But we make known to you, brethren, the grace of God that is given to the assemblies of Macedonia.

2. For in the many trials of their afflictions there was an abundance to their joy, and the depth of their poverty was made to superabound in the wealth of their generosity.

3. For I testify that according to their power and more than their power in the willingness of their soul,

4. They begged us with much entreaty that they might share in the grace of the ministry of The Holy Ones,

* Critical Greek has "**With much exhortation, entreating of us the favour and the fellowship of the ministry which was for the Saints**". The Greek here is vague; Did they want to serve or be served ? The Majority Greek adds, "**to receive**" after "**entreating of us**". The Majority Greek is closer to **The Peshitta** here, but both Greek texts lack the verb דנשתותפון -"that they may share", which has been turned into a noun - κοινωνιαν -"fellowship". I don't see either Greek text behind The Aramaic text; I do see omission and very loose paraphrase of the Aramaic text behind the Greek readings.

5. And not according to what we had hoped, but they offered themselves to Our Lord first and also to us in the will of God,

6.That we would seek from Titus, that as he started, thus he would complete also this grace in you.

7.But just as you abound in everything: in faith, in the word, in knowledge, in all diligence and in our love for you, so also, you shall abound in this grace.

8.I am not commanding simply to give you orders, but I am testing the truth of your love with the diligence of your companions.

9.For you know the grace of Our Lord Yeshua The Messiah, who for your sake became poor, when he was rich, so that you might become rich by his poverty.

10.But to counsel, I advise you this to help you, because from last year you began, not only to purpose, but also to do:

11.Finish now by works that thing which you desire, for as you had eagerness to desire, so you should complete by works from what you have.

12.For if there is a willingness, so it is accepted according to what one has; it is not according to what one does not have.

13.For it is not that others would have relief and you would have distress,

14.But that your abundance might come together at this time with their lack of these things, so that their abundance also of those things would be for your lack, that there would be equality.

15.As it is written: "He who increased took no surplus and he who took little was not deprived."

16.But thank God who gave this concern for you to the heart of Titus.

17.For he accepted our request and because he was greatly concerned, by his desire he went out among you.

18.But we sent our brother with him, whose praise in The Gospel is in all the churches.

19.In this way also he was truly chosen from the churches to go out with us in this grace of ministry from us for the glory of God and for our own encouragement.

20.But we fear in this lest anyone impute to us a flaw in this abundance that is ministered by us.

21.For we are concerned for what is right, not only before God, but also before men.

22.But we sent our brother with them, who had been proved by us, that he is diligent always in many things, but now he is all the more diligent by the trust of many concerning you.

23.If therefore Titus is my partner and helper among you, and if our other brethren are Apostles of the churches of the glory of The Messiah,

24.From now on show the demonstration of your love and our pride in you among them in the presence of all the churches.

Chapter 9

1.But concerning the ministration of the Saints, I make it redundant if I write to you.

2.For I knew the readiness of your minds and because of this I boasted of you to the Macedonians that Akaia was ready from last year and your zeal has excited many.

3.But I sent the brethren lest our boasting would be empty which we boasted about you concerning this matter, that as I have said, you would be prepared,

4.Lest Macedonia ns come with me and they find you unprepared and we would be ashamed; for we would not say that you would be ashamed by that boasting which we boasted.

5.Therefore it has been taken care of by me to ask of these my brethren to come beforehand to you and to prepare the blessing, which from the first was reported that it should be prepared in this way as a blessing, not to be according to greed,

6.But this, "Whoever sows frugally also reaps frugally, and whoever sows with bounty shall reap with bounty";

7.Every man according to what he is in his mind and not according to grief or of compulsion, for God loves the joyful giver.

8.But God is able to multiply every favor toward you that you may always have whatever is sufficient for you in all things and that you may superabound in every good work,

9.According to what is written: "He has dispersed and he has given to the poor, and his righteousness stands for eternity."

10.But he who gives seed to the sower and bread for food, he shall give and multiply your seed and increase the fruit of your righteousness,

11.That you may be enriched in all things with the entire right of an heir- that which perfects thanksgiving to God by us.

* פשיטותא –"Peshitutha" can mean "simplicity" or "the right of a plain heir"-(Jastrow's Targum Dictionary). It occurs again in v. 13, where its meaning is borne out.

12. Because the labor of this service not only satisfies the want of the Saints, but also abounds in much thanksgiving to God.

13. For because of the experience of this service, they glorify God that you submitted to the confession of The Gospel of The Messiah, and you became partners in your right of heirship with them and with every person.

14. And they offer prayer for you with the love of many because of the abundance of the grace of God which is upon you.

15. But thank God for his unspeakable gift.

Chapter 10

1. **B**ut I, Paul, beg of you by the serenity and gentleness of The Messiah, although when we are present, I am gentle with you, but when I am distant, I am bold toward you;

2. But I beg of you that when I come it is not necessary for me by the boldness that I have to dare to give counsel against those persons who regard us as if we walk in the flesh.

3. For even if we do walk in the flesh, on the other hand, we do not wage war according to the flesh.

4. The weapons of our warfare are not according to the flesh, but of the power of God, and by it we subdue rebellious fortresses,

5. And we pull down reasonings and every high thing that is exalted against the knowledge of God, and we take all minds prisoner to the obedience of The Messiah.

6. But we are prepared to execute the punishment of those who do not obey when your obedience is fulfilled.

7. Do you look upon appearances? If a man trusts upon himself that he is of The Messiah, let him know this from his soul, that as he is of The Messiah, so also are we.

8. For if I boast somewhat more of the authority that Our Lord gives to me, I am not ashamed, because he gave it to us for your edification and not for your destruction.

9. But I avoid it, lest it be supposed that I terrify you with my epistle,

* Greek mss. omit the phrase "**I avoid it**", making verse 9 a dangling modifier clause instead of a sentence: "**that I may not seem as if I would terrify you by my letters**".

10. Because there are many people who say, "The letters are weighty and powerful, but his bodily presence is weak and his speech contemptible."

11. But let him who speaks in this way consider this, that as we are in the message of our epistles when we are absent, so we are also in deeds when we are present.

12. For we dare not value or compare ourselves against those who flaunt themselves, for those among them who compare themselves are not wise.

13. But we do not boast beyond our size, but by the measure of the limits that God has distributed to us, to reach also as far as to you.

14. For it was not as if we did not arrive unto you, for we joined ourselves as far as unto you. We arrived with The Gospel of The Messiah.

15. And we do not glory beyond our measure in the labor of others. We have hope that when your faith increases we shall be magnified by you according to our measure, and we shall abound.

16. We shall boast also to preach The Gospel beyond you, not by measure of others whom we have already won.

17. But he who boasts, let him boast in THE LORD JEHOVAH.

18. For it is not he who praises himself who is approved, but he whom THE LORD JEHOVAH shall praise.

Chapter 11

1. **B**ut please be patient with me a little, while I speak foolishly, even if you are impatient with me.

2. For I am jealous over you with the jealousy of God, for I have betrothed you as a pure virgin to one Man, to present to The Messiah.

3. But I fear lest, as The Serpent deceived Eve by his craftiness, that your minds may also in this way be corrupted from the simplicity that is in The Messiah.

4. For if he who comes to you would preach another Yeshua to you, whom we have not preached to you, or you should receive another spirit which you have not received, or another gospel which you have not received, you may well be persuaded.

5. For I think that I have not come short in anything compared to those Apostles who greatly excel.

6. For although I am simple in my speech, yet I am not in my knowledge, but we have been open with you in all things.

7. Or have I committed a crime to humble myself that you may be exalted, and to preach The Gospel of God to you without charge?

8. And I robbed other assemblies and took expenses for your service.

9. And when I came among you and had need, I was not a burden to anyone of you, for the brethren who came from Macedonia satisfied my want, and in everything I kept myself and shall keep, lest I be a burden to you.

10. The truth of The Messiah is in me so that this boasting shall not fail me in the region of Akaia.

11. Why, because I do not love you? God knows.

12. But this that I do, I also shall do to cut off the accusations of those who seek a pretext, so in that by which they brag, they will be found like us.

13. For these are false Apostles and treacherous workers and they liken themselves to the Apostles of The Messiah.

14. And not to wonder at this, for if he who is Satan resembles an Angel of light,

15. It is not a great matter if also his Ministers imitate Ministers of righteousness, those whose end will be like their works.

16. But again, I say, no man should think of me as if I am a fool; otherwise, even as a fool receive me, so that I may brag a little.

17. Everything that I speak, it is not by Our Lord that I speak, but as in folly on this occasion of boasting.

18. Because many boast in the flesh, I also shall brag.

19. Are you of those who are listening to the stupid, while you are wise?

20. And do you submit to the one who is subject to you and to him who embezzles you and to him who takes from you and to him who exalts himself over you and to him who strikes you on your face?

21. I speak as one in dishonor, as if we are poor through stupidity. I say that in all things that a man presumes, I also presume.

22. If they are Hebrews, I am also; if they are Israelites, I am also; if they are the seed of Abraham, I am also.

23. If they are Ministers of The Messiah, in stupidity I say that I am greater than they, in more toil than they, with more wounds than they, in chains more than they, in death many times.

24. And I have been whipped by the Judeans five times with forty stripes minus one.

25. Three times I have been scourged with rods, one time I was stoned, three times I have been shipwrecked, a day and a night I have been in the sea without a ship,

26. On many journeys, in dangers of rivers, in dangers of robbers, in dangers from my kindred, in dangers from the Gentiles, in dangers in the city, in dangers in the desert, in dangers in the sea, in dangers by false brethren,

27. In toil and in fatigue, in many vigils, in hunger and in thirst, in many fasts, in cold and in nakedness,

28. Aside from much more, the crowds who are with me everyday, and my care which I have in my person for all the churches.

29. Who is suffering, and I do not suffer? Who has been subverted and I do not burn?

30. If it is fitting to boast, I shall boast in my sufferings.

31. God The Father of Our Lord Yeshua The Messiah, blessed to the eternity of eternities, knows that I do not lie.

32. In Dramsuq, the Captain of the Army of Aretus, The King, was guarding the city of the Damascenes to seize me,

33. And from a window in a basket they lowered me from a wall and I escaped from their hands.

Chapter 12

1. It is necessary to boast, but it is not beneficial, for I myself come to visions and revelations of Our Lord.

2. I knew a man in The Messiah more than fourteen years ago, whether in the body or without the body, I do not know, God himself knows, who was snatched up unto the third Heaven.

3. And I knew this man, if in a body or if without the body, I do not know, God himself knows,

4. Who was snatched up to Paradise and heard words that are unspeakable, because it is not authorized for a man to speak them.

5. Concerning this man I shall glory, but concerning myself I shall not glory, except only in sufferings.

6. For if I have wished to boast, I have not been misbehaving, for I speak the truth; but I

abstain, lest a man think of me more than what he sees in me and hears from me.

7. Lest I be lifted up by the abundance of revelations, a thorn for my flesh was handed over to me, an Angel of Satan to buffet me, lest I be lifted up.

8. And I begged of my Lord concerning this three times, to remove it from me.

9. And he said to me, "My grace is sufficient for you, for my power is perfected in weakness." I shall therefore joyfully boast in my sufferings, that the power of The Messiah may rest upon me.

10. Because of this, I am pleased with suffering, with disgrace, with distress, with persecution, with imprisonment, which is for the person of The Messiah, for when I am weak, then I am strong.

11. Behold, I was stupid in my boasting, because you compelled me, for you were indebted to testify for me because I lacked nothing of those Apostles who greatly excelled, even though I was nothing.

12. I performed the signs of an Apostle among you with all patience and with heroic deeds, with wonders and miracles.

13. For what did you lack of other churches, except only in this, that I was not a burden to you? Forgive me this wrongdoing!

14. Behold, this is the third time I am ready to come to you, and I shall not be a burden to you, because I do not seek yours, but you; for children ought not lay up treasure for the parents but the parents for their children.

15. But I cheerfully also shall spend and I would even give up my person for the sake of your souls, even though, the more I love you, the less you love me.

16. And perhaps I was not a burden to you, but as a crafty man I robbed you by treachery.

17. Did I greedily desire what was yours by the agency of another man whom I sent to you?

18. When I asked Titus and sent the brethren with him, was Titus greedily desiring what was yours? Did we not walk in the same spirit and in the same steps?

19. Do you again think that we make excuses to you? We speak before God in The Messiah, and all these things, my beloved, are for your edification.

20. For I fear lest I come to you and shall not find you as I like, and I may be found by you also as you do not like, lest there be fighting, envy, rage, contention, slander, murmuring, insolence and tumult,

21. Lest when I come to you, my God would humble me and I would grieve over many who have sinned and have not returned from defilement, from fornication and from lewdness which they have practiced.

Chapter 13

1. This is the third time I am coming to you. "By the mouth of two or three witnesses every word shall be established."

2. I had said this to you from the first and again beforehand I am saying it, as also the second time when I was with you I said it to you; even now, as I am absent, I write to these who have sinned and to all the others, whom, if I come again, I shall not spare,

3. Because you seek a proof of The Messiah that he speaks in me, he who is not weak among you, but is mighty among you;

4. For although he was crucified in weakness, yet he lives by the power of God; and we also are weak with him, but we are living with him by the power of God, who is in you.

5. Examine your souls, whether you stand in the faith. Tend to your souls, or are you not aware that Yeshua The Messiah is in you, and *that* if not, you are worthless?

6. But I hope that you will know that we are not worthless.

7. But I ask of God that nothing evil shall be in you, so that our proofs may appear, but that you would be doing good, and we may be as if worthless.

8. For we can do nothing against the truth, but for the cause of the truth.

9. But we rejoice whenever we are weak and you are strong; for we pray for this also, that you may be perfected.

10. Therefore, as I am absent I write these things, lest when I come, I deal severely according to the authority that my Lord gives to me for your building up, and not for your destruction.

11. From now on, my brethren, rejoice; be perfected and be comforted, and harmony and peace shall be in you, and The God of love and of peace shall be with you.

12. Greet one another with a holy kiss.

13. All of the Saints invoke your peace.

14. The Peace of Our Lord Yeshua The Messiah, the Love of God and the Fellowship of The Spirit of Holiness, be with all of you. Amen.

Greek has η χαρις του κυριου ιησου χριστου –
"**The grace of The Lord Jesus Christ**"; The Peshitta
has "**The peace of Our Lord Jesus The Messiah**".
"**Benefit**" in Aramaic can be תבתה . Peace is שלמה
. Let's compare the two in three Aramaic scripts:

Ashuri:
שלמה – "**Peace**"
טבתה- "**Benefit**", "**Goodness**"

DSS-Ashuri hybrid:
שלמה – "**Peace**"
טבתה - "**Benefit**", "**Goodness**"

Estrangela
ܫܠܡܐ- "**Peace**"

ܛܒܬܐ- "**Benefit**", "**Goodness**"

It appears that either the Ashuri or Dead Sea Scroll
scripts could account for the Greek reading of χαρις
. The DSS pair look the most alike. Three of the four
letters (**75%**) of each word look similar and could
have been confused. An argument could even be made
that the remaining letters ܫ and ܛ may be confused
one for another.

The Greek for "**Peace**" is ειρηνη ; Compare to χαρις
– "**Grace**" . Here they are in ancient uncial Greek
script:
EIPHNH "**Peace**" & XAPIΣ – "**Grace**". There is no
resemblance between them whatsoever. So how would
an Aramaean translating Greek into Aramaic see
XAPIΣ and translate as if he saw EIPHNH? Beats
me, but this is typical of the many differences between
The Peshitta and The Greek NT ; The Aramaic of The
Peshitta can account for many Greek readings where
they differ; the Greek cannot account very well , if at
all, for The Peshitta readings.

The data in Corinthians decidedly supports Peshitta
primacy -(The Peshitta as the original behind the
Greek texts).

The Epistle of The Apostle Paul to the Galatians

Chapter 1

1. Paulus an Apostle, not by the children of men, neither by a son of man, but by Yeshua The Messiah and God his Father, he who raised him from among the dead,

2. And all the brethren who are with me, to the assembly that is in Galatia.

3. Grace be with you and peace from God The Father and from Our Lord Yeshua The Messiah,

4. He who gave himself for the sake of our sins to set us free from this evil world, according to the will of God Our Father,

5. To whom be glory to the eternity of eternities. Amen.

6. I marvel how quickly you have been turned away from The Messiah, he who called you by his grace, unto another gospel

7. Which does not exist, but there are some who trouble you and wish to change The Gospel of The Messiah.

8. But even if we or an Angel from Heaven should evangelize you outside of that which we have evangelized you, we *or* he would be damned;

9. Just as I said to you from the first and now again I say to you, that if anyone evangelizes you outside of what you have received, he shall be damned.

10. Do I plead now before the children of men or before God, or do I seek to please the children of men? For if until now I have been pleasing men, I have not been a Servant of The Messiah.

11. But I notify you my brethren, that The Gospel that was preached by me was not from a human;

12. For I neither received nor learned it from a man, but by the revelation of Yeshua The Messiah.

13. For you have heard of my way of life, which from the first was in Judaism, that I was greatly persecuting the Church of God and destroying it.

14. And I was greatly surpassing many associates in Judaism who were of my people, and I was very zealous in the teaching of my ancestors;

15. But when he who separated me from my mother's womb chose and called me by his grace

16. To reveal his Son in me, that I would proclaim him among the Gentiles, immediately, I did not reveal it to flesh and blood,

17. Neither did I go to Jerusalem to the Apostles who were before me, but I went to Arabia and returned again to Dramsuq.

18. And after three years I went to Jerusalem to see Kaypha *, and I stayed with him fifteen days.

- Critical Greek has "Cephas"-the Aramaic name in Greek letters; most Greek mss. have "πετρον"-"Peter", which is the Greek translatyion of כאפא -"Kaypha", "a stone". We know this Apostle's name was the Aramaic Kaypha, given him by our Lord. Both Greek readings betray themselves as transcriptions or translations of Aramaic here and elsewhere. See 2:11 for the next example of this.

19. But I saw none of the other Apostles except Jacob, the brother of Our Lord.

20. But these things that I write to you, behold, before God, I do not lie.

21. After these things I came to the regions of Syria and Qiliqia.

22. And the churches in Judea, these who are in The Messiah, did not know me by face,

23. But they had heard only this: "He who from the first persecuted us, now, behold, he preaches that faith which from earlier times he had overthrown."

24. And they were praising God for me.

Chapter 2

1. But again, after 14 years, I went up to Jerusalem with BarNaba, and I brought Titus with me.

2. But I went up with revelation and I revealed to them The Gospel which I preached among the Gentiles. And I showed it privately to those who were considered to be something, otherwise I would have run in vain or might run in vain.

3. Even Titus, an Aramaean * who was with me, was not compelled to be circumcised.

* ארמיא – "**Aramaean**" or "**Syrian**" is ελλην – "**Greek**" in the Greek mss. "**Greek**"- ελλην, would not be translated as ארמיא "**Aramaean**". An Aramaean is an Aramaic speaking Gentile, but 20 times out of the 21 occurrences of "**Aramaean**" in **The Peshitta NT** , The Greek mss. have ελλην – "**Greek**"; once the word συρος – "**Syrian**" is used , which is an acceptable Greek translation. So the Greek NT has only the word "**Greek**" for "**Aramaean**" and "**Aramaic**". **The Peshitta NT** , on the other hand, has a dozen occurrences of "**Greek**" – יונית & יוניא. It certainly was not "cleansed" of references to "**Greek**" by changing them to "**Aramaic**". How can these things be, if The Peshitta is a translation of **The Greek NT** and **The Greek NT** is not a translation of The Peshitta? It does appear that the Greek books were "purged" of all reference to "**Aramaic**" and

The Holy Epistle of Paul The Apostle to The Galatians ✝ אגרתא קדישתא דפולוס שליחא דלות גלטיא

"**Aramaeans**" from Luke,
Acts,Romans,1Cor,Galatians,Colossians and
Revelation ! **The LXX** at least uses "συρος" *
"συριστι" ("**Syrian**" & "**Syriac**") for the Hebrew
ארמית & ארם ("**Aramaean**" & "**Aramaic**"). Syrians
are Aramaeans; Greeks are not Aramaeans. I detect
some funny business in this. See my web site
http://aramaicnt.com for an article on this subject
(Aramaic to Greek in The Greek NT).

4. But because of false brethren who came in to spy on the liberty that we have in Yeshua The Messiah, so as to enslave me,

* For "to enslave me"- Greek mss. have "**that they might bring us into bondage**":
Here is the Peshitta reading: דנשעבדונני ; "**to enslave me**"
Here is the Greek reading in Aramaic דנשעבדונן - "**that they might bring us into bondage**". The relevant variant parts are highlighted in blue.
In Dead Sea Scroll script, we have:
ר-ישעבדונני - "to enslave me".
ר-ישעבדונן - "that they might bring us into bondage".
Only one letter difference exists between these readings in this old Aramaic script.

In Greek the two readings are:
ΙΝΑ ΗΜΑΣ ΚΑΤΑΔΟΥΛΩΣΟΥΣΙΝ
ΙΝΑ ΕΜΕ ΚΑΤΑΔΟΥΛΩΣΟΥΣΙΝ

The Greek readings highlighted in blue differ in three of four letters of the critical words . It is unlikely that a Scribe translating Greek into Aramaic would mistake ΗΜΑΣ for ΕΜΕ. This same phenomenon occurs in Mark 9:22,Romans 8:35 & 39, Galatians 2:4, 1 Thess. 2:18 & [2 Tim. 1:18]. The suffix י (**Yodh**),meaning "**My**" was mistaken or not seen after the נ (**Nun**) . A final Nun often means "**Us**" or "**Our**". These all argue strongly for a Peshitta original of which the Greek text is a translation.

5. Not for a moment did we yield to their oppression, but that the truth of The Gospel may continue with you.
6. But those who were esteemed to be something (but who they were does not concern me) for God does not accept the persons of men, but those who are such have not added anything to me.
7. But on the contrary, for they saw that I was entrusted with The Gospel of uncircumcision as Kaypha was entrusted with the circumcision.
8. For he who encourages Kaypha in the Apostleship of the circumcision also encourages me in the Apostleship of the Gentiles.
9. And when they recognized the grace that is given to me, Jacob and Kaypha and Yohannan, those who were esteemed to be pillars, gave me and BarNaba the right hand of fellowship, because we *are* among the Gentiles and those *are* among the circumcision,

10. Only that we would remember the poor, and I had been concerned to do this.
11. But when Kaypha * came to Antiakia, I rebuked him to his face because they were tripped * up by him;

* Critical Greek has "Cephas"-the Aramaic name in Greek letters; most Greek mss. have "πετρον"-"Peter", which is the Greek translatyion of כאפא -"Kaypha", "a stone". We know this Apostle's name was the Aramaic "Kaypha", given him by our Lord. Both Greek readings betray themselves as transcriptions or translations of Aramaic here and elsewhere.

* Greek has "**he was to be blamed**". The Peshitta reading – "**They were stumbled**" is מתתקלין ܐܬܬܩܠܘ
מתחיבו means "**to be condemned**".Here are the two readings in Aramaic, one atop the other for easy comparison:
מתתקלין – "**They were stumbled**".
מתחיבו - "**To be condemned**". I have shaded similar corresponding letters in grey. 4 out of 6 in the second word match closely , or **67% correlation**.
In square Aramaic we have:
מתתקלין – "**They were stumbled**".
מתחיבו - "**To be condemned**". Again , here is **67% correlation**.
In Estrangela script:

ܡܬܬܩܠܝܢ

ܡܬܚܝܒܘ - Only 2 of 6 letters correspond- **33% correlation**.
The similarities may account for the Greek reading, which is not as clear a reading as the Aramaic. The Greek word for "**they were stumbled**" is ΕΣΚΑΝΔΑΛΙΖΟΝΤΟ- nothing like ΚΑΤΕΓΝΩΣΜΕΝΟΣ- "**he is condemned**". I see only one letter correlation here- 1/13 or **8% correlation**. Another possibility is the Greek word ΑΦΙΣΤΑΝΤΑΙ for "**They stumbled**, but that does not help Greek primacy prospects here at all. The Aramaic could not have come from the Greek reading.

12. For before people would come from the presence of Jacob, he was eating with the Gentiles, but when they came, he withdrew himself and separated, because he was afraid of those who were of the circumcision.
13. And others of the Judeans were also yielding with him in this; likewise also, BarNaba was led to accept persons.
14. And when I saw that they were not walking uprightly in the truth of The Gospel, I said to Kaypha* in the sight of all of them, "If you who are a Jew are living like a Syrian* and you are not living as a Jew, why do you compel Gentiles to live as Jews?

* "**to Kaypha**"- Most Greek mss. have "Πετρος"-"**Petros**"; Sinaiticus and Vaticanus (4th century Greek mss.) have "Κηφα"- Cephas (The Aramaic name) .
* "**as a Syrian**" or "**Aramaean**" – All Greek mss. have "εθνικως"- "**as a Gentile**". ארמאית ("**Arama-it**") can refer to the Aramaic language or the Aramaean people; The Syrians were the neighbors to Israel on the north and were probably the "**Arama-it**" referred to here.

15. For we who are by nature Judeans and not sinners of the Gentiles,

16. Because we know that a man is not justified by works of The Written Law, but by the faith of Yeshua The Messiah, we also believe in Yeshua The Messiah, that we should be made right by the faith of The Messiah, and not by the works of The Written Law, because no one is made right by the works of The Written Law.

*-"by the faith of Yeshua"- I think Paul's purpose is to magnify The Christ as our Savior, not our faith in The Christ. Our faith in Yeshua is a result of His grace toward us, not the other way around. Some have made faith into a work of man rather than the gift of God in Christ. Romans 3:22 , Gal. 2:20,3:22,Ephesians 2:8,9 , 3:12, Philipp. 3:9 and others have this same phrase "haymnutha d'Yeshua"(the faith of Jesus) or haymnutha d'Meshikha (The faith of The Messiah) as the cause of our justification. Our faith in Him must come from His faith (or faithfulness) or it is useless and false.

17. But if when we seek to be made right by The Messiah, we are found to be sinners, is then Yeshua the Minister of sin? God forbid!
18. For if I build those things again that I once destroyed, I have shown about myself that I violate The Covenant.
19. For I by The Written Law have died to The Written Law that I might live unto God.
20. And I have been crucified with The Messiah, and from then on I myself have not been living, but The Messiah is living in me, and this that I now live in the flesh, I live by the faith of The Son of God, he who has loved us* and has given himself for us*.

* "Us"- All Greek mss. seem to have "Me" in two places in this verse where the Peshitta has "Us". Here is "loved us" as **The Peshitta** has it in this verse:
דאחבן - "loved us"
Here is "loved me": דאחבני - "loved me"
• In Dead Sea Scroll script they are:
ﬦﬧﬧﬦ-"loved us"
ﬦﬧﬧﬦ-"loved me"
In Estrangela , they are : ܕܐܚܒܢ
ܕܐܚܒܢܝ
The DSS script seems most easily to account for the two readings-Peshitta and Greek. The final Nun ן and regular Nun נ are almost identical ; not so in square Aramaic or Estrangela. The Dead Sea Scroll script words have **84%** correlation.
No matter what Aramaic script is used, the differences are miniscule . The Greek for "Me" is ME and "Us" is HMAΣ.
"Loved me" in Greek Uncials would look like : ΑΓΑΠΗΣΑΝΤΟΣ ΜΕ.
"Loved us" in Greek Uncials would look like : ΑΓΑΠΗΣΑΝΤΟΣ ΗΜΑΣ. The 2 Greek pronouns have **25%** correlation at best.
"For us" in Aramaic is חלפין . "For me" is חלפי . In DSS script : חלפין & חלפי ; Estrangela : ܚܠܦܢ & ܚܠܦܝ . One letter difference !
That is **80%** letter correlation in any one of the 3 Aramaic scripts.

In Greek the same phrases are ΥΠΕΡΗΜΩΝ & ΥΠΕΡΕΜΟΥ. This kind of reading difference occurs not infrequently in The NT – far too often to be

accounted for by mistaking one Greek word such as **HMΩN** for **EMOY** . The Aramaic primacy theory best explains the Greek readings in such cases. The Greek cannot well account for the Aramaic. The words **HMΩN** & **EMOY** in Greek script have no more than **25%** correlation .

21. I do not reject the grace of God, for if righteousness is by The Written Law, The Messiah died for nothing.

Chapter 3

1. Oh stupid Galatians! Who has rivaled you? For behold, The Fashioner was portrayed * before your eyes, Yeshua The Messiah, when he was crucified.
* The large majority of Greek mss. have: "Who bewitched you not to obey the truth?" before "portrayed before your eyes". See the two readings in Aramaic and judge whether Aramaic came from Greek or vice versa:
אין דאתציר אומנא - "as he was portrayed The Artisan"
דלא תתפיסון - "that you would disobey"
Some spaces between letters are removed in the second reading, but everything is there. It looks feasible that a Greek translator double translated the Aramaic phrase shown on top, and misread it as the second phrase on the second take.This is not an uncommon phenomenon in the Greek NT, it seems.

2. This only I wish to know of you: Did you receive The Spirit by the works of The Written Law or by the hearing of faith?
3. Are you so foolish that you began in The Spirit and now you finish in the flesh?
4. Have you endured all these things for nothing? But oh, that it were for nothing!
5. Is he, therefore, who gives The Spirit among you, and does miracles among you, of the works of The Written Law, or of the hearing of faith?
6. Just as Abraham believed God and it was accounted to him for righteousness,
7. Know therefore that those who are of faith are the children of Abraham.
8. For because God knew beforehand that the nations are made right by faith, he preached The Good News to Abraham beforehand, as The Holy Scriptures say: "In you shall all the nations be blessed."
9. So then, believers are blessed with the believer Abraham.
10. For those who are of the works of The Written Law are under a curse, for it is written: "Cursed is everyone who shall not do all that is written in this Law."
11. But that a man is not made right with God by The Written Law, this is revealed, because it is written: "The just shall live by faith."

12. But The Written Law was not from faith, but, "Whoever shall do those things that are written in it shall live in them."

13. But The Messiah has redeemed us from the curse of The Written Law, and he became a curse in our place, for it is written: "Cursed is everyone who is hanged on a tree",

14. That the blessing of Abraham would be with the nations by Yeshua The Messiah, and we would receive The Promise of The Spirit by faith.

15. My brethren, I speak as among men, that a man does not reject or change anything in a man's covenant which has been confirmed.

16. But The Promise was promised to Abraham and to his seed, and he did not say to him, "To your seeds", as to many, but, "To your seed", as of one, who is The Messiah.

17. But I say this: The Covenant which was confirmed from the first by God in The Messiah, The Written Law which was four hundred thirty years years afterward, cannot cast off and cancel The Promise.

18. But if the inheritance is by The Written Law, it would therefore not be from The Promise to Abraham, but God gave it to him by The Promise.

19. Why therefore is there The Written Law? It was added because of apostasy until The Seed would come to whom The Promise belonged, and The Written Law was given by The Messenger in the hand of a Mediator.

20. A Mediator is not of one, but God is One.

21. Is therefore The Written Law contrary to The Promise of God? God forbid! For if a law had been given which was able to give life, truly righteousness would have been by The Written Law.

22. But the Scripture has shut all things up under sin, that The Promise by the faith of Yeshua The Messiah would be given to those who are believers.

23. But until the faith would come, The Written Law had kept us while we were closed off to the faith that was going to be revealed.

24. The Written Law was therefore a guide for us to The Messiah that we would be made right by faith.

25. But when the faith came we were not under a guide.

26. For you are all children of God by the faith of Yeshua The Messiah.

27. For those who have been baptized into The Messiah have put on The Messiah.

28. There is neither Jew nor Aramaean*, neither Servant nor Free person, neither male nor female, for all of you are one in Yeshua The Messiah.

* "Aramaean" is not in the Greek text; The Greek text has "Greek". All 21 references in the Peshitta to "Aramaic-Syrian" are "Greek" in the Greek texts, except in Luke 4:27, where we find "Συρος"-"Syrian". Here is Jastrow's Hebrew Aramaic Targum Dictionary entry for ארם – the root of ארמיא :

אֲרָם pr. n. (b. h.) 1) *Aram*, son of Shem. Targ. Gen. X, 22; a. e.—2) *Aramaea, Syria*. Targ. I Kings XX, 1; a. fr.—3) (a disguise for רוֹמָא) *Rome, Roman empire*

"A disguise for רומא -"Rome"! This is starting to make sense in explaining why **The Greek NT** has "Greek" in those 21 places where The Peshitta has "Aramaic" or "Aramaean". The Greek translator perhaps looked at ארמיא as code for "Roman" and wanted to disguise the fact by translating it as "Greek". There was good reason for that during the first century, especially during Nero the maniac's reign (circa AD 54-68), who was so paranoid about Christians that he declared open season on them in the empire for several years and had them set aflame to light his gardens at night! Here are two more entries from the same Dictionary:

אֲרַמָאָה, אֲרַמְאָה, אֲרַמְיָא, אֲרָמֵי, אֲרַמָאי h., ch. m. (=b. h. אֲרַמִּי) *Syrian*, in gen. *gentile, Roman*; comp. אֲרַמִי 2). Targ. O. Lev. XXV, 47.—Y.Shebi. IV,35ᵃᵇ (חֵר א׳ בּרוֹמִי (Y. Snh. III, 21ᵇ) a gentile in Rome. Ib. א׳ יְהוֹדָיֵי וכ׳ (prob. plur.) either be Jewish Jews (living as Jews ought to) or gentile gentiles (Roman Romans). Y. Ab. Zar. III, 41ᶜ top אֲרַמָאיָא וכ׳ the leather bottle of an Aramaean (or gentile) burst open. Yeb. 45ᵇ בַּר אַרְמָאָה son of a gentile. Hull. 97ᵃ; a. fr.—*Pl.* אֲרַמָאֵי. Targ. Y. Deut. XXXII, 24 (*Romans*); a. e.—Ab.Zar.31ᵇ.—Gitt.17ᵃ אֲרוֹמָאֵי (*Romans*). Gen. R. s. 63 אֲרַמָּאיִן. Koh. R. to VII, 11 אֲרַמָיֵי.—Num. R. s. 7 אֲרַמָאֵים (פְּבֵ׳׳ים); a. fr. [Lev. R. s. 34 אתון סארמאין, read מִידִוֹטָאֵיךְ, v. זְמַר.] —Fem. אַרְמָיָתָא. Yeb. l. c. V. אַרְמָי.

אֲרָם m., אֲרָמִית f. 1) (b. h.) *Aramaean, Aramaic, Chaldaic*. [Targ. II Kings XVIII, 26.]—א׳ לְשׁוֹן *Chaldaic*. Sabb. 12ᵇ; a. fr.—2) (=אֲרוֹם; v. אֲרַם 3) *Romish, Roman, heathen*. [Owing to Christian censors as well as timid Jewish copyists, many of the passages originally referring to Romans, Christians, &c., have been altered by substituting *Arammi, Kuthi, Goy* &c., so that only by keen criticism their real application can be ascertained.]—Fem. *gentile woman*. Ber. 8ᵇ (Ms.M. ארמאית). Snh. IX, 6; a. fr.—Y. Meg. I, 71ᶜ top ארמית *Latin*; v. בְּרָא.—*Pl.* אֲרַמִים Meg. 11ᵃ (some ed. פרסיים; Ms. M. רוֹמָיִים; Sifra B'hukk. Par. II, ch. 8 אססיריסס). V. אֲרוֹמָי.

The above notes in these entries confirm my previous suspicions that there was deliberate alteration of the original meaning (or apparent meaning) by disguising "Aramaith" & "Aram" as "Greek". The reason may have been as I stated above, or it may have been to create a decoy from Arameans and Aramaic Scripture by translation of the texts into Greek and affirming Greeks as the Gentile group being converted to The Christ and Greek manuscripts as the original text, whereas it was primarily Aramaic speaking peoples being converted, as the Holy Land and The Middle East was primarily populated with Arameans and Jews who had been speaking Aramaic for many generations and centuries. Greeks were a respected ethnic group as their culture and language were very popular with the Romans and had great influence in shaping Roman culture and the Latin language. The fact that the changes would exist in 21 out of 22 places throughout The NT from Luke to Revelation also confirms my former position that all 27 Greek books were translated before the end of Nero's reign in AD 68. Nero was paranoid of Christians and Christianity. He almost certainly would have gone after Aramaic scripture and Christians even moreso if he had thought that the Romans were the target of The Gospel for conversion. The Greek changes the word "Armaith" to "Greek". Nero would not have felt threatened by the

Greeks being converted. Revelation in Aramaic has a prologue attached to it that says it was written by the Apostle John who was exiled by **Nero Caesar** to Patmos. The number of The Beast of Revelation 13 is the number of Nero Ceasar in Hebrew letters נרון קסר , which letters' numerical values add up to 666.

29. And if you are of The Messiah, you are therefore the seed of Abraham and heirs by The Promise.

Chapter 4

1. I say that as long as the heir is a child, he is not distinct from the Servants, though he is Master over all of them;

2. But he is under guardians and stewards until the time that his father has appointed.

3. In this way also when we were children, we were enslaved under the principles of the world.

4. But when the end of time arrived, God sent his Son and he was from a woman and was under The Written Law,

5. That he would redeem those who *were* under The Written Law, and that we would receive the position of children.

6. But because you are children, God has sent The Spirit of his Son into your hearts, who cries, "Father, our Father".

* אבא –"Abba" is found in the Greek mss. transliterated as "Αββα". What is another Aramaic word doing in the Greek ms. presumably sent first to Greek speaking Galatians? "Αββα" is not a loan word in Greek; it is simply an Aramaic word written in Greek letters. We do not find the converse scenario ever in The Peshitta- i.e. , a Greek word simply written in Aramaic letters. There are some loan words, but that is to be expected at a time when Greek and Aramaic speakers had been neighbors in the Middle East for centuries. Greek and Latin loan words are found in Hebrew as well; they are not transliterations, but foreign words adapted and adopted in the borrowing tongue. Greek also has loan words from Aramaic and Hebrew. They should never be confused with transliterations, which abound in the Greek NT. **(Satan,Mammon,Korban,Gehenna,Messiah,Bar Jona, Bartholomew, Barabbas,BarNaba, Maranatha,Talitha cumi, Epatha,Eloi Eloi lama sebaqthani, Bethesda,Golgotha,Bethany,Mna,Keephas,Sadduce es,Pharisees, Pasca,Sabbath,Abba,Sabaoth,Raca,Rabboni,Hosan na,Boanerges, Bartimaius,Rabbi,Aceldama,Gabbatha,oua,Beelzeb ub,Bar-,amen,allelouia).** These words are found by the hundreds in toto in **The Greek NT**.

7. And therefore you are not Servants but children, and if children, also the heirs of God by Yeshua The Messiah.

8. For then when you had not known God, you served those which by their nature were not God.

9. But now that you have known God and especially that you are known by God, you have turned again to those sick and weak

principles, and you wish again to be subject to them.

10. You observe days and months and times and years.

11. I fear lest I have labored among you for nothing.

12. Be like me because I also have been like you, my brethren, I beg of you. You have wronged me in nothing,

13. For you know that in the illness of my flesh from the first I have preached The Good News to you.

14. And you did not ridicule, neither did you loathe the trial of my flesh, but you received me as an Angel of God and as Yeshua The Messiah.

15. Where is therefore your blessedness, for I testify of you that if it were possible, you would have plucked out and given your eyes to me?

* Most Greek mss. have "**What is your blessedness…?**" The Textus Receptus (KJV Greek text) and The Critical Greek text (Westcott & Hort 1881) have "**Where is your blessedness…?**". The Aramaic word איכו ("**Aykaw**") usually means "**Where is** ", but could have been construed to mean "**What is ?**"It is a compound word , made up of הו, "Is" + איכא "Where?" = איכו But איך "Ak" (ܐܝܟ in Estrangela) can also mean "**What**" . Here is **Smith's Compendious Syriac Dictionary** entry:

ܐܝܟ *as, as if, as it were, almost, about,* ܐܝܟ ܐܠܟܐ *about the first hour, about* 1 *o'clock. According to,* ܐܝܟ ܢܩܒܠ *as some think;* ܐܝܟ ܙܕܩ *in due form.* With ܕ and a verb expresses the subjunctive with *that* or *to, that I may, that thou mayest, &c.;* ܐܝܟ ܕܐܟܬܒܗ *as I may say, so to say, as is said;* ܐܝܟ ܕܢܗܡܐ *they may be permitted to build, they may build.* ܐܝܟ ܗܠܐ pl. ܐܝܟ ܗܠܝ *usually with* ܕ *prefixed, such, such as, what, how;*

- Notice the second to last word in the excerpt ("what"). So the Aramaic again explains two Greek readings, even if one of the Greek readings is a misreading of the Aramaic.

16. Have I become an enemy to you because I have preached the truth to you?

17. They imitate you, not for what is excellent but because they want to oppress you that you would imitate them.

18. But it is good that you would imitate excellence always, and not only when I am with you.

19. My children, those for whom I am in labor again until The Messiah shall be formed in you,

20. I wish to be with you now and to change my tone, because I am dumbfounded at you.

21. Tell me, you who wish to be under The Written Law, do you not hear The Written Law?

22. For it is written: "Abraham had two sons, one from a Maidservant and one from a Freewoman."

23. But he who was from the Maidservant was born of the flesh, but he who was from the Freewoman was by The Promise.

24. But these are illustrations of The two Covenants, the one that is from Mount Sinai begets to bondage, which is Hagar.

25. For Hagar is Mount Sinai that is in Arabia, and agrees with this Jerusalem and is serving in bondage and its children.

26. But that Jerusalem above is free, which is our mother.

27. For it is written: "Rejoice, barren one, she who does not bear, triumph and shout, she who does not give birth, because the children of the desolate have increased more than the children of a wife."

28. But we, my brethren, are children of The Promise like Isaac.

29. And as then, he who was born by the flesh did persecute him who was of the Spirit, so it is now also.

30. But what do the Scriptures say? Cast out the Maidservant and her son because the son of the Maidservant will not inherit with the son of the Freewoman.

31. We therefore, my brethren, are not children of the Maidservant, but children of the Freewoman.

Chapter 5

1. Stand therefore in that liberty with which The Messiah has set us free, and do not be yoked again in a yoke of bondage.

2. Behold, I Paul say to you that if you will be circumcised, The Messiah profits you nothing.

3. But I testify again to every person who is circumcised, that he is obligated to observe all of The Written Law.

4. You have been destroyed from The Messiah, those of you who are justified by that in The Written Law, and you have fallen from grace.

5. For we wait for the hope of righteousness by The Spirit who is of the faith.

6. For in The Messiah Yeshua, circumcision is not anything, neither is uncircumcision, only faith that is perfected* in love.

---

* Greek has ενεργουμενη - **working** ; The Peshitta reading is דמתגמרא – **that is perfected** " may have

been misinterpreted by a Greek translator. Aramaic words for "**working**" that may be relevant are :

Ashuri Aramaic:
דחפיטתא –"of work"
דמתחפטא -"which is worked"
דמתעבדא -"which is performed" (72% correlation)
דמתגמרא - "**which is perfected**" (Original Aramaic reading)
דמתעדרא -"which is helped"
דמתסערא -"which is done"

Dead Sea Scroll Aramaic:
דחפיטתא –"of work"
דמתחפטא -"which is worked"
דמתעבדא- "which is performed" (86% correlation)
דמתגמרא –"which is perfected" (Original Aramaic reading)
דמתעדרא –"which is helped"
דמתסערא -"which is done"

ܕܚܦܝܛܬܐ –"of work"

ܕܡܬܚܦܛܐ-"which is worked"

ܕܡܬܓܡܪܐ –"which is perfected" (Original Aramaic reading)

ܕܡܬܥܒܕܐ- "which is performed" (86% correlation)

ܕܡܬܣܥܪܐ-"which is done"

ܕܡܬܥܕܪܐ –"which is helped" The DSS script and Estrangela each have an **86% best correlation score** . I take the DSS to be the script in which this epistle was originally written, as 2:11 and 2:20 show that script to be the likely script used in those places.

"**Perfected**" in Greek would be τελειουται or καταρτισμενη ; Neither of these looks like the actual Greek reading ενεργουμενη. It appears that the Greek does not account for The Peshitta reading ; the correlation between Greek words here is very low: **33% at best**, and that is only in the verb endings, not in the root words.

Here is the Aramaic reading compared with what I believe a Greek translator construed the original to be:

דמתגמרא –**which is perfected**" (Original Aramaic reading)
דמתעבדא- "**which is performed**" (Hypothetical Base for Greek -86% correlation)

7. You were running well. Who agitated you to disobey the truth?

8. Your persuasion is not from him who has called you.

9. A little yeast ferments the entire lump.

10. I do trust in you by Our Lord that you will not entertain other things, and whoever troubles you will bear judgment, whoever he is.

11. But if I still preach circumcision, my brethren, why am I persecuted? Has the stumbling block of the crucifixion been eliminated?

12. But I would also that those who trouble you would be cut off.

13. But you have been called to liberty, my brethren, only let not your liberty be an

opportunity of the flesh, but you should be serving one another by love.

14. For all of The Written Law is fulfilled in one saying, by this: "You shall love your neighbor as yourself."

15. But if you bite and devour one another, beware lest you be consumed by one another.

16. But I say that you should be walking in The Spirit and the craving of the flesh you will never do.

17. For the flesh craves anything that opposes The Spirit and The Spirit craves whatever opposes the flesh, and they both are contrary one to another, lest you would be doing whatever you want.

18. But if you are led by The Spirit, you are not under The Written Law.

19. For the works of the flesh are known, which are fornication, impurity, whoredom,

20. The worship of idols, witchcraft, hate, contention, rivalry, rage, insolence, dissensions, divisions,

21. Envy, murder, drunkenness, reveling and all such things; those who are committing these things, as I said to you from the first, I say now also, that they shall not inherit The Kingdom of God.

22. But the fruits of The Spirit are love, joy, peace, patience, sweetness, goodness, faith,

23. Humility, endurance; the law is not set against these things.

24. But those who are of The Messiah have crucified their flesh with all its weaknesses and its cravings.

25. We shall live therefore in The Spirit and surrender to The Spirit,

26. And let us not be devoid of honor, disparaging one another and envying one another.

Chapter 6

1. My brethren, if any of you should be overtaken by a fault, you who are in The Spirit should restore him in the spirit of humility, and be cautious lest you also be tempted.

2. And bear the burdens of one another, for in this way you fulfill the law of The Messiah.

3. For if a man thinks he is something when he is not, he deceives himself.

4. But a man should prove his work and then he will have pride in himself and not in others.

5. For every person will carry his own luggage.

6. And let him who hears the word share in all good things with him who preaches to him.

7. Do not err; God is not put to shame, for anything that a man sows he reaps.

8. Whoever sows to the flesh reaps destruction from the flesh, and whoever sows to The Spirit shall reap eternal life from The Spirit.

9. And when we do what is good, let it not be tedious to us, for there shall be a time when we reap, and that will not be tedious to us.

10. Now therefore, while we have time, let us do good to every person, especially to the members of the household of faith.

11. Behold, I have written these writings to you with my hand.

12. Those who wish to boast in the flesh urge you to be circumcised only so that they would not be persecuted for the crucifixion of The Messiah.

13. Not even those who are circumcised keep The Written Law, but they want you to be circumcised so that they may take pride in your flesh.

14. But let it not be for me to take pride except in the crucifixion of Our Lord Yeshua The Messiah, in whom the universe has been crucified to me, and I have been crucified to the universe.

15. For the circumcision is not anything*, neither is uncircumcision; only the new creation.

* Most Greek mss. have τι ισχυει –"has any strength"; Critical Greek editions have, τι εστιν–"is anything." The 2 Greek readings have **42% correlation**.
Here are the two readings in DSS Aramaic:
מדם מחיל–"has any strength"
מדם איתוהי –"is anything"
88% correlation in Aramaic.

16. And those who agree to this path shall have peace and affection upon them and upon the Israel* of God.

* Paul is saying that the true Israel is the people of The New Creation who are led by The Spirit. See Romans 9:6-8.

17. A person therefore shall not put trouble upon me, for I have received* the scars of Our Lord Yeshua in my body.

* שקיל–"Received", strangely, is also used of crucifixion as "**lifted up**" on a cross.

18. The grace of Our Lord Yeshua The Messiah *is* with your spirit, my brethren. Amen.

The Epistle of The Apostle Paul to the Ephesians

Chapter 1

1. Paul, an Apostle of Yeshua The Messiah in the will of God, to those who are in Ephesaus, holy and faithful in Yeshua The Messiah.

2. Peace with you and grace from God our Father and from Our Lord Yeshua The Messiah.

3. Blessed is The God and The Father of Our Lord Yeshua The Messiah, he who has blessed us with all the spiritual blessings in Heaven in The Messiah.

4. Just as he chose us beforehand in him from before the foundation of the universe, that we shall be holy and without spot before him, and he ordained us beforehand in love for himself.

5. And he has constituted us as children by Yeshua The Messiah, as that is pleasing to his will,

6. That the glory of his grace may be praised, that which overflows upon us by his Beloved One.

7. For in him we have redemption, and the forgiveness of sins by his blood, according to the riches of his grace,

8. That which has superabounded in us in all wisdom and in all intelligence.

9. And he has taught us the mystery of his will, that which he had before ordained to perform in himself,

10. For the administration of the end of time, that all things which are in Heaven and in Earth would be made new again by The Messiah.

11. And we are chosen by him as he had before ordained us and willed to do all according to the counsel of his will,

12. That we would be those who first hoped in The Messiah, to the honor of his glory.

13. For you also heard by him the word of truth, which is The Good News of your salvation, and you believed in him, and you were sealed in The Spirit of Holiness who was promised,

14. Who is the pledge of our inheritance for the redemption of those who are living and for the glory of his honor.

15. Because of this, behold, I also, from when I heard of your faith in Our Lord Yeshua The Messiah and your love for all The Holy Ones,

16. I do not cease to give thanks for you and to remember you in my prayers,

17. So that The God of Our Lord Yeshua The Messiah, The Father of glory, would give you The Spirit of wisdom and revelation with his knowledge,

18. And that the eyes of your hearts would be enlightened, that you will know what is the hope of his calling and what is the wealth of the glory of his inheritance in The Holy Ones,

19. And what is the excellence of the greatness of his power in us, by those things which we believe, according to the action of the immensity of his power,

20. Which he performed in The Messiah and raised him from among the dead and set him at his right hand in Heaven,

21. Higher than all Principalities, Rulers, Powers, and Dominions, and higher than every name that is named, not only in this universe, but also in the one that is coming.

22. And he has put everything into subjection under his feet, and he has given him who is higher than all as The Head of the church,

23. Which is his body and the fullness of him who fills all in all.

Chapter 2

1. And *he fills* even you who were dead in your sins and in your stupidity.

2. And these things in which you walked from the first, you were in them according to the secular life of this world and according to the will of The Ruler of The Authority of The Air and of this spirit which is diligent in the children of disobedience.

3. We also were employed in those works from the first in the desires of the flesh, and we were doing the will of our flesh and of our minds, and we were entirely children of rage, as the rest.

4. But God who is rich in his compassion, because of his great love with which he loved us,

5. When we were dead in our sins, he gave us life together with The Messiah, and by his grace he saved us.

6. And he has raised us up with him and seated us with himself in Heaven in Yeshua The Messiah,

7. To show the coming ages the greatness of the riches of his grace and his sweetness, which has come upon us by Yeshua The Messiah.

8. For it is by his grace that we have been saved through faith, and this *faith* was not from you, but it is the gift of God,

9. Not of works, lest anyone should boast.

10. For we are his creatures who are created in Yeshua The Messiah for good works, those things which God had from the first prepared that we should walk in them.

11. Because of this, be mindful that you Gentiles from the first were of the flesh, and that you were called uncircumcision by that which is called circumcision and is a work of the hands in the flesh.

12. And you were at that time without The Messiah, and you were aliens from the government of Israel and strangers to The Covenant of The Promise and you were without hope and without God in the world.

13. But now you are in Yeshua The Messiah, when from the first you were distant, and you have come near by the blood of The Messiah.

14. For he is our peace who made the two one, and he destroyed the wall that was standing in the middle.

15. And he has canceled the hatred by his flesh and the law of commands in his commandments, that for the two, he would create in his Person one new man, and he has made peace.

16. And he has reconciled the two with God in one body, and in his crucifixion he has killed the hatred.

17. And he came preaching The News of Peace to you, to the distant ones and to those who are near,

18. Because in him, we both have access by One Spirit to The Father.

19. Therefore, you are not strangers, neither guests, but inhabitants of the city of The Holy One and children of the household of God.

* בני מדינתא דקדישא -"**Bnay mditta d'qadisha**" is literally "**children of the City of The Holy One(s)**" ; Greek has "συμπολιται των αγιων" –"**fellow citizens of The Holy Ones**", taking דקדישא – qadisha as plural; קדישא –qadisha can be singular or plural. Paul had already addressed the Ephesians as qadisha "**Holy Ones**" in the first verse of this epistle; it would be no great statement to then say they were "**fellow citizens of The Holy Ones**". <u>They were Holy Ones themselves, not fellow citizens of the holy ones!</u>

20. And you are built up upon the foundation of the Apostles and of the Prophets, and he is The Head of The Corner of the building- Yeshua The Messiah.

21. And the whole building is constructed by him and grows into a holy temple in **THE LORD JEHOVAH**,

22. While you also are built by him for the dwelling of God in The Spirit.

Chapter 3

1. **B**ecause of this, I Paul am the prisoner of Yeshua The Messiah for the sake of you Gentiles,

2. If you have heard of the administration of the grace of God, which is given to me among you.

3. For the mystery was taught me by revelation, just as I have written to you briefly.

4. As whenever you read, you can understand my knowledge in the mystery of The Messiah,

5. Which in other generations was not made known to the children of men as now it is revealed to his holy Apostles and to his Prophets by The Spirit:

6. That the Gentiles would be heirs and members of the body and of The Promise that was given in him by The Gospel,

7. That of which I have been a minister, according to the gift of the grace of God which is given to me by the action of his power;

8. To me, I who am the least of all The Holy Ones, this grace has been given, that I should preach The Good News among the Gentiles, the unsearched wealth of The Messiah,

9. And that I may enlighten every person by the administration of the mystery which was hidden from the world in God The Creator of all,

10. That by the church would be made known the full-diverse wisdom of God to Principalities and to Rulers who are in Heaven,

11. That which he had prepared from eternity and performed in Yeshua The Messiah Our Lord,

12. Him by whom we have boldness and access in the confidence of his faithfulness.

13. Because of this I request that you shall not grow weary of me by my afflictions which are for your sakes, for this is your glory.

14. And I bow my knees to The Father of Our Lord Yeshua The Messiah,

15. Him from whom every fatherhood is named, that is in Heaven and in Earth,

16. That he would grant you according to the riches of his glory to be confirmed by power in his Spirit, that in your inner person

17. The Messiah may dwell by faith, and in your hearts by love, when your root and your foundation shall be confirmed,

18. That you can discover with all the holy, what is the height and depth and length and breadth,

19. And you may know the magnitude * of the knowledge of the love of The Messiah and you may be filled in all the fullness of God.

* Greek has "**to know the love of Christ which surpasses knowledge**". Here is an excerpt from **Jastrow's Dictionary of The Targums , etc.** , for the Aramaic word , "רבותא" –"**Rabotha**" :

רְבֵי, רְבוּתָא f. 1) 1) *greatness, dignity, office ;* anointment. Targ. II Esth. VI, 10. Targ. Is. IX, 6. Targ. Deut. XXXII, 3 (Y. II רֵמֵי). Targ. Zech. IX, 4 (h. text יָקָר). Targ. Num. XVIII, 8 (h. text מָשְׁחָה). Targ. Ps. CXLV, 3 (some ed. רְבוּ). Ib. CL, 2, v. אֶתְרָא; a. fr.—

רְבוּתָא f. (denom. of רַבָּא) 1) *seniority.* Targ. O. Gen. XLIII, 33 כַּרְבּוּתֵהּ ed. Berl. (ed. כרביותה, corr. acc.).— 2) *superiority,* v. preced.

The Greek reading την υπερβαλλουσαν της γνωσεως , normally translated-"**surpassing knowledge**" may be translated simply "**excellence of knowledge**" , which is exactly the meaning of the Aramaic phrase in The Peshitta- מיתרא רבותא . The Greek after that takes on a new meaning with the word "αγαπην"-**agapayn** (form of "**agapay**")- then we have "**to know the love of Christ which surpasses knowledge**", which is nonsense. How can one know something that surpasses knowledge ? Another translation of the Greek is, "**to know the surpassing love of the knowledge of Christ**", but that is just as confusing or moreso than the other. I think a Greek translator put αγαπην- "love"- "agapay" in the wrong case (accusative instead of genitive) , which changes one letter at the end (αγαπην instead of αγαπης) . If that were the case, the Greek would have the same meaning as The Aramaic text here: "**the excellence of the knowledge of the love of The Messiah**".

20. But to him who is more than almighty to do for us and is greater than what we ask or imagine, according to his power that is active in us,

21. To him be glory by the church in Yeshua The Messiah to all generations of the eternity of eternities. Amen.

Chapter 4

1. I who am a prisoner in Our Lord request of you, therefore, that you walk just as it is suitable to the calling in which you are called,

2. In all humility of mind and quietness and patience, and that you would be patient one toward another in love,

3. And to be diligent to keep the harmony of The Spirit in the bonds of peace,

4. And that you would be in one body and One Spirit as when you were called in one hope of your calling.

5. For **THE LORD JEHOVAH** is One, and the faith is one, and the baptism is one,

6. And One is God The Father of all, and over all, and with all and in us all.

7. But to each one of us grace is given according to the size of the gift of The Messiah.

8. Therefore it is said, "He ascended to the heights and took captivity prisoner and he has given gifts to the children of men."

9. But that he ascended, what is it but that also he first descended to the lower regions of The Earth?

10. He who descended is the same who also ascended higher than all Heavens to restore all things.

11. And he gave some who are Apostles and some who are Prophets and some who are Evangelists and some who are Pastors and some who are Teachers,

12. For the perfecting of The Holy Ones, for the work of the ministry, for the building up of the body of The Messiah,

13. Until we all shall be one entity in the faith and in the knowledge of The Son of God and one perfect man with the dimensions of the stature of the maturity of The Messiah,

14. Neither shall we be children who are shaken and troubled for every wind of crafty teaching of the children of men, those who plot to seduce by their cunning.

15. But we have been firm in our love that all our affairs may increase in The Messiah, who is The Head,

16. And from him, the whole body constructed and joined in every joint, according to a gift given in measure to every member for his growth of the body, that his building may be completed in love.

17. But I say this and testify in **THE LORD JEHOVAH**, that from now on, you should not be walking as others of the Gentiles who walk in the emptiness of their minds,

18. And they are dark in their intellects and are aliens to the Life of God, because there is no knowledge in them and because of the blindness of their heart,

19. Those who have cut off their hope and handed themselves over to lewdness and to the cultivation of every impurity in their lust.

20. But you have not learned The Messiah in this way,

21. If truly you have heard him and you have learned of him, as whatever is truth is in Yeshua.

22. But you should put aside from you your first way of life, that old man, which is corrupted by deceitful desires,

23. And you should be made new in the spirit of your minds.

24. And you should put on the new man, who has been created by God in righteousness and in the purity of the truth.

25. Therefore, put aside from you lying and let a man speak the truth with his neighbor, for we are members one of another.

26. Be angry * and do not sin, and do not let the sun set on your anger.
(* "Ragza" has the basic meaning of "shake", "tremble" and applies to any strong human emotion or passion.)

27. Neither should you give place to The Slanderer.

28. But whoever has stolen, let him not steal from now on, but let him toil with his hands and produce good that he might have to give to the one who is in need.

29. Let not any hateful words come out of your mouth, but whatever is good and useful for improvement that you may give grace to those who hear,

30. Neither be grieving the Holy Spirit of God, for you have been sealed in him for the day of redemption.

31. Let all bitterness, fury, rage, clamor, and insults be taken away from you with all wickedness,

32. And be sweet one toward another and affectionate, and be forgiving one another, just as God in The Messiah has forgiven us*.
* Critical Greek ,The Textus Receptus (KJV Greek text) and The Latin Vulgate have "**You**". The Majority Greek text agrees with The Peshitta here.

Chapter 5

1. Be therefore imitators of God, as beloved children,

2. And walk in love, as also The Messiah has loved us and handed himself over for our persons, the offering and sacrifice to God, for a sweet fragrance.

3. But fornication, all impurity and greed are not even to be named at all among you, as is appropriate for Holy Ones,

4. Neither abusive language, neither worthless words, nor of disgrace, nor of nonsense- these things that are unnecessary, but in place of these, thanksgiving.

5. You have known this, that no person who is a fornicator or impure or a greedy person (who is an idol worshipper) has any inheritance in The Kingdom of The Messiah and of God.

6. Let no one deceive you with empty words, for it is because of these things the anger of God comes on the children of disobedience.

7. You should not therefore be partners with them.

8. For you were formerly darkness, but now you are light in Our Lord , therefore so walk as children of Light.

9. For the fruits of The Light* are in all goodness, righteousness and truth.

* Most Greek mss. have "**Spirit**" for "**Light**" (No capital letters exist in Aramaic).The Latin Vulgate and Critical Greek   text have "**Light**".

דנוהרא -"**Of The Light**" in Dead Sea Scroll script is
אֵרוּהֵנֵרדֵ .

דרוהא - "**Of The Spirit**" in Dead Sea Scroll script is
אֵהוֵרד .It is easy to see how the second DSS term may have been misread from the first , especially if the third and fourth letters וה were pushed together , looking like ה . We are not sure how the Resh ר and Nun נ looked ; They may have been as ר – נ or ר – נ . The former pair are more similar. Even without that supposition, there is **67%** correlation between the two words- enough to account for the majority Greek reading. If the וה letters were pushed together in the original Peshitta ms. from which Greek was being translated, that would give **80%** correlation.
The same in Estrangela script (used in all the oldest Peshitta mss.) is ܢܘܗܪܐ & ܪܘܚܐ. They are not quite as similar **(50%)** .
"**Of Light**" in Greek is Φωτος or ΦΩΤΟΣ ; "**Of Spirit**" is πνευματος or ΠΝΕΥΜΑΤΟΣ . That is a mere **33%** correlation. It is not very likely a translator would see ΠΝΕΥΜΑΤΟΣ and think ΦΩΤΟΣ . Peshitta primacy explains the Greek much better than the Greek can account for The Peshitta reading.

10. Distinguish what is pleasing before Our Lord.

11. Neither should you fellowship with the Servants * of darkness, because they have no fruit in them, but you should rebuke them.

* Greek mss. have "**works**" – εργοις or ΕΡΓΟΙΣ . The written Aramaic word for "**Works**" and "**Servants**" is the same (עבדא). The "**Works**" interpretation of Greek does not fit. A person does not fellowship with works or rebuke works; one fellowships with people and may rebuke people. The next verse confirms that the "**Servants**" meaning is the correct one.

12. For the thing that they* do in secret is an abomination to mention.

* Who are "**They**" , according to the Greek text of verse 11 ? "**They**" are "**The Servants of darkness**" according to The Peshitta. The "**works of darkness**" do nothing in secret or in public; they are what is done (object, not subject).Do not these facts concerning Aramaic strongly support the Aramaic original position and militate against a Greek original?

13. For all things are corrected by The Light and they are revealed, and everything that reveals* is light.

* Greek has a middle-passive verb φανερουμενον- "appears", "is revealed" . This is probably due to the fact that the Aramaic word גלא – can be active or passive -"reveals" or "is revealed", though the active sense is plainly intended. Light is what reveals something, not what is revealed. The Greek is incorrect.

14. Therefore it is said, "Awake, you who sleep, and arise from among the dead and The Messiah will illuminate you."

15. See therefore that you walk honorably, not as the fools, but as the wise,

16. Who redeem their opportunities because the days are evil.

17. Therefore do not be stupid, but understanding what the will of God is.

18. Neither be drunk with wine in which is debauchery, but be filled with The Spirit.

19. But speak to yourselves in Psalms and hymns and songs of The Spirit; be singing in your hearts to **THE LORD JEHOVAH.**

20. Be giving thanks always for the sake of every person in the name of Our Lord Yeshua The Messiah to God The Father.

* Greek has "ευχαριστουντες παντοτε υπερ παντων" -"**Give thanks for all things…**", though it could mean, **Give thanks for all** people"; it is ambiguous in Greek. The Aramaic is very clear. Scripture says ,"**In everything give thanks**", but that is a different proposition from , "**For everything give thanks**". I cannot see the Peshitta reading as a translation of the Greek.

21. Be subject to one another in the love of The Messiah.

22. Wives, be subject to your husbands as to Our Lord,

23. Because the man is the head of the woman just as The Messiah is also The Head of the church and he is The Savior of the body.

24. But just as the church is subject to The Messiah, in this way also wives are to their husbands in all things.

25. Husbands, love your wives, as The Messiah also loves his church and gave himself up for her sake,

26. To sanctify and purify her in the washing of water and in the word.

27. And he shall establish the church for himself when it is glorious, without blemish or wrinkle, neither any such things whatsoever, but it will be holy and without defect.

28. In this way men ought to love their wives as their bodies. Whoever loves his wife loves himself.

29. For no man ever hated his own body, but he nourishes and cares for his own, just as The Messiah does also for his church.

30. Because we are members of his body and we are of his flesh and of his bones.

31. Therefore, a man should leave his father and his mother and should cleave to his wife, and the two of them shall be one flesh.

32. This is a great mystery, but I am speaking about The Messiah and about his church.

33. Moreover, you also, everyone of you should in this way love his wife as himself; but the woman should revere her husband.

Chapter 6

1. Children, obey your parents in Our Lord, for this is right.

2. And this is the first commandment of promise: "Honor your father and your mother,

3. And it shall be well for you and your life shall be long on The Earth."

4. Parents, do not anger your children, but rear them in the discipline and in the teaching of Our Lord.

5. Servants, obey your Masters who are in the flesh with reverence and trembling and with simplicity of heart, as unto The Messiah,

6. Not publicly, as if you please the children of men, but as Servants of The Messiah, doing the pleasure of God.

7. And serve them with all your soul in love, as unto Our Lord and not as unto men,

8. As you know that anything a man does which is excellent will be repaid by Our Lord, whether he is a Servant or a Freeman.

9. Also you Masters, in this way do to your Servants; be forgiving offenses unto them, because you know that your Master also is in Heaven, and there is no favoritism with him. (Greek has, "**the same things, be doing towards them, forbearing your threat**…", a far cry from "**so do to your Servants, forgiving offenses to them**". The Greek texts seem to mitigate against being overly kind to slaves, here and in other verses. Compare Col 4:1 "**Masters, give unto your Servants that which is just and equal; knowing that ye also have a Master in Heaven**." from the Greek, with the Peshitta reading of the same verse: "**Masters, practice equality and justice with your Servants and be aware that you also have a Master in Heaven**." Giving what is equal and practicing equality are two vastly different things, it seems to me.

10. Therefore, my brethren, be strengthened in Our Lord and in the force of his power.

11. And put on all the armor of God, so that you can stand against the strategies of The Devil.

12. Because your fight has not been with flesh and blood, but with Principalities and

The Rulers and The Powers of this dark world and with wicked spirits which are under Heaven. * Greek has "**in Heavenly places**" – quite different from "**under Heaven**".

13. Because of this, put on all the armor of God that you shall be able to confront The Evil One, and when you are ready in all things, you shall stand.

14. Stand therefore and gird your waist with the truth and put on the breastplate of righteousness,

15. And shoe your feet with the readiness of The Gospel of peace,

16. And with these, take to you the shield of faith, that with it you may have the power to quench all of the blazing bolts of The Evil One.

17. Put on the helmet of salvation and grasp the sword of the Spirit, which is the word of God.

18. Pray with all prayers and with all desires always in The Spirit and be watching with him in prayer every moment as you pray constantly and make supplication for the sake of all The Holy Ones,

19. Also for me, that the word may be given to me by opening my mouth, that publicly I may preach the mystery of The Gospel,

20. That of which I am an Ambassador in chains, that I may speak it with boldness as it is necessary for me to speak it.

21. But so that you will know also each of my concerns and whatever I do, behold, Tukiqos, a beloved brother and trustworthy minister in Our Lord will inform you.

22. For I shall send him to you for this purpose, that you may know my affairs, and he will comfort your hearts.

23. Peace be with our brethren and love with faith, from God The Father and from Our Lord Yeshua The Messiah.

24. Grace be with all those who love Our Lord Yeshua The Messiah without corruption. Amen.

The Epistle of The Apostle Paul to the Philippians

Chapter 1

1. Paulus and Timotheus, Servants of Yeshua The Messiah, to all Holy Ones who are in Yeshua The Messiah, who are in Philippus with the Elders and the Ministers.

2. Grace be with you and peace from God our Father and from Our Lord Yeshua The Messiah.

3. I thank my God for the constant memory of you.

4. For in all my prayers for your sakes, as I rejoice, I make petitions

5. For your partnership in The Gospel from the first day, and until now,

6. Because I trust concerning this, that he who has begun good work in you will accomplish that until the day of Our Lord Yeshua The Messiah.

7. For it is right for me to think in this way about all of you, because you have been placed in my heart while I have been in my chains and in my defense for the truth of The Gospel, because you are my partners in grace.

8. For God is my witness, how much I love you with the affection of Yeshua The Messiah.

(Greek has, "**For God is my witness, how I long for you all in the bowels of Jesus Christ**." That just does not cut a straight line for me, especially compared to The Peshitta. By the way, "the bowels" as the seat of affection is a Semitic figure of speech, totally foreign to pre-Christian Greek. Greeks typically considered σπλαγχνα -"**splagcna**" in a literal sense or as the seat of violent emotion: "Rage,Jealousy,Grief". The positive sense originated as a result of translating the Hebrew idiom in religious literature, and as used in the NT, it reflects translation of the Aramaic idiom of "**Rakhma**" –"the bowels,mercy,love", as "**bowels**", the seat of affection.)

9. And I pray this, that your love may again increase and abound in knowledge and in all spiritual understanding,

10. That you would distinguish those things that are suitable, and that you may be pure, without an offense in the day of The Messiah,

11. And filled with the fruit of righteousness which is in Yeshua The Messiah, for the glory and honor of God.

12. I wish you to know my brethren, that my condition has come all the more to anticipate The Gospel;

13. So also my chains were revealed by The Messiah to the whole Praetorium and to everyone else.

14. A multitude of the brethren who are in Our Lord have been confident because of my chains and have been all the more defiant without fear to speak the word of God;

15. And some men are preaching The Messiah out of envy and contention, and some in good will and in love,

16. Because they know that I am appointed to defend The Gospel.

17. But those who preach The Messiah by contention, insincerely, only hope to add suffering to my imprisonment.

18. And in this I have rejoiced and do rejoice, that in every way, if in pretense or in the truth, The Messiah will be preached.

19. For I know that these things are found by me for life, by your prayers, and by the gift of The Spirit of Yeshua The Messiah,

20. Just as I hope and expect that I shall not be ashamed in anything, but openly as always, even now, The Messiah will be magnified in my body, whether in life or in death.

21. For my life is The Messiah, and if I shall die, it is gain for me.

22. But if also in this life of the flesh I have fruit in my work, I do not know what I shall choose for myself.

23. For two things are pressing upon me: I desire to depart that I might be with The Messiah, and this would be much better for me,

24. But also to remain in my body is pressing business for me because of you.

25. And this I know confidently, that I remain and continue for your joy and for the growth of your faith.

26. And when I come again to you, your boasting which is in Yeshua The Messiah alone will abound by me.

27. Be guided just as it is suitable to The Gospel of The Messiah, that whether I come to see you or whether I am absent, I may hear about you, that you stand in one spirit and one soul and that you are celebrated as one in the faith of The Gospel.

* Greek has συναθλουντες –"**striving together**"; Here is the Aramaic word in the Peshitta ומתנצדחיתון –"**& you are celebrated**". Here is the Aramaic for "**& you are striving**": ומתנצירתון . This is the original ומתנצדחיתון reading with one letter dropped-ה.What an amazing coincidence, is it not ? ומתנצדחיתון –"**& you are celebrated**" without the letter ה is ומתנצדיתון –"**& you are striving**" ! "**You are celebrated**" in Greek would be "αινεσθε" or "αινουμενοι".That looks nothing like συναθλουντες –"**striving together**". There is no evidence here to support the idea that The Peshitta was translated from Greek; on the other hand, the evidence for The Greek being a

translation of a Peshitta original is quite compelling here and elsewhere.

מתגצדהיתון –"**& you are celebrated**" (Peshitta)
מתגצירתון –"**& you are striving**" (Greek reading in Aramaic)
The two Aramaic words have **89%** letter correlation, with only one letter difference between them. The Peshitta mss. have no variant readings in this verse. The Greek words αινουμενοι & συναθλουντες have **17%** correlation at best. Is there any question that the Greek reading is derived from the Peshitta's Aramaic ?

28. And do not be shaken in anything by those who oppose us, as a demonstration of their destruction and of your life.
29. And this is given to you from God, that not only should you believe in The Messiah, but that you also will suffer for his sake.
30. And you will endure struggles, like those which you have seen in me and now hear about me.

Chapter 2

1. If you have, therefore, comfort in The Messiah, or the filling up of hearts with love, or communion of The Spirit, or tender care and mercy,
2. Fulfill my joy, that you would have one conscience, one love, one soul and one mind;
3. And you should not do anything with contention or empty glory, but in humility of mind, let every person esteem his neighbor as better than himself.
4. Neither let a man care for that which is his own unless every person *cares* also for that which is his neighbor's.
5. And reason in your souls this that also Yeshua The Messiah did:
6. He who, while he was in the form of God, did not esteem this as a prize, that he was the equal of God,
7. But he stripped himself and took the form of a Servant and was in the form of the children of men, and was found in fashion as a man.
8. And he humbled himself and was obedient unto death, even the death of being crucified.
9. Because of this, God has also greatly exalted him and he has given him The Name which is greater than all names,
10. That in The Name of Yeshua, every knee shall bow, which is in Heaven and in The Earth and which is under The Earth,
11. And every tongue shall confess that Yeshua The Messiah is **THE LORD JEHOVAH** to the glory of God his Father.

* The Name higher than all names is מריא "**MarYah**"- "**LORD JEHOVAH**" or "Lord Yahweh" , the Aramaic cognate of The Hebrew Old Testament Name - יהוה -"**Yehovah**" - The Name of God. The Greek texts have merely , "**Kurios**", which is not The highest name; it is not a name at all, merely a title which is used for landowners, merchants and nobles, and also is used of many pagan deities, as well as for the God of Israel in the Greek language. Greek has no name answering to The Tetragrammaton sacred Name "**YHWH**" as Aramaic does : מריא.

12. Therefore beloved, just as you have always obeyed, not when I am near to you only, but now when I am far from you, all the more, with awe and with trembling, do the service of your life *.

* Greek has "**Work out your own salvation**". This is not the meaning of the Aramaic- not by a long shot.

13. For God is carefully working in you both to desire and to do that thing which you desire *.

    * Greek has "**To do His pleasure**". The Aramaic is quite different.

14. Do everything without complaining and without division,
15. That you would be perfect and without blemish as purified children of God who dwell in a hard and crooked generation, and appear among them as lights in the world.
16. For you are in the place of life* to them, unto my boasting in the day of The Messiah, because I have not run for nothing, neither have I labored worthlessly.

* Greek has "**holding forth the word of life**".
Here is the Peshitta reading - "**You are to them in the place of life**" in **Dead Sea Scroll** Aramaic script:

Life   in the place to them   for you are

Here is "**You are holding forth to them the word of life**" in **Dead Sea Scroll** Aramaic script:

Life   the word to them for you are holding

The Peshitta mss. have no variant readings in this verse.
There is very little difference between the two readings in Aramaic. Part of the problem a first century translator may have had was poor lighting much of the time; couple that with reading someone else's handwriting in an age when eyeglasses were not available and there were no typewriters and word processors (and you must admit, the DSS script above has rather strange and distorted looking letters , many of which are very similar in appearance).Considering everything, the Greek translator did a very good job overall. The error rate in translation of the Aramaic is 0.4 % in 1 Corinthians by my estimation of 26 significant word errors in the Majority Greek text; that is **an accuracy rate of 99.6%** ! That is not too shabby! I doubt there are many today who could do as well at the same task, under 1st century circumstances.

17. But even if I am offered upon the sacrifice and service of your faith, I rejoice and triumph with all of you.

18. Rejoice and triumph with me in this way also.

19. But I hope in Our Lord Yeshua to send Timotheus to you soon, so that I may have refreshing when I learn about you.

20. For I do not have another here, who, like myself, is earnestly concerned for what is yours,

21. For they are all seeking what is their own and not what is of Yeshua The Messiah.

22. But you know the proof of this *man*, that as a son with his father, so he has worked with me in The Gospel.

23. But I hope to send this one to you soon, when I see my circumstances.

24. But I trust in my Lord that I also am soon coming to you.

25. But now a matter has compelled me to send Epaphroditus to you, a brother who is a helper and worker with me, but your Apostle and a Minister of my needs,

26. Because he was longing to see you all and he was grieved to know that you heard that he was ill.

27. For he was ill even unto death, but God had compassion upon him, and not upon him only, but also upon me, lest I would have sorrow upon sorrow.

28. Therefore, I diligently sent him to you, that when you see him again you will rejoice, and I shall have a little rest.

29. Receive him therefore in **THE LORD JEHOVAH** with all joy, and hold in honor those who are such.

30. For because of the work of The Messiah he approached death and scorned his life, to fulfill what you lacked in the ministry that was for me.

Chapter 3

1. Therefore, my brethren, rejoice in Our Lord; it is not tedious to me as I write these same things to you, because they protect you.

2. Beware of dogs; beware of evildoers; beware of the circumcisers.

3. For we are the circumcision, those who serve God in The Spirit, and we glory in Yeshua The Messiah, and we do not trust upon the flesh,

4. As I did have trust in the flesh, for if a man has hoped in his trust in the flesh, I have more than he:

5. Circumcised on the eighth day, of the family of Israel, from the tribe of Benjamin, a Hebrew, son of a Hebrew, in the Law, a Pharisee;

6. In zeal, a persecutor of the church, in righteousness of The Written Law I was without indictment.

7. But these things that were advantages to me, I have accounted losses for the sake of The Messiah.

8. I also consider all these things a loss for the majesty of the knowledge of Yeshua The Messiah, my Lord, him for whose sake I have lost everything, and I consider it all as a dung heap, that I may gain The Messiah,

9. And be found in him, while I do not have my own righteousness, which is from The Written Law, but that which is from the faith of The Messiah, which is the righteousness that is from God,

10. That by it I may know Yeshua and the power of his resurrection, and that I may share in his sufferings and be conformed with his death,

11. That perhaps I may be able to come to the resurrection from the place of the dead.

12. I have not yet received it, neither am I yet perfect, but I run so that I may obtain that thing for which Yeshua The Messiah apprehended me.

13. My brethren, I do not consider myself to have obtained it, but I know one thing: I have forgotten that which is behind me and I reach out before me,

14. And I run toward the goal to take the victory of the calling of God from on high in Yeshua The Messiah.

15. Let those who are perfected, therefore, be governed by these things, and if you are governed by anything else, God will reveal this also to you.

16. However, that we may arrive at this, let us follow in one path and with one accord.

17. Imitate me, my brethren, and observe those who walk in this way according to the pattern you have seen in us.

18. For many who walk differently, about whom I have told you many times, but now as I weep, I say that they are the enemies of the cross of The Messiah.

19. For their end is destruction, whose God is their belly and their glory is in their shame-these whose minds are in the dirt.

20. But our business* is in Heaven and from there we look for The Life Giver, Our Lord Yeshua The Messiah.

* Greek has "πολιτευμα"-"government", "citizenship"; I suspect that פולחנן (Business) was misread as פולוטין (Government) ; Look at these in DSS script: כוזהגנ : כוזומטנ-"government"; In Estrangela : ܦܘܠܘܛܝܢ

If you look carefully at the underlined letters- ח & ו , you can see ח appears as two letters put together – וו Zayin ,Waw , left to right . The letter to the left of ח is ן, which if pressed to the Zayin like half of ח "Khet" , looks like a Tau ת-ת. Tau ת and Tet ט sound very similar (T sound) ; If a Greek Scribe were reading and mentally pronouncing the word פולחנן as פולותינן or פולוטינן , he may have seen something like כוזהגנ (Business) as כוזוותנ and read it aloud and then translated from - כוזוטנ (Government). The evolution of this would look like:
1. כוזהגנ- "Our Business"
2. כוזוותנ –"(Khet broken into two letters- Zayin ו ,Waw ו)
3. כוזוותנ-"A phonetic spelling of "Paulautayan"(Tau -ת [T] sounds like Tet- ט [T]) ("Our Commonwealth")
4. כוזוטנ- "Paulautayan" (Our Commonwealth , the Aramaic base for "πολιτευμα"-"Government")
The Greek reading may have been based on sounding out word # 3 ("Paulautayan") and then writing it as #4 ("Paulautayan").
כוזהגנ - "Paulkhanan" -"Our Business" (Peshitta)
כוזוטנ - "Paulautayan" ("Our Commonwealth" , Aramaic for "πολιτευμα"-"Government")
The two have 72% correlation.
Some Greek words for "Business" are: λειτουργια & εργασια, λατρεια. "πολιτευμα"-"government" and "λατρεια"-"Service" are about as close as any two of the possible Greek pairs can be:
"ΠΟΛΙΤΕΥΜΑ"-"Government"
  "ΛΑΤΡΕΙΑ"-"Service"
These Greek words have 33% correlation.

21. For he will transform the body of our humiliation into the image of his glorious body, according to his great power by which everything has been made subject to him.

Chapter 4

1. Therefore, my beloved and precious brethren, my joy and my crown, so stand in Our Lord, my beloved.
2. I desire that Euodia and Suntyka be of one mind in Our Lord.
3. I also request of you, my true partner, that you will be helping these who labor with me in The Gospel, with Qlemas and with my other helpers, those whose names are written in The Book of Life.
4. Rejoice in Our Lord always, and again I say, rejoice.
5. And let your humility be known to every person; Our Lord is near.
6. Do not be worried for anything, but always in prayer and supplication with thanksgiving, let your requests be known before God,

7. And the peace of The God, Who is greater than every mind, will keep your hearts and your minds by Yeshua The Messiah.

This verse could be translated , "The peace of God which is greater than every mind…", but then that would include God's mind, would it not? Obviously, Paul was saying that God is supreme over all His creatures , not that His peace is greater than His own mind. The Greek has: "The peace of God which surpasses all understanding…",and presents a contradiction in terms which I am sure The apostle never would have written-(not to mention that The Holy Spirit would have never written).The Aramaic verse avoids the dilemma of the Greek verse. Most people would probably not object to the Greek reading, but our expectations from Scripture should be higher than that of mere common sense or conventional understanding. The Bible was written for all the ages to come and for eternity; It must be able to withstand the most rigorous assaults that logic can mount against it.

8. Therefore, my brethren, those things that are true, those that are honorable, those that are righteous, those things that are pure, those things that are precious, those things that are praiseworthy, deeds of glory and of praise, meditate on these things.
9. The things that you have learned and received and heard and seen by me, do these things, and The God of peace shall be with you.
10. But I have rejoiced greatly in Our Lord that you have come to be concerned for what is mine, just as you also were concerned, but you were not enabled;
11. But I said it, not because I had need, because I have learned that whatever I have will be enough for me.
12. I know how to be humbled, I know also what it is to abound; I am trained in everything and in all things, in fullness and in hunger, in excess and in poverty,
13. Because I master all things by The Messiah who empowers me.
14. However, you have done well in that you have shared with my afflictions.
15. But you Philippians know also that in the beginning of The Gospel, when I went out from Macedonia, not even one of the churches shared with me in an account of receiving and giving, but you only.
16. Because you also sent my necessities to me at Thessaloniqa, once and twice;
17. Not that I seek gifts, but I seek that fruit may abound to you.
18. I have received all things, and I have abundance and I am full, and I took all you sent to me by Epaphroditus, a sweet fragrance and acceptable sacrifice that pleases God.

19. And my God shall satisfy all your needs according to his riches in the glory of Yeshua The Messiah,

20. But to God Our Father is the glory and the honor to the eternity of eternities. Amen.

21. Invoke the peace of all The Holy Ones who are in Yeshua The Messiah. The brothers who are with me invoke your peace.

22. All The Holy Ones invoke your peace, especially these of the household of Caesar.

23. The grace of Our Lord Yeshua The Messiah be with all of you*. Amen.

* The Critical Greek text has "πνευματος υμων" - "**your spirit**". Below is a comparison of the Peshitta reading and the Greek reading in DSS Aramaic:

צלכון - "**you all**"

רוחכון - "**your spirit**"

The middle letter of the second word is the only significant difference in the appearance of two words; here are the two words with that one letter greatly diminished in size for illustration's sake:

צלכון - "**you all**"

רוחכון - "**your spirit**"

The same in Estrangela script looks like:

ܟܠܟܘܢ - "**you all**"

ܪܘܚܟܘܢ - "**your spirit**"

The Dead Sea Scroll Aramaic script looks like the best candidate for the original text of Philippians.

The Epistle of The Apostle Paul to the Colossians

Chapter 1

1. Paul, an Apostle of Yeshua The Messiah by the will of God, and brother Timotheus,

2. To those who are in Colossus, holy brethren and believers in Yeshua The Messiah: Peace with you and grace from God Our Father.

3. We always thank God, The Father of Our Lord Yeshua The Messiah, and we pray for you,

4. Behold, from the time we heard of your faith in Yeshua The Messiah and your love for all The Holy Ones,

5. Because of the hope which is kept for you in Heaven, that which from the first you had heard in the word of the truth of The Gospel,

6. That which was preached to you, as also to the whole world, and grows and yields fruit, just as also in you from the day when you heard and were taught the grace of God in the truth,

7. According to what you learned from Epaphra our beloved companion, who is a trustworthy Minister for you of The Messiah.

8. And he has made known to us your love, which is in The Spirit.

9. Due to this also, we, from the day when we heard, do not cease to pray for you and to request that you be filled with the knowledge of the pleasure of God in all wisdom and in all spiritual understanding,

10. That you would walk according to what is right, and that you may please God in all good works and yield fruit, and increase in the knowledge of God,

11. And that you would be empowered with all strength according to the majesty* of his glory with all patience, endurance and joy.

---

* Greek has κρατος –"Power,Dominion" ; Let's compare the Aramaic of The Peshitta reading - רבותא –"**Rabotha**" (**Greatness,Majesty**) with an Aramaic word for "Victory" – זכותא -"**Zakutha**" ; Here are the words in Dead Sea Scroll script : רבותא : זכותא . How about Estrangela script ? - ܪܒܘܬܐ : ܙܟܘܬܐ . Any one of these scripts could justify a misreading of the first word as the second, but I think the DSS is the most likely candidate as the source for the Greek reading (at least **80%** letter correlation).
In Greek, "**Greatness ,Majesty**" could be "μεγαλοσυνη", υπερβολη , μεγεθος , υπερεχον , μεγαλειοτητος. Which of these looks like κρατος – "**Power**" ?
The most similar in appearance is μεγεθος , which has only 2 letters corresponding to κρατος (**33%** correlation- a generous calculation). The Greek

primacy theory again suffers a defeat here. The Greek word κρατος –"**Power,Dominion**" is matched with זכותא –"**Zakutha**"(Victory) in Luke 1:51.

רבותא –"Majesty"(Peshitta)
זכותא –"Victory"(Aramaic for Greek reading ?)

12. I thank God The Father, who made us worthy for a part of the inheritance of the Saints in the light;

13. And he has saved us from the power of darkness and brought us into The Kingdom of his Beloved Son;

14. He in whom we have salvation and the forgiveness of sins;

15. He who is the image of The Unseen God and is The Firstborn of all creation.

16. By him was everything created which is in Heaven and in The Earth: everything that is seen and everything that is unseen, whether Thrones or Dominions or Principalities or Rulers; everything has been created by his hand and in him.

17. And he is The One who is before all, and all things exist by him.

18. And he is The Head of the body which is the church, for he is The Head and The Firstborn from among the dead , that he would be Preeminent in everything,

19. For in him All Fullness is pleased to dwell,

20. And to reconcile all things by him to Itself (All Fulness), and by him It (All Fulness) made peace by the blood of his crucifixion, whether of things that are in Earth or that are in Heaven. ("**All Fulness**" is The Godhead: God The Father, God The Son and God The Holy Spirit dwelling in the body of The Son. See 2:9.)

21. Even you from the first were aliens and enemies in your minds because of your evil works, and now he has given you peace,

22. By the body of his flesh and in his death, to establish you before him as Holy Ones without blemish and without an indictment,

23. If you continue in your faith while your foundation is true, and you are not moved from the hope of The Gospel which you heard, which has been preached in all creation under Heaven, of that of which I, Paulus, have become a Minister.

24. And I rejoice in the sufferings that are for your sake and I fill up the want of sufferings of The Messiah in my flesh for the sake of his body, which is the church,

25. Of which I am a Minister, according to the administration of God which is given to me among you, that I would fulfill the word of God,

26. That mystery which was hidden from the world and from generations but now has been revealed to his Holy Ones,

27. Those to whom God has chosen to make known what is the wealth of the glory of this mystery among the nations, which is The Messiah, who is in you, the hope of our glory,

28. Him whom we preach; and we teach and we educate every person in all wisdom, to confirm every person as perfected in Yeshua The Messiah;

29. For in this I also labor and fight with the help of the power that is given to me.

Chapter 2

1. **B**ut I want you to know what struggles I have for you and for those in Laidiqia and for those others who have not seen my face in the flesh,

2. And that their hearts may be comforted and that they may approach* by love all the wealth of assurance and understanding of the knowledge of the mystery of God The Father and of The Messiah,

- Greek has συμβιβασθεντων -"knit together"; The Aramaic is ונתקרבון -"& they may approach" ; Aramaic for "& they may be joined together" is ונתקטרון . The Greek for "approaching" is εγγιζοντων , which hardly looks like συμβιβασθεντων.
  Ashuri Aramaic script:
  ונתקרבון -"& they may approach" (Peshitta)
  ונתקטרון -"& they may be joined together" (Source for Greek reading ?)
  Dead Sea Scroll (Herodian) Aramaic:
  ונתקרבון -"& they may approach" (Peshitta)
  ונתקטרון -"& they may be joined" (Source for Greek reading ?)

Both Aramaic scripts exhibit 7 out of 8 letters the same, though it appears רב (Resh,Bet) in the original may have been switched to reverse order and then looked like טר in ונתקטרון -"& they may be joined". This works best in the DSS script, rather than Ashuri script. Correlations are at least 88% for the Aramaic scripts, possibly 95% with the DSS letter reversal.

3. Him in whom are hidden all the treasures of wisdom and knowledge.

4. But I say this: Let no man deceive you with persuasiveness of words.

5. For though I am separated from you in the flesh, yet I am with you in The Spirit, and I rejoice to see your organization and the stability of your faith which is in The Messiah.

6. Therefore, just as you have received Yeshua The Messiah Our Lord, walk in him,

7. Strengthening your roots while you are being built up in him, and you are being established in that faith which you have learned, in which may you abound with thanksgiving.

8. Beware lest any man rob you by philosophy, or by empty deception, according to the teaching of men and according to the principles of the world and not according to The Messiah,

9. For all The Fullness of The Deity dwells in him bodily.

10. And you also are completed in him, who is The Head of all Principalities and Powers.

11. And you are circumcised in him by circumcision that is without hands, in the putting off of the body of sins by the circumcision of The Messiah.

12. And you were buried with him in baptism, and in it you arose with him, because you believed in the power of God who raised him from among the dead.

13. And you, who had died by your sins and by the uncircumcision in your flesh, he has given you life with him and has forgiven us all our sins.

14. And he has blotted out by his authority the bill of our debts which was adverse to us and he took it from the midst and nailed it to his cross.

15. And by putting off his body, he stripped the Principalities and the Powers and shamed them openly in his Essential Self.

* Greek lacks "**By putting off His body**", which is a very significant phrase, indicating that the events in this verse would have occurred between the crucifixion and the bodily resurrection. This phrase in Aramaic did not come from Greek texts, as the Greek texts simply do not have it! Apparently a Greek translator simply missed it when translating the Aramaic.

* ארכוס -"**Arkas**" in one definition by Aramaean Christians and in their lexicons is "**The seventh order of Angels**". שליטנא and שלוטנא –"**Shultana**" , in its third definition is defined as "**The sixth order of Angels**". These are probably the meanings here, as the verse seems to describe The Messiah's spiritual activity after His physical death -"**Putting off His body**". Paul seems to use these words in this way in his epistles.

* קנומה –"**Qnoma**" is a word used only 15 times in The Peshitta NT; It may mean "**self**" , whether of a person or a thing, but it seems to indicate "**the essence of a thing**", according to Paul Younan, a native Aramaean and member of The Church of The East. With reference to Our Lord, it indicates, as here, His Divine Spirit as considered apart from His physical nature. Hebrews 1:3 (Peshitta) also refers to **The Qnoma** of The Son of God, as does John 5:26, Ephesians 2:15 & Hebrews 9:28. Hebrews 10:1 illustrates most clearly the meaning of the word: "**the very essence (qnoma) of the things**". The official doctrine of The Church of the East is that The Messiah has two qnomas (a Divine qnoma and a human qnoma), not to be confused with two natures, which according to that most ancient church are also possessed by The Messiah (called **Kayana**). I find no scriptural statements to the effect that Our Lord

possessed two **qnomas**. This verse and others mention only one, by which "**He purged our sins**" , "**put to shame the Principalities and Powers**" , "**made atonement for the sins of the many**", "**has Life in His qnoma**" as "**The Father has Life in His qnoma**" & "**in His qnoma He made of the two, one new man**". Hebrews 1:1-3 indicates that "**He Who purged our sins**" was The Divine Qnoma Who created all things and is The very Image of God's Being. Nowhere is there mention made of **two qnomas** existing in The Messiah. That concept is schizoid , it seems to me. No person or object can have two essential identities without being two persons or two objects. Our **LORD Yeshua Meshikha is One Person - One God Man, as One essence and nature, completely Divine in His Person and completely human in His nature, now glorified and raised to reign as Jehovah God, omnipresent, omnipotent and omniscient as He was from eternity.**

16.   Therefore let no man disturb you about food or about drink or in the distinctions of feasts and beginnings of months and Sabbaths,

17.   Because these things are shadows of those things that were future, but The Messiah is the body.

This verse is central to understanding Paul's teaching about the Old Covenant and The New Covenant. "**The Messiah is The Body**" of which the Old Covenant ordinances and precepts were mere " **shadows**".

18.   Let not a man wish by humility of mind to subjugate you to the worship of Angels to your condemnation, by which he presumes upon something that he does not see, and is emptily puffed up in his carnal mind,

19.   And is not holding The Head, from whom the whole body is constructed and settled in the joints and members, and grows with the growth of God.

20.   For if you have died with The Messiah to the principles of the world, why are you judged as if you live in the world,

21.   Namely, "Do not touch", "Do not taste", "Do not hold",

22.   Which are the things that need to be destroyed, and are the commandments and the teachings of the sons of men?

23.   And they appear to have in them a word of wisdom in the appearance of humility and worship of God and without sparing the body, not in things of honor, but in those things which are physical needs.

Chapter 3

1.   If therefore you are risen with The Messiah, seek that which is above, the place where The Messiah sits at the right side of God.

2.   Feed on that which is above and not that which is in The Earth,

3.   For you have died to yourselves and your lives are hidden with The Messiah in God.

4.   And whenever The Messiah, who is our life, is revealed, then you also will be revealed with him in glory.

5.   Kill therefore your members that are in Earth: fornication, impurity, diseases, wicked desires, and greed (which is idol worship),

6.   For because of these things, the anger of God comes upon his disobedient children.

Greek has "**The children of disobedience**". Romans 11:32 says "**God hath shut up all men in disobedience, that upon all men he might have mercy.**" The same phrase לא מתטפיסנותא –"**La mettapasnawtha**" is used in that verse. There is hope for the disobedient, for all of us were disobedient, but God has a plan of mercy for all people. Our hope is that "**God is The Father of all**", and deals with us all as His children.

7.   And you walked also in these things from the first, when you were employed in these things.

So this verse shows that God saves the disobedient; **who else is there to save ? Does he save the obedient ? of course not; the obedient have no need of salvation any more than the healthy need a physician.**

8.   But now put off from you all these things: anger, fury, wickedness, blasphemy, impure speech;

9.   Neither should you cheat one another, but put off the old man with all of his ways,

Greek has "**Having put off the old man**". The Peshitta text has a command: "**Put off the old man…**".

10. And put on the new, who is made new by knowledge in the image of his Creator,

11. Where there is neither Jew nor Aramaean*, neither circumcision nor uncircumcision, neither Greeks nor Barbarians, neither Servant nor Freeman, but The Messiah is all and in every person*.

* Greek has: "**Where there is not Greek and Jew, circumcision and uncircumcision, foreigner, Scythian, Servant, Freeman—but all things and in all—Christ.**"-(Rotherham's Emphasized Bible) The Peshitta lists a series of four contrasts; the Greek lists two contrasts, then "foreigner, Scythian"? , and then "Servant, Freeman". It just seems a bit incoherent or disjointed. The Greek has expunged all references to Aramaeans and Syrians from NT history, except for 1 reference to the ancient Naaman The Syrian in Luke 4:27. The Peshitta would not change "Greek" into "Syrian". "Greek" occurs intact 12 times in The Peshitta.

* "**The Messiah is all and in every person**", is the literal statement at the end of this Aramaic verse. The Greek has literally, "**Christ is all things and in all things**". It looks like a choice is between an apparent **Universalism** of The Peshitta text or apparent **Pantheism** of the Greek text !

12. Put on, therefore, as the chosen ones of God, holy and beloved, mercy and compassion, kindness and humility of mind, gentleness and long-suffering;

13. And be forbearing one to another and forgiving one another. But if anyone has an outrage against his neighbor, forgive just as The Messiah has forgiven you,

14. And with all these things, love, which is the bond of perfection.

15. And the peace of The Messiah* will govern your hearts, to which you are called in one body; and give thanks to The Messiah*.

* The Majority Greek has , "**And the peace of God..**" , and "**The Messiah**" is lacking at the end. The Critical has "**And the peace of Christ..**" & "**The Messiah**" is lacking at the end. The Aramaic text disagrees with both Greek texts here. The Critical reading at the beginning agrees with the Peshitta where The Majority Greek does not; both Greek texts disagree with The Peshitta at the end.

16. Teach and instruct your souls in the Psalms, that his word * may dwell in you richly in all wisdom, and sing in your hearts with grace to God * in praises and songs of The Spirit.

* Greek has "**The word of Christ**" which appears to be the transfer of the dropped "**Messiah**" at the end of the previous verse to the beginning of this verse: למשיחא at the end of The Peshitta verse 15 can mean,"**of the Messiah**". So the Greek text appears to have interpreted The Aramaic verse 15 as ending one word short of "**Messiah**", and then read the next sentence as starting with "למשיחא" –"**Of The Messiah**". The Aramaic reading cannot have come from any of the major Greek texts extant. The Greek, on the other hand, can be explained on the basis of the Aramaic.
* The Critical Greek has , "**to God**" , whereas the Majority Greek has "**to The Lord**".

17. And everything that you perform in word and in works, do in the name of Our Lord Yeshua The Messiah and give thanks by him to God The Father.

18. Wives, be subject to your husbands, as that is right in The Messiah.

19. Husbands, love your wives and do not be bitter toward them.

20. Children, obey your parents in all things, for thus it is pleasing before Our Lord.

21. Parents, do not anger your children, lest they lose heart.

22. Servants, obey your Masters of the body in all things, not outwardly as those who please men, but with a pure heart and in the awe of **THE LORD JEHOVAH.**

* The Critical Greek text has , "τον Κυριον" –"**The Lord**" ; The Majority Greek has "τον Θεον" –"**God**".

Each of these is a possible Greek translation of The Aramaic דמריא -"**D`MarYah**"- (of Jehovah).

23. And do all that you do with all your soul, as for Our Lord, and not as for the children of men.

24. And know that you will receive from Our Lord a reward in the inheritance, for you serve **THE LORD JEHOVAH** * The Messiah.

* "**For you serve <u>Jehovah The Messiah</u>**". No Greek ms. has this, nor could Greek have this.

25. But he pays the wrongdoer according to what he does wrong, and there is no favoritism.

Chapter 4

1. Masters, practice equality and justice with your Servants and be aware that you also have a Master in Heaven.

2. Persevere in prayer and be watching in it and giving thanks.

3. And pray also for us that God would open the door of the word to us to speak the mystery of The Messiah, for whose sake I am bound,

4. That I may reveal it and speak it just as I must.

5. Walk in wisdom toward outsiders and buy your opportunities.

6. And your words should always be with grace, as if seasoned with salt, and be aware how it is appropriate for you to answer each man.

7. Tukyqos, a beloved brother and a trustworthy Minister and our companion in **THE LORD JEHOVAH,** will inform you of my matters,

8. This one whom I sent to you to know your matters* and to comfort your hearts,

* Most Greek mss. have "**that he may know your state**"; some Greek mss. have , "**that you may know our state**".

9. With Onesimus, a trustworthy and beloved brother, who is from among you, to inform you of those matters that pertain to us.

10. Aristarchus, a captive who is with me, invokes your peace, and Marcus, son of the paternal uncle of BarNaba, about whom you have been directed; if he comes you, receive him,

11. And Yeshua, who is called Justus, these who are of the circumcision and those alone

who helped me in The Kingdom of God and those who are comforts to me.

12.   Epaphra, a Servant of The Messiah from among you, invokes your peace, laboring always for you in prayer, that you may stand perfect and complete in the whole pleasure of God,

13.   For I testify about him that he has great zeal for your sake and for those who are in Laidiqia and in Aerapolis.

14.   Luqa, our beloved Physician, invokes your peace, and Dema.

15.   Invoke the peace of the brethren in Laidiqia and of Numpha and of the church which is in his house.

16.   And whenever this letter is read to you, cause it to be read in the church of Laidiqia and read that which was written from Laidiqia.

17.   And tell Arkippus, "Remember the ministry that you have received in Our Lord, that you finish it."

18.   This greeting is in my own hand, who am Paulus. Remember my imprisonment. Grace be with you. Amen.

The First Epistle of The Apostle Paul to the Thessalonians

Chapter 1

1. Paulus and Sylvanus and Timotheus to the church of Thessaloniqa in God The Father and in Our Lord Yeshua The Messiah. Grace be with you and peace.

2. We thank God always for all of you, and we are reminded of you in our prayers constantly.

3. And we recall before God The Father the works of your faith, the labor of your love and patience of your hope, which are in Our Lord Yeshua The Messiah.

4. For we know your election, brethren, beloved of God,

5. Because our evangelism was not in words only, but it was to you also in power and in The Spirit of Holiness and in true conviction. You also know how we have been among you for your sakes.

6. And you imitated us and Our Lord, for you received the word in great affliction and in the joy of The Spirit of Holiness.

7. And you have been a model to all believers who are in Macedonia and in Akaia.

8. For the word of Our Lord has been heard from you, not only in Maqedonia and in Akaia, but in every place your faith in God is heard, so that we will not need to say anything about you.

9. For they relate what an introduction we had to you and how you were turned to God from the worship of idols to serve The Living and True God,

10. While you await his Son from Heaven, Yeshua, him whom he raised from among the dead; He is The One who delivers us from the fury that is coming.

Chapter 2

1. And you know, my brethren, that our introduction to you has not been for nothing.

2. But first we suffered and we were abused as you know, and then in a great struggle we spoke The Gospel of The Messiah* with you in the boldness of our God.

* Greek has "The Gospel of God"; I suspect that the Greek translator translated the Aramaic word סברתה - "Gospel" – 2nd to last word in the verse and then looked back to the preceding word דאלהן "of our God" instead of the following word דמשיחא-"of The Messiah" and translated του θεου -"of God" and finally באגונא –"in a struggle", which in the Peshitta verse is in the middle of the verse, but in Greek, is at the very end, so the Greek translator was accustomed to jumping around the Aramaic verses to accommodate the Aramaic syntax to a somewhat more idiomatic Greek syntax –(Though it does seem the Greek

normally follows Aramaic word order fairly closely, which testifies strongly for an Aramaic original).

3. For our comfort was not from deception nor from impurity, nor by treachery.

4. But as when we were tested by God to be entrusted with his Gospel, so we speak, not as if we would please the children of men, but God who tests our hearts.

5. For neither do we ever employ enticing speech as you know, neither an occasion for greed, God is witness,

6. Neither do we seek glory from the children of men; not from you, neither from others, when we could have been honored* as Apostles of The Messiah.

* Greek has "εν βαρει – "with a burden"; יקירא can mean "heavy,**burdensome,honored,dear,precious**". It appears a Greek mistranslated יקירא ; Paul spoke of not seeking שובחא –"glory" and not being יקירא – "honored" here, and of being מכיכא – "meek" in the next verse. **Thayers Greek-English Lexicon** has for "βαρει" a possible secondary meaning of "**authority**". I doubt Paul wanted to relinquish his authority as an apostle; that would have defeated his purpose as God's messenger. It also seems to me the Greek construction, "εν βαρει" belies the interpretations put upon it ; If Paul meant to convey the idea of being a burden (in Greek) , he would not have used the preposition εν – "in", "with" before βαρει- "burden". Even the Greek betrays a Semitic original; יקירא has a basic meaning of "**weight**"; the noun derivative of this verb is איקרא –"glory,honor,magnificence". Hebrew has a cognate word for יקר – "heavy" (the root of יקירא used in this verse) which is כבד –"kabad" –("be heavy", "get honor","get glory") and it has a noun form : כבוד –"Kabowd"- "weight,glory,honor". The Greek "εν βαρει" reflects the Semitic construction , "באיקרא" –"in honor" like theHebrew בכבוד –"in honor", both of which are based on the root word for "heavy".
So literally, εν βαρει is a Greek reflection of an Aramaic idiom whose literal sense is "in weight" – not a Greek concept at all, but definitely a Semitic one- **(Hebrew,Aramaic,Arabic,Ethiopic)**

7. But we were meek* among you, even as a nursemaid who cherishes her children.

* "**Humble**" is מכיכא ; Some Greek mss. have νηπιοι –"**Babies**", which is very close to the spelling in the Majority Greek text reading –"ηπιοι"- "**Gentle**" – just take the first letter off νηπιοι and you have ηπιοι.
"**Humble**" מכיכא in DSS script is Here is the Aramaic word in DSS script for "Babies"- . Another possibility is . Let's line them up, using -"mawlada"(birth,child) one atop the other in three different Aramaic scripts:

Ashuri		DSS	Estrangela	
מכיכא – "Humble"			– "Humble"	
מולדא –"Babies"			–"Babies"	

It appears the Dead Sea Scroll script pair are the most alike. I think four of the five letters in could have been read as they are in (shaded red & underlined); Lets compare them again in DSS script:

–"Babies"

– "Humble"

–"Babies"

In the grey shaded pair, each Aramaic corresponding letter is similar and could be read for the other- that is close to 100% correlation.

If there were only one Greek ms. with the silly reading, "Babies", I would chalk it up to a misreading of the Greek majority reading in an uncial manuscript, in which the preceding letter N was read as the first letter of the following word "HΠIOI"- "**Gentle**" , forming "NHΠIOI"- "**Babies**"; Uncial mss. in Greek have no spaces between words , so this kind of error would have been easy to make. An uncial ms. would have looked like this in verse 7:

ΑΛΛΕΓΕΝΗΘΗΜΕΝΗΠΙΟΙΕΝΜΕΣΩΥΜΩΝΩΣ
ΑΝΤΡΟΦΟΣΘΑΛΠΗΤΑΕΑΥΤΗΣΤΕΚΝΑ

"HΠIOI"- "**Gentle**" is highlighted red and underlined; Adding the previous letter N makes it
NHΠIOI – "**Babies**".
However- there are too many early and diverse witnesses to this absurd reading to write it off as a Greek misreading error. Here are the witnesses for the reading NHΠIOI – "Babies" : P[65] (3rd century),ℵ,B,C,D,G,I,Ψ, Ten Italic mss (5th cent. - 10th), Latin Vulgate , Coptic 4th cent. Mss, Clement (2nd cent, Origen (3rd cent.) , and other church fathers of the 3rd and fourth centuries, including **Ephraim** the Syrian of the fourth century..
The fact that there are witnesses to Aramaic here-(**Codex D** quite often follows **Peshitta readings**- and **Ephraem the Syrian** used **Aramaic mss.** as his authority), says that this error occurred very early and was widely copied into many languages in a widespread geographical area from Egypt to **Syria** to Rome. Even **P[65]**, the earliest Greek ms. listed here, disagrees often with the other Greek mss. cited here in The Epistles. The fact that all these bear witness to this absurd reading is testament to an authority higher than a Greek uncial (no existing Greek uncial is followed closely by any group of Greek mss. in any book of The NT). I submit that the authority behind all these witnesses was a Peshitta manuscript. There apparently was an early Aramaic ms. which had the above error as illustrated in DSS Aramaic and was translated into Greek in the first century and thence into the several languages- Coptic, Latin, Italic, Ethiopic. So it was not properly a translation error, but an error of transcription in Aramaic into an early Aramaic manuscript of the first century. The error would not have survived in Peshitta mss, as the Aramaean Scribes would have easily detected and rejected it; a Greek translator was not in the business of textual criticism ; he would merely translate what he saw and pass it on. So there is widespread –though still a minority- witness to this early error in an Aramaic ms.

The fact remains that Greek mss. have these two readings, both of which may be explained as being derived from Aramaic. The Peshitta has no variant reading here among its mss. .(v. Juckel:Ms. Schoyen 2530/Sinai Syr. 3 & The NT Peshitta- Hugoye :Journal of Syriac Studies)

8. In this way also we cherish and long to give you, not only The Good News of God, but our lives also, because you are our beloved.
9. For you remember, brethren, that we were toiling and laboring in the works of our hands by night. And by day, that we might not be a burden to anyone of you,

* Greek adds to the end of this : εκηρυξαμεν εις υμας το ευαγγελιον του θεου -"**We preached to you The Gospel of God**".

Apparently they worked by night and preached by day. The Greek includes the preaching in this verse to clarify that. Actually, the two verses should be combined , as they are one continuous sentence and thought: "**For you remember, brethren, that we were toiling and laboring in the works of our hands by night; and that we might not be a burden to anyone of you,you and God are witnesses, how we preached by day The Good News of God to you, purely and rightly, and we were without a fault toward all the believers.**"

10. You and God are witnesses, how we preached The Good News of God to you purely and rightly, and we were without a fault toward all the believers.

Greek has " ως οσιως και δικαιως και αμεμπτως υμιν τοις πιστευουσιν εγενηθημεν" – "**how holily and righteously and blamelessly we became to you believers**". I hate to sound like a stickler for correct grammar, but you can't have a string of adverbs describing a verb of being, which εγενηθημεν is ; It is incorrect to say : "**we were blamelessly**", or "**we were righteously**" . In The Aramaic text, the first two adverbs describe their preaching, which is fine grammar: they "**preached purely and rightly**". The following phrase is an adjective, not adverb, in Aramaic: "**without fault we were**" ; that too is perfect Aramaic grammar. These things are explained by Aramaic primacy; Greek primacy is being increasingly clobbered by the facts and statistics.

11. Just as you know that we have been like a father to each one of you, pleading with his children, and we comfort your hearts and charge you
12. To walk as it is suitable to God, who has called you into his Kingdom and into his glory.
13. Because of this, we also thank God constantly that you have received the word of God from us, not as if you received the word of the children of men, but just as it is truly the word of God, and which is working among you by deeds in those who believe.
14. But you, my brethren, imitated the churches of God that are in Judea, these who are in Yeshua The Messiah, so that you suffered also by the children of your nation just as they did also of the Judeans,
15. Those who murdered Yeshua The Messiah our Lord, and they have persecuted their own Prophets, and us, and they do not please God and have become opposed to all people.
16. For they forbid us to speak with the Gentiles, that they may live to fulfill their sins always, but fury has come upon them until the end.
17. But we, brethren, were bereaved for a short time of your presence, but not in our hearts,

and we took all the more pains in much love to see your faces.

18. And we wished to come to you, I Paul, once and twice, and Satan hindered me.

* Greek has "**Satan hindered us**"; עוכני is "hindered **me**"; עוכן is "hindered **us**"; Here are the two words in DSS script: עוכני & עוכן ; In Estrangela script: ܥܘܟܢܝ & ܥܘܟܢ . A Yodh is the smallest letter in Aramaic and easily missed. The Greek for "**me**" is με or εμε ; "Us" is "ημας". In uncial (capital Greek letters used in ancient mss.) they are:
"me" is ME or EME ; "Us" is "HMAΣ". These are not easily confused, hence the Aramaic may account much more easily for the Greek reading than vice versa.

עוכני-"hindered **me**"
עוכן-"hindered **us**"

19. For what is our hope and our joy and the crown of our glory, but you alone, before Our Lord Yeshua at his coming?

20. For you are our glory and our joy.

Chapter 3

1. And because we did not resist, we chose to remain in Athens by ourselves,

2. And we sent Timotheus our brother to you, a Minister of God and our helper in The Good News* of The Messiah, that he might strengthen you and inquire* of you concerning your faith,

* סברתה - "**Sbartha**" comes from a root word "Sbar" which means "To be bright". From this are derived the meanings: "**Hope,Think,Look for, Be pleasant, Be intelligent, Conclude, Argue, Plan, Have an idea, Preach good news.**" All these are light shedding activities.
* Greek has παρακαλεσαι –"to comfort" where The Peshitta has "inquire". Compare the Aramaic for "may inquire" with "may comfort":
Ashuri Aramaic
בבעא "**may inquire**"(Peshitta)
בביא "**may comfort**"(Greek reading in Aramaic)
In Estrangela
ܢܒܥܐ - "**may inquire**"(Peshitta)
ܢܒܝܐ - "**may comfort**"(Greek reading in Aramaic)
In Dead Sea Scroll script
נבעא - "**may inquire**"(Peshitta)
נביא - "**may comfort**"(Greek reading in Aramaic)
The Aramaic pair in each script have approx. **75%** correlation.
The Greek for "**to inquire**" closest in appearance to παρακαλεσαι –"**to comfort**" is πυνθανεσθαι. Let's line them up like the Aramaic pair, in Uncial script:

ΠΑΡΑΚΑΛΕΣΑΙ –"to comfort"
ΠΥΝΘΑΝΕΣΘΑΙ-"to inquire"
The Greek pair have **54%** correlation.
It again appears that the Greek reading, though different from the Aramaic, may be explained as a misreading of one letter of the Aramaic reading. The two Greek words differ in five out of eleven letters in each.

3. Lest any of you should lose hope by such sufferings, for you are aware that we are appointed to this.

4. For also when we were with you, we said to you before that we would be persecuted, just as you know it happened.

5. Because of this I also did not resist until I sent to know your faith, lest the tempter would tempt you and our labor would be worthless. (This verse and the next confirms the Peshitta reading of verse 2 –"Inquire" as correct, as opposed to the Greek "Comfort".)

6. But now since Timotheus has come to us from your midst and he gave us good news concerning your faith and about your love, and that you have a good commemoration of us in every place and you desire to see us, just as we also do you,

7. Therefore we were comforted by you, brethren, concerning all our adversities and in our afflictions, because of your faith.

8. And now we live, if you will abide in Our Lord.

9. For what thanks can we pay on your behalf to God, for every joy with which we rejoice because of you,

10. Except that before God, we pray all the more earnestly, night and day, to see your faces, and perfect whatever is lacking in your faith?

11. But God Our Father and Our Lord Yeshua The Messiah shall direct our way to you,

12. And may he multiply and increase your love one toward another, and that to every person, just as we love you,

13. And establish your hearts without a fault in holiness before God Our Father at the arrival of Our Lord Yeshua The Messiah with all of his Holy Ones.

Chapter 4

1. Therefore, my brethren, we beg of you and pray earnestly for you in Our Lord Yeshua that as you have received of us how you must walk and please God, that you may grow all the more.

2. For you know those commandments which we gave to you by Our Lord Yeshua.

3. For this is the will of God: your holiness, and that you be separate from all fornication,

4. And that each one of you know to possess his vessel in holiness and in honor,

5. And not in the passion of lust, as others of the Gentiles who do not know God;

6. Neither should you presume to violate and take advantage, anyone, of his brother in this matter, because Our Lord is the avenger of all such, just as we have said before and testified to you,

7. For God has not called you to impurity but to holiness.

8. Therefore, whoever defrauds, does not defraud a man, but God, he who gives his Spirit of Holiness among you.

9. But you do not need to have written to you concerning love of the brethren, for you yourselves are taught by God to love one another.

10. You also are doing so to all the brethren who are in all Macedonia, but I beg of you, my brethren, that you superabound,

11. And that you would be diligent, peaceable and occupied with your business, working with your hands just as we commanded you,

12. That you would be walking in good form toward outsiders and that you would be dependent on no man.

13. I* want you to know* my brethren, that you should not have sorrow for those who are asleep, as do the rest of mankind who have no hope.

* Greek Textus Receptus (behind The English King James Version), has "ου θελω δε υμας αγνοειν" – "**I would not have you to be ignorant**", however, most Greek mss.(Critical Greek texts and Byzantine alike) have ,"ου θελομεν δε υμας αγνοειν" –"**We would not have you to be ignorant**". "**I want**" in Aramaic here is צבא אנא ; "**We want**" would be צבין חנן. In DSS – אנא אצי̈ ‎ -"**I want**"-Peshitta reading; ‎ ץH ‎ ‎ -̈ "**We want**"; Other forms for "**We wish**" are עבי̈נ , ‎ עצֻי̈ ‎ , אHאḦ ‎ . This last one is the most similar to the actual reading in Aramaic; let`s compare just those two: In DSS אנא אצי̈ "**I want**" ‎ ‎ ‎ ‎ ‎ "**We want**"; Possibly an early Peshitta manuscript had the form ‎ אנאצי̈-"**I want**" (Eastern and Western Peshitta mss. sometimes write pronouns differently) and a Greek translator saw this as ‎ -"**We want**". I am inclined to think not, however, and to go with the 1st pair listed, which I show below again:

אנא אצי̈-"I want"
‎ ‎ ‎ -"We want"

* Another difference between the Greek and Aramaic texts here and in more than ten other places in The Gospels and The Epistles, is the use in Greek of a double negation ("**I would not have you to be ignorant**") where the Peshitta has a simple positive – "**I want you to know**". **The LXX** does employ this construction in The Apocrypha a couple times and once in Hosea 4:15 where the Hebrew text does not have anything like it. I have some thoughts on this, but they are mere conjecture at this point.

14. For if we believe that Yeshua died and arose, in this way also God shall bring with him those who have fallen asleep in Yeshua.

Another possible translation is: "**For if we believe that Yeshua died and arose, in this way God, by Yeshua, shall bring with Him those who have fallen asleep.**"

15. But this we say to you by the word of Our Lord, that we, those who remain at the coming of Our Lord, we who have life, shall not overtake those who are asleep;

16. Because Our Lord shall descend from Heaven with a command and with the voice of the Archangel and with the trumpet blast of God, and the dead who are in The Messiah shall rise first;

17. And then we who remain, who have life, we shall be carried away with them together in clouds to a meeting of Our Lord in the air, and in this way, we shall always be with Our Lord.

18. Therefore, comfort one another with these words.

Chapter 5

1. But you do not need to be written to about times and seasons, my brethren,

2. For you truly know that the day of Our Lord so comes as a thief in the night.

3. When they shall say, "There is peace and quiet", then suddenly destruction shall arise upon them as labor pains upon a pregnant woman, and they shall not escape.

4. But you, my brethren, you are not in darkness that the day should overtake you as a thief.

5. For you are all children of light and children of the day and you* are not children of the night, neither children of darkness.

● Greek has "**& we are not**" where The Peshitta has "**& you are not**". "**We are**" is הוין , הוינן or איתין & "**You are**" is הויתון ; In DSS script : ‎ ‎ -"We are" ‎ ‎ -"You are"

Peshitta mss. do not have variants in this verse as they should if the Aramaic is based on Greek. There are Greek mss. with the Peshitta reading :**D** (5th cent.) ,**G** (9th cent.) as well as The Itala Version (Latin,2nd cent.).

6. Let us not sleep therefore as the rest, but let us be watchful and sensible.

7. For those who sleep, sleep at night, and those who are drunk are drunk at night.

8. But we are the children of the day; let us be vigilant in our minds and put on the breastplate of faith and of love and let us take the helmet of the hope of Life,

9. Because God has not appointed us to wrath, but to the possession of Life in Our Lord Yeshua The Messiah,

10. He who died for our sake, that whether we are awake or asleep, we shall live together with him.

11. Because of this, comfort one another and build one another up just as you have done.

12. But we beg of you, my brethren, that you will recognize those who labor among you and have standing among you in Our Lord and teach you,

13. That they should be esteemed by you in greater love, and be at peace with them because of their works.

14. But we beg of you, my brethren, correct wrongdoers, encourage the feeble souls, bear the burdens of the weak and be patient with every person.

15. Beware lest anyone of you reward evil for evil, but always run after the good with each and every person.

16. Rejoice at all times.

17. Pray without ceasing.

18. Give thanks in everything, for this is the will of God in Yeshua The Messiah among you.

19. Do not quench the Spirit.

20. Do not reject prophecy.

21. Examine everything and hold what is excellent.

22. Flee from every evil matter.

23. But The God of peace shall make all of you perfectly holy and shall keep your whole spirit, soul and body without fault for the arrival of Our Lord Yeshua The Messiah.

24. Faithful is he who has called you; it is he who shall perform it.

25. Pray for us, my brethren.

26. Invoke the peace of all our brethren with a holy kiss.

27. I bind you with an oath by Our Lord, that this letter will be read to all the holy brethren.

28. The grace of Our Lord Yeshua The Messiah be with you. Amen.

The Second Epistle of The Apostle Paul to the Thessalonians

Chapter 1

1. Paulus, Sylvanus and Timotheus, to the church of the Thessalonians which is in God Our Father and Our Lord Yeshua The Messiah.

2. Grace be with you and peace from God Our Father and from Our Lord Yeshua The Messiah.

3. We are indebted to give thanks to God for you always, my brethren, as it is necessary, because your faith grows all the more and the love of each and every one of you increases toward his neighbor,

4. As we also will boast of you in the Assemblies of God for your faith and for your endurance in all your persecutions and your sufferings that you endure,

5. For a demonstration of the just judgment of God, that you may be worthy of his Kingdom, for whose sake you suffer.

6. And truly it is just before God to reward suffering to your tormentors,

7. And you who are tormented he shall save* with us by the revelation of Our Lord Yeshua The Messiah who is from Heaven, with the armies of his Angels,

---

* The Greek mss. have αvεσιv – "Rest" ; The explanation for this is very simple:
Here is the Aramaic word for "Rest": ניחא ;
       Here is "He shall save": נחא ;
The Yodh י is in "Rest"- ניחא and not in "He shall save" – נחא . The Greek for "He shall save" is "σωσει", nothing like "αvεσιv". Another possibility is ζωοποιησει ("He will give life")- even less like "αvεσιv".
Of course, one might object that an Aramaean might have translated Greek αvεσιv -"Rest"- נחא , simply omitting the "Yodh"- י , which would be easy enough . There are several problems with that hypothesis, however, one of which is that The Peshitta NT should have demonstrable errors in it somewhere, if it were a translation; no one has produced any, to my knowledge. The Peshitta mss. have no variants in this verse to support a Greek original behind it.(Based on Gwilliam-Pinkerton's collation of Peshitta mss. of Paul's epistles).

8. Whenever he executes vengeance in blazing fire on those who do not know God and on those who have not recognized The Good News of Our Lord Yeshua The Messiah,

9. For they will be paid in judgment: eternal destruction from the face of Our Lord and from the glory of his power,

10. Whenever he comes to be glorified in his Holy Ones, he will show his wonders in his believers, because you believed in our testimony that was for you in that day.

11. Because of this we always pray for you that God would make you worthy of your calling, and all the pleasure of goodness and the works of faith in power would fill you entirely,

12. That the name of Our Lord Yeshua The Messiah would be glorified in you and you in him, according to the grace of our God and Our Lord Yeshua The Messiah.

Chapter 2

1. But we beg of you, my brethren, concerning the arrival of Our Lord Yeshua The Messiah and concerning our assembling unto him,

2. That you would not be soon shaken in your minds, neither be troubled, either from word, nor from a spirit, neither from an epistle that is as if from us, namely, that, "Behold, The Day of Our Lord has arrived."

3. Let no man deceive you by any means, to the effect that surely no revolt will first come and The Man of Sin, The Son of Destruction, be revealed,

4. He who opposes and exalts himself against everything that is called God and religion, just as he will sit in the Temple of God, as God, and will show concerning himself as if he is God.

5. Do you not remember that when I was with you, I said these things to you?

6. And now you know what controls, that he may be revealed in his time.

7. The mystery of evil has even now begun to work within, only if that which now controls will be taken from the midst;

8. And then that Evil One will be revealed, whom Our Lord Yeshua will consume with a breath of his mouth, and will destroy him by the revelation of his coming.

9. For the coming of that one is in the activity of Satan in all power, signs and false wonders,

10. And in all the error of evil which is in the perishing, because they did not receive the love of the truth in which they would have Life.

11. Because of this, God sent them the activity of delusion that they would believe lies.

12. And all those who believed not the truth, but chose evil, will be judged.

13. But we are indebted to thank God always for your persons, brethren, beloved of Our

Lord, that God has chosen you from the beginning for Life by sanctification of The Spirit and by belief of the truth,

14. For he has called you to these things by our evangelism, that you would be* glory to Our Lord Yeshua The Messiah.

* Greek has "εις περιποιησιν δοξης" – "**for possession of the glory**" ; The Aramaic construction דתהוון תשבוחתא למרן has two possible meanings; in an idiomatic sense, (דתהוון) may have been read as דתהין - a 3rd person fem. singular future, matched with "**Glory**"- fem. sing.) it means "**that Our Lord may have glory**"; In a more straightforward sense,(taking דתהוון as 2nd person plural masculine future – "That **you would be**"), it means "**that you would be glory**". The Greek seems to favor the first sense, though it is misleading, implying the glory of Jesus may go to the believer. The Greek seems to be an incorrect and awkward translation of the Aramaic here. I doubt an Aramaean would get the Peshitta reading from the Greek reading.

15. Therefore, my brethren, be established and hold the commandments fast that you have learned, whether by discourse or by our epistle.

16. But Our Lord Yeshua The Messiah, and God Our Father, who has loved us and has given us eternal comfort and good hope by his grace,

17. Comfort your hearts and be occupied in every word and every good work.

Chapter 3

1. From now on, brethren, pray for us, that the word of Our Lord would run and be glorified in every place as it is with you,

2. And that we would be saved from evil and vicious men, for the faith does not belong to everyone.

3. But **THE LORD JEHOVAH** is faithful, who will keep you and deliver you from evil.

4. But we trust you in Our Lord, that whatever we command you, you do and you will do.

5. And Our Lord will direct your hearts into the love of God and to the Gospel preaching of The Messiah.

6. But we command you, my brethren, in the name of Our Lord Yeshua The Messiah, that you will be separate from every brother who walks wickedly and not according to the commandments that they received* from us,

* The Majority (Byzantine) Greek text mss. has "They received"; The Critical Greek has "**You received**"(plural) ; The Textus Receptus Greek has , "**He received**".
* The Aramaic for "**They received**"(Peshitta reading) is דקבלו ; "**You received**" is דקבלתון ; "**He received**" is דקבל
  Interestingly, The Eastern Peshitta differs here from the Western mss. and has דקבל – "**He received**". The Western Peshitta reading seems to

stand between the other two and best explains the Greek and The Eastern reading:
קבלתון – "**You received**" – (Critical Greek reading)
קבלו –"**They received**" (This Peshitta edition's reading , Majority Greek & Latin Vulgate)
קבל – "**He received**" –[Eastern Peshitta and Textus Receptus Greek(1 manuscript?) (KJV)]
There are four Greek readings:παρελαβετε παρελαβον παρελαβε παρελαβοσαν- all very similar, with 3,3,& 3 letters difference from the majority reading.
Add two letters to the Peshitta reading in this edition and you have the Critical Greek reading; Take off the last letter of the original reading and you have the Eastern reading and the reading of The Textus Receptus in The King James Version. Let the reader decide which best explains the other - The Peshitta's Aramaic or The Greek.

7. For you know how it is right to imitate us, for we have not walked wickedly among you,

8. Neither have we eaten the bread of any of you without charge, but we were working with labor and toil, by night and by day, that we would not be a burden to anyone of you,

9. Not because we did not have authority, but that we might give you an example by our lives, that you may imitate us.

10. For when we were with you, we had commanded you this, that no one who is unwilling to work shall eat.

11. For we hear that there are some among you who walk wickedly and do not labor at all, but are worthless;

12. But such we command and beseech them in Our Lord Yeshua The Messiah, that they shall work quietly and eat their bread.

13. But you, my brethren, do not be weary to do what is excellent,

14. And if a man disobeys these words in this letter, let this one be separated from you, neither take part with him, that he may be ashamed,

15. And do not hold him as an enemy, but admonish him as a brother.

16. But The Lord of peace give you peace always in everything. Our Lord be with all of you.

17. Greetings, in the writing of my own hand. I, Paulus, have written what is the sign which is in all my epistles; I write in this way:

18. The grace of Our Lord Yeshua The Messiah be with all of you. Amen.

The Eastern Peshitta has "**all of you my brothers. Amen.**" No Greek text has that reading. See how similar the Aramaic words "**Amen**" and "**Brothers**" are:

אמין-"**Amen**"
אחין- "**Brothers**"

Perhaps an early Scribe read "**Amen**" twice , the first time as אחין-"**Brothers**" and the second as אמין– "**Amen**". The word "אחין –"**Brothers**" also may be spelled in a shorter and common form - **אחי** "Akhay", which would explain why the final Nun) is missing in The Eastern Peshitta - **אחי** "Akhay". (In Estrangela , the common script of Peshitta mss. since the second century AD, it is - ‎) "Akhay".

Here is a photo of these last two words from the Khabouris Manuscript (an Eastern Peshitta ms. copied from a fourth century ms.):

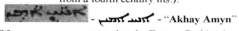 - ‎ - "Akhay Amyn"

Of course, one may argue that the Eastern Peshitta is correct and that a Scribe simply skipped **אחי** "Akhay" and went to the following and similar **אמן**–"Amen". There are several problems with that position; first, there is no Greek manuscript with the reading "**Brothers**". That is a bit of a problem for both Greek primacists and for Aramaic primacists -(those who support an Eastern Peshitta original) . There are however, many Peshitta readings without Greek witnesses, so this is not a major problem by itself. In conjunction with the fact that the Western Peshitta tradition lacks the word "**Brothers**" here, the lack of Greek witnesses becomes significant. It is reasonable that Aramaic primacists would expect that if all Greek mss. support one Aramaic reading where there is a variant reading in The Peshitta NT , that this would settle the matter . There are not many places where the two Peshittas differ. The argument that The Peshitta was based on or revised to the Greek standard is simply nonsense and has no foundation in the textual evidence. Neither The Western nor The Eastern Peshitta can be shown to conform to any Greek standard, whether Byzantine, Alexandrian or Western. More often than not, it differs with all Greek readings, where Greek variants occur.

Another argument for the originality of the text presented in this edition (Gwilliams-Pinkerton 1920 critical edition of The Peshitta) is that this is practically identical with the edition in which the author has discovered eight long codes that extend throughout The NT several times and one that covers 96% of The NT , some in Hebrew and some in Aramaic. The codes are spelled out by skipping many thousands of letters at a time (17,000 up to 99,000) to form sentences of 25 to 191 letters. **What is significant about these codes for Textual Criticism is that if one letter were to be added to the Peshitta edition tested, or one letter were deleted, none of the codes would exist at all !** No other edition of the several I have tested of The Peshitta has any such codes. I have also performed an exhaustive experimental search of The Peshitta (two editions) for 95 Hebrew and Aramaic Divine names and titles as codes. The resulting data is several million words of information called **Equidistant Letter Sequences** which demonstrate statistically that the Peshitta NT was deliberately coded with many of these Divine names and titles. They cannot be due to random occurrences; none of the control texts tested shows positive results, and they were tested alongside The Peshitta , word for word, skip number for skip number, in exactly the same way as it was.

I believe Gwilliams & Pinkerton did a magnificent work in compiling this edition of The Peshitta Pauline epistles. It is practically impeccable ,as is The Gwilliams-Pusey edition of The Gospels before it.

The First Epistle of The Apostle Paul to Timothy

Chapter 1

1. Paulus, an Apostle of Yeshua The Messiah, by the commandment of God Our Lifegiver, and of The Messiah Yeshua, our hope,

2. To Timotheus, a true son in the faith: Grace, mercy and peace from God Our Father and The Messiah Yeshua, Our Lord.

3. I requested of you when I went to Macedonia that you remain in Ephesaus and that you command certain men that they would not teach diverse doctrines,

4. And that they would not give heed to fables and to accounts of endless genealogies; these things produce all the more contentions and not edification in the faith of God.

5. But the sum of The Commandments is love from a pure heart, from a good conscience and from true faith.

6. Some of them have strayed from these things and have turned people away to empty words,

7. In that they seek to be teachers of The Written Law, while they do not understand anything that they say, neither anything about which they contend.

8. But we know that The Written Law is good if a man will be led by it, according to The Written Law,

9. While he knows that The Written Law was not appointed for the righteous, but for the evil, the rebellious, the wicked, for sinners, for the vicious, for those who are impure, for those who strike their fathers, those who strike their mothers, for murderers,

* Greek has "πατραλωαις και μητραλωαις ,ανδροφονοις"- "**father killers, mother killers, murderers**"? This makes little sense, especially when compared to The Peshitta reading: "**Those who hit their fathers and those who hit their mothers, and murderers.**"

10. For fornicators, for males who lie down with males, for kidnappers of free men, for liars, for oath breakers and for all things opposed to the sound teaching

* The Aramaic has "**males lying with males**" (as the word is a masculine participle, it refers to masculine subjects) ; the Greek mss. use "αρσενοκοιτης", which is a compound word not found in Greek literature, made of the words "αρσην"(**male**) and "κοιτη" (**copulation**) . The Greek word is unclear in meaning: "**Male copulation**" , or "**Copulation with males**" ? Κοιτη , the base word of this compound word, never refers to "**a copulator**" but to "**a bed**" or "**to lying down**" or "**copulation**". In the context, the Greek is disjointed . The Peshitta has: "**The Law was written for fornicators, for males who lie down with males, for kidnappers** , etc.", whereas the Greek has: "The Law was written for fornicators, **lying down with men**, kidnappers, etc..". The Law was written for certain people, not for certain activities. So the Greek word focuses on one activity –" **lying down with men**", along with people-"**fornicators**", "**kidnappers**", etc.. rather than the people who perpetrate it; this is an error in a grammatical sense as well as a theological sense and contextual sense; The Law's purpose was for people, not certain sins people commit. In this light, the Peshitta reading is clearly superior to the Greek. There are many apparent Greek word inventions in The Greek NT which look like compound words in which two or three Aramaic words in the text are combined. This is one example, in my view.

11. Of The Good News of the glory of the Blessed God, with which I have been entrusted.

12. And I thank him who has empowered me, Our Lord Yeshua The Messiah, who accounted me trustworthy and has put me into his ministry,

13. Me, I who from the first was a blasphemer and a persecutor and abusive, but I obtained mercy, because I did not know what I was doing, without faith.

14. But the grace of Our Lord abounded in me, and faith and love, which are in Yeshua The Messiah.

15. This is a trustworthy saying and worthy of acceptance: "Yeshua The Messiah came to the universe to save sinners, of whom I am the foremost."

16. But because of this he showed me mercy, that Yeshua The Messiah might show in me first all his patience, as the example of those who are going to believe in him unto eternal life.

17. But to The King of the universe, to him who is indestructible and unseen, who is The One God*, be honor and glory to the eternity of eternities. Amen.

* The Majority Greek text (most Greek mss.) have "μονω σοφω θεω" –"Only wise God". "Who is Only Wise" in Aramaic is חד דחכים הד ; "Who is One". In DSS script it is חד ד אטדי - "Who is Only Wise"; חד דחיו - "Who is One".

Here are comparisons in three scripts :

Translation	Dead Sea Scroll	Estrangela	Ashuri
"Who only wise"	חד דאטדי הד	ܗܢܟܢܬ ܢܚ	דחכימהד
"Who is One"	חד דחיו	ܐܠܘܗܐܗܕ	דהויוהד

The DSS pair has **80% correlation** between the words דאטדי -"Who Wise" and דחיו -"Who is". Neither the Ashuri nor the Estrangela pair have near the letter correlation the Dead Sea Scroll script pair presents. The Critical Greek reading agrees with The Peshitta reading, with " ΜΟΝΩ ΘΕΩ"- "**Only God**". Here is the majority Greek reading lined up in Uncial Greek script: "ΜΟΝΩ ΣΟΦΩ ΘΕΩ" –"**Only wise God**". Correlation there is much lower , considering the 4 letters in ΣΟΦΩ –"**Sopho**"(Wise) in the Majority Greek which is lacking in the Critical Greek.

18. I commit this decree to you, my son, Timotheus, according to the former prophecies which were concerning you, that you may wage this excellent warfare by them,
19. In faith and in good conscience, for those who have rejected this from themselves have been emptied of faith,
20. Like Humenayus and Alexandros, those whom I have delivered to Satan* that they may be instructed not to blaspheme.

* Greek has σατανα -"Satana", which is not a Greek word; it is an Aramaic word transliterated into Greek from the Aramaic NT **35** times in **12** books from The Gospels,Acts,Pauls Epistles and Revelation. 14 times, Greek has "**Διαβολος,-εω**" (**Diabol[os],-ew**) –"**The Devil**," "**slanderer**", "**slander,**" where the Aramaic ܣܛܢܐ "**Satana**" occurs. So 35 of the 49 occurrences of ܣܛܢܐ – "**Satana**"- are paralleled by Greek σατανα "**Satana**",while the other 14 occurrences are matched with "**Διαβολος**" –"**The Devil**," "**Slanderer**". Aramaic does have a term for "**Διαβολος**" –"**The Devil**," "**Slanderer**"; it is קרצא אכל – "**Akal Qartsa**"-"**The Devil**", "**Slanderer**";This occurs 27 times in The Peshitta Nitwit seems unlikely that "Satana" in The Peshitta would be a translation of the Greek "**Diabolos**", since "**Akal Qartsa**"-"**The Devil**" would be the likely translation term. Also, the Greek transliteration "**Satana**" seems not to occur outside of the NT except in the Greek of **Sirach**, which was probably composed in Aramaic in the 2ⁿᵈ cent. BC.

* **The LXX** translation has "**Διαβολ**..."- **Diabol**. root **19** **times** for the Hebrew Bible's **27 occurrences (70%)** of שטן –"**Satan**"! So there was a precedent set for translating the Semitic name "**Satan**" as "**Διαβολος**" (**Diabolos**) –"**The Devil**", though in the 3ʳᵈ century BC Greek translation from Hebrew, the ratio of "**Satan**" being translated to "**The Devil**" was 70%, and by the 1ˢᵗ century AD, the ratio of Aramaic "**Satana**" being transliterated to "**Satana**" in Greek was 70% and "**The Devil**" had 30%.

Chapter 2

1. Therefore, I beg of you that before all things, you will offer supplications to God, prayers, intercessions and thanksgiving, for the sake of all people,
2. For the sake of Kings and Rulers, that we may lead a quiet and tranquil way of life in complete reverence to God and purity.
3. For this is pleasing and acceptable before God Our Lifegiver,
4. He who wills that all people shall have Life, and shall be converted to the knowledge of the truth.

5. For God is One, and The Mediator of God and the sons of men is One: The Son of Man, Yeshua The Messiah,
6. Who gave himself a ransom in the place of every person, a testimony that has come in its time,
7. That of which I am appointed a Preacher and an Apostle of the truth. I say and I do not lie, that I am the Teacher of the Gentiles in the belief of the truth.
8. I desire, therefore, that men would pray in every place, lifting their hands in purity without rage and without scheming;
9. Likewise also the women shall be modest in fashion of dress, their adornment shall be in bashfulness and in modesty, not in braiding with gold or with pearls or in gorgeous robes,
10. But with good works, just as it is suitable for women who profess the worship of God.
11. Let women learn in silence with all submission,
12. For I do not allow a woman to teach, neither to usurp over a man, but she should be quiet;
13. For Adam was formed first, and then Eve.
14. And Adam was not deceived, but the woman was deceived and violated the commandment;
15. But she lives by her children, if they continue in faith and in love, in holiness and in modesty.

Chapter 3

1. This is a trustworthy saying, that if a man desires Eldership, he desires a good work.
2. And an Elder ought to be one in whom no fault is found and is the husband of one woman, is of a vigilant mind, sober, orderly, loves strangers and is a teacher;
3. And he does not transgress concerning wine and his hand is not swift to strike*, but he should be humble, not contentious, neither a lover of money,

* The Majority Greek text has μη αισχροκερδη –"**no filthy gain**". It is a senseless reading consisting of two words combined to form a compound word: αισχρος (**filthy**) + κερδης (**gain**) – there is no verb with this reading, like "**being greedy**" or "**given to**", not to mention that "**without love of money**" is at the end of the verse :"αφιλαργυρος". Below is a comparison of the Peshitta reading , "**swift of hand to strike**" with the Aramaic for "**lover of filthy gain**" in three different Aramaic scripts: **Ashuri script:**
רהטא אידה לממחא –"his hand is swift to strike"
רחמא יותרן טנפתא-"lover of filthy gain"
69% letter correlation

Dead Sea Scroll Script:
רהטא אידה לממחא "his hand is swift to strike"
רחמא יותרן טנפתא-"lover of filthy gain"

77% letter correlation

Estrangela Script:

ܐܝܕܗ ܩܠܝܠܐ ܠܡܡܚܐ –"his hand is swift to strike"

ܪܚܡܝ ܝܘܬܪܢܐ ܛܢܦܐ -"lover of filthy gain"

54% letter correlation

The Dead Sea Aramaic Script – (למפחא היד אאחד
(דשטא again looks like it was the original New Testament script from which the Greek epistle was translated in the first century.

4. And he governs his house well, and holds his children in subjection with all purity.

5. For if he does not know how to lead his own household well, how can he lead the Church of God?

6. Neither should he be a young disciple*, lest he be lifted up and would fall into the judgment of Satan*;

* **Greek has** "νεοφυτον" –**"Neophyte" (Lit. "new plant"). The Aramaic refers to a new disciple.** "of Plant" in Aramaic is-דנצבתה or יורקתה or עסבא ; In DSS script: עסב א or יורקתא or דנצבתא "of his discipleship" is תולמדה -DSS- תגלמדה;

Let's place the two readings in DSS Aramaic side by side in enlarged script:

תגלמדה טליא -"a young disciple"
דנצבתא טליא -"a young plant"

* Greek here and in verse 7 has "Διαβολος" –"The Devil"; Aramaic has "Satan" in both verses. Διαβολος is a Greek word; "Σατανα" –"Satan" is not, it is Aramaic. The Greek NT does have this word (See 1:20), though in one third of references in which The Peshitta has "Satana" , the Greek word used is "Διαβολος". In **The LXX** (Greek OT) , 19 of 27 references to Satan are translated as Διαβολος – **Diabolos** –"The Devil". On the other hand, an Aramaean would most likely translate Διαβολος as אכל קרצא – "The Devil", "Slanderer".

7. He ought to have an excellent testimony from outsiders, lest he fall into shame and into the trap of Satan.

8. In this way also, Ministers should be pure and should not double-speak, neither be inclined to much wine, neither love defiled riches,

9. But they should hold the mystery of the faith in a pure conscience.

10. And those who are such should be first proved and then let them serve, being without fault.

11. In this way also, the wives should be modest and alert in their minds and shall be faithful in everything and should not be slanderers.

12. A Minister should be one who has one wife and leads his children and his household well.

13. For those who serve well purchase a good rank for themselves and much boldness in the faith of Yeshua The Messiah.

14. I have written these things to you, as I hope that I shall soon come to you,

15. But if I delay, that you may know how it is necessary to behave in the household of God, which is the church of **THE LIVING GOD**, the pillar and foundation of the truth.

16. And this Mystery of Righteousness is truly great, which was revealed in the flesh and was justified in The Spirit; He appeared to Angels and was preached among the Gentiles; He was trusted in the world and he ascended into glory.

N * Most, if not all Greek mss. have "ευσεβειας" – "of Godliness" ; In Aramaic, "Godliness" would be דחלתא or דחלת אלהא . **The Peshitta has** דכאנותא ("of righteousness") .There seems to be another explanation for this, beside word similarity in Aramaic, as כאנותא occurs four times in 1 Timothy matched in Greek with the word "ευσεβεια" – "Godliness". Since "God" is implied in "Godliness" , **and since the most common Aramaic match for this Greek word is** דחלת אלהא - "fear of God", we should look for an Aramaic indication of "God" in the text which leads the Greek translator to translate with "ευσεβεια" –"Godliness" four times in this book and four times it also matches דחלת אלהא -"Fear of God". I believe I have found that "God" is in the text in every case, but in code form in the plain text. For more on this, see my book, **Divine Contact** , the chapter on **Alep-Tau** codes, available at http://aramaicnt.com

Chapter 4

1. **But** The Spirit speaks plainly that in the last time they shall depart one by one from the faith and they shall go after deceiving spirits and after the teachings of demons,

2. These *persons* who deceive by false appearances* and speak lies and sear their consciences;

* Greek has "υποκρυσει"-"Hypocrisy"; In Aramaic, "Hypocrisy" is usually "מסב אפא"; (אפא also). Compare with the word in this verse for "in appearances" – באסכמא ; Here they are, one atop the other, in three Aramaic scripts:

Ashuri:

דבאסכמא דגלא -"In false appearances"
דבמסבא באפא -"In hypocrisy"

Dead Sea Scroll:

דבאסכמא דגלא-"In false appearances"
דבמסבא באפא-"In hypocrisy"

Estrangela:

ܕܒܐܣܟܡܐ ܕܓܠܐ -"In false appearances"

ܕܒܡܣܒܐ ܐܦܐ-"In hypocrisy"

Here is The Peshitta reading,

דבאסכמא דגלא – d'baskama d'egla- "In false appearances".

DSS script shows promise in the words

דבמסבא באפא -"Mesaba b'apha"-"In hypocrisy", as the supposed source for the Greek reading "υποκρυσει"-"Hypocrisy". There is **73% correlation (8 of 11 letters)** with the Peshitta reading.

Greek for appearances is σχημασι which is not very like υποκρυσει (22% similarity).

3. And they forbid to be married and they abstain from foods which God has created for use and thanksgiving for those who believe and know the truth.

4. For every creation is beautiful to God, and there is nothing to be rejected if it is received with thanksgiving,

5. For it is sanctified by the word of God and by prayer.

6. If you will teach your brethren these things, you will be a good Minister of Yeshua The Messiah, as you have been brought up in the words of faith and in the good teaching with which you have been taught.

7. But abstain from insipid fables of old women and train yourself in righteousness;

8. For exercise of the body profits a little for this time, but righteousness profits in everything, and it has the promise of life for this time and of the future.

9. This is a trustworthy saying and is worthy of acceptance.

10. For because of this we toil and we are reproached*, because we hope in THE LIVING GOD, who is the Lifegiver of all of the children of men, especially of believers.

* Critical Greek has αγωνιζομεθα -"we struggle" ;The Majority Greek text agrees with The Peshitta ονειδιζομεθα-"we are reproached". Compare the Aramaic מתחסדינן –"We are reproached", with מתחסמינן" – "Compete zealously" ; the two words are identical but for one letter! Here are the two words enlarged and one atop the other:

Ashuri script:
מתחסדינן – "We are reproached"
מתחסמינן – "We compete zealously"

DSS Script :
בתחדסﬞﬞ–"We are reproached"
בתחדסמﬞﬞ– "We compete zealously"

Estrangela :
ܡܬܚܣܕܝܢ–"We are reproached"

ܡܬܚܣܡܝܢ – "We compete zealously" .

It hardly matters which Aramaic script is used, though the DSS and Estrangela pairs are a bit more alike than the Ashuri script pair. The differences in each pair are those between a **Dalet** and a **Mem** (underlined letters) . In DSS , there are two strokes and a bit of an up stroke difference between the two letters-ﬧ & ﬦ . In Estrangela , there are three strokes and a dot difference-ܕ & ܡ In Ashuri, there are two strokes and two humps on the **Mem** מ that distinguish it from **Dalet** ד . Each Aramaic script presents at least **88% letter to letter correlation** between each word pair.

The two Greek words involved in the variants are: αγωνιζομεθα & ονειδιζομεθα. There are four & five letters distinctly different here in each, and they are the

most vital – the root words of each Greek word; these would not be confused one for another.

Greek Uncial (All CAPS) :

ΑΓѠΝΙΖΟΜΕΘΑ
ΟΝΕΙΔΙΖΟΜΕΘΑ The probability seems small that Greek was translated to Aramaic here. On the contrary, The Peshitta seems to account for the two Greek readings. The Greek words show 58% letter correlation.

11. Teach and command these things.

12. Let no man despise your youth, but be an example to believers in word and in behavior, in love, in faith and in purity.

13. Until I come, be diligent in reading, in prayer and in teaching.

14. Do not despise the gift that is in you, which is given to you by prophecy and by the laying on of the hands of the Eldership.

15. Meditate on these things and abide in them, that you may be known to every person before whom you come.

16. Pay attention to your soul and to your teachings; persevere in them, for when you do these things you will bring life to your soul and to those who hear you.

Chapter 5

1. Do not rebuke an elder, but petition him as a father, and those who are young as your brothers,

2. And elder women as mothers, and those who are younger, as your sisters in all purity.

3. Honor those widows who are widows indeed;

4. And if there is a widow who has children or grandchildren, let them learn first that they should be assigned to children of their households, and they should pay compensation to their parents, for this is acceptable before God.

5. But whoever is truly a widow and is alone, her hope is upon God and continues in prayer and in supplication, night and day;

6. But she who worships the Arena* is dead while she lives. *(אסטרניא is defined by **Jastrow's Targum Dictionary** as "The Theatre", "The Arena", "Gladiatorial shows";p. 92) :

אצ', איס', אסטריא, אסמריה, אסטריא

איצ'א f. (also אסטרא m.) cacophemistic appellations of all kinds of gentile sports; cmp. the use of θέατρον and θέατρίζετν in Ad Corinth.,I, IV, 9, a. Hebr. X, 33; אסטרא &c., as if a denomin. of סרד, cmp. Syr. אסטרניא אצטרניא, P. Sm. 304 a. cit. ibid.; אצטריבא, as if fr. צרב; אסטריון (v. next w.) as if fr. ד. אצ, v. אירצטין; cmp. אבידר) theatre, arena, gladiatorial shows, &c. Ab. Zar. I, 7 (16ᵃ) גרדום

איס', איצ', אצטריא, אצטריה, אצטריא f. (סרד, cmp. אסטרניא אצטריא א P. Sm. 304 a. quot. ibid.; cmp. אבידן) place of debauchery, an opprobrious name for the theatres, arenas &c. of the Romans, and a phonetic perversion of theatrum, θέατρον. Ab. Zar. I, 7 (16ᵃ) you must not build . . . . 'כו אצטרייא גרדום (Ms. M. אצטריבא,

cmp. Syr. אצטרניא, אסטרניא, P.
אִיטְצ׳, אִיס׳, אִיצְטַרִין, אֶסְטָרִין (אצטרטון,
אִצטַרְדִּין, אִיצטַרְיִן), also with rejection of א after pre-
fixes) m. (pl. of אסטרא, v. preced.; used as sing., sub.
שור בית ה־ &c.) arena, theatre. B. Kam. IV, 4 (39ᵃ)
אִיס׳, אִיצ׳, אסטרין, אצטרין [אִיצטַרין] v. preced.
end] f. (prop. pl. of אסטרא אסטרא, v. preced., used as
sing.) same. B.Kam.IV,4 (39ᵃ) שור חאיצטרין Ms.M. (ed.
אצטדין, Ms.H.a. R. a. Mish.Nap. אסטדין, Y. ed. איסטרין)
an ox of the arena (that killed a person). Tosef. Ab. Zar.
II, 7 וב׳ חיושב באסטרין Var. (ed. Zuck. אסטריון, ed.
איסטרין) he who attends the arena as a spectator is like
a murderer (countenancing bloodshed); Y.ib.I,40ᵇ חיושב

7. You shall command these things to them that they might be without fault.
8. For if a man does not take care of those who are his own, especially those who are members of the household of faith, this one has renounced the faith and is worse than those who are unbelievers.
9. Therefore you shall choose a widow who is not less than sixty years old, who had one husband,
10. And she has a testimony of good works, if she has raised children, if she has received strangers, if she has washed the feet of the Saints, if she has relieved the afflicted, if she has walked in every good work.
11. But avoid those widows who are younger, for these separate from The Messiah and seek to have a husband;
12. And their judgment is set, for they have rejected their former faith;
13. But they learn laziness while going around house to house, and not only laziness, but also to increase talking, to take up vanities and speak that which is inappropriate.
14. I am willing therefore that the younger ones marry, bear children, lead their households and do not give any occasion of contempt to the enemies;
15. For even now they have begun, one by one, to turn after Satan.
16. If male or female believers have widows, let them support them, and do not let them burden the church, so that it may have enough for those who are truly widows.
17. Those Elders who lead well deserve double honor, especially those who toil in the word and in teaching.
18. For the Scriptures say, "Do not muzzle the ox while it is treading", and, "The laborer deserves his wages."
19. Do not accept an accusation against an Elder, but upon the mouth of two or three witnesses;
20. Those who sin, rebuke before everyone, so that the rest of the people may fear.

21. But I testify to you before God and Our Lord Yeshua The Messiah and his chosen Angels, that you will observe these things and not let your mind be prejudiced for anything and do nothing by favoritism.
22. Lay hands quickly on no man, and do not share in the sins of strangers; keep yourself in purity.
23. Do not drink water from now on, but drink a little wine because of your stomach and because of your chronic illness.
24. There are people whose sins are known, and they precede them to the place of judgment, and some follow them.
25. In this way also, good works are known, and those which are otherwise cannot be concealed.

Chapter 6

1. Let those who are under the yoke of bondage hold their masters in all honor that the name of God and his teaching be not blasphemed.
2. Let those who have believing masters not despise them, because they are their brothers, but let them rather serve them, because they are believers and beloved, by whom they are at peace in their service. Teach these things and implore them.
3. But if there is a man who teaches another doctrine and does not attain to the sound words of Our Lord Yeshua The Messiah and the teaching of the reverence of God,
4. This one is lifted up as he knows nothing, but he is ineffective in disputes and debates of words, from which come envy, contention and blasphemy, and establishes evil thoughts,
5. And the misery of the children of men who corrupt their minds and are cheated of the truth, and they think that making money is the worship of God; but stay away from these things,
6. For our profit is great, which is the worship of God while *having* the necessities, for we have enough.
7. For we have brought nothing into the universe, and we know that we can take nothing out of it;
8. Because of this, food and clothing is enough for us.
9. But those who desire to be rich fall into temptations and into traps, and into many foolish and harmful desires, and they sink the children of men into corruption and destruction.

10. But the root of all these evils is the love of money, and there are some who have desired it and have erred from the faith and have brought themselves many miseries.

11. But you, Oh man of God, escape from these things, and run after righteousness, after justice, after faith, after love, after patience and after humility.

12. And fight in the good contest of faith and seize eternal life, to which things you are called, and you have professed a good profession before many witnesses.

13. I testify to you before God, he who gives life to all, and Yeshua The Messiah, he who testified an excellent testimony before Pontius Pilate,

14. That you keep the commandments without defilement and without blemish until the revelation of Our Lord Yeshua The Messiah,

15. He who is going to reveal himself in his time, The Blessed God and Only Mighty One*, The King of Kings and the Lord of Power, * אלהא מברכא –Alaha mbarka-"The Blessed God" is a term used by Paul in chapter 1, verse 11.)

16. He who alone is uncorrupted and dwelling in light that a human cannot approach and which none of the children of men has seen, nor can see, to whom be honor and authority to the eternity of eternities. Amen.

17. I command the rich of this world that they not be lifted up in their minds and that they would not trust upon wealth because there is no certainty concerning it, but upon THE LIVING GOD, who gives richly to us all for our comfort,

18. And that they should do good works, should be rich in good deeds, and should be ready to give and to share,

19. And they shall lay up for themselves a good foundation for what is future, that they may seize upon true life.

20. Oh, Timothy*, guard that which is committed to you and escape from empty echoes* and from the perversions of false knowledge.

טימתאא – "Timothy" here is strangely similar to the Greek vocative form used in this verse. This occurs with the name "Theophilus" as well, in Luke 1:3 and Acts 1:1. In Greek "Timothy" in 1 Tim. 1:18 is vocative, though the Peshitta does not have this form there. "Timothy" & "Theophilus" are Greek names; both were probably from Syria, where like Luke, they spoke Aramaic and Greek , at least in Antioch and its environs. In these three places, it seems that the rare Greek form is orally transliterated in The Peshitta's Aramaic text. It appears that the Aramaic form is not copied from the Greek text, as the Greek vocative form used in 1:18 does not occur in the Peshitta text of that

verse. The Greek name "Petros" also occurs three times for "Simeon Kaypha" ("Simon Peter") in 1 & 2 Peter and Acts as an acknowledgment of that apostle's fame for being the first Jewish apostle to preach to Gentiles and make converts. The Greek "Petros" occurs 162 times in the Greek NT. The Gentiles would call "Kaypha"- "Petros"(Greek) or "Petrus"(Latin).

Another evidence that this verse is original in Aramaic is the idiom "Bnayth qala sriqta" ("Daughters of the voice of vanity") "Bnayth qala" means "echo" , "sound" or "saying". The Greek is understandable as a translation of Aramaic , but the Aramaic is an idiom that looks original and an unlikely translation of the Greek- "profane & vain babblings"-βεβηλους κενοφωνιας as a source for this Aramaic idiom . Far more likely is a Greek translation of this Aramaic idiom.

Here follows another bit of Peshitta primacy evidence in this verse: טנף is "profane"; בנת is "daughters", found in this verse; Here are the two words: טנף : בנת. Here they are in DSS script: "טנף: בנת; in Estrangela we have ܒܢܬ ܛܢܦ. How about a hybrid Ashuri & DSS script ?: טנף בנת. Another word for "profane" is חלת (a very loose association grammatically) ; In DSS -חלת: The pair for comparison: בנת חלת;
In Estrangela : ܒܢܬ ܚܠܬ.

The DSS pair בנת חלת are the most similar - 66% correlation. Not bad for two three letter words. Now try to envision rotating the first letter of בנת -B'nath (the letter ב) 90 degrees counterclockwise ( ) and compare it to the first letter of the word חלת -ח. & ח . Then we would have the word חנת ; Compare that to חלת –"Profane". That would seem even more like "Khelath" ("Voice").

The following are comparisons in Aramaic of the two readings, "Opposition" & "Perversions"

ܣܩܘܒܠܐ-"Opposition"
ܕܓܠܬܐ -"Perversions"(Peshitta)

Now look at a slight variation of the word for "Opposition" which means "Complaint", compared to "Perversions":

ܩܒܠܬܐ-"Accusation", "Complaint"
ܕܓܠܬܐ-"Perversions" (Peshitta)

These two words are very similar in appearance, possibly accounting for a Greek mistranslation of Aramaic;They have 80% letter correlation.

21. For those who profess it have themselves gone astray from the faith. Grace be with you. Amen.

The Second Epistle of The Apostle Paul to Timothy

Chapter 1

1. Paulus, an Apostle of Yeshua The Messiah, by the will of God, and by The Promise of life, which is in Yeshua The Messiah,
2. To beloved son Timotheus: Grace, love and peace from God The Father and from Our Lord Yeshua The Messiah.
3. I thank God, whom I serve from my forefathers with a pure conscience; I constantly remember you in my prayers, night and day,
4. And I long to see you and I remember your tears, so that I am filled with joy
5. By the recollection which I have of your true faith, which began first in your mother's mother,* Lois, and in your mother Euniqay, and I am convinced that it is in you also.

* Greek has **μαμμη** – "**Mammee**" , which means "**Mother**" or "**Grandmother**". The Peshitta has "**your mother's mother**".

6. Because of this, I remind you to rouse the gift of God that is in you by laying on of my hands.
7. For God has not given us a spirit of fear, but of power and of love and of instruction*.

* Greek has σωφρονισμος – "**sound mind**" ; The Aramaic word "**Instruction**"- ("**Martinotha**") - מרתינותא & מרעינותא –"**Reasoning**" are very similar; only one letter difference exists between them. These words come from different roots and are unrelated to each other. It appears a Greek translator looked at ודמרעינותא and saw ודמרתינותא , which has a **88%** correlation for the 8 letters (underlined) of each of the two words. "**Sound mind**" is ודנכפותא , though that is not as good a match (**50% ?**); ודמתקנותא is "**Stability**" (**63%** match) , so there are several possible Aramaic words which could account for the Greek reading. Greek for "**Instruction**" in the genitive case is παιδειας ; "**Exhortation**" is παρακλησεως; these are not similar at all to σωφρονισμος. Here are the two Aramaic words "**Instruction**" and "**Reasoning**" for comparison :

ודמרתינותא-"**& of instruction**"
ודמרעינותא-"**& of reason**"

8. Therefore do not be ashamed of the testimony of Our Lord, neither of me his prisoner, but bear evils with The Gospel by the power of God,
9. He who has given us life and has called us with a holy calling, not according to our works, but according to his will and the grace which has been given to us in Yeshua The Messiah before the time of the world,

* Greek has "προ χρονων αιωνιων" – "**before eternal times**" , which, frankly , is a ridiculous phrase. Time and Eternity are opposites; there is no such thing as an eternal time, nor can eternity or the eternal be measured with a timepiece, as eternity is timeless. "**While we look not at these seen things, but at those not seen; for these seen things are time related, but those not seen are eternal.**" -2 Cor. 4:18 .Titus 1:2 also has this Greek phrase -προ χρονων αιωνιων. In both places, the Peshitta has קדם זבנא דעלמא – "**Before the time of the world**". דעלמא is "**of the world**" ; "**Eternal**" in Aramaic is דלעלמא – one letter added , so possibly a Greek translator misread דעלמא ("**of the world**") as דלעלמא -"**Eternal**" in these two places.

10. And is now revealed by the revelation of Our Lifegiver, Yeshua The Messiah, who has destroyed death and has displayed life and indestructibility by The Gospel,
11. He by whom I am appointed a preacher, an Apostle and a teacher of the Gentiles.
12. Therefore, I endure these things, and I am not ashamed, for I know in whom I have believed and I am convinced that he is able to keep my trust for me until that day.
13. Let the sound words which you have heard from me be a model for you in the faith and love which are in Yeshua The Messiah.
14. Keep the good trust by The Spirit of Holiness, who dwells within is,
15. For you know this, that all those who are in Asia have turned away from me, of whom are Pugelos and Hermogenes.
16. May Our Lord give compassion to the house of Onesiphorus, who many times has refreshed me and was not ashamed of the chains of my bondage;
17. But also when he came to Rome, he sought me with diligence and found me.
18. May Our Lord grant that he find mercy with Our Lord in that day; and how that he ministered to me, especially in Ephesaus, you know.

Chapter 2

1. You therefore, my son, be strengthened in the grace which is in Yeshua The Messiah,
2. And those things which you have heard from me by many witnesses, entrust those things to trustworthy men, who are able also to teach others.
3. And endure hardships as a good Soldier of Yeshua The Messiah.
4. Is not a Soldier bound in matters of the world to please him who has chosen* him?

* Greek has στρατολογησαντι –"**enlister**" ; "**His Enlister**" in Aramaic is מפלחהי .

דגביהי-"Who has chosen him"
דמפלחהי-"His enlister"
דגביהי-"Who has chosen him"
דמפלחהי-"His enlister"
𐡃𐡂𐡁𐡉𐡄𐡉-"Who has chosen him"

ܐܬܠܘܓܠܗ-"His enlister"

The underlined pair are in Dead Sea Scroll Aramaic script. They are the most likely explanation for the Greek ; Those two have a possible 72% letter correlation.

וחי צאי - "Who has chosen him"
אהלוגגצ -"His enlister"

"Him who has chosen him" in Greek would probably be the participle - εκλεξαντι ; This hardly looks like στρατολογησαντι –"enlister" . I give εκλεξαντι a score of 27% correlation. Here are the two Greek words in uncial script for comparison: ΣΤΡΑΤΟΛΟΓΗΣΑΝΤΙ
ΕΚΛΕΞΑΝΤΙ

5. And if a man competes, he is not crowned if he does not compete by the rules.

6. It is fitting for the plowman who toils that he first be sustained by his crop.

7. Consider what I say. May Our Lord give you wisdom in everything.

8. Call to mind Yeshua The Messiah, who arose from the place of the dead, he who is from the seed of David according to my Gospel,

9. In which I suffer evil things, even unto chains, as an evildoer, but the word of God is not chained.

10. Because of this, I endure everything for the sake of The Elect Ones, that they also may find the life which is in Yeshua The Messiah with eternal glory.

11. And this word is trustworthy, for if we have died with him*, we shall also live with him,

* Greek has "If we died together"; "With Him" is lacking both times in this verse in the Greek, making its meaning ambiguous.

12. And if we suffer, we shall also reign with him, but if we renounce him, he will also renounce us.
* Greek has "we shall reign together"; "With Him" is lacking in this verse , as is "Him" after "we reject", in the Greek, making its meaning ambiguous.

13. And if we shall not have believed in him*, he continues in his faithfulness, for he cannot renounce himself.
• Greek has "If we disbelieve"; "in Him" is lacking in this verse in the Greek versions.

14. Remind them of these things, and charge them before Our Lord that they should not dispute about words without profit, to the overthrow of those who hear such things.

15. And take care of yourself, that you present yourself perfectly before God, a laborer without shame, who preaches* the word of truth straightforwardly.

* Greek has **ορθοτομουντα** - "to cut straight" ; The idea seems to be "ploughing a straight

furrow". Here is the Aramaic word for "preaches"- מכרז ; Here is the word for "ploughing"- מכרב ; Here they are in order in DSS script: מצ רו מצרב.

In Estrangela : **ܡܟܪܒ ܡܟܪܙ** ; Ashuri Aramaic script:

מכרב מכרז . Any of these three scripts shows a 75% correlation between these two words. I therefore hypothesize that the Greek reading came from a misreading of the Aramaic word מכרז as מכרב . The Greek has no word similar to

ορθοτομουντα - "to cut straight" that means "to preach straight" . The Greek words for "to preach" would commonly be, "**κηρυσσων**", "**ευαγγελιζομενος**",or perhaps "**αναγελλιζων**". It appears the Greek cannot account for the Peshitta reading; The Peshitta can account for the Greek.

Ashuri Aramaic
דמכרז – "who preaches" (Peshitta)
דמכרב – "who ploughs"(Greek reading in Aramaic)
80% correlation !

Dead Sea Scroll Aramaic
וחי צאי – "who preaches" (Peshitta)
צאי – "who ploughs" (Greek reading in Aramaic)
80% correlation !

Estrangela Aramaic
ܕܡܟܪܙ– "who preaches" (Peshitta)
ܕܡܟܪܒ– "who ploughs" (Greek reading in Aramaic)
80% correlation !

16. And avoid empty words in which there is no benefit, for they will all the more add to the wickedness of those who converse in them,

17. And their speech will seize many like a consuming cancer, and one of them is Humenayus, and another, Philetus,

18. These who have wandered from the truth, while saying that the resurrection of the dead has occurred, and overthrow the faith of some.

19. But the foundation of God stands firm, and it has this seal: "And **THE LORD JEHOVAH** knows those who are his, and let everyone who calls on the name of **THE LORD JEHOVAH** separate from evil."

20. But in a great house, there are not only vessels of gold or silver, but also of wood and of pottery, some of them for honor and some for dishonor.

21. If a man therefore will purify himself from these things, he is a pure vessel for honor, suitable for the use of his Lord and ready for every good work.

22. Escape from all lusts of youth and run after righteousness, faith, love, and peace,

with those who call on Our Lord with a pure heart.

23. Abstain from the disputes of fools who are without instruction, for you know that they generate conflict.

24. But a Servant of Our Lord ought not to fight, but to be humble toward every person, instructive and long-suffering,

25. That he may instruct with humility those who dispute against him. Perhaps God will give them repentance and they will know the truth,

26. And they will remember their souls and break loose from the trap of Satan by whom they were captured for his pleasure.

Chapter 3

1. **B**ut you should know this, that in the last days hard times will come.

2. And people will be lovers of themselves, lovers of money, boasters, proud, blasphemers, disloyal to their people, rejecters of grace, wicked,

3. Slanderers, captives to desire, cruel, haters of the good,

4. Traitors, impulsive, arrogant, loving lust more than the love of God,

5. Who have a form of God-worship and are far from his power; remove from you those who are such.

6. For some of them are these who crawl house to house and capture women buried in sins and are led to various lusts,

7. Who are always learning and are never able to come to the knowledge of the truth.

8. But just as Jannes and Jambres arose against Moses, in this way also they have withstood the truth; persons who corrupt their minds and are rejected from faith.

9. But they will not proceed to their advancement, for their madness is known to every person, just as theirs was also known.

10. But you have gone after my teaching and after my customs, after my love, after my endurance, after my desire and after my faith, after my long-suffering,

11. After my persecutions and after my suffering; and you know those things which I endured in Antiakia, Iconiun and Lystra, what persecutions I endured, and my Lord delivered me from all of them.

12. But also, all those who choose to live in the worship of God in Yeshua The Messiah are persecuted.

13. But evil men and deceivers will add to their evils, as they go astray and deceive.

14. But you should abide in those things that you have learned and of which you are assured, for you know from whom you have learned them,

15. And because from your childhood you were taught The Holy Scrolls which can make you wise unto the life in the faith of Yeshua The Messiah.

16. Every writing which is written by The Spirit* is profitable for teaching, for correction, for direction and for a course in righteousness,

---

* *Greek has "Θεοπνευστος," –"God breathed". This word, like many other Greek words in The Greek of Paul's epistles, occurs nowhere in Greek literature or in The LXX, just one time in The NT Greek. They seem to combine two adjacent Aramaic words into compound Greek words. The Aramaic has, "*דברוחא אתכתב*" –"which is written by The Spirit". Here is "God breathed" in Aramaic:* דבאלהא אתנשב*; now let's see the two phrases in Dead Sea Scroll script:*

אתכתב   דברוחא –*which is written by The Spirit*
אתנשב   דבאלהא –*which is breathed by God*

*Nine of the eleven corresponding letters in each phrase are identical or almost identical. This similarity is roughly a 75% letter correlation between the two readings in Aramaic. The most similar Greek match for "Θεοπνευστος," –"**God breathed**" which also means "**written by The Spirit**" would be "πνευμαγραφητος". This word would be unique in Greek literature, as is "Θεοπνευστος," –"God breathed", and the two have a correlation of about 25%. It would be very difficult to account for The Peshitta reading on the basis of Greek. The Dead Sea Scroll Aramaic above can easily account for the Greek reading.*

17. That the man of God will be perfect and perfected for every good work.

Chapter 4

1. **I** charge you before God and Our Lord Yeshua The Messiah, he who is going to judge the living and the dead at the revelation of his Kingdom:

2. Preach the word and stand with diligence, in season and out of season; reprove and rebuke with all long-suffering and teaching.

3. For there will be a time when they will not obey sound teaching, but they will multiply teachers to themselves, according to their desires, and with an itching of their sense of hearing,

4. And they will turn their ears from the truth and turn aside unto fables.

5. But you, be watchful in all things and endure hardships; do the work of an Evangelist and fulfill your ministry.

6. For now I am offered as a sacrifice and the time of release has arrived.

7. I have fought an excellent fight; I have finished my race and I have kept my faith.

8. And now a crown of righteousness is kept for me, which my Lord shall award to me in that day when he shall judge the just, but not only to me, but also to those who will have loved his revelation.

9. Let it be your concern to come quickly to me.

10. Dema has abandoned me and loves this world and he has gone to Thessaloniqa, Qrisqus to Galatia, Titus to Dalmatia.

11. Only Luqa is with me. Take Marcus and bring him with you, because he is suitable to me for the ministry.

12. I have sent Tukiqus to Ephesaus.

13. When you come, bring the bookcase* and the books that I left in Troas with Qarpus, especially the parchment scrolls.

● * Greek has "**Cloak**" –φελονην, instead of "**Book case**".

"**Cloak**" in Aramaic could be מרטוטא or נחתא or בירונא –

In DSS script:"**Cloak**"-נחתא, or מרטות א, or ברונגא.

"**Book case**" in DSS script is כתבא .The word for "**Book**"-"**kthava**" looks very similar to "**Cloak**"-"**nyakhta**" in DSS (Dead Sea Scroll script) ; both are underlined. The Greek translator apparently glossed over "**Bayt**" ("**Place**") and translated כתבא as נחתא. Three of the four letters of each word are very similar or identical (**75%** correlation).The two in Estrangela are: ܟܬܒܐ ,

ܢܚܬܐ . The DSS pair are the most similar; it appears that the Peshitta reading accounts for the Greek reading here, as in so many other places. Consider also that the Greek φαιλονην is found nowhere in Greek literature and is , according to Thayer's Greek English Lexicon is a misspelled transposition of φαινολην - referring to a " traveling coat, for protection against stormy weather". According to this interpretation, Paul was asking for a raincoat from prison ! Add to this that most Greek mss. have φελονην – equally strange and unprecedented in Greek literature and not really a word at all. And neither φαιλονην nor φελονην resembles Βιβλον , Βιβλιον -"Book" or γραμματα - "writings". Here again are the two readings –"**Books**" and "**Cloak**" in the Aramaic script used in Dead Sea Scrolls Israel 2000 + years ago:
כתבא –"**The Book**" (Peshitta)
נחתא – "**The Cloak**" (Source for Greek reading?)

14. Alexandros the Blacksmith showed me great evil. May Our Lord pay him according to his works.

15. Beware of him also, for he is very arrogant against our words.

16. At my first defense, no man was with me, but they all abandoned me. May this not be accounted to them.

17. But my Lord stood with me and empowered me, that the preaching might be fulfilled by me, and the Gentiles would all hear that I was delivered from the mouth of the lion.

18. And my Lord will deliver me from every evil work and will give me life in his Kingdom in Heaven, for to him is the glory to the eternity of eternities. Amen.

19. Give greeting to Prisqila and to Aqilaus and to the house of Onesiphorus.

20. Erastus stopped in Qorinthus, but Trophimus I left while he was sick in the city of Miletus.

21. Be careful to come before winter. Eubulus invokes your peace, and Pudas, Linus, Qlaudia and all the brethren.

22. Our Lord Yeshua The Messiah be with your spirit. Grace be with you*. Amen.

* The Eastern Peshitta has "**with us**"- עמן as compared to עמך. Two late Greek mss. and a few Latin Vulgate mss. have "**with us**", but this is out of character with Paul's salutations ; he never prays grace to himself in his writings, and all his closings confer grace upon others, not himself.

The Epistle of The Apostle Paul to Titus

Chapter 1

1. **P**aulus a Servant of God and an Apostle of Yeshua The Messiah, in the faith of The Chosen Ones of God and the knowledge of the truth which is in the awesomeness of God,

2. Concerning the hope of eternal life, which The True* God promised before the times of the world*.

* Greek has αψευδης –"not lying". Quite often the Greek has a double negative construction where The Peshitta has simply a positive statement: "not lying" = "True" ; "Not ignorant" = "Knowing". See also Luke 1:37,Mat. 17:20, Mat. 13:57, Mark 6:4, Heb. 7:20,Heb. 9:7.

* Greek has "προ χρονων αιωνιων" – **before eternal times**" , which , frankly , is a ridiculous phrase. Time and Eternity are opposites; there is no such thing as an eternal time, nor can eternity or the eternal be measured with a timepiece, as eternity is timeless. "**While we look not at these seen things, but at those not seen; for these seen things are time related, but those not seen are eternal.**" -2 Cor. 4:18 .1 Timothy 1:9 also has this Greek phrase -προ χρονων αιωνων. In both places, the Peshitta has קדם זבנא דעלמא – "**Before (antecedent to) the time of the world**".

דעלמא is "**of the world**" ;

דלעלמא is "**Eternal**"

– The 2ⁿᵈ is the 1ˢᵗ with one letter added, so possibly a Greek translator misread דעלמא ("**of the world**") as דלעלמא - "**Eternal**" in these two places. **In Pesher Habakkuk DSS:**

ﬡﬢﬥﬠﬢ is "of the world" ;

ﬡﬢﬥﬠﬥﬢ is "Eternal"

3. And he has revealed his word in his time by our preaching, with which I was entrusted by the commandment of God Our Lifegiver.

* "**Lifegiver**" is the literal sense of מחינא; it can also have the sense of "**Savior**", referring to Him Who gives eternal life, not merely the natural life of the body. Either translation would be acceptable, though I believe Paul's emphasis was on salvation, not natural life, so I have in the interlinear translation "**Lifegiver**" as the literal meaning in most of the 16 places where it occurs in The NT. מחינן ("**Our Lifegiver**") occurs six times just in Titus. Usually, Jesus is mentioned as "**our Lifegiver**" just after "**God Our Lifegiver**" is mentioned. See the next verse.

4. To Titus, a true son in the inner faith: Grace and peace from God The Father and from Our Lord Yeshua The Messiah, Our Lifegiver.

* Most Greek mss. have, "χαρις ελεος ειρηνη" – "Grace,mercy,peace". טיבותא may mean "grace" or "loving kindness". It may very well be that this word was double translated by the translator who produced the Majority Greek text. * The Critical Greek (Alexandrian) text omits "**Our Lord**".

5. For this reason I had left you in Crete, that you might set right those things that are lacking, and ordain Elders in each city just as I ordered you:

6. One who is without fault and has been the husband of one wife, and has believing children who are not abusive and not insubordinate in immorality.

7. For an Elder ought to be without faults as a steward of God, and not led by his own mind, neither bad tempered, neither excessive with wine, neither should he be quick to strike with his hand, neither loving filthy riches,

8. But he should love strangers, love goodness, should be modest, just, holy, and keep himself from lusts.

9. He should care* for the teaching of the word of faith, as to be able also to comfort by his sound teaching, and rebuke those who are contentious.

* Greek has "αντεχομενον" – "**holding to, supporting**"; The Peshitta has בטיל –"**He cares**". Here is an Aramaic word meaning, "**to bear, to carry**": טען ; In Dead Sea Scroll Aramaic script, it is: ﬡﬠﬢ ; adding a waw proclitic to בטיל –"**He cares**" is - (ובטיל); טען becomes וטען . Let's see these two in DSS script and enlarged:

ﬥﬢﬠﬢﬥﬢ -"**& he cares**"(Peshitta)

ﬡﬠﬢﬥﬢ -"**& he bears**"(Source of Greek reading ?)

I see **80%** correlation (four out of five letters) between these two words in this script (The two Waw's- ﬢﬢ ,Two Yodh's-ﬢﬢ , Lamedh & Final Nun- ﬥﬡ ; Even the ﬤ "Bet" and ﬥ "Tet" have similar shapes) .

10. For there are men who are not submissive and their words are empty; they deceive the minds of people, especially those who are of the circumcision,

11. Those whose mouths must be stopped up, for they destroy many households and teach what is not right for the sake of filthy riches.

12. One man among them, their own Prophet said, "The children of Crete are always liars, wicked beasts and idle bellies."

13. And he has brought this testimony truthfully; therefore, rebuke them severely that they might be sound in the faith.

14. And they should not yield to fables of the Judeans and commands of men who hate* the truth.

* Greek has "**who turn away**". "**Hate**" is דסנין . דתפנין is "**Turn**" ; In DSS script: ﬡﬠﬡﬢ : ﬡﬥﬤﬢ ;

Estrangela: ܗܦܟܝܢ ܕܡܗܦܟܝܢ .Another word for "**turn away**" is:הפכין . In DSS script: ﬡﬡﬥﬤﬢ The DSS Aramaic script in shaded grey seems to be the Aramaic script behind the base Greek translation. **DSS Script**

אֶפֶׁגּוּן- "Who Turn"(Source of Greek reading?)

וּאֲמֵךְ- "Who Hate"(Peshitta)

וּדְפֶגּוּן- "Who Turn"(Source of Greek reading?)

Ashuri Script

הפכין- "Turn"(Source of Greek reading?)

דסנין- "Who Hate"(Peshitta)

דפנין- "Who Turn"(Source of Greek reading?)

Estrangela

ܦܟܝ̈ܢ - "Turn"(Source of Greek reading?)

ܣܢܝ̈ܢ - "Who Hate"(Peshitta)

ܦܢܝ̈ܢ - "Who Turn"(Source of Greek reading?)

The Ashuri and Estrangela pairs each have **80%** correlation. The Greek reading αποστρεφομενων -"**who turn away**"; & The Greek reading μισουντων-"**who hate**" have **21%** correlation at best for the Greek pair. It seems unlikely the Greek reading gave rise to the Aramaic.

15. For to the pure everything is pure, but to those who are defiled and unbelieving nothing is pure, but their mind and conscience is defiled.

16. And they profess that they know God, but by their works they reject him; they are enemies, disobedient and worthless concerning every good work.

Chapter 2

1. **But** speak what is fitting for sound teaching.

2. And teach that Elders would be watchful in their minds, modest, pure, sound in faith, in love and in patience,

3. And the elder women, in this way also, to be fitting in appearance for the worship of God and not to be slanderers, neither subservient to much wine, and to be teachers of excellence.

4. And chasten those who are young women to love their husbands* and their children*,

* **Greek has** φιλανδρους **(Philandrous)–"Men lovers"** (we get the English word "**Philanderer**" from this Greek word), and *φιλοτεκνους **(Philoteknous)–"Children lovers"**. Lack of possessive pronouns makes the Greek rather generic and even counterproductive. I know Paul did not intend for women believers to be "**men lovers**" - "**Philanderers**", but to love their husbands. This Greek wording is unworthy to be the inspired original word of God.

5. And to be chaste and holy, taking good care of their households and obeying their husbands, lest anyone blaspheme the word of God.

6. And in this way beseech those who are young men to be serious.

7. But show yourself in all things *as* a model in all good works, and in your teaching let your speech be wholesome,

8. Serious, uncorrupted*, and let no man despise it, so that he who opposes us may be ashamed, as he will be unable to say anything disgraceful against us.

*Greek has "ακαταγνωστον" –"**that cannot be impeached**", which is nowhere else in **The LXX OT** or **The Greek NT**, but once in the Apocrypha – "ακαταγνωστοι" in 2 Maccabees 4:47.The Peshitta reading ,"**not corrupt**" - לא מחבלא , certainly did not come from the Greek reading.The Greek for "**incorruptible**" is αφθαρτον , not much like ακαταγνωστον at all (**33%** correlation). An Aramaic word meaning "**impeached**" is מקבילא or מתקבלא . In DSS : קבל͏ܐ or קܒܠ͏ܐ ; "**Corrupt**" is מחבלא ; In DSS script: מܚܒ͏ܠܐ ; Now let's compare the two most similar forms of these two Aramaic words:

מܚܒܠܐ –"**Corrupt**"
מܬܩܒܠܐ –"**Impeached**"

I see only a one letter difference between these two words in DSS script; That is **83% correlation** between these two readings in Aramaic! That seems pretty strong evidence that The Peshitta's Aramaic is the base from which the Greek ακαταγνωστον was translated.

9. Let Servants be subject to their Masters in all things and be pleasing, and let them not resist;

10. Neither let them steal, but in all things let them show their good loyalty, to adorn the doctrine of God Our Lifegiver in all things.

11. For the all saving* grace of God has been revealed to all men;

* מחית "**Mekhayth**" is from the same root as מחינא –"**Mekhayna**" (see above note at 1:3). It refers to God's salvation in giving eternal life to people.

12. And it leads us to reject wickedness and the lusts of the world and to live in this world in purity, in righteousness, and in the worship of God,

13. While we look for the blessed hope and the revelation of the glory of The Great God and Our Lifegiver, Yeshua The Messiah,

14. Who gave himself in our place to redeem us from all evil and to purify a new* people for himself, which is zealous of good works.

* Greek has "**peculiar**"- "περιουσιον". חדתא- "**New**" is very similar to חדא – "**One**","**Singular**","**Particular**".

חܕܬܐ -"**New**"
חܕܐ -"**Singular**"

Possibly "**New**" was misread as "**Singular**" by a Greek translator. "**New**" in Greek is καινη or νεος – Nothing like περιουσιον.The Peshitta reading did not come from Greek.

15. Speak these things; beseech and rebuke with all authority, and no man should despise you.

Chapter 3

1. Charge them to obey Rulers and Authorities and to submit and be prepared for every good work,

2. And not to insult any person, neither to be contending, but they should be humble and show their sweetness in all things to all people.

3. For we also from the first were without intelligence and without conviction. We were deceived and Servants to changing lusts and were employed in wickedness and in envy. We were despicable and hating one another.

4. But when the sweetness and the loving kindness of God Our Lifegiver was revealed,

5. Not by works of righteousness that we had done, but by his own love he gave us life, through the washing of the new birth and the renewing of The Spirit of Holiness,

6. Whom he poured upon us richly by Yeshua The Messiah Our Lifegiver,

7. That we would be made right by his grace and we would be heirs by the hope in eternal life.

8. But the saying is trustworthy, and I want you also to be assuring them in these things, that they who have believed in God would be concerned to cultivate good works, for these things are good and beneficial for the children of men.

9. But abstain from foolish debates, from tales of genealogies, from contentions and from the contests of The Scribes, for there is no profit in them and such things are worthless.

10. Avoid a man who is a heretic after the first and second admonitions,

11. And be aware that he who is such is perverse and a sinner and is self condemned.

12. When I have sent to you Artemis or Tukyqos, be diligent to come to me to Niqopolis, for I have set my mind to winter there.

13. But concerning Zena the Scribe and concerning Apollo, be diligent to attend well to them, that they would lack nothing,

14. And they will teach those who are ours also to cultivate good works in matters of distress, lest they should be fruitless.

15. All those who are with me invoke your peace. Invoke the peace of all those who love us in the faith. Grace be with all of you. Amen.

The Epistle of The Apostle Paul to Philemon

1. Paul a prisoner of Yeshua The Messiah, and brother Timotheus, to beloved Philemon and our companion laborer,

2. And to Aphia our beloved* and to Arkippus our fellow laborer and to the church that is in your house.

* A few Greek mss. have , "& to Apphia our sister..". Most Greek mss. have ,"& to Apphia the beloved..". "Our Beloved" in Aramaic is חביבתן ; Our sister is חתן ; In DSS script they are : חתן - חביבתן ; In Estrangela : ܚܬܢ - ܚܒܝܒܬܢ . "Our beloved" has all the letters of "Our sister", which are highlighted in blue (in the color edition) and also underlined (1st, 5th and 6th from the right), which, in that order, spell "Our sister" in the Aramaic language. A careless and bleary eyed Scribe might skip a few letters in translating, from time to time, (The Critical Greek mss. Vaticanus and Siniaticus are famous for omissions) especially when the omission of three letters still leaves a coherent and contextually fitting word. Hence, the Aramaic primacy hypothesis (I believe I have accumulated enough supporting evidence in The NT to establish it as a theory) explains many Greek readings; the Greek for "Beloved" is ΑΓΑΠΗΤΗ ; "Sister" is "ΑΔΕΛΦΗ". Only the first and last letters are the same, which letters have no meaning by themselves, neither is either word mistakable for the other. It is very difficult to see how, if the Greek were the original, an Aramaean translator would misread ΑΔΕΛΦΗ ("Sister") as חביבתן ("Beloved"), if that were the original reading.
Certainly The Peshitta agrees here with the Majority Byzantine reading much more closely than with the Critical Greek text, as it generally does, however it also differs here and in many places radically from all Greek readings. Besides, if Greek were the original, and Aramaic the translation thereof, we would expect the variant readings to occur in the translation language (Aramaic), not in the original. There are practically no variant readings to speak of in The Peshitta mss, but The Greek mss. abound with them ! Too large a number of these are traceable to the Peshitta text for this to be coincidental. I hope that anyone reading the voluminous evidence shown in Gospels and Epistles of this interlinear will see that **The Greek NT** is a translation of **The Peshitta NT** text.

3. Grace be with you and peace from God Our Father and from Our Lord Yeshua The Messiah.

4. I thank my God always, and I remember you in my prayers,

5. Behold, from the time that I heard of your faith and love which you have toward Our Lord Yeshua and toward all The Holy Ones,

6. That the sharing of your faith would produce fruit in works and in the knowledge of every good thing which you have in Yeshua The Messiah.

7. For we have great joy* and comfort, for by your love the affections of the Saints have been refreshed.

● The Critical Greek has "**I had great grace**" where the Majority Greek and The Peshitta has "**We have great joy**". "Joy" in Greek is "χαραν", whereas "Grace" is "χαριν", so the Critical Greek reading is probably a misreading of "χαραν" as "χαριν", only one letter α (**Alpha**) being mistaken for ι (**Iota**) . The change of subject from "**We had**" to "**I had**" may be explained on the basis of misreading one letter in Aramaic : לן - "**to us**" & לי - "**to me**" . These words are part of an idiom in Aramaic describing possession or ownership. The final **Nun** (ן) in לן is sometimes mistaken for **Yodh** י if the bottom stroke is faint or missing. Here are the words at issue in DSS script : ן : ; In Estrangela: ܠܢ : ܠܝ . Either the square Ashuri Aramaic, DSS or Estrangela may account for the variant Greek reading. In Greek, the word "**We have**" is εχομεν ; "**I had**" is εσχον .

ן טבותא אית לי - "I have grace"
ן טבותא אית לן - "We have joy"

8. Because of this, I have great freedom in The Messiah to command you those things that are right.

9. But for love's sake, I beg of you, I Paul, who am The Elder, as you know, and now also a prisoner of Yeshua The Messiah,

10. I beg of you concerning my son Onesimus, whom I begot in my bondage,

11. He who was not useful to you at times, but now also is very useful to you and to me,

12. And I sent him to you, so receive him as my son*.

* Greek mss. have σπλαγχνα- "bowels" . In Aramaic, that would be רחמא- "**Rakhma**" (**mercy,affection,friend,love**).
Here are the actual Aramaic readings: דלילדא - "Son" and דלרחמא- "**Rakhma**" in Dead Sea Scroll Aramaic script: ; If you will notice the second word's fourth letter from the right , ח (**Khet**) , you may notice that it looks like two letters just barely touching at the top . If I take the letters of the other word and compress them together, you might mistake them for a ח ("Khet") or a מ "Mem". I propose that a Greek Scribe did both ! First he saw as ל (as if it were rotated counterclockwise a bit, then compressed as ח (I think the copy he had must have been illegible at this place and he was deciphering, letter by letter here) , then he looked back at the same letters and saw as מ ; hence became.
Even discounting my letter theory, these two words have a **66%** letter correlation.
The Greek word for "son" is υιος or "τεκνον"; Compare those with σπλαγχνα- "bowels". How would an Aramaean translating from Greek mistake σπλαγχνα for τεκνον or υιος? This would be the scenario if The Peshitta were translated from Greek. That theory is not supported by the facts here. Peshitta primacy wins in Philemon, hands down.
Great Isaiah Dead Sea Scroll script
-"Son"
- "Mercy,Affection,Friend,Love"
Pesher Habakkuk DSS script
-"Son"
-"Mercy,Affection,Friend,Love"

Depending on how one sees the letter correlation in the above two words, there is **66-84 %** correlation between the two words.

13. For I was willing to keep him with me to minister to me on your behalf in the bondage of The Gospel.

14. But I did not want to do anything without your counsel, so that your benefit would not be by necessity, but by your will.

15. But perhaps also for this cause he departed for a time, so that you may have him for eternity,

16. Not as a Servant from now on, but more than a Servant; as my particularly beloved brother, how much moreso yours, both in the flesh and in Our Lord?

17. If, therefore, you are my partner, receive him as mine.

18. And if you lack anything or he owes you a debt, put it to my account.

19. I, Paul, have written with my hand; I myself will pay, without saying to you also that you owe me your soul.

20. Yes, my brother, I am refreshed by you in Our Lord. Satisfy my love in The Messiah*.

⬤   Most Greek mss. have "**In The Lord**" ; Critical Greek texts. have "**In Christ**", agreeing with The Peshitta... The likely Aramaic for "**In The Lord**" would be "במרן" or "במריא".

"**In The Messiah**" is במשיחא.
"In THE LORD JEHOVAH" is במריא which is much more similar, with **66%** letter correlation.

DSS script: בגמשיחא- "**In The Messiah**"

במריא "**In The LORD**"

66% letter correlation

Estrangela script:

66% letter correlation

The Greek for "**Christ**" is Χριστω
"**Lord**" is Κυριω .

That gives **a 16% correlation** for the two Greek words. The Aramaic copy translated into Greek must have been unclear at this place in the letter, so that two letters in במשיחא were unreadable; ח was not read; ש was read as ר .

21. Because I trust that you will listen to me, I have written to you and I know that you will do more than what I have said.

22. But prepare for me at once a dwelling place, for I hope soon to be given to you by your prayers.

23. Epaphra, a fellow captive in Yeshua The Messiah, invokes your peace,

24. And Marcus, Aristarchus, Dema and Luqa, my helpers.

25. The grace of Our Lord Yeshua The Messiah be with your spirit. Amen.

The Epistle of The Apostle Paul to the Hebrews

Chapter 1

1. From the first, in all parts and in all forms, God spoke with our fathers by The Prophets,

2. And in these last days he has spoken with us by his Son, whom he ordained The Heir of all things, and by him he made the universe.

3. For he is The Brilliance of his glory, The Image of his Being, and upholds all* things by the power of his word; and he in his Essential Being has accomplished the purification of our sins, and he sat down at the right hand of the Majesty on high. *

("Akhyd koll" is literally "Holding all things" and is an Aramaic idiom meaning, "Almighty". It occurs 10 times in the NT. The other 9 are in Revelation. See Rev. 1:8 for the next one.)

4. And This One is altogether greater than the Angels, according to how much more excellent than theirs is **The Name*** which he possesses.

שמא (Shema) "The Name" is "Ha Shem" – השם - in Hebrew , which is the common Title for **God** in Hebrew liturgy. This verse in Aramaic makes much better sense than the Greek text which says , "..He has inherited a more excellent name than they" – as if The Christ is greater than Angels because of an inheritance rather than His very nature and Person as God! The context of verses 1-12 bears this out; The Name "MarYah Yeshua Meshika" is Divine and higher than every name because He is absolute Deity of absolute Deity- **The LORD GOD** of The Heavens and of The Earth by His very eternal nature.

5. For to which one of the Angels did God* ever say, "You are my Son; today I have begotten you", and again, "I shall be to him The Father and he shall be to me the Son."?

* Greek lacks "God" in this verse, and says, "To Whom did He ever say, You are my Son…" Did Who ever say ? The verse before is referring to The Messiah. To omit "God" leaves a misleading and confusing statement.

6. Again, when he brings The Firstborn into the universe, he says, "All the Angels of God shall worship him."

7. But he spoke in this way about the Angels: "He makes his Angels the wind and his Ministers the burning fire."

8. But concerning The Son, he said, "Your throne, oh God, is to the eternity of eternities. A straight scepter is the scepter of your Kingdom."

9. "You have loved righteousness and you have hated evil; because of this, God, your God, has anointed you with the oil of a joy beyond your companions."

10. And again, "You have laid the foundation of The Earth from the beginning and the Heavens are the work of your hands."

11. "Those shall pass away and you remain, and they all shall wear out like a robe,"

12. "And you shall fold them up like a cloak; they shall be changed, and you are as you are* ; your years shall not end."

* ואנת איך דאיתיך אנת (Literally, "**You are as you are**") is very like **AHIAH ASHAR HIGH**" in Exodus 3:14 ("**I AM WHO I AM**") and אנא אנא –"**Ena Na**"- "**I AM**"- a proclamation of The Eternal Deity, which **Jehovah** used in The OT and as **MarYah Yeshua** used some 30 times in The Peshitta NT – "**I AM THE LIVING GOD**".

13. But to which of the Angels did he ever say, "Sit at my right hand until I put your enemies as a footstool under your feet"?

14. Behold, are they not all spirits of service, who are sent into service for the sake of those who are going to inherit life?

Chapter 2

1. Because of this, we are indebted that we should be all the more attentive to whatever we have heard, lest we fall*.

* Greek reads μηποτε παραρρυωμεν – "**Lest we glide aside**" (Young's Lit. Translation); Rotherham's has : "**Lest we drift away**". These sound rather entertaining compared to The Aramaic , "**Lest we fall**".

2. For if a word spoken by Angels was established and everyone who heard it and violated it received a reward by justice,

3. How shall we escape if we despise those things which are our life, those which began to be spoken by Our Lord and by those who heard from him among us, and were confirmed,

4. While God testified concerning them with signs, wonders and various miracles, and by gifts of The Spirit of Holiness, which were given according to his will?

5. For it was not to Angels that he subjected the future world, about which we are speaking;

6. But as The Scripture* testifies and says, "What is a man, that you remember him, and the son of man that you care for him?"

* Greek mss. have "**one in a certain place testified**". That seems rather vague and non-authoritative compared to The Peshitta reading.

7. "You have brought him a little lower than The Angels. You have placed glory and honor on his head and you have authorized him over the works of your hands."

8. "You have subjected all things under his feet." But by this, that 'He subjected everything to him', it does not leave anything which is not subjected; but now, we do not yet see that everything is subjected to him.
9. But we see that he is Yeshua, who became a little lower than the Angels for the suffering of his death, and glory and honor are placed upon his head, for God himself, by his grace, tasted death in the place of every person.

 * The Eastern Peshitta differs considerably here; it reads : "**But we see that He is Jesus - He Who was a little lower than the Angels for the suffering of His death , and glory and honor are placed on His head, for He , apart from God, tasted death in the place of everyone**". The Greek mss. agree with the Western Peshitta (& my interlinear). The Western Peshitta **could** be translated as the Greek texts have it: "**By the grace of God He tasted death for everyone**", though the Aramaic בטיבותה אלהא is not the normal construction used for that sense :The norm in Paul's writing and in Hebrews would be בטיבותה דַאלהא – The red underlined letter is a Dalet proclitic. That is the norm for genitive constructs with **Alaha (God)**. The only apparent exception I can find in the epistles is דחלת אלהא –"**the fear of God**", which is not a true genitive construct, for the true sense in that expression is "**fear toward God**" , which disqualifies it as a genitive, in which case the Dalet proclitic ד would not be used and would be incorrect. The Greek text of 2:9 is apparently a mistranslation of the Aramaic in that sense. I don't believe Paul would have written אלהא -"**God**" if he had meant דאלהא - "**of God**". That would only create confusion for the reader. I also cannot accept the Eastern Peshitta version of this verse for several reasons, the first of which I cannot go into here, but recommend my first book, **Divine Contact-Discovery of The Original NT** for an explanation of how I found the original text of The whole NT.
 The second reason is doctrinal ambiguity. The Eastern reading implies that Jesus either was separated from God: "**For He , apart from God, tasted death for everyone**" or that "**He tasted death for everyone but God**". I cannot accept that Paul stated either proposition. The first possibility is simply contrary to The Gospels, in which Jesus asserted His eternal unity with God His Father, without Whom He could do nothing and Whose actions He imitated and Whose words He repeated (See John 5:19 and 10:30). If The Christ could do not the least thing without His Father, He certainly could not do the greatest thing, which was His death for a lost world as atonement for sin. Consider also that He saw His Father dying :
 And Jesus answered, and said to them: Verily, verily, I say to you: The Son can do nothing of his own pleasure, but what he seeth the Father do: for what things the Father doeth, these in like manner doeth the Son. (Murdock)
 Nothing but what He sees The Father do ? If that is what He said, and I believe it is, then Our Lord's death was truly not unique to His Person in The Godhead; He saw The Father dying and followed His example ! They truly died together as One just as they did everything in Life. This is the mystery of The Gospel: God The Father, God The Son and God The Holy Spirit died as One in The Messiah for the sin of the world. That was the end of the old creation, as it could not endure without its Living Creator God. God also arose from the dead, not on the third day in the physical resurrection of Yeshua, but on the cross before His physical death. The atoning death and the resurrection occurred on the cross before He said, "It

is finished!" and "Father, into Thy hands..." and He bowed His head and expired. "**If The One died for all, then all died with Him. And he died for all, that they who live should not live to themselves, but to him who died for them and rose again. And therefore, we know no person after the flesh: and if we have known the Messiah after the flesh, yet henceforth we know him no more.**" (2 Cor. 5:14-16)
.
 We must see the world in a new light- the light of the atoning death of God The Creator and His regenerating resurrection. "**Whoever therefore is in the Messiah, is a new creature: old things have passed away**"; And Who is The Messiah ? He is The Yahweh of Israel, The Creator of The Heavens and The Earth- Omnipotent,Omniscient,Omnipresent,Eternal. Who is not in the Omnipresent One, Who is " **all and in all and fills all in all**" ?We must see all people as in The Messiah and as His new creatures, created by Him for good works. All their sins have passed away. We must believe The Gospel if we are to ask others to believe it. "**Old things have passed away**". "**We must think anew and act anew**", said Abraham Lincoln; never are such words more appropriate than when applied to The Good News of Yeshua Meshikha's Death,Burial and Resurrection. Let us discard "old thinking"- that is, thinking based on the unbelief that we live in the old fallen world, riddled with sin, misery and death. "**And all things are made new, by God; who hath reconciled us to himself by the Messiah, and hath given to us the ministry of reconciliation**". No qualification is made to these statements. It does not say, "**the believer's old things have been passed away**". It does **not** say, "**All things are new in the believer**"; it is a universal and unqualified truth – unqualified except by "**whoever (or whatever) is in The Messiah**", which is all- inclusive. "**For it was God by the Messiah who hath reconciled the world with his majesty, and did not reckon to them their sins; and who hath placed in us the word of reconciliation.**" What Jesus did on the cross, God did. There was no suffering of The Messiah that His Father did not endure as well. The Godhead as a whole suffered death in becoming sin;Lamsa's translation of 2 Cor. 5:21 says: "**He who knew no sin has made Himself to be sin for us…**" That is the death God died. In The death of The Creator, all creation died. In His resurrection, all things were raised from the dust of oblivion into New Heavens and a New Earth- justified by The Divine blood, bathed and regenerated by The Divine Spirit of Holiness, sanctified by The Word of God The Son: "**If I be lifted up from The Earth, I will draw all people unto Myself**". John 12:32.
 Jesus said to them: Verily I say to you, that, as for you who have followed me, when the Son of man shall sit on the throne of his glory in the new world, ye also shall sit on twelve seats, and shall judge the twelve tribes of Israel.- Matthew 19:28
תרעסר כורסון ותדונון תרעסר שבטא דאיסראיל
ברה דאנשא על תרנוס דשובחה תתבון אף אנתון על
לכון דאנתון דאתיתון בתרי בעלמא חדתא מא דיתב
Mt 19:28 אמר להון ישוע אמין אמר אנא
 3 Who being the brightness of his glory, and the express image of his person, and upholding all things by the word of his power, when he had by himself purged our sins, sat down on the right hand of the Majesty on high;
דוכיא דחטהין ויתב על ימינא דרבותה במרומא
ואחיד כל בחילא דמלתה והו בקנומה עבד
3 דהויו צמחא דשובחה וצלמא דאיתותה
 1Co 10:11 All these things which befell them, were for an example to us; and they are written for our instruction, on whom the ends of the world hath come.
מטל מרדותא דילן דהרהתהון דעלמא עלין מטת
הלין דין כלהין דגדש להון לטופסן הוי ואתכתב
1Co 10:11
.
 Heb 9:26 otherwise, he must have suffered many times, since the commencement of the world; but now

in the end of the world, he hath once offered himself in a self-sacrifice, to abolish sin.

הו זבן קרב נפשה בדביחותה דנבטליה לחטיתא
מן שוריה דעלמא השא דין בחרתה דעלמא חדא
Heb 9:26 ואן לא חיב הוא דזבנתא סגיאתא נחש

And he that sat upon the throne said, Behold, **I make all things new**. And he said unto me, Write: for these words are faithful and true.

כתוב הלין מלא מהימנתא ושרירתא איתיהין
דיתב על כורסיא הא חדתא עבד אנא כל מדם לי
5 ואזלת ואמר לי

6 And he said unto me, **It is done**. I am Alpha and Omega, the beginning and the end. I will give unto him that is athirst of the water of life freely.
לדצהא אנא אתל מן עינא דמיא חיא מגן
6 ואמר לי הוי אנא אלף ואנא תו רישיתא ושולמא
Rev. 21:5,6

22 But <u>ye have come to Mount Zion, and to the city of the living God, the Jerusalem that is in Heaven</u>; and to the assemblies of <u>myriads of Angels</u>;

23 and <u>to the church of the first-born, who are enrolled in Heaven and to God the judge of all; and to the spirits of the just, who are perfected</u>;

24 <u>and to Jesus,</u> the Mediator of the new covenant; and <u>to the sprinkling of his blood</u>, which speaketh better than that of Abel.

25 <u>Beware, therefore, lest ye refuse to hear him who speaketh with you.</u> For if they escaped not, who refused to hear him who spake with them on The Earth, how much more shall we not, if we refuse to hear him who speaketh with us from Heaven?

(Let everyone reading this consider the results of refusing to hear these, His words.)

10. For it was fitting for him by whom are all things and for whom are all things, and bringing many children into the glory, that The Prince of their life would perfect himself by his suffering.

11. For he who makes holy and they who are made holy are all of one, therefore, he is not ashamed to call them his brothers,

12. When he said, "I shall announce your name to my brethren and within the church I shall glorify you."

13. And again, "I will trust in him", and again, "Behold, I and the children whom God has given me."

14. For because the children shared together in flesh and blood, he also shared in these things in the same form, so that by his death he would destroy the one who had held the authority of death, who is Satan,

15. And he would free those who, by the fear of death, all their lives were subjected to bondage.

16. For death was not authorized* over the Angels, but death was authorized over the seed of Abraham.

* In this verse The two Peshittas (Eastern & Western) differ considerably: The Eastern Peshitta has : "**He took not from Angels but He took from the seed of Abraham.**" The Greek mss. agree with the Eastern Peshitta, though either seems awkward at best.

The Western reading here is coherent and fits the context of the verses before and after. The Greek and Eastern readings seem out of joint with the context as well as being an incomplete statement. Considering that in verse 9 also there is a major and famous variant between the two Peshitta's about the death of Christ, I suspect a doctrinal controversy (Nestorian vs. Monophysite) was behind that verse's variants. The **Nestorians** believed (and still do) that The Messiah had two **natures** -"Kyana's" and two "Qnoma's" (**consciousnesses** ?)- a Divine and human one of each . The death of The Messiah was physical only and involved only His human qnoma. The Divine nature and qnoma are impassible –incapable of suffering. The **Monophysites** ("**One nature**") branch of the Aramaean church had held that the nature and Person of The Messiah was simply Divine and nothing more. They had no problem with the concept of God suffering and dying, since Jesus was and is God and the Scriptures plainly state that He died.

Personally , I disagree with both positions in this matter, though I believe the Western readings are correct in Hebrews 2:9 and Acts 20:28 (Another "Death of The Messiah" reading) and that the Nestorian doctrine was not developed until the fifth century and resulted from these few early alterations in the Peshitta text. **Below I list the Eastern reading of this verse in interlinear form**:

(for) גיר (it was) הוא (not) לא 16
| (He received *) נסב (the Angels) מלאכא (from) מן
(the seed) זרעה (from) מן (but) אלא |
(He received *) נסב (of Abraham) דאברהם
"**For He received not from Angels but He received from the seed of Abraham.**"

Here is The Western Peshitto reading from my **Aramaic-English Interlinear New Testament**:

(the angels) מלאכא (over) על (for) גיר (it was) הוא (not) לא
(but) אלא (death *) מותא (was) הוא (authorized *) משלט
(of Abraham) דאברהם (the seed) זרעה (over) על
(it was) הוא (authorized) משלט

The light highlighted words were omitted and the grey highlighted were altered in the Eastern text. Possibly "**Authorized**" משלט was changed to נסלט phonetically by mispronouncing Shin ש (Sh) as Semkat ס (S) , so **Mashlat** became **Maslat**. The Mim מ was distorted to Nun נ the Lamed dropped, and the Tet ט rotated 45 degrees counterclockwise and read as Bet ב, transforming משלט into נסב. Honestly, I cannot be confident of this explanation, as the translator in question would have had to misread the two different words, twice each. Possibly the Peshitta manuscript being translated was severely smudged in this verse or damaged and unreadable at the words in question, or perhaps it was poorly written there. It seems to me that there was physical damage in the manuscript and that the translator had no other copy with which to compare it, so he did the best he could and came up with the Greek reading found now in all Greek mss. The same Peshitta manuscript from which he translated also became the chief copy used in the Eastern Church, from which all other Eastern Peshitta mss. were derived. This is my personal opinion, and has no bearing on the orthodoxy or unorthodoxy of either reading or the adherents of either text. Both Peshittas are in almost perfect agreement textually and doctrinally. Generally, omissions are far more common errors in copying, than addition, so the longer reading is generally the original. There are exceptions to this rule, of course.

17. Because of this, it was right that he would become like his brethren in all things, that he would be a compassionate and trustworthy High Priest in what is God's, and would make atonement for the sins of the people.

(It would seem that this statement- "**Because of this**", supports the Western reading of the previous verse, referring to "**Death was authorized over the seed of Abraham**", so that it was "**necessary**" (another translation of "**zadaq**") for **The Prince of Life** to become like his Jewish brethren in every sense, by His incarnation, in order to suffer and die for their sakes. If the other reading were the original, we would have a non sequitur in v. 17, because verse 16 would essentially give no reason for the statement in 17; Verse 17 would be saying , in essence: "**Because He became human, in the line of Abraham, he had to become human in the line of Abraham.**" Since He had become human in the line of Abraham, he would of necessity be subject to temptation, suffering and death. There was no additional change necessary by which He could become like his brethren. **The incarnation was not the cause of the incarnation. Death was the cause of the incarnation**; it was incumbent upon Our Lord to become mortal and to die in order to free us from death.)

18. For in this, because he has suffered and was tempted, he can help those who are tempted.

Chapter 3

1. Therefore my holy brethren, who are called with a calling from Heaven, consider This Apostle and High Priest of our confession, Yeshua The Messiah*,

* The Critical Greek mss. and Latin Vulgate lack "**The Messiah**" . In 2:7 , the Critical Greek text agrees with The Peshitta reading whereas the Byzantine Majority Greek mss. omit a significant portion of the verse. If the Peshitta were a translation of Greek, in 2:7 it would be a translation of the Critical Greek and here in 3:1 it would be a translation of the Byzantine Greek text. But this is a phenomenon often found in the NT, which does not favor Greek primacy and rather supports Peshitta primacy. Quite often, The Peshitta agrees with no known Greek reading (See 2:6 and 2:16).

2. Who is faithful to The One who appointed him, as Moses in his entire household.
3. For the glory of This One is much greater than that of Moses, as much as the honor of the builder of the house is greater than his building.
4. For every house is built by some man, but he who built all things is God.
5. And Moses as a Servant was entrusted with the entire household for the testimony of those things that were going to be spoken by him,
6. But The Messiah as The Son over his house; and we are his house, if we will hold the confidence and the pride of his Gospel until the end;
7. Because The Spirit of Holiness said, "Today, if you will hear his voice,
8. Do not harden your hearts to anger him* , like the rebellious, and as the day of temptation in the wilderness

* No Greek mss. have "**to anger Him**" . How would this reading have come from Greek ? The Aramaic למרגזותה ,however,could loosely be interpreted "**in the provocation**" , but it ignores the pronoun enclitic "ה"(Him,His) and forces the proclitic to mean "in", which is very rare.This reading also occurs in verse 15. The Hebrew of Psalm 95:8 has "**In Meribah**" ;"**Meribah**",which means "**provocation**", was the place where Moses smote the rock and brought water out for Israel. He named the place "**Massah**" (**Temptation**) & "**Meribah**" (**Provocation**).The place name was not transliterated in **The Peshitta OT** or in **The LXX**; it was translated, as the meaning was more important than the name. The Hebrew of Ps. 95:8 has ,"**In Meribah in the day of Massah**".

9. When your fathers tempted me and they proved and saw my works forty years.
10. Because of this, I was weary with that generation, and I said, 'That is a people which deceives their heart, and they have not known my ways.'
11. And I swore in my anger, 'They shall not enter my rest.'"
12. Beware therefore, my brethren, lest there be an evil, unfaithful heart in any of you, and you depart from THE LIVING GOD;
13. But inquire of yourselves every day, until the day that is called today, lest anyone of you should be hardened by the deception of sin.
14. For we have been joined with The Messiah, if we shall hold fast to this true Covenant from the beginning to the end,
15. Just as it was said, "Today, if you will hear his voice, do not harden your hearts to anger him."
16. For who were those who heard and angered him? Was it not all of these who went out from Egypt by Moses?
17. And with whom was he wearied forty years, but with them who sinned and whose bones fell in the wilderness?
18. And concerning whom did he swear that they would not enter his rest, but those who were unconvinced?
19. And we see that they could not enter, because they did not believe.

Chapter 4

1. Let us fear, therefore, lest, while The Promise of entering into his rest stands, any of you should be found to come short of entering.
2. For we also were evangelized as they were, but the word did not benefit those who heard, because it was not joined with faith by those who heard it.

3. But we who believe enter into rest, but just as he said, "As I swore in my anger, they shall not enter my rest." For behold, the works of God have existed from the foundation of the world,

4. According to what he said about the Sabbath* : "God rested on the seventh day from all his works."

* For שבתא ("Sabbath") , the Greek mss. have εβδομης ("Seventh") ; "Seven" in Aramaic is שבעא . Let's see these words in DSS script:

שבתא - ("Sabbath")
שבעא - ("Seven")

In Estrangela script: ܫܒܬܐ ܫܒܥܐ . Either Aramaic script shows **75% correlation**. The Peshitta reading "Sabbath" explains the Greek "Seventh" much more credibly than the Greek "Seventh" can explain the "Sabbath" reading. Here are the respective Greek words: σαββατα – εβδομης and in Greek uncial script:

ΣΑΒΒΑΤΑ – ΕΒΔΟΜΗΣ - (0% correlation) !

5. And here again he said: "They shall not enter my rest."

6. Because, therefore, there has been an opportunity for each person to enter and those who were first evangelized did not enter, in that they were not persuaded,

7. Again he appointed another day, after much time, just as it is written above that David said, "Today, if you listen to his voice, do not harden your hearts."

8. For if Yeshua, son of Nun*, had given them rest, he would not afterward have spoken of another day.

* "Yeshua son of Nun" in the Greek mss. is simply ιησους "Jesus" , which seems very confusing. This actually refers to **Joshua** (Hebrew- "Yeshua") **son of Nun** , who wrote the OT book of Joshua. One would assume the Greek text speaks of The Son of God (Jesus) here, because it is not specific and does not distinguish who is meant. The Greek does not look like the inspired original.

9. So then, it remains for the people of God to keep the Sabbath.

* **For** למשבתו -"**to keep the Sabbath**" , Greek mss. have "σαββατισμος"; this word occurs nowhere else in Greek literature and is an obvious reworking of the Aramaic למשבתו "**Lamshebatu**"- (**to keep Sabbath**) in Greek letters with grammatical noun ending. The word "σαββατον" occurs 68 times in the Greek NT, including in Acts,1 Corinthians and Colossians.

10. For whoever enters his rest has rested from his works as God has from his own.

11. Let us take pains, therefore, to enter that rest, lest we fall in the manner of those who were not persuaded.

12. For the word of God is living and all-efficient*, and much sharper than a double edged sword, and it pierces to the separation of soul and spirit and of joints, marrow and of bones*, and judges the reasoning and conscience of the heart.

* "**All efficient**" & "**And of the bones**" do not occur in the Greek mss. Where did these phrases come from? A translation of Greek would not have produced these phrases in the Peshitta.

13. And there is no created thing hidden from before him, but everything is naked and open before the eyes of him to whom we give an account.

14. Because we have therefore a great High Priest, Yeshua The Messiah*, The Son of God, who has ascended to Heaven, let us hold fast to his* confession.

* Greek lacks "**The Messiah**" and also "**His**" in "**His confession**" .

15. For we do not have a High Priest who cannot suffer with our weaknesses, but One who was tempted in all things like we *are*, apart from sin.

16. Let us come therefore publicly to the throne of his grace to receive mercy, and we shall find grace to help in a time of suffering*.

*Greek mss. have Ευκαιρον -"**in a convenient time**". Ευκαιρον literally means "**good time**" – just the opposite of the Peshitta reading -"**time of suffering**" ! Who asks for help in the good times? It may make for a fine sounding sermon to exhort people to do so, but it is superfluous to ask for help after one has just been helped, and for blessing while one is awash in blessings. We need help in an inconvenient time and time of trouble. I am more and more impressed with The Peshitta text as compared to the Greek, the more I read and compare them.

Chapter 5

1. For every High Priest of the children of men was appointed for the sake of men over the things that are of God, to present offerings and sacrifices for the sake of sin,

2. Who can humble himself and suffer with those who are ignorant and erring because he is also clothed with weakness,

3. And he owes a debt for his own sake, that as for the people, in this way also for his own sake, he will make an offering for his sins.

4. And it was not for himself that a man took the honor, but he who was called by God, just as Aaron.

5. So neither did The Messiah glorify his soul to be High Priest, but he who said to

him, "You are my Son; today I have begotten you",

6. As he said in another place, "You are a Priest for eternity in the image of Melchizedek."

7. While also he was clothed in the flesh, he offered prayers, supplications, strong shouting and tears to him who was able to give him life from death, and he was obeyed.

8. And although he is The Son, he learned obedience by the fear and the suffering which he endured;

9. And in this way he was perfected and became the cause of eternal life to all those who obey him.

10. And he was named The High Priest by God, in the image of Melchizedek.

11. But about this Melchizedek we have much to say, but it is hard to explain it because you have bad hearing.

12. For you ought to be teachers, because of the time you have had in the doctrine, but now, again, you need to learn those things which are the primer letters of the first words of God, and you have need of milk and not of solid food.

13. But every person whose food is milk is unacquainted with the word of righteousness, because he is an infant.

14. But solid food is for the mature, those whose senses are instructed to distinguish good and evil, because they practice.

Chapter 6

1. Because of this, let us leave the beginning of the message of The Messiah, and let us go on to perfection; or are you laying again another foundation for conversion from dead works and for faith in God,

2. For the teaching of baptism, the laying on of hands, for the resurrection from among the dead, and for eternal judgment?

3. We shall do* this if THE LORD JEHOVAH permits.

* Many Greek mss. have "ποιησωμεν"- "We should do", an aorist active subjunctive verb; Many also have "ποιησομεν" –"We shall do", an future active indicative verb. The Aramaic verb נעבד can have either meaning. All Aramaic imperfect tenses may be translated variously as future-"shall"-verb, optative-"may"-verb, hortatory-"let"-verb, purpose-"should"-verb, habitual present verb or as an imperative verb-"Thou shalt-verb, "Do"-verb, etc.. Many Greek variant readings may be traced to this Aramaic verb phenomenon as their source. Aramaic

participles also have considerable flexibility in that they may be translated as present tenses , future tense or past tense, depending on the context (very much like Hebrew).

4. But those who have descended once to baptism and tasted the gift from Heaven and received The Spirit of Holiness,

* למעמודיתא "Baptism" is similar to למנהרנותא "Enlightenment", which the Greek mss. all have. Here are the terms in DSS script:

למעמודיתא - "Baptism
למנהרנותא - "Enlightenment"

There are only two dissimilar letters in the two Aramaic words above.
In Estrangela they are ܠܡܥܡܘܕܝܬܐ ܠܡܢܗܪܢܘܬܐ .
not quite as similar as in DSS script, with 66% correlation ; DSS script words have 78% correlation . I fail to see how this and the previous verses were taken from the Greek . The Greek word for "enlightened" is φωτισθεντας; "Baptized" is βαπτισθεντας; Here are the two in uncial script: ΦΩΤΙΣΘΕΝΤΑΣ & ΒΑΠΤΙΣΘΕΝΤΑΣ. The Greek endings are standard and long for passive participles (6 letters long here) , hence the words are very similar, but not as similar as their Aramaic Estrangela counterparts. Assuming the

Greek ΦΩΤΙΣΘΕΝΤΑΣ ("Enlightened") is original , ΒΑΠΤΙΣΘΕΝΤΑΣ ("Baptized") represents 82% correlation, however, the first letters of a word are the most important for recognition; the first

two of ΦΩΤΙΣΘΕΝΤΑΣ are nothing like the first letters of ΒΑΠΤΙΣΘΕΝΤΑΣ. The rest of each word in Greek is basically an added ending for the particular masculine accusative plural of the aorist passive participle of a verb with an "izo" ending, which "Baptizo" and "Photizo" are. **The root words are the most critical in distinguishing one word from another**. These are the first part of the word, usually three to five letters long. I doubt therefore that a translator of Greek would mistake the root Φωτ- "Phot-" as ΒΑΠΤ- "Bapt-". (Yes , the English "Photo" and "Baptize" come from these Greek roots.) Notice also The Peshitta has the word "**descended**" נחתו before "**baptism**" . The Greek does not have this.
This same word discrepancy occurs in Hebrews 10:32 ! See note below at that place.

5. And tasted the good word of God and the power of the future world,

6. Who would sin* again and again crucify The Son of God, and become contemptible, cannot be renewed to conversion.

* Greek mss. have "παραπεσοντας" –"falling away" . I suspect a Greek translator looked at the Aramaic נחטון -"they sin" and saw נפלון ("falling"). Here are those two Aramaic words in three different scripts:

Ashuri: נחטון -"they sin"
נפלון -"falling"

Dead Sea Scroll: נחטון-"they sin"
נפלון-"falling"

Estrangela: ܢܚܛܘܢ -"they sin"
ܢܦܠܘܢ -"falling"

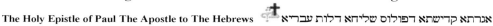

אגרתא קדישתא דפולוס שליחא דלות עבריא

The Estrangela pair are the most similar, which may indicate Estrangela was the original script used in composing Hebrews, or at least used in the copy translated into Greek. The letter correlation in that pair is **80%**. The others have 60% correlation.

The Peshitta here says that a true believer in The Messiah cannot sin and be reconverted. 1 John 3:6-10 goes even further and says a person born of God cannot sin at all! See also Hebrews 10:26.

7. But The Earth that drinks rain that comes to it often, and makes vegetation grow that is useful for those for whom it is cultivated, receives blessing from God.

8. But if it should produce thorns and thistles, it would be rejected and not far from curses, but its end is burning.

9. But we are persuaded concerning you, my brethren, those things that are excellent and that accompany life, even though we speak in this way.

10. For God is not evil, that he would disregard your works and your love which you have shown in his name, which you have ministered to the Saints and you do minister.

11. But we desire that each one of you have this diligence for the perfection of your hope until the end,

12. And that you should not lose heart, but that you would be imitators of those who by faith and patience have become heirs of The Promise.

13. For when God made a promise to Abraham, because there was no greater than he by whom to swear, he swore by himself,

14. And he said, "Blessing, I shall bless you, and multiplying, I shall multiply you."

15. And in this way he was patient and received The Promise.

16. For among men, they swear by that which is greater than they, and concerning every dispute which they have had among them, a sure end of it has come by an oath.

17. Because of this, God was all the more willing to show the heirs of The Promise that his Promise would not change, and he bound it with an oath,

18. That by two unchangeable matters, because God cannot lie about them, we who have sought refuge in him have great comfort, and we may seize the hope which was promised to us,

19. Which we have as an anchor that holds fast in our soul, which will not be moved, and has entered inside the veil,

20. Where Yeshua entered before for our sake and has become The Priest for eternity in the image of Melchizedek.

Chapter 7

1. This Melchizedek is The King of Shalim, Priest of The Most High God, and he met Abraham when he returned from the massacre of Kings and blessed him. ("Shalim" is translated "Salem" in the Greek & English Bibles; Salem is ancient Jerusalem.)

2. And Abraham distributed to him a tenth of everything that he had with him; but his name is interpreted , "King of Righteousness" and again "King of Shalim", which is, "King of Peace",

3. Without _his_ father and _his_ mother _being written in_ the genealogies, neither _having_ beginning of _his_ days nor end of _his_ life, but _in_ the likeness of The Son of God, _his_ Priesthood remains for _eternity_.

The Greek mss. have: (YLT) Without father, without mother, without genealogy, having neither beginning of days nor end of life, and being made like to the Son of God, doth remain a Priest continually.

The Peshitta text has ten more words of information than the Greek text. These are underlined in my translation to illustrate what is fairly typical in the NT comparisons of Greek and Aramaic versions. Translation normally involves a loss of information ("Lost in translation") , not adding of information. This phenomenon of less info. in the Greek texts supports Peshitta primacy and mitigates strongly against a Greek original for NT books. See my book **Divine Contact** for several experiments in which this phenomenon is analyzed statistically throughout the NT. The resulting thousands of data all support Peshitta primacy (an Aramaic original NT) unanimously.

4. But see how much greater This One is than the man Abraham, Chief of The fathers, to whom he gave the tithe of the best.

5. For those of the sons of Levi who received Priesthood had a commandment of The Written Law to take a tenth part from those people of their brethren, as also they had come forth from the loins of Abraham.

6. But This _Man_ who is not written in their genealogies received the tithe from Abraham and blessed him who had received The Promise.

7. But without dispute, he who is lesser is blessed by him who is greater than he.

8. And here the children of men who die receive tithes, but there, he about whom the Scriptures testify that he lives.

9. And as a man, let us say about him that by Abraham, Levi, who receives tithes, was caused to tithe.

10. For he was yet in the loins of his father when he met* Melchizedek.

 * The Greek has συνηντησεν αυτω ο μελχισεδεκ - "when Melchizedek met him"; not a major difference, but explainable on the basis of the Aramaic, which literally says," he met him Melchizedek".This could be construed to say "when Melchizedek met him", but only by forcing the grammar unnaturally.So the Greek could be explained as a translation of the Peshitta, but not vice versa.

11. If perfection therefore is by Priesthood of Levi, (for by it The Written Law was established to the people), why was another Priest needed to arise in the image of Melchizedek? But does it say that he would be in the image of Aaron?

12. But just as there was a change in The Priesthood, in this way there was also a change in The Law.

13. For he about whom these things were said was born from another tribe, from which a man never ministered at the altar.

14. For it is revealed that Our Lord arose from Judah, about which tribe Moses never said anything concerning Priesthood.

15. And moreover, again, it is apparent by this that he said that another Priest arises in the image of Melchizedek,

16. He who was not by the law of carnal commandments, but by the power of an indestructible life.

17. For he testified about him, "You are The Priest for eternity in the image of Melchizedek."

18. But there was a change in the first testament because of its impotence, and there was no benefit in it.

19. For The Written Law perfects nothing, but hope, which is greater than it, entered in its place, by which we approach God.

20. And he confirmed it to us by an oath.

 * All Greek mss. have "And inasmuch as it is not apart from oath"as the whole of the verse! This is not even a sentence in Greek, but a dangling modifier clause. The Greek seems to be a long winded paraphrase of the Aramaic with the double negative "not without" instead of the straightforward positive "He confirmed it". This occurs in The Gospel of Mark, Romans,1 & 2 Cor. , 1 Thess. and elsewhere not a few times.

21. For they were Priests without an oath, but this one, with an oath, as he said to him by David: "THE LORD JEHOVAH has sworn and will not lie, that you are The

Priest for eternity in the image of Melchizedek."

 * The critical Greek text lacks ,"In the image of Melchizedek". The OT Peshitta agrees with the reading here in The Peshitta: "in the image of Melchizedek". The Hebrew text of Psalm 110:4 can mean "in the order of Melchizedek" or "in the manner of Melchizedek" , the latter of which fits the word בדמותה –"badmutha".

22. This Covenant, of which Yeshua is The Guarantor, is entirely better.

23. And there were many Priests because they were dying and were not permitted to continue.

24. But This One's Priesthood, because he is Eternal, does not pass away.

25. And he can give life for eternity to those who come near to God by him, for he lives always and offers prayers for our sakes.

26. For because this Priest also was right for us: pure, without malice and without defilement, who is separate from sin and exalted higher than Heaven,

27. And he has no compulsion every day as The Chief Priests to offer sacrifice, first for his sins and then for the people, for This One did it one time by his Life which he offered.

28. For The Law establishes weak men as Priests, but the word of the oath which was after The Law, The Son, who is perfect for eternity.

Chapter 8

1. But The Summit of all these things that we have: The High Priest who sits at the right hand of the throne of The Majesty in Heaven.

2. And he is the Minister of The Holy Place and The True Tabernacle, which God set up, and not man.

3. For every High Priest is appointed to offer gifts and sacrifices, and because of this it was right also for This One to have something to offer.

4. And if he were on Earth, he would not be a Priest, because there have been Priests who have been offering gifts according to what is in The Law,

5. Those who serve the form and the shadow of these things that are in Heaven, as it was said to Moses when he made The Tabernacle, "See and do everything by the image that appeared to you on the mountain."

6. Now Yeshua The Messiah* has received the Ministry which is better than that, as The Covenant of which he is made The

Mediator is better, and it is given with better promises than that.

** The Greek mss. lack "**Jesus The Messiah**" , which leaves Moses as the closest subject (v.5). That is misleading, to say the least.*

7. For if the first one had been without fault, then there would have been no place for this second one.

8. For he found fault with them, and he said, "Behold, the days are coming, says **THE LORD JEHOVAH**, and I will perfect a New Covenant for the family* of the house of Israel and for the family* of the house of Judah."

** (of the house) דבית (the family) ביתא - "Baytha d'bayth" occurs twice, and is an Aramaic idiom here- definitely original and not from Greek. The Greek has simply, "**the house of Israel; the house of Judah**".*

9. "Not like that Covenant that I gave* to their fathers in the day when I took their hands and brought them from the land of Egypt, because they did not continue in my Covenant; I also rejected them, says **THE LORD JEHOVAH**."

** Greek has "**covenant I made with their fathers**"; it also has "**I neglected them**"; Compare these to The Peshitta's , "**covenant I gave to their fathers**" and "**I rejected them**". The Greek obviously loses something in translation here, and generally throughout the NT.*

10. "But this is The Covenant that I shall give to the family of the house of Israel: After those days, says **THE LORD JEHOVAH**, I shall put my law in their minds and upon their hearts I shall write it, and I shall be to them a God, and they shall be to me a people."

11. "And a man will not teach a citizen of his city, neither his brother, and say, 'Know **THE LORD JEHOVAH**', because they shall all know me, from their little ones and unto their Elders."

12. "And I shall purge* them of their evils, and I shall not remember their sins again."

** **Greek mss. have** "ιλεως εσομαι"-"**Merciful I will be**" . The Aramaic word אחוס ,from חוס , can mean "**I shall have mercy**" ; the form of the word used here is אחסא , from חסי – "**to make atonement, to pardon,to purge**". The Greek seems to have come from the very similar word - אחוס –"**to pity,have mercy**".*

אחוס – "to pity,have mercy"
אחסא "to make atonement, to pardon,to purge"

13. In that he said, "New", he has made the first old, and that which is outdated and old is near destruction.

Chapter 9

1. But in the first there was an order of ministry and a worldly sanctuary.

2. For the first Tabernacle that was made there had the Manorah and the table of showbread, and it was called The Holy Place.

3. But the inner* Tabernacle from within the second veil was called The Holy of Holies.

** Greek mss. have δευτερον-"**Second**". "**Second**" in Aramaic would probably be דתרין ; Compare that with דלגו – "**Inner**".
Have a look at these in Dead Sea Scroll script: דתרין :: דלגו and you can see a probable explanation for the Greek reading. Here they are in Estrangela: דתרין : דלגו . The DSS script pair have at least **66% correspondence**. If תרין "Two" were the mistaken reading interpreted by a Greek translator, we would have this comparison:*

*תרין -"**Second**"*
*דלגו -"**Inner**"*

*The Greek for "**Inner**" is εσωτερον, which has three letters difference from δευτερον-"**Second**". These two words have **60%** correlation, though the differences between the Greek words are more distinct than those between the Aramaic words. The DSS seems to explain the Greek.*

4. And there was in it the golden place of incense and The Ark of the Covenant, all overlaid with gold, and it had a pot of gold in which was manna and the Rod of Aaron which budded, and The Tablets of The Covenant.

5. And above, the cherubim of glory, which shrouded over the mercy seat; but there is no time for us to speak about each one of these things which were thus fashioned.

6. But The Priests were always entering the outer* Tabernacle and performing their ministry,

** Greek mss. have πρωτην-"**First**". "**At the first**" in Aramaic would probably be בריש ; Compare that with בריא –"**Outer**", and you can see the probable explanation for the Greek reading. Greek for "**Outer**" here would be εξωτεραν. This has 3 of 8 letters similar to πρωτην-"**First**" (**38%** similarity).*

Dead Sea Scroll Script:
*בריא-"**Outer**" (Peshitta)*
*בריש – "**At the first**" (Source of Greek?)*
75% Aramaic letter correlation

7. But The High Priest would enter the inner * Tabernacle once a year by himself with blood, which he was offering in the place of his soul and in the place of the evil doing * of the people.

** Greek mss. have δευτεραν-"**Second**". "**Second**" in Aramaic would probably be דתרין ; Compare that with דלגו –"**Inner**".
Have a look at these in Dead Sea Scroll script: דתרין :: דלגו and you can see a probable explanation for the Greek reading. Here they are in Estrangela: דתרין : דלגו . The DSS script pair have at least **66% correlation**. If תרין "Two" were the mistaken reading interpreted by a Greek translator, we would have this comparison:*

*תרין -"**Second**"*
*דלגו -"**Inner**"*

The DSS seems to explain the Greek.

* Greek has αγνοημα – agnoayma, "ignorance".
The Aramaic has סכלותה - "**saklawtha**" means
"foolishness". "evil doing", "offense". It is a mistake
to say The High Priest sacrificed for the ignorance of
the people. The Greek appears to me to be a
mistranslation of the Aramaic.

8. But by this The Spirit of Holiness had
taught that the way of holiness had not yet
been revealed, as long as the first Tabernacle
was standing.

9. And this was a symbol for that time in
which gifts and sacrifices were offered, which
were not able to perfect the conscience of him
who offers them,

10. Except in food and drink only, and in
various washings, which are ordinances of the
flesh that are established until the time of
reformation.

11. But The Messiah who has come has
become The High Priest of the good things
that he did*, and he entered The Great and
Perfect Tabernacle which is not made with
hands, and was not from these created
things.

- Majority Greek has "**things to come**" –
μελλοντων- "**mellontone**" . The Aramaic דסער -
"that He did" looks similar to דעתיד , "that is
coming". In DSS , they are: דעתיד : דסער .
Personally, the square Aramaic pair look more similar
than DSS: דעתיד דסער . I see **60% correlation** here
in these three letter pairs: דעתיד דסער out of the five
of the longer word of the pair- דעתיד (3/5 = 60%). It
is also noteworthy that the word עביד occurs in this
verse and has essentially the same meaning as דסער
and also looks even more like עתיד .
Critical Greek (P⁴⁶ is a 2ⁿᵈ-3ʳᵈ Century Papyrus ; it
and **Codex B**- 4ᵗʰ Cent.) has the following reading in
the place of μελλοντων : γενομενων ("**things which
happened**"). This word is quite in keeping with The
Peshitta reading דסער , which can have the sense **of**
"happening". Here is the Syriac definition exerpt:

> fut. , act. part. ,
> pass. part. , , . a) *to visit, inspect, look
> after, care for, provide, heal* ;
>
> b) *to do, deal, commit, act, effect, perform* ;
> *to treat* ; *to exact* ; *who deal,
> effect* ; *His power which
> worketh in us.* c) *to be, happen, come to pass* ;

The part c) meaning is based on the Ethpeel (Passive)
form of the verb not used in The Peshitta, but another
passive form meaning of this verb ("to be") is used
with the active form and is so confirmed by the Greek
version in 1 Cor. 12:29 (δυναμεις-"can be") .Quite
often a passive form meaning is a reflection of the
active form as well in Aramaic.

Based on this, דסער can mean "b) **to do**" or "c) to be,
happen, come to pass". The Aramaic can explain both
Greek readings: "**things to come**" –μελλοντων &
γενομενων ("things which happened").

12. And he did not enter with blood of
yearling goats and of calves, but with his own
blood he entered the holy place one time and
has achieved eternal redemption.

13. For if the blood of kids and of calves and
the ashes of a heifer were sprinkled on those
who were defiled and it sanctified them for
the purifying of their flesh,

14. How much more therefore, will the blood
of The Messiah, who by The Eternal Spirit
offered himself without blemish to God,
purify our conscience from dead works that
we may serve **THE LIVING GOD**?

* The Majority Greek has "**Your conscience**"; The Critical
Greek has "**Our conscience**", agreeing with The Peshitta.
תארתן is "**Our conscience**" ;
תארתכון is "**Your conscience**",
with the two additional letters underlined.

15. Because of this, he is The Mediator of
The New Covenant, for in his death he is
salvation to those who violated The First
Covenant, that we, those who were called to
eternal inheritance, would receive The
Promise.

16. For where there is a testament, it shows
the death of him who made it;

17. But it is only valid concerning one who is
dead, because as long as he who made it lives,
there is no use for it.

18. Because of this, not even the first was
established without blood.

19. For when the entire ordinance which was
in The Law had been commanded by Moses
to all the people, Moses took the blood of a
heifer and water with scarlet wool, and
hyssop, and sprinkled upon the scrolls and
upon all the people.

20. And he said to them, "This is the blood of
The Covenant which was commanded you by
God."

21. Also he sprinkled blood upon the
Tabernacle and upon all the vessels of the
ministry,

22. Because all things are purged by blood in
The Written Law, and without the shedding
of blood there is no forgiveness.

23. For it is necessary that these things which
are symbols of the Heavenly are purified by
these things, but the Heavenly by better
sacrifices than these.

24. For it was not The Holy Place made by
hands that The Messiah entered, and which
was the symbol of the real one, but he entered
Heaven to appear before the face of God in
our place;

25. And not that he should offer himself many times, as The High Priest was doing and entered The Holy Place every year with blood that was not his;

26. Otherwise, he ought to have suffered many times from the beginning of the world, but now in the end of the world, he has offered himself one time to destroy sin by his sacrifice.

27. And just as it is appointed to the children of men to die once, and after their deaths the judgment,

28. In this way also, The Messiah was offered one time and he slaughtered in his Person the sins of the many, but the second time he appears without our sins, for the life of those who expect him.

Chapter 10

1. For The Written Law had a shadow in it of good things that were coming. It was not the essence of those matters; because of this, while they were offering those sacrifices every year, they could never perfect those who offered them.

2. For if they had perfected *them*, doubtless, they would have ceased from their offerings, because their conscience would not have been buffeted by sin once they had themselves been purged;

3. But by those sacrifices they remember their sins every year,

4. For the blood of oxen and of yearling goats cannot purge sins.

5. Because of this, when he entered the universe, he said, "Sacrifices and offerings you did not want, but you have clothed me with a body * ",

---

* The Hebrew of Psalms 40:6 has, אזנים כרית לי –"Ears You have opened for Me". The Peshitta OT has the same reading. The Clementine LXX has , "ωτια δε κατηρτισω μοι" – "ears You have prepared for Me". Another LXX version has :σωμα δε κατηρτισω μοι – "a body You have prepared for Me".The OT text followed here certainly was not The standard Massoretic nor The Peshitta OT text. The LXX represents another Hebrew text which was known in the first century AD. We see it here and there in the quotes from the OT in the Peshitta NT, which quotes are certainly not conformed to any one standard OT text known.

6. "And burnt peace-offerings for sins you have not demanded.

7. And I said, 'Behold, I come', because in the beginning* of The Writings* it is written of me, 'to do your will, oh God.'"

---

* The Hebrew Scriptures are arranged into "The Law", "The Prophets" (Major & Minor) and "The Writings". "The Writings"-כתובים –"Kethuvim" start with "The Psalms".There are twelve books (in the Hebrew reckoning) in

---

"The Writings".This verse is a quotation from Psalms 40:7-9. The Aramaic word for this section of The Old Testament is כתבא –"Kthavay". The Greek phrase in this reading is "κεφαλιδι Βιβλιου" –("In the heading of the book") which really does not make sense with regard to this quotation; neither does the translation "In the volume of the book…" fare much better. What book? It is too vague to carry much authority, as there is no reference to the authority of Scripture in the Greek.

The Peshitta OT version is essentially the same as this quotation in The Peshitta NT, with the exception of the verb form in "Behold, I come"; there the OT Peshitta has , " אתית דהא" –"Behold, I have come" instead of " אנא אתא אנא דהא" –"Behold, I come" and the last verb , דאעבד -"to do", where The OT version has למעבד –"to do".There is also an additional verb at the very end of The OT version : צבית –"I delight". This NT Peshitta verse does not appear to be taken from The Peshitta OT version; neither does it agree with the Massoretic Hebrew text or the LXX version. The Greek NT version does appear identical to the LXX of Psalms 40:7. I present both here for the reader:

LXX :τοτε ειπον ιδου ηκω εν κεφαλιδι βιβλιου
γεγραπται περι εμου του ποιησαι
το θελημα σου ο θεος μου εβουληθην

NT : τοτε ειπον ιδου ηκω εν κεφαλιδι βιβλιου
γεγραπται περι εμου του ποιησαι
ο θεος το θελημα σου

The red underlined words at the end of The LXX verse are omitted in the NT quote, probably as extraneous to the point of the quotation. Everything else is the same except for the word order of the last phrase –
"το θελημα σου ο θεος" -
"ο θεος το θελημα σου" , both of which have the same meaning- "Your will, O God."

8. Above, he said, "Sacrifices and offerings and burnt peace offerings for sins you did not want"; those that were offered were by The Written Law.

9. And afterward he said, "Behold, I have come to do your will, oh God." In this he abolishes the first to establish the second.

10. For in this, his will, we are made holy in the offering of the body of Yeshua The Messiah, once.

11. For every High Priest who has stood and served those with those sacrifices every day was offering those things which were never able to purge sins.

12. But This One offered one sacrifice for the sake of sins, and he sat down at the right side of God for eternity.

13. And he waits from then on until his enemies are put as a footstool under his feet,

14. For by one offering he has perfected those who are sanctified by him for eternity.

15. But The Spirit of Holiness also testifies to us, who says:

16. "This is the covenant that I shall give them after those days, says THE LORD JEHOVAH: I shall put my law into their minds, and I shall write it upon their hearts,

17. And their evils and their sins I shall not remember."

18. But where there is forgiveness of sins, no offering for sins is needed.

19. Therefore brethren, we have boldness in the entrance of the holy place by the blood of Yeshua.

20. And the way of The Life who made us new is now within the veil which is his flesh.

21. And we have The High Priest over the house of God.

22. Let us approach therefore with a true heart and the confidence of faith, while our hearts are sprinkled and purified from a wicked conscience and having bathed our bodies in pure water;

23. And let us grasp firmly the confession of our hope and not waver, for he who has promised us is faithful.

24. And let us pay attention to one another in the encouragement of love and of good works.

25. And we should not be forsaking our meetings, as is the custom for each person, but plead with one another all the more, as long as you see that day drawing near.

26. For if a man shall sin by his will after receiving the knowledge of the truth, there is no sacrifice to be offered afterward for sins,

27. But that terrible judgment is ready and the zeal of fire which consumes the enemies.

28. For if any violated the law of Moses, he would die without mercy by the mouth of two or three witnesses.

29. How much more do you think he will receive capital punishment, he who has trampled upon The Son of God and esteemed the blood of his covenant to be like that of every person, who also was made holy by it, and he has despised The Spirit of grace?

30. For we know him who said, "Vengeance is mine, and I shall give payment." And again, "THE LORD JEHOVAH will judge his people."

31. It is very terrible to fall into the hands of THE LIVING GOD.

32. Remember therefore the first days in which you received baptism* and endured a great contest of suffering with reproach and affliction.

---

* למעמודיתא "baptism" is similar to למנהרנותא "enlightenment", which the Greek mss. all have. Here are the terms in DSS script:
למעמודיתא - "Baptism"
למנהרנותא - "Enlightenment"
The Aramaic words above differ significantly in only two letters of the nine letters in each word. The others are identical or very similar in appearance.

In Estrangela they are ܠܡܥܡܘܕܝܬܐ & ܠܡܢܗܪܢܘܬܐ, not quite as similar as in DSS script, with **66%** correlation ; DSS script words have **78%** correlation.
I fail to see how this and the previous verses were taken from the Greek . The Greek word for "enlightened" is φωτισθεντας; "Baptized" is βαπτισθεντας; Here are the two in uncial script:
ΦΩΤΙΣΘΕΝΤΑΣ & ΒΑΠΤΙΣΘΕΝΤΑΣ. The Greek endings are standard and long for passive participles (6 letters long here) , hence the words are very similar, but not as similar as their Aramaic counterparts. Assuming the Greek ΦΩΤΙΣΘΕΝΤΑΣ ("Enlightened") is original , ΒΑΠΤΙΣΘΕΝΤΑΣ ("Baptized") represents 82% correlation. **The first letters of a word are the most important for recognition**; the first two of Φ**Ω**ΤΙΣΘΕΝΤΑΣ are nothing like the first letters of ΒΑΠΤΙΣΘΕΝΤΑΣ. The rest of each word in Greek is basically an added ending for the particular masculine accusative plural of the aorist passive participle of a verb with an "izo" ending, which "Baptizo" and "Photizo" are. **The root words are the most critical in distinguishing one word from another**. These are the first part of the word, usually three to five letters long. I doubt therefore that a translator of Greek would mistake the root ΦΩΤ- "Phot-" as ΒΑΠΤ- "Bapt-". (Yes , the English "Photo" and "Baptize" come from these Greek roots.)

33. And you became a spectacle, and you were also made associates with people who endured these things.

34. And you were grieved concerning those who were imprisoned and you endured with joy the robbery of your possessions, because you know you have a possession in Heaven which is greater and does not pass away.

35. Therefore do not throw away the boldness which you have, for a great reward is coming for it.

36. For you must have patience to do the will of God and receive The Promise,

37. "Because there is little time, and very little, when he who is coming will come and will not delay."

38. "But the righteous one shall live by my faith, and if he gives it up, my soul is not pleased with him." (See Habakkuk 2:3,4 LXX. This quote agrees with The LXX reading of The O.T, unlike other quotes in Peshitta Hebrews.)

39. But we are not of despondency which leads to destruction, but of the faith that imparts to us our soul.

Chapter 11

1. Now faith is the conviction concerning those things that are in hope, as if it were these things in action*, and the revelation of those things that are unseen;

* Greek omits "as if it were those things in action". Where did The Peshitta get this phrase, if it is a translation of Greek?

2. And by this there was a testimony concerning the ancients.

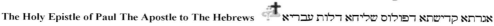
3. For by faith we understand that the worlds were fashioned by the word of God, and these things that are seen came into being out of those things which are unseen.

4. By faith, Abel offered to God a sacrifice much better than that of Cain, and because of it there is a testimony concerning him that he was righteous, and God testifies concerning his offering; and because of it, although he died, he also speaks.

5. By faith, Enoch was transported away and he did not taste death, neither was he found, because God transported him away; for before he was to transport him, there was this testimony concerning him: "He pleased God."

6. But without faith, no one can please God, for whoever is brought near to God must believe that he exists and that he is the rewarder of those who seek him.

7. By faith, Noah worshiped, when those things which had not been seen were spoken to him, and he made the Ark for the lives of his children in his household, by which he condemned the world, and he became the heir of the righteousness which is in faith.

8. By faith, Abraham, when he was called, obeyed to go out to the place that he was going to receive for an inheritance, and he went out when he did not know where he was going.

9. By faith he became an inhabitant in that land which was promised to him, as in a foreign land, and he dwelt in tents with Isaac and Jacob, his heirs of The Promise.

10. For he was looking for The City which has foundations, whose builder and maker is God.

11. By faith also Sarah, who was sterile, received power to conceive seed, and she who was not in the time of her years gave birth, for she was sure that he who promised her was faithful.

12. Because of this, from one who was failing in old age* were born as many as the stars in the Heavens, and as the sand which is upon the seashore, which has no measure.

---

* Greek has, "νενεκρωμενου" –"who had become dead" , where The Peshitta has דבטל בסיבותא-"who was failing in old age". Have a look at במיתותא – "in death", "in mortality". Here are the comparisons in three scripts:

בסיבותא-" in old age"
במיתותא-" In mortality"

[Estrangela script]-" in old age"
[Estrangela script]-" In mortality"

[Estrangela script]-" in old age"

[Estrangela script]-" In mortality" .

The first pair have a letter to letter correlation of **86%**. ס & מ are very similar and could easily be confused one for another; the other letters except for ב & ת are identical ; The DSS pair have close to that 86%, though ס & מ are not quite as similar as the same letters in Ashuri script : ס & מ . The Estrangela pair are least alike, with 72% letter correlation. Any of these scripts presents a much better basis for the Greek reading than vice versa. Here is "**old age**" in Greek : γηρει ; compare that to νενεκρωμενου –"**who had become dead**". See any resemblance? Here are the Greek words, side by side:

γηρει **&** νενεκρωμενου

0% correlation for the Greek pair.
Here are the two Aramaic words again in Ashuri Aramaic:

בסיבותא -"In old age"
במיתותא -"In mortality"

I see Greek primacy lagging far behind Peshitta primacy.

13. These died in faith, all of them, and they did not receive their promise, but they saw it from a distance and rejoiced in it and confessed that they were foreigners and nomads in The Earth.

14. But those who say these things show that they seek their City.

15. And if they had been seeking that city which they had left, they had time to return again to it.

16. Now it is apparent that they longed for better than that, which is in Heaven; because of this, God is not ashamed to be called their God, for he has prepared a City for them.

17. By faith, Abraham offered Isaac during his testing, and laid his only son on the altar, whom he had received by The Promise.

18. For it was said to him, "In Isaac your seed shall be called."

19. And he accepted in his soul that God was able to raise him from the dead, and because of this, he was given to him in a simile.

20. By the faith of what was future, Isaac blessed Jacob and Esau.

21. By faith, when Jacob was dying, he blessed each one of the sons of Joseph and bowed on the top of the staff.

22. By faith, when Joseph was dying, he related the exodus of the children of Israel and gave orders about his bones.

23. By faith, the parents of Moses hid him for three months when he was born, when they saw that the boy was beautiful, and they were not afraid of the King's commandment.

24. By faith, Moses, when he became a man, renounced being called the son of Pharaoh's daughter.

25. And he chose to remain in affliction with the people of God and not to enjoy sin for a short time.

26. And he considered that the reproach of The Messiah was much greater wealth than the treasures of Egypt, for he was attentive to the payment of the reward.

27. By faith he forsook Egypt and was not afraid of the rage of The King and he endured as if he had seen God, who is unseen*.

* The Greek texts have , "τον γαρ αορατον ως ορων" –"As seeing the invisible one". "God" is missing. This seems to be short on information, as all spirit beings are invisible.

28. By faith he observed Passover and sprinkled the blood, lest he who was destroying the firstborn should touch them.

29. By faith, they passed through The Sea of Reeds* as upon dry land, and the Egyptians were swallowed up by it when they dared to enter it.

* The Greek NT uses the word "ερυθρος"- (eruthros) - "Red", here and in Acts 7:36, for "The Red Sea". The Hebrew OT uses the term, "Yam - Suuph" – "Sea of Reeds" 28 times. "Yam Suuph" never means "Red Sea".("Yamma d'suuph" here in Aramaic). "Red" is a mistranslation. The "Sea of Reeds" was much larger 3500 years ago than it is today. A major earthquake has shifted the Euro-Asian plates which meet at a fault line that ran under that Sea in Moses' time and drastically changed the coastline to what it is today. The Peshitta reading in Acts and here cannot be from Greek. **The Greek LXX** also has ερυθρα θαλασση-(eruthros Thalassay-Red Sea) throughout the OT . It mistranslated the Hebrew text consistently.The actual crossing point for the Hebrews was an inlet about 10 miles wide near Lake Timnah at the northern extension of what is called The Red Sea, based on The LXX translation. The Hebrews called it "**Yam Suuph**". This verse and Acts 7:36 is strong support for Peshitta primacy and Divine inspiration and opposition to Greek primacy and inspiration.The Peshitta did not get this reading from Greek, though the Greek LXX consistently translated "**Yam Suph**"-("Sea of Reeds") as ερυθρα θαλασση-(eruthra Thalassay-Red Sea), and the Greek NT seems to have followed suit here and in Acts 7:36.

30. By faith, the walls of Jericho fell, after it was walked around for seven days.

31. By faith, Rahab the harlot did not perish with those who disobeyed, for she received the spies in peace.

32. And what more shall I say? For I have little time to recount about Gideon and about Baraq, about Samson, about Jephthah, about David, about Samuel and about the other Prophets:

33. Those who by faith conquered Kingdoms and wrought justice, received promises and shut the mouths of lions;

34. They quenched the power of fire, were delivered from the edge of the sword, were strengthened out of weakness, became strong in battle and overturned enemy camps.

35. And they gave women their children by resurrection of the dead, and others died by torture and did not expect to be delivered, that they would have a better resurrection;

36. Others entered mockings and scourgings; others were handed over to chains and to prison cells;

37. Others were stoned; others were sawn in half; others died by the edge of the sword; others traveled wearing skins of sheep and of goats, and were needy, afflicted and beaten;

Greek mss. have , "They were stoned, they were sawn asunder, <u>they were tempted</u> -(not in Peshitta) , in the killing of the sword they died…"
"**They were sawn in half**" is אתנסרו. אתנסין is "**They were tempted**".Here are these two in DSS:אתן נסרו
אתן נסין

In Estrangela : ܐܬܢܣܪ̈ܘ   ܐܬܢܣܝܢ . The DSS pair is most similar , with **almost 100% correlation**; even the last two letters , 1ٹ- & ٹٹ- are very similar in this script. The Estrangela script pair are the least similar , with 66% correlation. I calculate about **84% correlation** for the Ashuri script . **Apparently a Greek Scribe read אתן נסרו-" twice , once correctly as אתן נסרו-"They were sawn in half', and again as אתן נסין – "They were tempted".**The Critical Greek has the two interpretations in reverse order to The Byzantine Greek text. The Greek words involved are : ΕΠΡΙΣΘΗΣΑΝ & ΕΠΕΙΡΑΣΘΗΣΑΝ. These have **75% correlation** , which is higher than other Greek examples, but still not as high as Ashuri and DSS Aramaic pairs. Here is the Greek pair, one atop the other: ΕΠΡΙΣΘΗΣΑΝ–"They were sawn in half' ΕΠΕΙΡΑΣΘΗΣΑΝ-"They were tempted"

Here is the Aramaic pair, one atop the other: אתן נסרו -They were sawn in half' אתן נסין -"They were tempted"

– "Worth a thousand words".

38. Persons of whom the world was not worthy; and they were as wanderers in desert places and in mountains and in caves and caverns of The Earth.

39. And all of these, concerning whom there is a testimony of their faith, did not receive The Promise.

40. Because God provided for our advantage that they would not be made perfect without us.

Chapter 12

1. Therefore, we also, who have all of these witnesses who surround us like clouds, let us throw off from us all the weights of the sin which is always ready for us, and let us run with patience this race that is set for us.

2. And let us gaze at Yeshua, him who is The Author and The Perfecter of our faith, who for the joy that was his, endured the

cross and ignored the shame, and he sits upon the right side of the throne of God.

3. Behold, therefore, how much he endured from sinners, those who were themselves opponents to their own souls, so that you do not become careless in yourselves, neither weaken your souls.

* The Critical Greek text agrees here with The Peshitta: "**opponents to themselves**"; The Majority Byzantine Greek text has αμαρτωλων εις αυτον αντιλογιαν –"**contradiction of sinners against himself**".

4. For you have not yet come as far as to blood in the struggle against sin.

5. And you have strayed from the teaching which speaks to you as to sons: "My son, turn not away from the course of THE LORD JEHOVAH, neither neglect your soul when you are rebuked by him."

6. "For whomever THE LORD JEHOVAH loves, he instructs, and draws aside* his children with whom he is pleased *."

* נגד – "Nagad" can mean -"**Draw,lead,attract,draw aside,beat,scourge,extend,prolong**". The Greek reading μαστιγοι ,"scourges", is out of context with the Aramaic word phrase לבניא אילין דהו צבא בהון –"**Children with whom He is Pleased**". A good human father does not scourge his children at all, in my opinion; Much less would he scourge those with whom he is pleased. * The Greek reading παραδεχεται – paradechetai -"receives", seems a misreading of the Aramaic צבא – "Tsava" (Pleased) . In other places where reading παραδεχεται – paradechetai -"Receives" occurs , the Aramaic verb קבלא "Qaval" ("Received") is used in The Peshitta. Here are the Aramaic verbs for "Pleased" and "Received" in DSS script: ‏קפא : צבא .

In Estrangela script: ‎ܨܒܐ ܩܒܠ .

The Aramaic verb צבא – "Tsava" (Pleased) has a form מצטבא which means , "Accepted". The two Aramaic words in Estrangela script are ‎ܨܒܐ ܡܨܛܒܐ

. It appears that the Greek readings in this verse are based on The Peshitta's Aramaic. It also appears that in the two Greek readings mentioned here, the Greek translator selected an incorrect meaning among the possible interpretations of the two Aramaic words נגד – "Nagad" and צבא – "Tsava".

Now here is an interesting fact. The Greek word προσδεχεται – prosdechetai comes from the same root as παραδεχεται – paradechetai –"Receives" and can have the same basic meaning: "Receive" , and this Greek word parallels the Peshitta's Aramaic word סבא –"Expect,Wait,Look for".Another Aramaic candidate for the base behind the Greek reading παραδεχεται – paradechetai –"Receives" , is נסבא ("Take,Receive"). Ashuri Aramaic script: 1. צבא & 2. סבא & 3. נסבא :

Estrangela Aramaic script: 1. ‎ܨܒܐ & 2. ‎ܣܒܐ & 3.‎ܢܣܒܐ : Dead Sea Scroll Aramaic script : 1. ‏צבא

& 2. ‏סבא & 3. ‏נסבא.

צבא – "Tsava" (Pleased) & נסבא "Nsava" ("Take,Receive") are very similar phonetically. It is possible that a Greek translator relied on dictation at this point or simply pronounced the word "Nsava"

instead of "Sava" and translated it παραδεχεται – paradechetai -"receives" accordingly.

‏צבא – "Tsava" ("Pleased")
‏נסבא –"Nsava" ("Take,Receive")

The above DSS pair have about **70%** letter correlation. The Greek for "**Pleased**" is ευδοκησα, or αρεσκειν , neither of which looks anything like the reading παραδεχεται – paradechetai -"Receives". The Greek reading –"**and scourges every son whom He receives**", cannot credibly account for the Peshitta's Aramaic reading, nor when compared to The Peshitta reading, does it commend itself as the original. The Peshitta can account for the Greek.

7. Therefore endure the discipline, because God deals with you as with children; for who is the son whom his father does not discipline?

8. And if you are without the discipline by which every person is disciplined, you are strangers * and not children.

⬤ The Greek reading is "voθοι" – nothoi- "illigitimate". The Aramaic for this would be גורא לבני "benay gora" ("sons of adultery") ; In DSS script ‏בני גורא ; In Estrangela : ‎ܒܢܝ ܓܘܪܐ . Compare לבני גורא with לכון נוכריא -"Strangers" ‎ܠܟܘܢ ܢܘܟܪܝܐ :‏בני גורא with ‎ܒܢܝ ܓܘܪܐ & ‎ܠܚܡ ܢܘܟܪܝܐ . The grey highlight marks the Aramaic letters in the actual **Peshitta** reading that are quite similar to the hypothetical Aramaic behind the Greek. The letters are in the same order as in the hypothetical reading for "**illegitimate**".Here they are in Ashuri script with three letters removed after the hypothetical reading: לכון נורא - לבני גורא (88% match) . In Estrangela: ‎ܒܢܝ ܓܘܪܐ & ‎ܠܚܡ ܢܘܟܪܝܐ ; In DSS :‏בני גורא with ‏בני גורא . The Ashuri script presents the greatest similarities in the words גורא & נורא (extracted from נוכריא). Estrangela script is close behind with ‎ܓܘܪܐ and ‎ܢܘܪܐ (from ‎ܢܘܟܪܝܐ). The DSS falls short as a candidate here , with ‏גורא & ‏נורא. It is most likely Paul wrote to the Hebrew Christians in the DSS script; they would have probably been unfamiliar with Estrangela unless they lived in Persia or perhaps Syria. The DSS may have been used beyond Israel, since the scattered Christians from Palestine would have been familiar with it. Greek for "Strangers" is "ξενοι".

⬤ Here are the two Greek words for "**Illigitimate**" & "**Strangers**":

"voθοι" - nothoi-"Illigitimate"
"ξενοι" -Xenoi-"Strangers"

The two Greek words have 40% correlation. It is doubtful that voθοι " nothoi - "illigitimate"would be translated נוכריא -"Nukraya"- "Strangers" by an Aramaean translator. When separating the letters in the Peshitta reading to match up with the Greek reading, the DSS script looks very similar in the two:

Dead Sea Scroll Script
‏לכון נוכריא -"You strangers" (Peshitta reading)
‏לבני גורא -"Sons of adultery" (Greek reading)
70% correlation

Ashuri Script
לכון נוכריא -"You strangers" (Peshitta reading)
לבני גורא -"Sons of adultery" (Greek reading)
70% correlation

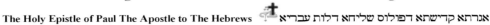
And since when are illigitimate children not children?
And can God have illigitimate children? And if he could, whose fault would that be?
The Peshitta primacy theory is strongly buttressed here; Greek primacy suffers another resounding defeat.

9. And if our fathers who are in the flesh have disciplined us and we did revere them, how much more therefore ought we submit to The Father of Spirits and live?

10. For they, for that short time, disciplined us as they pleased, but God, for our benefit, that we may share in his holiness.

11. But no discipline in its time seems to be joyful, but it is sorrowful; but in the end it yields the fruit of peace and of righteousness to those who have been trained by it.

12. Therefore strengthen your hands and set your shaky knees firmly.

13. Make straight paths for your feet, that the lame member may not fail, but that it may be healed.

14. Run after peace with every man, and after holiness, without which no one shall see Our Lord.

15. And be watchful, lest anyone among you be found lacking the grace of God, or lest the root of bitterness produce vines and harm you, and many be defiled by it,

16. Or lest a man be found among you *as a* fornicator, or debauched, like Esau, who for one meal sold his birthright.

17. For you know that afterward he desired to inherit the blessing and was rejected, for he found no place of restoration, while he sought it in tears.

18. For you have not approached the fire* that burned and was tangible, neither to the darkness and dark fog and the tempest,

* Most Greek mss. (The Byzantine class) have ορει -"**The mount**"; The Critical Greek agrees with **The Peshitta** reading-"**The fire**". Here is the Aramaic for "Mountain": טורא ; Compare "**Fire**"- נורא . Here are the words in Estrangela: ܢܘܪܐ ܛܘܪܐ In DSS script: נורא טורא .

Any more evidence needed to see where the Greek "Mount" came from?
Another possibility is that a Greek Scribe saw: (the fire) לנורא (you have approached) אתקרבתון and translated אתקרבתון , then looked back at verse 22 to the **verb** in :(to the mountain) לטורא (you have come) אתקרבתון , which is identical to that in verse 18, and then saw לטורא instead of לנורא and translated ορει -"**The mount**". He then resumed work in the next word in verse 18 (that burned) דיקדא , etc..

נורא -"**Fire**"(Peshitta)
טורא -"**Mountain**"(Greek reading in Aramaic)
75% correlation
Greek for "Fire" is πυρ or in uncial- ΠΥΡ
"The Mount" is ορει or in uncial- ΟΡΕΙ
0% correlation

* Byzantine mss. have σκοτος –"**Darkness**" ; The Critical Greek mss. have ζοφω , a word meaning ,"**Darkness , Mist**".It just so happens that the Aramaic word, ערפלא , the

corresponding word in Western Serto script ܥܪܦܠܐ in Smith's Syriac Dictionary is defined –

ܥܪܦܠܐ, ܥܪܦܠܐ pl. ܥܪܦܠܐ f. a) *dark fog* or *mist*, *thick darkness*. b) ܥܪܦܠܐ ܕܥܝܢܐ *a white film* on the eyes. DERIVATIVES, ܥܪܦܠܢܐ b, ܡܥܪܦܠ.
ערפלא-"**Dark fog**" (Critical Greek reading)
ערפלא-"**Thick darkness**" (Majority Greek reading)
100% correlation

σκοτος –"**Darkness**"
ζοφω-"**Darkness , Mist**"
0% correlation

So it does appear that two different Greeks translated this Aramaic word each with a different Greek word meaning "Darkness". Of course, one may argue The Peshitta could have translated either Greek reading. Greek word as ערפלא , and that is theoretically possible, however, The Peshitta has only one reading here, while the Greek mss. have two readings. The Peshitta's textual integrity overall and the Greek mss.' wide variety of readings throughout the NT are not consistent with Greek primacy and a Peshitta translation. The data support and account for the Greek NT as a translation of Aramaic words in The Peshitta NT in so many places, including also Greek variants of many sorts and places, while the Greek readings can scarcely provide convincing evidence to the contrary anywhere that I am aware of in The Peshitta NT. The vast bulk of evidence supports Peshitta primacy, not a Greek original at all.

19. Neither the sound of the trumpet and the voice of words, which those who heard it refused, so that no more would be spoken with them.

20. For they were not able to endure anything that was commanded: "If even an animal shall approach the mountain, it shall be stoned."

21. And so terrible was the sight that Moses said, "I am afraid and fainthearted."

22. But you have come to The Mountain of Zion and to The City of **THE LIVING GOD**, to The Jerusalem which is in Heaven, and to the assembly of myriads of Angels;

23. And to the church of the firstborn ones who are written in Heaven, and to God The Judge of all, and to the spirits of the righteous who are made perfect,

24. And to Yeshua, The Mediator of The New Covenant, and to the sprinkling of blood, which speaks better than that of Abel.

25. Beware therefore, lest you refuse him who speaks with you, for if those were not saved who refused him who spoke with them on Earth, how much less are we if we shall refuse him who speaks with us from Heaven?

26. Whose voice shook The Earth, but now he has promised and said, "One more time, I shall shake, not only Earth, but also Heaven."

* Most Greek mss. have σειω -"I shake" –present tense. Critical Greek has σεισω -"I shall shake". The Aramaic verb אזיע can have either present , past or future meaning in this form.

27. But this that he said: "One time", indicates the change of those things that are shaken, because they are made, that those things which are not shaken may remain.

28. Therefore, because we have received The Kingdom that is not shaken, we shall receive grace by which we shall serve and please God in reverence* and in awe*.

* Critical Greek has ευλαβειας και δεους – "fear and shamefacedness"; The Byzantine Greek mss. (Majority Text) has

"αιδους και ευλαβειας" – "shamefacedness and fear". Both Aramaic words - דחלתא & תחמצתא (The last two in the verse) have several meanings: תחמצתא - "Takhmatsta" means "reverence , bashfulness, modesty". דחלתא- "Dakhlatha" means, "fear,reverence,worship,awe,piety". Here are the entries for these words from **Smith's Compendious Syriac Dictionary**:

In Western Serto script - [Syriac script]

[Syriac] rt. [Syriac]. f. *bashfulness, modesty, reverence;* [Syriac] *honour among thieves;* [Syriac] *impudent.*

[Syriac] pl. m. [Syriac], f. [Syriac], rt. [Syriac]. generally f. a) *fear, dread,* pl. *panics.* b) generally constr. or emph. *awe, worship, religion* often used of false or mistaken religion, of a heresy or sect; [Syriac] *the fear of God;* [Syriac] *piety, reverence towards God, true religion;* [Syriac] or [Syriac].

The Majority Greek Text probably follows the Peshitta reading ("Fear" is matched with דחלתא – [Syriac] in Estrangela , the last word in The Peshitta verse.The Critical Greek , however, may simply follow the same text with alternate translations of the same words. "αιδους" in Greek has two meanings: "Shamefacedness" or "Reverence". "Ευλαβειας" also has more than one meaning:"Fear", "Reverence, "Piety", "Fear of God", "Caution". So both Greek readings could be explained by The Peshitta reading.

29. For our God is a consuming fire.

Chapter 13

1. Let the love of the brethren continue among you.

2. And do not forget kindness to strangers, for by this, some who, while they were unaware, were worthy to receive Angels.

3. Remember those who are imprisoned, as if you are imprisoned with them. Call those to mind who are afflicted, as if you are the people who wear their bodies.

4. Marriage is honorable with all and their bed is pure, but fornicators and adulterers God judges.

5. Let not your mind love money, but let whatever you have suffice for you, for **THE LORD JEHOVAH** has said, "I shall not forsake you *, neither shall I let go * of your hand."

* The two verbs ארפא & אשבקך are used together in The Peshitta OT several times, and are translated by Lamsa as ,"I will not fail you (ארפך) , nor forsake you - אשבקך." ארפא + is an idiom meaning "to let go", "to lose hold of". ארפא by itself could mean, εγκαταλειπω -"forsake", but it is part of an Aramaic idiom which is more specific in meaning, as shown above. This idiomatic phrase (the hand) אידיא (of you) בך (shall I let go *) ארפא did not come from the Greek "σε εγκαταλειπω" –"forsake you". It does appear the Greek came from one definition of ארפא, which I show here:

left as a legacy. APH. [Syriac] a) *to leave, let alone;* [Syriac] *give us seven days' respite;* [Syriac] *leave me to my misery;* [Syriac] *let it settle;* [Syriac] *they will leave nothing behind.* Often with [Syriac] *to loose hold, let go, allow; to weaken;* with [Syriac] *and* [Syriac] *to lose hold of, to become weak.* b) *to leave, desert, renounce;*

Actually, the Greek reading seems to have its last two verbs reversed from The Peshitta order: the second to last Greek verb is ανω, from ανημι **aniemi** an-ee'-ay-mee , from 303 and hiemi (to send); TDNT-1:367,60; v
AV-loose 2, forbear 1, leave 1; 4
1) to send back, relax, loosen
2) to give up, omit, calm

[Syriac] PEAL only part. adj. [Syriac], [Syriac], [Syriac]. a) *loose, porous, friable, soft* as air, earth, *unstable* as water; *flabby* as flesh. b) *loose, slack, effeminate, dissolute;* [Syriac] *slack harpstrings;* [Syriac] *badly built ships;* [Syriac] *we are not to be idle nor slack and ineffectual.* PAEL [Syriac] a) *to loosen, slacken, relax; to weaken, enfeeble;* [Syriac] *his body was en-*
3) to leave, not to uphold, to let sink . This conforms generally to the last Aramaic verb ארפא from רפא

[Syriac] fut. [Syriac], act. part. [Syriac], [Syriac], pass. part. [Syriac], [Syriac], [Syriac]. a) *to leave, go away;* [Syriac] *the fever left her.* With [Syriac] *to let blood;* with [Syriac] *to expire;* also [Syriac] *his soul departed.* Otiose with verbs of motion : [Syriac] *they went away, took leave;* [Syriac] *he went out;* [Syriac] *he took to flight.* b) *to leave over, leave behind, leave by will;* [Syriac] *he left none remaining;* [Syriac] *I shall leave a good example;* [Syriac] *the riches his parents had left him.* c) *to give leave, allow, let alone;*

The last Greek verb καταλειπω ("Forsake") conforms to the second to last Aramaic verb אשבקך , from שבק :

6. And it is for us to say confidently, "The Lord is my helper; I shall not fear what anyone does to me."

7. Be mindful toward your Leaders who have spoken with you the word of God. Consider the results of their conduct and imitate their faith:

8. Yeshua The Messiah; He is yesterday, today and forever.

9. Do not be led to strange and changeable teaching, for it is good that we strengthen our hearts by grace and not with foods, because

those who have walked* in them have not been helped.

*The Critical Greek text has the present participle περιπατουντες –peripatountes ("walking"); The Majority Greek agrees with The Peshitta reading, "**have walked**".

10. But we have an altar from which those who minister in The Tabernacle have no authority to eat.

11. For the flesh of these animals, whose blood The High Priest brought to The Holy Place for the sake of sins, was burned outside of the camp.

12. Because of this, Yeshua also suffered outside of the city to sanctify his people by his blood.

All major Greek texts have εξω της πυλης "**Outside the gate**". "**From the Gate**" in Aramaic is, מן תרעא ; מדינתא is "City". These words in Estrangela are ܬܪܥܐ ܡܢ & ܡܕܝܢܬܐ . DSS has תרעא מן & מדינתא . **Papyrus 46** and **Uncial P** has περεμβολης –"**Camp**"; the Aramaic for "**Camp**" is משריתא which occurs in the verses before and after this one . Let's compare "**City**" with "**Camp**" in Aramaic: משריתא מדינתא . In Estrangela script: ܡܫܪܝܬܐ ܡܕܝܢܬܐ . In either script, these words look similar.DSS script: משריתא : מדינתא . All three have **83%** letter correlation.The DSS pair appear the most similar to me, given the Yodh-Resh (ᐱ-ᒥ) similarity as well as an almost dyslexic Yodh- Nun (ᐱ-ᒧ) similarity. Even the Shin-Dalet (ᗯ-ᕼ) look strangely dyslexically related. Dead Sea Scroll Aramaic may have been the original for Hebrews.
The definition for the Greek word περεμβολη follows :
3925 παρεμβολη parembole par-em-bol-ay'

from a compound of 3844 and 1685; ; n f

AV-castle 6, camp 3, army 1; 10

1) an encampment
1a) the camp of Israel in the desert
1a1) used for the city of Jerusalem, inasmuch as that was to the Israelites what formerly the encampment had been in the desert
1a2) of the sacred congregation or assembly of Israel, as it had been gathered formerly in camps in the wilderness
1b) the barracks of the Roman Soldiers, which at Jerusalem were in the castle of Antonia
2) an army in a line of battle

The Greek word πυλη is defined by Thayers Lexicon as follows:
4439 πυλη pule poo'-lay

apparently a primary word; TDNT-6:921,974; n f

AV-gate 10; 10

1) a gate
1a) of the larger sort
1a1) in the wall of either a city
1a2) a palace
1a3) a town
1a4) the temple
1a5) a prison

Here are the parallel Greek words used :
ΠΥΛΗΣ = "Gate"
ΠΟΛΕΩΣ = "City"
ΠΕΡΕΜΒΟΛΗΣ = "Camp"

"Gate" and "City" in Greek have a **50%** letter correlation. It seems the Aramaic מדינתא was mistaken by at least two Greek Scribes as משריתא. It also appears that the first Greek translator put πυλης for "מדינתא" – "City" as metonymy (A part of speech using a part of something to stand for the whole)- Gate=City. Here are the two Ashuri Aramaic words in question, one atop another, for comparison:
מדינתא = "City" (Peshitta reading)
משריתא = "Camp" (Greek reading)
In Estrangela script: ܡܕܝܢܬܐ ."City" (Peshitta reading)
ܡܫܪܝܬܐ ."Camp" (Greek reading)
DSS script: מדינתא - "City" (Peshitta reading)
משריתא - "Camp" (Greek reading)
The two Aramaic words for "**City**" and "**Camp**" have **83%**.

The above facts show that it is very likely that the Greek readings in this verse came from The Peshitta reading. The fact that there are no Peshitta variant readings here makes it unlikely that the Greek is behind The Peshitta text.

13. We also, therefore, should go out to him outside of the camp, while we bear his reproach.

14. For we have no city here that abides, but we look for that which is coming.

15. And through him let us offer sacrifices of praise always to God, which is the fruit of the lips giving thanks to his name.

16. And do not forget charity and sharing with the poor, for with these sacrifices a man pleases God.

17. Obey your Leaders and submit to them, for they watch for the sake of your souls, as persons who give an account, so that they may do this with joy and not with groans, because that is not advantageous to you.

18. Pray for us, for we trust* that we have a good conscience, for we desire in all things to conduct ourselves well.

* The Majority Greek text has a perfect tense verb πεποιθαμεν ."**We have trusted**".The Critical Greek agrees with The Peshitta's present tense verb תכילינן with πειθομεθα -"**We trust**".

19. I especially seek of you to do this, that I may return quickly to you.

20. Now The God of peace, who brought forth from the place of the dead The Great Shepherd of the flock, Yeshua The Messiah Our Lord, by the blood of the eternal covenant,

21. Perfect you in every good work to do his will and perform in us whatever is excellent before him by Yeshua The Messiah, to whom is glory to the eternity of eternities. Amen.

22. I beseech of you, my brethren, to be patient in your spirit with the word of exhortation, because I have written to you with brevity.

23. But know that our* brother Timotheus has been released, and if he comes soon, I shall see you with him.

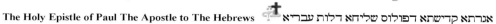
* The Majority Greek text omits the possessive pronoun "**our**".
The Critical Greek has it.

24. And invoke the peace of all your Leaders and of all The Holy Ones. All of those who are from Italy invoke your peace.
25. Grace be with all of you. Amen.

The Epistle of The Apostle James

Chapter 1

1. Yaqob the Servant of God and of Our Lord Yeshua The Messiah to the twelve tribes which are scattered among the nations: Peace.

2. May you have every joy, my brethren, when you enter various and many temptations,

3. For you know that the trial of faith imparts to you patience.

4. But patience will have a complete work for itself that you would be perfected and complete, and that you would be lacking nothing.

5. But if anyone of you lacks wisdom, let him ask from God who gives to everyone simply, and does not reproach, and it will be given to him.

6. But let him ask in faith, without wavering, for he who wavers is like the waves of the sea which the wind troubles,

7. And let not that man think he will receive anything from **THE LORD JEHOVAH.**

8. Whoever wavers in his mind is troubled in all his ways.

9. But let the poor brother boast in his exaltation,

10. And the rich man in his humiliation, because as a blossom of the grass, so he passes away.

11. For the sun rises with its heat and shrivels the grass and the blossom falls and the beauty of its appearance is destroyed. So also the rich man fades in his ways.

12. Blessed is the man who endures temptation, for when he has been tested, he will receive a crown of life, which God has promised to those who love him.

13. A man should not say when he is tempted, "I am tempted by God", for God is not acquainted with evil and he does not tempt a man.

14. But each man is tempted from his own desire, and he lusts and he is seduced.

15. And this desire becomes pregnant and gives birth to sin, but sin, when it has matured, gives birth to death.

16. Do not go astray, my beloved brethren.

17. Every good and perfect gift descends from above, from The Father of lights with whom there is no change nor a shadow of variation.

18. He was pleased and gave birth to us by the word of the truth, that we would be the first fruits of his creation.

19. And you, my beloved brethren, everyone of you should be quick to hear, slow to speak and slow to anger.

20. For the rage of man does not perform the righteousness of God.

21. Therefore put away from you all abomination and the multitude of evils and in humility accept the word which is planted in our nature*, which is able to save these souls of yours.

* "And receive the word which is planted in our nature". This is not in the Greek texts anywhere, hence it is extremely unlikely that it would have come from Greek.

22. But be a doer of the word and not only a hearer, and do not deceive yourselves.

23. For if a man will be a hearer of the word and not a doer of it, this one is like one who sees his face in a mirror,

24. For he sees himself and passes by and forgets how he was.

25. But everyone who gazes into The Perfect Law of Liberty and continues in it, he is not a hearer who heard what is forgotten, but is a doer of the works, and this one shall be blessed in his work.

26. And if a man thinks that he serves God, and does not hold his tongue, but deceives his heart, this person's service is worthless.

* Greek mss. lack "serve God" and have θρησκος – "Religious". The Majority Greek adds "εν υμιν" – "among you".

27. For pure and holy ministry before God The Father is this: to take care of orphans and widows in their affliction, and for a man to keep his soul without defilement from the world.

Chapter 2

1. My brethren, do not hold the glorious faith of Our Lord Yeshua The Messiah with acceptance of persons.

2. For if a man will enter your assembly with a gold ring or fine clothing and a poor man enters in dirty clothing,

3. And you have regard for him wearing fine clothing, and you say to him, "Sit well here", and you say to the poor man, "Stand over there or sit here before our* footstool.",

* Greek has "my footstool"; כובשא דרגלין is "our footstool"; כובשא דרגלי is "my footstool"– one letter difference ! The difference in Greek is between ημων "our" and μου "my"; In Greek uncial script,

these pronouns , "our" & "we" are HMωN and MOY . In fact, here is a photo of the Codex Vaticanus from James 2:3, with the words -EKEI YΠO TO YΠOΠOΔION MOY OY ΔIEKPIΘHTE EN- "here before my footstool. Do ye not make distinctions among?":

E KEIⲨⲚⲞⲦⲞ⳨ⲚⲞⲠⲞⲆⲀⳠ
ⲘⲞⲨⲆⲒⲉⲔⲢⲒⲞⳠⲦⲈⲈⳠⲈ

The Greek pronouns HMωN and MOY have **25% correlation** (1 of 4 letters).

| Here | under | the | footstool | My | not you |
| EKEI | YΠO TO | | YΠOΠOΔION | MOY | OY |

make distinctions? among
ΔIEKPIΘHTE   EN

The **Aramaic words** for the two readings have **80% correlation** :

Ashuri Aramaic Script
כובשא דרגלין is "our footstool" (Peshitta)
כובשא דרגלי is "my footstool" (Source of Greek reading ?)

Dead Sea Aramaic Script
ꓩ∧|∧ꓹ ⳑꓤ צꓑ.ꙅ.ꙅ - "our footstool"(Peshitta)
∧|∧ꓹ ⳑꓤ צꓑ.ꙅ.ꙅ - "my footstool"(Source of Greek reading ?)

The Aramaic words explain the Greek reading quite well- one letter was dropped or missed from the Peshitta reading, making it read , "**My footstool**" to a Greek translator.The Greek cannot so easily account for The Peshitta reading.

4. Behold, are you not divided in your souls and have you not become expositors of wicked reasonings?
5. Hear, my beloved brethren: Is it not the poor of this world, however, who are rich in faith? God has chosen them to be the heirs in that Kingdom which God has promised to those who love him.
6. But you have despised the poor. Behold, do not the rich have dominion over you and drag you to court?
7. Behold, do they not slander The Worthy Name by which you are called?
8. And if you fulfill The Written Law of God in this, as it is written: "You shall love your neighbor as yourself", you are doing well.
9. But if you show partiality, you are sinning, and you are reproved by The Written Law as violators against The Written Law.
10. For whoever keeps the whole Written Law and slips in one thing, he is condemned by the entire Law.
11. For he who said, "Do not commit adultery", also said, "You shall not murder." But if you are not committing adultery, but you have murdered, you have become a violator of The Law.
12. So be speaking and acting as a person who is going to be judged by The Law of Liberty.

13. The judgment is without mercy against him who does not practice mercy, but with mercy, you have dominion over judgment*.

* Greek has "mercy rejoices against judgment"- κατακαυχαται ελεον κρισεως . "Rejoices" in Aramaic could be
מסתבחין or מתחתרין , fitting the grammatical form of the actual Peshitta verb.
משתעלין is "have dominion" –the Peshitta reading.
In Dead Sea Scroll script, these are ꓕ.ꓴ.ꓕ∧ꓩꓩ or
ꓕ.ꙇ.∧Ⴟꓴꙅ –"Rejoices"
ꓕ.ꙇ∨Ⴟꓴꙅ - "Have dominion"is the Peshitta reading.
In Estrangela script, these are
ܡܫܬܥܠܝܢ - "Have dominion"
or
ܡܣܬܒܚܝܢ–"Rejoices"
"Have dominion" - ܡܫܬܥܠܝܢ is the Peshitta reading. Whichever Aramaic script is used, the Peshitta reading and the second reading for "**Rejoices**"- משתעלין have **72% correlation**.Here are the Ashuri Aramaic words for comparison:

משתעלין –"**Have dominion**" (Peshitta)
משתבחין –"**Rejoice,Glory**" (Base to Greek reading ?)
72% correlation

The Greek for "has dominion" most similar to "Rejoices" is κατακυριευσει. Let's compare the two Greek words:
    KATAKYPIEYEI-"Has dominion"
    KATAKAYXATAI–"Rejoices"
Six out of twelve letters are the same or similar in the two Greek words, which is **50% correlation**.

14. What good is it my brethren, if a man says, 'I have faith', and he does not have deeds? Can his faith save him?
15. And if a brother or sister is naked and lacking daily food,
16. And any of you will say to them, "Go in peace, be warm, be full", and he would not give them the bodily necessities, what good is that?
17. So also faith alone without works is dead.
18. For a man may say to you, "You and I have faith*; I have works. Show me your faith without* works, and I shall show you my faith by my works."

* Greek has a shorter reading : "**You have faith**…" instead of "**You and I have faith**"…
* The Majority Greek has "εκ των εργων"-literally ,"**out of works**"; The Critical Greek text has "χωρις των εργων" – "**apart from works**". The Majority Greek text has additionally : "**your works**" ; The Critical Greek text at the end has , "**faith**" instead of "**my faith**".

19. You believe that God is One; you do well; the demons also believe and tremble.
20. Are you willing to know, oh feeble man, that faith without works is dead*?

* Critical Greek has "αργος"-"**Lazy**".
Dead Sea Aramaic Script

 אגרתא דיעקוב שליחא

כאדתא –"Dead"(Peshitta)
כאטדא –"Staggering,Tottering"(Base for Greek?)

The DSS pair have **75% correlation**. Greek for "Dead" is "νεκρος" ; Compare with "αργος"- "Lazy". They have **40% correlation** at best.

21. Was not our father Abraham justified by works when he offered up Isaac his son upon the altar?
22. Do you see that his faith upheld his deeds and by deeds his faith was perfected?
23. And the Scripture was fulfilled which said,"Abraham believed in God, and it was accounted to him for righteousness", and he was called the friend* of God.

(See Genesis 15:6 & 2 Chronicles 20:7 in Hebrew and Peshitta Version; The Peshitta text of Gen. 15:6 is almost identical to the quote here, except there the name Abram is used instead of Abraham. The Peshitta O.T. in Chronicles has "Rakhma" –"Friend", the same Aramaic word used here.)

24. You see that by works a man is justified and not from faith alone.
25. In this way also, was not Rahab the harlot justified by works when she received the scouts and sent them out by another way?
26. Just as the body without the spirit is dead, so also faith without works is dead.

Chapter 3

1. There should not be many teachers among you, my brethren, but you should know that we will incur greater judgment,
2. For all of us stumble much. Everyone who does not slip in his speech is a perfect man who can subdue also his whole body.
3. And behold, we put a bridle in the mouths of horses, so that they will submit to us and we turn their whole bodies.
4. Also, mighty ships, which are steered by the wind and a hard small piece of wood, are driven to wherever the will of the helmsman determines.
5. In this way, also, the tongue is a small member and has dominion; even a small fire kindles a great forest.
6. And the tongue is a fire and a world of sin; it is like a jungle. And that tongue by itself, while it is among our members, defiles our whole body and sets on fire the successions of generations, which roll on like wheels; it also burns with fire*.

* Greek has υπο της γεεννης –"by Gehenna"(Hell ?). Gehenna in Aramaic is גהנא ; "By Gehenna" would be בגהנא ;
Compare the actual Peshitta Aramaic reading with "By Gehenna" :

Ashuri Aramaic:
בנורא--"with fire"

בגהנא–"by Gehenna"
60% correlation

In DSS script :
--"with fire"
--"by Gehenna"
60-80% correlation

Estrangela script:
--"with fire"
--"by Gehenna"
60% correlation

I am inclined to accept the DSS script as the base script of the original from which Greek James was translated, as practically all examples studied in The NT favor that script as the original, or a hybrid Ashuri-DSS script. The Ashuri **Gamal** - may have been used rather than the DSS and the Ashuri **Nun** – rather than DSS . If so, the correlation would be **80%** for the hybrid script. Taking DSS as is and comparing letters Nun –Gamal and (Waw,Resh) with Khet , one can see how the word pair would be confused.

In DSS-Ashuri script :
--"with fire"
--"by Gehenna"
80% correlation

The Greek for fire is πυρος ; This does not compare well with γεεννης ; correlation is only 16% between these two, demonstrating that it is very unlikely an Aramaean translator would mistake γεεννης - "Gehenna" for πυρος -"Fire" in an hypothetical translation of Greek to The Peshitta's Aramaic.

7. And all kinds of animals, birds and creeping things of the sea and of the land are tamed by the nature of humanity,

* "**& of the land**" is not in the Greek versions. Where did The Peshitta get these words ?

8. But the tongue no man is able to tame, this evil which is uncontrolled; It is full of deadly poison.
9. With it we bless **THE LORD JEHOVAH*** and The Father; with it we curse the children of men who are made in the image of God.

* There are two different Greek readings here: The Critical Greek text (א,B, etc.) has τον Κυριον- "Lord" and
The Majority Greek text has τον Θεον , -"God" . This may very well represent two different attempts to translate מריא – **MarYah**, which is the Aramaic cognate for **Yahweh**. "MarYah" - מריא , is two root words combined: **Mar** - "Lord" + **Yah** –short form of "Yahweh". "Kurios" is the most common translation in Greek , but only represents the first root of the word, ignoring the second part –"Yah". "Theos" - Θεον is probably an attempt to convey the meaning of the second and most significant part of the word "Mar**Yah**" as God, which **Kurios**- Κυριος, simply cannot do.

10. From the mouth proceeds blessing and cursing, my brethren. These things ought not so to be done.
11. Is it possible that from one spring, sweet and bitter waters go out?

12. Or can a fig tree, my brethren, produce olives, or a vine, figs? So neither can salt water be made sweet.

13. Who of you is wise and instructed? Let him show his works in a beautiful way of life in the wisdom of meekness.

14. But if you have bitter envy or contention in your hearts, do not be puffed up against the truth and lie.

15. Because this wisdom does not descend from above, but is earthly, from the thoughts of the self and from demons.

16. For where there is envy and contention there is also chaos and every evil thing.

17. But the wisdom that is from above is pure, filled with peace, meek and attentive, filled with love and good fruit, without division and does not show partiality.

18. But the fruits of righteousness are sown in peace by those who make peace.

Chapter 4

1. From where is war and contention among you? Is it not from the lusts which war in your members?

2. You lust and you do not possess; you murder and envy and you have no power. You fight and you do battle and you have not because you ask not.

3. You ask and you do not receive, because you ask wickedly so that your lusts may be fed.

4. Adulterers! Do you not know that the love of this world is hatred toward God? Therefore whoever chooses to be a friend of this world is an enemy of God.

5. And perhaps you think the Scripture says in vain, "The spirit that dwells within us lusts with jealousy." (* Who knows what scripture James was quoting here?)

6. But Our Lord gives us more grace; therefore, he said, "God humbles the proud and he gives grace to the humble."

7. Submit therefore to God and stand against Satan, and he will flee from you.

8. Draw near to God and he will draw near to you. Purify your hands, you sinners; sanctify your hearts, doubting souls.

9. Be humble and make lamentation and let your laughter be turned to mourning, and your joy to grief.

10. Be humble before **THE LORD JEHOVAH**, and he will exalt you.

11. Do not speak against each other, my brethren, for he who speaks against his brother or judges his brother speaks against The Written Law, and judges The Written Law; if you judge The Written Law, you are not a doer of the law, but its judge.

12. One is he who lays down The Written Law and judgment, who is able to give life and to destroy. Who are you who are judging your neighbor?

13. But what shall we say about those who say: "Today or tomorrow we shall go to a city, where we shall also work one year; there we shall earn wages and make profits?"

14. And they do not know what tomorrow is. What are our lives except a vapor that appears for a little while and vanishes and passes away?

15. Therefore, they should say, "If **THE LORD JEHOVAH** pleases, and we live, we shall do this or that."

16. They boast in their pride. All such boasting is evil.

"**They boast**" is משתבהרין ; Greek has "**You boast**", which could be משתבהריתון in Aramaic.Greek for "**they boast**" is καυχωνται ; "**You boast**" is καυχασθε – That is **50% correlation** in the Greek word pair. The Aramaic word pair have **80% correlation** in all three scripts.

Greek Uncial
ΚΑΥΧΩΝΤΑΙ-"**They boast**"
ΚΑΥΧΑΣΘΕ-"**You boast**"
50% correlation

Ashuri Script
משתבהרין -"**They boast**"(Peshitta)
משתבהריתון -"**You boast**"(Hypothetical Base for Greek)

Dead Sea Script
-"**They boast**"(Peshitta)
-"**You boast**"(Hypothetical Base for Greek)

Estrangela Script
-"**They boast**"(Peshitta)
-"**You boast**"(Hypothetical Base for Greek)
80% correlation

17. Whoever knows the good and does not do it, to him it is sin.

Chapter 5

1. Oh rich men, wail and weep over the miseries which are coming upon you!

2. For your wealth is decayed and stinks, and your garments are eaten by moths.

3. Your gold and your silver has corroded itself and their corrosion will be for a witness against you and will consume your flesh. You have gathered fire to yourselves for the last days.

4. Behold, the payment of the laborers which you swindled, who have reaped your land,

cries out, and the cry of the reapers has entered the ears of THE LORD JEHOVAH of Hosts*.

* The Greek has σαβαωθ – "Sabaoth" which is a Hebrew word; it is also found in The Aramaic Targums just as it is here in The Peshitta – צבאות and in Hebrew: Here is the note from **Thayer's Greek English Lexicon** :
4519 σαβαωθ sabaoth sab-ah-owth`
of Hebrew origin 06635 צבאות in feminine plural; ; n indecl
AV-sabaoth 2; 2
    1) "Lord of Sabaoth"
    1a) Lord of the armies of Israel, as those who are under the leadership and protection of **Jehovah** maintain his cause in war.

The LXX has the word σαβαωθ 61 times as a transliteration of צבאות . צבאות occurs twice in The Peshitta NT & σαβαωθ twice in The Greek NT. It certainly is not Greek, anymore than these Aramaic terms in the Greek NT are Greek: **Sabbata,Mammona,Rabbi,Kepha,Pascha,Satana, Boanerges, Messias,Abba,Maranatha,Talitha Cumi,Eli Eli lama sabacthani, Ephatha, Rabboni,Beelzebub,Abaddon,** and many others. The total occurrences of the above amount to over 200 occurrences; Other terms occur many times in The Greek NT, such as "Christos", declared in John 1:41 Greek text to be a **translation** of "μεσιαν"(Messiah) in the phrase: μεσιαν ο εστιν μεθερμηνευομενον χριστος – "**The Messiah, which is translated, "The Christ".**
The International Standard Bible Encyclopedia has this "μεσιαν" as "Aramaic" .
μεθερμηνευομενον – " 3177 μεθερμηνευω methermeneuo meth-er-mane-yoo`-o from 3326 and 2059; ; v AV-being interpreted 6, be by interpretation 1; 7   1) **to translate into the language of one with whom I wish to communicate**, to interpret".
"**Messiah**" is the term by which Yeshua was called; this is Aramaic, in agreement with The language of first century Israel. "Christos" occurs 563 times in The Majority Byzantine Greek NT. Those 563 occurrences are therefore each and all translations of the Aramaic "משיחא" (**Meshiha**). Along with John 1:41, John 4:25 in Greek has the woman at the well , a Samaritan, using the phrase, μεσιας ερχεται ο λεγομενος χριστος – "**The Messiah, who is called The Christ.**" Was she speaking Hebrew? No, a Samaritan woman would not be speaking Hebrew. Μεσιας- "**The Messiah**". She obviously was not speaking Greek.The Greek transliterates the Aramaic "משיחא" (**Meshiha**) with the same word "μεσιας" used in John 1:41, to represent what Andrew said to Simon Peter. In both places, the word χριστος is shown to be the Greek for the Aramaic word, transliterated as Μεσιας.There is both transliteration and translation at work in both places (as in four others).

5.   For you have made merry upon The Earth, and you have been gluttons. You have nourished your bodies as for a day of slaughter.
6.   You have condemned and murdered The Righteous One and he has not opposed you.
7.   But you, my brethren, be patient until the coming of THE LORD JEHOVAH, like a farmer who waits for the precious crops of the ground; he is patient over them until he receives the early and late rain.
8.   In this way also, be patient and strengthen your hearts, for the coming of Our Lord draws near.
9.   Do not complain one against the other, my brethren, lest you be judged, for behold, The Judge is standing before the gate.

10. Take the example of The Prophets to yourselves, those who spoke in The Name of THE LORD JEHOVAH, my brethren, for patience in your afflictions.
11. For behold, we give a blessing to those who have endured. You have heard of the endurance of Job, and you have seen the result which THE LORD JEHOVAH made for him, because THE LORD JEHOVAH* is merciful and caring.
    * The Majority Greek lacks the last reference to "The Lord" ("Jehovah" in Peshitta) .
12. But above all things, my brethren, do not be swearing vows, neither by Heaven, neither by The Earth, neither by any other oath, but let your word be, 'Yes, yes' and 'No, no', lest you be condemned under the judgment.
13. And if any of you is in suffering, let him pray, and if rejoicing, let him sing songs.
14. And if one is ill, let him call The Elders of the church, and let them pray over him and anoint him with oil in the name of Our Lord.
15. And the prayer of faith heals the one who is ill and Our Lord raises him up; and if sins were done by him, they are forgiven him.
16. But be confessing your offenses* one to another, and pray one for another to be healed, for the power of the prayer which a righteous person prays is great.

* Critical Greek has "**Sins**". Majority Byzantine Greek has "**faults**". The Aramaic word סכלותא (ܣܟܠܘܬܐ) in Serto Script) – "**Saklutha**" can mean "Folly" or "Sin". Here is the entry from The Comprehensive Aramaic Lexicon:
sklw, sklwt (sak̲lū, sak̲lūt̲ā) n.f. folly

1 folly Syr.
2 sin Syr.
LS2: 473.
Smith's Compendious Syriac Dictionary has this entry:
ܣܟܠܘ, ܣܟܠܘܬܐ pl. ܣܟܠܘܬܐ rt. ܣܟܠ. f. *folly, transgression, evil-doing, offence;* ܠܐ ܣܟܠܘܬ *innocent, innocently;* ܚܣܝܪܘܬ ܣܟܠܘܬܐ *want of reason, senselessness, folly.* Hence, the Aramaic can account for why some Greek mss. have παραπτωματα (offenses,trespasses) and some have αμαρτιας (sins).

Ashuri Aramaic script:
סכלותכון –"Your offenses"(Peshitta & Byz.)
סכלותכון –"Your sins" (Critical Greek reading)
There is 100% correlation between the two readings in Aramaic.
παραπτωματα & αμαρτιας are the two Greek readings. There is no similarity there (0% correlation).

If The Peshitta were the translation, why does the Greek have hundreds (if not thousands) of variant readings that are simply alternate translations or misreadings (often of a single letter) of a single Aramaic word found in the Peshitta reading of the same verse and in the grammatically corresponding parallel word? This phenomenon does not cut both ways. The Peshitta, for all intents and purposes, has no variant readings to speak of.

17. Elijah was a man subject to suffering like we, and he prayed that it would not rain on the land, and it did not come down for three years and six months;

18. And he prayed again, and the skies gave rain and the land yielded its fruit.

19. My brethren, if any of you will stray from the way* of truth, and a man restore him from his error*,

   * Greek lacks "**the way**" & "**from his error**".

20. Let him know that he who turns a sinner from the error of his way gives life to his soul from death and blots out the multitude of his sins.

The First Epistle of The Apostle Peter   אגרתא קדמיתא דכאפא שליחא

The First Epistle of the Apostle Peter

Chapter 1

1. Petraus, an Apostle of Yeshua The Messiah, to The Chosen Ones and Pilgrims who are scattered in Pontus and in Galatia, in Qapadoqia, in Asia and in Bithynia;

2. Those who have been chosen in the prior knowledge of God The Father by sanctification of The Spirit, for obedience and for the sprinkling of the blood of Yeshua The Messiah. Grace and peace be multiplied to you.

3. Blessed is God The Father of Our Lord Yeshua The Messiah, he who in his great pity has begotten us again by the resurrection of Yeshua The Messiah to the hope of life,

4. And to an inheritance which is indestructible, undefiled and unfading, prepared for you in Heaven,

5. While you are kept by the power of God and by the faith, for the life which is ready to be revealed in the last time;

6. In which life you shall rejoice for eternity, although at this time you are a bit weary with various temptations which suddenly come upon you,

7. So that the proof of your faith may appear, which is worth more than refined gold tried in the fire, for glory and honor and praise at the revelation of Yeshua The Messiah,

8. Him whom you have not seen and yet you love, and in his faith* you greatly rejoice with glorious joy which cannot be spoken,

---

* Greek has "εις ον αρτι μη ορωντες" –"upon whom now not looking" ; לא ובחזיתוניהי could conceivably mean, "**& while you have not seen Him**". <u>The actual Peshitta reading is here</u>: לה ובהימנותה -"**Him & by His faith**". I see possible **64% correlation** in **The Ashuri** script phrase comparisons if the Nun-Waw pair נו in the Peshitta reading is reversed in one set to be ונ in the hypothetical Aramaic base for the Greek reading. Correlating letters are color coded (in color version).

Ashuri Aramaic script:
ובחזיתוניהי-לא -"**& while you have not seen Him**" Base for Greek reading
לה ובהימנותה- -"**Him & by His faith**". Peshitta reading
64% correlation in Ashuri.
Dead Sea Scroll script has:
ובחזיתוניהי אל -"**& while you have not seen Him**"-Base for Greek reading
ובהימנותה הל -"**Him & by His faith**"-Peshitta reading
73% correlation in DSS.

Estrangela script:
ܘܒܚܙܝܬܘܢܝܗܝ ܠܐ -"**& while you have not seen Him**"-Base for Greek reading
ܘܒܗܝܡܢܘܬܗ ܠܗ -"**Him & by His faith**"-Peshitta reading
55% correlation in Estrangela script

Apparently a Greek translator double translated "**Lah wavahimnothah**" - לה ובהימנותה , first inaccurately as "εις

ον αρτι μη ορωντες" –"**upon whom now not looking**" as shown above in the first Aramaic reading –"**La wavakhazaythwan**; then he looked away and translated and looked back and reread it accurately as πιστευοντες –"**believing**".

9. That you may receive the reward of your faith: The Life of your souls;

10. About which Life The Prophets have investigated, when they prophesied about the grace that was going to be given to you.

11. And they searched for what time The Spirit of The Messiah who dwelt in them revealed, and testified that the sufferings of The Messiah were coming, and his glory which was after that;

12. And it was revealed to all those who were searching, because they were not inquiring for themselves, but for us they were prophesying of those things belonging to us, which now are revealed to you by those who have evangelized you in The Spirit of Holiness, who is sent from Heaven, into which things the Angels have also desired to gaze.

13. Because of this, gird up the loins of your mind, be perfectly attentive and hope for the joy which is coming to you in the revelation of Our Lord Yeshua The Messiah,

14. As obedient children, and do not be partaking again of your former lusts, which you were lusting without knowledge.

15. But be Holy Ones in your entire way of life, as he who has called you is holy,

16. Because it is written: "**Be holy, just as I also am holy.**"

17. And if you call upon The Father, he who has no respect of persons and judges every person according to his works, live your life in reverence in this time of your pilgrimage,

18. As you know that you were redeemed from your worthless works which you received from your fathers, not with silver which wears out, neither with gold,

19. But with the precious blood of The Lamb, who has no blemish or defilement in him, who is The Messiah.

20. He was appointed beforehand to this before the foundation of the world and was manifested at the end of times for you;

21. You, who by him have believed in God, who raised him from among the dead and has given him the glory, that your faith and hope would be upon God,

22. So that your souls would be sanctified in obedience to the truth and that they be filled with love without partiality, that you would be loving one another from a pure and perfect heart,

23. As persons who have been born again, not from fallible seed, but that which is infallible, by the living word of God which stands for eternity.

24. Because all flesh is grass and all its beauty as the blossom of the field*; the grass withers and the blossom fades.

* Greek has "**flower of the grass**". "**Of the Grass**" in DSS Aramaic can be : ᚠᚷᚪᚫᚱᚪ, ᚪᚫᚲᚫᚠᚷ, ᚪᚱᚩᚲ

The Peshitta reading –"**Field**" is ᚪᚱᚾᚦᚷ.
In Ashuri , The Peshitta reading , "**of the Field**" is דחקלא .
The 3 "**of the Grass**" Aramaic words are : דעמירא , דעסבא , דארעא . **The shaded Aramaic words have at least 60% correspondence.**
Greek for "**of the Grass**" is χορτου.
Greek for "**of the field**" is αγρου. These two have **50% correlation** at best.

Greek Uncial script
XOPTOY–"of the grass"
AΓPOY–"of the field"
50% correlation
Ashuri-DSS Aramaic script
דחקלא –"of the field"
דעסבא–"of the grass"
75% correspondence?
Estrangela Aramaic script

ᚺᚢᚾᚫ –"of the field"

ᚺᚢᚾᚫᚷ–"of the grass"

Which word pair is the more similar and thus more likely to account for the other language version?
Let the reader judge.

25. And the word of our God* stands for eternities. And this is that word by which you have been evangelized.

* Greek has "of The Lord"–tou Kuriou. The Peshitta reading of verses 24,25 conforms to The Hebrew & LXX O.T. , and exactly with The Peshitta O.T. reading of Isaiah 40:8 (employing excerpts). The Greek text agrees with none of these in its reading.

Chapter 2

1. Therefore, put away from you all wickedness, all treachery, partiality, envy and slander,

2. And be as nursing* infants, and yearn for the word as for pure and spiritual* milk by which you shall grow strong for life*,

* The Majority Greek lacks "**for life**"; The Critical Greek has "**into salvation**" -εις σωτηριαν , which is a typical Greek rendering of the Aramaic "**Khaya**"- חיא , whose essential meaning is "**Life**", but can also at times refer to salvation. "Salvation" is entirely out of place in this verse; we do not "**grow into salvation**" as the Critical Greek states it, which is a theological heresy and absurdity. This Greek reading does support the Peshitta primacy model, however. The Peshitta does not follow any Greek text, as it contains more information than they do : "**nursing children**" , "**as for milk**" , "**& spiritual**", "**for life**". The Greek can be derived from the Aramaic (primarily by omission of words) but the Aramaic cannot be derived from the Greek texts.

3. If you have tasted and you have seen* that **THE LORD JEHOVAH** is good,

* Greek lacks "**& you have seen**". The Peshitta verse is an obvious allusion to Psalms 34:8:

Yahweh good that & see Taste
טעמו וראו כי-טוב יהוה Hebrew.–"**Taste and see that Jehovah is good.**"
Here is the Peshitta OT version of that Psalms verse:
MarYah good that & see Taste
טעמו וחזו דטב מריא Aramaic.–"**Taste and see that Lord Jehovah is good.**"("**MarYah**" means "**LORD JEHOVAH**") See the similarities in the Hebrew and Aramaic? It appears the Greek translator (I assume the Greek is a translation in this interlinear, due to all the evidence I have compiled supporting that position) saw טעמתון and translated it "εγευσασθε" –"**You have tasted**" and inadvertantly skipped the next Aramaic word וחזיתון –"**& you have seen**" because it has the same ending as the previous word טעמתון ; he then proceeded to translate the next word דטב –"**that good**", etc..

4. He to whom you draw near, The Living Stone, whom the children of men have rejected, and is chosen and precious to God.

Verse 4 is a description of The subject of verse 3 –"**The LORD**"- "**Yahweh**" in Psalms 34:8 , as made plain in The Peshitta text and in the Aramaic cognate "**MarYah**" – מריא. Shimeon Kaypha (Peter) the Apostle presents **Yeshua** as **Jehovah** – The "**YHWH**" of Israel .

5. And you also, as living stones, be built up and become spiritual temples and holy Priests to offer spiritual sacrifices acceptable before God by Yeshua The Messiah.

6. For it is said in the Scriptures, "Behold, I lay down in Zion an approved and Precious Stone at the head of the corner, and whoever believes in him will not be ashamed."

* This is a quotation from Isaiah 28:16 from a text not quite The Hebrew Massoretic text (Hebrew has "**a sure foundation**" & "**shall not make haste**") nor The LXX reading :("**costly,choice corner stone,choice..**") nor Peshitta OT :("**shall not be afraid**"). This is typical of Peshitta NT quotes from the OT; no one known OT text type is represented . Some sort of hybrid text was used which was somewhere between The Massoretic Hebrew and a Hebrew text like that behind The Greek LXX..
Greek : ιδου τιθημι εν σιων λιθον ακρογωνιαιον εκλεκτον εντιμον και ο πιστευων επ αυτω ου μη καταισχυνθη
LXX : ιδου εγω εμβαλω εις τα θεμελια σιων λιθον πολυτελη εκλεκτον ακρογωνιαιον εντιμον εις τα θεμελια αυτης και ο πιστευων επ αυτω ου μη καταισχυνθη
You can compare the Greek verse (Majority text) with the LXX and see that the Greek text is not a verbatim quote of The LXX, but probably is an edited version of the Peshitta text & then revised according to The LXX.

7. This honor is given therefore to you - those who believe, but to those who are disobedient,
* Greek has additionally a quote from Psalms 118:22 -λιθον ον απεδοκιμασαν οι οικοδομουντες ουτος εγενηθη εις κεφαλην γωνιας – (**The stone which the builders rejected, the same is become the head of the corner**.)-identical to The LXX text of that verse. This insertion (I do not give my reasons here for asserting this as an insertion) garbles the sense of the sentence given in this and the following verse.

8. He is a stone of stumbling and a rock of offense, and they stumble on it, in that they

do not obey the word, for they are appointed to this.

9. But you are a chosen race who serve as Priests for The Kingdom, a holy people, a redeemed assembly; you should proclaim the praises of him who called you from darkness into his excellent light.

10. You are those who at the first were not considered a people, but now are the people of God, neither were mercies upon you, but now mercies are poured out upon you.

11. Beloved, I beg of you, as wayfarers and as foreigners, depart from all these desires of the body that make war against the soul,

12. And let your way of life be beautiful before all children of men*, those who speak wicked words of you, that they may see your beautiful works and praise God in the day of examination.

---

* Greek has εθνεσιν -"**the Gentiles**","**Nations**". The Peshitta has אנשא –"**Men**"; Here is "Gentiles" – עממא. In DSS script they are אעממא:אנשא . In Estrangela script: ܐܢܫܐ: ܥܡܡܐ. The Ashuri pair look more alike than those in the other scripts. **Other Aramaic words for** "Nations" or "Gentiles" are: חנפא אומתא , אמון , אומון
In Estrangela script:

ܚܢܦܐ - "Pagans" ,"Gentiles"

ܐܢܫܐ –"Men"

ܥܡܡܐ -"Gentiles"

Ashuri Aramaic
חנפא- "Pagans", "Gentiles"
אנשא–"Men"
עממא-"Gentiles"
DSS Aramaic
חנפא- "Pagans", "Gentiles"
אנשא –"Men"
עממא-"Gentiles"

The Estrangela , Ashuri & DSS shaded pairs have at least **50% letter correlations** (2 out of 4); The DSS pair are closer in appearance than the Ashuri,with **75%** correlation.

Greek for "Men" is usually "Ανθρωποις" ; "Nations – Gentiles" is εθνεσιν. In Greek Uncial script:
ΑΝΘΡΩΠΟΙΣ –"Men"
ΕΘΝΕΣΙΝ-"Gentiles"

I see no correlation (**0%**) in the two Greek words whatsoever. It looks highly unlikely that The Peshitta reading came from Greek, as a translator looking at εθνεσιν- "**Nations –Gentiles** would not be at all prone to translate it as אנשא –"**Men**".

---

13. Submit to all the sons of men* for the sake of God; to Kings, because of their authority,

---

* Greek has "υποταγητε παση ανθρωπινη κτισει" – "**Submit to every human creation**". The Aramaic "בני אנשא" is "**Sons of men**" "**children**" – בני may be interpreted "**building**" as from בנא (Bna) instead of the obvious root ברא -"**Bra**" –"**Son**".The Greek is an obvious error.We are not to submit to any human creation; submission indicates an attitude of humility and service which can only be expressed toward another person, not toward things or institutions. If Peter had "**ordinances**" or "**laws**" in mind, he would have plainly said so; he would not have used a word that refers to "**creation**" and always (in OT LXX and Greek NT) refers to God's creation, never man's.

Incidentally, this verse does not teach absolute obedience to men; submission is not necessarily obedience."**Whether it is right before God to hear you rather than God, you judge.**" Acts 4:19

14. And Judges, because they are sent by him for the punishment of wrongdoers and for the praise of the workers of good.

15. For it is the will of God in this way that by your excellent works you may shut the mouths of fools - those who do not know God,

16. As free children, and not as persons who make their liberty a cloak for their evil, but as Servants of God.

17. Honor every person, love your brethren, worship God and honor Kings.

18. To those who are Servants among you: Submit to your masters in reverence, not only to the good and to the meek, but also to the severe and to the perverse;

19. For such *servants* have grace before God who, for the sake of a good conscience, endure distresses which come upon them by The Evil One.

20. But what honor is it to those who endure suffering because of their foolishness? But when you do what is good and they afflict you and you endure, then it magnifies your honor with God.

21. For you are called to this, for even The Messiah died for our sake and left us this example, that you would walk in his steps,

22. He who did no sin, neither was deceit found in his mouth;

23. He who was insulted and did not insult, and he suffered and did not threaten, but he handed his judgment over to The Judge of righteousness.

24. And he took all of our sins and lifted them in his body to the cross, for as we are dead to sin, we shall live in his righteousness, for by his scars you have been healed.

25. For you had gone astray like sheep, and you have returned now to The Shepherd and The Caregiver of your souls.

Chapter 3

1. In this way, also, you women, submit to your husbands, that you may win without labor those who do not obey the word by your beautiful way of life,

2. When they see that you conduct yourselves in reverence and discretion.

3. Do not be adorned with outward ornaments of your hair braids or of gold jewelry or fine clothing,

4. But be adorned in the secret person of the heart and in a humble spirit which is uncorrupted, an excellent ornament before God.

5. For in this way from the first, the holy women who hoped in God were adorning their souls and they submitted to their husbands.

6. Just as Sarah was subject to Abraham and was calling him, "My lord", whose daughters you are by good works, when you are not shaken with any fear.

7. And you men, in this way dwell with your wives by knowledge, and hold them in honor as weaker vessels, lest you be subverted in your prayers, because they also inherit the gift* of eternal life with you.

* Greek has χαριτος –"**Grace**" ;
The Peshitta has מוהבתא –"**Mawhabta**"-"**The gift**";

"Grace" in Aramaic is usually טיבותא –"**Taybutha**".
Here are the words in Dead Sea Scroll Aramaic script:

ﬡﬡﬡﬡ –"**The Gift**" (Peshitta)
ﬡﬡﬡﬡ –"**Grace**" (Base of Greek reading ?)

These two words have **84%** letter correlation. The Greek for "Gift" in correct grammatical form for this passage is χαρισματος or δωρου ; χαρισματος & χαριτος have **70%** correlation, which is relatively high for Greek word pairs, but is still significantly lower than the Aramaic word pair correlation.The Greek words differ in letter number by three; the Aramaic pair differ in only one letter and have the same number of letters in each word !The Aramaic text obviously is not derived from Greek (no Greek text has "Eternal life") and none has "the gift". The Greek is easily accounted for as a translation of the Aramaic in which the word "**eternal** was simply dropped and ﬡﬡﬡﬡ –"**Mawhabta**"-"**The gift**" was misread as ﬡﬡﬡﬡ –"**Taybutha**"-Grace".

8. But the conclusion is that you should all be in harmony; suffer with those who are suffering, love one another, be merciful and humble.

9. And you should not repay a person evil for evil, neither insults for insults; but to the contrary of these things, give blessings, for you are called to this, that you would inherit blessing.

10. Therefore, whoever desires life and loves to see good days, let him keep his tongue from evil and his lips that they do not speak deceit.

11. Let him move away from wickedness and let him do good; let him seek peace and run after it.

12. Because the eyes of **THE LORD JEHOVAH** are upon the righteous and his ears hear them; the face of the Lord is against the evil.

13. And who is he who will do evil to you if you will be zealous for good?

14. And if you suffer for the sake of righteousness, you are blessed, and you should not be afraid of those who terrorize you, and be not provoked.

15. But hallow **THE LORD JEHOVAH** The Messiah in your hearts, and be ready to return a defense to everyone who requests a statement from you about the hope of your faith, in meekness and in reverence,

16. As you have a good conscience, so that those who speak against you as against evil people, may be ashamed as people who reject your beautiful way of life, which is in The Messiah.

17. For it is an advantage to you that when you are doing good works, you suffer evil, if it is thus the will of God, but not while you are doing evil.

18. Because The Messiah also died once for the sake of our sins, The Righteous One in the place of sinners, to bring you to God, and he died in body and lived in his Spirit.

19. And he preached to those souls who were held in Sheol,

20. These who from the first were not convinced in the days of Noah when the long-suffering of God commanded that there would be an ark, upon the hope of their repentance*, and only eight souls entered it and were kept alive by water. * ("**Upon the hope of their repentance**" is not in the Greek versions".)

21. For you also are saved in it by that simile in baptism, not when you wash the body from impurity, but when you confess* God with a pure conscience, and by the resurrection of Yeshua, The Messiah,

*Greek has "συνειδησεως αγαθης επερωτημα εις θεον δι αναστασεως ιησου χριστου" - "**but the request unto God, for a good conscience, through the resurrection of Jesus Christ**". The Greek has salvation coming by "**requesting a good conscience**"; The Peshitta says it is through "**confessing God with a pure conscience**", which comports with other scripture : "**And if you shall confess with your mouth Our Lord Jesus, and shall believe with your heart that God has raised Him from the dead; you shall have life.**" Romans 10:9

22. He who has been escorted into Heaven, and he is upon the right hand of God, and the Angels and the Principalities and the Powers are subjected unto him.

Chapter 4

The First Epistle of The Apostle Peter ✝ אגרתא קדמיתא דכאפא שליחא

1. If therefore The Messiah has suffered in your place in the flesh, be you also equipped with the same mind, for everyone who has died * in his body has ceased from all sins; * (Greek has, **"the one who has suffered in the flesh has ceased from sins."** Please excuse my boldness, but that is sheer nonsense! One Aramaic word for "**suffered**" is חאש. "Died" is מאת.

DSS script:
חאש-"Suffered"
מאת-"Died"
There is **67%** letter correlation (2/3) between the two Aramaic words in DSS. Greek for "**he who died**" is τεθνηκως. "**Suffered**" is παθων. Those two share two letters but they do not correspond in order of placement, and one word has 5 letters and the other has eight, so they are not similar at all in appearance, as you can see. I would generously give them **25%** letter correlation.

2. Therefore he shall not live for the desires of men, as during the time that he was in the body, but for the will of God.

3. For that past time was enough in which you served the pleasure of The Pagans, in debauchery, drunkenness, in whoredom, in orgies and in the worship of demons.

4. And behold, now they marvel and insult you because you do not run riot with them in this former debauchery,

5. Those who give an account to God, who is going to judge the dead and living.

6. For because of this, The Good News was proclaimed also to the dead that they would be judged as children of men in the flesh and they would live in God by The Spirit.

7. The end of all things has arrived, therefore sober up and wake up to prayer.

8. And before everything, have a severe love for each other, for love covers a multitude of sins.

9. And love strangers without murmuring.

10. And let each one of you serve his neighbor with the gift he has received from God, as good stewards of the unique grace of God.

11. Everyone who speaks, let him speak according to the word of God, and everyone who ministers, according to what power God gives to him, that God may be glorified in all that you do, by Yeshua The Messiah, whose glory and honor is truly to the eternity of eternities.

12. Beloved, do not be astonished at the temptations that will come upon you, as if something strange happened to you, for they are for your proving.

13. But rejoice that you share in the sufferings of The Messiah, for in this way also you shall rejoice and be jubilant in the revelation of his glory.

14. And if you are reproached for the sake of the name of The Messiah, you are blessed, because The Glorious Spirit of God rests upon you.

Majority Greek has more: " in regard, indeed, to them, he is evil-spoken of, and in regard to you, he is glorified";

15. Only let none of you suffer as a murderer, or as a thief, or as an evildoer.

16. But if anyone suffers as a Christian, let him not be ashamed, but let him praise God for this name.

17. For it is time that the judgment will begin from the house of God; but if it begins from us, what is the end of those who are not convinced of The Good News of God?

18. And if the righteous have life in hardship, where is an evil man and a sinner found?

19. Therefore, let those who suffer according to the will of God commit their souls to him by excellent works, as to a faithful Creator.

Chapter 5

1. But I beg the Elders who are among you, I, your fellow Elder and witness of the sufferings of The Messiah and a sharer of his glory, which is going to be revealed:

2. Shepherd the flock of God that follows you and give care spiritually, not by compulsion, but with pleasure, not by defiled profit, but with all your heart,

3. Not as lords of the flock, but as excellent examples to them.

4. And when The Chief Shepherd will be revealed, you shall receive a crown of glory from him that does not fade away.

5. And you younger men, submit to your Elders and be closely garbed with humility of mind toward each, because God is opposed to those who are proud and he gives grace to the humble.

6. Be humbled, therefore, under the mighty hand of God, that he may exalt you at the right time.

7. And cast all your cares on God, for he takes care of you.

8. Be alert, be reflective, because your enemy Satan roars like a lion and is walking and seeking whom he may devour.

9. Stand against him, therefore, being firm in your faith, and know also that sufferings come against your brethren who are in the world.

10. But it is The God of grace who has called us to his eternal glory by Yeshua The Messiah, who gives us, while we shall endure

these small afflictions, to be empowered,
confirmed and established in him to eternity;
11. To him is the glory, the dominion and the
honor to the eternity of eternities. Amen.
12. As I consider these few things, I am
writing to you by a trustworthy brother,
Sylvanus; I am convinced and I testify that
this is the true grace of God in which you
stand.
13. The chosen church which is in Babylon
invokes your peace, and Marqus, my son.
14. Invoke the peace, one of another, with a
holy kiss. Peace be with all those who are in
The Messiah. Amen.

The Second Epistle of The Apostle Peter

* The Epistle of 2nd Peter is not included in The Peshitta ; neither is 2nd John, 3rd John, Jude or Revelation. Those books are supplied in John Gwynn's edition of the General Epistles from The Crawford Aramaic manuscript and others of these books. These books have been included in the Western Canon of The Syrian Orthodox Church, The Maronite Church and others which use the Aramaic NT, however, the General Epistles in those churches have been based on <u>The Harklean Syriac Version</u> , which is a translation from the Greek NT into Aramaic done in AD 616. **The text used by John Gwynn is not The Harklean Version**. The texts of the two editions are quite diverse in many places, & Gwynn characterizes the Crawford & Palestinian Aramaic texts used as very Peshitta-like –"as idiomatic as The Peshitta"- and of a high quality, unlike the Harklean's Aramaic, which is quite crude and stilted, -"has systematically done violence to the Syriac" - very obviously a literal translation of Greek. *(See John Gwynn's introductions to <u>Remnants of The Later Syriac Versions of The Bible</u> & <u>The Apocalypse of St John</u>. Gwynn was not a Peshitta primacist, however; he believed the Syriac NT was entirely translated from Greek.)*

Chapter 1

1. **S**himeon Petraus, a Servant and an Apostle of Yeshua The Messiah to those who, equal in honor* with us, were worthy* for the faith by the righteousness of Our Lord* and Our Savior Yeshua The Messiah.

* * All Greek mss. have ισοτιμος – "equally precious" in place of these two Aramaic words; ισοτιμος **is a compound word** ισο – "equal" + τιμος –"precious". Interestingly , the Aramaic words באיקרא & שׁוית can mean "in worth" & "equally".
* All the Greek mss. have λαχουσιν –"they obtained by lot" ; The Aramaic אשׁתויו –"were worthy" is very similar to another verb אשׁתיו which means "they imbibed, they received". I posit that the word אשׁתויו –"were worthy" was read as אשׁתיו -"they imbibed, they received" and translated λαχουσιν –"they obtained by lot".The Greek for "they were worthy" or "they were esteemed worthy" is αξιοι ησαν or αξιωθησονται or καταξιωθησονται . Which of these looks like λαχουσιν –"they obtained by lot" ? So is it unlikely the Aramaic reading אשׁתויו – "were worthy"came from Greek reading , λαχουσιν –"they obtained by lot". It looks far more likely that the Greek came from the Aramaic text. (By the way: Does God cast lots?)
   Here are the two readings in Aramaic:
   אשׁתויו –"They were worthy" (Gwynn's Edition)
   אשׁתיו –"They received" (Hypothetical base for Greek reading)

* Greek has του θεου ημων -"of our God", as does The Harklean.

2. Grace and peace be multiplied to you by the teaching of Our Lord Yeshua The Messiah,

3. As The One who has given all things which are of the divine power, with The Life and Awesomeness of God by his teaching, who has called us into his glory and majesty,

4. Who has granted you* by these great and precious declarations to be sharers of the divine nature, when you flee from the corruption of desires which are in the world.
   Greek has ημιν "to us".

5. And when this has happened, bring all diligence and add to your faith virtue and unto your virtue, knowledge,

6. But unto knowledge, perseverance, and unto perseverance, patience, and to patience, the worship of God,

7. But unto the worship of God, the affection of the brotherhood, but unto affection of the brotherhood, love.

8. For when these things are found in you and abound, they prove you are not lazy nor fruitless in the teaching of Our Lord Yeshua The Messiah.

9. For he in whom these things are not found is blind, because he does not see that he has forgotten the purification of his former sins.

10. And all the more my brethren, take pains concerning this, that by your good deeds you shall make your calling and your election sure, for when you are doing these things, you will never fall.

11. For in this way an entrance of the eternal Kingdom of Our Lord and Our Savior Yeshua The Messiah is richly given to you.

12. And for this reason I do not weary of reminding you concerning this, truly, even though you know these things well and are established on this truth,

13. But it seemed good to me, that as long as I am in this body, to awaken your memory,

* Greek has "σκηνωματος"- "Tent". Aramaic for "Tent" is במטללא –"Matlala" or במשכנא –"Mashkna". The actual Aramaic reading is בפגרא –"b'pagra "- "in body this".
   In DSS script, the actual Aramaic reading is בפגרא ,Again,this is בפגרא
   DSS Aramaic for "in a Tent " –"Matlala" is במטללא;& –"Mashkna"במשכנא . The firstAshuri pair have **66%** correlation.The Greek for body would be "σωματος "; Compare Greek -"σκηνωματος"- "Tent".One is seven letters and one is ten letters. One other fact mitigates against the Aramaic being derived from the Greek- The Greek word σκηνωματος is traditionally often used metaphorically for "the body " as a "tent " for the soul, according to Greek philosophy and theology. The Aramaic word does not carry that usage. Hence it seems much more likely the Greek is a translation of the Aramaic than vice versa. It is not likely an Aramaean would have translated σκηνωματος "tent" as בפגרא –"body ".
Here is an excerpt from <u>Thayer's Greek English Lexicon</u> for σκηνωμα :
4638 σκηνωμα skenoma skay'-no-mah

from <u>4637</u>; TDNT-7:383,1040; n n

AV-tabernacle 3; 3

1) a tent, a tabernacle
   1a) of the temple as God's habitation
   1b) of the tabernacle of the covenant
   1c) metaph. of the human body as the dwelling of the soul

The same Greek word occurs in the next verse, where the Aramaic has דפגרי – "**of my body** ".

14. As I know that the departure from my body is soon, just as Our Lord Yeshua The Messiah has informed me.

15. But I take pains that you may also constantly have a record by which to do these things after my departure.

16. For we have not gone after craftily made fables to inform you of the power and the coming of Our Lord Yeshua The Messiah, but we were eyewitnesses of his Majesty.

17. For when he received from God The Father honor and glory, when this voice came to him from the splendid glory in his Majesty: "This is my Son, The Beloved, he in whom I delight",

18. We also heard this voice from Heaven, which came to him when we were with him in The Holy Mountain.

19. And we have also the true word of prophecy, upon which you do well to gaze, as at a lamp that shines in a dark place, until the day will shine and the Sun* will rise in your hearts,
  * Greek has φωσφορος –"**phosphoros**"-"**light bearer**", "the planet Venus", "day star".

20. While you first know this: No prophecy is its own exposition of the Scriptures.

21. The prophecy came not by the will of man in the ancient times, but when holy men of God spoke, being compelled by the Holy Spirit.

Chapter 2

1. But there were also lying Prophets among the people, as there shall be lying teachers also among you, those who bring destructive heresies and deny the Lord who bought them, while bringing upon themselves speedy destruction.

2. And many will go after their abominations, because of which, the way of truth will be blasphemed.

3. And by greed and fictitious accounts they will make profit among you, these whose judgment from the first has not been idle and their destruction does not sleep.

4. And if God did not spare the Angels who sinned, but cast them down in chains* of darkness into the lowest depths* and handed them over to be kept for the judgment of torment*,
  * Greek has ταρταρωσας –"**Tartarused**", "**Cast into Tartarus**"? – a participle from "**Tartarus**" not found

anywhere else in Greek literature. The noun form – "Ταρταρος" is found in The LXX (Job 40:20) where it refers to "the quadrapeds in **the deep**". This use of the noun is much more in keeping with the meaning of the Aramaic in this verse תחתיתא (tekhtytha)-"**the depths**".
  * There are two Greek readings here: Most mss. have- εις κρισιν τηρουμενους –"**unto judgment being kept**" and the two old uncials (א-4th cent & .A -5th cent.) have - εις κρισιν κολαζομενους τηρειν –"**unto judgment being punished to be kept**". Each of these is represented in the Aramaic text –"**to be kept for judgment of torment**". Both of these can be derived from the Aramaic; it would be very difficult to maintain that the Aramaic interpolated these two readings into one to form a translation into Aramaic. This kind of split reading and split translation in Greek from Aramaic occurs in so many places and with all possible text types and even individual Greek uncials that it is almost inconceivable to argue that the Aramaic was based on all Greek ms. readings in so many places in The NT.

5. And he did not spare The First World but he preserved Noah, the eighth man, a Preacher of righteousness, when he brought a flood over the world of the wicked,

6. And when he burned the cities of Sadom and Amorah and condemned them in an overthrow, when he set an example to the wicked who were to come,

7. Also he delivered righteous Lot who suffered the indignity and the abominable* way of life of those who were lawless *,
  * *Greek has: και δικαιον λωτ καταπονουμενον υπο της των αθεσμων εν ασελγεια αναστροφης ερρυσατο- "**And He did rescue righteous Lot, worn down by the conduct in unbridled lust of the wicked.**"
The Aramaic language is an upgrade in information and intensity from the Greek, which is typical for The Peshitta compared to the Greek. Another term for this is lower entropy (higher information and organization content) ; a translation will have less information and detail than its original. The Greek consistenty exhibits this trait compared to The Aramaic text and hence exhibits the traits of a translation whereas The Peshitta-Aramaic NT exhibits the traits of an original document.

8. For while seeing and hearing, the righteous man dwelling among them from day to day, his righteous soul was tormented by lawless deeds,

9. THE LORD JEHOVAH knows to deliver from suffering those who reverence him, but he keeps the evil for the day of judgment while they are being tormented,

10. But especially those who go after the flesh and desire of defilement, and preach against authority, *being* insolent and proud, who do not tremble in the presence of dignitaries when they blaspheme;

11. Whereas The Angels who are greater than they in power and strength do not bring against them a judgment of blasphemy from THE LORD JEHOVAH;

12. But these, like dumb animals, are by nature* for the knife and destruction*, as they slander those things which they do not understand and by their corruption they will be destroyed.

** Greek has γεγεννημενα φυσικα εις αλωσιν και φθοραν –"**born natural for capture and corruption**".

13. They are those with whom the payment for evil is evil. A daytime banquet of defilement is considered by them a pleasure, and they are filled with defects. When they celebrate in their love feasts, they indulge themselves,

14. Having eyes that are full of adultery and sins that never end, as they seduce souls who are unstable and have a heart that is trained in greed, children of the curse.

* Greek has "οφθαλμους εχοντες μεστους μοιχαλιδος" – "**having eyes full of an adulteress**".This does not look good for the Greek text. Most English translations cover this glaring error over by translating it as "**adultery**", which is not the correct translation of the Greek word.Rotherham's translation is one of a few honest translations of this verse in the Greek, which I quote above.

15. And when they abandoned the straight way, they strayed and went in the way of Balaam, son of Beor*, he who loved the wages of evil;

* Greek has two readings: P[72](3rd cent.),C + Majority has Βοσορ – "Bosor"; The Critical Greek text has βεωρ – "Beor", which agrees with the Aramaic reading.Here are the two in Aramaic:

Ashuri script
בעור –"Beor"
בצור – "Bosor"
90% correlation
DSS script
ב ע ור –"Beor"
ב צ ור – "Bosor"
90% correlation
Estrangela script
ܒܥܘܪ –"Beor"
ܒܨܘܪ – "Bosor"
75% correlation

Both Aramaic names are found in the OT Peshitta; The Greek LXX has the two Greek names Βεωρ – "**Beor**" & Βοσορ – "**Bosor**" matched with the Aramaic names as shown. The two in Aramaic are very similar in Ashuri and in Dead Sea Scroll scripts; Estrangela spellings are not quite as similar, though still more so than in the Greek spellings.

Greek uncial script
ΒΕΩΡ –"Beor"
ΒΟCΟΡ –"Bosor"
Sinaiticus: ΒΕΩΟΡCΟΡ
Vaticanus ΒΕΩΡ
Sinaiticus has both readings combined in one-ΒΕΩΟΡCΟΡ –"Beoorsor"
Vaticanus has ΒΕΩΡ –"Beor". Greek shows **40%** letter correlation.

16. But the reproof of his violation was a dumb donkey which spoke with the voice of men, restraining the madness of the Prophet.

17. These are fountains without water, clouds which are driven by a hurricane, for whom the gloom of darkness is reserved.

18. For when they utter empty horrors, they seduce by filthy desires of the flesh those who had just escaped from those who were employed in deception.

19. They promise liberty to them when they are servants of corruption; for that by which anyone is conquered, to the same he is also a slave.

20. For if when they have fled the abominations of the world by the teaching of Our Lord and our Savior, Yeshua The Messiah, they are again entangled in these things, they are overcome again, and their end is worse than the beginning.

21. For it were better for them not to have known the way of righteousness than that when they knew, they would turn away afterward from the holy decree that was delivered to them.

22. But these things have happened to them of the true proverb: "The dog that returned to its vomit, and the pig that was washed to the wallowing of the mud."

Chapter 3

1. Now, beloved, this second epistle I write to you- these things by which I awaken your pure minds by memory,

2. That you may remember the words that were spoken before by the holy Prophets and the commandments of Our Lord and our Savior, which were through the Apostles,

3. And as you knew this first, that in the end of days, scoffers would come who scoff while they walk according to their own lusts,

4. And they say, "Where is The Promise of his coming? For from when our forefathers fell asleep, everything continues in the same way from the beginning of creation."

5. For they disregard this when they please: That the Heavens which were from the first, and The Earth, from the water and by the water, arose by the word of God,

6. By which the world which then was, lay in water and was destroyed.

7. But the Heavens and The Earth which are now, by his word are stored up as for fire and are kept for the day of judgment and of the destruction of wicked people.

8. But you shall not disregard this one thing, beloved: "One day is to **THE LORD JEHOVAH** as a thousand years, and a thousand years is as one day."

9. **THE LORD JEHOVAH** does not delay his promises as people consider delay, but he is patient for your sakes, and because he is

not willing that any person would perish, but that every person would come to conversion.

10. But the day of **THE LORD JEHOVAH** comes as a thief in which the Heavens suddenly pass away, but the elements being set on fire shall be destroyed and The Earth and the works that are in it shall be discovered*.

* The Majority Greek text has , γη και τα εν αυτη εργα κατακαησεται - "**The Earth and its works shall burn up**" . The Critical Greek text agrees with The Peshitta here : γη και τα εν αυτη εργα ευρεθησεται -"**The Earth and its works shall be discovered**". The Aramaic תשתחי could mean, "**will melt**", "**will be refined**". The actual Peshitta reading תשתכח is very similar to that.

Ashuri Script

תשתכח-"**shall be discovered**"(Peshitta reading)

תשתחד-"**shall melt**" (Hypothetical Aramaic for Greek reading)

80% correlation

DSS Aramaic Script

ℵℶℵℷℵℸ-" **shall be discovered**"(Peshitta reading)

ℵℸℵℶℵℷ-"**shall melt**" (Aramaic for Greek reading)

80% correlation

Estrangela Script

ܢܫܬܟܚ-" **shall be discovered**"(Peshitta reading)

ܢܫܬܚܕ-"**shall melt**" (Aramaic for Greek reading)

80% correlation

The Estrangela script here looks like the most likely candidate for the original Aramaic script from which the Majority Greek text was translated. Apparently, the Critical Greek was translated from the Dead Sea Scroll or Ashuri Script in 2 Peter.

11. As therefore all these things are to be destroyed, it is right for you to be in your way of life as those who are holy and in the worship of God,

12. While you expect and eagerly desire the coming of The Day of God in which the Heavens, being tested by fire, shall be dissolved, and the elements, when set on fire, shall melt.

13. But according to his promise, we look for The New Heavens and The New Earth, in which dwells righteousness. (Verses 10-13 are not referring to physical destruction by fire, but spiritual renovation, according to Zephaniah's prophecy:

3:8,9 ¶ **Therefore wait ye upon me, saith the LORD, until the day that I rise up to the prey: for my determination *is* to gather the nations, that I may assemble the kingdoms, to pour upon them mine indignation, *even* all my fierce anger: <u>for all the earth shall be devoured with the fire</u> of my jealousy.**

For <u>then will I turn to the people a pure language, that they may all call upon the name of the LORD, to serve him with one consent</u>. The prophecies about fire devouring the earth are truly about spiritual transformation and salvation, otherwise, there would be no people left on earth, as there obviously will be, making "**a New Heaven and New Earth in which righteousness dwells.**"

14. Therefore beloved, as you expect these things, take pains that you shall be found without spot and without defect before him in peace.

15. And you shall consider that the patience of **THE LORD JEHOVAH** is salvation, just as our beloved brother Paul wrote to you, according to the wisdom that was given to him,

16. Just as in all of his letters he spoke about these things, in which are things difficult for the intellect, which those who are without teaching and unstable, pervert, as also the other Scriptures, to their own destruction.

17. You therefore, beloved, as you have known beforehand, guard your souls, lest you go after the deception of those who are without The Law and you fall from your own stability.

18. But grow in grace and in the knowledge of Our Lord and Our Savior, Yeshua The Messiah, and of God The Father, to whom the glory is now and always, even to the days of eternity. Amen.

The First Epistle of The Apostle John

Chapter 1

1. **We** evangelize to you that which was from the beginning, that which we have heard and we have seen, that which we have perceived with our eyes and we have touched with our hands- him who is The Word of Life.

2. And The Life was revealed and we perceived and we testify and we proclaim to you the Life Eternal, that which was with The Father and was revealed to us.

3. And the thing which we have seen and heard we show also to you, that you will have communion with us, and our communion is with The Father and with his Son Yeshua The Messiah.

4. And these things we write to you that the joy which we have in you may be complete.

5. And this is The Good News that we have heard from him and we evangelize to you: God is Light, and there is no darkness at all in him.

6. And if we say that we have communion with him and we walk in darkness, we are lying, and we are not informed of the truth.

7. But if we walk in The Light as he is in The Light, we have communion with each other and the blood of Yeshua his Son purges us from all of our sins.

8. And if we shall say we do not have sin, we deceive ourselves, and the truth is not in us.

9. But if we confess our sins, He is faithful and righteous to forgive us our sins, and he will purge us from all our evil.

10. And if we say that we have not sinned, we make him a liar and his word is not with us.

Chapter 2

1. **C**hildren, I write these things to you so that you will not sin, and if a person will sin, we have "The Redeemer of the accursed"* with The Father - Yeshua The Messiah, The Righteous One.

* Greek has παρακλητος – **Paracletos** ,"**Comforter**","**Advocate**". Some think this Aramaic word פרקלטא ("**Parqlayta**") is a loan word from Greek. The reverse is probably true; פרקלטא is a compound of two words: פרק-**Praq** , "**Redeemer**" + לטא –**Layta**, "**The accursed**". The word in Aramaic indicates a **Savior** , which is perfectly fitting and descriptive of The Messiah here and in chapter 5, as well as in John 15, where The Holy Spirit is called "**Khrayna Parqlayta**" –"**Another Savior**" . The Greek word is rather tepid by comparison; a "comforter" or "advocate" does not bespeak the power and perfection of Our Lord's role and that of The Holy Spirit in our redemption. "In times like these, we need a **Savior**", says the famous hymn "**The Solid Rock**". Nothing less will do.

2. For He is The Atonement who is for the sake of our sins, and not in our place only, but also in the place of the entire universe.

3. And by this we sense that we know him, if we keep his commandments.

4. For he who says, "I know him", and does not keep his commandments, is lying and the truth is not in him.

5. But he who keeps his word, in this one truly the love of God is perfected, for by this we know that we are in him.

6. He who says, "I am in him", must walk according to his walk.

7. Beloved ones, I am not writing a new commandment to you, but an ancient commandment which you had from the beginning; but the ancient commandment is that word which you have heard*.

* The Majority Greek adds "απ αρχης" –"**from the beginning**"; The Critical Greek does not.

8. Again, a new commandment I am writing to you, that which is true in him and in you, for the darkness has passed and the true light begins to appear*.

* Greek has "ηδη φαινει" –"**already shines**".

9. Whoever says, therefore, that he is in the light and hates his brother, is in darkness still.

10. But he who loves his brother dwells in light and there is no violation in him.

11. But he who hates his brother is in darkness and walks in darkness and does not know where he is going, because the darkness has blinded his eyes.

12. I write to you, children, that your sins have been forgiven you because of his Name.

13. I write to you, fathers, that you have known him who is from the beginning. I write to you, young men, that you have conquered The Evil One. I write to you children, that you have known The Father.

14. I have written to you, fathers, that you have known him who is from the beginning. I have written to you, young men, that you are strong, and the word of God dwells in you and you have conquered The Evil One.

15. Do not love the world, neither the things that are in it, for whoever loves the world does not have the love of The Father in him.

16. For everything that is in the world: the desire of the body and the lust of the eyes and the pride of temporal life, these are not from The Father but these are from the world.

17. The world is passing and its lust, but he who does the will of God continues for eternity.

18. My children, it is an end time, and according to what you have heard that The False Messiah comes, already there have been many false messiahs, and by this we know that it is an end time.

19. They went out from us but they were not of us, for if they had been of us, they would have remained with us; but they went out from us to disclose that they were not of us.

20. And you have an anointing from The Holy One, and you discern every person.

21. I have not written to you because you do not know the truth, but because you do know it, and that no lie is from the truth.

22. Who is a liar but whoever denies that Yeshua is The Messiah? Such a person is a false messiah. He who denies The Father denies also the Son.

23. He who denies The Son also does not believe* in The Father; whoever confesses The Son confesses* The Father also.

*Greek reads εχει –"have,has"; The Majority Greek lacks the second half of the verse; The Critical Greek has it (א,B,A) : ο ομολογων τον υιον και τον πατερα εχει –"He that confesseth the Son, hath, the Father also."

* The only difference from the Aramaic is the verb εχει –"has", where the Aramaic has "Mawdey"-"confesses".

24. And anything which you have heard from the first, let remain with you, for if that which you have heard from the first remains with you, you also remain in The Father and in The Son.

25. And this is The Promise which he has promised us: Eternal Life!

26. But I have written these things to you because of those who seduce you.

27. And if The Anointing will remain with you which you have received from him, you do not need anyone to teach you, but as The Anointing who is from God* is teaching you about everything, and is true, and there is no falsehood in him, even as he has taught you, abide* in him.

* Greek lacks "from God".
* Majority Greek has "you shall abide"; Critical has "abide".

28. And now my children, abide in him, that when he is revealed, we shall not be ashamed before him, but we shall have boldness at his arrival.

29. And if you know that he is righteous, know also that everyone who does righteousness is* from him.

• Greek has γεγενηται-"has been born". "Born" in Aramaic would be "אתיליד". Compare to איתוהי-"is":

DSS script :
איתווניד - "Is"
אתוליד - "Born"
84% correlation
Ashuri (with DSS Lamed)
איתוהי - "Is"
אתיליד - "Born"
66% correlation

Estrangela

⟨aramaic⟩ — "Is"
⟨aramaic⟩ — "Born"
33% correlation

A careful look at the first pair of words shows a close resemblance in all 5 letters of the second word (underlined and highlighted in color version) with four of the first word. Essentially, all was needed to read the first word as the second, was to drop two- Yodh's -י, which would be the easiest to miss, as they are the smallest of Aramaic letters.

Chapter 3

1. And behold how much the love of The Father abounds to us, that he has called us and also has made* us children; because of this, the world does not know us, because it does not know him.

* Critical Greek has "και εσμεν" –"& we are". Most Greek mss. lack this. It looks like a comment on the Aramaic reading - אף עבדן –"also He made us" , which probably refers to the fact that God has called us children and has made us children; the Critical Greek (א,A,B,C,P,Ψ) interprets this as -"& we are".

2. Beloved, now we are the children of God, and it has not been revealed until now what we are going to be, but we know that when he has been revealed, we shall be in his likeness, and we shall see him just as what he is.

3. And everyone who has this hope upon him purifies himself, just as he is pure.

4. But whoever commits sin commits evil, for sin is entirely evil.

5. And you know that he was revealed to take away our sins and there is no sin in him.

6. No one who remains in him commits sin, and no one who sins has seen him, neither has he known him.

7. Children, let no one deceive you; he who does righteousness is righteous even as The Messiah* also is righteous.
* Greek lacks "The Messiah".

8. He who commits sin is from Satan*, because Satan* is a sinner from the beginning. The Son of God appeared for this reason: To destroy the works of Satan*.

• Greek has ο διαβολος – "The Devil" three times in this verse & once in verse 10; The Peshitta has ܣܛܢܐ – "Satan" in those places. The LXX uses διαβολος almost exclusively (25 out of 27 occurrences) to translate the Hebrew שטן –"Satan".Aramaic has another word for "The

Devil" – "AkalQartsa". If The Peshitta were a translation of the Greek text, it would most likely translate ο διαβολος – "**The Devil**" with אכלקרצא- AkalQartsa , not סטנא – **Satana**. אכלקרצא- **AkalQartsa** and διαβολος – "**The Devil**" both mean "The Slanderer"; סטנא –**Satana**. means "The Adversary".
As it stands in the Majority Greek text , Σατανα –"Satan" (a transliterated Aramaic word in Greek letters) occurs 37 times in The NT (counting one Hebrew spelling- "Σαταν") and Διαβολος in all forms occurs 38 times. Sixteen of the 38 places in which Διαβολος occurs, The Peshitta has סטנא – **Satana – in eight books of the NT (Matthew,Luke,John,1 Tim,2 Tim,Hebrews,James,1 Peter,1 John).**
The data suggests an Aramaic original; the LXX model translation of Hebrew confirms this.

9. No one who is begotten from God commits sin, because his seed is in him and he is not able to sin because he has been begotten from God.

10. By this the children of God are distinguished from the children of Satan: No one who does not do righteousness, neither loves his brother, is from God.

11. For this is the commandment that you have heard from the first: "You shall love one another",

12. Not like Cain who was from The Evil One and murdered his brother; and why did he murder him? Only because his works were evil and those of his brother were righteous.

13. Do not be surprised, my brethren, if the world hates you.

14. We know that we have departed from death into life by this: Because we love the brethren. He who does not love his brother remains in death.

15. For everyone who hates his brother murders a person, and you know that eternal life cannot abide in anyone who murders a person*.
  * Greek has ουκ εχει ζωην αιωνιον εν αυτω μενουσαν – "**has not eternal life abiding in him**".

16. By this we know his love toward us, for he gave his Life in our place, and it is right for us that we also would give our lives for the sake of our brothers.

17. Whoever has worldly possessions and sees his brother who has a need and withholds his compassion from him, how is the love of God in him?

18. Children, let us not love one another with words and with speech, but in deeds and in truth.

19. And by this we are made known that we are from the truth, and we assure our hearts before he comes*. * Greek lacks "**before He comes**".

20. For if our heart condemns us, how much greater is God than our heart? And he knows all things.

21. Beloved, if our heart does not condemn us, we have boldness before God.

22. And we shall receive all the things that we ask from him, because we keep his commandments and we do good before him.

23. And this is his commandment: that we believe in The Name of his Son, Yeshua The Messiah, and we should love one another, as he commanded us*.
* The Majority Greek lacks "**us**".The TR (KJV Greek) and Critical Greek has it.

24. And whoever keeps his commandments is kept* by him and he dwells in him, and by this we perceive that he lodges in us, from his Spirit, that one whom he has given to us.
  * Greek has "en autw μενει" –"**remains in Him**".

Chapter 4

1. Beloved, do not believe all spirits, but be distinguishing between the spirits whether they are from God, because many false Prophets have gone out into the world.

2. The Spirit of God is known by this: every spirit who confesses that Yeshua The Messiah has come in the flesh is from God.

3. And no spirit that does not confess that Yeshua has come in the flesh is from God, but this is from that False Messiah, him whom you have heard that he will come, and already he is in the world.

4. You are from God, children, and you have conquered them, because he who is in you is greater than he who is in the world.

5. And these are from the world, therefore they speak from the world and the world listens to them.

6. But we are from God and he who knows God listens to us and he who is not from God does not listen to us; by this we perceive The Spirit of Truth and the spirit of deception.

7. Beloved, let us love one another, because love is from God, and everyone who loves is born of God and knows God,

8. Because God is love, and everyone who does not love does not know God.

9. In this the love of God is known to us: for God sent his only Son to the world so that it shall live by him.

10. In this is love: it was not that we loved God, but he has loved us, and he sent us his Son, the atonement for the sake of our sins.

11. Beloved, if God loves us in this way, we are indebted also to love one another.

12. No person has ever seen God, but if we love one another, God abides in us, and his love is fulfilled in us.

13. In this we know that we abide in him and he abides in us, because he has given us of his Spirit.

14. And we see and do testify that The Father has sent his Son, The Savior for the world.

15. And everyone who confesses Yeshua, that he is The Son of God, God dwells in him and he dwells in God.

16. And we believe and we know the love that God has for us, for God is love, and everyone who dwells in love dwells in God. (Greek adds "and God in him".)

17. By this, love is fulfilled with us, that we may have boldness in the day of judgment, because as he is, so also are we, in this world.

18. There is no fear in love, but perfect love casts out fear, because fear is by suspicion, but he who fears is not grown up in love.

19. Therefore we shall love God because he first loved us.

20. But if a man will say, "I love God", and he hates his brother, he is lying; for he who does not love his brother who is visible, how is it possible for him to love God who is invisible?

21. And we have received this commandment from him: "Everyone who loves God shall love his brother also".

Chapter 5

1. Everyone who believes that Yeshua is The Messiah is born from God, and everyone who loves him who begot, loves also the one who is begotten of him.

2. And by this we know that we love the children of God, whenever we love God and we do his commandments.

3. For this is the love of God: to keep his commandments; and his commandments are not burdensome.

4. Because everyone who is born from God conquers the universe; and this is the victory that conquers the universe - our faith.

5. Who is he who conquers the universe but he who believes that Yeshua is The Son of God?

6. This is he who came by water and blood, Yeshua The Messiah; it was not by water only, but by water and blood.

7. And The Spirit testifies because The Spirit is the truth.

8. And there are three testifying: The Spirit and the water and the blood, and the three of them are in one.

9. If we receive the testimony of men, how much greater is the testimony of God? And this is the testimony of God which he testifies about his Son:

10. Everyone who believes in The Son of God has this witness in his soul. Everyone who does not believe God makes him a liar because he does not believe the testimony that God testifies concerning his Son.

11. And this is the testimony: God has given us Eternal Life, and that life is in his Son.

12. Everyone who lays hold of The Son lays hold also of The Life, and everyone who does not lay hold of The Son of God does not have The Life in him.

13. These things I have written to you that you will know that you have Eternal Life, you who believe* in the name of The Son of God.

* The Majority Greek & TR has "and **that you may believe in the Name of The Son of God**.." דהימנתון –D'himnathown can be translated : "**That you believe**" or "**Because you believe**" or "**You who believe**". Apparently the translator of the Majority Greek text read it as "**That you believe**" and the Critical Greek translator read it as "**Who believe**". Both Greek readings further buttress Peshitta primacy in this place and for 1 John as a whole.

14. And this is the confidence which we have toward him: Everything that we ask him according to his will, he hears for us.

15. And if we are convinced that he hears us concerning whatever we ask from him, we trust that even now we receive the things that we desire which we ask from him.

16. If a man sees his brother who sins a sin that is not worthy of death, let him ask, and Life will be given to him for those who are not sinning unto death; for there is mortal sin; I do not say that a man should pray for this.

17. For every evil is sin, and there is sin that is not mortal.

18. And we know that no one who is born from God commits sin, for he who is born from God keeps his soul and The Evil One does not touch it.

19. We know that we are from God, and the whole world lies in The Evil One.

20. And we know that The Son of God has come and he has given us a mind to know The True One and to be in The True One- in his Son, Yeshua The Messiah. This One is The True God and The Life Eternal.

21. My children, keep yourselves from the worship of idols.

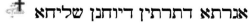

The Second Epistle of The Apostle John

1. The Elder to The Elect lady and her children, those whom I love in the truth, but it is not I only, but also all those who know the truth,

2. Because of the truth which dwells in us and is with us for eternity.

3. May grace, mercy and peace be with us, from God The Father and from Our Lord, Yeshua The Messiah, The Son of The Father, in truth and in love.

4. I rejoiced much when I found some of your children walking in truth, according to the commandment which we have received from The Father.

5. And now I would persuade you Lady, not according to the new commandment I wrote to you, but that which we had from the beginning, that we love one another.

6. And this is love, that we walk according to his commandment; this commandment is according to what you have heard from the beginning, in which you have been walking.

7. For many deceivers have gone out into the world, those who do not confess that Yeshua The Messiah has come in the flesh; such a person is a deceiver and antichrist.

8. Pay attention to your souls, that you do not lose anything which you have cultivated, but that you may receive a full reward.

9. No one who is a violator and does not continue in the teaching of The Messiah has God in him. He who continues in his teaching, this one has The Father and The Son.

10. If a man comes to you and does not bring this teaching, do not receive him into the house and you shall not say to him, "You are welcome."

11. For he that says to him, "You are welcome", is a partaker with his evil deeds.
(John is likely referring to a house church and telling them not to receive heretics into the fellowship.)

12. As I had much to write to you, I did not want to speak with parchment and ink, but I hope to come to you and we shall speak face-to-face, that our joy may be complete.

13. The children of your Elect sister invoke your peace. Amen.

The Third Epistle of The Apostle John ✠ אגרתא דתלת דיוחנן שליחא

The Third Epistle of The Apostle John

1. The Elder to beloved Gaius, whom I love in truth.

2. Our beloved, I pray for you that you will prosper in all things and be well, just as your soul prospers.

3. For I rejoice much that the brethren came and testified about your faithfulness, how you walk in the truth.

4. For I have no greater joy than this, that I hear that my children are walking in the truth.

5. Our beloved, by faith you do that which you do to the brethren, and especially those who are strangers,

6. Those who have testified of your love before all the church. You did well when you gave them necessities, as is becoming to God.

7. For the sake of his name they went out, not taking anything from the Gentiles;

8. Therefore we are indebted to receive such as these, that we may be helpers for the truth.

9. I desired* to write to The Assembly, but he who loves to be their number one, Diotrephis, does not receive us. * No Greek text has "**I desired**" here.

10. Therefore, if I come, I will remember his works, which he did when he slandered us with wicked words; and when that was not enough for him, he did not receive the brethren, and those who do receive them, he forbids and throws out of the church.

11. Our beloved, do not imitate evil, but the good. One who does good is from God. One who does evil has not seen God.

12. Concerning Demetrius, he has a testimony from everyone and that of the assembly, as well as that of the truth, and we also testify, and you know* that our testimony is true. * The Majority Greek text and The Harklean Syriac version have the plural "**you know**" (2nd person plural), whereas this edition of Gwynn has the singular "**you know**" (2nd person singular). The Critical Greek text agrees here with this Peshitta edition of the General Epistles.

13. I have much to write to you, but have not desired to write to you* with ink and pen. * The Majority Greek lacks "**to you**" here. The Critical Greek has it.

14. But I hope that I shall see you soon, and we shall speak face-to-face*.
  • Literally,"**Mouth to mouth**", which is an Aramaic idiom meaning "**openly**" or "**in person**". Hebrew has the same idiom; I doubt that Greek has such an idiom; its occurrence in Greek here and in 2 John , as well as in The LXX of Numbers 12:8 indicates a Semitic original behind the Greek.

15. Peace be with you. The friends invoke your peace. Invoke the peace of the friends, each person by name.

The Epistle of The Apostle Jude

1. Yehuda, the Servant of Yeshua The Messiah and the brother of Yaqob, to the Gentiles called by God The Father, beloved ones, and kept by Yeshua The Messiah.

2. Mercy, peace and love be multiplied to you.

3. Beloved, when I gave all diligence to write to you about our common life, it was necessary for me to write to you, as I am to persuade you to compete for the faith, which was once delivered to The Holy Ones.

4. For men have obtained entrance, who from the beginning were written with this guilty verdict: "Evil men who pervert the grace of our God into an abomination and deny him who is the only **Lord God** and Our Lord Yeshua The Messiah."

5. I wish to remind you, as you all know, that God, when once he had brought the people out from Egypt, afterward destroyed those who did not believe.

6. And those Angels who kept not their Principality, but abandoned their own way of life, he has kept to the great Day of Judgment in unseen chains under darkness,

7. Just as Sadom and Amorah and their surrounding cities, in which, like these, they committed fornication and went after other flesh, are subject* to demonstrations of eternal fire while they are condemned to judgment.

*   Here the Greek has: "**are set forth for an example, suffering the punishment of eternal fire**." Here are the two readings in Aramaic, first in Ashuri Aramaic script, then in Dead Sea Scroll Aramaic script:

•

סימן תחת תחויתא דנורא דלעלם-"**Subject to demonstrations of eternal fire**" -Peshitta
סימן תחוי תבעתא דנורא דלעלם-"**Appointed an example, vengeance of eternal fire**"-Greek reading in Aramaic

-"**Subject to demonstrations of eternal fire**" -Peshitta
-"**Appointed an example, vengeance of eternal fire**"-Greek reading in Aramaic

"**Demonstrations**" is תחויתא; "**Subject**" is סימן תחת

"**Vengeance**" is תבעתא ; "**Appointed example**" is סימן תחוי

It seems likely that the Greek reading came from The Aramaic text, and not vice versa. The Greek words for Vengeance and Demonstration are δικη & δειγμα. Only two letters out of the six in δειγμα are similar there, which is **33%** correlation. The Aramaic words illustrated above have **60%** and **75%** correlations, showing that they are more likely to be confused, one for another, than the Greek words. Greek primacy does not stand up in the face of the evidence.

8. In this likeness, these also lust in *their* dreams, who defile the flesh, reject Lordship and slander The Glory.

9. But Michael the Archangel, who, when he was speaking with The Devil about the body of Moses, did not speak to bring a slanderous judgment against him, but he said, "**THE LORD JEHOVAH** will rebuke you."

10. But these things which they do not know, they slander, and those things which they desire naturally, like dumb animals, in them they are corrupted.

11. Woe to them who have gone in the way of Cain, and have run riot after the deception of Balaam for wages, and they have perished in the rebellion of Korah.

12. These are those who are defiled in their feasts and run riot while feeding themselves without fear, clouds without rain that wander with the wind; trees, whose fruit has died, who are without fruit, which have died twice and they pull-up by the roots,

13. Strong surges of the sea that show their shame by their froth. These are wandering stars, for whom the gloom of darkness is reserved for eternity.

14. But Enoch, the seventh from Adam, prophesied to these as he said, "Behold, **THE LORD JEHOVAH** comes with myriads of his Holy Ones,

15. To do judgment on all and to reprove all souls, because of all the works of those who did wickedness, and because of all of the hard words which evil sinners have spoken."

16. These are those who murmur and complain in every matter while they walk according to their desires, their mouth speaks guiltiness, and they flatter persons for profit.

17. But you, beloved, remember those words that were spoken before by the Apostles of Our Lord Yeshua The Messiah,

18. Who said to you, "In the last time there shall be those who mock and by their own desires go after wickedness."

19. These are those who distinguish the animal nature, because they do not have The Spirit.

20. But you beloved, be encouraged again in your holy faith, praying in The Holy Spirit,

21. But let us keep ourselves in the love of God as we look for the mercy of Our Lord Yeshua The Messiah unto our eternal life.

22. And snatch some of them who are from the fire.

23. And when they repent, show pity upon them with respect, while you hate also the tunic that is defiled by the flesh.

24. But to him who can keep us without offense and without defilement and present *us* without a flaw

25. Before his glory in joy (He alone is God our Savior by Yeshua The Messiah Our Lord); to him is the praise, dominion, honor and majesty, even now and unto all ages. Amen.

The Original Aramaic New Testament in Plain English
The Revelation of Yeshua The Messiah ✝ גלינא דישוע משיחא

The Revelation of Yeshua The Messiah

(From The 12th century Crawford Manuscript)

גלינא
על יוחנן מסברנא מן אלהא בפטמון
דהוא
גזרתא דאשתדי לה מן נארון קסר

The Revelation
which came to John The Evangelist
from God in Patmos
the island to which he was exiled by
Nero Caesar

Introduction

The Date of Authorship

Sir Isaac Newton wrote the following concerning the date of the writing of Revelation. Isaac Newton, one of the greatest scientists of all time, wrote voluminously on the subject of Bible prophecy, especially of the books of Daniel and Revelation:
"Irenaeus introduced an opinion that the Apocalypse was written in the time of Domitian; but then he also postponed the writing of some others of the sacred books, and was to place the Apocalypse after them: he might perhaps have heard from his master Polycarp that he had received this book from John about the time of Domitian's death; or indeed John might himself at that time have made a new publication of it, from whence Irenaeus might imagine it was then but newly written. Eusebius in his Chronicle and Ecclesiastical History follows Irenaeus; but afterwards [a] in his Evangelical Demonstrations, he conjoins the banishment of John into Patmos, with the deaths of Peter and Paul: and so do [b] Tertullian and Pseudo-Prochorus, as well as the first author, whoever he was, of that very antient fable, that John was put by Nero into a vessel of hot oil, and coming out unhurt, was banished by him into Patmos. Tho this story be no more than a fiction, yet was it founded on a tradition of the first churches, that John was banished by him into Patmos in the days of Nero. Epiphanius represents The Gospel of John as written in the same time of Domitian, and the Apocalypse even before that of Nero. [c] Arethas in the beginning of his Commentary quotes the opinion of Irenaeus from Eusebius, but follows it not: for he afterwards affirms the Apocalypse was written before the destruction of Jerusalem, and that former commentators had expounded the sixth seal of that destruction. With the opinion of the first Commentators agrees the tradition of the Churches of Syria, preserved to this day in the title of the Syriac Version of the Apocalypse, which title is this: *The Revelation which was made to John the Evangelist by God in the Island Patmos, into which he was banished by Nero the Caesar*. The same is confirmed by a story told by [d] Eusebius out of Clemens Alexandrinus, and other antient authors, concerning a youth whom John some time after his return from Patmos committed to the care of the Bishop of a certain city. The Bishop educated, instructed, and at length baptized him; but then remitting of his care, the young man thereupon got into ill company, and began by degrees first to revel and grow vitious, then to abuse and spoil those he met in the night; and at last grew so desperate, that his companions turning a band of high-way men, made him their Captain: and, saith [e] Chrysostom, he

continued their Captain a long time. At length John returning to that city, and hearing what was done, rode to the thief; and, when he out of reverence to his old master fled, John rode after him, recalled him, and restored him to the Church. This is a story of many years, and requires that John should have returned from Patmos rather at the death of Nero than at that of Domitian; because between the death of Domitian and that of John there were but two years and an half; and John in his old age was [f] so infirm as to be carried to Church, dying above 90 years old, and therefore could not be then suppos'd able to ride after the thief. This opinion is further supported by the allusions in the Apocalypse to the Temple and Altar, and holy City, as then standing; and to the Gentiles, who were soon after to tread under foot the holy City and outward court. 'Tis confirmed also by the style of the Apocalypse itself, which is fuller of Hebraisms than his Gospel. For thence it may be gathered, that it was written when John was newly come out of Judea, where he had been used to the Syriac tongue; and that he did not write his Gospel, till by long converse with the Asiatick Greeks he had left off most of the Hebraisms. It is confirmed also by the many false Apocalypses, as those of Peter, Paul, Thomas, Stephen, Elias and Cerinthus, written in imitation of the true one. For as the many false Gospels, false Acts, and false Epistles were occasioned by true ones; and the writing many false Apocalypses, and ascribing them to Apostles and Prophets, argues that there was a true Apostolic one in great request with the first Christians: so this true one may well be suppos'd to have been written early, that there may be room in the Apostolic age for the writing of so many false ones afterwards, and fathering them upon Peter, Paul, Thomas, and others, who were dead before John. Caius, who was contemporary with Tertullian, [g] tells us that Cerinthus wrote his Revelations as a great Apostle, and pretended the visions were shewn him by Angels, asserting a *millennium* of carnal pleasures at Jerusalem after the resurrection; so that his Apocalypse was plainly written in imitation of John's: and yet he lived so early, that [h] he resisted the Apostles at Jerusalem in or before the first year of Claudius, that is, 26 years before the death of Nero, and [i] died before John."-
Sir Isaac Newton
The Nature of The Crawford Manuscript

John Gwynn has written at length concerning this unusual manuscript in his The Apocalypse of St. John, in a Syriac Version Hitherto Unknown .Gwynn believed the manuscript to be a copy of an early 7th century translation from Greek, yet significantly and radically different from The Harklean Syriac Version translated in A.D. 616 . He notes that the book contains more Hebraisms than any other NT book and that it is idiomatic- Aramaic used throughout, unlike The Harklean Version which is Graecianized (conformed to Greek language). He also is of the opinion that the writer was thoroughly familiar with the Peshitta O.T. and used its vocabulary and style extensively, listing dozens of words peculiar to that version found only in Crawford Revelation and not in The Peshitta N.T. .

I have a different view of the nature of this text which Gwynn's findings support; for instance, Hebraisms (or Aramaisms) would not come from Greek, they would come from Hebrew or Aramaic. Aramaic idioms, of which Gwynn lists a considerable number specifically, are evidence of original Aramaic, not Greek. The Peshitta O.T. vocabulary is Aramaic, not Greek, so the abundant usage of its style and vocabulary strongly indicates that The Crawford is an Aramaic original, not a translation from Greek.Greek primacy has ruled Western Biblical scholarship for so long that even the suggestion of an Aramaic original New Testament has been laughed out of the court of scholarship every time it has been proposed. I have uncovered evidence recently which overwhelms all Greek primacy claims

*and proves (and I use that word as appropriately as it can be used) that the original New Testament was written in Aramaic.I cannot present the case here, but refer the reader to my book, **Divine Contact-Discovery of The Original New Testament** , available at* http://aramaicnt.com .
Suffice it here to say that The Peshitta NT plus Gwynn's edition of The General Epistles and Revelation are demonstrated to be the original autographs of the Apostles. That claim may be ridiculed and regarded as suspect on the face of it, but the evidence is irrefutable , and the evidence isn't going away; neither is The Aramaic NT.
*The Aramaic text presented in **The Aramaic-English Interlinear NT** is what I believe is the letter perfect Divinely written original word of **The Living God**. Everyone who reads it will be judged by what he reads and is accountable before God to accept and obey it as His word and revelation. I count it a high honor and privilege to read it for myself and also to present this English translation of God's original utterance to The Apostle John on The Isle of Patmos circa AD 55. May you experience the revelation of Yeshua The Messiah from The Spirit of The God Who gave it to His Only Son. Amen.*

Chapter 1

1. The Revelation of Yeshua The Messiah, which God gave to him, to show his Servants what had been given to soon occur, and he symbolized it when he sent by his Angel to his Servant Yohannan,

* "He symbolized" – שודע - "Shooda" is an important key for unlocking the meaning of Revelation. Symbolic language and imagery is used throughout to represent eternal realities and future events, very similar to the prophesies of Daniel and Ezekiel and the visions Joseph had interpreted in Genesis. Here is Smith's Syriac Dictionary entry for the word – שודע - "Shooda" in the Shaphel mode:

> acknowledged. SHAPHEL ܐܫܘܕܥ to make clear, explain, teach ; to mean, notify, indicate, signify esp. symbolically , to symbolize, typify, prefigure,

2. Who witnessed the word of God and the testimony of Yeshua The Messiah - everything whatever he saw.

3. Blessed is the one who reads and those who hear the words of this prophecy and keep those things that are written in it, for the time is near.

4. Yohannan to the seven assemblies that are in Asia: Grace to you and peace from The One Who is, and was, and is coming, and from The Seven Spirits which are before his throne,

C * Most Greek mss. have απο θεου ο ων και ο ην και ο ερχομενος - "from God who is, and who was, and who is coming"; Some omit "God"; **all** the Greek readings here are a mess grammatically; three nominative (subject) cases are used where 3 genitives should be used as the object of απο –"from". This is an introduction to the quality of Greek in **The Apocalypse**, which is rather shoddy. I give here an exerpt from Charles Torrey:

"It has long been recognized that the New Testament is written in very poor Greek grammar, but very good Semitic grammar. Many sentences are inverted with a verb > noun format characteristic of Semitic languages.

Furthermore, there are several occurrences of the redundant "and". A number of scholars have shown in detail the Semitic grammar imbedded in the Greek New Testament books. (For example: Our Translated Gospels By Charles Cutler Torrey; Documents of the Primitive Church by Charles Cutler Torrey; An Aramaic Approach to The Gospels and Acts by Matthew Black; The Aramaic Origin of the Fourth Gospel by Charles Fox Burney; The Aramaic Origin of the Four Gospels by Frank Zimmerman and Semitisms of the Book of Acts by Max Wilcox)

In addition to the evidence for Semitic grammar imbedded in the Greek New Testament, the fact that serious grammatical errors are found in the Greek New Testament books may be added. Speaking of the Greek of Revelation, Charles Cutler Torrey states that it "...swarms with major offenses against Greek grammar." He calls it "linguistic anarchy", and says, "The grammatical monstrosities of the book, in their number and variety and especially in their startling character, stand alone in the history of literature." Torrey gives ten examples listed below:

1. Rev. 1:4 "Grace to you, and peace, from he who is and who was and who is to come" (all nom. case)
2. Rev. 1:15 "His legs were like burnished brass (neut. gender dative case) as in a furnace purified" (Fem. gender
sing. no, gen. case)
3. Rev. 11:3 "My witness (nom.) shall prophesy for many days clothed (accus.) in sackcloth."
4. Rev. 14:14 "I saw on the cloud one seated like unto a Son of Man (accus.) having (nom.) upon his head a golden
crown."
5. Rev. 14:19 "He harvested the vintage of The Earth, and cast it into the winepress (fem), the great (masc.) of the
wrath of God."
6. Rev. 17:4 "A golden cup filled with abominations (gen.) and with unclean things" (accus.)
7. Rev. 19:20 "The lake of blazing (fem.) fire (neut.).
8. Rev. 20:2 "And he seized the Dragon (accus.), the old serpent (nom.) who is the Devil and Satan, and bound
him."
9. Rev. 21:9 "Seven angels holding seven vessels (accus.) filled (gen.) with the seven last plagues."
10. Rev. 22:5 "They have no need of lamplight (gen.) nor of sunlight (accus.)."'''

The Aramaic text of The Crawford ms. has no such grammatical problems. Are we to believe the **original was written with poor Greek grammar** and that **the Aramaic translation is flawless ?** Some may believe just that; as for myself, I find no precedent for that position in any other book of scripture, in either OT or NT, nor does the Christian doctrine of inspiration of scripture allow for such a poor original text. The best objection one may offer is that we are left with poor copies of Revelation whose original Greek text was free from all such errors. It would be passing strange to find that not one manuscript or group of manuscripts remains with original readings and that only the errors in all the above cases survived. Aramaic primacy clears up the problem quite easily; **The Greek text is a translation of an Aramaic original.**

5. And from Yeshua The Messiah, the Trustworthy Witness, the Firstborn of the dead and The Ruler of the Kings of The Earth- him who loves us and has loosed* us from our sins by his blood.

** The Critical Greek text also has "**loosed us**"; The Majority Greek has "**washed us**".*
In DSS Aramaic script, these two readings may be: ܘܫܪܐ -"& loosed"

ܘܐܫܝܓ-"& washed"

Even though the Aramaic words above differ by scarcely one letter, this example is not decisively pro-Aramaic original, as the Greek readings are just as similar as the two in Aramaic: λουσαντι-"**Washed**" & λυσαντι-"**Loosed**", however, only the Greek mss. have variant readings here, and the Aramaic can account for both Greek readings. If the Aramaic were a translation of Greek, it bears no evidence in the form of variant readings (though Crawford ms. is the only one of its kind of Revelation) or in supporting any one Greek text type consistently or even with a semblance of uniformity, either here or in any lengthy portion of Revelation or any other part of the New Testament.

6. And he has made us The Priestly Kingdom to God and his Father; to him be glory and Empire to the eternity of eternities. Amen.

7. Behold, he comes with clouds and every eye shall see him, even those who pierced him, and all the families of The Earth shall mourn for him; yes and amen!

8. I am The Alap and The Tau, says THE LORD JEHOVAH God, he who is and has been and is coming, The Almighty.

* I submit an excellent article on this verse by Chris Lancaster, a long time Peshitta researcher and Peshitta primacy advocate"

The Greek:

εγω εμι το αλφα και το ω λεγει κυριος ό θεος ό ων και ό ην και ό ερχομενος ό παντοκρατωρ

(/ego emi to **alpha** kai to **o** legei kurios ho theos ho on kai ho en kai ho erchomenos ho pantokrator/)

Translation:

"I am the **Alpha** and the **O(mega)**, says the Lord God, who is and who was and who is to come, the Almighty."

Chapter 21 Verse 6

The Greek:

και ειπεν μοι γεγονα εγω το αλφα και το ω ή αρχη και το τελος ωγο τω διψωντι δωσω εκ τες πηγης του υδατος της ζωης δωρεαν

(/kai eipen moi gegona ego to **alpha** kai to **o** he arche kai to telos ogo to dipsonti doso ek tes peges tou udatos tes zoes dorean/)

Translation:

"And he said to me, They are come to pass. I am the **Alpha and the O(mega)**, the beginning and the end. I will give to him that is athirst of the fountain of the water of life freely."

Chapter 22 Verse 13

The Greek:

εγω το αλφα και το ω ό πρωτος και ό εσχατος ή αρχη και το τελος

(/ego to **alpha** kai to **o** ho protos kai ho eschatos he arche kai to telos/)

Translation:

"I am the **Alpha** and the **O(mega)**, the first and the last, the beginning and the end."

In the vast majority of Greek manuscripts, they state:

το αλφα και το ω (/to **alpha** kai to **o**/ : The Alpha and the O(mega))

αλφα (/alpha/ : Alpha) being the first letter of the Greek alphabet, and ω (omega), the last.

One VERY strange thing of note:

αλφα (/alpha/ : Alpha) is spelled out while ω (omega) is simply the single letter ω (omega).

All of the Aramaic texts of Revelation that survive to date:

'aléf 'af téu : The Alap, also the Tau)

[Note: in the above picture, the circled word on the left is the word for Tau in Aramaic. Aramaic is written from

right to left - Chris]

Alap is the first letter of the Aramaic alphabet, where Tau is the last, in parallel with the Greek Alpha and Omega.

How similar a lone ωμεγα (/omega/ : Omega) (or ω) looks like Tau [ܐܬ – Chris] in Estrangelo script!

Taking a look at how ωμεγα (/omega/ : Omega) was written at the time of the New Testament, we get a good idea

of what shape was recognized. The similarity is rather striking between Omega and the letters of Tau [ܐܬ –

Chris]

closely written together.

Since copies of this book were written by hand, if ܐܬ :

Tau was written closely together, it would be easily indistinguishable from an ωμεγα (/omega/ : Omega). The translators then must have simply thought to transliterate it, thinking that it was an ωμεγα (/omega/ : Omega) in the first place. Arguably this error can only go in one direction

9. I Yohannan am your brother and companion in suffering and in the patience which is in Yeshua*. I was in the island that is called Patmos, because of the word of God and because of the testimony of Yeshua The Messiah.

• Most Greek mss. have "**tribulation, Kingdom** and **patience**".

  * The Majority Greek adds "Χριστω"-"**Christ**"

10. And I was in The Spirit on the first day of the week*, and I heard behind me a loud voice like a trumpet,

* Greek has "κυριακη ημερα"-"**Lord's day**", which was a newly coined phrase when it was first written in the Greek of this verse. It is found nowhere else in non-Christian Greek lit..The Aramaic has simply **"first of the week"**, which is the word for "**Sunday**". The Aramaic would hardly have been a translation of the Greek.

11. Which said, "Those things which you have seen, write in a book and send to the seven assemblies: to Ephesaus, to Zmurna, to Pergamaus, to Thawatyra, to Sardis, to Philadelphia and to Laidiqia.

  * Byzantine Greek manuscripts add "**in Asia**";Critical Greek agrees here with the Aramaic text.

12. And I turned to know* that voice which spoke with me, and when I turned around, I saw seven menorahs of gold;

* Greek has "βλεπειν"-"**to see**".This word is somewhat misleading, since it emphasizes vision rather than understanding, whereas the Aramaic word למדע means "**to know**", which is much more to the point when "**a voice**" is the object.

13. And in the midst of the menorahs as the likeness of a man, and he wore an ephod* and he was girded around his chest with a golden wrap.

אפודא –"Ephoda" is not a translation of the Greek text, which has "ενδεδυμενον ποδηρη" – "clothed to the foot". Have a look at The LXX use of the word ποδηρη in Exodus alongside the Hebrew text it translates. The LXX and Hebrew has each its own English translation parallel to it:

Ex 25:7 και λιθους σαρδιου και λιθους εις την γλυφην εις την επωμιδα και τον ποδηρη
Ex 25:7 (LXXE) and sardius stones, and stones for the carved work of the breast-plate, and the full-length robe.
Ex 25:7 אבני-שהם ואבני מלאים לאפד ולחשן (BHS)
Ex 25:7 (AV) Onyx stones, and stones to be set in the ephod, and in the breastplate. (Aramaic Peshitta-ברסמא-breastplate)

Ex 28:4 και αυται αι στολαι ας ποιησουσιν το περιστηθιον και την επωμιδα και τον ποδηρη και χιτωνα κοσυμβωτον και κιδαριν και ζωνην και ποιησουσιν στολας αγιας ααρων και τοις υιοις αυτου εις το ιερατευειν μοι
Ex 28:4 (LXXE) And these are the garments which they shall make: the breast-plate, and the shoulder-piece, and the full-length robe, and the tunic with a fringe, and the tire, and the girdle; and they shall make holy garments for Aaron and his sons to minister to me as Priests.
Ex 28:4 ועשו בגדי-קדש לאהרן אחיך ולבניו לכהנו-לי יעשו חשן ואפוד ומעיל וכתנת תשבץ מצנפת ואבנט ואלה הבגדים אשר (BHS)
Ex 28:4 (AV) And these [are] the garments which they shall make; a breastplate, and an ephod, and a robe, and a broidered coat, a mitre, and a girdle: and they shall make holy garments for Aaron thy brother, and his sons, that he may minister unto me in the Priest's office.

Ex 28:31 και ποιησεις υποδυτην ποδηρη ολον υακινθινον
Ex 28:31 ¶ (LXXE) (28:27) And thou shalt make the full-length tunic all of blue.
Ex 28:31 ועשית את-מעיל האפוד כליל תכלת (BHS)
Ex 28:31 ¶ (AV) And thou shalt make the robe of the ephod all [of] blue.

Ex 29:5 και λαβων τας στολας ενδυσεις ααρων τον αδελφον σου και τον χιτωνα τον ποδηρη και την επωμιδα και το λογειον και συναψεις αυτω το λογειον προς την επωμιδα
Ex 29:5 (LXXE) And having taken the garments, thou shalt put on Aaron thy brother both the full-length robe and the ephod and the oracle; and thou shalt join for him the oracle to the ephod.
Ex 29:5 ואת-האפד ואת-החשן ואפדת לו בחשב האפד והלבשת את-אהרן את-הכתנת ואת מעיל האפד ולקחת את-הבגדים (BHS)
Ex 29:5 (AV) And thou shalt take the garments, and put upon Aaron the coat, and the robe of the ephod, and the ephod, and the breastplate, and gird him with the curious girdle of the ephod: (Aramaic Peshitta-ארוזא-girdle)

Ex 35:9 και λιθους σαρδιου και λιθους εις την γλυφην εις την επωμιδα και τον ποδηρη
Ex 35:9 (LXXE) (35:8) and sardine stones, and stones for engraving for the shoulder-piece and full-length robe.
Ex 35:9 ואבני-שהם ואבני מלאים לאפוד ולחשן (BHS)
Ex 35:9 (AV) And onyx stones, and stones to be set for the ephod, and for the breastplate.

Eze 9:2 και ιδου εξ ανδρες ηρχοντο απο της οδου της πυλης της υψηλης της βλεπουσης προς βορραν και εκαστου πελυξ εν τη χειρι αυτου και εις ανηρ εν μεσω αυτων ενδεδυκως ποδηρη και ζωνη σαπφειρου επι της οσφυος αυτου και εισηλθοσαν και εστησαν εχομενοι του θυσιαστηριου του χαλκου
Eze 9:2 (LXXE) And, behold, six men came from the way of the high gate that looks toward the north, and each one's axe was in his hand; and there was one man in the midst of them clothed with a long robe down to the feet, and a sapphire girdle was on his loins: and they came in and stood near the brazen altar.
Eze 9:2 וקסת הספר במתניו ויבאו ויעמדו אצל מזבח הנחשת ואיש כלי מפצו בידו ואיש-אחד בתוכם לבש בדים אנשים באים מדרך-שער העליון אשר מפנה צפונה והנה ששה (BHS)
Eze 9:2 (AV) And, behold, six men came from the way of the higher gate, which lieth toward the north, and every man a slaughter weapon in his hand; and one man among them [was] clothed with linen, with a writer's inkhorn by his side: and they went in, and stood beside the brasen altar. (Peshitta ברצא-fine white linen)

Eze 9:3 και δοξα θεου του ισραηλ ανεβη απο των χερουβιν η ουσα επ αυτων εις το αιθριον του οικου και εκαλεσεν τον ανδρα τον ενδεδυκοτα τον ποδηρη ος ειχεν επι της οσφυος αυτου την ζωνην
Eze 9:3 (LXXE) And the glory of the God of Israel, that was upon them, went up from the cherubs to the porch of the house. And he called the man that was clothed with the long robe, who had the girdle on his loins;
Eze 9:3 אל-האיש הלבש הבדים אשר קסת הספר במתניו מעל הכרוב אשר היה עליו אל מפתן הבית ויקרא וכבוד אלהי ישראל נעלה (BHS)
Eze 9:3 (AV) And the glory of the God of Israel was gone up from the cherub, whereupon he was, to the threshold of the house. And he called to the man clothed with linen, which [had] the writer's inkhorn by his side. (Peshitta ברצא-fine white linen)

Eze 9:11 και ιδου ο ανηρ ο ενδεδυκως τον ποδηρη και εζωσμενος τη ζωνη την οσφυν αυτου και απεκρινατο λεγων πεποιηκα καθως ενετειλω μοι
Eze 9:11 (LXXE) And, behold, the man clothed with the long robe, and girt with the girdle about his loins, answered and said, I have done as thou didst command me.
Eze 9:11 הקסת במתניו משיב דבר לאמר עשיתי כאשר צויתני והנה האיש לבש הבדים אשר (BHS)
Eze 9:11 (AV) And, behold, the man clothed with linen, which [had] the inkhorn by his side, reported the matter, saying, I have done as thou hast commanded me. (Peshitta ברצא-fine white linen)

Zec 3:4 και απεκριθη και ειπεν προς τους εστηκοτας προ προσωπου αυτου λεγων αφελετε τα ιματια τα ρυπαρα απ αυτου και ειπεν προς αυτον ιδου αφηρηκα τας ανομιας σου και ενδυσατε αυτον ποδηρη
Zec 3:4 (LXXE) (3:5) And [the Lord] answered and spoke to those who stood before him, saying, Take away the filthy raiment from him: and he said to him, Behold, I have taken away thine iniquities: and clothe ye him with a long robe,
Zec 3:4 ראה העברתי מעליך עונך והלבש אתך מחלצות לאמר הסירו הבגדים הצאים מעליו ויאמר אליו ויען ויאמר אל-העמדים לפניו (BHS)
Zec 3:4 (AV) And he answered and spake unto those that stood before him, saying, Take away the filthy garments from him. And unto him he said, Behold, I have caused thine iniquity to pass from thee, and I will clothe thee with change of raiment.

In Exodus 28:31, the Hebrew word אפוד "Ephod" (compare the Aramaic word in Rev. 1:13 אפודא "Ephod") may have been translated with the Greek word ποδηρη ; ποδηρη parallels the following Aramaic words in The OT (In Dead Sea Scroll script): אפודא-ephod, כרסא-breastplate, אפוד-ephod , כרובא-girdle, בוצא-fine white linen. אפודא is matched in The Harklean Syriac Version by פודרא –Pawdara-"A long Priestly garment down to the feet". Here is a comparison of two Aramaic words in Ashuri script:

אפודא –"Ephod"
בוצא-"Fine linen"

DSS script:
אפודא –"Ephod"
בוצא -"Fine linen"

These two words in DSS script are strangely similar **(80% correlation)**.

Estrangela script:
ܐܦܘܕܐ –"Ephod"
ܒܘܨܐ -"Fine linen"

They are not nearly as similar in Ashuri or Estrangela scripts.

The second word בוצא-"Bawtsa" is represented in The LXX by the Greek ποδηρη in several places. Thus the Greek reading ποδηρη may be explained on the basis of the Aramaic reading אפודא –"Ephod". The Aramaic word is not from the Greek ποδηρη -"down to the feet". The word "Ephoda" is a Semitic word which occurs once in The Peshitta OT (Hosea 3:4) and once in The Aramaic NT –right here.

14. And his head and his hair were white as wool and like snow, and his eyes were like flames of fire.
15. And his feet were in the form of the brass of Lebanon* which is heated in a furnace, and his voice was like the sound of many waters.

* The Greek of Westcott & Hort's edition has χαλκολιβανω ("Burnished brass"- neuter noun, dative case) matched with πεπυρωμενης ("Burning"- feminine noun , genitive case) ` this is a grammatical "no , no" in Greek. Both case & gender should agree for these two words. The Greek χαλκολιβανω seems also to be an invented word, not occurring elsewhere in Greek lit. It appears a translator made a compound Greek word out of two Aramaic words "Brass" & "Lebanon", which did not exist before and confused all the translators. Most translations of the Greek have, "Burnished brass" as the meaning. The Greek of **The Apocalypse** ("**Gilyana**" in Aramaic) seems to contain many new compound words like χαλκολιβανω which combine two Aramaic words to form a new Greek word.

16. And he had in his right hand seven stars, and a sharp lance* proceeded from his mouth, and I saw* him like the Sun appearing in its strength.

* רומחא – "Rawmkha" is used in Luke 2:35 and here in The NT. It is a feminine noun, contrary to Smith's Syriac Dictionary, and is accompanied by a feminine verb in Luke 2:35 and by a feminine adjective here (חריפתא – "Kharripta- "Sharp"). Greek has "ρομφαια διστομος οξεια"-"a sword double edged sharp" (Literal word order). Here is the Aramaic for "Double" : תרינתא –"Trayyanita";

Compare the Aramaic here for "**Sharp**"- חריפתא. It seems that here and in Rev. 19:15, חריפתא - "**Kharripta**- "Sharp" was read doubly as both "double" and "sharp".
Here are both words in Dead Sea Scroll script:

חריפתא-"Sharp"
תרינתא-"Double"

Ashuri Aramaic Script:
חריפתא-"Sharp"
תרינתא-"Double"

Estrangela Aramaic Script
ܚܪܝܦܬܐ-"Sharp"
ܬܪܝܢܬܐ-"Double"

The two words are even more similar in Ashuri script than in DSS script. You can see how even the **Nun-Yodh** pair- נ could have been mistaken for **Pe-** פ. It seems our Greek translator's vision was not too "sharp" and instead was seeing "double"! The Ashuri pair have at least **90%** letter correlation
   * Greek has οψις αυτου -"**His appearance**" .
Here is the Aramaic Crawford reading : וחזתה – "**& I saw Him**".
Compare the Aramaic for the Greek reading: וחזוה "**& His appearance**"-
Here is the Aramaic Crawford reading in DSS script: וחזתה –"**& I saw Him**".
Compare the Aramaic for the Greek reading in DSS script: וחזוה "**& His appearance**"-
Here is the Aramaic Crawford reading in Estrangela script: ܘܚܙܬܗ –"**& I saw Him**".
Compare the Aramaic for the Greek reading in Estrangela: ܘܚܙܘܗ "**& His appearance**"-

Any of these Aramaic scripts presents at least **80% correlation** between Aramaic word pairs.

Greek for "**I saw**" would be ειδον – not very like οψις – "**appearance**" .The Greek does not seem to account for the Aramaic reading; The Aramaic can account for the Greek.

17. And when I saw him, I fell at his feet like a dead man, and he laid his right hand upon me saying, "Do not be afraid, for I am The First and The Last;
18. I am he who lived and died, and behold, I am alive to the eternity of eternities, amen, and I have the key of Death and of Sheol.
19. Write, therefore, whatever you have seen and those things that are, and *that* are going to come to pass after these things.
20. The mystery of the seven stars which you saw in my right hand and the seven menorahs: the seven stars are the Messengers of the seven assemblies, and the seven menorahs of gold which you saw* are the seven assemblies.
   * A group of Greek mss. has "**which you saw**" , including the Textus Receptus , are in agreement with the Crawford ms. here.

Chapter 2
1. And to The Messenger of the assembly of Ephesaus write: Thus says he who holds the

seven stars in his hand, he who walks among the menorahs of gold:'"

2. "I know your works, your toil and your patience, and that you cannot tolerate evil ones, and you have tested those who claim to be Apostles, and they are not, and you have found them false."

3. "And you have patience and you have endured because of my name and you have not tired."

4. "But I have something against you, because you have left your former love."

5. "Remember from where you have come out and do the former works; but if not, I will come against you and I will remove your menorah, unless you repent.

6. But you have this, that you hate the works of the Naqolaytans, those things which I also hate.

7. He who has an ear to hear, let him hear what The Spirit is speaking to the assemblies, and I shall give to the victor to eat of the tree of life, which is in The Paradise of God.

8. And to The Messenger of the assembly of Zmurna, write: "Thus says The First and The Last- he who was dead and lives:"

9. "I know your suffering and your poverty (but you are rich) and the blasphemy of those who call themselves Jews of the Judeans, when they are not, but are the synagogue of Satan."

10. "Be afraid in none of those things that you will suffer; behold The Devil will throw some of you into prison to be tested and you will have suffering for ten days; be faithful unto death, and I will give you a crown of life."

11. "He who has an ear, let him hear what The Spirit says to the assemblies. 'Whoever overcomes will not be hurt by the second death.'"

12. And to The Messenger who is in the assembly of Pergamum, write: 'Thus says he who has the sharp sword of two edges.'"

13. "'I know where you dwell: the place of Satan's throne, and you keep my name and have not denied my faith, and in the days when you and my faithful witness* contended for the sake of all my faithful witnesses, he was murdered among you.'"

Greek translator who seems to have also played the role of editor as well. A second phrase – "**for the sake of all My witnesses**" is missing in the Greek texts; after careful inspection , I saw that "**for the sake of all**" – "**Mettul d'col**" was probably translated as the Greek name Αντιπας -"**Antipas**", which strange to say, means "**For the cause of all**", from two Greek words, αντι –"**for,instead of, for the cause of**" + πας -"**all,every**". So may the Greek translator have put a name to "**My witness**" as "**Antipas**".

The Aramaic from the verse:-
(of all) דכל (for the sake) מטל
(faithful) מהימנא (My) דילי (witnesses) סהדא

using the hypothetical Greek method above could be rendered: "**Antipas my faithful witness**". סהדא "sahda" can be plural or singular –"witnesses" or "witness".

Why would a translator add all the information in the Aramaic (underlined words in prose translation) if the Greek were the original ? Why also would he have not simply copied "**Antipas**" instead of translating it into a phrase "for the sake of all" ? Invention and addition are not the signs of normal translation; omission and simplification are; therefore the Greek evinces evidence of being a translation here as in many other places in Revelation and in other NT books.

14. "But I have a few things against you, for you have there those who hold the doctrine of the Balaam, him who taught Balaq to cast a stumbling block before the children of Israel, to eat sacrifices of idols and to commit fornication."

15. "So you also have those who hold the doctrine of the Naqolaytans, likewise.

16. Repent therefore, or else I shall come upon you at once, and I shall make war with them with the sword of my mouth."

17. "And he who has an ear, let him hear what The Spirit speaks to the assemblies: 'To the one who is victorious I shall give of the manna which is hidden, and I shall give him a white pebble, and upon the pebble, a new name in writing that no man knows except he who receives.'"

18. "And to The Messenger who is in the assembly in Thawatyra, write: 'Thus says The Son of God, he who has eyes like flames of fire and his feet like the brass of Lebanon."

19. "I know your works, your love, your faith, your service and your patience, and your latter works are more than the first."

20. "I have much against you, because you are tolerating your wife* Jezebel who says about herself that she is a Prophetess, and teaches and seduces my Servants to commit fornication and to eat the sacrifices of idols."

---

* Greek has "**of Antipas**". "**Antipas**" in Aramaic would be אנתיפס , אנטיפס or אנתיפאס. Frankly this does not look like any Aramaic word in the text, so I don't see the explanation for the Greek reading based on word similarity in Aramaic. I do see that the Aramaic verse speaks of "**My witness**" and does not name him. This may have presented a problem to a

* The Byzantine Greek mss. (Majority text) agrees with "**your wife**" whereas the Critical and TR Greek have simply "την γυναικα"-"**woman**".

21. "And I gave her time for repentance, and she did not choose to turn from her fornication."

22. "Behold, I shall cast her into a coffin*, and those who commit adultery with her into great suffering, unless they repent of their deeds."

* Greek has κλινην "a bed". The Aramaic ערסא can refer to " a bed" , "a litter" or "a bier". "A bed" makes no sense in this context.

23. "And I shall kill her children by Death, and all the assemblies will know that I search the kidneys and the hearts, and I shall give to everyone of you according to your works."

24. "I say to you and to the rest who are in Thawatyra, all of those who do not have this doctrine, those who have not known the depths of Satan, as they say: I shall not lay upon you any other burden."

25. "That which you have, therefore, hold fast until I come."

26. "To him who is victorious and keeps my works, I shall give authority over the nations,"

27. "To Shepherd them with a rod of iron, and like the vessels of a potter you shall shatter them, for in the same manner I have also received of my Father."

28. "And I shall give him the Star of the Morning."

29. "He who has an ear, let him hear what The Spirit is saying to the assemblies."

Chapter 3

1. "And to The Messenger who is in the assembly of Sardis write: Thus says he who has The Seven Spirits of God and the seven stars: I know your works and the name that you have, and that you are alive and are dying."

2. "Be vigilant and confirm what remains of those things that are ready to die, for I have not found you *such* that your works are perfect before God."

3. "Remember how you have heard and received; take heed and return. But if you do not wake up, I shall come upon you as a thief, and you will not know which hour I shall come upon you."

4. "But I have a few names in Sardis, those who have not defiled their garments, and they walk before me in white and they are worthy."

5. "He who overcomes in this way is garbed with a white garment, and I shall not blot out his name from The Book of Life, and I shall

confess his name before my Father and before his Angels."

6. "Whoever has an ear, let him hear what The Spirit speaks to the assemblies."

7. "And to The Messenger of the assembly in Philadelphia write: 'Thus says The Holy One, The True One, he who has the key of David, The One who opens and there is none who shuts, and he shuts and there is none who opens:"

The Crawford text of this verse conforms more closely to The Peshitta reading of Isaiah 22:22 than does the Greek or The Harklean Aramaic text, and also to the Hebrew present participles-"**who shuts**", "**who opens**", more closely than the Greek does. Even the Aramaic phrases (& there is none who closes) דאחד ולית & (& there is none who opens) ולית דפתח are identical in **The Peshitta of Isaiah** where the black highlighted letters are shown in bold type, while the Harklean has לא אנש אחד -"no man shuts" and פתח לא אנש -"no man opens", conforming to the Greek readings.Here is the Hebrew verse of Isaiah 22:22 in interlinear form:

(& I shall place) ונתתי
(of house of David) בית-דוד (key) מפתח
(on his shoulder) על-שכמו
(opens) פתח (& none) ואין (& he shuts) וסגר (shuts) סגר (& none)ואין (& he opens) ופתח
Isa 22:22

8. "I know your works, and behold, I have set an open door before you which no man can shut, because you have a little power, and you have kept my word and have not denied my name."

9. "And behold, I grant some of the synagogue of Satan, of those who say about themselves that they are Jews and are not, but they are lying, behold, I shall make them come and worship before your feet and to know that I love you."

10. "Because you have kept the word of my patience, I also shall keep you from the trial that is going to come over the entire inhabited world, to test the inhabitants of The Earth."

11. "I come at once. Hold fast whatever you have, lest someone take your crown."

12. "And I will make the overcomer a pillar in The Temple of God and he will not go outside again, and I shall write upon him The Name of my God, and the name of The City, The New Jerusalem, which descends from my God, and my new Name."

13. "Let him who has an ear hear what The Spirit says to the assemblies."

14. "And to The Messenger of the assembly of the Laidiqians* write: "Thus says The

Eternal, The Trustworthy and True Witness, and The Source of The Creation of God:"

● **T.R.** The Greek mss. (Byzantine Majority + The Critical Greek text) have - εν λαοδικεια –"**in Laodicea**"; The Textus Receptus (KJV Greek text base) has λαοδικεων –"**of Laodiceans**". This agrees with the Aramaic reading here. The Textus Receptus has a good number of readings which differ from other Greek (Byzantine and Critical) texts and which agree with The Peshitta and Crawford ms. . The Aramaic Crawford ms. does not follow The TR Greek text or any other Greek text known. All Greek texts are supporting witnesses derivable from The Crawford Aramaic text.

● An interesting note in **Thayer's Greek-English Lexicon** under the entry for λαοδικεια -"**Laodicea**" documents that Laodicea, Colossae and Hierapois were destroyed by an earthquake in AD 66 . Laodicea was not rebuilt until 120 years later by Marcus Aurelius. This little known fact is extensively documented by Bishop Lightfoot in His commentary on Colossians and Philemon, pp 274-300. This says volumes about the date for The Book of Revelation, does it not ? It must have been written before AD 66 , else there had been no Laodicea left to which John could write! Tacitus, the Roman historian, wrote that Laodicea "**without any relief from us,recovered itself from its own resources.**"Tacitus wrote this in the early second century. Another source says that Laodicea "**lay in ruins for quite a period of time" until the Roman emperor Hadrian, at the beginning of the second century (reigned AD 117-138) revived it after he visited the place.** "It was almost totally rebuilt during the reign (AD 188-217) of Marcus Aurelius Antoninus (Nicknamed Caracalla)." There was apparently no major rebuilding of Laodicea before the second century and it is highly unlikely that this destruction should go unmentioned if a letter to its church were written after AD 66 to a place in ruins and which furthermore boasts ,"**I am rich and affluent and have need of nothing**" (v. 17). It is amazing that modern Bible commentators seem to be completely ignorant of this historical information, dating the writing of Revelation at AD 95- an absurdly late date.

15."I know your works; you are neither cold nor hot; because it is necessary that you be either cold or hot,"
16."And you are lukewarm and neither cold nor hot, I am going to vomit you from my mouth."
17."Because you said that you are rich, and, 'I have prospered, and I lack nothing', and you do not know that you are sick and wretched and poor * and naked,"

Greek mss. have τυφλος –"**Blind**" after "**Poor**", which The Aramaic Crawford does not have. The Aramaic for "**Blind**" is usually סמיא . Have a look at this word and "**Poor**" – מסכנא in **DSS Aramaic script** :

א⋏רסמ-י-"& Blind"
אנרסמ-י-"& Poor"
Estrangela script:
ܣܡܝܐ-"& Blind"
ܡܣܟܢܐ-"& Poor"

The DSS Aramaic **Simkat** ס & **Mim** מ (each word has both letters in corresponding places) appear more similar to each other than the Estrangela counterparts
ܣ & ܡ ,thus making it more likely a translator would

confuse the DSS script words than the Estrangela script words. The DSS letters ⋏ -**Yodh** & נ **Nun** are also much more similar (⋏ -**Yodh** & **Kap** - כ also) than in other scripts.
Another possible explanation for the "**Blind**" reading is a double reading of the word דויא (Dawya)– "**Wretched**". Below are the readings for "Blind" & "Wretched" in 3 Aramaic scripts:

Ashuri:
עורא (Awar)-"Blind"
דויא (Dawya)-"Wretched"
Estrangela:
ܥܘܪܐ (Awar)-"Blind"
ܕܘܝܐ (Dawya)-"Wretched"
Dead Sea Scroll:
אꞱꞱꟼ (Awar) -"Blind"
אꟼꟼꞱ (Dawya)-"Wretched"

Notice again how the DSS script pair looks most similar. Just a slight turning of ⋏ -(Yod) in אꟼꟼꞱ and you have a ר —(Resh) in אꞱꞱꟼ . The first letter in each also look very similar - ע (Ayin) & ד (Dalet); just a little tilt to the Dalet, and you have Ayin.

I do not pretend to ignore the possibility that an Aramaen might have translated this text from Greek and simply omitted a word ("**Blind**") , which is much more common than the addition of words in translation. I simply offer an explanation in support of the converse theory of Aramaic primacy here, of which this author is fully convinced.
Frankly, the Greek text of Revelation is rather poor, as shown in the extensive notes above. The original Greek scribe was most likely working under several handicaps:
1.He was probably copying in secret, for fear of his life under Nero's mad hatred for all people and things Christian. 2. He would have copied at night, most likely, under poor light conditions.
3. He was probably not extremely conversant with the difficult and obscure Aramaic script John used from Israel (Herodian-Dead Sea script).
4. We don't know how good his eyesight was, he may have suffered from mild dyslexia, as I see several places where it appears he may have reversed letter positions within words, and
5. He does not seem to have been too keen with Greek grammar, hence, Greek was probably not his native language. All things considered, he did a commendable translation job, overall!

18."I counsel you to buy gold from me, proved by fire, that you may prosper, and white garments to put on, lest the shame of your nakedness be revealed, and eye salve to apply that you may see."
19."I rebuke and discipline those whom I love. Be zealous therefore and return."
20."Behold, I stand at the door and I shall knock. If a man listens to my voice and will open the door, I also shall come in and I shall have supper with him, and he with me."
21."And I shall grant the overcomer to sit with me on my throne, just as I have overcome and I sit with my Father on his throne."
22."Whoever has an ear, let him hear what The Spirit says to the assemblies."

Chapter 4

1. After these things I saw, and behold, a door opened in Heaven, and a voice which I heard like a trumpet speaking with me saying, "Come up here, and I shall show you whatever is granted to happen after these things."

2. And at once I was in The Spirit, and behold a throne fixed in Heaven, and upon the throne sat he;

3. And he who sat was as the likeness of the appearance of Jasper red quartz stone and of red and white Sardius, and a rainbow of the clouds which encircled the throne was like the appearance of an emerald;

4. And around the throne, twenty four thrones, and upon those thrones, twenty four Elders who sat wearing white garments and crowns of gold upon their heads.

5. And from the throne proceed thunders and lightnings and voices, and seven lamps were burning before that throne, which are The Seven Spirits of God.

6. And before the throne, a sea of glass as the likeness of crystal, and in the midst of the throne and around the throne, four beasts that were full of eyes, front and back.

7. The first beast was like a lion; the second had the likeness of a calf; the third beast had a face like a man and the fourth beast, the likeness of a flying eagle.

8. Each one of these four beasts stood and had from its appendages and over it six surrounding wings, and from within they are full of eyes and are not silent day or night, saying, "Holy, holy, holy, LORD JEHOVAH God Almighty, he who is and has been and is coming."

* מריא –"Marya" is Aramaic for "Yahweh" and occurs 14 times as such in this ms. of Revelation. The first is 1:8 and the last is 22:20 , where Jesus is addressed as "Marya Yeshua" – "Yahweh Jesus". It appears 239 times in The Aramaic NT – in all but 7 books (not in Gal, 1 Thess, Titus, Philemon, 1st, 2nd, 3rd John). None of The Greek NT books has this or any word like it, as Greek has no equivalent for "Yahweh".

9. And when these four beasts give glory and honor and thanks to him who sits upon the throne and to The One Living to the eternity of eternities, amen,

10. The twenty four Elders fall down in front of him who sits upon the throne and worship The Living One for the eternity of eternities, amen, and cast their crowns before the throne saying,

11. "You are worthy, Our Lord and Our God, to receive the glory and the honor and the power, because you have created all things, and by your pleasure they exist and were created."

Chapter 5

1. And I saw in the right hand of him who sits upon the throne, a scroll inscribed from the inside and from the outside, and sealed with seven seals.

"Sealed seven seals" in Aramaic is "Tabaya taba shaba", which is really a play on words and poetic in Aramaic. There is more of this in Revelation, as you will see. The poetic element is strong evidence for an Aramaic original. The Greek does not exhibit this trait as does The Peshitta-Crawford Aramaic NT text.

2. And I saw another mighty Angel preaching with a loud voice: "Who is worthy to open the scroll and to loosen its seals?"

3. And there was none able in Heaven or in Earth, nor any under The Earth, to open the scroll and to open its seals and look upon it.

"L'kethava w'lamashra
Tabaway w'lamakhzay"
is more poetry (two couplets) in the last four Aramaic words of the verse. Not only does the Greek not have this poetic element, but The Harklean Syriac version (translated from Greek mss.) also lacks it here.

4. I was weeping much because none was found worthy to open the scroll and to loosen its seals,

5. And one of the Elders said to me, "Do not weep; behold, The Lion from the tribe of Judah, The Root of David, has prevailed to open the scroll and its seals."

6. And I saw in the midst of a throne and of The Four Beasts and of the Elders, a Lamb, which was as if it were slain, and it had seven horns and seven eyes, which are The Seven Spirits of God sent into the whole Earth.

7. And he came and took the scroll from the hand * of him who sat on the throne.

* Greek lacks "the scroll" ;Greek also has "out of the right of Him".

8. And when he had received the scroll, The Four Beasts and twenty four Elders fell down before the Lamb, while each one of them had a stringed instrument and a vessel of gold full of sweet spices, which are the prayers of The Holy Ones,

9. Singing a new hymn of praise, and they were saying, "You are worthy to take the scroll and to loosen its seals, because you were slain and you have redeemed us by your

blood to God from every tribe, nation and people,"

10. "And you have made them a Kingdom, Priests and Kings to our God, and they shall reign over The Earth."

11. And I saw and heard as *it were* the voices of many Angels around the throne and of The Beasts and of the Elders, and their number was ten thousand ten thousands and thousands of thousands.

12. And they were saying with a loud voice, "Worthy is the slain Lamb to receive power, wealth, wisdom, strength, honor, glory and blessing."

13. And every creature which is in Heaven and in Earth, under The Earth, in the Sea and all that is in them, I also heard saying to him sitting upon the throne and to the Lamb: "Blessing and honor and glory and dominion for the eternity of eternities."

14. And when The Four Beasts said, "Amen", The Elders fell down and worshiped.

Chapter 6

1. And I saw when The Lamb opened one of the seven seals, and I heard one of The Four Beasts speaking like the sound of thunder: "Come and see*."

* The Critical Greek omits "**& see**".The Majority Greek has this phrase.

2. And I heard and I saw and behold, a white horse, and he who sat upon it had a bow, and a crown was given to him, and he went out and gave victory, and was conquering and would conquer.

* Greek lacks the words , "**& I heard**".This verse has a Semiticism which would never come from Greek- the same verb root is used three times in a row in different modes and tenses as predicate to the same subject ("he who sat") -**Zkay,Zka,D'nezka-"giving victory,conquering, to conquer**". The Greek has only two verbs where The Aramaic has three.

3. And when he opened the second seal, I heard the second Beast which said, "Come."

4. And a red horse went out, and to him who sat upon it was given to take peace from The Earth and to kill each one, and a great sword was given to him.

5. And when he opened the third seal, I heard the third Beast saying, "Come*", and behold, a black horse, and he who sat upon him had a balance scale in his hand.

* The Majority Greek adds "**& see**".The Critical Greek lacks this phrase.

6. And I heard a voice from among The Beasts, which said, "A two-quart measure of wheat for a denarius and three two-quart measures of barley for a denarius, and you shall not harm the wine and the oil."

* **Denarius** – A denarius was roughly an average day's wage.

7. When he opened the fourth seal, I heard the voice of a Beast saying, "Come*."

* The Majority Greek adds "**& see**".The Critical Greek lacks this phrase.

8. And I saw a pale horse, and the name of him who sat upon it was Death, and Sheol joined him and authority was given to him over a fourth of The Earth to kill with the sword, with starvation, with Death, and by the animals of The Earth.

9. And when he opened the fifth seal, I saw under the altar the souls of those who had been murdered for the word of God and for the testimony of Yeshua* which they had.

* The Majority Greek has "of The Lamb".The Critical Greek lacks this phrase.The Crawford has "of Yeshua".Ten Byzantine mss. have "**Ihsou Cristou**"- "**of Jesus Christ**".

10. And they cried with a great voice, and they were saying, "How long, LORD JEHOVAH, holy and true, do you not judge and avenge our blood upon the inhabitants of The Earth?"

11. And to each and every one of them was given a white robe, and it was said that they should rest for a little season of time until their companions and their brothers were also perfected, who were going to be killed, even as they had been.

12. And I saw when he opened the sixth seal, and there was a great earthquake, and the Sun was blackened like sackcloth of hair, and the whole moon became like blood.

13. And the stars of the Heavens fell upon The Earth, like a fig tree casting its figs when it is shaken by a strong wind.

14. And the Heavens were parted like scrolls being rolled up, and every hill and all the islands were moved from their places.

15. And the Kings of The Earth and The Princes and Captains of thousands and the rich and the mighty and every Servant and every Free Person, hid themselves in caves and in the rocks of the mountains,

16. And they said to the mountains and rocks, "Fall on us and hide us from before the face of the Lamb,"

17. "Because the great day of his* anger has come, and who is able to stand?"

*Critical Greek has **"Their anger"**;Majority Greek has **"His anger"**.

דרוגזהון – "d'rugzahown" is literally "their anger", which grammatically refers to the plural אפוהי - "faces" in verse 16. The Greek of verses 16 & 17 has "hide us <u>from the face of Him Who sits on The Throne and</u> from <u>the wrath</u> of The Lamb, for the great day of [Their] His wrath is come….The underlined words are not found in The Crawford ms.. (I believe the Aramaic of these verses can account for the Greek readings. Rev. 5:13 has "**unto Him Who sits on The Throne and unto The Lamb**", so the phrase was probably selected to correct what appeared to be a problem in the Aramaic text, recreating a familiar phrase. The plural pronoun in"**their** anger" was confusing to a Greek translator who did not relate it to the plural "**faces**"(אפא –"Apha"is always used in the plural form,even when singular in meaning), so he inserted ,"**Him Who sits upon The Throne**", before "**The Lamb**" to give a plural reference point for דרוגזהון - d'rugzahown -"of Their anger".(אפא – "Apha" is technically feminine, though it can have masculine predicates).

אפוהי –"His nostrils", from אפא - ("Apha"-"Nostrils,Face,Presence") is very similar to the Hebrew אף –("Aph"–"Anger,<u>Wrath</u>,Face,Nostrils").The Greek translator apparently translated אפוהי as the Aramaic word אפא –"Face" once in "the face of Him …" and then again he translated it with a Hebrew meaning –"Wrath" in אפוהי דאמרא -"the wrath of the lamb". These facts can explain the Greek readings , "**Him Who sits on The Throne**", "**the wrath of The Lamb**" , and "**His anger**" (Byzantine & Textus Receptus) which reflects the Aramaic reading here, referring to **The Lamb** in v. 16 , as well as the Greek reading , "**Their anger**" (Critical text of Westcott & Hort) .

Chapter 7

1. And after this, I saw four Angels standing over the four corners of The Earth and holding the four winds, that the winds would not blow on The Earth, neither on the Sea, neither on any tree.

2. And I saw another Angel ascending from the dawning of the Sun and having the seal of **THE LIVING GOD**, and he cried with a loud voice to the four Angels to whom it was given to harm The Earth and the Sea,

3. And he said, "Do not harm the land, neither the Sea, nor the trees, until we seal the Servants of God on their foreheads."

4. And I heard the number who were sealed - one hundred forty-four thousand, from all the tribes of Israel:

5. From the tribe of Yehudah, twelve thousand; from the tribe of Reuben, twelve thousand; from the tribe of Gad, twelve thousand;

*רוביל –"Rubil" is the spelling of The Peshitta OT (found 72 times in Genesis to Ezekiel) also found in The Crawford Aramaic here for ראובן -"Reuben".

6. From the tribe of Asher, twelve thousand; from the tribe of Naphtali, twelve thousand; from the tribe of Menashe, twelve thousand;

7. From the tribe of Shimeon, twelve thousand; from the tribe of Issachar, twelve thousand; from the tribe of Levi, twelve thousand;

8. From the tribe of Zebulon, twelve thousand; from the tribe of Joseph, twelve thousand; from the tribe of Benjamin, twelve thousand sealed.

9. After this I saw many multitudes which were impossible to count, which were of all people, generations, nations* and languages, standing before the throne and before the Lamb, and wearing white garments and with palms in their hands.

*אמון "Amwan" , plural of אומתא "Ummta" means "Nations","Communities" , "Peoples","Classes".

10. And they shouted with a great voice, and they were saying, "Salvation to our God, and to him Who sits upon the throne, and unto the Lamb!"

And they shouted in a great voice
and they were saying ,
"Salvation to our God
and to Him sitting upon the throne
and unto The Lamb".

The Greek text may be so translated , or "**Salvation to our God sitting upon the throne and to The Lamb**".The Aramaic verse is clearly Trinitarian.

11. And all of the Angels were standing around the throne and The Elders and The Four Beasts, and they fell before the throne on their faces,

12. Saying, "Amen! Glory and blessing and wisdom and thanksgiving and honor and power and strength to our God for the eternity of eternities! Amen!

13. And one of The Elders responded and he said to me, "Who are these wearing white garments and from where have they come?"

14. And I said to him, "My Lord, you know." And he said to me, "These are those who came from great suffering and they have purified their garments and whitened them in the blood of The Lamb."

15. "Because of this, they are before the throne of God, and they serve him day and night in the Temple and he who sits on the throne will dwell with them."

16. "They will not hunger, neither will they thirst, and the Sun will not assail them, neither any heat."

17. Because The Lamb who is in the midst of the throne will shepherd them and will lead

them unto Life and beside fountains of water, and he will wipe away every tear from their eyes.

    * Greek lacks "**beside life**" and has "**God** shall wipe away.." The verb ונלחא "w'nalha"("wipe away") is very similar to the Aramaic ואלהא "w'Alaha"("& God") and may have been read twice, once as the verb and once as "God"; this double reading phenomenon is referenced elsewhere in Revelation.(See 3:17 & 1:16)

Ashuri script:
ונלחא –" & He will wipe away"
ואלהא –"& God"

DSS script:
–" & He will wipe away"
–"& God"

Estrangela script:
–"& He will wipe away"

–"& God"

Verse 17 is a poem reminiscent of the 23ʳᵈ Psalm. I present this below in interlinear form and a prose translation.

Revelation 7:17 (The Aramaic Crawford Manuscript)

The Throne in the midst of The Lamb For
kursya d`vemesath d`emra mettul

מטל דאמרא דבמצעת כורסיא

beside life them & shall guide them He shall shepherd
hayay seed ennown oo`nashwal ennown nera

נרעא אנון ונשבל אנון ציד חיא

of waters springs & beside
d`mayya ayntha oo`seed

וציד עינתא דמיא

their eyes from tears all & He shall wipe
aynechown min damaa kole oo`nalha

ונלחא כל דמעא מן עיניהון

Like sounding words are colored the same (in color version);Black words do not rhyme.

Mettul d'amra d'vemesath kursya
Nera ennown oo'nashwal ennown seed hayay
Oo'seed ayntha d'mayya
Oo'nalha koll damaa min ayneehown

The end of every line rhymes with every other line (lines 1 & 3;lines 2 & 4).Rhyme, however, is not the feature to look for in Semitic poetry;look for meter and metaphor, parallel words and imagery. This has all of these elements. First, it recalls Psalm 23-a Song about The Shepherd guiding the sheep (notice the irony of The Lamb being The Shepherd) beside still waters. Here, the waters represent Life itself, which His people may drink directly. The Aramaic words עינא -ayna - "**Eyes**" and עינתא -ayntha -"**Fountains**" are the same word in different genders and applications. We have "**Waters**" and "**Tears**" as parallel words; **Lamb** & **Shepherd** are also parallel and yet present a paradox; indeed each parallelism is a paradox: Eyes are fountains, but the springs of water comfort the grief that produces tears from the eyes.The tears represent sorrow;the waters represent life and joy; The Lamb represents a helpless victim and sacrifice for sin;The Shepherd represents The **LORD** Himself-both are The same Messiah Yeshua."**Emra**"-"**Lamb**" & "**Nera**"-"**Shepherd**" are two of the first rhyming words at the beginning of the first two lines. "**Nalha**"-"**Wipes away**" also rhymes with "**Nera**" & "**Emra**", and is the first word on the last line, and is the second of two actions performed by **The Lamb** in this verse.

The Harklean Aramaic translation from Greek does not have the poetic arrangement of The Crawford ms. text.The Greek text certainly does not present a poem here.

This is very poetic,not something to be expected from a translation!

Rev 7:17- English Translation

Because The Lamb
Which is in the midst of The Throne
Shall shepherd them
And shall guide them beside Life
And beside springs of water
And He shall wipe all tears from their eyes.

Chapter 8

1. **A**nd when he opened the seventh seal, there was stillness in Heaven for about half an hour.

2. I saw seven Angels who were standing before God, to whom were given seven trumpets.

3. And another Angel came and stood over the altar and had a golden censor, and much incense was given to him to offer with the prayers of all The Holy on the altar which was before the throne.

4. And the smoke of the incense went up with the prayers of The Holy Ones from the hand of the Angel before God.

5. And the Angel took the censor and filled it with fire which was upon the altar and cast it over The Earth. And there were thunders and voices and lightnings and earthquakes.

6. And the seven Angels, with whom were the seven trumpets, prepared themselves to sound.

7. And the first sounded, and there was hail and fire mixed with water*, and they were cast upon The Earth, and the third of The Earth was burned, and a third of the trees burned, and all the grass of The Earth burned.

    * Greek has "**with blood**". Here is "**with blood**" in Aramaic : בדמא .
    Compare that to the Aramaic reading- "**with water**"- במיא .

DSS script:
–"with water"
–"with blood"

Estrangela script:
–"with water"

–"with blood"

The DSS pair are the most similar in appearance, with perhaps **66%** letter correlation.
The Greek reading YΔATI- "**water**" is not as similar to AIMATI –"**blood**" (**50%**).

8. And the second* sounded, and there was as a great burning mountain falling into the sea and a third of The Sea became blood.
> * Greek has "**second angel**", though "**angel**" is not in verse 7, simply, "**the first**".

9. And a third of all creatures that were in the Sea that had breath, died, and a third of ships was destroyed.

10. And the third* sounded, and a great burning star fell from the sky like a blaze and it fell on a third of the rivers and upon the springs of water,
> * Greek has "**third angel**", though "**angel**" is not in verse 7, simply, "**the first**".

11. And the name of the star is called Absinthian and a third of the water became like Absinthe and a multitude of people died because the waters were made toxic.
> "Apsythna" is the Aramaic name for "**Absinthium**" – "An Aromatic plant yielding a bitter extract used in making absinthe and in flavoring certain wines".

12. And the fourth* sounded and a third of the Sun was devoured and a third of the moon and a third of the stars, and a third of them became dark, and a third of the day did not appear, and the night likewise.
> * Greek has "**fourth angel**", though "**angel**" is not in verse 7, simply, "**the first**".

13. And I heard an eagle flying in the sky, which said, "Woe, woe, woe, to the inhabitants of The Earth from the sound of the trumpets of the three Angels who are going to sound!"

Chapter 9

1. And the fifth* sounded, and I saw a star that fell from the sky to The Earth, and the key of the pit of The Abyss was given to it.
> * Greek has "**fifth angel**", though "**angel**" is not in 4:7, simply, "**the first**".

2. And smoke came up from the pit like the smoke of a great furnace which was heated, and the Sun and the air were darkened by the smoke of the pit.

3. And from the smoke, locusts went out over The Earth, and power was given to them which the scorpions of The Earth have.

4. And it was told them not to harm the grass of The Earth, neither any greenery, nor the trees, but only the people who do not have the seal of God on their foreheads.

5. And it was given to them not to kill them, but that they would suffer pain for five months, and their torment was like the torment of a scorpion when it attacks a man.

6. And in those days people will seek death and will not find it, and they will long to die and death will flee from them.

7. And the form of the locusts was like the form of horses prepared for battle, and upon their heads as crowns of the likeness of gold, and their faces were like the faces of men.

8. And they had hair like hair of women and their teeth were like those of lions.

9. And they had breastplates like breastplates of iron and the sound of their wings was like the sound of the chariots of many horses running to battle.

10. And they had tails like scorpions and a sting in their tails, and their authority is to hurt people for five months.

11. And there is a King over them, the Angel of The Abyss, whose name in Hebrew is Avadu*, and in Aramaic* his name is Shareh.

> * "Avadu" in Judean Aramaic is the command- "**Work**"; "**Shareh**" has several possibilities, the most likely being , "**Be strong**" or "**Be faithful**".I believe the Greek text has it wrong here with its Hebrew "Abaddon"(Destruction) and the Greek interpretation of "Apollyon" (Destroyer). The Angel of The Abyss must be given authority and released from the pit; he also does no destruction, only causes pain. Nothing and no one is killed.The locusts cannot harm a blade of grass. This is not the work of The Destroyer.
> * The Greek says that "Hebrew" and "Greek" are the languages in which the name of the Angel is given; the Crawford says "**Hebrew**" and "**Aramaic**" are the two languages. The Peshitta has 21 other references beside this one to Aramaic & Aramacans; **the Greek has no reference whatsoever to Aramaic or Aramaeans in The NT**; in every place where the Peshitta has such a reference, the Greek has the word ελλην or ελληνικη (Both mean "**Greek**"). The Peshitta also has ten references to Greek, so it is not a matter of The Peshitta expunging references to Greek.

The Greek NT is suspiciously devoid of all reference to Aramaic culture, people and language, as if they did not even exist in the first century. I call this a **literary genocide**. It probably had a reasonable cause at the time, but the effects of this "purge" are still with us today. Scarcely anyone even knows that Aramaic was the dominant language and Aramacan the dominant culture of the Middle East and the Holy Land from the 7th century BC until the 3rd century AD. The language continued to be spoken in that region until the seventh century. The notion that the NT was written in Aramaic is commonly dismissed in favor of Greek with nary a trace of historical evidence to support a Greek original. See Josephus' Wars of The Jews and Antiquities for background info.

12. One woe is gone; behold, again two woes are coming.

13. After these things, the sixth Angel sounded, and I heard one voice from the four horns of the altar of gold, which is before God,

14. Which said to the sixth Angel that had a trumpet: "Loose the four Angels imprisoned at the great river Euphrates."

15. And those four Angels were released who were prepared for an hour and for a day and for a month and for a year, to kill a third of the children of men.

16. And the number of the army of the horsemen was two-ten thousand ten thousands (200 million), and I heard their number.

17. And in this way I saw the horses in a vision, and those sitting upon them had breastplates of fire and Chalcedony brimstone, and the heads of the horses were like the heads of lions, and fire and brimstone and smoke proceeded from their mouths.

18. And by these three scourges a third of the children of men were killed: by the fire, by the brimstone and by the smoke that proceeded from their mouths,

19. Because the power of the horses was in their mouths, and also in their tails*.

* Greek adds, "γαρ ουραι αυτων ομοιαι οφεσιν εχουσαι κεφαλας και εν αυταις αδικουσιν" – "for their tails were like unto serpents, and had heads, and with them they do hurt".

20. And the rest of the children of men who were not killed by the scourges did not turn from the work of their hands to not worship Devils and idols of gold, of silver and of brass, and of wood and of stone, which do not see, neither hear, nor are able to walk.

21. And they did not turn from their murders or from their witchcraft or from their fornication*.

N * Greek has an additional phrase at the end: και εκ των κλεμματων –"and of stolen things". "Thefts" in Aramaic is גנבותא ; adding the possessive pronoun "their" at the end gives גנבותהון –"Their thefts". Compare the actual reading at the end – זניותהון- "Their fornication". Here they are one atop the other:

Ashuri
זניותהון-"Their fornication"
גנבותהון–"Their thefts"

Now let's see them in DSS script:
-"Their fornication"
–"Their thefts"

And Estrangela Script:
-"Their fornication"
–"Their thefts"

All scripts show strong similarity between the two words, with 7/8 or **87% correlation** for DSS; Ashuri and Estrangela have **74%**.
Double translation of certain Aramaic words seems to have occurred in the Greek of Revelation by misreading some words after they were correctly translated once, though I suspect something more deliberate was occurring. See my notes see my book, **Divine Contact** , the chapter on **Alep-Tau** codes, available at http://aramaicnt.com for more on strange

deliberate "**Kabbala**" techniques used in producing certain parts of the Greek NT from Aramaic.

Chapter 10

1. And I saw another Angel* who descended from Heaven and he wore a cloud and a rainbow of the sky on his head and his appearance was like the Sun, and his legs like pillars of fire.

* Greek has "**a mighty angel**" and "**a rainbow upon his head**". It also has "**face**" instead of "**appearance**".

2. And he had a small scroll opened in his hand and he placed his right foot on the Sea, but the left on The Earth;

3. And he shouted with a loud voice like a roaring lion, and when he shouted, seven thunders spoke with their voices.

4. And when the seven thunders spoke, I was ready to write, and I heard a voice from The Seventh* Heaven, which said, "Seal that which the seven thunders spoke and do not write it."

* This can be "**The seventh Heaven**" or a reference to "**The seventh angel**" speaking to John. This Aramaic word "**Seventh**" occurs exactly seven times in the Crawford text of Revelation. All forms of "**seven**" occur 35 times , or 5x7 times.(The Aramaic word Shemaya –"**Heaven**" occurs 56 times in Revelation (Crawford) which is 7x7 + 7.)

5. And the Angel whom I saw was standing on The Sea and upon the dry land, raising his hand to Heaven.

6. And he swore by him who lives to the eternity of eternities, him who created Heaven and that which is in it, and The Earth, and that which is in it: "Time shall be no more."

7. "But in the days of the seventh Angel, when he shall sound, the mystery of God is completed, which he evangelized to his Servants The Prophets."

8. And I heard a voice from Heaven again speaking with me and it said, "Go take the little scroll that is in the hand of the Angel who stands on the land and upon the Sea."

9. And I went to the Angel and I told him to give me the little scroll and he said to me, "Take and eat it and your belly will be bitter to you, but it will be like honey in your mouth."

10. And I took the little scroll from the hand of the Angel and I ate it and it was like sweet honey in my mouth and when I had eaten it, my belly was bitter.

11. And he said to me, "A time is given to you again to prophesy unto the nations and peoples and languages and many Kings".

Chapter 11

1. And a reed was given to me like a rod and the Angel was standing and said, "Rise and measure the Temple of God and the altar and those who worship in it,"

2. "And the inner court of the Temple leave out and do not measure it, because that is given to the Gentiles, and they will trample The Holy City forty two months.

This reading (the inner court) is very different from the Greek reading, which has "**the outer court**".If The Revelation was written in Nero's reign (AD 54-67), as I have discussed in the intro. to Revelation, then this passage about The Temple still standing makes sense, whereas if the conventional date of AD 95 is assigned, it makes no sense, since the Temple was destroyed AD 70. Accepting the early date means this verse is a prophesy about the siege and destruction of the Temple, and this verse in the Crawford is especially shocking in that it says the very inner court of the Jews would be destroyed and that there would be a 42 month (3 and a half years) siege of Jerusalem, which is exactly what happened in AD 67 till AD 70. Josephus recorded it and was there when it happened. The outer court was for the Gentiles anyway, so the Greek reading is pointless.

3. "And I shall grant my two witnesses to prophesy twelve hundred and sixty days while wearing sackcloth."

4. "These are the two olive trees and the two menorahs, which stand before the Lord of the whole Earth*."

 * The Critical Greek and Majority Greek text have "**The Lord**"-"**tou Kuriou**". The TR and a good number of miniscules have **tou Yeou**-"**God**".

 * Zechariah 4:11-14 is alluded to here: It says "Then answered I, and said unto him, What are these two olive trees upon the right side of the candlestick and upon the left side thereof ? (AV) And he answered me and said, Knowest thou not what these be? And I said, No, my lord. Then said he, These are the two anointed ones, that stand by the Lord of the whole Earth".
 The Majority Greek text & Critical Greek of v. 4 omits "**of the whole**" ; The Aramaic is closer to The OT text of Zechariah in this regard.

5. "And whoever seeks to harm them, fire comes out of their mouths and consumes their enemies and those that choose to harm them; so it is given to them to be killed."

6. "And these have authority to close up the sky that the rain would not descend in the days of their prophecy, and they have authority to change water to blood and to strike The Earth with all plagues as much as they wish."

7. "And when their testimonies are complete, The Beast that will ascend from the Sea* will make war with them and will conquer them and kill them."

 * Greek has, "from the Abyss".See 13:1

8. "And their corpses came into the street of The Great City, which spiritually is called Sadom and Egypt, where their Lord was crucified."

9. "And then they of the peoples and generations, languages and nations will look upon their corpses three and a half days, and they will not allow their corpses to be placed in tombs."

10. "And the inhabitants of The Earth will rejoice over them and they will celebrate and they will send gifts to each other, because of the two Prophets who tormented the inhabitants of The Earth."

11. "And after three and a half days, The Living Spirit from God entered into them and they stood on their feet and The Spirit of Life fell upon them and great fear came over those who saw them."

 * A whole phrase of this verse ("**The Spirit of Life fell upon them**") is absent from the Greek text.

12. "And they heard a great voice from Heaven that said to them, "Come up here." And they went up to Heaven in a cloud and their enemies gazed at them."

13. "And in that hour there was a great earthquake and one out of ten cities fell, and the names of men who were killed in The earthquake were seven thousand, and the rest were in fear and gave glory to God who is in Heaven."

14. "Behold, two woes are gone and, behold, the third woe comes at once."

15. And the seventh Angel sounded, and there were great voices in Heaven that said, "The Kingdom of the world has become our God's* and his Messiah's, and he shall reign to the eternity of eternities."

* Greek has "**Our Lord's**"; Here is the Aramaic reading דאלהן –"**our God's**"
                                       compared to the
Aramaic דמרן - **Our Lord's** .
In DSS script they are –"**our God's**"
                 & - **Our Lord's** .
 "Our Lord" almost always refers to Jesus The Messiah, so the Greek would seem out of place referring to "Our Lord" and "His Messiah". Actually these readings do not seem to be the kind that would be easily mistaken for each other, either in Greek or in Aramaic.
Nevertheless I show them here enlarged for the reader:
                Aramaic in DSS script
               –"**Our God's**"
               –"**Our Lord's**"
                Greek uncial script
          ΘΕΟΥ ΗΜΩΝ –"**our God's**"
          ΚΥΡΙΟΥ ΗΜΩΝ–"**Our Lord's**"

The Aramaic pair have a **60% correlation** using the actual Aramaic reading as the basis of comparison for the alternate Greek reading in Aramaic. The first and last letters are identical in each and the He ה and Resh ר are not dissimilar; absent the small bottom left stroke in the ה , they are practically identical, so 3 out of 5 letters in the base word are conceivably interchangeable with the alternate word. The Greek does not fare as well, with 2 letters of the base word **KYPIOY** –**"Lord" being found to match with the alternate reading ΘEOY** –"God"; 2 out of 6 is **33% correlation**.

The Aramaic primacy model is a much more plausible basis for the Greek readings, generally, than the Greek primacy model is for the Aramaic.

16. And the twenty four Elders who sit before God on their thrones fell on their faces and worshiped God,

17. Saying, "We thank you, **LORD JEHOVAH** God Almighty, who is and has been, for you have taken your great power and you have reigned."

18. "And the nations were angry and your anger has come, and the time of the dead to be judged, and you shall give reward to your Servants the Prophets and to The Holy Ones and to those who reverence your name, to the small with the great, and you shall destroy those who have corrupted* The Earth."

* דחבלו -d'khablu comes from חבל –khbal –"to twist,writhe,travail,be in labor, pervert,corrupt,destroy".This verb is used twice in this verse and here it is in the past tense –"**who have corrupted**". "**Destroyed**" would not fit here. The Greek text has a present participle , which is a possible derivation of the Aramaic perfect tense, but the Aramaic perfect tense is not a likely derivation of a Greek present participle; rather a participle in Greek would most likely be translated with a participle in Aramaic.

19. And the Temple was opened in Heaven, and the Ark of his covenant appeared in the Temple, and there were lightnings, thunders, voices, earthquakes and large hail.

Chapter 12

1. And a great sign appeared in Heaven: a woman who was wearing the Sun, and the Moon was under her feet, and a crown of twelve stars on her head;

2. And she was pregnant and she cried out and was in labor; she was also in anguish to give birth.

3. And another sign appeared in Heaven and, behold, a great fiery* Dragon that has seven heads and ten horns, and upon its heads seven diadems.

* **Critical** Greek and Textus Receptus Greek has πυρρος "red", "fire colored"; The Majority Greek text (about 100 mss.of Revelation) have πυρος "of fire".The Aramaic word דנורא can mean "**fiery**". נורא is "**Fire**" and דנורא is "**of fire**" or "**fiery**".

Even the Aramaic Harklean Version (translated from Greek) has the same reading The Crawford ms. has; the Greek has two variant readings, and why? **The answer here seems to be the same as for many other places in The NT where Greek has variant readings- The Aramaic cognate word in the Aramaic text has several meanings or can be easily mistaken for another similar Aramaic word which translates to the pertinent Greek reading.**

If some Greek readings are simple copyist errors involving one letter difference, as here, the sum total of hundreds of Aramaic words being very similar to the Aramaic word corresponding to a Greek reading which is unlike an alternate Greek reading (I know that's a mouthful) tips the balance decidedly in favor of Aramaic primacy and against Greek primacy. This kind of evidence does not occur for Greek primacy-(An original Greek New Testament model).

4. And its tail dragged the third of the stars that are in the Heavens and cast them upon The Earth; and the Dragon was standing before the woman who was ready to give birth, that when she had delivered, it would devour her Son.

5. And she delivered the Son, the Male* who was to Shepherd all the nations with a rod of iron. And her Son was caught up to God and to his throne.

* Greek has "υιον αρσεν" – "**son male**" which is a literal rendering in line with the Aramaic text; this rendering is not Greek language but Semitic (Hebrew-Aramaic-Arabic-Ethiopic are Semitic languages). The Hebrew Bible has this expression in 1 Sam. 1:11 and Jer. 20:15 - זרע אנשים- "**-men** seed" & בן זכר - "**son** seed" .There are many Semiticisms in the Greek version of Revelation, strongly indicating a Semitic original.

6. And the woman fled to the wilderness, where she had a place prepared by God where she would be sustained twelve hundred and sixty days.

7. And there was war in Heaven: Michael and his Angels fighting with the Dragon; and the Dragon and its Angels fought

8. And did not prevail, neither was a place found for them in Heaven.

9. And the great Dragon was cast down, that Chief Serpent, which is called The Devil and Satan, which deceives all The Earth, and it was cast down unto The Earth and its Angels were cast down with it.

10.And I heard a great voice from Heaven that said, "Now is the deliverance and the power and The Kingdom of our God, for The Accuser of our brethren is cast down, which accused them night and day before our God,"

11."And they were victorious by the blood of The Lamb and by the word of his testimony* and they did not love their lives unto death."

* Greek has "of their testimony"; Only The testimony of The Lord Yeshua has power to defeat Satan. "Our testimony" is irrelevant. "His testimony" is found in Mark 14:61,62 :

But He was silent and did not answer anything, and again The High Priest asked Him and said, "Are

You The Messiah, The Son of The Blessed One ?" But Jesus said to him, "I AM The Living God, and you shall behold The Son of Man sitting at the right hand of The Power of God and coming on the clouds of Heaven".

The Peshitta alone has the full force of Our Lord's confession under oath to The High Priest. His answer was not "Yes, I am The Son of God". His answer was "Ena Na"-"I am The Living God…".This answer was given to a cohort of hundreds of Soldiers who came to arrest Him in the Garden of Gethsemane, and the entire cohort fell backward to the ground (See my Interlinear of John 18:5,6).

12."Therefore Heavens, celebrate, and those who dwell in them; woe to The Earth and to the Sea, for The Devil, who has great fury, has descended to them, as he knows that he has little time."

13.And when the Dragon saw that it had been cast down to The Earth, it persecuted the woman who had given birth to The Male.

14.And two wings of a great eagle were given to the woman to fly into the wilderness to her place, to be sustained there for a time, times, and half a time, from before the face of The Serpent.

15.And The Serpent cast water like a river out of its mouth after the woman, to cause her to be taken by the waters.

16.And The Earth helped the woman, and The Earth opened its mouth and swallowed that river which the Dragon had cast from its mouth.

17.And the Dragon raged against the woman and went to make war with the remnant of her Seed*, these who keep the commandments of God and have the testimony of Yeshua. (*"her seed" is singular and refers to her Son; "Seed" in the singular always refers to male offspring- a son.)

Chapter 13

1. And I stood on the sand of the Sea, and I saw a beast ascending from the Sea, which had ten horns and seven heads, and upon its horns, ten diadems, and upon its heads the name* of blasphemy.

* Greek has "names" – ονοματα . The Aramaic שמא -"Shma" is singular. Whoever penned the original Crawford Aramaic text was highly expert in the language; if he was translating from Greek, he would have known easily the difference between the singular Greek ονομα and the plural ονοματα ; no known Greek ms. has the singular ονομα – "name".The fact that the Crawford has שמא - "Shma"-"Name" mitigates strongly against a Greek original behind it; if it were a translation of Greek, it would have שמהא -"Shmahey" –"names" or שמהין - "Shamhayn"-"names", as does the Harklean Syriac Version -(שמהא -"Shmahey").

Whoever penned the Greek version of Revelation was not nearly as competent in Greek as the writer of the original Crawford text was in Aramaic; of that I am confident.

2. And The Beast that I saw was like a leopard, and its feet like those of a wolf and its mouth like that of lions, and the Dragon gave its throne, its power and great authority to it.

3. And one of its heads was as if it had been crushed to death and its mortal wound was healed, and all The Earth marveled after The Beast.

4. And they worshiped the Dragon that gives authority to The Beast, and they worshiped The Beast saying, "Who is like this Beast, and who is able to war with it?"

5. And a mouth that speaks great things and blasphemy was given to it, and authority was given to it to work forty two months.

6. And it opened its mouth to blaspheme before God, to blaspheme The Name and the dwelling of those who dwell in Heaven.

7. And it was granted to make war with The Holy Ones and to conquer them, and it was given authority over all generations, peoples, languages and nations.

8. And all the inhabitants of The Earth will worship it, those who are not written in The Book of Life of The Lamb slain before the foundation of the world.

9. He who has an ear, let him hear.

10. Whoever leads into captivity goes into captivity and those who murder with the sword will be killed with the sword. Here is faith and the endurance of The Holy Ones.

11. And I saw another Beast that ascended from the ground, and it had two horns and was like The Lamb and was speaking like The Dragon.

12. And it will exercise all the authority of the former Beast before it and will make The Earth and those living in it also to worship the first Beast, whose mortal wound was healed.

13. And it will perform great signs so as to make fire descend from Heaven on The Earth before the people.

14. And it will seduce those living on The Earth by the signs that were given to it to perform before the Beast, to tell the dwellers on Earth to make an image to the Beast, which had the wound by the sword and lived.

15. And it was given to it to give spirit to The Image of the Beast and to cause that all who would not worship the image of the Beast would be murdered.

16. And it will cause all, small and great, rich and poor, Masters and Servants, to be given a mark on their right hands or on their foreheads,

17. That no one may buy or sell again except one who has the mark of the name of the Beast on him, or the number of its name.

18. Here is wisdom, and whoever has a mind in him, let him calculate the number of the beast, for it is the number of a man: six hundred and sixty-six.

Chapter 14

1. **A**nd I saw and behold, The Lamb standing on the Mount Zion, and with him one hundred forty-four thousand who have his name upon them and the name of his Father written on their foreheads.

2. And I heard a sound from Heaven as the sound of many waters and as the sound of a great thunder; the sound which I heard was like a harpist playing on his harp.

* Greek has "harpists". The Aramaic קיתרודא can be singular or plural and the last word בקיתרודהי could be mistaken for a plural (not so with the verb דנקש), though I cannot be confident in the expertise of the translator who would do so.

3. And they were singing as a new hymn of praise before the throne and before The Four Beasts and before the Elders, and no one was able to learn the hymn but the one hundred forty-four thousand redeemed from The Earth.

4. These are those who have not been defiled with women, for they are virgins who cleave to the Lamb wherever he goes. These were redeemed from men, the firstfruits to God and to the Lamb.

5. And there is no falsehood found in their mouths as they are without fault.

6. And I saw another Angel flying in the midst of Heaven and he had with him The Eternal Good News to preach unto the dwellers of Earth and unto all people, nations, generations and languages,

7. Saying with a great voice, "**S**tand in awe of God and give him glory, because the hour of his judgment has come, and worship him who made the Heavens and The Earth and the Sea and the springs of water."

8. And another, the second one, followed him and said, "Fallen, fallen, Babylon the Great, who gave all nations to drink of the passion* of her fornication!"

* Greek has "Wine of passion". The Aramaic words for "Passion" and "Wine": חמתא & חמרא. Just one letter difference!

9. Another, the third Angel, followed them saying with a great voice, "**W**hoever worshiped The Beast and its Image and received its mark on his forehead

10. Shall also drink from the wine of the passion of **THE LORD JEHOVAH**, which is mixed* without dilution* in the cup of his rage, and he will be tormented by fire and brimstone before the holy Angels and before the Lamb."

** Wine was normally mixed with some water; this wine was "mixed without mixing" which means it was served "straight up".

11. "**A**nd the smoke of their torment ascends for the eternity of eternities, and there is no rest, day or night, for those who worship The Beast and its Image and for him who takes the mark of its name."

This verse does not affirm everlasting punishment, though it gives that impression. If it were meant to teach that, the language would be more straightforward. Smoke may rise to eternity even after the fire is extinguished in a Heaven without a ceiling. The smoke represents the effect of the punishment – or purging; eternity of eternities signifies the eternal realm of souls of all people who are also affected by the torment and purging of sin, which fire and brimstone represent. "**There is no rest**" to those who worship (present tense) The Beast…. It is important to note the tense of the verb. It does not say **there will never be rest to them**, nor does it say there is no rest for those who **worshiped** The Beast. All of us worshiped The Beast at one time; that does not mean there is no salvation possible for us. Revelation is written in symbolic terms, not literal language. "**No rest**" signifies that the torment of the wicked is primarily internal and mental anguish, not literal physical pain caused by literal fire burning flesh. If the torment were the burning of bodies in fire and molten sulphur, "rest" would not be the remedy needed by the tormented. They would need serious medical attention at the least; what they really would need is a Divine Savior. The Bible does not anywhere say that there are some for whom Jesus The Messiah is not a Savior or whom He cannot or will not save. It does say that some go into eternal torment; it does not say they cannot or will not come out from it.

A major stumbling block for many is the concept of the word "eternal" and "eternity" being confused with "everlasting". According to The Bible, that which is eternal is timeless- without reference to time (See 2 Cor. 4:18). "**Everlasting**" indicates an infinite or endless period of time. According to Paul's definition of "**Eternal**", דלעלם –**D'lalam** , The word "Everlasting" is a violation and contradiction against eternity, where time has no reference point and is therefore meaningless. One cannot describe or define eternity as an infinitely long time; it is not time at all , nor can it be measured at all by a time piece. We must find a new frame of reference for eternity outside of time and time concepts. It is God's frame of reference, Whose Name is "**I AM**".

12. Here is the patience of The Holy Ones, those who keep the commands of God and the faith of Yeshua."

13. And I heard a voice from Heaven that said, "Write, 'Blessed are the dead, from now on, who have departed in Our Lord; Yes, says The Spirit, because they shall rest from their labors.'"

14. And behold, a white cloud, and upon the cloud sat the likeness of a man, and he had on his head a crown of gold, and in his hand a sharp sickle.

15. And another Angel went out from the Temple and shouted with a great voice to him sitting on the cloud, "Send your sickle and reap, because the hour to reap has come."

16. And he who sat on the cloud thrust his sickle unto The Earth and The Earth was reaped.

17. Another Angel went out from The Temple which is in Heaven, and there was with him a sharp sickle.

18. Another Angel went out from the altar, who had authority over fire, and he shouted with a great voice to him who had the sharp sickle with him: "Send your sharp sickle and gather of the clusters of the vineyards of The Earth, because its grapes are large."

19. And the Angel thrust his sickle unto The Earth and gathered the vines of The Earth and cast into the great winepress of the passion of God.

20. And the winepress was trodden outside the city and blood came out of the winepress unto the bridle of the horses for twelve hundred * stadia.

* Greek mss. have χιλιων εξακοσιων "a thousand, six hundred stadia";The Greek ms. Aleph (ℵ, 4th cent.) has χιλιων διακοσιων –"a thousand two hundred".
Here is a photocopy of The Sinaiticus at this place in the verse : .

ϹΤΑΛΙ ϹϽΝ ΧΙΛΙϢΝϵჳΛ
ΛΙΙ ΚΟϹΙϢΝΚΛΙϹ

The letters in Greek uncial script are –

ϹΤΑΔΙϢΝΧΙΛΙϢΝ[ΕΞΑ]
σταδιων χιλιων[εξα] "stadia thousand [six]

ΔΙΑΚΟϹΙϢΝΚΑΙΕ
διακοσιων και ε two hundred. And "

If the Aramaic is the original, how did most Greek mss. get 600 instead of 200 ? Ah, but the Aramaic ומאתין **is 600 and 200! How?** The Aramaic language uses letters for numbers as well as words. ומאתין can mean "and two hundred" (which it most likely does) or it can be interpreted as "(hundreds) מאתין (six) ו since ו –(Waw) is also used for the number six.
The Greek interpretation may have been influenced by the Hebrew form for "hundreds"- מארת ; The correct Aramaic form would be מאא .
The more accurate use of this method would actually give –"six- two hundreds" which is exactly what The

Sinaiticus has ! [Greek does not have a six -two hundreds.]
So The 4th century Greek Sinaiticus bears witness to the Aramaic text of Revelation (The only Greek ms. with 1200 stadia in this place) as does The Majority Greek Text with its subtle but sloppy use of Gematria to obtain 1600 stadia.

ומאתין - "**And two hundred**"
(Crawford & Greek Sinaiticus)
ו-מאתין- "**Six** -hundreds" (Greek reading base ?)

Chapter 15

1. **A**nd I saw another great and wonderful sign in Heaven: Angels which had the seven last plagues with them, for in them the anger of God is finished.
  Mic 7:18 Who is a God like unto thee, that pardoneth iniquity, and passeth by the transgression of the remnant of his heritage? he retaineth <u>not</u> <u>his</u> <u>anger</u> for <u>ever</u>, because he delighteth in mercy.

2. And I saw as a sea of glass mingled with fire, and those who were victorious over The Beast and over its Image and over the number of its name, and they stood over the sea of glass and had with them the stringed instruments of God.
  * harp,lute,cithern,guitar, sheminith,lyre,asor,viol,sackbut,zither.

3. And they sang the song of Moses the Servant of God and the song of The Lamb. They were saying: "Great and marvelous are your works, **LORD JEHOVAH** God Almighty. Just and true are your works, King of the universe."

4. Who will not reverence you, **LORD JEHOVAH**, and glorify your name? For you alone are holy. Therefore, all the nations will come and will worship before you, because you are true."

5. But after these things, I looked, and the Temple of the Tabernacle of the Testimony was opened in Heaven.

6. And the seven Angels went out from the Temple, who had with them the seven plagues, while wearing pure and bright linen* and bound around their chests with a golden wrap.

* Most Greek mss. have λινον-"**linen**". Westcott and Hort's Greek edition has λιθον –"**stone**".

Estrangela	Dead SS Aramaic script
ܟܬܢܐ – Linen : צ ת נ א	
ܟܐܦܐ – Stone: א פ א צ	

7. And one of The Four Beasts gave to the seven Angels seven vessels full of the passion of God, who is The Life for the eternity of eternities. Amen.

8. And The Temple was full of the smoke of the glory of God and of his power, and no one was able to enter the Temple until the seven plagues of the seven Angels would be finished.

Chapter 16

1. And I heard a great voice from the Temple that said to the seven Angels: "Go and pour out the seven vessels of the passion of God on The Earth."

2. And the first went and poured his vessel upon The Earth, and there were severe and painful abscesses over the people who have the mark of The Beast upon them and *over* those who worship its image.

3. And the second Angel poured his vessel into The Sea and The Sea became as dead, and every living animal in the sea died.

* Greek mss. have : εγενετο αιμα ως νεκρου -"**it became blood, as of a dead man**" . The Crawford ms. has "**Sea**" twice;the Greek has "**Blood**" in place of the second "**Sea**".
Here is the word "**Sea**" in Aramaic: יכמא ; Here is "**Blood**" : דמא .
Now look at them in DSS script:
ꓕꓓꓵ (Yamma-"Sea")
ꓕꓓꓵ (Dma-"Blood")
Estrangela
ܝܡܐ (Yamma-"Sea")
ܕܡܐ (Dma-"Blood")
The DSS script seems the more similar pair.
The Greek for "**Blood**" is αιμα ; The Greek for "**Sea**" is θαλασση .They are not at all similar.
I submit that the Aramaic explains the Greek, but the Greek does not explain the Aramaic reading.

4. And the third Angel poured his vessel into the rivers and into the springs of water, and they became blood.

5. And I heard the Angel of the waters saying, "You are righteous, who are and have been, and you are holy, who have decreed these things,

6. Because they have shed the blood of the Prophets and of The Holy Ones, and you have given them blood to drink. They deserve *it*."

7. And I heard the altar saying: "Yes, **LORD JEHOVAH** God Almighty, true and righteous are your judgments." (Greek and Latin Vulgate also have, "I heard the altar saying".)

8. And the fourth Angel poured his vessel over the Sun, and it was given him to scorch people with fire.

9. And the children of men were scorched with great heat, and they blasphemed the name of God who has authority over these plagues, and they did not repent to give him glory.

10. And the fifth Angel poured his vessel over the throne of The Beast, and its Kingdom became darkness, and they were gnawing their tongues from the pain.

11. And they blasphemed the name of The God of Heaven due to their pains and due to their sores, and they did not repent of their works.

12. And the sixth Angel poured his vessel over the great river Euphrates, and its waters dried up that the way of the Kings from the East may be prepared.

13. And I saw from the mouth of The Dragon and from the mouth of The Beast and from the mouth of The False Prophet, three foul spirits like frogs,

14. For they are the spirits of Demons* who performs signs, which go into the Kings of the habitable Earth, to gather them to the war of that great day of God Almighty.
* Aramaic words for "**Demon**" are at least two: שארא –"**Shada**" and דיוא –"**Daywa**". Greek has only one word for "**Demon** –(δαιμονιον "**Daimonion**"). In Revelation, the Greek has but one word, δαιμονιον, where the Aramaic has both שארא –"**Shada**" and דיוא –"**Daywa**". (See 9:20 & 18:2 as here). The Harklean Syriac Version (translated from Greek) has only דיוא –"**Daywa**" in Revelation. If The Crawford were a translation of Greek , as is commonly supposed, why would it use two different Aramaic words for the same Greek word? This phenomenon occurs with other words as well.

15. "Behold, I come like a thief. Blessed is he who watches and keeps his garments, lest he walk naked, and they see his shame."

16. And he shall gather them to the place called, in Hebrew ,"Megiddo".

17. And the seventh Angel poured his vessel into the air, and a great voice went out from The Temple from before the throne, which said, "It is done."

18. And there were lightnings and thunders and there was a great earthquake, the like of which earthquake there has not been since people have been upon The Earth, it was so great.

19. And the great city became three parts, and the cities of the nations fell and Babylon The Great was remembered before God, to give it the cup of the wine of his passion and of his wrath.

20. And every island fled and the mountains were not found.

21. And great hailstones, about a talent, fell from the sky on the children   of men, and the children of men cursed God because of

the plague of   hail, because his plague was very great.

* A talent (Kakra) was both a monetary weight of gold , silver or brass (worth as much as 125 British pounds) , or a measure of sheer weight (94 lbs.)

Chapter 17

1. And one of the seven Angels who had with them the seven vessels, came and spoke with me saying, "Follow me; I shall show you the judgment of The Harlot who sits on many waters,"

2. "For the Kings of The Earth committed fornication with her and all Earth dwellers are drunk with the wine of her fornication."

3. And he brought me to the wilderness in The Spirit, and I saw a woman who sat on a blood-red beast full of blasphemous names, which had seven heads and ten horns.

4. And the woman was wearing purple and scarlet gilt with gold and precious stones and pearls and had a cup of gold in her hand, and it was full of abominations and the filth of her fornication.

5. And upon her forehead was written: "Mystery Babylon The Great, The Mother of Harlots and of the Filth of The Earth."

6. And I saw the woman who was drunk with the blood of The Holy Ones and with the blood of the witnesses of Yeshua, and I was stunned with a great astonishment when I saw her.

7. And the Angel said to me, "Why are you stunned? I shall tell you the mystery of The Woman and of The Beast that bears her, which has seven heads and ten horns."

8. "The Beast which you saw, existed and is not, and is about to come up from the Sea, and is going to destruction. And the inhabitants on Earth will marvel, whose names are not written in The Book of Life from the foundation of the world, when they see The Beast which was, and is not, and is approaching."

9. "Here is the meaning for one having wisdom: the seven heads are seven mountains, upon which The Woman sits."

10. "And there are seven Kings; five have fallen and one is*, and there is another not yet come, and when he comes, a little remaining time is given to him."

* Nero was the sixth Caesar of Rome ("**One is**"), Julius Caesar being the first. This confirms my view that Revelation was written during Nero's reign (A.D. 54-68).

The first eleven Caesars:
Julius, Augustus, Tiberius, Caligula, Claudius, Nero, G alba, Otho, Vitellius, Vespasian, Titus.
Some think the seven Kings are reference to seven Kingdoms:
Assyrian, Babylonian, Persian, Greek, Roman, Split Roman (East & West), Holy Roman. Jerusalem fell during **Vespasian's** reign, AD 70.

11. "And The Dragon*, and The Beast which it brought* and is not, also is the eighth, and is of the seven, and is going to destruction."
* דאיתיה –Can mean "which is", or "which he brought". The latter makes sense in connection with The Dragon, which brought The Beast to power and prominence -See 13:2. No Greek ms. has the reading of "The Dragon" & "The Beast which it brought" as does The Crawford ms. in this verse.

12. "And the ten horns of The Beast are ten Kings, whose Kingdoms they have not yet received, but take authority as Kings for one hour with The Beast."

13. "These have one will, and their power and authority they give to The Beast."

14. "These will make war with The Lamb and The Lamb will conquer them, because he is The Lord of Power and The King of Kings, and because his people are called, chosen and faithful."

15. And he said to me, "The waters that you saw, upon which The Harlot sat, are the nations, multitudes, peoples and languages."

16. "And the ten horns that you saw on The Beast will hate The Harlot and will make her desolate and naked and will devour her flesh and will burn her in fire."

17. "For God gave into their hearts to perform his pleasure and to do their one purpose and will give their Kingdom to that Beast until the words of God are fulfilled."

18. "And The Woman which you saw is that Great City, which has rule over the Kings of The Earth."

Chapter 18

1. And after these things I saw another Angel from Heaven, who had great authority, and The Earth was brightened by his glory.

2. And he shouted with a great voice: "Fallen, fallen, Babylon the Great! And it is become the abode for Demons and a prison to every impure and detestable spirit."

3. "Because she mixed of the wine of her fornication for all the nations, and the Kings of The Earth committed fornication with her, and the merchants of The Earth have become rich by the power of her infatuation."

4. And I heard another voice from Heaven that said, "Come out from within her my

people, lest you share in her sins, that you would not receive from her plagues."

5. "Because the sins in her have touched Heaven, and God has called her evil to mind."

6. "Pay her just as she also has paid, and give her double for her deeds. In the cup which she has mixed, mix her a double".

7. "Because of that in which she glorified and exalted* herself, give such suffering and sorrow, for she said in her heart, 'I sit a queen, and I am not a widow and I shall not see sorrow."

* Greek here and in verse 9 has εστρηνιασεν – "partying", "reveling"; possibly this is because a translator construed אשתעלית – "exalted herself" as אשתעלית (from עולא – "do evil, be lawless") or from אשתבית from the verb שנא – "be frenzied, infatuated". It is not difficult to see how the Greek came from the Aramaic; it is difficult to see the reverse scenario happening. Greek for "exalted herself" is ΕΠΗΡΕΤΟ or ΥΨΩΘΗ or ΥΨΩΘΕΙΣΑ or ΥΨΩΝ or ΥΨΩΘΗΣΕΤΑΙ. Does any of these look like ΕΣΤΡΗΝΙΑΣΕΝ? Hardly.

8. "Because of this, in one day there will come upon her plagues, death, sorrow, and starvation, and she will burn in fire, because **THE LORD JEHOVAH** is powerful who judges her."

9. And the Kings of The Earth, who committed fornication with her and exalted themselves, will weep and wail concerning her, when they see the smoke of her burning,

10. As they stand opposite from fear of her punishment, and they will say, "Woe, woe, woe, the great city Babylon! The Mighty city! For in one hour your judgment has come!"

11. And the merchants of The Earth will weep and grieve over her, and there is no one buying their cargo again:

12. Cargo of gold and silver and of precious stones, of pearls, of fine linen, of purple, of silk, of scarlet, of every fragrant wood and every ivory vessel, every precious wooden vessel, and brass, iron and marble,

13. Cinnamon, spices, ointments, frankincense, wine, oil, fine white flour, sheep, horses, chariots and the bodies and souls of the children of men.

14. And your own pleasant fruits have departed from you, and everything luxurious and splendid is gone from you and you will not see* them again."

● Greek has two different readings: μη ευρης (Byzantine) –"you (singular) shall not find" and μη ευρησουσιν "they shall not find" (Critical Greek) .The Byzantine reading seems to reflect the Aramaic verb תחזין –"you will see" (2nd person singular)

whereas the Critical Greek skips to the next verb in the next verse- נשכחון –"they shall find", and does not have it in the next verse at all. Apparently the next verse in Aramaic is where the Greek got this verb - "they shall find" but the Majority Greek modified it to be singular in agreement with the Aramaic verb in this verse- תחזין-"you shall see".
Greek for "You will see" is οψει or οψη, ιδης or βλεψη. The Greek word closest to : ευρης is ιδης. The letter correlation here is **40%**.

Ashuri Script
תחזין-"you shall see"
תשכחון-"you shall find"

Dead Sea Scroll Script
תחזין-"you shall see"
תשכחון-"you shall find"

Estrangela Script
ܬܚܙܝܢ-"you shall see"

ܬܫܟܚܘܢ-"you shall find"

All three scripts show **66%** letter correlation between the two readings in Aramaic.

15. And the merchants of these things, who grew rich by her, will not find them, and they will stand opposite from fear of her punishment, weeping and lamenting,

16. And saying, "Alas alas, the great city that wore fine linen and purple and scarlet gilt in gold and precious stones and pearls!

17. For the wealth is lost in one hour!" In this way also, every ship Navigator, everyone traveling in a ship to places, and the ship Captains, and everyone who does business at sea, stood from a distance,

18. And they lamented her when they saw the smoke of her burning and they were saying, "Who is like The Great City?"

19. And they cast earth upon their heads and shouted as they wept and lamented and they were saying, "Alas, alas, Great City, by which those who had ships in the sea grew rich from her magnificence, which is destroyed in one hour!"

20. "Rejoice over her, Oh Heaven, Holy Ones, Apostles and Prophets, because God has executed your judgment upon her!"

21. And one of the Angels took a mighty stone, great as a millstone, and cast it into the sea and said, "In this way with violence, Babylon The Great City will be thrown down, and it will not exist again!"

22. 'And the sound of stringed instruments and of trumpets and the various singers and shouting will not be heard in you again!"

23. "And the light of a lamp will not appear to you again, and the voice of a groom and the voice of a bride will not be heard in you again, because your merchants had been great ones of The Earth, for by your sorceries you deceived all the nations!"

24. And in her was found the blood of The Prophets and Holy Men who were murdered on Earth.

Chapter 19

1. And after these things, I heard a great sound of many multitudes in Heaven saying, "Hallelujah! Redemption, glory and power to our God!

    * The Majority Greek has η σωτηρια και η δυναμις και η δοξα του θεου ημων - "**salvation,& power & glory of our God**"; the Critical Greek has the Aramaic word order, η σωτηρια και η δοξα και η δυναμις του θεου ημων - "**salvation, glory and power of our God**"; some Byzantine mss. and TR Greek (KJV) have , η σωτηρια και η δοξα και η τιμη και η δυναμις κυριω τω θεω ημων - "**salvation and glory & honor & power of our God**". The Aramaic תשבוחתא –"**Tishbokhta**" can mean

ܬܶܫܒ݁ܽܘܚܬ݁ܳܐ rt. ܫܒ݁ܚ. f. pl. ܬܶܫܒ݁ܚܳܬ݂ܳܐ, ܬܶܫܒ݁ܚܳܬ݂ܳܐ

a) *praise, honour, glory, magnificence; a hymn,*
-
-**Smith's Compendious Aramaic Dictionary**: It appears that this Aramaic word was double translated by one translator-a phenomenon not uncommon in Revelation's Greek apparently.(See previous notes on this.)
The Harklean Syriac Version has –
To our God & honor & glory & power redemption

לאלהן פורקנא וחילא ותשבוחתא ואיקרא

"Redemption & power & glory & honor to our God"
This is a revision of the Peshitta (in my opinion) based on the Majority (Byzantine) Greek text type. It retains many unique readings of The Peshitta NT with many revisions of that text based on translation of Greek into Aramaic. This reading in verse one shows that the Greek text used was similar to the TR reading of this verse.
    I don't see the different Greek texts as completely separate translations of the Aramaic text, but I see one original Greek translation (The Majority-TR type Greek text) and several revisions of that based on the Aramaic original. A revision would not be a fresh translation but a new edition of the original Greek version in which many words were retranslated, but the vast majority of the text was left intact. Many differences in the Greek texts are due to copyist errors which have nothing to do with different translations of Aramaic words.

2. For his judgments are true and just, because he has judged The Great Whore, who corrupted The Earth with her whoredom and he has required the blood of his Servants from her hand.

"**Required the blood ...from her hand**" is a Semitic idiom used in The Old Testament -2 Samuel 4:11 - **Hebrew interlinear (my translation):**
    (from your hand) מידכם 2 Samuel 4:11
    (his blood) את-דמו - (I shall require) אבקש
The Peshitta OT has:
-2 Samuel 4:11
    (your hand) אידיכון (from) מן

(his blood) דמה (I shall require) אתבע

The Peshitta OT of this verse 2 Sam. 4:11 has the same verb used in this verse 2 of Revelation and the same idiom, which idiom indicates that equal payment (life for life) is required of the criminal for the crime of murder.
The LXX Greek of 2 Samuel has :εκζητησω το αιμα αυτου εκ χειρος υμων –" **I will seek his blood from your hands**".
The Greek of this Revelation verse has: "εξεδικησεν το αιμα των δουλων αυτου εκ χειρος αυτης –"**He will avenge the blood of his Servants from her hand.**"
The point is that these words in the Greek reflect a Semitic original; These words in Greek do not reflect a Greek original.

3. Again, they said*, "Hallelujah!" And her smoke ascends to the eternity of eternities.
    * Majority Greek has "**he said**".

4. And the twenty four Elders and the four Beasts fell down and worshiped our God who sits on the throne, and they were saying, "Amen! Hallelujah!"

5. And *there was* a voice from the throne that said, "Praise our God, all his Servants and worshipers of his name- all of them, the small with the great!"

6. And I heard a sound like that of many multitudes, and like the sound of many waters and like the sound of mighty thunders saying, "Hallelujah! For **THE LORD JEHOVAH** God Almighty reigns!

7. We rejoice and celebrate! We give him glory, because the wedding of the Lamb has come, and his bride has prepared herself!"

8. And it was given to her to wear fine linen, pure and bright, for the fine linen is the uprightness of The Holy Ones.

9. And they said to me, "Write, 'Blessed are they who are called to the wedding supper of the Lamb!'" And one said to me, "These are the true words of God."

10. And I fell before his feet and worshiped him, and he said to me, "No!* I am your fellow Servant and of your brothers who have the testimony of Yeshua. Worship God, rather, for the testimony of Yeshua is the spirit of prophecy."

    * Greek has ορα μη –"**See not**"- not a meaningful statement. Translators usually insert the words "**that you do it**" between these two words in a lame attempt to make up for the apparent shortcomings of this Greek reading.

11. And I saw Heaven opened and behold, a white horse, and he who sat upon it is called trustworthy and true, and in righteousness he judges and he makes war.

12. And his eyes were like flames of fire, and many diadems were upon his head and he had The Name written, which no one knew but he alone.

13. And he wore a garment soaked with blood, and his name is called The Word of God.

14. And the army of Heaven were joined to him on white horses and were wearing linen white and pure.

15. And sharp swords came out of their mouths by which they will kill the nations, and he will shepherd them with a rod of iron and he treads the winepress of the wrath of Almighty God.

* The Greek has "εκ του στοματος αυτου εκπορευεται ρομφαια" –"a sharp sword proceeds from His mouth". The Aramaic text has an army of Warriors with swords from their mouths!

* The Majority Greek has διστομος οξεια –"double edged sharp".The Critical Greek and TR lacks - διστομος –"double". Here is the Aramaic for "Double" תרינתא –"Trayyanita"; Compare the Aramaic here for "Sharp"- חריפתא. It seems that here and in Rev. 2:16, חריפתא -"Kharripta- "Sharp" was read doubly as both "double" and "sharp".Here are both words in **Dead Sea Scroll Aramaic script:**

חריפתא-"Sharp"
תריניתא-"Double"

Ashuri Aramaic Script:
חריפתא-"Sharp"
תרינתא-"Double"

* Greek has παταξη -"will smite"; The Aramaic reading for "will smite" is נמחון . The Crawford Aramaic reading is נקטלון . Here are the two words in

DSS script:
נקטלון -"will kill"
נמחון -"will smite"

These two have at least **60%** letter correlation.

Ashuri
נקטלון-"will kill"
נמחון-"will smite"
66% correlation

Estrangela
ܢܩܛܠܘܢ-"will kill"
ܢܡܚܘܢ-"will smite"
66% correlation

Greek for "he will kill" is ΑΠΟΚΤΕΝΕΙ.This looks nothing like ΠΑΤΑΞΗ -"smite".If the Aramaic were a translation of the Greek, it would not likely contain the reading "kill" when the original had "smite".

16. And he has on his garment over his thigh the name written: "The King of Kings and The Lord of Power".

17. And I saw another Angel standing in the sun and crying with a loud voice, and he said to the birds flying in the midst of the sky, "Come, gather to the great supper of God",

18. "To eat the flesh of Kings and the flesh of Captains of thousands and the flesh of Warriors and the flesh of horses and of those sitting upon them, and the flesh of Freemen and of Servants, and of small and of great."

19. And I saw The Beast and its armies and the Kings of The Earth and their Soldiers who gathered to make war with him who sat upon the horse, and with his Soldiers.
This verse in Greek omits the Beast's armies.

20. And The Beast was captured and The False Prophet with it, who did signs before it by which he seduced those who received the mark of The Beast, and those who worshiped its image; and both went down* and were cast into The Lake of Fire that burns also with brimstone.

* Greek has ζωντες - "alive" .In Aramaic,"& they descended"is ונחתו .
"& they were alive" in one form would be ונחיתו .
Let's see these compared to נחתו –"descended" in DSS script :
ונחתו – "& they descended"
ונחיתו– "& were alive"

The Ashuri and the Dead Sea Scripts both show 80% letter correlation in the above word pairs.
The Greek for "They went down" is κατεβησαν .
Compare ζωντες - "alive".
See any resemblance?
How about in uncial script: ΚΑΤΕΒΗΣΑΝ-"They went down" ΖΩΝΤΕΣ - "Alive" ?
Neither do I.

21. But the rest were killed with the sword of him who sat upon the horse, by that which proceeded from his mouth, and all the birds of prey were filled with their flesh.

Chapter 20

1.And I saw another Angel from Heaven who had with him the key of   The Abyss and a great chain in his hand.

2. And he seized The Dragon and The Ancient Serpent, which is The Devil and Satan, and bound him for a thousand years;

3. And he cast him into The Abyss and shut and sealed the top of it so that he would not again seduce all the nations; after these things it is granted to release him for a little season.

4. And I saw seats, and they sat upon them, and judgment was given to them, and these souls who were cut off for the testimony of Yeshua and for the word of God, and because they did not worship the Beast, neither its Image, nor received a mark between their eyes or on their hands, they lived and reigned with The Messiah for one thousand years;

5. And this is the first resurrection.

6. Blessed and holy is he, whoever has part in the first resurrection, and the second death

has no authority over these, but they shall be Priests of God and of The Messiah, and they shall reign with him one thousand years.

7. And whenever the one thousand years are finished, Satan will be released from his imprisonment,

8. And he will go forth to seduce all the nations in the four corners of The Earth: Gog and Magog, to gather them to war, those whose number is as the sand of The Sea.

9. And they went to war upon an open place of The Earth and surrounded the city of the camp of The Holy People and of The Beloved City, and fire descended from Heaven from God and consumed them.

10. And their Seducer, The Devil, was cast into The Lake of Fire and Brimstone where The Beast and The False Prophet are, and they shall be tormented day and night for the eternity of eternities.

11. And I saw a Great White Throne and him sitting at the top of it, from whose face Earth and Heaven fled away, and no place was found for them.

12. And I saw the dead, great and small, who stood before the throne, and scrolls were opened, and another scroll was opened, which is of The Judgment, and the dead were judged from those things that were written in the scrolls, according to their works.

Greek has της ζωης -"of Life". Here is "of Life" in Aramaic : דהיא or דהייא- "of Life"
Here is the Crawford reading :
דדינא- "of Judgment"

Here is "of Life" in Dead Sea Scroll script: ﬧﬧﬡﬤ or ﬧﬧﬡﬤ- "of Life"
Here is the Crawford reading :
ﬡﬧﬤﬤ- "of Judgment"
Here is "of Life" in Estrangela script :

ܚܝܐ or

ܕܝܢܐ - "of Judgment"

The Crawford reading : ܕܝܢܐ - "of Judgment".

The Dead Sea Scroll (DSS) is the most promising script candidate for explaining the two readings in Aramaic and Greek. It appears that ﬡﬧﬤﬤ –"of Judgment" was read as ﬧﬧﬡﬤ "of Life" by a Greek translator reading an Aramaic manuscript. He would have misread two letters of the five: ﬤ as a ﬨ , and ﬤ as a ﬧ ; each is quite a plausible mistake as these letters are quite similar in this script.
The Dead Sea script pair has at least **80%** correlation.
The Greek for "of Judgement"- κρισεως and ζωης-"of Life" have 14% correlation.

13. And the Sea yielded the dead which were in it, and Death and Sheol yielded the dead which were with them, and they were judged, one by one, according to their works.

14. And Death and Sheol were cast into The Lake of Fire- this which is the second* death.

Interestingly , the Aramaic word here for "**the second**", "**repeated**"-"**Tanayna**", has the same consonantal spelling as the word for "**The Dragon**". See also v. 14 and 21:8.("Death of the Dragon" ?) *
Most Greek mss. add , "**The lake of fire**" again after "**The second death**".

15. And whoever was not found inscribed in The Book of Life was cast into The Lake of Fire. (The Book of Life is mentioned in Philip. 4:3, Rev. 3:5, 13:8, 17:8.)

Chapter 21

1. And I saw new Heavens and a new Earth, for the former Heavens and the former Earth had departed, and the Sea was no more.

2. And I saw The Holy City, New Jerusalem, descending from Heaven from beside God, prepared like a bride adorned for her husband.

3. And I heard a great voice from Heaven that said, "Behold, the Tabernacle of God is with the children of men, and he dwells with them and they shall be his people and the same God is with them and shall be their God*. * (Greek Textus Receptus –[KJV Greek] has "their God"; most Greek mss. do not.)

4. And he* shall wipe away every tear from their eyes, and from now on there shall not be death, neither grieving, nor clamor, neither shall there be disease again, for His sake*. * (Greek Textus Receptus –[KJV Greek] has "God"; see note at 7:17 where Greek has "God shall wipe away" and The Aramaic has, "He shall wipe away", refering to The Lamb of God.)

* Greek has "**for the first things departed**", instead of "**for his sake**." The last two Aramaic words ,אפיה, על-"for His sake" plus the next word in v. 5- ואזלת, could be construed as, "**because its former departed**", אפיה –"**before it**" and ואזלת –"**& it departed**" (3rd fem. Singular) . It is poor Greek translation, nevertheless.

5. And I walked and he who sat on the throne said to me, "Behold, I make all things new." And he said to me, "Write: These words are trustworthy and true."

6. And he said to me, "They are done. I am Alap and I am Tau, The Source and The Fulfillment. I shall give to the thirsty one from the fountain of the water of life without charge."

7. "And he who is victorious shall inherit these things, and I shall be his God and he will be my son."

8. "But to the timid, the unbelievers, the evil, the defiled, murderers, sorcerers, fornicators, idol worshipers and all liars: their part is in the burning Lake of Fire and Brimstone, which is the second death."

9. And one of the seven Angels who had with them the seven vessels full of the seven last plagues, came and he spoke with me

saying, "Come; I shall show you the bride, the wife of the Lamb."

10. And he carried me in The Spirit to a great and high mountain and he showed me The Holy City Jerusalem, coming down from Heaven from the presence of God,

11. And it had the glory of God and its light was as the likeness of precious stones, like Jasper red quartz, as the appearance of crystal.

12. And it had a wall, great and high, and it had twelve gates, and at the gates, twelve Angels, and names written which are the names of the twelve tribes of Israel;

13. From the East, three gates, from the North, three gates, and from the South, three gates, and from the West, three gates.

14. And the wall of the city has twelve foundations, and on them, the twelve names of the Apostles of The Son*.

* Greek has του αρνιου -"of The Lamb" ; Here are the readings , "of The Son" (Crawford ms.) and "of the Lamb" in DSS Aramaic:

Ashuri script

אמרא-"of the Lamb"

דברא- "of The Son"

דערבא-"of the Sheep"

DSS script

אמרא -"of the Lamb"

דברא - "of The Son"

דערבא-"of the Sheep"

Estrangela script

ܐܡܪܐ-"of the Lamb"

ܒܪܐ- "of The Son"

ܥܪܒܐ-"of the Sheep"

The Greek readings αρνιου-"of The Lamb" & υιου -"of The Son" are not sufficiently alike to explain the Aramaic reading. Here they are in Greek uncial script with all spaces removed to simulate what fourth century Greek and earlier would have looked like:

APNIOY-"of The Lamb"
YIOY –"of The Son"

As you see, the actual Greek reading has three letters (APN-) which are unlike those in the second reading ;the first is six letters and the second four letters, with only three letters the same out of the six. If Greek were the original and Aramaic the translation of the Greek reading, it is difficult to see how the Aramaic was derived from Greek. There is only **50% correlation** between YIOY & APNIOY . The pair of underlined DSS Aramaic readings above show much better correlation than the Greek words (75% or more) ב and ב may be confused one for the other in this script, as may א & ד , indicating that an Aramaic original probably gave rise to the Greek text rather than vice versa.

15. And he who spoke with me had with him a measuring reed of gold to measure the city and its wall.

16. And the city was laid out four-sided, and its length like its width. And he measured The City with the reed, with twelve thousand stadia its length; its width and its height are equal.

17. And he measured its wall one hundred forty-four cubits by the measure of a man, that is, of the Angel.

18. The building of the wall was Jasper Quartz, and the city was of pure gold, in the likeness of pure glass.

19. And the foundation of the wall of the city is adorned with precious stones; and the first foundation, Jasper red-blue-yellow Quartz, and the second, Sapphire, and the third, white Chalcedony, and the fourth, Emerald,

20. And the fifth, red and white Sardius and banded Onyx, and the sixth, red and white Sardius, and the seventh, Goldstone, and the eighth, Beryl, and the ninth, Topaz, and the tenth, green and gold Chrysoprasus, the eleventh, dark blue Jacinth, the twelfth, Amethyst,

21. And twelve gates and twelve pearls, one to each, and everyone of the gates was of one pearl, but the street of the city of pure gold, as if there was glass in it.

22. And I saw no Temple in it, for **THE LORD JEHOVAH** God Almighty, he is its Temple*. (Greek adds, "and the Lamb" from the beginning of the next verse in Aramaic.)

23. And The Lamb and The City do not need the Sun or the Moon to illuminate it, for the glory of God illuminates it, and The Lamb is its lamp.

24. And the nations* walk in its light and the Kings of The Earth bring glory* to it.

* The Textus Receptus Greek (KJV Greek) has , "**The nations of the saved**…". Most Greek mss, Byzantine and Alexandrian, agree with The Aramaic reading of The Crawford ms. used here.
* The Majority Greek has "glory and honor"; the Critical Greek agrees here with The Aramaic Crawford ms.
The Aramaic תשבוחתא –"**Tishbokhta**" can mean -

ܬܫܒܘܚܬܐ pl. ܬܫܒܚܢ, ܬܫܒܘܚܬܐ rt. ܫܒܚ. f.
a) *praise, honour, glory, magnificence; a hymn*,
-**Smith's Compendious Aramaic Dictionary**;
It appears that this Aramaic word was double translated by one translator-a phenomenon not uncommon in Revelation's Greek apparently.(See previous notes on this; also note at 19:1.)

25. And its gates shall not be shut by day, for there shall be no night there.

26. And they shall bring to it the glory and honor of the nations.

27. There shall not be anything defiled there, or one who makes defilement or lies, but only those who are written in The Book* of the Lamb.

* Greek has "the book of life of The Lamb".

Chapter 22

1. And he showed me a river of the water of life, pure and clear as crystal, and it went out from the throne of God and of the Lamb.

2. And in the center of the street on this side and on that, upon the river, The Tree of Life which produces twelve fruits, and every month it gives its fruits and its leaves for the healing of the peoples.

3. And no curse shall be there, and the throne of God and of The Lamb shall be in it, and his Servants shall serve him.

4. And they shall see his face and his Name shall be upon their foreheads.

5. And there shall be no night there and neither will they need lights,* lamps, or the light of the Sun, because **THE LORD JEHOVAH** God gives them light, and he is their King* for the eternity of eternities.

Critical Greek has "χρειαν φωτος λυχνου και φως ηλιου" –"need of light of lamp, neither light of sun" ; there is a grammatical boo boo in this reading in the word φως –"light" ; it is in the wrong case (accusative) , whereas it should be genitive- φωτος . The Majority Greek **has** χρειαν ουκ εχουσιν λυχνου και φωτος ηλιου –"not have need of lamp, neither light of sun", correct in grammar, but apparently skipping the first of two "lights" in the Aramaic verse.
Greek has "they shall reign forever", which does not ring as true as "He is their King forever".And over whom would all people reign? It sounds like "all chiefs and no indians". The nations walk in its light, therefore The **LORD** God Himself will be King over all The Earth and Heaven.

6. And he said to me, "These words are trustworthy and true, and **THE LORD JEHOVAH,** God of The Spirit of The Holy Prophets, has sent his Angel to show his Servants what is granted to happen soon."

7. "And behold, I come soon. Blessed is he who keeps the words of the prophecy of this book."

8. I am Yohannan, who saw and heard these things. And when I saw and heard, I fell to worship before the feet of the Angel who was showing me these things.

9. And he said to me: "Seer, no! I am your fellow Servant and of your brothers the Prophets and of those who observe these words of this book. Worship God!"

Greek has "ορα μη" – **See –not** . I can find this phrase in one other place (Joshua 9:7) in The LXX &

in Rev. 19:10. It does not make good sense.The Aramaic phrase does make sense: חזי לא -**"Seer ,no !"** John was definitely a **"Seer"** and is addressed as such elsewhere in Revelation according to Murdock's translation of the previous verse. The word for **"Seers"** is used in verse 15 as well.

10. And he said to me, "Do not seal the words of the prophecy of this book, for the time is near."

11. "And he who does evil, will do evil again; he who is foul, again will be polluted; the righteous again will do righteousness and the holy will again be hallowed."

12. "Behold, I come at once, and my reward is with me, and I shall give to every person according to his work."

13. "I am Alap and I am Tau, The First and The Last, The Origin and The Fulfillment."

The Greek mss. are split (approx.100 each group) between "**The First and The Last and The Beginning and The End**" & "**The Beginning and The End and The First and Last**".
What is truly interesting is that the Aramaic words in The Crawford text ושולמא ושוריא ואחריא קדמיא – the last four words in the verse all have double meanings. קדמיא –**Qadmaya** can mean "**First**" or "**Beginning**"; אחריא –**Akhraya** can be "**The last**" or "**The end**". שוריא -**Shuraya** can be "**Beginning**", "**Origin**", "**Introduction**" and שולמא –**Shawlama** –is "**End**", "**Completion**","**Consummation**".It is easily conceivable that a Greek translator and a later reviser or translator using the same Aramaic text would translate these words differently, thus producing the two major Greek readings here.

14. "Blessings to those who are doing his Commandments; their authority shall be over The Tree of Life, and they shall enter The City by the gates."

15. "And outside are fornicators, murderers, idol worshipers, the defiled, sorcerers and all seers* and workers of lies."

Most Greek mss. have "πας φιλων και ποιων ψευδος" - **"every one loving and doing falsehood"**. Here is the Aramaic חזיי -**"Seers"** in DSS script: חזיﬀ ;
Here is חובי- **"beloved"**, **"Friends"** in DSS : חוﬀב.
DSS script
Lets enlarge and align them for close comparison:
חזיﬀ – **"Seers"**
חוﬀב – **"Friends"**
The DSS pair have at least **75%** similarity.
It looks quite likely that the Greek translator saw חזיﬀ -"Seers" and translated it as if he saw חוﬀב -"friends" .

The Greek **LXX** manages to translate the Hebrew for "**Seer**" - חזה & ראה as προφητην – "**Prophet**"(several times), ορωντα – "**Seer**" (7 times) , βλεποντος –"**Seer**" (6 times). ανακρουομενω – "**Chief player**", αυτος-"**He**" , Nine times out of 28 it leaves the Hebrew untranslated or mistranslated.It seems the Greek translators had some difficulty with this ancient Semitic concept of "**One who sees**" as an official title and office. The Greek word φιλων occurs 6 times in the Greek NT ; 3 times (50%) it is translated "Friends". Φιλων in this verse is a singular participle verbal form whereas φιλων , where it is translated "**friends**" , though identical in form, is a plural adjective.

The Greek for "**Seers**" in this verse would most likely be ορωντες or βλεποντες . Here are the two most similar Greek words meaning "**Seers**" and "**Friends**":

Greek Uncial script
ΟΡΩΝΤΕΣ – "**Seers**"
ΦΙΛΩΝ – "**Friends**"

I see two letters in the second Greek word that are the same as two in the first word; that is two out of seven, or **28%** correlation.

It seems highly unlikely the Aramaic of this verse ("חזוי – "**Seers**") came from Greek (ΦΙΛΩΝ – "**Friends**") as the Greek words above are so dissimilar as to cancel the Greek primacy theory here as in practically every other place where the two theories are compared to the data of the Greek and Aramaic texts.

16. I, Yeshua, have sent my Angel to testify these things among you before the assemblies. I AM THE LIVING GOD, The Root and The Offspring of David, and his Companion, and The Bright Morning Star."

No Greek ms. has "**& his Companion**". This is a totally uncontrived and very poignant description of Our Lord's relationship to David. It speaks for the originality of the reading by its own merits.

17. "And The Spirit and The Bride are saying, 'Come', and let him who hears, say, "Come", and let him who thirsts* come and take the water of life without charge."

Greek has "**Whosoever will, let him take the water of life freely**". Here , as in quite a few other places, it appears a Greek translator double translated an Aramaic word.

In this case, ודצהא –"**he who thirsts**" was read correctly and then reread as ודצבא –"**& he who will**". Each of the three Aramaic scripts presents **80% letter correlation** between the two words.

Ashuri Aramaic script
ודצהא -"**& he who thirsts**"
ודצבא -"**& he who will**"
DSS Aramaic script
(DSS script) -"**& he who thirsts**"
(DSS script) –"**& he who will**"
Estrangela Aramaic script
(Estrangela script) -"**& he who thirsts**"
(Estrangela script) –"**& he who will**"

18. "I testify to everyone who hears the word of the prophecy of this book: Whoever will place upon these things, God shall place upon him the plagues that are written in this book."

19. "And whoever subtracts from the words of the Scripture of this prophecy, God shall subtract his part from The Tree of Life and from The Holy City, those things which are written in this book."

20. And when he testified these things, he said, "Yes*, I am coming soon." "Come, LORD JEHOVAH Yeshua." *Critical Greek omits "Yes".*

21. The grace of Our Lord Yeshua The Messiah be with all of his Holy Ones. Amen.

Epilogue

I encourage the reader to read my **Aramaic-English Interlinear New Testament**, from which this English translation is derived. I have also written **Divine Contact-Discovery of The Original New Testament** which documents how I discovered by scientific experiment that The Peshitta New Testament was written by God Himself and that The Greek New Testament is a first century translation of The Aramaic Peshitta New Testament books. There are free articles, excerpts and book links available at aramaicnt.com

Those discoveries are what led me to translate the Peshitta and to publish it. After thirty years of searching for the original New Testament among the Greek texts, I have found it in the Aramaic manuscripts of The Peshitta, which has been faithfully and meticulously copied and preserved by Assyrian and Syrian Scribes, who have been counting the words and letters of each book for over 1900 years and have always held to its text as the original word of God to the Apostles.
Every time the Western church has approached nearer to the original words of the Apostles and those words have been disseminated, there has been reformation, renewal and revival of the Christian faith.

The Peshitta is as close to the original as possible, as **it is the original written New Covenant**. The reformation that will result from the dissemination and translation of the original New Testament will be greater than any that has hitherto come upon The Earth, for its Truth is eternal and infallible.

I encourage the reader to share this knowledge and Testament with others in every way practicable. We shall go from a famine of hearing the word of God (Amos 8:11) to an age of feasting on manna from Heaven.

My people are destroyed for lack of knowledge...Hosea 4:6
 Where *there is* no vision (Divine revelation), the people perish: but he that keepeth the law, happy *is* he. Proverbs 29:18
    The Lord gave the word: great *was* the company of those that published *it*. Psalm 68:11

 For The Earth shall be filled with the knowledge of the glory of the LORD, as the waters cover the sea. Habakkuk *2:14*

Appendix

Pericope de Adultera
(Syriac Peshitta New Testament 1905)

The above is probably what the Gospel of John looked like when it was first written. The script is the same as found in the Dead Sea Scrolls and was used in Hebrew and Aramaic writing from about 100 B.C. to A.D. 135 in Israel and Syria. It may have been used in Mesopotamia as well, though there Estrangela probably replaced the script after A.D. 100. Peshitta manuscripts, like most Bible mss., have generally the same number of letters on each line and are uniform, line to line, page to page, unlike the sample above. There were no verse numbers in the manuscripts.

The passage is the story of the woman taken in adultery, found in most Greek mss. of John's Gospel (7:53-8:11) and in 8 Aramaic mss., as well as in most ancient Bible versions and in numerous references by the church fathers to the Gospel of John. The Peshitta mss. do not contain the passage, however, but have 7:52, then continue with 8:12, without ever so much as a space between.

The following is an explanation of the omission by The Peshitta and consequently, of the omission by a relatively small number of Greek mss. (howbeit, ancient). Almost all of the 900+ Greek mss. of John have the account in its traditional place.

The first century Jewish writers used scrolls, not books as we do. The above passage would have been written in block sections.

Have a look at the start of the passage and of the start of the verse following it in Aramaic:

Pesher Habbakuk Dead Sea Scroll Script

ᵁᴶᴴ ᵁᴵᴷ ᴰᴷᴾ ᴷᴸ – End of v.52; Beginning of v. 53
ᴶᴼᴿ ᴳᴶᴴ ᴶᵁᴰᴷᴴ ᴷᴸ – End of v. 11; Beginning of v. 12

(Great Isaiah Dead Sea Scroll Script (Herodian

ᴶ^ᴶᴴ ᴶᴵᴷ ᴰᴷᴾ ᴷᴸ – End of v.52; Beginning of v. 53
ᴶ^ᴴ ᴴᴶᴸ ᴶ^ᵁᴰᴴ ᴷᴸ – End of v. 11; Beginning of v. 12

Estrangela Script

[Estrangela script] – End of v.52; Beginning of v. 53
[Estrangela script] – End of v. 11; Beginning of v. 12

Ashuri Aramaic Script

אזל הכיל
תוב דין

Pesher Habbakuk-Herodian Hybrid Script

ᴶ^ᴶᴴ ᴶᴵᴷ ᴰᴷᴾ ᴷᴸ – End of v.52; Beginning of v. 53
ᴶ^ᴴ ᴴᴶᴸ ᴶ^ᵁᴰᴴ ᴷᴸ – End of v. 11; Beginning of v. 12

A scribe copying a Peshitta ms. in the 1st century, perhaps the first and only one of two or three to make a copy of the original, may have been finishing verse 52 and had looked ahead to v.53 and had seen ᴶ^ᴶᴴ ᴶᴵᴷ -"went therefore", and when he had finished v. 52, his eye went back to the manuscript and fell on v. 12 of chapter 8 (though the chapter and verse divisions did not exist then) where he saw ᴶ^ᴴ ᴴᴶᴸ -"But again" instead of ᴶ^ᴶᴴ ᴶᴵᴷ -"went therefore".

ᴶ^ᴶᴴ ᴶᴵᴷ -"went therefore" Beginning of v. 53
ᴶ^ᴴ ᴴᴶᴸ -"but again" Beginning of v. 12

The two phrases are generally similar, though there are a couple of problems; the first is Alap and Tau, the 1st letter of each of the two phrases, respectively.

Below is a chart showing 1st century Aramaic letters Alap (called "Aleph" in Hebrew) and Tau taken from photos of Dead Sea Scrolls.

The Alphanumeric System Of First Century A. D.

Alphabetic Numerals: Hebrew Aramaic[5]
Far right & far left are modern forms; hand written forms are like some from 1st Century

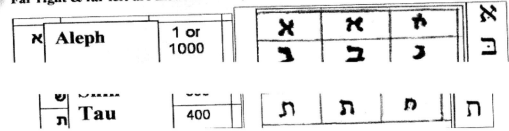

There are variations in handwritten forms for each letter; 3 are shown for each letter. I display Alap and Tau in two forms most similar to each other:

-Alap

-Tau

    Let's put these in the 2 phrases:

ﾉ^ﾊ ﾉﾑ -"went therefore"

ﾉ^ﾤ ﾉﾑ -"but again"

Now there is but one major difference remaining- the letter He (ﾊ) in the 4 letter word ﾉ^ﾊ – "hakyl", with 3 letters in the matched ﾉ^ﾤ -"dyn" . If the Lamed ﾉ in ﾉﾑ & ﾤ in ﾉﾑﾤ do not look similar enough, how about ﾤ & ﾤ? Let's put these in as well:

ﾉﾑﾊ ﾉﾑ -"went therefore"

ﾉ^ﾤ ﾉﾑﾊ -"but again"

Alphabetic Numerals: Hebrew Aramaic[5]

Far right & far left are modern forms; hand written forms are like some from 1st Century

		Value				
א	Aleph	1 or 1000				א
ב	Beth	2				ב
ג	Gimel	3				ג
ד	Daleth	4				ד
ה	He	5				ה
ו	Waw	6				ו
ז	Zayin	7				ז
ח	Heth	8				ח
ט	Teth	9				ט
י	Yodh	10				י
כ ך	Kaph or Final Kaph	20				כ
ל	Lamedh	30				ל
מ ם	Mem or Final Mem	40				מ
נ ן	Nun or Final Nun	50				נ
ס	Samekh	60				ס
ע	Ayin	70				ע
פ ף	Pe or Final Pe	80				פ
צ ץ	Sadhe or Final Sadhe	90				צ
ק	Qoph	100				ק
ר	Resh	200				ר
ש	Shin	300				ש
ת	Tau	400				ת

[5] Compare Editors, Francis Brown, S. R. Driver, & Charles A. Briggs, *The New Brown, Driver, and Briggs English Lexicon of the Old Testament* (Grand Rapids, Michigan: Baker Book House, 1981); *Numerology - Gematria: The Mathematics of the Torah*, ©5760-5765 (2000-2005) by Gal Einai Institute: http://www.inner.org/gematria/gematria.htm

With such modifications, the two phrases show high letter correlations- about 11/14, or 77% correlation.

It is very interesting that the beginnings of v. 53 and verse 12 show these similarities in the Dead Sea Scroll Herodian script, because these are the very verses bordering the controversial passage of the woman taken in adultery and would account for a scribe accidentally omitting the entire passage of 12 verses!

I have inserted the two highlighted phrases as I have portrayed them in the passage (at 7:53 and 8:12) using the Herodian Aramaic script letter photos to illustrate how they may have appeared to the first Peshitta copyist as he looked at the original Aramaic Gospel of John.

The Peshitta original with the passage of the adulteress can account precisely for the present Peshitta with an erroneous omission of it (though eight Aramaic mss. do have this passage). We cannot account for its existence in almost all Greek Gospel mss. and ancient versions as a fabrication. That is highly improbable. Omission is far more likely than fabrication and addition of spurious accounts on the part of an Aramaean Christian scribe.

What is very surprising is that The Peshitta mss. do not have the passage, which would indicate that the Peshitta mss. existing today are all copies of one copy of the original, not the original itself, and some of the other Aramaic mss. which do have it, may actually be traced to another copy of the original, or perhaps to the original itself! If the Peshitta mss. are copies of a second generation ms., then no matter how carefully those mss. were copied, we may expect other copyist errors to exist in all of them, due to the errors of the first copyist. If other Aramaic mss. represent another rescension of another copy, or of the original itself, and we should assume one or the other to be the case, then we should give equal consideration to those of that rescension when significant differences exist between the two text types. This is especially relevant where there is a verse or reading in one text which is missing in the other; it should be assumed in such a case that the error is one of omission and not of addition; omission is an easy mistake for an honest scribe to make, and the integrity of New Testament scribes should be assumed; addition of new material not found in the manuscript being copied is not an honest mistake, it is deliberate and corrupt and should be ruled out as an explanation wherever there is doubt.

Aramaean Christian scribes are famous for their accuracy and integrity in their work and reverent devotion to the scripture text "written by The Spirit" –(2 Timothy 3:16). They would as likely cut off a finger as to deliberately omit a word or letter of scripture. They also kept a record of important statistics for each ms. so as to compare it with its original and keep copying errors to an absolute minimum.

There is no such Massora tradition to be found among the Greeks and their Greek mss., hence, the number of transcription errors are multiplied by a factor of ten for Textus Receptus mss., compared to Eastern Peshitta mss., all the way up to 70 to 100 times as many variants in the Alexandrian and other ancient Greek Uncials and papyri, between any two mss..

I have yet to encounter a better accounting of the omission of this passage, or of its addition in John's Gospel. The close visual similarity of the two phrases in exactly the places where they occur in the critical edition of The 1905 Syriac Peshitta NT shows an almost 100% correlation of 4 out of 7 letters in the longer of the two phrases (the shorter has 6 letters) and a quite high correlation between the remaining 2 corresponding letters. An error of the eye in glancing back at the manuscript after copying what is now known as verse 7:52

and looking for ܐܙܠ ܠܗ ܗܟܝܠ -"went therefore" (beginning 7:53)
and finding   ܬܘܒ ܕܝܢ -"but again"   (beginning 8:12)
seems to exactly account for the Peshitta not having this passage of twelve verses between 7:52 and 8:12.
It is safe to say that with the letter variations considered, the letter correlations are in the 80-85% range for the two Aramaic phrases.
The Greek text for the beginning of the two verses in question is:
παλιν ουν αυτοις ελαλησεν- "Again he said to them" 7:53
και επορευθησαν εκαστος-"And they went each one" 8:12

How about the endings of verses 7:52 and 8:11?
ουκ εγειρεται-"does not arise" -7:52
μηκετι αμαρτανε –"no longer sin"- 8:11

Neither of these Greek phrase pairs looks alike, nor do they sound alike. I can see no
explanation based on Greek for the omission of the passage in ten ancient Greek mss.

The correlation of the Greek phrases is a generous 3/8 for the last words of the two verses:
εγειρεται-"arise"
αμαρτανε-"sin"

3/8 is 38% correlation between the two Greek words, and the correlation is between letters in the endings of the words, which are least significant for identifying a word in Greek. The Majority Greek text does not seem to offer a valid explanation for the omission of the passage from the other Greek mss..

The 1905 Syriac Peshitta New Testament critical edition, based overall on 70 mss., can account for the omission in The Peshitta manuscripts as well as in the Greek mss. which omit it, on the basis of Peshitta primacy- the idea that The Peshitta Aramaic NT is the original from which the Greek NT was translated. There is abundant documentation to support that position contained in The Aramaic-English Interlinear New Testament and in The Original Aramaic New Testament in Plain English. Both of these are available from my web site: aramaicnt.com

I also have compiled the evidences in a 180 page book titled , Jegar Sahadutha-"Heap of Witness". This is also for sale as a printed book or as an E- book download. All my books are available in both printed editions or download files.

Bibliography:
In writing this interlinear I used or consulted MS Word, Dragon Naturally Speaking 9.0 software, Adobe Acrobat 5.0 , CutePDF Writer, Online Bible ME (with many Bible versions, including The 1905 Syriac Peshitta New Testament, Murdock's translation of The Peshitta, Hodges-Pierpont Majority Greek NT-1993, Westcott and Hort's 1881 Greek NT,The Latin Vulgate) Smith's Syriac Dictionary, Nestle-Aland Novum Testamentum-25th edition, Jastrow's Targum Dictionary, The Comprehensive Aramaic Lexicon (web site), W.M. Thackston's Introduction To Syriac , The New Covenant Aramaic Peshitta Text with Hebrew Translation-1986 , The Syriac Bible-1979, Paul Younan's Interlinear Translation of The Peshitta Gospels and Acts, The Holy Bible from the Ancient Eastern Text-George M. Lamsa's translation from the Aramaic of The Peshitta, Codefinder software of Research Systems Inc, Biblia Hebraica Stuttgartensia (Leningrad Hebrew Old Testament ms.), 1769 Authorized Version, The Arabic Bible, Rahlfs' Greek Septuagint , 1851 Brenton's English Septuagint, Greek Septuagint Apocrypha, The Emphasized Bible by Rotherham, Young's Literal Translation of The Bible, 1899 Douay-Rheims American Version , Remnants of The Later Syriac Versions of The Bible and The Apocalypse of St John by John Gwynn.

Manufactured by Amazon.ca
Acheson, AB